Acts of Conscience

Critical Perspectives on Disability
Steven J. Taylor, Arlene Kanter, *and* Beth A. Ferri, *Series Editors*

Syracuse University Press is proud to announce the launch of our new series, Critical Perspectives on Disability, with the publication of Steven J. Taylor's book, *Acts of Conscience: World War II, Mental Institutions, and Religious Objectors*. Books in this series will explore the place of people with disabilities in society through the lens of disability studies, critical special education, disability law and policy, and international human rights. The series publishes books from such disciplines as sociology, law and public policy, history, anthropology, the humanities, educational theory, literature, communications, the study of popular culture, and diversity and cultural studies.

Acts of Conscience

World War II, Mental Institutions, and Religious Objectors

Steven J. Taylor

SYRACUSE UNIVERSITY PRESS

Copyright © 2009 by Syracuse University Press
Syracuse, New York 13244-5160

All Rights Reserved

First Edition 2009

09 10 11 12 13 14   6 5 4 3 2 1

The paper used in this publication meets the minimum requirements
of American National Standard for Information Sciences—Permanence
of Paper for Printed Library Materials, ANSI Z39.48–1984.™∞

For a listing of books published and distributed by Syracuse University Press,
visit our Web site at SyracuseUniversityPress.syr.edu

ISBN-13: 978-0-8156-0915-5   ISBN-10: 0-8156-0915-9

Library of Congress Cataloging-in-Publication Data

Taylor, Steven J., 1949–
Acts of conscience : World War II, mental institutions, and religious objectors /
Steven J. Taylor. — 1st ed.
p. cm.
Includes bibliographical references and index.
ISBN 978-0-8156-0915-5 (cloth : alk. paper)
1. Psychiatric hospitals—United States—History—20th century.   2. People with
mental disabilities—Education—United States—History—20th century.
3. World War, 1939–1945—Conscientious objectors—United States.
4. Civilian Public Service—History.   I. Title.
RC443.T39 2009
362.2'1—dc22
2009004376

Manufactured in the United States of America

To Betsy, Jeff, and Lea, with love

Steven J. Taylor, Ph.D., is Centennial Professor of Disability Studies and codirector of the Center of Human Policy, Law, and Disability Studies at Syracuse University. He has published widely on disability policy, the sociology of disability, and qualitative research methods. He has been the recipient of the Research Award from the American Association on Mental Retardation, the Syracuse University Chancellor's Citation for Exceptional Academic Achievement, and the first annual Senior Scholar Award from the Society for Disability Studies.

Contents

Illustrations

Acknowledgments

I want to take the opportunity to acknowledge all of those who contributed directly or indirectly to this book.

This book was made possible through a research sabbatical granted by Syracuse University in the spring of 2007. Thanks to Dean Doug Biklen for supporting my sabbatical and to Cyndy Colavita, Rachael Zubal-Ruggieri, Pam Walker, Arlene Kanter, Beth Ferri, Perri Harris, Sari Biklen, and Bob Ciota for filling in for me while I was on leave. Rachael and Cyndy also gave me invaluable assistance on many aspects of my research and writing throughout the process. Ben Ware, dean of the Graduate School at Syracuse University, awarded me a generous grant that helped me conduct the research on which this book is based. With the support of university chancellor Nancy Cantor and vice chancellor Eric Spina, Doug Biklen appointed me Centennial Professor of Disability Studies in July 2008, and this appointment provided time and resources that enabled me to put the finishing touches on the book.

The Mennonite Church USA Historical Committee and Archives (MCA) at Goshen, Indiana, the Swarthmore College Peace Collection (SCPC) at Swarthmore, Pennsylvania, and the Brethren Historical Library and Archives (BHLA) at Elgin, Illinois, are national treasures. There are endless books to be written based on the rich historical documents maintained at these archives. I want to express my appreciation of Dennis Stoesz, Rich Preheim, and Cathy Hochstetter of the MCA, Wendy Chmielewski of the SCPC, and Kenneth Shaffer of the BHLA for welcoming me during visits to their archives, helping locate documents and materials, and making it possible for me to reproduce many of the photographs in the book. Dennis Stoesz of the MCA and Mary Beth Sigado of the SCPC arranged to scan photographs for me. Paul D. Leichty of the Anabaptist Disabilities Network and indirectly Bill Gaventa helped me identify the MCA initially. John Thiesen of the Mennonite Library and Archives at North Newton, Kansas, generously loaned me CDs of audiotaped interviews conducted with former conscientious objectors (COs) and other knowledgeable persons. Lynn K. Lucas of the Adriance Memorial Library in Poughkeepsie provided me with newspaper articles on conscientious objectors at Hudson River State Hospital, and Milton Botwinick helped me identify stories on the National Mental Health Foundation and Philadelphia State Hospital published in Philadelphia papers. Heather T. Frazier generously granted me permission to quote liberally from the oral histories contained in her coedited book with John O'Sullivan, "*We Have Just Begun to Not Fight.*" Sarah Jones of Mental Health America gave me permission to quote from *Out of Sight, Out of Mind.*

Former World War II COs or their family members who spoke to me about their experiences own my deep respect and appreciation: Jack Allen, W. Forrest Altman, Evert Bartholomew, John Bartholomew, Samuel Burgess, Gilbert Goering (a Korean War conscientious objector whose brothers served in the Civilian Public Service), Neil Hartman, Curtis Johnson, Charles Lord, William March, Caryl Marsh, Ward and Alice Miles, Stuart Palmer, Richard Ruddell, Warren Sawyer, and Florence Siegel. Warren Sawyer was kind enough to arrange for me to visit Medford Leas, New Jersey, where I interviewed him and eight other former COs.

I owe a special debt of gratitude to former World War II COs and their family members who loaned me their personal papers, which helped fill in the blanks of the story of the Civilian Public Service and efforts to reform institutions: Warren Sawyer, Ward Miles, Robert and Eleanor Cox, Neil Hartman, and Harold and Philip Wik.

Marvin Weisbord was kind enough to speak with me about his memories of interviewing the founders of the National Mental Health Foundation for his book *Some Form of Peace.* Christine Conway Reese shared her memories of her former husband, CO and mental health reformer Justin Reese.

John O'Brien, Don Forrest, and Steven Mcfayden-Ketchum explained their philosophies for becoming COs during the Vietnam War. Michael Schwartz gave me insights into the oral method of instruction for deaf students. Sari Biklen helped me understand the religious and political philosophies of members of the Society of Friends, or Quakers.

Carol and Jerry Berrigan made time to speak with me about Dorothy Day and the Catholic Workers as well as the leaders of the antiwar movement during Vietnam. Jerry and Carol, along with Kathleen Rumpf, continue to teach me about how human beings should act toward each other.

Many colleagues contributed to this book. Arlene Kanter and Beth Ferri supported the idea behind this book for the Syracuse University Press Critical Issues in Disability series on which we serve as coeditors. Bob Bogdan, John O'Brien, and Wolf Wolfensberger helped me think through some of issues discussed in the book. Wolf also loaned me some hard-to-find publications relevant to this book.

Portions of this book relating to the reform movement in intellectual and developmental disabilities that started in the 1960s were supported, in part, by a subcontract awarded to the Center on Human Policy at Syracuse University by the Research and Training Center on Community Living and Employment at the University of Minnesota. The Research and Training Center is funded by the National Institute on Disability and Rehabilitation Research (NIDRR) under Grant no. H133B080005. The opinions expressed in this book are mine, and no endorsement by the University of Minnesota or NIDRR should be inferred. Thanks to Charlie Lakin for his continued support of my work.

I want to thank members of Syracuse University Press for their support of and enthusiasm for this book and the Critical Perspectives on Disability series: Alice Randel Pfeiffer, director; Ellen S. Goodman, former assistant to the director; John Fruehwirth, former managing editor; Lisa Kuerbis, marketing coordinator; Kay Steinmetz, editorial and production manager; and Lynn Hoppel, design specialist, who designed the cover of this book. Annette Wenda did a fine job copyediting the original manuscript of this book.

Finally, I want to acknowledge and thank my wife, Betsy Edinger, and my children, Jeff and Lea, for their love and support. Betsy read and commented on early drafts of this book and spent countless hours listening to me talk about what I was learning about the story of the World War II COs and how I wanted to tell it. Betsy, Jeff, and Lea also tolerated stacks of archival documents spread over just about every available surface of our kitchen as I was researching and writing this book. I dedicate this book to them.

Abbreviations

ACCO	Association of Catholic Conscientious Objectors
ACLU	American Civil Liberties Union
AFSC	American Friends Service Committee
APA	American Psychiatric Association
BHLA	Brethren Historical Library and Archives
BSC	Brethren Service Committee
CO	Conscientious objector
CPS	Civilian Public Service
CPSU	Civilian Public Service Union
FOR	Fellowship of Reconciliation
GAP	Group for the Advancement of Psychiatry
MCA	Mennonite Church USA Historical Committee and Archives
MCC	Mennonite Central Committee
MHP	Mental Hygiene Program
MLA	Mennonite Library and Archives
NAMH	National Association for Mental Health
NCMIH	National Committee for Mental Hygiene
NMHA	National Mental Health Association
NMHF	National Mental Health Foundation
NSBRO	National Service Board for Religious Objectors
SCPC	Swarthmore College Peace Collection
WRL	War Resisters League

Acts of Conscience

Introduction

One may differ, as I do, with the views that led these young men to take up a difficult and unpopular position against service in the armed forces. But one cannot help but recognize their honesty and sincerity in reporting upon the conditions they found in the hospitals to which they were assigned.

—ALBERT Q. MAISEL, "Bedlam, 1946: Most U.S. Mental
Hospitals Are a Shame and a Disgrace"

In the mid- to late 1940s, a group of young men rattled the psychiatric establishment by beaming a public spotlight on the squalid conditions and brutality in our nation's mental hospitals and training schools for people with psychiatric and intellectual disabilities. They brought about exposés reported in newspapers across the country and major carriers of popular culture and led a reform effort to change public attitudes, revise institutional commitment laws, and improve the pay, status, and training of institutional staff. Their efforts prompted major psychiatric and mental hygiene organizations to acknowledge the failures and deficiencies in how states cared for the "mentally ill" and "mental defectives."

These young men were among the 11,996 World War II conscientious objectors assigned to the Civilian Public Service as an alternative to serving in the military. The CPS was an outgrowth of the efforts of the "historical peace churches"—the Mennonites, Brethren, and Friends or Quakers—to enable their members to act on their pacifist beliefs by conducting "work of national importance under civilian direction." Once the CPS was established, it attracted men from more than 120 religions. The majority of CPS men were Mennonites, Brethren, Friends, and Methodists, but their ranks also included Catholics, Jews, and African American Muslims, in addition to some secular objectors.

The CPS was jointly operated by church committees, the Selective Service (SS), and administrative agencies, including the U.S. Forest Service, the National Park Service, and the Soil Conservation Service. Men were initially assigned to government work camps, where they maintained parks and nurseries; constructed roads, bridges, and truck trails; dug ditches; fought forest fires; and engaged in other public works projects. The men were not paid for their work, and church committees paid for their living expenses. Owing to the desires of many men to perform more humanitarian public service and pressing labor shortages caused by the war, the Selective Service eventually approved the assignment of CPS men to "detached units," where they worked on alternative projects. A number of men volunteered to work on dairy farms or public health projects in the rural South. Some served as "human guinea pigs" in medical experiments conducted at some of the nation's leading universities and medical centers and were infected with hepatitis, malaria, or pneumonia; exposed to parasites; and subjected to extreme temperatures, high and low altitudes, or semistarvation diets. Approximately 3,000 men served at state mental hospitals and training schools, where they worked as attendants or performed other jobs.

Conditions at public institutions for people with psychiatric or intellectual disabilities were far from ideal prior to World War II. The war had a devastating impact on the institutions. Many male staff members were drafted, and both male and female workers left the institutions for jobs in higher-paying defense industries. The institutions were left with few workers, sometimes 1 attendant on duty for as many as more than 140 patients. Of those staff members who were left, many were drifters who oversaw institutional wards with a closed fist, or worse—clubs and hoses filled with buckshot. The use of straitjackets and other forms of restraining devices was commonplace. Clothing, cleaning materials, and other essentials were usually in short supply.

For most CPS men, work at the mental hospitals and training schools was difficult and stressful. Ten-hour workdays were commonplace. As few as 1 to 3 men were in charge of as many as 350 patients, including those individuals with the most severe disabilities. The harsh and sometimes brutal treatment of patients by regular attendants challenged the humanitarian and pacifist beliefs of many of the young COs. On terribly understaffed and overcrowded wards, the COs often had to resort to physical restraints and coercion to keep patients safe and to maintain control and order. The COs often debated among themselves the appropriateness and morality of using force to protect themselves or the patients under their care.

Shocked by institutional conditions and the treatment of patients, some COs brought complaints to the attention of local community leaders, public officials, and the press. Widely reported media exposés flared up at Eastern State Hospital in Williamsburg, Virginia; Mount Pleasant State Hospital in Iowa; Cleveland State Hospital in Ohio; Hudson River State Hospital in Poughkeepsie, New York; and elsewhere. Sometimes civic leaders and newspapers joined the COs in calling for reforms of the institutions. Often, state officials and local veterans' groups denounced the COs as troublemakers and slackers.

At Philadelphia State Hospital, commonly known as Byberry, four COs—two Methodist, one Jewish, and one Baptist—developed an ambitious plan to reform the nation's system of caring for people with psychiatric and intellectual disabilities. With the support of church committees and the approval of the Selective Service, they created the Mental Hygiene Program of the CPS. CPS officials set one condition on the establishment of the Mental Hygiene Program: it had to operate under the supervision of medical experts. The National Committee for Mental Hygiene agreed to sponsor the program and oversee its activities, along with a panel of national experts. The National Committee itself had been founded to reform mental hospitals by Clifford Beers, author of *A Mind That Found Itself*, in 1909, but had since turned its attention to other priorities.

The Mental Hygiene Program began to publish a newsletter and training materials for attendants on the proper care of patients. One member of the program's staff started to research state commitment laws to prevent the unnecessary institutionalization of mental patients. The program also solicited reports on conditions from COs working at other state institutions. More than one thousand accounts were eventually received. The founders of the Mental Hygiene Program secretly planned the release of a report on the state of public institutions across the nation.

As the CPS drew to a close in 1946, the COs who founded the Mental Hygiene Program planned to launch a new national organization to improve the care of mental patients. The men had little faith in the ability of either the National Committee for Mental Hygiene or the American Psychiatric Association, the other national mental health organization, to do what needed to be done to reform institutions. Both the National Committee and the APA were loath to expose institutional conditions publicly. For these COs, only a national organization controlled by laypersons could lead a successful reform movement.

At the same time the four Byberry COs were planning a new organization, they were working with investigative reporters to bring national attention to the plight of the nation's mental patients. Albert Deutsch of New York's *PM* newspaper and Albert Q. Maisel of *Life* magazine visited the Mental Hygiene Program's offices to review the reports of institutional conditions recorded by COs at state mental hospitals and training schools. Deutsch published exposés of Philadelphia State Hospital and Cleveland State Hospital in April 1946. On May 6, 1946, Maisel wrote a scathing indictment of state mental hospitals based largely on CO reports in *Life*. That same day, the formation of the National Mental Health Foundation, the successor to the Mental Hygiene Program, was announced in the *Philadelphia Inquirer*.

The National Mental Health Foundation got off to an auspicious start. The *Philadelphia Inquirer* story was picked up by the Associated Press and published in the *New York Times, New York Post, Baltimore Sun*, and elsewhere. The story reported that former U.S. Supreme Court justice Owen J. Roberts would serve as national chairman of the new organization. Before long, other prominent Americans would lend their names in support of the foundation's efforts. Eleanor Roosevelt, who had become aware of the Mental Hygiene Program's activities, was an early supporter of the new foundation and put its leaders in contact with others who could help establish its credibility. Eventually, American Civil Liberties Union founder Roger Baldwin, author Pearl Buck, actress Helen Hayes, civil rights activist Mary McLeod Bethune, First Lady Bess Truman, Howard University president Mordecai Johnson, and other religious, civil, and political leaders would be listed as national supporters or board members of the National Mental Health Foundation. Reform-minded psychiatrists and others agreed to serve as professional advisers to the new organization.

The negative publicity surrounding institutions forced leaders in psychiatry and mental hygiene to publicly acknowledge the significant shortcomings of state institutions. At meetings and in publications, representatives of the National Committee for Mental Hygiene and the American Psychiatric Association admitted that the care of patients in public mental hospitals was all too often woefully inadequate. In the ensuing years, a number of states significantly increased funding for their mental hospitals.

For the next four years, the National Mental Health Foundation received public acclaim for its efforts to improve mental patient care. A book based on the accounts of the COs, *Out of Sight, Out of Mind*, was published in 1947, and received a glowing review by Eleanor Roosevelt in her popular "My Day" newspaper column. Stories on the foundation's activities were published in *Time, Newsweek,* and newspapers across the country. Radio broadcasts sponsored by the foundation and narrated by celebrities were heard by listeners in many cities in North America. President Harry Truman wrote Chairman Justice Owens a letter commending the foundation for its accomplishments.

Despite its successes, the National Mental Health Foundation struggled financially almost from the start. It had trouble meeting its payroll, which had grown with the addition of new staff members, and its leaders sometimes went without pay. Over time, the foundation, which had been established as a staff-run organization, came to be dominated by its Board of Directors. Many of the original board members and supporters were replaced by Philadelphia business and civic leaders who had little knowledge of the foundation's history and original mission. Then, what had started as a joint fund-raising effort among national mental health organizations evolved into discussions of a merger between the National Mental Health Foundation, the National Committee for Mental Hygiene, and the

Psychiatric Foundation, a fund-raising arm of the American Psychiatric Association. The board of the National Mental Health Foundation led the merger effort. In 1950, the three organizations merged to become the National Association for Mental Health. By that time, three of the founders of the national foundation had left the organization. At least two of them were skeptical about the two other organizations and feared domination by medical professionals.

The newly formed National Association for Mental Health took on the identity of the previous National Committee for Mental Hygiene. It lacked the passion and zeal of the COs who had established the Mental Hygiene Program of the CPS and the National Mental Health Foundation. Institutional reform was not a priority of the new organization. The institutions became out of sight, out of mind, once more.

The World War II COs were not the first persons to expose conditions at public institutions in America, and they would not be the last. What distinguishes the COs from institutional reformers of other eras is that their efforts have been largely forgotten or ignored in the professional history and the public realm. Their contributions and activities have faded from the professional and popular memory.

This book tells their history. It is a history about pacifism and national service, disability in America, the nature of reform movements, and the complexity of social change.

PART ONE

"We Won't Murder"

—PAUL COMLY FRENCH, 1940

1

"Work of National Importance under Civilian Direction"

It was January 1940, and war was on the horizon. In Europe, Germany had invaded Poland the previous September, leading Great Britain and France to declare war against the Nazi regime. Sensing that Nazis and fascists in Europe would only "respect force and force alone," President Franklin Delano Roosevelt had begun calling for increases in defense spending, despite strong isolationist sentiments in the United States.[1] Meanwhile, in the East, tensions were increasing between the United States and Japan, as Japan sought to solidify its control over China and Southeast Asia.[2]

Mindful of the treatment of conscientious objectors during World War I, representatives of the "historic peace churches"—the Friends or Quakers, Mennonites, and the Brethren—requested a meeting with Roosevelt to discuss the handling of COs in the event of a draft. During the First World War, the 1917 conscription act exempted members of recognized peace churches from combat, but required them to serve in noncombatant roles.[3] The conscientious objector provision in the 1917 law read: "Nothing in this act contained shall be construed or compel any person to serve in any of the forces herein provided for, who is found to be a member of any well-recognized religious sect or organization at present organized and existing and whose creed or principles forbid its members to participate in war in any form and whose religious convictions are against war or participation therein in accordance with the creed or principles of said religious organizations, but no person so exempted shall be exempted from service in any capacity that the President shall declare to be noncombatant."[4]

Although the law exempted Friends, Mennonites, Brethren, and members of lesser-known peace churches such as the Moravians (Hutterites) and Schwenkfelders from combatant service, the exemption did not apply to members of other religions whose beliefs permitted, but did not require, conscientious objection to war or to those individuals who opposed war on humanistic grounds.[5] As stated by Congressman Newton of Minnesota, the law was written to prevent

"pro-Germans, I.W.W., political Socialists, and cowardly slackers" from qualifying as conscientious objectors.[6] Further, for the peace churches and many of
their members, *any* form of participation in the military violated their religious
principles. At a special meeting called to discuss the war on January 9, 1918, the
General Conference of the Church of the Brethren issued the following statement:
"We . . . urge our Brethren not to enlist in any service which would, in any way,
compromise our time-honored position in relation to war; also that they refrain
from wearing the military uniform. The tenets of the church forbid military drill-
ing, or learning the art or arts of war, or doing anything which contributes to the
destruction of human life or property."[7]

Throughout World War I, members of peace churches qualifying for an
exemption from combat were expected to report to military training camps upon
being drafted and to perform service under military direction. Many members
of the peace churches did, in fact, enter the military and served in combatant or
noncombatant roles. Others who refused to cooperate with military authorities
were subjected to mistreatment and abuse. One Mennonite described the treatment of conscientious objectors at a military camp in Virginia: "We were cursed,
beaten, kicked, and compelled to go through exercises to the extent that a few
were unconscious for some minutes. They kept it up for the greater part of the
afternoon, and then those who could possibly stand on their feet were compelled
to take cold shower baths. One of the boys was scrubbed with a scrubbing brush,
using lye on him. They drew blood in several places."[8]

More than 500 conscientious objectors were court-martialed and sent to federal prisons.[9] Seventeen were sentenced to death and 142 to life imprisonment.[10]
The death sentences were never carried out, and in 1933, Roosevelt issued a proc-
lamation of pardon to the objectors.

Through the efforts of Rufus Jones of the American Friends Service Committee and others, Congress passed a law authorizing conscientious objectors
opposed to any military service to be furloughed from the military for agricultural service or foreign relief work, in exceptional circumstances, toward the end
of the war. The law was passed too late to make a difference for most conscientious objectors and did not "free the absolute conscientious objector from the ten-
tacles of the military machine."[11]

◆   ◆   ◆

Between the world wars, representatives of the Brethren, Mennonites, and
Friends held occasional conferences and discussions to discuss plans in the event
of another national draft. With the increasing militarism of Germany in Europe
and Japan in Asia, a delegation of the three peace churches met with Roosevelt in

1937 to present their own statements on war. It was not until 1939, and the clear prospects of war, however, that the historic peace churches hammered out a joint position statement to present to Roosevelt. Then on January 10, 1940, Rufus Jones and Walter C. Woodward for the Society of Friends, Rufus D. Bowman and Paul H. Bowman for the Church of the Brethren, and P. C. Hiebert, Harold S. Bender, and E. L. Harshbarger for the Mennonite Church presented the statement to the president of the United States. The statement expressed appreciation of Roosevelt for his attempts to avoid war: "We desire, first of all, to express our deep appreciation for your repeated effort to prevent the European war, our warm support of your confident insistence that the United States shall not be drawn into this conflict, and our hope that opportunity will arise for our nation to co-operate with other neutral nations in offering mediation or other peace-promoting techniques toward the earliest possible establishment of peace." Yet the statement also recognized that war might be all but inevitable:

> If, in spite of all efforts to maintain neutrality, the tragic day should come when our beloved nation is drawn into war, we expect to continue our work for suffering humanity, and to increase its scope because of the greater need at home and abroad. Such service would permit those whose conscientious convictions forbid participation in war in any form to render constructive service to their country and to the world. We appear today chiefly to discuss with you plans to provide for this alternative service as it may relate to possible conscription.

The statement concluded by pledging cooperation with the government and reaffirming the loyalty of the historic peace churches: "Our desire is to co-operate in finding the best solution to the problem of the conscientious objector, and it is even more to render as loyal citizens the highest type of constructive service we can to our country and to the world."[12]

After presenting Roosevelt with the initial statement, the group then gave him a more specific proposal on how conscientious objectors should be handled in the event of a draft. This had been more difficult for the representatives of the peace churches to work out. The Friends had wanted a provision for "absolutist" objectors: persons opposed to cooperation with conscription and any form of involuntary service. The Mennonites and the Brethren, on the other hand, believed that objectors owed some form of service to the country in times of national emergency.[13] Although the final version of the proposal requested consideration of the absolutist position, it was specific on only three agreed-upon points: that a civilian board be established to make determinations about conscientious objector status and to authorize nonmilitary service projects, that draft boards be directed to route objectors to this civilian board, and that the historic peace churches be permitted to set up and administer service projects for objectors.[14] Roosevelt responded amicably to the delegation, and the representatives left the meeting believing that it had been a success. Yet Roosevelt paid scant attention to the issue of conscientious objection until late 1940.[15]

In the spring of 1940, Congress considered a draft law. On June 20, soon after Germany's invasion of France, the Burke-Wadsworth Bill was introduced in the Senate.[16] The proposed law was nearly identical to the 1917 conscription act. Its exemption from combatant service applied only to members of historic peace churches and did not excuse conscientious objectors from serving in noncombatant roles. Throughout the summer, representatives of the peace churches, joined by members of other churches and secular peace groups, lobbied members of Congress and the administration to dramatically revise the proposed law. The Friends, who were more inclined, if not compelled, to intervene in the affairs of government than the Mennonites and Brethren, led the charge.

◆   ◆   ◆

From July 10 to August 2, 1940, the House Military Affairs Committee held hearings on the Selective Training and Service Bill.[17] On July 10 and 11 the Senate Military Affairs Committee sponsored hearings on the same bill. The hearings focused attention on some of the critical issues at stake. A recurring question raised by some members of Congress boiled down to what would happen if everyone in the country refused to protect the privileges claimed by certain religious groups. The chairman of the House committee asked Amos S. Horst of Akron, Pennsylvania, who represented the Mennonite Church, the following question: "Now suppose that all of our people were thus conscientiously opposed to war and Mr. Hitler should come to town with a few tanks and guns, and mechanized troop divisions: what could we do about it?" Horst deftly turned the question around: "Now, your question was, if all were like that, then the question may be reversed: if all were that way, then the possibility might not be." One response to the "What if everyone believed the way you do?" question was "If everyone believed the way I do, we wouldn't have a problem to begin with." Abraham Kaufman, executive secretary of the War Resisters League, an organization representing non—peace church and nonreligious objectors, approached the question in a different way. Citing the methods of Gandhi, Kaufman explained to the House committee that his group did not reject defense but, rather, rejected military defense. He argued, "We do not guarantee this nonviolent method as being a success, but neither can the supporters of military defense guarantee success for their methods." Similarly, Harold Evans of the Society of Friends testified at the Senate committee hearings:

"We fought one war to make the world safe for democracy but as we see it, the world has not been made safe for democracy."[18] The "war to end all wars" had failed to end war.

Another issue during the hearings related to who should be exempt from military service. Representative John J. Starkman of Alabama questioned Maj. Lewis B. Hershey, who would become director of the Selective Service in July 1941, on the wording of the original Burke-Wadsworth Bill: "I was reading the provision about the conscientious objector, and it appears to me on that that he is required to be a member of some religious group which has as its doctrine or principles objection to participation in war. Do you not believe that the bill ought to be changed so as to take care of the individual conscientious objector?" Hershey replied:

> You are speaking of something that I have a great deal of sympathy with, but I have not arrived at, perhaps, the best solution. Unquestionably if we could find the man and know that he is, in fact, whether he belongs to a creed or whether he does not, a conscientious objector, we should try the utmost to do something about it. We have had quite a little dealing with several of these people that have met us and discussed the matter with us and I think that they are very honest about it. Of course, on the other hand, you have this great group of people who are not honest, that are trying to run in under the tent if someone else puts it up, and somewhere in there I think that we should contrive a solution, but it is a little difficult.[19]

Testifying at the Senate committee hearings, Harold Evans explained the Society of Friends' position that individual conscience, not membership in any particular religion, should be the basis for granting exemption from military service: "We ask for the same treatment for all conscientious objectors, regardless of membership in any historic peace church, because we feel that this is a matter not of membership in the Society of Friends, of Mennonites, or Dunkards, but is a matter of the individuals' conscience."[20] Both the Mennonites and the Brethren (sometimes referred to as the Dunkards) took a similar position.

The testimony of Dorothy Day during the Senate committee hearings highlighted the problem of limiting exemptions to members of the historic peace churches. Day was a founder of the Catholic Workers movement, along with Peter Maurin, in 1933, and was the editor of the *Catholic Worker*. The Catholic Workers were committed to nonviolence, social justice, and hospitality to the poor. Questioned by Senator Edward R. Burke of Nebraska about whether the wording "well recognized religious sect whose creed or principles forbid its members to participate in war in any form" contained in the original Burke-Wadsworth Bill would protect persons aligned with Day's beliefs, she answered:

It does not protect the Catholics; no. It may protect the Quakers, the Mennonites, the Dunkards, but not Catholics. After all it is not part of our creed. Our creed takes care of matters not having to do with this. This is a matter of opinion. There has been no Papal pronouncement on war and peace. There has been many a pronouncement on armament and conscription, and there has been no pronouncement—I mean that puts people under pain of mortal sin. We can express ourselves, for instance, and many Catholics will disagree with us, a great many, but it is not a matter or morals; it is a matter of opinion. . . . So there is nothing in the Catholic creed which would entitle us to that exemption. It does not deal with Catholics.[21]

The Catholic Workers movement was one of a fair number of odd groups out in the pacifist movement in the 1940s. Their own church had never taken a position on the immorality of war or conscription. In Day's words, it had never pronounced participation in war as a mortal sin that could condemn sinners to an eternity in hell. So the Catholic Workers were forced to rely on individual conscience to support their pacifism. The influence of the Catholic Workers was limited during World War II. Their time would come during another war, when Catholics inspired by Dorothy Day became leaders of an antiwar movement.

A final issue that came up during the hearings had to do with alternatives to combatant service. In the questioning of Paul Comly French, a member of the Society of Friends, during the House hearings, the chairman asked:

Let me ask you a question. Somebody representing the conscientious objector here today said that they would have no objection to performing such service as driving an ambulance and taking care of the wounded and that is humanitarian employment. What difference is there in the man at the front with a gun aimed on his fellowman to shoot him and the fellow who is back in the warehouse somewhere packing the cartridges and sending them to him to continue shooting?[22]

French replied:

According to the Quaker view point, there is no difference. That is why we are particularly anxious to see a provision in the bill for alternative civilian service. . . . We are perfectly willing, and the Friends are perfectly willing to do anything on any constructive job there is to be done. At the present time we have work camps around the country where boys are paying their own expenses for the summer, to do a physical job of labor to help people that need it. We think that is a constructive piece of American citizenship, and we would like to do that.[23]

Both the Mennonites and the Brethren would later acknowledge the leadership of French and the Friends in successfully lobbying for a more acceptable conscription law.[24]

◆   ◆   ◆

When Roosevelt was approached by the historic peace churches in early 1940, he had little interest in proposing a conscription law. Isolationism ran strong in the country, and Roosevelt would be up for reelection that fall. After his nomination by the Democratic Party in July, however, he gave his support to the Burke-Wadsworth Bill, on August 23.[25] Also, in August, the Republican candidate for president, Wendell Wilkie, endorsed compulsory military conscription in his acceptance speech.[26] Conscription would not become a controversial issue in the presidential campaign.

A final version of the Selective Service law more amenable to conscientious objectors was passed by the House and Senate on September 14.[27] President Roosevelt signed the Selective Training and Service Act into law on September 16, 1940. It was the first peacetime draft law in the history of the United States.

The Selective Training and Service Act of 1940, the 783rd law passed by the Seventy-sixth Congress, second session, included the following provision:

> Nothing contained in this act shall be construed to require any person to be subject to combatant training and service in the land or naval forces of the United States who, by reason of religious training and belief, is conscientiously opposed to participation of war in any form. Any such person claiming such exemption from combatant training and service because of such conscientious objections whose claim is sustained by the local board shall, if he is inducted into the land or naval forces under this act, be assigned to noncombatant service as defined by the President, or shall, if he is found to be conscientiously opposed to participation in such noncombatant service, in lieu of such induction, be assigned to work of national importance under civilian direction.[28]

From the perspective of the historic peace churches, the final version of the law was vastly superior to the 1917 conscription act and the original version of the Burke-Wadsworth Bill. It expanded exemptions to cover not only members of historic peace churches but also anyone conscientiously opposed to combatant or noncombatant service based on religious training and belief, provided for work of national importance under civilian direction, and created an appeals process under the Department of Justice as opposed to military tribunals. To the disappointment of the Friends, in particular, it failed to include provisions for absolutists—persons conscientiously opposed to participation in the conscription system itself.

Like most laws, the Selective Training and Service Act of 1940 contained ambiguous concepts open to different interpretations: "noncombatant service," "religious training and belief," "work of national importance under civilian direction." It would be up to administrative agencies under the president or federal courts to define these concepts.

◆   ◆   ◆

With the Selective Training and Service Act in place, representatives of the historic peace churches turned their attention to the administration and funding of the program for "work of national importance under civilian direction." In the fall of 1940, numerous meetings were held among representatives of the peace churches and between them and government officials. Government officials were slow to direct attention to the specifics of the program. On October 2, Hershey, who would later become director of the Selective Service, told Paul Comly French to prepare a "detailed plan, for submission to him, which would cover precisely what we want in relation to civilian service."[29]

In addition to coming up with proposals for the civilian service program, the Mennonites, Friends, and Brethren were faced with the question of how to represent themselves in dealings with the government. Hershey had asked French if he spoke for all of the peace churches and suggested that the Friends take over the administration of civilian public service projects.[30] When the Friends proposed to the other two major historic peace churches that the American Friends Service Committee play the central role in the public service program, the Mennonites and Brethren expressed their preference for the creation of an independent organization to coordinate efforts. The Mennonites were uneasy about collaborating with the other groups in the first place.[31] At a meeting held among representatives of the three churches on October 5, it was agreed that the Brethren, Mennonites, and Friends would cooperate in forming a new organization.[32] The National Council for Religious Objectors was formed that October, with M. R. Zigler of the Brethren as chairman, Orie O. Miller of the Mennonites as vice chairman, and Paul Comly French, Friend, as executive secretary. Zigler later recalled that AFSC executive secretary Clarence Pickett was unhappy with the selection of Zigler as chairman of the new group and walked out of the meeting.[33] In November, the National Council became the National Service Board for Religious Objectors.

◆   ◆   ◆

Throughout the history of what was to become the Civilian Public Service, NSBRO occupied an ambiguous position. It compiled information and issued reports, served as a liaison with the Selective Service system in negotiating CPS

1. Executive Committee of the NSBRO Board of Directors *(from left):* M. R. Zigler (Brethren), Orie Miller (Mennonite), Paul Furnas (Friends), and Charles Boss (Methodist). (Brethren Historical Library and Archives, Elgin, Illinois)

policies, and acted as a troubleshooter when problems arose. Yet NSBRO never exercised any control over the myriad of religious organizations and government and private agencies involved in the CPS, let alone the Selective Service. At most, French, as executive secretary—in essence, the staff director—could use his moral authority and skills as a negotiator to try to influence the course of events. French met frequently with Selective Service officials to try to resolve problems that had arisen with the CPS and to present the positions of the church committees and COs. In a 1945 report, French recalled the history of NSBRO: "The U.S. Government asked that the representatives of the pacifist organizations form one single office to discuss the problems of COs with the government. On Oct. 4, 1940 a National Council for Religious Conscientious Objectors was formed by the Friends, Brethren and Mennonites. Later the name was changed to the National Service Board for Religious Objectors and other groups were invited to participate."[34]

By 1945, NSBRO could list a hodgepodge of historic peace churches, local or regional churches, religious splinter groups, and secular peace groups among its members and affiliates:

American Baptist Home Mission Society

Assemblies of God, General Conference

Brethren Service Committee

Catholic: Association of Catholic Conscientious Objectors

Christadelphian Central Committee

Christadelphian Service Committee

Church of God, Indiana

Church of God, Seventh Day

Congregational Christian Committee for Conscientious Objectors

Disciples of Christ Department of Social Welfare

Dunkard Brethren Committee

Dutch Reformed Church

Episcopal Pacifist Fellowship

Evangelical and Reformed Church: Commission on Christian Social Action

Evangelical Church, Board of Christian Social Action

Evangelical Mission Covenant

First Divine Association in America, Inc.

Friends: American Friends Service Committee

Jewish: Central Conference American Rabbis, Jewish Peace Fellowship, and Rab-
    binical Assembly of America

Lutheran: Augustana Lutheran FOR and Lutheran Peace Fellowship

Mennonite Central Committee

Methodist: Commission on World Peace

Mogiddo Mission

Molokan Advisory Committee

Pacifist Principle Fellowship

Pentacostal Church, Inc.: Committee on Presbyterians in Civilian Public Service

Seventh Day Adventists, War Service Committee

Unitarian Pacifist Fellowship

United Brethren

United Lutheran Church in America, Board of Social Missions

Women's International League for Peace and Freedom

Young Men's Christian Association

Consultative members were the Federal Council of Churches in Christ and the Fellowship of Reconciliation.[35]

NSBRO's name was later changed to the National Interreligious Service Board for Conscientious Objectors (NISBCO). In 1996, NISBCO published a directory of members of the Civilian Public Service in World War II. Today, the organization is named the Center on Conscience and War. The center remains affiliated with religious peace organizations.

◆　◆　◆

In late October 1940, the National Council for Religious Conscientious Objectors, which was soon to become NSBRO, came up with a plan for the operation of the civilian public service program. Under the plan, COs could work with government agencies, with the government paying maintenance and pay for the men, or with private agencies, which would pay for all costs, provided that the men and the agencies were mutually agreeable.[36] Shortly afterward, the President's Advisory Committee on Selective Service recommended to the Selective Service a revised version of this plan that would include government-run camps, camps run jointly by government agencies and church groups, with the government paying wages, and private camps run and paid for by church groups. President Roosevelt vigorously rejected the plan.

In December, NSBRO and representatives of the peace churches met with Clarence Dykstra, who had been appointed director of the Selective Service, and other government officials to try to work out a plan that might be acceptable to the government and the president. Dykstra had been president of the University of Wisconsin. He lasted as Selective Service director for only a brief period of time. Facing poor health and discontent at his university, he resigned effective April 1, 1941.[37] Dykstra proposed that the churches administer and underwrite the costs of civilian public service projects. Congress had not appropriated funds for the Civilian Public Service, and Dykstra advised NSBRO and the churches that if the Selective Service went to Congress to request an appropriation, it might result in complete government administration of projects, with no involvement of the churches. In addition, neither Congress nor the president was likely to approve payment of COs for their service. During the remaining months of peace and throughout the war, there was strong opposition to paying COs among political figures. Even Eleanor Roosevelt, who would later support COs at state mental hospitals, expressed opposition to payment of COs in a 1944 article in *Ladies' Home Journal* and her "My Day" columns.[38]

The peace churches were reluctant to take government funds for the operation of the CPS and were willing to accept Dykstra's advice to avoid asking Congress for an appropriation. As early as October 2, French had told Hershey that the Friends would probably prefer not to take government funds. At the October 5 meeting among the peace churches that formed what would become NSBRO, the sentiment was against accepting government funds: "It was declared that any program of work camps would cost heavily, but that we should attempt to strain ourselves to do it without government money. Conscription is likely to be of long duration and some kind of church-directed program should be started now and kept out of government hands. If government financial support is sought, there is bound to be political control of the work by the government, therefore we should try to finance the program ourselves."[39] On December 20, French wrote Dykstra that the groups involved with NSBRO would be willing to administer and pay for COs assigned to service projects on a six-month experimental basis.[40] The "experiment" was to last more than five years.

In cooperating with the government in arranging for alternative public service, the historic peace churches had in mind a wide range of activities, including humanitarian and relief projects designed to address human suffering at home and abroad. Government officials had in mind work projects modeled after the Civilian Conservation Corps (CCC), a public works program designed to put unemployed men to work under Roosevelt's New Deal.

On December 20, 1940, Dykstra sent President Roosevelt a memorandum outlining a plan for the assignment of COs to "civilian camps for soil conservation and reforestation work."[41] Dykstra's memo started out by indicating that no appropriation had been made by Congress for COs to perform work of national importance under civilian direction and referring to the "difficulties to both the armed services and the law enforcement agencies" presented by COs "far out of proportion to the numbers involved" during the previous war. Throughout the Civilian Public Service, first Dykstra and then Hershey consistently defended the program by arguing that it would spare the armed forces the practical and morale problems posed by men unwilling to serve in the military. Dykstra explained that the secretary of war, the secretary of agriculture, the secretary of the interior, and the director of the Selective Service had informally agreed on a five-point plan, subject to the president's approval:

1. The War Department would furnish cots, bedding, and camp equipment as feasible and necessary.

2. The Departments of Agriculture and the Interior would provide technical supervision for soil conservation and similar projects as well as tools and necessary equipment to the extent practicable.

3. The Federal Security Agency would cooperate and, if possible, make abandoned Civilian Conservation Corps camps available and perhaps tools and equipment.

4. The Selective Service would furnish general administrative and policy supervision and inspection and pay men's transportation costs to the camps.

5. The National Council for Conscientious Objectors, representing church groups, "has agreed for a temporary period to undertake the task of financing

and furnishing all other necessary parts of the program, including actual day-to-day supervision and control of the camps (under such rules and regulations and administrative supervision as is laid down by Selective Service), to supply subsistence, necessary buildings, hospital care, and generally all things necessary for the care and maintenance of the men." This point also indicated that admittance to the camps would not be dependent on membership in the church groups sponsoring them.

The memo added that the government could modify the program at any time or take it over entirely.

Dykstra sketched out what would become the program for "work of national importance under civilian direction" authorized by the Selective Training and Service Act of 1940. Although the specifics of the program would be modified over the years, the basic structure of the program—with responsibility spread among the Selective Service, religious groups, and agencies providing technical supervision of the work—would remain intact throughout the war and the aftermath. The only exception would be the establishment of government-operated camps beginning in 1943 to deal with problems encountered in the program.

On February 6, 1941, President Roosevelt issued Executive Order 8675, "Authorizing the Director of Selective Service to Establish or Designate Work of National Importance under Civilian Direction for Persons Conscientiously Opposed to Combatant and Noncombatant Service in the Land or Naval Forces of the United States."[42] The Executive Order gave the director of the Selective Service wide-ranging authority to determine work of national importance, make assignments to such work, use the services of other government agencies or accept the voluntary services of private organizations and individuals, and prescribe rules and regulations to carry out the president's order.

The Civilian Public Service program had been established. The first CPS camp was opened by the American Friends Service Committee at Patapsco State Forest outside of Baltimore on May 15, 1941—almost seven months before the declarations of war against Japan on December 8 and Germany on December 11.

2

"Religious Training and Belief"

In World War II, 10,110,104 men were drafted into the armed forces.[1] At least 37,000 draft-age men were exempted from combatant or military service as conscientious objectors, or COs, under the Selective Training and Service Act. At least 25,000 men served in noncombatant roles in the military under an "I-A-O" draft classification. The number of I-A-O objectors could have been as high as 50,000, although precise statistics were not kept.[2] Between 11,500 and 11,996 were classified as "IV-E" in the draft and assigned to perform alternative service in the Civilian Public Service.[3] An additional 6,086 men were imprisoned for failing to accept any form of service.[4]

◆　◆　◆

For most Americans, conscientious objection cannot be separated from opposition to specific wars and government policies. The growing unpopularity of the Iraq War was based not on moral opposition to war but on a lack of confidence in the reasons for going to war and in how it had been conducted. Iraq was increasingly viewed as the wrong war in the wrong place at the wrong time. Of course, the Iraq War was being fought by an "all-volunteer army," with the support of civilian contractors and a relatively small number of troops from other countries. There were few COs during the Iraq War. They were people who initially volunteered for military service and then decided, for one reason or another, that they could no longer participate in the war effort.

Even after more than thirty-five years, the Vietnam War lingers in the public consciousness and continues to serve as fodder in political debates. Vietnam seemed to define what it meant to be "antiwar." Hundreds of thousands of young men refused to enter the military. To be sure, Vietnam-era COs and war resisters included members of the historic peace churches. War was no more morally acceptable to Mennonites, Friends, and Brethren during Vietnam than during earlier wars. Yet in the Vietnam era, many COs did not come from churches with a pacifist history and did not even oppose war on grounds associated with organized religions. In *United States v. Seeger,* the Supreme Court ruled in 1965 that one did not have to profess belief in the existence of God to qualify as a conscientious objector.[5]

At least in the public arena, opposition to the Vietnam War was led by "New Left" intellectuals and students, "Old Left" radicals and pacifists, including World War II resisters such as A. J. Muste and David Dellinger, and activists from a church lacking a strong tradition of pacifism—Catholics. Religious opposition to the Vietnam War had a Catholic public face.

Inspired by Dorothy Day of the Catholic Workers and Catholic theologian Thomas Merton, the Berrigan brothers—Daniel, a Jesuit priest, and Philip, a Josephite priest—made national headlines and graced the covers of magazines such as *Time* for their protests against the Vietnam War.[6] In October 1967, Philip Berrigan along with Tom Lewis, David Ebenhardt, and Jim Mengel were arrested for pouring their blood over draft records in Baltimore. Then, in a 1968 incident receiving widespread national attention, the so-called Catonsville Nine— Daniel Berrigan, Philip Berrigan, David Dorst, John Hogan, Tom Lewis, Marjorie Melville, Thomas Melville, George Mische, and Mary Moylan—removed hundreds of draft records from a Selective Service office in Maryland and burned them with homemade napalm to protest the war.[7] In court, the defendants made statements later recorded in Daniel Berrigan's play *The Trial of the Catonsville Nine*. Daniel Berrigan stated:

> Our apologies good friends
> for the fracture of good order the burning of
> paper
> instead of children   the angering of the orderlies
> in the front parlor of the charnel house
> We could not so help us God do otherwise
> for we are sick at heart   our hearts
> give us no rest for thinking of
> the Land of
> Burning
> Children.[8]

The nine were convicted on November 9, 1968.

Gordon Zahn, a World War II CO who would later become a sociologist and author of a number of books on war and peace, explained the activism of the Berrigans as part of a "Great Catholic Upheaval" that questioned the Catholic Church's long-standing "just war" doctrine attributed to Saint Augustine and elaborated upon by Thomas Aquinas and others.[9] Under that doctrine, war was justified when certain conditions were met, and Christians should grant the "presumption of justice" to war-making authorities in cases of doubt. A 1983 pastoral letter from the U.S. bishops provided one of the clearest formulations of the just war doctrine:

There must be a *just cause*, a "real and present danger." Both Popes Pius XII and John XXIII added limitations that basically restrict "just" wars to wars of defense because of the nature of modern war;

Only a war declared and conducted by *competent (legitimate) authority* can be considered "just";

Comparative justice requires that, in the absence of a truly international authority, no state should assume or claim absolute justice for its cause;

There must be a *right intention* (always the search for a just peace);

War must be a *last resort*; all other options must have been tried and must have failed for war to be "just";

There must be reasonable *probability of success*;

Proportionality requires that the war's costs and harmful effects not be greater than the good to be achieved.

Only just means may be used—that is, strategies and weapons which *discriminate* between the guilt and the innocent (noncombatant immunity) and are limited so that no greater injury or harm is done (even to the guilty) than is necessary.[10]

Like the historic peace churches, Dorothy Day and the Catholic Workers movement had long opposed all war and the just war doctrine. As Day wrote in a 1969 reflection: "How can we show our love by war, by the extermination of our enemies? If we are followers of Christ, there is no room for speaking of the 'just war.' We have to remember that God loves all men, that God wills all men to be saved, that indeed all men are brothers. We must love the jailer as well as the one in prison. We must do that seemingly utterly impossible thing: love our enemy." The Catholic Workers' pacifism had a profound influence on the Berrigans: "More than any other institution or individual, the *Catholic Worker* movement influenced Dan and me, especially with its tradition of nonviolent direct action."[11]

Despite the prominence of the Berrigans and other Catholic activists in the antiwar movement in the Vietnam era, the Catholic hierarchy in the United States never embraced the Catholic Workers' position during the Vietnam era. Many bishops, in fact, expressed opposition to the Berrigans' protests and attempted to silence them, although the Catholic Church had become more open to conscientious objection after the Second Vatican Council.[12]

Many, if not most, antiwar protesters and COs during the Vietnam era were not pacifists in the strict sense of the term. Opposition to the Vietnam War was based not only, or always, on opposition to warfare but rather on opposition to that *specific* war. Even for radical pacifists like the Berrigans, there was an intensity and vehemence to the opposition to the Vietnam War, reflecting the nature of the war and the belief that the war grew out of long-standing injustices in the United

States. Philip Berrigan wrote: "The war in Southeast Asia was our country's paranoia and racism metastasized into genocidal madness. Not a mistake. Not a misunderstanding. A campaign to exterminate, not liberate, the Vietnamese. Vietnam was the Puritans hacking their Native American benefactors to pieces. Vietnam was the Christian church sanctioning the slave trade. Vietnam was dropping the atomic bomb on a country already on its knees."[13]

When the rate of draftees claiming CO status rises dramatically over the course of a war, it most likely reflects opposition to the specific war itself rather than changes in beliefs about war in general. Citing Selective Service statistics, Heather T. Frazier and John O'Sullivan reported striking increases in the percentage of draftees classified as COs during the Vietnam War:

> As the war in Vietnam heated up, and as opposition to it intensified, the ranks of conscientious objectors grew rapidly. In 1968, the number of selective service registrants classified as conscientious objectors rose to 8.5 percent of those inducted into the military. The following year it reached 13.5 percent, in 1970 25.6 percent, and in 1971 42.6 percent. In 1972, with the phasing down of American forces in Vietnam and the winding down of the draft, for the first time in history more men were classified as conscientious objectors, 33,041, than those inducted, 25,273.[14]

◆　◆　◆

World War II was different from Vietnam or Iraq. The war was not welcomed, by any means, but after Nazi aggression in Europe and the Japanese bombing of Pearl Harbor, it was not controversial. The nation rallied around the war effort, and citizens accepted sacrifices. There were no mass protests against the war.

Studs Terkel referred to World War II as "the good war," although he admitted that "the adjective 'good' mated to the noun 'war' is so incongruous." Terkel wrote: "The crowning irony lay in World War Two itself. It had been a different kind of war. 'It was not like your other wars,' a radio disk jockey reflected aloud. In his banality lay a wild kind of crazy truth. It was not fratricidal. It was not, most of us profoundly believed, 'imperialistic.' Our enemy was, patently, obscene: the Holocaust maker. It was one war that many who would have resisted 'your other wars' supported enthusiastically. It was a 'just war,' if there is any such animal." More recently, in the 2007 Public Broadcasting System series *The War*, Ken Burns characterized World War II as the "necessary war."[15]

The construct of a "good war" or "necessary war" becomes meaningful only when contrasted with the construct of a "bad war" or "unnecessary war." It was probably the nation's experience with Vietnam that has made memories of World

War II so popular among the American people. A nation whose confidence as the beacon of democracy had been shaken during the Vietnam era has welcomed reminders that it had saved the world by defeating the forces of fascism during World War II.

Not only is World War II remembered as a good, just, or necessary war, but the persons who planned, fought, and supported it are also nostalgically thought of as heroes who confronted the forces of evil and won. This sentiment is captured by the titles of former NBC News anchor Tom Brokaw's books *The Greatest Generation* and *The Greatest Generation Speaks: Letters and Reflections*. Brokaw did not attempt to hide his profound admiration and respect for those who fought the war and supported the war effort:

> These men and women came of age in the Great Depression, when economic despair hovered over the land like a plague. They had watched their parents lose their businesses, their farms, their jobs, their hopes. They had learned to accept a future that played out one day at a time. Then, just as there was a glimmer of economic recovery, war exploded across Europe and Asia. When Pearl Harbor made it irrefutably clear that America was not a fortress, this generation was summoned to the parade ground and told to train for war. . . .
>
> They answered the call to help save the world from the two most powerful and ruthless military machines ever assembled, instruments of conquest in the hands of fascist maniacs.
>
> They faced great odds and a late start, but they did not protest.[16]

If the men and women who served in the military or supported the war from home in "the good war" represented "the greatest generation," then what are we to make of those who not only refused to bear arms but would not even support the troops in nonviolent ways during World War II? To understand the majority of COs in World War II and the churches that supported them, one cannot view them in terms of a good or bad, just or unjust, or necessary or unnecessary war. Nor can one view them through the lens of antiwar movements during the Vietnam or Iraq wars.

◆   ◆   ◆

Pacifists are not all alike in their philosophies. Although the historic peace churches shared a commitment to pacifism and collaborated in the CPS before and during World War II, the three major churches—the Friends, Mennonites, and Brethren— had significantly different religious philosophies and traditions. Even within the peace churches there were separate branches that had different customs, if not belief systems.

The Mennonites and Brethren, as well as the Hutterites (Moravians), traced their roots to the Anabaptist reformation in Europe, and specifically Switzerland, Germany, Austria, and Holland, in the sixteenth century.[17] Among the beliefs of the Anabaptists ("rebaptizers") was that baptism should occur only upon confession of faith, since the Bible did not mention infant baptism. This, among other things, placed the Anabaptists at odds with both the Catholic Church and the Protestant Reformation initiated by Martin Luther, John Calvin, and Huldrych Zwingli.

The beginning of the Mennonite Church is set at 1525 in Zurich, Switzerland, when a group of adults refused to have their children baptized, in defiance of a decree by the city council, and baptized each other. The name of the religion comes from Menno Simons, a Dutch Catholic priest who had joined the Anabaptists in 1536.

Mennonites migrated to the United States and Canada in the eighteenth and nineteenth centuries and settled first in Pennsylvania. The largest number of Mennonites can be found today, as during World War II, in Pennsylvania, Ohio, Indiana, and Kansas.

Since the first half of the twentieth century, there have been a relatively large number of separate Mennonite conferences, which change as branches merge or split apart. Titus William Bender reported that twelve Mennonite branches participated in the CPS. Brethren M. R. Zigler, who would become the chairman of NSBRO, recalled that seven Mennonite branches were present at a 1940 meeting to discuss formal cooperation among the three peace churches. The roster of men at the CPS unit at Mount Pleasant, Iowa (Unit 86), sponsored by the Mennonite Central Committee during World War II, included these groups: Old Mennonite, General Conference Mennonite, Church of God in Christ Mennonite, Mennonite Brethren, and Full Gospel.[18] Other units had Conservative Mennonites, Mennonite Brethren in Christ, Amish Mennonites, and Old Order Amish Mennonites. The Mennonite conferences varied in their beliefs, traditions, and lifestyles.

The Amish are related to but separate from the Mennonites. They broke from the Swiss Brethren Mennonites in the late 1600s and were named after their leader, Jacob Amman. The Amish are known for their simple lifestyle, plain clothes, and rejection of technology. The Amish made the national news in October 2006 when a gunman broke into West Mines Amish School and brutally murdered five young girls. The compassion of the Amish community in offering condolences and aid to the wife and family of the murderer has been heralded by Mennonites as a "teaching moment for all of us who seek to be true followers of Christ."[19] In contrast to the Amish, most Mennonites today do not seek to avoid involvement in society and the rest of the world.

Since the sixteenth century, Mennonites have renounced war and violence. A key principle of faith among Mennonites has been "nonresistance," from Christ's teaching "Resist not evil." This principle is radically different from the principle of nonviolent resistance practiced by Gandhi and others. Especially in the World War II era, nonresistance was apolitical and meant that Mennonites should avoid confrontation with and active involvement in the state.[20] A 1943 statement of the Mennonite Central Committee read: "The Mennonites do not consider themselves 'pacifists' in the accepted modern sense of the term, since these groups frequently base their philosophy and action programs on humanitarian or general moral and religious considerations, rather than exclusively on the New Testament, and since they often resort to political activity and pressure in their efforts to attain their objectives."[21]

In contrast to the Friends and other pacifists, Mennonites did not oppose conscription during the war as long as they were not required to serve in the military. The Mennonite position before and during the war was that the church was against conscription but would not refuse to cooperate with it.[22] This position later shifted from political nonresistance to active opposition to all forms of militarism, including conscription.

When Amos S. Horst testified before the House Committee on Military Affairs in 1940, he presented a written statement containing a resolution adopted by the Mennonite Conference the previous year. The resolution stated, "We are constrained as followers of Christ to abstain from all forms of military service and all means of support of war," and listed a series of specific commitments: no part in carnal warfare or conflict between nations or strife between classes, groups, or individuals; no involvement during wartime with civilian organizations temporarily allied with the military in the prosecution of war; no part in the financing of war bonds or contributions in support of military efforts; no participation in the manufacture of munitions or weapons; no involvement in military training; no activity that tends to promote ill will or hatred among nations; and no pursuit of profit out of war. A portion of the resolution titled "Our Attitude During Wartime" endorsed commitments to peace and nonresistance: "If our country becomes involved in war, we shall endeavor to continue to live in a quiet and peaceable life in all godliness and honesty; avoid joining in the wartime hysteria of hatred, revenge and retaliation, manifest a meek and submissive spirit, being obedient unto the laws and regulations of the government in all things, except in such cases where obedience to the government would cause us to violate the teachings of the Scriptures so that we could maintain a clear conscience before God (Acts 5:29)."[23]

The Mennonites have a long tradition of mutual aid, not only to fellow Mennonites but to all peoples. The front page of the February 16, 2007, issue of the

Syracuse Post-Standard had this headline: "Storm-Struck Mexico Is Blessed by Mennonites." Mexico is located north of the city of Syracuse in the Snow Belt region of upper central New York. Lake-effect snow dumps on this area. Mennonites from throughout the region, which does not have a large Mennonite population, came to Mexico to shovel snow off the roofs of farmers' barns so that they would not collapse under the snow's weight. One Mennonite said, "It's as much a blessing for us as those we help."

In 1922, the Mennonite Central Committee was established to coordinate mutual-aid efforts.[24] In the fall of 1940, Orie Miller informed the other peace churches that the MCC would represent all Mennonites in NSBRO and would administer Mennonite CPS camps and units.[25] The MCC also agreed to represent the Old Order Amish, who did not have a conference in the Mennonite Church.[26] Conservative Mennonites would later accuse Orie Miller as well as "liberal Old Mennonites" and "liberal General Conference Mennonites" of dominating the MCC and imposing an "ecumenical" atmosphere in Mennonite camps and units.[27] G. Richard Culp argued: "Orie O. Miller had claimed, in the Chicago MCC meeting, that 'the government does not wish to deal with more than one organization representing the Mennonites.' This gave him a free hand to mix Mennonites of all shades of doctrine and belief in the camps. Thus Old Order Amish, Old Order Mennonites, Old Mennonites, General Conference Mennonites, and Mennonite Brethren were thrown together. As indicated previously, the positions of influence were filled by the more educated Old Mennonites and General Conference Mennonites."[28]

Culp's position was endorsed by a number of conservative Mennonites, including Wilbert Kropf, bishop of the Western Conservative Mennonite Fellowship, who wrote: "Bro Culp has given a true picture of the ruinous result of becoming organizationally involved with liberal programs." Despite these criticisms of Miller and the MCC, there is little evidence of discord within MCC camps and units, which ran extremely smoothly in comparison with AFSC, Brethren Service Committee, and government-administered camps. While a CO at Hudson River State Hospital in Poughkeepsie, New York, Culp wrote a summary of his experiences at the unit.[29] He commented that religious life was often crowded out by other things and recommended that conservative and liberal Mennonites have separate units, but did not describe any problems among men within the Poughkeepsie unit.

The Church of the Brethren traces its origins to Schwarzenau, Germany, where it was founded in 1708 under the leadership of Alexander Mack.[30] Like the Mennonites, the Brethren practiced rebaptism of adults who had been baptized in other faiths, in the tradition of Anabaptism. The Brethren were often referred to as

the Dunkards up until the middle of the twentieth century. "Dunkards" was originally a derogatory name that referred to the practice of total immersion during
baptism. Zigler stated that representatives of five Brethren branches participated
in a critical 1940 meeting among the historic peace churches.[31] At least one branch
continued to use Dunkard in its name.

The Brethren first came to the United States in 1719. The first congregation of
twenty families settled in Germantown, Pennsylvania. In 1729, another 120 Brethren, including founder Alexander Mack, joined the original group. In the 1700s,
Brethren settled throughout the East Coast and by the mid-1800s had spread to
midwestern and other states.

Especially in their early years, the Brethren's religious philosophy was similar
to the Mennonites. The Brethren believed in peace and nonresistance. According
to Albert N. Keim and Grant M. Stoltzfus, peace for the Brethren meant "opposition to war, no coercion in religion, and no litigation in court." In a 1918 statement,
the Church of the Brethren pledged its obedience to government, as long as government acted in accord with the Word of God: "We are taught that Governments
are ordained of God, and that the administrators of Government are ministers of
God. As such we are to be in subjection to them. . . . The word and authority of
God, however, must be final and supreme overall. And when the demands of men
and of government conflict with the Word of God, we are then bound by the latter,
regardless of consequences."[32]

Between World War I and World War II, the position of the Church of the
Brethren shifted from nonresistance to nonviolent resistance.[33] By 1938, the church
pledged its commitment to influencing the government, especially in matters of
peace and war: "We ought to labor constantly to put the ideals of Christ into our
government." As Carl D. Bowman put it, "Quite simply, traditional nonresistance
had required Brethren to wash the dirt of the world's streets from their feet. Yet
now that they were spending more time in those streets, they worried less about
washing and more about clean streets."[34] The Brethren would no longer try to be
separate from the affairs of government.

In a statement before the House Committee on Military Affairs in 1940, Paul
H. Bowman presented the position of the Church of the Brethren. He first mentioned the close association between the Brethren and the Mennonites and Society
of Friends, "especially our work for world peace and the relief of human suffering." Explaining the position of the Brethren on their relationship with the state,
he stated, "The Brethren regard their supreme citizenship as being in the commonwealth of God to which they yield their greatest loyalty, but they do accept
constructive and creative leadership in the state. They exercise the right of suffrage
and approve the holding of public office where principles of love and nonviolence

are not violated. Political government is regarded as ordained of God through the collective judgment of its citizenry but the Brethren deny the right of the majority to conscript or suppress the consciences of the minority."[35]

The Brethren Service Committee was formed in 1939 to coordinate the church's peace and relief efforts. The BSC was later assigned responsibility for administering the Brethren's CPS camps. The types of alternative service acceptable to the Brethren were relief to war sufferers, relief of refugees, reconstruction of war-stricken areas, refugee resettlement, reclamation and forestry, relief and reconstruction in the United States, medical and health service, and farm service.[36]

The origin of the Religious Society of Friends—best known as the Quakers, originally a derogatory term that has come into common usage—is traced to George Fox in 1652 in England.[37] Like the Mennonites and Brethren, there are different branches of Friends. According to Zigler, five branches of Friends participated in the 1940 meeting among the historic peace churches.[38] The main difference among Friends is whether their congregations hold "programmed" or "unprogrammed" meetings. Programmed meetings are held under the leadership of a pastor, whereas unprogrammed meetings are held among worshipers who wait quietly for messages from God.

The migration of Friends to the United States began soon after the founding of the religion. The role of Philadelphia Quakers in the Pennsylvania colony and the establishment of the United States is well known in American history. Under William Penn, Pennsylvania established a reputation for acceptance and tolerance. Penn welcomed the Mennonites, Brethren, and other persecuted religious groups in Europe to settle in Pennsylvania. As early as 1688, Quakers in Germantown protested American slavery.[39] Starting in the mid-1700s, the Friends spread from the East Coast to the Midwest and eventually states across the country.

The Friends did not have churchwide doctrines or organize general conferences to communicate the "church's position."[40] The core religious construct of the Friends was the "Inner Light," the belief that within each person there is a "light" that reflects Christ himself. Christ exists within all people.[41] Friends could experience the will of God through inner searching. As Mulford Q. Sibley and Philip E. Jacob wrote, for Friends, God works through an informed mind and sensitive conscience.[42]

If Christ—God—exists in every person, then the value of all human beings must be respected. This underlies the Friends' long-standing commitment to pacifism. In the 1940 Senate Military Affairs Committee hearings, Harold Evans testified, "For almost 300 years the Society of Friends, commonly called Quakers, have maintained their testimony against all war and for freedom of conscience and religious liberty. They have believed that lasting good can be accomplished not by war and violence but only by service and an appeal to the divine spark in the life of every man. . . . Especially have they been opposed to military conscription, because it violates their deep-seated belief in the sacredness of the personality of every individual and of the principles which Jesus lived and taught."[43]

Because Friends experienced God directly through inner searching, however, then a person could rely on individual conscience to decide to participate in the military, according to many Friends.[44] During World War II, Brand Blanshard, the head of the Department of Philosophy and Religion at the Friends' Swarthmore College, received national publicity when he argued that an extreme emphasis on pacifism was inconsistent with Quakerism: "What the Light reveals is left to the individual conscience; it is not imposed on us from outside. If this is correct, the attempt to prescribe the pacifist dogma is clearly inconsistent with that tolerance which the great doctrine implies."[45]

Historically, the Friends have not believed in a clear separation between the secular and the religious. The Friends have long been involved in public matters and the affairs of the state and have actively tried to change government policies. Their belief in resisting immoral government policies and actions stood in contrast to the Mennonite principle of nonresistance during World War II. The contrast in these stances would be seen in the actions of CPS units sponsored by these churches during the war.

Like the Mennonites and Brethren, the Friends had a long history of involvement in relief work. Friends could give "testimony" to God through acts aimed at alleviating the suffering of other human beings. In 1917, the American Friends Service Committee was established to coordinate Friends' relief efforts. Rufus Jones, who was later instrumental in the establishment of the CPS, was the first chairman of the American Friends Service Committee.

The AFSC administered the CPS program on behalf of the Friends. Although the AFSC opposed conscription, it supported cooperation in constructive public service:

> The participation of the American Friends Service Committee in the Civilian Public Service does not imply its approval of conscription. We continue to believe that the entire war system, including its conscription of our lives and service of men, is morally wrong.
>
> We recognize a responsibility, however, for something more than protest. . . . We believe that the provisions of the Selective Training and Service Act of 1940 regarding the treatment of conscientious objectors, although they do not provide full recognition of conscience, do represent a real advance over the legal provisions made during the first world war, and have gone far towards maintaining

our country's democratic heritage of religious freedom throughout the extent of this war.[46]

Various branches of the peace churches raised funds for the respective service committees. The MCC listed eighteen conferences, including the General Conference of Mennonites, the Old Order Amish, the Conservative Amish Mennonites, the General Conference of Mennonites, and the Old Order Mennonites, that donated money to the MCC for the CPS.[47]

As the CPS wore on, a handful of other religious groups joined the peace churches in sponsoring camps and units. By the end of the CPS, two units were sponsored by the Methodist World Peace Commission, two by the American Baptist Home Mission Society, one by the Disciples of Christ, one by the Committee on Christian Social Action of the Evangelical and Reformed Church, and four by the Association of Catholic Conscientious Objectors.

The Methodist Church was not a pacifist church, but a sizable number of COs in the CPS were Methodists. The Methodist Church of America's position adopted in 1939 held that the government should not compel individual Methodist conscientious objectors to perform military service:

> The Methodist Church, true to the principles of the New Testament, teaches respect for properly constituted civil authority. It holds that government rests upon the support of its conscientious citizenship, and that conscientious objectors to war in any or all of its manifestations are a natural outgrowth of the principle of good will and the Christian desire for universal peace; and that such objectors should not be oppressed by compulsory military service anywhere or at any time. We ask and claim exemption from all forms of military preparation or service for all conscientious objectors who may be members of the Methodist Church.[48]

At least some Baptist and Evangelical and Reformed churches held a similar position. On May 23, 1936, the Northern Baptist Convention indicated: "We reaffirm our belief in the right of conscience to refuse to bear arms or submit to military training." Similarly, the International Convention of the Disciples of Christ endorsed the right of individuals to exercise conscience on war in 1939: "As a free and democratic fellowship, the Disciples of Christ recognize the right of individuals to follow their own consciences in matters of practical conduct. Inasmuch as convinced Christian pacifists constitute an unpopular and misunderstood minority, we reaffirm at this time our respect for them and their position, and pledge our assistance to any who may face persecution or privation because of their pacifist convictions."[49]

The Association of Catholic Conscientious Objectors was independent of the Roman Catholic hierarchy. The vast majority of American Catholics were hostile toward COs. The ACCO was closely identified with the Catholic Workers. According to Gordon Zahn, the ACCO was the "organizational front" for the movement's peace activities. Dorothy Day's and the Catholic Workers' pacifism was based on the Sermon on the Mount and Christ's campaign to love God, neighbor, and self.[50] Although Day did not believe in the CPS and opposed cooperation with conscription, she did not stand in the way of those individuals organizing the ACCO.[51] In fact, the Catholic Workers provided financial and moral support to the ACCO. The letterhead of the ACCO listed its address as Mott Street, where the Catholic Workers were located, and Dorothy Day as a member of its Advisory Council.

Each of the churches and religious groups sponsoring CPS units had a distinct philosophy underlying its opposition to war. The sentiments of individual COs were not necessarily the same as the bodies supporting them.

◆   ◆   ◆

World War II conscientious objectors were incredibly diverse, representing more than 120 and as many as 200 churches and religious denominations as well as nonreligious persons.[52] Their backgrounds and philosophies varied greatly from each other.

During the war, there were 6,422 county-based draft boards responsible for inducting men into the military or granting exemptions from service.[53] Of the many millions of men registering for the draft, a minuscule number—72,354—applied for noncombatant or civilian public service.[54] An estimated 37,000 were eventually granted CO status by their draft boards. The remaining claimants were either found to be physically or mentally unfit for military service or inducted into the military.

To be classified as a CO, men had to file the "Special Form for Conscientious Objector" (DSS Form 47).[55] On the form, the registrant first (Series I) had to claim exemption from combatant service, being willing to participate in noncombatant service (I-A-O classification), or any form of service under the direction of military authorities (IV-E). This was followed by a long series of questions about the registrant's beliefs and backgrounds, including:

1. Describe the nature of your belief that is the basis of your claim made in Series I above.

2. Explain how, when, and from whom or from what sources you received the training and acquired the belief that is the basis of your claim made in Series I above.

3. Give the name and present address of the individual upon whom you rely most for religious guidance.

4. Under what circumstances, if any, do you believe in the use of force?

5. Describe the actions and behavior in your life that in your opinion most conspicuously demonstrate the consistency and depth of your religious convictions.

6. Have you ever given public expression, written or oral, to the views herein expressed as the basis for your claim made in Series I above? If so, specify when and where.

7. Have you ever been a member of any military organization or establishment? If so, state the name and address of same and give reasons you became a member.

8. Are you a member of a religious sect or organization? (Yes or No) . . .

9. Describe your relationships with and activities in all organizations with which you are or have been affiliated, other than religious or military.

10. Give the names and other information indicated concerning persons who could supply information as to the sincerity of your professed convictions against participation in war.

Each local draft board judged CO claims differently. Some draft boards, especially the ones located in communities with large concentrations of Mennonites, Brethren, and Friends, were sympathetic toward COs and granted exemptions liberally. Jack Allen, a Friend CO drafted from Moorestown, New Jersey, explained that his draft board included Quakers and friends of his. Other draft boards were unsympathetic or even hostile toward COs. Neil Hartman, a Methodist who later became a Quaker, was drafted from Cedarville, Ohio. He recalled that his draft board viewed left-wing students at nearby Antioch College as "Communists" and was not inclined to approve CO exemptions. Like several thousand other COs, Hartman's claim was denied, and he had to pursue appeals established by the Selective Training and Service Act before his exemption was approved. Catholic Gordon Zahn from Milwaukee, Wisconsin, also had to appeal his draft board's decision before being granted an exemption. His local board included a Catholic pastor who believed that no Catholic could be a conscientious objector. In 1941, Selective Service director Hershey had overruled his own appeal panel's determination that Catholics could not be COs since the church had no official teaching on pacifism.[56]

According to a breakdown of the religious affiliations of CPS men compiled by NSBRO, the largest number by far were Mennonites: 4,665, or almost 39 percent.[57] Members of the Church of the Brethren totaled 1,353 men, or roughly 11 percent of the CPS. The Society of Friends had 951 men in the CPS, or nearly 8 percent of the total. After the historic peace churches, the Methodists had the largest number of men in the CPS: 673. The remainder of the CPS included men from religions rang-ing from the well known to the obscure.

Quite apart from their specific religions, CPS men fell into five broad categories according to their backgrounds and philosophies. "Born-and-Raised Peace Church Objectors" included men who had grown up pacifist as members of historic peace churches. For many members of traditional Friend, Mennonite, and Brethren com-munities, conscientious objection was the natural course of action. Friend Stuart Palmer explained why he had entered the CPS: "I'm a Birthright Quaker. . . . It was pretty much expected from the beginning." Birthright Friends were those born of two Friends parents and who were automatically accepted into their par-ents' meetings at birth. Old Order Amish Mennonite Uriah Mast explained why he became a CO: "Oh, I would say probably the knowledge I had of the teaching of the church. . . . And then the parents' feeling that this was the right thing to do. . . . But as far as having deep religious convictions from the Bible, I couldn't quite say that. It was mostly deep religious convictions which were embedded in my back-ground of the family and the church really. . . . I more or less took the attitude that if you belong to the Amish church, then you comply to Amish rules." Mennonite John Hostetler gave a similar reason for joining the CPS: "It was the knowledge that it was the right thing to do, of course, which came from experience with my church, my local church, and the teaching I'd received."[58]

After the war, CO Gordon Zahn received his Ph.D. in sociology from Catholic University in 1953. His dissertation was titled "A Descriptive Study of the Social Backgrounds of Conscientious Objectors in Civilian Public Service During World War II."[59] Like other sociologists who studied the COs,[60] Zahn viewed conscien-tious objection as a form of social deviance. He distinguished between "'encour-aged deviants' (men who took the conscientious objector stand in response to pressures initiated by their religious community or who received definite support in their stand from that community) and 'resister deviants' (men who took the conscientious objector stand without the benefit of such support)."[61]

Especially in the 1940s and '50s, the sociological construct of deviance car-ried a negative meaning and tended to be overly simplistic.[62] It implied that the sociologist could identify societal norms by examining government laws or pub-lic opinion and then tag violators of those norms as deviant. In a pluralistic and heterogeneous country, laws and public opinion do not necessarily reflect societal norms or agreed-upon rules for living and acting in civil society, but rather the influences of dominant groups or power structures. Otherwise, any ethnic or reli-gious minority could be deemed deviant.

Despite the shortcomings of the sociological construct of deviance, Zahn's dis-tinction is useful for understanding how members of different religious groups responded to wartime fervor and public and political support for conscription during World War II. Some men were surrounded by family members and religious communities who expected or supported the rejection of military service. Others went against the grain in expressing conscientious objection to entering the military.

Zahn's concept of "encouraged deviants" fitted "Born-and-Raised Peace Church Objectors." In various degrees, the Mennonites, Brethren, and Friends provided community support—and in some cases exerted social pressure—for young men to become COs. The CO position was affirmed in their families and communities, religious and otherwise. Zahn argued that the Mennonites represented the extreme form of encouraged deviance, with the Brethren next in order. With their religion's emphasis on individual conscience and resistance to doctrine, many Friends could choose noncombatant or even combatant service without facing ostracism from their communities. The Friend CO would be supported by his meeting, but many young men took a different course of action without jeopardizing their standing in the church.

The Church of the Brethren had consistently held that "all war is sin." The 1935 "Restatement Concerning War and Peace" reiterated this stance. In 1939, although the church again stated that "one who enlisted in military service is not in full accord with the faith and practice of the general brotherhood," it also preached "brotherly love and forbearance" for Brethren who entered the military.[63] Brethren who served in the military could remain members of the church.

Many Mennonites received strong expectations to follow the church's pacifist teachings. Ivan Amstutz, an Old Mennonite, stated that even noncombatant service was "really out of the question" because it was "kind of frowned on." Paul Frank Webb reported on an interview with the wife of a Mennonite man who served as a medical corpsman during World War II and was shunned by his community, eventually leaving the religion. John Hostetler recalled that two-to-one members of his community went into the CPS and that the ones who went into the military lost their membership in the church.[64]

Despite their religions' traditions of pacifism, a sizable number of Mennonites, Brethren, and especially Friends entered the military during the war. The draft census study of Mennonites inducted prior to December 1944 by the Mennonite Central Committee found that 45.9 percent entered the CPS, 14.5 percent accepted noncombatant service under the I-A-O classification, and 39.6 percent served in the regular military, although there was wide variation among different Mennonite conferences and districts.[65] In contrast to the dominant Mennonite philosophy, some individual churches even encouraged entrance into the military. Loris Habegger, a member of the Mennonite General Conference from Beine, Indiana, reported that his pastor preached that the I-A-O classification in the medical corps was the "Mennonite Way." Marvin Wasser, whose brother served as a bombardier during the war, recalled that ten of the twelve men drafted from his church chose to enter the military, and only two entered the CPS.[66]

Of the Brethren in the 1940s, Carl Bowman reported, "In spite of strong denominational statement against war, 80% of young Brethren opt for combatant military service; only 10% choose alternative service." Allen Smith described the dismay of pacifist Friends when roughly 90 percent of eligible men served in the armed forces during World War II. Paul Comly French reported on a survey of 8,460 draft-age men at 600 Friends meetings.[67] Only 560 men (6.62 percent) entered the CPS, while 620 (7.33 percent) entered the military under an I-A-O noncombatant classification and 40 (0.47 percent) went to prison. A total of 5,012 (59.24 percent) entered the military. The rest were deferred for other reasons.

When men from the historic peace churches entered the military, it was not so much individual deviation from the main teachings of their churches. Rather, it tended to reflect the influences of the men's congregations, or branches or meetings, as well as their families. Culp, who was critical of liberal Mennonite conferences, reported that the "plain" Mennonite groups—the Old Order Mennonites, Old Order Amish, Holdeman Mennonites, Reformed Mennonites, and Hutterites—all had more than 90 percent of their young men in CPS camps, whereas only one conference among the Old Mennonites, the "plainest" and "strictest in the country," reached the 90 percent figure.[68] Although Mennonites, in particular, who accepted an I-A or I-A-O classification might be shunned by traditional conferences or congregations, the opposite was not true. Even in the most worldly or mainstream congregations, COs from the peace churches tended to be accepted and supported by their families and churches. They were not criticized for following the CPS path. This was what made the peace churches different from most other religions.

"Convinced Peace Church Objectors" were those men, overwhelmingly Friends, who had converted to a peace church. In contrast to "Birthright Friends," "Convinced Friends" had joined the Religious Society of Friends because they were attracted to its spiritual teachings or social activism. Many of them were drawn to the Friends because of the religion's tradition of pacifism.

Convinced Friends found support for their conscientious objection among their congregations, or meetings, but often experienced disapproval or even rejection by their own families. Warren Sawyer grew up as a non-Friend in Aurora, New York, but had become a Quaker as a young adult. For more than three years, he served at a CPS unit at Byberry, Philadelphia State Hospital, in Pennsylvania. In letters written to his aunts during his time in the CPS, he described the often stormy relationship with his father, who had remarried and moved to Philadelphia. On October 25, 1942, he wrote:

> On my day off this week I went thru quite a siege. Of course, I was at dad's and I am glad that this came to a head. . . . I said we were working for world brotherhood, etc., and dad flew right there. He asked me if I really thought that I could have a brotherhood with the Germans, those dirty, rotten stinking bastards, he said. Of course my answer was that there is that of God in every man and a few other quotations such as "Love thy neighbor." That made him hotter. Then I proceeded to point out that . . . Hitler is a by-product of the stupidity of the allies of the last war. He proceeded to tell me that we must hold them down tighter so that they will never rise again. I suggested that this country is then defeating the very thing for which it is fighting, democracy. They preach democracy but do not give it to others. There he hit the ceiling. He told me, "If you ever mention the dirty stinking rats in this house again I shall kick you out and chase you around the block."[69]

"Nonpacifist Church Religious Objectors" included men who came from religions that accepted conscientious objection as an act of individual conscience, such as the Methodist Church, and those religions that did not. For these men, conscientious objection was an act of individual conscience based on their interpretation of the Bible or spiritual teaching.

Harold Barton was a Baptist from Eugene, Oregon, who also served at Byberry and would become one of the leaders of the COs' mental health reform movement. He explained his reason for becoming a CO: "By association and training in the First Baptist Churches of *Grants Pass*, Oregon, *Medford*, Oregon, *Eugene*, Oregon and *Butte*, Montana had resulted in my becoming a deeply convinced objector to war based on New Testament Christian Teachings. Under no stretch of the imagination could I envisage Jesus putting on a military uniform. As His follower it was equally impossible for me." Evert Bartholomew described himself as a very religious Methodist who became a CO because of his religious beliefs: "If I was going to believe that Jesus was my mentor, I could not have gone to war."[70]

Some men based their opposition to war on a combination of religious belief and political philosophy. Many members of the Fellowship of Reconciliation, a religious pacifist society founded in Great Britain, objected to war on general religious and political grounds.[71] Samuel Burgess, who was a Unitarian and later became a Friend, explained his position:

> I became convinced [that] one of the prime causes of war was economic, and I became a convinced socialist, and soon joined the Socialist Party. I also started attending meetings of the world-wide religious pacifist organization, the

Fellowship of Reconciliation, and soon joined, a membership that I have maintained to this day. . . .

. . . Then in College, we found many sympathetic students at the Brown Christian Association, and my opinions which had been mostly political and a matter of personal morality, now became more and more centered on personal religious convictions.

The conclusion that I reached was that war is just plain wrong, and military service is immoral. It is wrong to kill anyone, and this goes for capital punishment, as well. To accept the uniform of a military organization is to become part of the killing machine, whether or not you actually carry and fire a gun. Therefore, I could not accept the concept of service in the medical corps or the chaplain corps. Military service is inconsistent with any religious principle I hold. It is directly contrary to the words and spirit of Christ.[72]

COs from nonpacifist religions had varied experiences with their families and churches. Some were accepted or at least tolerated; others were rejected. According to M. R. Zigler, many mainstream religions were antagonistic to COs: "I'll say this word: that even to today I would rather go to Congress to get consideration for the conscientious objector on a religious basis than I would the National Council of Churches representing 32 major denominations."[73]

"Secular Objectors" constituted a striking minority among members of the CPS, especially in view of the fact that the Selective Training and Service Act required that COs demonstrate "religious training and belief" as the basis for their conscientious objection. Methodist Evert Bartholomew remembered a group of agnostic secular humanists in the CPS and questioned how they got their CO classification. Bartholomew was influenced by these men and eventually became a secular humanist himself, although he also retired to a Friends continuing-care community and considered himself a "Quaker fellow-traveler."[74]

Secular objectors were a diverse group of men who opposed war, or at least World War II, on a broad range of political and philosophical grounds.[75] They included socialists, anarchists, adherents to Gandhi's philosophy of nonviolence, and what some COs referred to as "oddballs."[76] CO J. Benjamin Stalvey recalled meeting quite a few COs who professed no religion at a CPS camp, including Aaron Orange, an active socialist, who proclaimed, "Marxism is my religion."[77]

The War Resisters League, which was founded in 1923, represented the "secular and left wings of the pacifist movement" prior to and during World War II.[78] Many of the most radical COs in the CPS and those men who chose to go to prison were members of the WRL.

Many secular objectors did not reject religion. Rather, their conscientious objection was not based, first and foremost, on religion. Nathaniel Hoffman, a

Jewish CO, explained the influence of the War Resisters League on his beliefs: "Joining the War Resisters League at that time, and the fact that many of them were Jewish—although they weren't drawing on that necessarily—gave me a center which was actively opposed to war, actively helping COs. Without that, I don't know that I would have known how to or would have had the strength to push ahead on my own."[79]

Another Jewish CO, Leonard Edelstein, was one of the four men at the AFSC Byberry mental hospital unit in Philadelphia who initiated the national mental health reform movement. An obituary published in the June 11, 2006, *San Francisco Chronicle* reported that he had died on June 2 at the age of ninety: "Notable: Attended the 1929 Boy Scout Jamboree in England, where he became lifelong friends with Kioshi Yagi of Japan, who inspired his commitment to pacifism and declaration of conscientious objection during WWII." The obituary was published for Leonard Cornell. Edelstein had changed his name after the war: "Loved the graciousness and human-ness of the Friends, intensely disliked the 'Brotherly Love' of Philadelphia which my wife Betty and I experienced in seeking housing while I was acting as Executive Director of the National Mental Health Program. Hence the name change from Edelstein to Cornell."[80]

Like other "resister deviants" whose stance was not based on membership in a historic peace church, secular COs often perplexed, embarrassed, or angered their families.[81] Hoffman recalled his family's reaction: "It was almost a total inability to understand how a Jewish person could not go along with what the country needed, or Jewish people needed, in terms of what Hitler was doing. I can't say that I was supported, but I was a favored son, and they were embarrassed by it, quite embarrassed, but didn't take any active opposition." Edward Burrows, raised Episcopal and Presbyterian from South Carolina, described his parents' response when a newspaper reported that he was one of two COs registered in the state: "They were horrified."[82]

"Nonpacifist Religious Objectors" represented the final group of COs and war resisters. These men were members of religions that did not renounce force or war but had other reasons for opposing military service in World War II. Jehovah's Witnesses rejected both pacifism and conscientious objection, but claimed that they should be exempted as ministers, since all were expected to preach the Word of God.[83] For Jehovah's Witnesses, the only battle they could participate in was Armageddon. Although a sizable number of Jehovah's Witnesses, 409, did enter the CPS, many more chose to go to prison rather than perform military or civilian public service. Of the 4,363 men sentenced to prison for refusing military or civilian public service as of June 30, 1944, 3,079 were Jehovah's Witnesses.[84]

Another nonpacifist religious group that opposed military service during the war was composed of African American Muslims who believed that World War II did not represent a "holy war" consistent with the teachings of the Koran.[85] NSBRO did not report statistics on African American COs in the CPS, but did indicate that 155 members of Muslim groups were prosecuted for refusing military or civilian public service as of June 30, 1944.[86] The AFSC reported under "Reasons for Conviction," as of December 7, 1943, 141 "Negro Moslems claiming allegiance to 'Islam,' and similar sects." A May 1, 1943, *Time* article on the draft referred to "Negro 'Moslems'" as the "most exotic group of convicted objectors." At least some African American Muslims did choose to enter the CPS. Albert N. Keim published a photo of Aleem Whitson, wearing a tattered sweater, and identified him as a "Negro Moslem" at an AFSC camp at Merom, Indiana, in his 1990 book. The CPS directory published by the National Interreligious Service Board for Conscientious Objectors, formerly NSBRO, listed a Nazeer Aleem. Aleem was identified as a Muslim from Cleveland, Ohio, who served at Merom, Indiana, and three other CPS units. A picture of Aleem appeared first in a photo album of members of the AFSC unit at New Hampshire State Hospital.[87] Aleem, who bore a striking resemblance to "Whitson" in Keim's book, was neatly dressed in a white shirt and tie.

Catholic COs who viewed World War II as an unjust war as well as followers of Catholic priest and radio personality Charles Coughlin and his fascist views would be included in this group of nonpacifist religious objectors. As Zahn noted, the Coughlinites would have felt morally compelled to go to war against the Soviet Union.[88] COs identified with the Catholic Workers, like Zahn, were inclined to be pacifists who opposed all war.

Administration of a CPS composed exclusively of members of the historic peace churches would have been a complex undertaking, given the churches' differences in philosophy and approach. The great diversity among the COs in their religious and political beliefs would make administering the CPS a daunting task for the Selective Service, the peace churches, and NSBRO. Toward the end of the war, the CPS came close to falling apart because of the vast differences among CPS men.

3

"An Experiment in Democracy"

From the time of his appointment as director of the Selective Service in 1941 until the end of the draft, then brigadier general Lewis Blaine Hershey was a staunch supporter of the Civilian Public Service. The CPS represented a reasonable solution to the "problem" of the CO. On the one hand, the CPS would spare the conscription system, the military, and law enforcement authorities from dealing with the headaches posed by men who could be sent to remote camps. On the other hand, Hershey was sympathetic with COs who based their position on religious grounds. He referred to the CPS as an "experiment in democracy . . . to find out whether our democracy is big enough to preserve minority rights in a time of national emergency."[1] Former National Service Board for Religious Objectors chairman M. R. Zigler described Hershey as a "very good man" and perhaps "the finest exponent of religious liberty that I've ever met."[2] Hershey was regarded as a congenial man who liked to remind representatives of COs of his Mennonite ancestry.[3] At a meeting in Washington, D.C., he joked with Loris Habegger, director of an MCC CPS unit at Marlboro mental hospital in New Jersey: "We could not have had World War II without the Mennonites. . . . It furnished me out of my background to direct the Selective Service. It furnished General Eisenhower to direct the allied forces. And it furnished the conscientious objectors."[4]

Throughout the CPS, Hershey and the Selective Service system played a political balancing act to keep the CPS out of the public spotlight and to protect it from congressional backlash. During the war, the American Legion and the Veterans of Foreign Wars actively lobbied to dismantle the CPS and became embroiled in public controversies when COs led exposés of state mental hospitals. In Congress, COs had few, if any, supporters.[5] At Senate subcommittee hearings on August 19, 1942, Senator Styles Bridges commented:

> I think that perhaps most people—in fact, I know most people—have a tendency
> to look on them as slackers rather than as conscientious objectors. There is a very
> deep feeling in this country on this subject. The correspondence I have received

indicates that there is a deep feeling, for instance, in my state. There is a small group of people located there that I know feels very deeply on the rights of the conscientious objector. On the other hand, I would say, from the evidence you get through correspondence and personal contact, that the feeling is very bitter the other way—very bitter.[6]

In 1943, Senator Elmer Thomas of Oklahoma introduced an amendment to eliminate the classification of conscientious objectors, including those men serving in noncombatant roles, from the Selective Training and Service Act, in response to a petition from the national legislative committee of the American Legion.[7] The amendment never made it out of the Senate Military Affairs Committee.

Hershey and the Selective Service went to great lengths to avoid the impression that the service was coddling CPS men in any way. Despite the appeals of NSBRO, church representatives, and COs themselves, the Selective Service refused to support payment for CPS work. Col. Lewis Kosch, chief of the Camp Operations Division of the Selective Service system, testified at a Senate subcommittee hearing in August 1943, "We have been against payment of any kind. . . . We feel that as soon as you set up a pay scale for these people that is in any way comparable to that of the army, then the slacker will say: 'Well, that is a good place for me to get in'; and we feel by not making payment is one of the ways we have of sorting the slackers out from the conscientious objectors."[8]

"Public relations" was a constant concern for the Selective Service and, hence, NSBRO and the CPS church agencies. The Selective Service was intent on keeping COs out of public view and political controversies. In approving CPS projects, the Selective Service required NSBRO to answer five major questions:

1. Was the project important to the government in the emergency, considering the man power available, and was the project the most important thing that could be done at that time? Would it continue to be important with the probable changes in the situation?

2. Would the conscientious objectors be willing to do this work?

3. Would the public tolerate the objector in the community where the project was to be located?

4. Would other employable labor be displaced?

5. Would it raise political controversy?[9]

Throughout the CPS, the Selective Service issued its harshest directives when the actions of CPS men threatened to bring negative publicity or public reaction to the program. NSBRO and the administering committees of the churches, in

2. NSBRO meeting with Col. Lewis Kosch *(end of table)* and Gen. Lewis Hershey *(only his ear is visible)*. (Brethren Historical Library and Archives, Elgin, Illinois)

turn, expected directors of CPS camps or units to alert them to potential public incidents and to routinely report on public relations in their areas.

General Hershey would remain director of the Selective Service long after the end of World War II and the CPS. During the Vietnam War, Hershey became a lightning rod for antiwar and antidraft efforts for his policy of canceling deferments and ordering early induction of young men who burned their draft cards or joined protests.[10] He was removed from his position by President Richard Nixon in 1970. By the end of his career, he had become the only four-star general in army history to achieve that rank without ever serving in a combat position.[11] He died in 1977 at the age of eighty-three.

◆　◆　◆

The CPS was a complex program, involving hundreds of federal and state government bodies, private agencies, and church-related committees and groups. The Selective Service system exercised overall authority over the program. It approved CPS projects and activities, developed rules for unit operations, and required detailed reports on the work of CPS men. Although the Selective Training and Service Act specified "work of national importance under civilian direction" for COs opposed to military service, most Selective Service officials in charge of the CPS were military men. Col. Lewis F. Kosch, who had been in the National Guard with General Hershey, served as head of camp operations in the Selective Service and was responsible for administration of the CPS.[12] Kosch signed Selective Service correspondence "Colonel, Field Artillery" along with "Assistant Director, Camp Operations."[13]

According to NSBRO, as of March 1, 1945, the CPS had cost the Selective Service $2,435,393.58, including more than $160,000 for travel of the CPS men to camps, $438,000 for oversight of camp operations, and $1,800,000 in subsidies to the Departments of Agriculture and the Interior for their involvement in the CPS program.[14]

NSBRO formally represented the peace churches and other religious groups in dealings with the Selective Service, although the Mennonites, Brethren, and Friends sometimes communicated with the Selective Service directly. The 1947 CPS directory published by NSBRO listed eleven members on its Board of Directors, including M. R. Zigler of the Brethren, Orie Miller of the Mennonites, and Paul Furnas of the Friends, who had been selected at the start of the CPS.[15] That same directory listed Paul Comly French as the executive secretary, the same position he had held at the start of NSBRO, and more than one hundred other personnel, including a large number of CPS men.

3. NSBRO meeting: Paul Comly French *(seated, third from left)*. (Brethren Historical Library and Archives, Elgin, Illinois)

NSBRO was initially organized into three sections, the Camp Section, the Complaint Section, and the Assignment Section. The Camp Section was responsible for selecting locations of camps and coordinating arrangements to make the camps operational. A Special Projects Section was later added to handle "detached units" such as mental hospitals and training schools. The Assignment Section decided where men would be sent and maintained records on their placements. The Selective Service required that men be assigned at least one hundred miles from the locations from which they had been drafted. The Selective Service had the authority to disapprove camps or units and assignments. The Complaint Section handled cases in which men contested their Selective Service classifications. NSBRO later added an Advisory Section, which was concerned with men sentenced to or in danger of being sent to prison, and a Financial Section, which worked with non–historic peace churches to secure contributions for the expenses of their members in the CPS. According to Melvin Gingerich, in early 1943, these non–historic peace churches funded 40 percent of the expenses of their members in the CPS. NSBRO also published a monthly magazine, the *Reporter*, which published articles on COs and the CPS.[16]

The participating church groups funded NSBRO. Between March 1, 1941, and February 28, 1948, the BSC had contributed $125,954 for NSBRO, in addition to the costs of the service committee's own operations and CPS projects and men.[17]

◆ ◆ ◆

Initially, CPS camps, or units, were jointly administered by church and federal agencies. The MCC, AFSC, BSC, Association of Catholic Conscientious Objectors, Methodist World Peace Commission, American Baptist Home Mission Society, Disciples of Christ, and Committee on Christian Social Action supervised camp life, while federal and, later, state and private agencies provided technical supervision of the camps and directed the work of CPS men. The first camps were operated under agencies in the federal Departments of Agriculture and the Interior and specifically the Soil Conservation Service, Forest Service, and National Park Service. Technical supervision was later provided by the Fish and Wildlife Service, Farm Security Administration, Bureau of Reclamation, General Land Office, Public Health Service, Coast and Geodetic Survey, Weather Bureau, Office of Scientific Research and Development, Surgeon General of the U.S. Army, Veterans Administration, and Puerto Rican Reconstruction Administration (PRRA) as well as individual hospitals, training schools, agricultural stations, and other special units.[18]

The list of CPS camps would eventually number 151, although some of them were never opened.[19] Some numbered camps included projects such as medical experiments at multiple locations. Except for some public health projects in Florida and Mississippi, camps and mental hospitals in Virginia, a mental hospital in Louisiana, and a National Park Service camp and hospital unit in North Carolina, no CPS camps or units were located in the South or Southwest of the United States, regions of the country where COs might create "public relations" problems.

The church agencies operated independently of NSBRO. The Mennonites and the Friends, in particular, stressed their independence from NSBRO and other churches. A policy adopted by the MCC in September 1943 read:

> Accepting the requirement of Selective Service that one representative office be set up through the C.P.S. administrative agencies shall deal with the S.S. as a unit, the Mennonite Central Committee has participated in setting up, operation, and financial support of the National Service Board for Religious Objectors. It recognizes this board as the servant of the C.P.S. administrative agencies and as the proper place to review and co-ordinate such common or joint policies as are necessary in C.P.S. It does not consider the N.S.B.R.O. to have any jurisdiction in the administration of C.P.S. or in the formulation or operation of policies governing the life of the men under the administration of the M.C.C. The M.C.C. is happy to note the advantageous functioning of the N.S.B.R.O. and the relation of mutual respect and confidence which has obtained among the administrative agencies represented on the N.S.B.R.O. However, its participation in the N.S.B.R.O. is not to be construed as necessarily signifying agreement with the other agencies or members of N.S.B.R.O. in points of social or religious philosophy or administrative policy.[20]

The AFSC's policy stated, "The National Service Board for Religious Objectors is the representative of the administering religious agencies, designed to perform representative and coordinating functions and is not an administrative organization. The religious agencies, rather than NSBRO, are the sponsoring bodies and determine final policy."[21] Especially as the CPS wore on, the AFSC became more and more independent of NSBRO and distanced itself from the other peace church committees.

Clarence Pickett was the most influential member of the AFSC, although Paul Furnas was executive director of the AFSC CPS program. Pickett wanted to deal directly with the Selective Service rather than going through NSBRO.[22] He was close with Eleanor Roosevelt and often had dinner at the White House. He frustrated both Hershey of the Selective Service and French of NSBRO by going directly to the president or Mrs. Roosevelt to raise CPS issues.[23] French, a member of the Society of Friends himself, thought it was more difficult to work with Pickett and the Friends than any other group: "It is so strange that the Friends talk so much about cooperation and yet are so hard to work with." French even wondered whether Pickett felt personal hostility toward him.[24]

4. Mennonite Central Committee CPS Directors Conference, 1945. (Mennonite Church USA Historical Committee and Archives, Goshen, Indiana)

The MCC, BSC, and AFSC each maintained large staffs to administer and coordinate the CPS program. These workers included supervisors, educational specialists, publicists and newsletter editors, accountants and bookkeepers, and clerks and secretaries. The BSC spent $78,910 for its CPS operations in Elgin, Illinois, as of the end of February 1948.[25]

The historic peace churches incurred substantial expenses for the CPS. Under the arrangement with the Selective Service, the church agencies assumed responsibility for COs' room and board, medical care, and other routine expenses. CPS men were asked to contribute $30 per month for their living expenses whenever possible. The church agencies covered the expenses of the vast majority of men who could not afford this amount. According to Sibley and Jacob, the peace churches raised $7 million to pay the expenses of CPS men.[26] Eighteen Mennonite conferences contributed almost $2.9 million to the MCC.[27]

The MCC, AFSC, BSC, and other administering religious agencies paid the expenses for all CPS men in their camps, not just members of their churches. As of March 1945, the CPS had cost churches $5,137,728.[28] Of this figure, the MCC, AFSC, and BSC had paid $4,554,213, with the remainder coming from other religious bodies sponsoring camps or from other churches who paid the CPS religious agencies for men in their camps. The peace churches underwrote the costs of a significant number of men who did not come from their churches:

AFSC: Friends in CPS camps: $426,272
Non-Friends in AFSC camps: $787,991
BSC: Brethren in CPS camps: $671,793
Non-Brethren in BSC camps: $616,269
MCC: Mennonites in CPS camps: $1,836,543
Non-Mennonites in MCC camps: $215,325

The Association of Catholic Conscientious Objectors had the most difficult time paying for the costs associated with its camps. Because it was not supported by the Catholic Church and had to rely on the financially strapped Catholic Workers, it was constantly in debt. Zahn wrote: "An internal NSBRO memo dated August 23, 1945, records what it described as 'the Catholic dope': the total cost of the Catholic men inducted from the beginning to that date amounted to $44,973.17; the total contributions received toward their support, $3760.54; the 'uncared for' balance, $41,212.63. That ninety-plus deficit serves as the most fitting summary of the Catholic CPS experience." In a letter to Miss E. S. Brinton at the Friends' Swarthmore College Library dated July 22, 1942, Dwight Larrowe, director of an ACCO camp in Stoddard, New Hampshire, stated, "We have scraped and scrimped in every way to save. Our meals cost us 12 cents a plate, and our total expenses run about $16 per man per month. In other camps the total cost is about $35. Certainly that is evidence that the men have gone without—have sacrificed many things." The letter concluded with a plea: "We have prayed to St. Joseph and to our Mother Mary for help—we know we will not be refused. We know that they, through your generosity, will help us. We thank you for all you have done in the past, and beg your prayers for us in the future." Colonel Kosch of the Selective Service wanted the Catholic camp at Warner, New Hampshire, closed because the men did not have sufficient food to eat.[29]

The service committees of the historic peace churches were magnanimous in accepting and supporting men who were not from their religions in their camps. Final assignments to camps were made by the Selective Service, but COs could indicate their preferences regarding religious sponsorship. Men receiving a IV-E classification were sent a four-page questionnaire from NSBRO. The questionnaire asked men about their religious, educational, and vocational backgrounds and enabled them to check whether they preferred to serve in an AFSC, BSC, MCC, or ACCO camp. After receiving recommendations from NSBRO, the national headquarters of the Selective Service sent state headquarters DSS Form 49, "Assignment to Work of National Importance," with instructions to forward this form to the local draft board. The local board then sent COs DSS Form 50, "Order to Report for Work of National Importance":

GREETING:

    Having been found acceptable for work of national importance under civilian direction, you have been assigned to _____ Camp located at _____ in the State of _____.

    You are ordered to report to the local board at _____ m. on the _____ day of _____, 194_, where you will be furnished transportation and given instructions to proceed to camp.

    You are ordered to report to the camp pursuant to the instructions of the local board, to remain in the camp, and to perform your prescribed duties until such time as you are released or transferred by proper authority.[30]

The Friends and Brethren, in particular, ended up with a large number of men in their camps who were not from their religions. In AFSC units, Friends represented a clear minority. Only about one-fourth of the COs in AFSC units were members of the Society of Friends. From May 1941 to the end of December 1944, 3,046 men had been enrolled in AFSC camps and units; 951 Friends served in the CPS during its entire history.[31] Of the 2,104 COs who served in the Brethren CPS, a bit over half, 1,119, were Brethren.[32] By contrast, the vast majority of COs in MCC camps were Mennonites. At the peak of the CPS in September 1945, there were 3,754 Mennonites in the CPS, and 534 non-Mennonites in the MCC CPS.[33] Their relative religious homogeneity made the MCC camps run fairly smoothly. Especially as the CPS wore on, the religious and political diversity of AFSC and BSC work camps, but not mental hospital and training school units, created tensions among men who resented the outlooks of the AFSC and BSC and their cooperation with the Selective Service.

◆ ◆ ◆

When the peace churches agreed to participate in the CPS, it was because they did not want their members to be forced to be under government control. As the CPS came into form, however, the Selective Service strengthened its control over the program, to the dismay of many church leaders as well as individual COs.[34] The CPS was not so much a "church-state partnership" as a Selective Service program assisted by other governmental, religious, and private bodies.[35]

As early as 1941, Colonel Kosch of the Selective Service made it clear that the CPS was not a partnership and that the Selective Service exercised total control:

Tom Jones, president of Fisk University and first director of Friends Civilian Public Service, recounted a trip he made to the Friends camp at Merom, Indiana, in 1941 in the company of Colonel Louis Kosch, deputy to the newly appointed director, Lewis Hershey.

As Jones spoke enthusiastically about what he hoped could be accomplished through Civilian Public Service, Colonel Kosch interrupted him with "Who do you think you are? Don't you know I'm in charge of these camps under Selective Service?"

Jones replied that he thought the historic peace churches were promised complete autonomy.

"My dear man," said Kosch, "the draft is under United States government operation. Conscientious objectors are draftees just as soldiers are. Their activities are responsible to the government. The peace churches are only camp managers."[36]

In a widely reported statement in late 1942, Lt. Col. Franklin A. McLean attempted to "remove certain misunderstandings" held among COs assigned to the CPS. The statement read, in part:

Realizing that many conscientious objectors are as strongly opposed to engaging in what is commonly called defense work as to military service it is the policy of Selective Service to choose projects as unrelated to the war effort as possible and to operate them through those agencies that are distinctly civilian in character. But, since the determination of what constitutes defense is a matter of opinion, and since there is no distinction under the law, it is impossible to promise an assignee, officially or otherwise, that he will not be obliged to do defense work. . . . These decisions are powers of the Director of Selective Service and must remain in his hands.

. . . The program is not being carried on for the education or development of individuals, to train groups for foreign service or future activities in the post-war period, or for the furtherance of any particular movement. Its purpose is to do work of national importance as selected by the Director. There is no obligation to provide an assignee with work for which he has been particularly prepared, wished to do, or regards as socially significant. Neither is there any intention of engaging in what has generally been called the social welfare field except as it may enter into the regular projects. Assignees can no more expect choice of location or job than can men in the service or a great many civilians. . . .

During nonworking hours assignees are under the control of the Camp Director. This individual serves in a dual capacity being the representative of the church sponsoring the camp and also of Selective Service. As agent of the church he is responsible for the physical and spiritual welfare of men in camp.

For Selective Service he carries out and enforces certain regulations such as the granting of leave and furlough, accounts for the men assigned to the camp and prepares various reports. As far as Selective Service is concerned the Camp Director is in charge of the camp. The impression that camps are democracies to be run by the assignees is entirely erroneous. . . .

From the time an assignee reports to camp until he is finally released he is under control of the Director of Selective Service. He ceases to be a free agent and is accountable for all of his time, in camp and out, twenty-four hours a day. His movements, actions and conduct are subject to control and regulation. He ceases to have certain rights and is granted privileges instead. These privileges can be restricted or withdrawn without his approval or consent as punishment, during emergencies or as a matter of policy. He may be told when and how to work, what to wear and where to sleep. He can be required to submit to medical examinations and treatment and to practice rules of health and sanitation. He may be moved from place to place and from job to job, even to foreign countries, for the convenience of the government regardless of his personal feelings or desires.[37]

The "experiment in democracy" was not to be run democratically.

4

"A Significant Epoch in Your Life"

Around the time COs received the order to report to the Civilian Public Service from the Selective Service, they received a letter welcoming them from the religious service committee sponsoring the camp to which they had been assigned. COs assigned to Brethren Service Committee camps received a letter from W. Harold Row, director of the Brethren CPS: "Your entrance into a Civilian Public Service Camp marks a significant epoch in your life—just how significant no one can tell at this moment."[1] The letter provided brief descriptions of the CPS and the philosophy of the BSC. Attached to the letter were a list of clothing men should bring to camp and a short summary of the camp.

Shortly after the establishment of the AFSC–National Park Service camp in Patapsco, Maryland, in May 1941, CPS camps were opened in Grottoes, Virginia (MCC–Soil Conservation Service), and Largo, Indiana (BSC–Soil Conservation Service).[2] The first ACCO or Catholic conscientious objector camp was opened in Stoddard, New Hampshire, in August of that year. By the end of 1941, twenty-one CPS Forest Service, National Park Service, and Soil Conservation Service work camps were in operation in California, Maryland, Virginia, Colorado, Indiana, Arkansas, Ohio, Massachusetts, New York, New Hampshire, Pennsylvania, Michigan, Iowa, North Carolina, Oregon, and Illinois. The locations of the initial camps were generally based on the availability of former Civilian Conservation Corps facilities that could be refurbished.

Work at the camps was supervised by project superintendents from the government agencies. Men typically worked eight to ten hours a day, including transportation time to work sites. Work at the camps varied greatly and included firefighting; erosion control; ditch digging; road construction; raising and planting seedlings; building dams and reservoirs; removing dead trees; maintaining parks; constructing roads, bridges, and truck trails; surveying; maintaining nurseries; building wood or stone fences; making firebreaks; constructing fire lookout towers, garages, and sanitary facilities; and similar kinds of outdoor labor. The CPS men occasionally also performed work such as emergency farm labor or searching for missing persons. On May 17, 1943, CPS men joined the

5. CPS Camp no. 21, Cascade Locks, Oregon. (Brethren Historical Library and Archives, Elgin, Illinois)

search for Doris Dean, a four-year-old girl lost in the Blue Ridge Mountains near Grottoes, Virginia.[3] They found her after she had spent five days and five nights lost in the forest. In April 1943, COs from the nearby Mennonite Denison Soil Conservation camp helped save Council Bluffs, Iowa, from being flooded by the Missouri River.[4]

One of the most challenging and interesting camps was based at Missoula, Montana, which opened in May 1943 under the Forest Service and the MCC.[5] It was a "smoke jumpers" camp at which men were trained to parachute into remote wilderness areas to fight forest fires. COs at this camp were selected from existing AFSC, BSC, and MCC camps. In contrast to other work camps, the Forest Service provided food and housing and a maintenance fee to the men. After the men's initial training, they were sent to locations in Montana, Oregon, and Idaho. The smoke jumpers unit brought welcomed positive publicity to the CPS. A January 25, 1943, article in *Time* announced the planned opening of the camp: "Conscientious objectors who want courageous, if noncombatant, wartime work learned last week

6. CPS men outside barracks, CPS Camp no. 21, Cascade Locks, Oregon. (Brethren Historical Library and Archives, Elgin, Illinois)

that they might get it. In June, Selective Service will start giving some 60 conchies the stiff Army and Marine parachute training course. The purpose: to fight forest fires. They will probably be stationed at Missoula, Mont., regional Forest Service headquarters, center of a rugged and remote fire area."[6] Before long, the Bureau of Reclamation, Fish and Wildlife Service, Weather Bureau, and other federal agencies provided technical supervision at CPS work camps and projects.

Like most things in the CPS, COs' labor was carefully recorded and reported. Project superintendents filed monthly reports with the Selective Service. By the end of the CPS, the Selective Service could report, for example, that COs had contributed 1,213,000 man-days in thirty Forest Service camps and 1,112,000 man-days in nineteen Soil Conservation Service camps.[7] The work was further broken down by jobs as well as number, mile, cubic yard, feet, acre, pound, and similar measurements.[8] For instance, Selective Service records indicated that COs had spent 4,312 man-days moving and planting 1,104,650 trees.

Some CPS men enjoyed the physical labor in the camps, got along well with government project superintendents and foremen, and liked working outdoors and living in sometimes picturesque parts of the country. Especially on the eastern

7. CPS men fighting the "Goose Creek Fire" at a Forest Service camp in Idaho. (Swarthmore College Peace Collection, Swarthmore, Pennsylvania)

seaboard and in the Northwest, camps were located in beautiful, if not spectacular, mountainous locations.

However, there was a pervasive feeling among CPS men that their work in camps fell far short of being "work of national importance" and represented little more than make-work. In an August 1945 report on the CPS, the peace churches, and the Selective Service, Kenneth Keeton and Don Elton Smith at the BSC camp at Cascade Locks, Oregon, identified many of the problems with the program that would be written about by commentators years after the war. Keeton and Smith commented on the Forest Service: "The Forest Service has always favored reasonably stern and rigid work hours since the work is in lieu of military service. . . . It is quite apparent that the Forest Service is chiefly time centered in its attitude toward the work. That is, it is more concerned about the men's spending a certain amount of time at work than it is about how much work is done."[9]

In its 1945 report on the CPS, the AFSC was critical of the "wasteful use of conscientious objectors": "We believe that the service of conscientious objectors has in many instances been wasted on projects of little immediate value, when it could have been better directed to meet pressing public needs growing out of the war

8. CPS men working on a rock wall, CPS Camp no. 21, Cascade Locks, Oregon. (Brethren Historical Library and Archives, Elgin, Illinois)

emergency and demanding the kind of training and skills which CPS men have to offer." The AFSC acknowledged the long-term value of some forms of forestry and conservation work, but questioned the importance of many of the projects to which CPS men had been assigned: "Most of the Park Service work, however, much of the forestry work, especially where firefighting is needed only during a limited season of the year, and some of the soil conservation programs we feel to be of minor significance under present conditions and incapable of utilizing effectively the men which have been placed at their disposal."[10]

CPS men were not paid for their work and did not receive worker's compensation or care for dependents. Although Congress had authorized payment of CPS men not in excess of the amount paid to men inducted into the army, the Selective Service refused to request funds to pay them. Selective Service officials maintained that nonpayment would separate "slackers" from legitimate conscientious objectors and believed that the CPS program would be more acceptable to the public if men were not paid. As Keeton and Smith at Cascade Locks wrote in 1945, "C.O.s are regarded by S.S. as wards, not employees of the government."[11] In addition to paying the costs of supporting CPS men in camps, the AFSC, MCC, and BSC allocated a small maintenance fee to COs to help them pay for clothing, toiletries, and personal items. The MCC initially gave men $1.50 per month, while the AFSC and BSC gave them $2.50 per month. The BSC, if not the other church committees, later increased the monthly fee to $3.50.

In 1942, the Selective Service did ask Congress to provide for accident compensation for CPS men. Testifying before the Senate Committee on Military Affairs, Colonel Kosch explained that if CPS men were injured in their work, society would have to take care of them anyway: "If they are not taken care of in this way, they will still be wards of society; they will have to be taken care of, because their injury or disability has been received in the service of their country." In response to Kosch, Senator Styles Bridges of New Hampshire asked a rhetorical question: "Colonel, how much of an obligation do you think the citizens of the country have to a man who refuses to fight for his country when his country is in jeopardy and everything is at stake?" In one of his better moments, Kosch replied:

> Well, I don't think my personal opinion on that would have anything to do with it. Under the law as set up there are certain rights for this man and certain places to which he is allowed to go; it is considered service to his country, and he is just complying with that law.
>
> I am not a conscientious objector myself. In fact, I have had 32 years of service, and this is just a job that has been given me to do, and I feel I have to look after the rights of the people I am representing here and the things I am running, and try to protect the Government in every way we can in the future.[12]

When the bill came up for consideration on the floor of the Senate, Senator Kenneth McKeller of Tennessee stated, "What bothers me is that I do not think conscientious objectors during a war, especially such a war as that in which we are now engaged, should be encouraged. I think that if we continue to throw safeguards around them and make everything easy for them, the next proposal will be to pay them salaries or compensation for all work done, to pay for their upkeep, and everything of the kind, and we will have an army of conscientious objectors. I do not feel very kindly about it."[13] Despite some senators' reservations about the bill, the Senate passed it in late August 1942. The bill died when the House of Representatives failed to consider it that year.[14]

The churches attempted to compensate injured CPS men in emergency situations and to provide for their dependents whenever possible. NSBRO reported that a rough survey of 8,000 CPS men indicated that 2,347 had wives and 833 had children and that the churches had provided aid to roughly 600 families in the amount of $158,700.[15] The AFSC reported that as of early 1945, one-third of the men in its program were married, one-third of whom had children. It also stated that it had helped 293 families and provided a total of $20,000 in cash allotments to 94 families. The AFSC concluded: "We believe that care for CPS dependents is the clear responsibility of the government. Since conscience is not a crime, why penalize the families of conscientious objectors?"[16]

◆   ◆   ◆

Each work camp had a camp director who was responsible to both the Selective Service and the sponsoring church committee. Initially, the camp directors were non-CPS members of the churches. Later, they were CPS men selected by the church committee or, in some instances, elected by the CPS men in the camp or unit. In at least some instances, the Selective Service claimed the authority to approve appointments of camp directors.

The camps were allocated what was called "overhead," a quota of men excused from forest, park, soil conservation, or other work to help run the camps. Overhead might have included camp directors, educational or recreational directors, cooks, laundry workers, and others. Eisen reported that there were 23 "overhead" men in a BSC camp of 125 men and 27 in a camp of 175.[17]

Women also might be assigned by a church to help in the camps as nurses or dieticians. The MCC camps typically had women serving as matrons, and in BSC and AFSC camps directors' wives sometimes played this role.[18] For women from peace churches, who were not subject to the draft, serving in CPS camps and later in women's mental hospital units was a way to "witness" against war.

Many wives and children followed CPS men to their camp assignments. One traveling MCC camp matron stated that she found between 15 and 55 wives who had moved near camps.[19] Some lived in nearby communities. Other wives and children lived in cabins or tents located next to the camps.[20] A photo album prepared by Herbert Michael at the BSC camp at Cascade Locks, Oregon, showed a series of family shacks dubbed "Hersheyville."

The presence of wives and families created problems for camp directors, especially at MCC units. Melvin Gingerich noted, "Hundreds of wives followed their husbands to camp and obtained jobs in the nearby cities. Camp directors were divided in their reaction to this trend. Married men whose wives lived near by found it difficult to enter into the off-work hours' program of the camps. As often as they possibly could, many obtained liberties and leaves even when this meant missing classes, programs by visiting lecturers, and religious services."[21]

When mental hospital and training school units were opened, the number of CPS men with wives living nearby greatly increased. Not only was it easier for wives to move to and obtain jobs in towns and cities near CPS units, but the men were also more likely to meet and marry women met at church women's hospital units or in the surrounding area. The rights or privileges claimed by married CPS

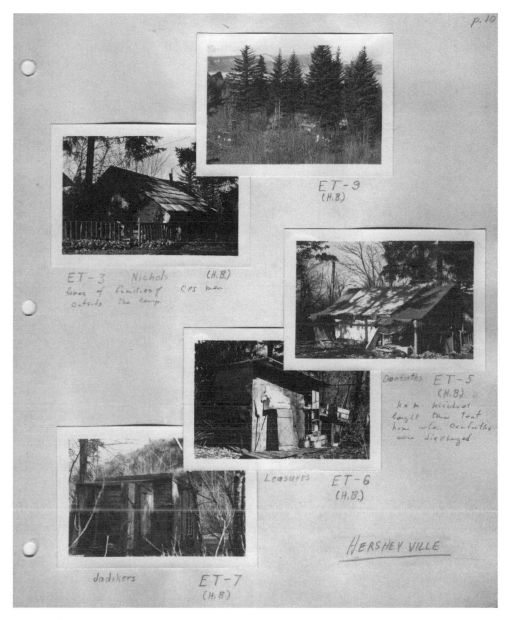

9. "Hersheyville." Photo album showing shacks of family members of CPS men outside of CPS Camp no. 21, Cascade Locks, Oregon. (Brethren Historical Library and Archives, Elgin, Illinois)

men at mental hospitals and training schools would create public relations problems for the CPS and lead to a crackdown by the Selective Service.

Most camps were barracks containing dormitories, cafeterias, and areas for education, recreation, and religious services. Mennonite Aden Horst, who was originally assigned to the Grottoes, Virginia, camp, stated, "There were many

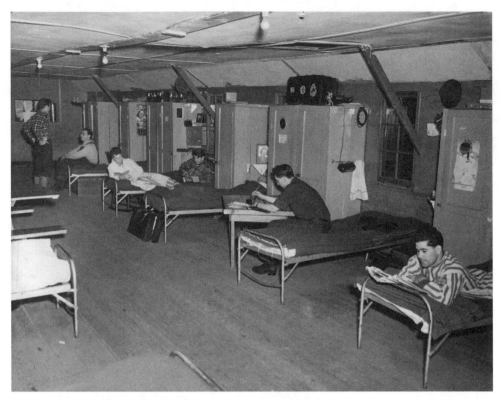

10. CPS men inside camp barracks. (Brethren Historical Library and Archives, Elgin, Illinois)

of these abandoned CCC camps across the U.S. and they were available to serve as base camps for the CPS program. The camps were basically all designed the same—dormitories, dining hall, director's quarters, laundry facility, chapel, government headquarters, infirmary (with several beds for confined patients), and recreation facilities."[22]

Camp directors and other administrative personnel were required to submit monthly time and work reports on standardized forms summarizing information required by the Selective Service. Four copies of the reports were prepared. One was kept by the camp, one was submitted to the sponsoring church agency, and two were sent to NSBRO, which forwarded a copy to the Selective Service. By March 1942, the workdays in CPS camps had been standardized. The instructions for "NSB 105a Camps' Time Record" read:

> Effective March 1, 1942, a new work schedule was instituted. This came as a result of the wide variance among camps in the number of work hours, travel time, lunch hours, etc. Camps working in cooperation with the Soil Conservation Service, Forest Service, and National Park Service are now following this schedule.

Assignees will be available for turnover to technical agencies at 7:30 A.M. daily. They will be under the supervision of the technical agency until they are returned to camp at 5:00 P.M. The hours 7:30 A.M. to 5:00 P.M. daily include all necessary travel time, the three-quarters of an hour should be allowed for lunch.

On Saturdays the hours of work shall be from 7:30 a.m. to noon, but the Superintendent may turn back to the camp director not to exceed twenty-five per cent of the men turned over at work call for camp duties, and the superintendent may use such additional men as he sees fit for project work at the camp site. Men turned over to the camp director for camp duties will work the same hours as the men in the field, and their labor will be properly supervised by the camp director or his authorized representative.

The foregoing hours of labor will in no way affect the liability of assignees for emergency calls by the project superintendent at any hour of the day or night for work of an emergency nature.[23]

The reports also covered arrivals, transfers, and discharges; absent-without-leaves (AWOLs), leaves (non–working days), furloughs (a maximum of thirty days per year furloughed from working days), and sick in camp or hospitalized (sick leaves were not permitted); men assigned to administrative duties or overhead; and an accounting of government equipment.

The MCC, BSC, AFSC, ACCO, and other religious agencies that would end up sponsoring camps or units also required camp directors—or assistant directors, as they would be called when CPS men moved into detached units in mental hospitals, training schools, and other projects—to maintain records and submit reports on camp operations and finances. The MCC prepared a sixty-nine-page manual on camp records, financing, and procedures that addressed such reports as the "Weekly Report of Receipts and Disbursements," "Semi-annual Inventories Report," "Food Cost Calculation Report," and "Food Consumption Report." Educational directors at MCC units were required to file quarterly reports summarizing educational activities, outside speakers, special meetings, library additions, and other information.[24]

Most camps published regular newsletters reporting on upcoming educational and religious activities, administrative decisions, announcements, and church or CPS news. Newsletters might also contain articles on religious philosophy and public service. The MCC's *Educational Director's Manual* described the camp paper: "The camp paper can be of great service to the campees and to the constituency. It should offer editorials, feature articles and book reviews relating to the basic objectives and program of the camp, particularly peace education. For some, the camp paper may be their sole channel of information about CPS. This wider reading public should be kept in mind in the editing of each issue." Examples of MCC camp papers included the *Pike View Peace News, Olive Branch,* and *Vanguard.*[25] BSC *(Compass)* and AFSC units *(Scribe)* published newsletters with similar names.

MCC camp newsletters were relatively apolitical and contained little criticism of the Selective Service, NSBRO, or the MCC.[26] Especially during the latter part of the CPS, newsletters from BSC and AFSC camps were likely to contain articles critical of the government, the Selective Service, NSBRO, and the church agencies. After the establishment of CPS mental hospital and training school units, newsletters would play an important role in informing units of reform efforts at other institutions.

◆   ◆   ◆

Camps sponsored by the different church agencies varied greatly from each other. This difference reflected not only the orientation of the churches but the composition of men in their camps as well.

MCC camps were the most structured and were viewed as authoritarian compared to other camps.[27] They also tended to be homogenous in comparison with other camps, although there was wide variation in the Mennonite conferences from which the men had come.

11. CPS men on Soil Conservation Service work crew, CPS Camp no. 46, Big Flats, New York. (Swarthmore College Peace Collection, Swarthmore, Pennsylvania)

Based on a random analysis of Selective Service records, Gordon Zahn compared the social backgrounds of a sample of CPS men from different religious backgrounds. Nine out of every ten Mennonites came from a rural area, 60 percent had been engaged in agricultural work at the time they entered the CPS, and only 15.8 percent had any education beyond high school.[28] Adrian E. Gory and David C. McClelland reported higher levels of educational attainment among Mennonite CPS men: 21.4 percent had attended at least one year of college, and 6.7 percent had completed college or done postgraduate work. Of course, statistics can obscure differences in any group of people. Mennonite Paul Goering noticed a tendency among college-educated men at Grottoes to spend more time with each other.[29]

The camp directors and other appointed administrators were expected not only to ensure the smooth operation of the camps but also to help "our young men grow in character and in the Christian faith as a result of this experience."[30] As early as October 1941, the MCC established a set of educational objectives for Mennonite camps. The main objectives, with subobjectives listed under them, included:

1. Appreciation of our Mennonite Heritage and Mission in the World.
2. Understanding the Christian's Relation to the State and the Community.
3. Deepening Christian Experience.
4. Promoting Personal Growth.

12. CPS men on Soil Conservation Service work crew, CPS Camp no. 46, Big Flats, New York. (Swarthmore College Peace Collection, Swarthmore, Pennsylvania)

Camp administrators were responsible for scheduling regular prayer meetings and religious services and enforcing "discipline" over the personal lives of their men. Ministers and church leaders regularly visited the camps to conduct services or give talks. Drinking alcohol, smoking, and card playing were frowned upon or punished, although Goering recalled that smoking was not uncommon at the Grottoes camp.[31]

Conservative Mennonites would later criticize what they saw as the lax administration of the camps and the negative influences of liberal Mennonites on Old Order Amish and Old Order Mennonite young men. Elmer Showalter, a former minister of the Lancaster Mennonite Conference, believed that the CPS program was "devastating" to the church: "A few were helped, but the majority lost conviction and a minority revealed their condition by smoking, off-color stories, and movie attendance."[32] However, in a report on the Amish in the CPS written at the time, Eli J. Bontrager, who was Amish himself, expressed satisfaction with the MCC's administration of the CPS:

> The organization known as the M.C.C. is not exactly what some of our brethren think it should be and also some of the more conservative Mennonites do not like the idea of being so closely associated with some of the more liberal branches. However, the work of the M.C.C. in C.P.S. is solely in the line of non-resistance and in this respect the different branches are practically all in accord. Difference as to non-conformity are [sic] never mentioned and the work of the M.C.C. in C.P.S. does not interfere in any way with the rules and regulations and practices of any of the branches. Each branch is respected in its position and the stand it takes. The directors of the C.P.S. camps strongly urge assignees to live up to the rules and regulations of his own church and they discourage debating or discussing their differences.[33]

Leaders of some conservative Mennonite churches advocated for the establishment of separate camps for members of different conferences or branches.[34] Although most Amish CPS men were spread throughout MCC camps and units, one Amish camp was opened for thirty-two men in Boonesboro, Maryland.[35] A Mennonite Church unit for men from conservative conferences also was established in Malcolm, Nebraska.[36] There was little interest among CPS men in separate camps, however, and the movement to separate men by conference collapsed.

Some former CPS men recalled tensions between conservative and liberal Mennonites in the camps.[37] For many Mennonite COs, however, time spent in the camps and CPS gave them a deeper appreciation of the church and the range of beliefs of men from different conferences and congregations.[38] Men at all CPS camps regularly held "bull sessions" to discuss religion and politics. Edwin

Schrag, who had served at MCC camps at Denison, Iowa, and North Fork, California, recalled that arguments over religion were a "favorite past time." There was also good-natured bantering among men from different conferences. Aden Horst told this story about Grottoes: "There were two boys from Lancaster County, Pennsylvania who believed it was a sin to laugh. Some of us would say and do silly things in an attempt to make them laugh. One of the boys would occasionally break into a smile, but the other one never did." A controversy arose at the Grottoes camp when a conservative Mennonite bishop was scheduled to visit. Mennonites from other conferences would be denied the opportunity to participate in communion.[39] After a number of conservative Mennonite men objected, communion was canceled.

Whatever differences there were in MCC camps, they did not experience the unrest that would characterize many other CPS camps. Mennonites from all conferences tended to accept the authority of the camp director and the MCC itself. The minority of men who were not Mennonites could transfer out of the camps if they did not like how they were administered. There is almost always an exception to any generalization. Paul Comly French recorded one extremely unusual incident told to him by Henry Fast of the MCC: "Henry Fast discussed with me the two Mennonite boys at Downey, Idaho, who had tarred and feathered the camp director. From the conversations he had with them and the government officials there, it certainly sounds like a real exhibition of non-resistance on the part of the camp director who permitted the boys to strip him, paint him with tar, and then sprinkle feathers over him."[40] French did not say if the camp director was tarred and feathered for being too strict or too lax.

Compared to MCC camps, AFSC camps were unstructured and freewheeling. The AFSC administered the camps but gave CPS men a say in policy making and selecting camp directors. The AFSC intended the camps to be run in the tradition of Friends' religious and business meetings.[41] In this tradition, meetings were held in silence until someone felt inspired to speak, consistent with the Friends' emphasis on inner searching. Business meetings would be held to consider issues or concerns. The group assembled would not vote but would reach decisions based on the "sense of the meeting."

Friends were a distinct minority in AFSC camps.[42] These camps attracted a relatively large number of political or secular objectors as well as members from "mainstream" religions. Although many non-Friends appreciated the sponsorship of the AFSC—and some even became Quakers during or after the CPS—a number resented being under the authority of any religious organization or being subjected to the teachings of the Friends. In a study of two AFSC camps, H. Otto Dahlke reported that many non-Friends resented what they perceived to be the subtle proselytizing of the Friends.[43] Because most men in AFSC camps were not Friends, it was difficult for the camps to conduct business in accord with the "sense of the meeting." At the same time, the Friends' nonauthoritarian approach created expectations that everything would be decided democratically, when, in fact, camps were administered under the control of the Selective Service.

As early as October 1941, Colonel Kosch of the Selective Service expressed concern over the administration of AFSC camps and opposition to the idea that they should be run democratically. French wrote in his diary:

> Col. Kosch called me this afternoon and asked me to come over to talk with him. As soon as I walked in his office, he said he was greatly concerned about the Quaker camps and had recommended to General Hershey that the Government take them over in a month or six weeks unless we were able to demonstrate more ability in administration. . . . He said he was sure we could not continue to function on the basis of all of the boys in the camp making all of the major decisions and that we would have to support our directors or they would be compelled to take them over. He said he felt from the beginning that our democratic plan would not work but was willing to give us a chance to experiment with it. Now, he said, he was of the opinion that most of the men were not conscientious objectors but were objectors to all rules and regulations and everything pertaining to organized system.[44]

French next spoke with General Hershey and sensed that Hershey shared Kosch's position that something had to be done about the Friends' camps. The next day French spoke about the situation with Clarence Pickett of the AFSC, who seemed to acknowledge that administrative changes were needed in the AFSC camps. Paul Furnas was later appointed executive director of the AFSC-CPS. AFSC camps would present problems to the Selective Service throughout the CPS. The 1942 "Selective Service Statement of Policy" by Lieutenant Colonel McLean— "The impression that camps are democracies to be run by the assignees is entirely erroneous"—was almost certainly directed at men in AFSC camps.

Like other camps, AFSC camps had organized religious meetings, guest speakers, and educational activities. Some subgroups within AFSC camps resisted involvement in camp-sponsored events and held their own services and activities.

"Bull sessions" at AFSC camps were intellectually stimulating for many men. Friends tended to come from urban areas and to be relatively highly educated. Zahn reported that two-thirds of the Friends in his sample came from urban areas, and almost three-fourths had some college education. Gory and McClelland found that 68.4 percent of Friends in the CPS had completed at least one year of college education, and 40.5 percent had college degrees. A report by the AFSC indicated that 89 percent of Friends had graduated high school and 69 percent had attended college, with 20.5 percent graduating. AFSC camps also attracted more non-Quaker intellectuals and educated persons than other camps. Methodist Neil Hartman, who became a Friend, explained, "I went to a Quaker camp. We spent all our time talking about what Christians should do in a time of war." Evert Batholomew, also a Methodist upon entering the CPS, said, "I was very religious when I went to CPS. I met other men who were just as religious as I was. But I met some guys who were intellectually superior. . . . They were deep into science, deep into philosophy. They started feeding me books. . . . I entered as a religious CO, but left as a secular humanist."[45]

Of the service committees of the peace churches, the AFSC was more critical of the CPS and the nature of the work assigned at camps. An AFSC report read:

> The majority of the jobs within CPS camps are non-technical and require no particular skill or experience. 50% of the men in camps have been assigned to simple, manual tasks. Only 10% have been used in technical or professional work. This is not surprising, as the pattern for the camps was set by the Civilian Conservation Corps, established to utilize young men who usually had no professional training and limited occupational experience. But the waste that has resulted from the placing of many highly trained and skilled men in this pattern has been very great.[46]

As in the case of many things involving the CPS, BSC camps fell somewhere between the AFSC and MCC in the administration of the camps. In the first communication with COs assigned to BSC camps, BSC-CPS director W. Harold Row stressed democratic ideals, pacifism, and cooperation, not religious beliefs or church involvement:

> These camps have been set up in cooperation with the United States government to give an opportunity through cooperative good will to find a constructive public service. This alternative service is vital and necessary to maintain a democracy. The American way of life was developed out of the ideals of equal opportunity, sacrificial good will and cooperation. While others seem conscientiously to feel they must protect our national life and freedom with armies and offer their lives to do so; we believe we should give our lives to demonstrate that democracy is the fruit of good will and self-discipline in recognizing the rights and needs of others. Upon you falls a responsibility, in recognizing the rights and needs of others. Upon you falls a responsibility, not only for personal development, but also for continuance and growth of the values in the Civilian Public Service Movement. Many people are waiting to see what you and your associates are going to make of this experiment, an experiment new in the whole experience of mankind. Not only your loved ones and those identified with C.P.S., but also a host of students,

church leaders, and those vitally interested in minority rights are counting on you to come through creatively. In a very real way you represent all of these folk in your camp experience. It is therefore expected that you will cooperate and sacrifice to make this program and your camp a success.[47]

Approximately 53 percent of CPS men in BSC camps were Brethren. BSC camps stood between MCC and AFSC camps in the number of men from outside of its church. Similarly, Brethren COs tended to be more highly educated than the Mennonites but less highly educated than the Friends.[48] Gory and McClelland reported that 38.5 percent of Brethren men in the CPS had finished at least one year of college, and 18 percent had completed college.[49]

The initial camp directors were selected by the central office of the BSC. Like the MCC and AFSC, the BSC eventually turned to assignees to serve as camp directors. According to Leslie Eisen, the administration of the camps became more democratic and participatory over time.[50] By 1944, the BSC used a "conference method" to select camp and unit directors. Conferences composed of the central office, assignees, and Brethren in the region selected administrators through a consensus process.

A sixteen-page report, "Development of Techniques of Administration in CPS #21," in the Cascades, Oregon, camp by Don Elton Smith described the evolution of camp administration and the complexities of decision making at CPS camps. Cascades, Oregon, was originally established in late 1941 as a jointly operated BSC and MCC camp, an unusual arrangement. Its first director was Mark Schrock, a Brethren minister, and the assistant director was a Mennonite CO. Both had been appointed by the committees' central offices. According to Smith, "The attitude of director Schrock differed from the published viewpoint of Selective Service in that he wanted the men to have a part, though a limited one, in camp government." At general meetings led by Schrock soon after the opening of the camp, a president of the camp was chosen who appointed committees on religion, education, and recreation, and a camp council composed of the president and representatives of the four camp barracks was formed. The committees and the council worked in cooperation with administrators appointed by the church agencies. "It was a sort of benevolent administration those first few months in camp," wrote Smith. "The policy of the religious administrative agencies seemed to be one of caution."[51]

The MCC withdrew from administration of the camp in May 1942. Smith wrote, "The Mennonites had consistently been the most conservative bloc in camp, taking the view that the director should administer the camp and that there should not be any representative government of the assignees." In the following months, the camp experienced a series of disputes regarding the administration of the camp. Some COs argued that they should make all of their own rules and not accept Selective Service rules and policies, a position certain to place them at odds with the government and the BSC. Others objected to decisions made by a majority of the assignees, feeling that they coerced minorities in the camp. Discussions were held about whether unanimity or 90 percent or 75 percent should be required for any camp policies or positions. Still other assignees believed that the camp should not be administered by any religious group and that the camp director should be elected from and by the assignees; camp administrators continued to make decisions without involving the men. By early 1943, the camp committee structure had broken down: "A majority of things camp government dealt with were petty and without significance. Many an hour was spent debating the precise camp limits or at what hour lights should be extinguished."[52]

A new camp director and codirector were subsequently chosen by representatives elected by the men in camp and representatives of the BSC. The new camp director was Robert Case, and the codirector was Charles Davis. Both were Presbyterians. After that time, camp administration moved to what Smith called a "functional government." Under this system, committees and interest groups were established to make decisions regarding the assignment of men to camp overhead positions and other matters that had been previously decided upon by camp administrators, with or without the involvement of assignees. At the same time, decision making was based on consensus. Smith concluded: "Men who are not free cannot bargain; they can only ask favors. In accepting CPS men are no longer in a position to develop administrative techniques beyond the confines of Selective Service regulations or bargain with the Forest Service for more significant work. . . . The early paternalism of the Brethren Service Committee has been largely cleared away within the camp with the recognition of the rights of the men to decide upon what activities they wish to engage."[53]

The ACCO officially administered two Forest Service camps, one in Stoddard, New Hampshire, and one in Warner, New Hampshire. However, the Stoddard camp closed in October 1942, the same month the Warner camp opened, and Dwight Larrowe served as director of both. The name Camp Simon, which was selected by the COs, was used for both. The ACCO also operated a general hospital unit in Chicago, which was later turned over to the BSC, and a state training school unit at Rosewood, Maryland.

Camp Simon was intended to be operated on what camp director Larrowe called "functional authoritarianism":

We are operating under a sort of functional authoritarianism. The Director is ultimately responsible for the whole camp and so has supreme authority. Other officers have authority according to their responsibility. The cook is responsible for and has authority in the kitchen; the nurse is responsible for and has authority in the infirmary, and so on.

Responsibility and authority are inseparable, though they should be as decentralized as possible; responsibility must be moral as well as financial and political. We believe that discipline is essential and must, when necessary, be enforced.[54]

Yet Zahn characterized Camp Simon's history as turbulent and described how the diverse group of men there resisted authoritarian governance.

Zahn, like any good sociologist, presented a typology of COs at Camp Simon.[55] The first three types were supporters of the camp administration, and most closely shared its Catholic identity: the Chapel Group (who were most actively involved in the camp's religious program and subscribed to the just war theory), the Catholic Workers (who identified with Dorothy Day's pacifist and social justice philosophy), and the Coughlinites (who followed Roman Catholic priest Charles Coughlin and shared his fascist, anti-Semitic sympathies). Other types were the College Boys and Intellectuals (who based their pacifism on philosophical or ideological grounds), the Artists (who were "individualistic and independent spirits"), the Disrupters (who were uncooperative by nature and held the camp administration and other COs in disdain), the Workers (who were quiet, steady, willing to work, and uninterested in political or ideological controversies), and the Oddballs (who just seemed to be "misfits").

If one substituted the first three Catholic divisions with groups from other religions, this typology would probably have applied to most of the AFSC and some of the BSC camps. Most camps had proadministration "company men," antiadministration disrupters, and men who put in their time and ignored camp politics. Catholics in one of the two AFSC camps Dahlke studied were among the most vehement in denouncing the Friends and resisting the camp administration. Neil Hartman recalled that in his camp experience, Catholics "were the ones agitating" and "didn't want to have anything to do with the Quakers." Charles Lord mentioned problems at an AFSC unit in Trenton, North Dakota: "We even had some Catholics. We had some problems with them. They put a sign on their door: 'Beware anyone who enters.' They were not pacifists."[56]

The camps administered by the church agencies and the National Park Service, Forest Service, and Soil Conservation Service represented the Selective Service's idea of what the CPS should be: work camps where COs could be confined in relatively remote locations. Before long, however, the appeals of NSBRO, the churches, and COs for more meaningful service and wartime labor shortages would lead the Selective Service to approve projects separate from the original base camps.

5

"Detached Units"

When leaders of the peace churches first contemplated alternative public service, humanitarian projects were high on their list of priorities. The alleviation of human suffering was central to the missions of the Mennonites, Friends, and Brethren.

Toward the end of World War I, the army released ninety-nine COs to the Friends to do relief work in France.[1] The Friends, Brethren, and Mennonites hoped that their men could perform similar service as an alternative to entering the military after passage of the Selective Training and Service Act of 1940.

Soon after the establishment of the Civilian Public Service, the AFSC and the Brethren planned to send COs to England and China to do relief work in war-torn areas.[2] The Selective Service stalled on approving the plan. Then, on February 13, 1943, President Roosevelt approved a relief unit to go to China in a letter to AFSC executive secretary Clarence Pickett: "I approve your request to obtain seventy volunteers from civilian work camps for medical relief, sanitation and public health work in China and I have taken the matter up with the Secretary of War. He tells me that he has discussed this matter with you and that at his request the National Director of Selective Service has agreed to cooperate with you in securing the volunteers you desire and in procuring passports for them."[3] Eleanor Roosevelt was a supporter of foreign relief work by the COs.

At the same time the service committees were planning foreign relief efforts, colleges associated with the peace churches were preparing to establish foreign relief training programs. The draft age was being lowered from twenty-one to eighteen. An MCC pamphlet explained that the lowering of the draft age would deplete colleges of young men, limit the supply of college-trained men available for foreign relief, and tempt Mennonite young men to select military service over civilian public service because of college programs sponsored by the army and navy. Paul Comly French of NSBRO, Orie Miller of the MCC, and some college presidents worked on securing Selective Service approval for CPS relief training programs.[4] Plans to establish training programs at four Mennonite colleges, four Friends colleges, and four Brethren colleges were approved by the Selective Service. COs would receive up to twelve months of college training and pledge to perform foreign relief service for the duration of the war and afterward. The first college programs were opened in the spring of 1943 at Brethren Manchester College, Mennonite Goshen College, and Friends colleges at Swarthmore, Haverford, Guilford, and Earlham.[5] Courses at Goshen College included Christian Life and Mennonite Heritage; Contemporary World Relief Needs, Central Europe, South America, and China; History and Philosophy of Mennonite Relief; Social Factors and Christian Personality; Community Hygiene; and Community Nutrition.[6]

Soon after the foreign relief service and college training programs were reported in the media, there was an immediate backlash. According to Paul Comly French, the American Legion expressed its strong opposition to the programs: "The American Legion Executive Committee has asked that Congress investigate the approval by Selective Service of the use of CPS in China and the approval of the CPS Training Corps. Legion officials have discussed the program with Selective Service and pointed out that they feel it is absurd that men should be permitted to go to China and to prepare for relief services in college when there is a critical need for men to perform farm service in this country."[7]

A paragraph in the War Establishment Appropriation Bill for 1944 addressed transportation of COs to foreign lands to provide relief service. At hearings before a subcommittee of the House Committee on Appropriations on June 10, 1943, Representative Joe Starnes of Alabama read into the record two recently published newspaper articles.[8] The first article, published on June 4 in the *Washington Daily News,* described foreign relief service by COs in relatively positive terms:

> The first group of conscientious objectors scheduled for work outside the United States will be sent within a few days to do relief work in Chungking, China, which has received an average of two bombings a day for 4 years.
>
> First contingent will consist of 10 young men. Some 60 others will follow. All have been training for several months at Haverford College, Quaker school in Pennsylvania, in public health, first aid, mass feeding, maintenance of motor vehicles, and background and languages of the area in which they will work. . . .
>
> The service board plans to send some 40 to 50 men to each of 4 or 5 colleges for such training. These men agree to serve for the duration of the war plus 2 years. All expenses are borne by the churches. They receive nothing from the government.
>
> The Chungking project was approved by President Roosevelt and it is reported to have been the brainchild of Mrs. Roosevelt, who has many Quaker friends.[9]

The other article, "While Saving the World," which was written by Frank C. Waldrop and published in the *Washington Times-Herald* on May 8, was full of inaccuracies and all but attacked the foreign relief service program. The writer rattled off a series of "facts" that he said were provided by Col. Lewis F. Kosch of the Selective Service and Paul C. French of NSBRO, whom he described as "a civilian aide of his who will supervise the program in detail." Waldrop wrote that the COs would be educated at "Harvard, Yale, Princeton, Swarthmore, the University of Pennsylvania, and perhaps one or two more eastern colleges." By throwing in the names of Ivy League universities Harvard, Yale, Princeton, and Penn, none of whom would be involved in relief training, he left the impression that this service was an elitist program for pampered COs. He questioned how much the COs would be paid and whether they would repay the government for the education given to them: "On the face of it, they are just being set up in good jobs, perhaps for life." Waldrop concluded by quoting the reaction of "a lady to whom this writer told the following facts yesterday" and asking a series of rhetorical questions:

> She has two sons in the army. One of them volunteered within a week after Pearl Harbor. The other followed as soon as he recovered from a major operation he had to undergo before he was physically qualified to pass the army tests.
>
> Said she: "My boys would like to go to college too. They would like safe jobs for 18 months to 2 years after the war in something like this. . . . I hope I see my boys after this war is over, and I hope I never have to sit in judgment on these other cases."
>
> What do you think is the right way to handle these conscientious objectors? Should they be sent out . . . ? Should they be ordered into noncombatant work of the army—doing clerical, medical, and quartermaster duty?
>
> Or should they be left where they are? Let's see some reactions in the Voice of the People.[10]

Representative Starnes gave his reaction at the House subcommittee hearings. Commenting on the Selective Training and Service Act of 1940, Starnes said, "I fully admit the culpability of Congress in passing such legislation. I regret that such legislation was ever enacted in the first place, and in the second place, after it was enacted, I regret that these people should be set up as a separate class and given a college education in a special civilian organization and then transported abroad in army transportation."[11]

On June 18, the House Appropriations Committee reported a bill containing language prohibiting any expense, direct or indirect, for COs for "compensation of military or civilian personnel, transportation on any kind of conveyance belonging to or operated by or at the expense of the War Department, and instruction, education, or training of any kind."[12] The committee made this statement after adding this language to the bill: "It would be incongruous, the committee feels, to use such funds upon persons possessing convictions or beliefs that relieve them from the foremost obligation of every citizen of his country." The House passed the bill without discussion. The final version of the Military Establishment Appropriations Act passed by both houses of Congress contained language prohibiting the use of funds for instruction, education, or training of IV-E COs in colleges, the service of COs outside of the United States and its territories and possessions, transportation of COs to and from such colleges or any such service, and the compensation of military or civilian service personnel for these purposes.[13] An article in the July 8, 1943, *Chicago Tribune Press* with the title "Kill Scheme of Mrs. F. D. R. for Objectors" read:

> A scheme sponsored by Mrs. Eleanor Roosevelt for giving several hundred conscientious objectors special college training and sending them abroad on foreign relief work has been abandoned under orders from Congress, it was disclosed today. A spokesman for selective service headquarters said abandonment of the plan has resulted in the recall of six conscientious objectors who were on their way to China and the withdrawal of an additional 200 from training courses in eastern and middle western colleges. . . .
>
> Selective service sources said they were not in sympathy with the program to begin with but that it was pushed by the "White House" after Mrs. Roosevelt had proposed it. The program, which was thus quietly started several months ago, ran into opposition from members of congress and officials of the American Legion who got wind of it.[14]

This act of Congress ended CPS foreign relief service and training. College training programs were discontinued by September.[15]

Religious agencies continued to offer foreign relief training as an after-hours program at CPS units at Alexian Brothers Hospital in Chicago; Duke University Hospital; Howard, Rhode Island; Ypsilanti, Michigan; Beltsville, Michigan; Orlando; Denison, Iowa; Minneapolis; and Poughkeepsie, New York, to prepare COs for service following the war.[16]

After the war, COs who had spent as many as four years in the CPS volunteered for relief projects sponsored by church agencies. Areas in Europe, Asia, and Africa had been devastated during the war. Some countries were on the brink of mass starvation. In 1946, the daily food ration in Austria was twelve hundred calories, in Hungary people subsisted almost entirely on bread, with a daily ration of five ounces, while the food supply in Bulgaria was a little more than eight ounces a day.[17] According to a newsletter published by the BSC, the situation was dire in some countries: "*Yugoslavia:* Disease and starvation will increase greatly unless grain imports improve sharply. *Romania:* Famine is apparent everywhere and deaths reported daily. People eating acorns or corn mixed with grass."

Friend Warren Sawyer was a "sea-going cowboy" on one of the Brethren "cattle boats," which delivered horses, cattle, and other livestock to nations devastated by the war. Methodist Neil Hartman, who later became a Friend, went to Japan as part of a relief unit. Mennonites Marvin Wasser and Edwin Scrag, who had been trained in the Poughkeepsie foreign relief program, served respectively in relief units in France and China after the war. Methodist-turned-Friend Dick Ruddell and his wife went to China as part of a Friends ambulance unit. Baptist Harold Wik, who had been accepted into the ill-fated Goshen College foreign relief training program, spent three years in a Mennonite relief unit in China and then continued relief work there under other church auspices.[18] Each of these men had served in CPS work camps and then state mental hospitals. Many other COs served humanity in church-sponsored foreign relief units after their time in the CPS.

◆ ◆ ◆

At the same time that the peace churches were trying to have foreign relief work and training approved as forms of alternative service under the CPS, they wanted to expand the CPS to include service outside of the work camps. Many COs questioned whether work at Forest Service, National Park Service, and Soil Conservation Service camps qualified as "work of national importance." The AFSC, in particular, argued that the education and skills of many COs were wasted at the work camps. As late as 1945, the AFSC would write, "Included on a typical work crew clearing logs and stumps from a drainage canal were a machinist, a mechanical engineer, a research physicist, two YMCA boys' secretaries, a personnel manager, a turpentine distiller, a piping engineer as well as an assortment of farmers, lawyers and students."[19]

From the start of the CPS, the Selective Service wanted to place COs in remote locations where they would be out of sight and out of mind. General Hershey believed that COs should be kept out of the military, where they could be uncooperative and disruptive, and out of the public limelight: "The conscientious objector, by my theory, is best handled if no one hears of him."[20] His predecessor as director of the Selective Service, Clarence Dykstra, had testified at House hearings: "It is contemplated that the conscientious objectors will be segregated from their respective communities and placed in camps similar to those of the Civilian Conservation Corps."[21] Selective Service officials not only worried that COs could create public relations problems for the CPS by being too visible in society but also feared that they could hurt the war effort by spreading their pacifist views.

At hearings of a subcommittee of the Senate Committee on Military Affairs on August 19, 1942, Colonel Kosch testified:

> We are not setting up projects that puts them in a position where they can do it, like social-welfare work, teaching schools, and so forth. We have had pressure put on us to put them in to teaching schools where they are short of funds, and so forth, but we have refused to do it, because we do not believe that the government should be a party to helping these men spread their pacifist propaganda. Around these camps you find there is a certain amount of it done due to the fact that if the churches invite the people in to talk we can't say "no" to it. However, if the churches do not ask them in, there is no particular way they have of spreading their propaganda on these jobs, because they are work jobs; and, as I say, we are opposed to setting up any type of project which would lend itself to the spreading of their propaganda.[22]

NSBRO and church agencies pressed the Selective Service to approve social service and other projects for COs outside of the work camps and proposed projects to be tried on an experimental basis. With all-out war and the military draft, the country also faced severe labor shortages in agriculture and key industries. Congress considered a labor draft to complement the military draft. Senator Claude Pepper of Florida and other members of Congress questioned whether the CPS was using COs effectively. Pepper would later lose his seat in the Senate and then serve in the House of Representatives. He would become the leading advocate for elderly people in Congress from the 1960s until his death in the late 1980s. After the war, he would lend his name as a sponsor of the National Mental Health Foundation, established by former COs to reform state hospitals and training schools.

Perhaps with the encouragement of NSBRO and the AFSC, government and private agencies began requesting that the Selective Service assign COs to fill job vacancies or address labor needs. In a letter dated September 15, 1942, for example, John Tucker, chairman of the Board of Directors of the Nursery and Child Home of Maryland, wrote General Hershey to request the assignment of CPS men to serve as teachers or house fathers.[23]

In 1942, the Selective Service finally approved the establishment of "detached units" or "special service units" separate from CPS work camps. Before entering detached units, CPS men had to spend at first sixty and then ninety days in work camps or base camps, as they were eventually called. For men who worked at hospitals, mental hospitals, and training schools as well as dairy farms and some other projects, the institutions or farmers paid for the services of the men. Consistent with Selective Service policy, however, the men were not permitted to be paid.

The money went to the religious agency, which, after deducting the maintenance expenses for the men, sent the remainder to NSBRO, which in turn forwarded it to a special account at the U.S. Treasury.

The first special service units were opened at Alexian Brothers Hospital in Chicago under the ACCO, and a series of public health projects in Florida under the BSC, the MCC, and the AFSC, in March 1942.[24] Other hospital units would be opened at Presbyterian Hospital in New York under the AFSC in September 1942 and Duke University Hospital under the Methodist Commission on World Peace in December of that year. In the hospitals, COs worked as orderlies, attendants, and technical or support staff.

Another public health project would be established in Gulfport, Mississippi, under the MCC in February 1945. The public health projects were conducted in primarily rural, largely African American areas. Hookworm, an intestinal parasite, was spread by a lack of sanitary facilities. It was rampant in parts of the South during the period, and an estimated 33 percent of the population in one Florida county suffered from hookworm infestation.[25] To fight hookworm and other parasites and diseases, COs constructed privies, installed wells, and built septic tanks and other sanitary facilities. Other work included screening houses to keep out mosquitoes, conducting health surveys, and performing public health and community education projects.

In July 1945, BSC, MCC, and AFSC units were opened in Puerto Rico and the Virgin Islands under the Puerto Rican Reconstruction Administration. The PRRA had been established by President Roosevelt in 1935 to fight disease and parasite infestation.[26] COs worked with the PRRA to build medical facilities and provide medical and social services.

The first mental hospital unit was opened by the AFSC at Eastern State Hospital in Williamsburg, Virginia, in June 1942. During World War II, mental hospitals and training schools faced severe labor shortages. Attendants had been drafted for the military or had taken higher-paying jobs in defense industries. In a letter dated April 8, 1943, to Colonel Kosch of the Selective Service, Charles Zeller, superintendent of Philadelphia State Hospital, known as Byberry, described the situation: "As of this date, we have one hundred and ten vacancies out of one hundred and seventy-three male attendant positions. We have one paid attendant on duty on each shift per one hundred and forty-four patients."[27]

The first CPS unit at a training school for people with intellectual disabilities opened in Mansfield, Connecticut, under the BSC in March 1943. Eventually, CPS units would be established at forty-four mental hospitals in twenty states and fifteen training schools in twelve states. Approximately three thousand COs would serve at mental hospitals and training schools, primarily as attendants.

One of the earliest mental hospital units planned for the CPS experienced the first of what would be many "public relations" problems at state institutions. Brethren M. R. Zigler had worked with the mental hospital located in Elgin, Illinois, the home of the headquarters of the Brethren Church, to establish a CPS unit there. Zigler reported being humiliated by what happened:

> Everything worked so neatly, and I thought we'd be the first one to get into the mental hospital deal. Colonel [Lewis] Kosch [director of the Selective Service's Camp Operations Division] came out; he thought everything had worked out all right. The American Legion didn't like it, and when he came out there to finalize the program, he had to meet with the American Legion. And he called me at two o'clock in the morning and said he couldn't do a thing with them, and they'd just have to postpone working on the project then.[28]

A CPS unit never opened in Elgin.

The AFSC administered a unit at Cheltenham School for Boys, a "school for Negro juvenile delinquents," in Maryland. In January 1943, about a month after it had opened, the unit included a cook, an attendant, social workers, clinical psychologists, and an accountant.[29] The unit was racially integrated.

In May 1943, the first dairy farm and dairy herd testing projects were established under the general authority of the Department of Agriculture, in cooperation with state and other agencies. COs worked directly for farmers on dairy farms or traveled from farm to farm to test the quality of cows' milk. CPS men also were assigned to state agricultural experiment stations.

◆   ◆   ◆

The first of what were called CPS "human guinea pig experiments" started in October 1943 under the U.S. Office of Scientific Research and Development or the Office of the Surgeon General.[30] Along with the mental hospital and training school units, the human experiments were highlighted as major contributions of the CPS. According to the AFSC, "We feel that the service performed by CPS men in mental institutions and as human 'guinea pigs' in medical research has proved of particular significance to national and human welfare."[31]

Medical experiments were conducted on approximately five hundred COs by researchers from many of the leading universities and hospitals in the nation, including Harvard, the University of Pennsylvania, Yale, the University of Chicago, Massachusetts General Hospital, Stanford University, the University of Minnesota, and others.[32] CPS men were infected with malaria, hepatitis, and pneumonia; exposed to parasites; and subjected to extreme temperatures, high and low

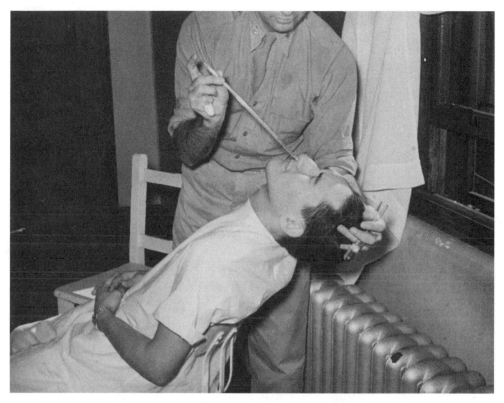

13. CPS "human guinea pig" in mononucleosis medical experiment, CPS Unit no. 68, Norwich, Connecticut. (Brethren Historical Library and Archives, Elgin, Illinois)

altitudes, and various diets.[33] At a Forest Service CPS camp in New Hampshire, insecticide powders were tried out on thirty COs who wore lice-infested clothes for several weeks, while continuing to work nine-hour days building roads. The experiment was designed to halt the spread of typhus caused by lice.

An experiment conducted on COs at the University of Minnesota was designed to study rehabilitation from a semistarvation diet. Under the sponsorship of the BSC, medical researcher Ancel Keys subjected thirty-six COs to a semistarvation diet averaging 1,570 calories per day. The thirty-two men who made it through the six months of the starvation phase of the experiment lost an average of just over thirty-seven pounds, or 24.29 percent of their body weight.[34] During the rehabilitation phase of the experiment, men were divided into different groups who received varying amounts of additional calories over the semistarvation diet. The Minnesota starvation experiment was heralded as a pioneering study in nutrition, although it took a physical and psychological toll on the men who participated in it.

The Minnesota experiment was advertised to COs as an opportunity to contribute to knowledge that would aid in the rehabilitation of starvation victims in

14. CPS "human guinea pig" in semistarvation medical experiment, University of Minnesota, Minneapolis. (Swarthmore College Peace Collection, Swarthmore, Pennsylvania)

Europe. To recruit COs, W. Harold Row of the BSC and Paul Furnas of the AFSC sent a set of brochures to CPS directors or unit leaders.[35] Their recruitment letters were identical: "The Brethren Service Committee [or American Friends Service Committee] is anxious that this project succeed, and will appreciate your help." The recruitment procedure also had CPS men who had participated in previous vitamin experiments at the Minnesota unit contact friends to apply to be part of the semistarvation experiment: "Immediately prepared mimeographed materials for unit members to write to friends with, to get interested. Underground in CPS is wonderful."[36] A one-page flyer dated September 1943, *Will We Know How to Feed*

Europe When the Time Comes? read: "It would give us something about which to be concerned as a group and provide an alternative to the blank-wall we have met in making our witness in the international relief field." The AFSC and the BSC approved and, as the Minnesota experiment illustrated, often actively supported the guinea pig experiments. The BSC contributed financially to the Minnesota experiment. The MCC and Mennonites were marginally involved in medical experimentation.[37]

Ward Miles, Neil Hartman, Warren Sawyer, Charlie Lord, Michael Marsh, Richard Ruddell, Forrest Altman, and other COs assigned to the Byberry mental hospital unit in Philadelphia participated in jaundice experiments at the University of Pennsylvania.[38] CPS Unit 140, which was operated under the auspices of the Office of the Surgeon General and the AFSC and the BSC, sponsored the jaundice, or hepatitis, experiments (Unit 140 was previously Unit 115 under the Office of Scientific Research and Development). Like many other experiments conducted on COs, the hepatitis experiments grew out of problems encountered during the war. In Italy, in particular, hepatitis was rampant among U.S. troops. More men had contracted hepatitis than had been killed or wounded during battle. The hepatitis experiments were led by Drs. John Neefe and Joseph Stokes at the University of Pennsylvania. Many of the subjects of the experiments were COs at Byberry. Some COs, such as Warren Sawyer, were recruited for the experiments from Byberry. Others, like Charles Lord, first volunteered for the experiments and then applied to work at Byberry after moving to Philadelphia. Byberry superintendent Charles Zeller supported the experiments and arranged for COs at the institution to be part of them. One article published by the researchers acknowledged Zeller's cooperation.[39] COs involved in the experiments lived either at a former fraternity house on the Penn campus or in the housing for COs at Byberry.

The Penn experiments involved both hepatitis A and hepatitis B, then known as infectious and serum hepatitis. In one serum hepatitis experiment, nine men were inoculated with one of two forms of plasma or yellow fever vaccine tainted with hepatitis. Blood and urine tests were conducted at regular intervals, and the men's physical symptoms were closely monitored. Eight of the men definitely contracted hepatitis, and one, Warren Sawyer, probably did. Figures in the journal article charted each man's serum bilirubin, urine bilirubin, brosullphalein, cephalin FLOCC, vitamin A, and other levels pre- and postinoculation, over a period of 160 to 230 days. Each figure contained the man's initials, and an acknowledgment at the end of the article listed the men by name. One figure reported on the blood or urine levels of one man, "W.F.A." (most likely W. Forrest Altman), who served as an uninoculated control. A brief section of the article reported that two hospital employees "who were in exceptionally close contact with one of the volunteers at

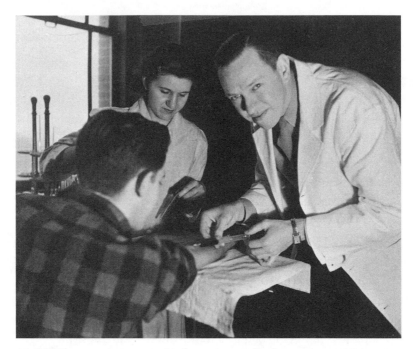

15. CPS "human guinea pig" in hepatitis medical experiment, University of Pennsylvania, Philadelphia. (Swarthmore College Peace Collection, Swarthmore, Pennsylvania)

a time when he was showing evidence of mild hepatitis" developed moderately severe hepatitis.[40] Based on this experiment, the researchers concluded that plasma or serum could transmit hepatitis, that the time of onset of serum hepatitis was shorter than previously believed, and that hepatitis could occur without jaundice.

Another experiment was designed to determine whether different treatments of contaminated water could prevent the occurrence of hepatitis.[41] Hepatitis viruses could pass through filters that retained bacteria and had proven resistant to treatment methods that controlled bacteria. COs ingested water specimens contaminated with feces from a person with hepatitis. There were different treatment conditions according to whether the specimens had been coagulated, filtered, or passed through activated carbon or treated with varying levels of chlorine. Some specimens also contained E. coli. Some of the treatment conditions were controls with untreated specimens. Each CO drank 2.75 liters of the specimen over a period of twenty-four hours. Neil Hartman referred to these concoctions as "milk shakes."[42] None of the men who had ingested specimens treated with a certain level of chlorine came down with hepatitis. In the other treatment or control groups as many as five of six men contracted hepatitis. The researchers concluded that chlorine treatment could inactivate the virus. In an acknowledgment at the end of the article, they thanked the Selective Service, NSBRO, the AFSC, Philadelphia State Hospital, and CPS Unit 140.

COs who contracted hepatitis experienced malaise, weakness, anorexia, nausea, vomiting, muscle pains, headaches, chills, upper respiratory infections, or abdominal pain. Men's symptoms ranged from mild to severe. Years later, Charles Lord recalled, "I got so sick. . . . My future wife visited me and I told her, 'I wish I could die.'" At the time, Warren Sawyer wrote, "I was really sick on Thanksgiving day. I really thought I had jaundice and that I would die. About four in the morning I was very cold and nauseated. I thought that I would choke to death. . . . My nose and throat were filled. I couldn't swallow. I vomited and was stuffed with muscous [sic]."[43]

Sometime after the experiments, liver biopsies were conducted on some of the COs to see if any lasting damage had been done to their livers. Neil Hartman reported that C. Everett Koop, who would be appointed surgeon general in the Reagan administration, conducted the biopsies. Koop served as assistant surgeon at the hospital of the University of Pennsylvania in 1947 and then surgeon in chief at the Children's Hospital of Philadelphia beginning in 1948. Hartman said that he wrote Koop years later after he had read a book by Koop. Koop wrote back almost right away: "He said if he had known then what he knew now, he wouldn't have done it. He thought it was too dangerous. . . . He claimed one person died."[44]

COs had various motivations for volunteering to participate in medical experiments. Many believed that this was a way to serve humanity. Warren Sawyer said, "That's all that occurred to me—serving mankind." Many years later, COs felt that the experiments had been important and that they would volunteer again if they had to make the same decision. For some COs, it got them away from Byberry, if only for period of time. Ward Miles, who went on to become a medical doctor and considered the experiments necessary, commented that they "got me away from B Building." (B Building was a notorious "violent ward" at the institution.) Miles continued: "I would spend three days at Byberry and three days at the jaundice unit. It was very stressful." Some men participated in the experiments to prove that they were not cowards, as COs were often called. Evert Bartholomew, who was a human guinea pig in malaria experiments at Goldwater Memorial Hospital in New York City, explained, "I could say that I was eager to demonstrate that we COs were not afraid of danger and doing something for humanity and here was my chance." Neil Hartman expressed a similar sentiment: "We were called yellow bellies and things like that. I wanted to prove that I wasn't afraid to take risks if it did good. I would not take risks to kill people, but if it would save people. . . . Actually I was happy that I had the opportunity to show the world I was willing to take risks."[45]

COs involved in the medical experiments were aware that they were taking risks, but they did not always know the nature of those risks. Hartman later recalled, "They didn't tell us the dangers of it," and Sawyer agreed: "No information. They just told us, 'Volunteer.'" At the time of the experiments, Sawyer wrote, "Yesterday I was told that the jaundice unit would start and it did. . . . What I know about jaundice is small. They have tried to experiment on animals but they don't seem to be able to react to the disease. . . . I have asked five doctors about the possibility if my having recurring jaundice also about the possibility of upsetting my internal anatomy. Chances all of them said were very slight. I shall probably never have jaundice again and there will be nothing ruined on my innards. Mortality rate if [*sic*] low."[46]

After participating in one experiment, Sawyer was approached to be in another:

> Friday down at the jaundice unit Dr. Neefe asked me if I would like to be injected with some more jaundice. This would be a different kind. It would be with some of Ben's blood. Most of the men that have been, in fact all of the men that were injected with Ben's blood were sick with symptoms of jaundice within 24 days. Dr. Neefe wants to see if I am immune to that. He says he could learn more from me if I got injected with this than he could from any other man. I haven't made up my mind as yet. Of course, I realize he was shooting me the old wahoo to get me to do it.[47]

For the public relations–conscious Selective Service, NSBRO, and religious agencies, the guinea pig experiments were a boon for the CPS. A *Life* magazine article on July 30, 1945, was titled: "Men Starve in Minnesota: Conscientious Objectors Volunteer for Strict Hunger Tests to Study Europe's Food Problem." Characteristic of *Life,* the article included a photo spread showing emaciated men at rest, on a treadmill, or being measured or tested. That same issue contained a photographic essay on displaced persons in Europe. It showed refugees on trains and in displaced-persons centers and transient camps. An October 19, 1942, *Time* magazine article described the New Hampshire CO study of typhoid-carrying lice: "This new method of typhus control might save millions of lives in the next few years."[48] Articles and editorials about the human guinea pig experiments appeared in the *New York Times,* Philadelphia papers, and many other newspapers across the country.[49]

In the 1940s, the human guinea pig experiments conducted on COs were not regarded as ethically problematic. The experiments were conducted by well-respected researchers and at leading universities and medical centers. The Selective Service, NSBRO, and the church committees not only approved medical experimentation on COs but sometimes actively cooperated in recruiting men to participate in the studies. At a time when COs were looked down upon in society, the experiments brought favorable publicity to the CPS. The COs themselves saw the experiments as an opportunity to serve humanity and demonstrate their altruism.

Nazi researchers who conducted human experimentation on concentration camp and mental hospital inmates during World War II were tried for war crimes during the Nuremberg Trials.[50] Sixteen were condemned to death. Many of the experiments were similar to the ones conducted on COs, including experimentation on typhus, malaria, seawater consumption, and extreme pressure and temperatures. German researchers also carried out hepatitis experiments on mental hospital patients and Jewish children at a concentration camp.[51]

Based on the Nazi medical experiments, the Nuremberg Code was established in 1949 to guide the conduct of research on humans. The World Medical Association later issued the Helsinki Declaration in 1964 to refine protections for humans involved in research.[52] Then, following exposés of unethical medical experiments in the United States, the federal government acted in 1974 to establish ethical guidelines and regulations for the conduct of human research. Among the controversial experiments attracting public attention in the United States was hepatitis research conducted on children at Willowbrook State School in Staten Island, New York.[53] A research team led by Saul Krugman infected children at Willowbrook with hepatitis in an attempt to find a vaccine for the disease. In 1979, the National Commission for the Protection of Human Subjects of Biomedical and Behavioral Research released the *Belmont Report,* containing ethical principles and guidelines for the protection of human research subjects. The key ethical principles in the report were respect for persons, beneficence (that is, minimize harms and maximize benefits to subjects), and justice. Federal regulations governing research were designed to build on the *Belmont Report*'s principles.[54]

The ethical standards of one era cannot necessarily be imposed on the activities in another era. Certainly, medical researchers in the 1940s could not have been expected to adhere to today's federal regulations and guidelines, which are largely procedural in nature and emphasize documentation and record keeping. Yet the human guinea pig experiments conducted on the COs call into question the ethical standards of the researchers involved in the studies. The COs were referred to as "volunteers" in the experiments, but they volunteered for the studies only in the sense that they chose participation in research over other forms of required service. They were not free of undue influence to become human guinea pigs. It is doubtful whether most of the experiments could have been conducted if they had been forced to rely on subjects who were not under government control. The experiments offered no benefits to the COs and often placed them in direct harm. The hepatitis experiments could have not only caused acute illness but resulted in long-term liver damage and even death as well. A key ethical principle that has emerged in human research is informed consent. People should be informed of research procedures and the benefits and risks of research before participating in experiments. The idea of consent is not new. Walter Reed fully informed subjects of known risks in yellow fever research in 1900.[55] COs did not always understand the experiments or their risks. In the Minnesota semistarvation experiments, Keys apparently told men of the dangers of the research, although the dangers were not fully known.[56] In the hepatitis experiments at Penn, the risks appeared to have been minimized or glossed over. The risks did not only involve men who participated in the experiments. At least two other people were believed to have been infected with hepatitis from one of the COs in the experiments. Samuel Burgess was a CO at a camp in Cooperstown, New York, and a mental hospital unit at Williamsburg, Virginia. He later became a pathologist. Burgess's brother worked for the AFSC and was responsible for approving medical experiments in which the COs participated. Many years later, Burgess stated about his brother, "If he knew then what he knew later, he would never have approved that hepatitis experiment. A number of people who were in the hepatitis experiment never were well again."[57]

The ethics of the human guinea pig experiments with COs might be questioned or even challenged. Reflecting on the experiments, the subjects themselves tended to be proud of their participation and their service to humanity.

◆   ◆   ◆

To the frustration of NSBRO and the religious agencies, the Selective Service turned down a large number of domestic social welfare, educational, and humanitarian projects. The AFSC listed more than one hundred social and welfare agencies that requested and were denied the assignment of CPS men.[58] These organizations included the Indiana Department of Public Welfare, the Pittsburgh School for the Deaf, the Children's Aid Society in New York City, the Federal Public Housing Authority, the County of Los Angeles Health Department, the Iowa School for the Blind, Nebraska Central College, American Youth Hostels in Massachusetts, and the American Red Cross for New York, Philadelphia, and Boston. Presumably, these projects threatened to cause political controversy or provide COs with the opportunity to spread their "pacifist propaganda," whereas projects with dairy farmers, the "mentally ill" and "mentally defective," "Negro" juvenile delinquents, medical researchers, Puerto Ricans, and the rural poor in the South would not.

By early 1944, the number of CPS men in detached units exceeded the number in work camps.

◆ ◆ ◆

The detached service units brought to light a long-simmering issue in American society: race. The CPS was interracial and integrated in an era in which the U.S. military and many social institutions in both the South and the North were segregated. The number of nonwhite COs in the CPS does not appear to have been reported by the Selective Service or NSBRO. The Selective Service "Special Form for Conscientious Objector" (DSS Form 47) for CO claims did not ask for information about race or ethnicity, although its "Conscientious Objector Report" (DSS Form 48) for CPS assignments and discharges did have a question about race. NSBRO's personnel records for CPS men did not include any questions about race or ethnicity.[59]

Although it is difficult to say how many nonwhite or non-Euro-American men served in the CPS, some African Americans clearly served. Muslim Nazeer Aleem was a CO at Marom, Indiana; Trenton, North Dakota; Coshocton, Ohio; and Concord, New Hampshire. CO J. Benjamin Stalvey recalled a group of African American First Century Christians at the Trenton, North Dakota, camp. Photos maintained at the archives of the Swarthmore College Peace Collection, the Mennonite Church USA at Goshen, Indiana, and the Church of the Brethren at Elgin, Illinois, show an occasional African American in CPS units. A photo of six Brethren COs who made up the CPS Staff Advisory Council in the Church of the Brethren archives includes an African American, Glen Evans.[60] The *CPS Directory* published by NISBCO in 1996 had an entry for a Glenn L. Evans, identified as a Baptist from Roanoke, Texas.

The Friends were among the first and strongest opponents of slavery in America and had a long history of advocating for racial justice. In his book *The Good War*, Studs Terkel cited a published quote by a Japanese American who remembered that the AFSC offered assistance to Japanese Americans to avoid going to relocation camps during World War II.[61]

In March 1946, the BSC issued a general statement on the CPS. The statement contained a section on minorities: "The problem of minorities is of special significance in C.P.S. Idealistically the B.S.C. works for religious tolerance, racial equality, and political freedom. In assisting in the placement of assignees, the B.S.C. considers qualifications of the men without regard to race, creed or politics. In spite of our striving, however, this ideal is not practically attained in all of our projects. When an assignee feels he cannot remain on a project under such conditions, the B.S.C. will seek to effect satisfactory transfer to another assignment."[62]

The policy acknowledged that the BSC did not always live up to its ideals. In a memo sent to CPS men at five units on December 8, 1944, Morris Keeton,

16. Brethren Service Committee CPS Staff Advisory Council. (Brethren Historical Library and Archives, Elgin, Illinois)

educational secretary of the BSC, asked for volunteers to conduct a study of race relations in the Brethren CPS:

> We all agreed that we should investigate facts on causes of discrimination and non-assimilation among racial groups in BCPS [Brethren Civilian Public Service] units with a view to finding the most effective points on which to take action. We did not agree upon where the personnel for this study would be found. Someone must be found in BCPS to take responsibility for this study. It should be someone who expects to make his life work in matters related to this. It might be a person who wants to get sociology credit toward a degree or write a doctoral dissertation through this investigation and accompanying study.[63]

The BSC sponsored a "School of Race Relations" at Camp Kane in Pennsylvania from May to September 1944. The school offered weekly forum lectures, with discussion sessions, seminar meetings, and independent studies. The scope of work for one seminar included studying "the anthropological, sociological and psychological facts about race and race groupings and the theories and myths about race that have grown up in modern times." A second seminar had this purpose: "This study group will deal with the specific racial problems in the United States of America: in particular, Negro-white relations, American Indian–white relations, Oriental-white relations, Mexican-American-white relations."[64] African American COs represented approximately 12 percent of the men at Camp Kane.

The Mennonite Church had a philosophy of tolerance and "love thy neighbor," but was silent on the matter of race. Mennonites neither held slaves in early America nor worked for the abolition of slavery.[65] Further, because they often came from rural areas of Pennsylvania and the Midwest, most Mennonites had limited contact with members of other races or ethnicities other than Native Americans.

NSBRO and the committees of the historic peace churches would tread lightly on the issue of race when it arose in CPS camps and units. Sensitive to negative public relations that could harm the CPS program and even the existence of individual units, they were reluctant to confront blatant or subtle racism when it reared its ugly head. It would be left to individual COs to take aggressive stands against the racism pervasive in American society.

Some COs identified with the religious pacifist organization the Fellowship of Reconciliation, which strongly opposed racial discrimination. In November 1945, the New England Fellowship of Reconciliation held a fall conference, "The Pacifist Task in the Post-war World."[66] The registration fee was one dollar for regular participants and fifty cents for students and CPS men. The morning of the first full day of the conference held concurrent round-table discussions on foreign policy and domestic policy. The session on domestic policy was titled "How Can We Improve Our Race Relations?" One of the speakers in this session was Talcott Parsons, a professor of sociology at Harvard. His 1951 book, *The Social System*, which presented society as a well-oiled machine composed of interrelated parts, would be heralded as a sociological classic. Parsons later coedited *The Negro American* with Kenneth Clark, a leading African American psychologist, in 1966. Clark's research with his wife, Mamie Phipps Clark, on the preferences of African American children for white or black dolls would be influential in convincing the Supreme Court of the detrimental effects of school segregation in the famous case *Brown v. Board of Education.*[67]

In 1942, the Fellowship of Reconciliation established the Committee of Racial Equality that would later be named the Congress of Racial Equality (CORE).[68] Under the leadership of James Farmer, Bayard Rustin, and others, CORE would become a major civil rights organization in the United States in later years.

Out-of-the-way work camps were not likely to experience race-related public relations problems. None of the Forest Service, Soil Conservation Service, or Park Service camps was located in the Deep South, which would not have been friendly territory for CO camps in the first place. Yet racial issues pervaded American society, and when they did arise in camps, individual CPS men often organized to confront them.

George Yamada was a CO at the BSC Forest Service camp in Cascade Locks, Oregon. Entering the CPS on December 5, 1941—two days before the attack on Pearl Harbor—Yamada was a Japanese American. Smith explained what happened:

> When evacuation of all people of Japanese ancestry on the Pacific coast was ordered, Yamada was ordered through Selective Service to report to a War Relocation Authority camp. Yamada protested the order, as did a majority of the men in camp on the grounds of racial discrimination and a violation of civil liberties. [Camp director] Schrock refused to sign the necessary papers for the transfer. For several weeks men conducted a vigorous campaign, promising non-violent direct action if Yamada was forced to go to a relocation center. The action nearly resulted in Selective Service taking over direct administration of the camp.[69]

In a less-than-ideal compromise negotiated by NSBRO with the army, which was approved by the Selective Service, Yamada was offered a transfer to a CPS camp in Colorado Springs, outside of the restricted zone for Japanese Americans. Yamada accepted the compromise, and the matter was put to rest.

In other CPS camps, men protested when fellow African American COs were denied service or discriminated against by area establishments when they left camp grounds.[70]

The detached units brought COs into greater contact with the public and governmental and social institutions. In the context of a segregated society, the CPS and COs were forced to confront deeply held prejudicial beliefs and entrenched discriminatory practices.

Public health hookworm projects administered by the MCC in Mulberry and the AFSC in Orlando created controversies when the units offended the segregationist sentiments of white public officials and citizens in Florida. At the MCC Mulberry project, COs soon became aware of racism in the South and sought Christian ways to deal with it.[71] CO Harry Van Dyck explained that the camp newsletter ran articles on race: "Camp newsletters were a major outlet for expressing our ideals. At Mulberry, our camp newsletter, *Box 96,* ran a series of essays on race relations written by individual campers. My contribution to the series was a lengthy piece entitled 'Psychology of Race Prejudice.' In it I spoke of 'our race problem' as a 'social abscess which we cannot long endure.'" The camp invited African American pastors and educators to speak to the COs, and the camp quartet sang at local African American churches.[72] Two of the COs introduced themselves to noted educator Mary McLeod Bethune, founder of Bethune-Cookman College and a leader in African American organizations. When former COs established the National Mental Health Foundation in 1946, McLeod Bethune would sit on its Board of Directors.

The Mulberry unit sponsored a conference on black and white cooperation in May 1945, and in February 1946 more than a dozen COs made a weekend trip to Bethune-Cookman, where they met with faculty, played in a softball game with African American students, and attended Sunday church services.[73] Van Dyck recalled the visit to Bethune-Cookman:

> I recall two major impressions. One was the poverty-stricken condition of the campus and its facilities. The buildings were small and plain, and the appointments inside them were drab. The campus lacked sidewalks and attractive landscaping. The other impression I had was of the awkwardness of our interactions with members of the college community—faculty and students alike. They were gracious and hospitable, and we tried to be casual, but I felt that no one was fully at ease. I suspect that they were puzzled, perhaps even embarrassed, by a group of white COs descending in their midst. For them, the situation probably was too irregular, the event too contrived.[74]

Before the COs departed Bethune-Cookman, they attended the college's weekly Sunday-afternoon program for students and the public. They were introduced by the president of the college, and one of the men gave brief remarks.[75] They were overshadowed that day by an address by a reporter from the *Pittsburgh Courier,* a prominent black newspaper, and the presence of a young African American baseball player who had just been signed by Branch Rickey to play for the Brooklyn Dodgers, Jackie Robinson.[76] For their involvement with the African American community, the COs from the Mulberry unit were called "Nigger lovers" by members of the local white citizenry.[77]

A public controversy that drew in the AFSC erupted at the Orlando public health camp. In May 1944, white COs gave a party for the graduating class of an African American high school.[78] The county commissioners responded by calling for the withdrawal of the CPS unit. At least twenty COs asked the AFSC to determine whether the unit should be continued. The AFSC reached a compromise with state and local officials that the unit could stay if the COs agreed not to engage in racial mingling. Individual COs unwilling to agree to this directive would be given the opportunity to transfer out of the unit. Camp director Chris Ahrens later recalled, "I was director of the Orlando, Florida, Hookworm Control Project unit. We worked with a black high school, improving facilities. For giving a party for the graduating class and mixing races, the KKK went for our scalps and insisted that we all leave. Lou Schneider came down from [the AFSC in] Philadelphia to negotiate and reached an agreement with the Klan leaders to let those stay who would obey local mores. Thus I got the chance to work two years in Puerto Rico."[79] It was not one of the AFSC's finer moments.

Another public health project sponsored by the MCC in Gulfport, Mississippi, created an uproar within the CPS.[80] The unit was planned in cooperation with the state board of health, the U.S. Public Health Service, the state director of the Selective Service, the MCC, NSBRO, and others. It even received the endorsements of representatives of the local Chamber of Commerce, the American Legion, and elected officials, rarities in the history of the CPS. Soon after the camp was announced, men at AFSC and BSC camps began to question whether the unit would be racially integrated. An article by a CO at the MCC camp in Mulberry, Florida, who supported the opening of the camp, described the protests prompted by the Gulfport unit:

> Most widely publicized of these was that of the Lyons, N.J. group in which seventy-one men addressed themselves to the NSBRO criticizing a reply from NSB's Claude Shotts to their earlier queries as to whether the proposed Mississippi Unit was to be freely interracial or Jim Crow.
>
> The statements of Mr. Shotts that drew the most fire were: "As far as I know there has been no CPS project either in the south or the north where there has been advance agreement that men will be received without race distinction. It is exceedingly unfortunate that we cannot carry out religious ideals on race along with our religious convictions about war." The Lyons men feel that by ignoring the race question the NSB is not accurately representing the concerns of the historic peace churches. They also feel that to live consistently we can tolerate no condition short of equality for all, and that if we do accept such conditions we are making a deal with race-baiters and are denying the basic Christian principle of the Fatherhood of God and the brotherhood of man. So they oppose the opening of the Mississippi unit.[81]

In the detailed "Analysis and Criticism of the Handling of the Conscientious Objector in World War II," Sanford Rothman and Max Ginsberg, Jewish COs at the BSC camp at Cascade Locks, Oregon, faulted NSBRO: "Its stand on discrimination is very weak and definitely not in accord with the feelings of the great majority of men in CPS. Rationalization has been used to carry a point when it was felt serious opposition would be encountered." The critique pointed specifically to the problem of discrimination in the selection of detached CPS units: "In the past units have been approved by Selective Service and the NSBRO with a disregard for discrimination factors (both as to people served and membership restrictions within the unit); examples are Cheltenham, Maryland, southern camps generally, Delaware Agricultural Station."[82]

Despite the internal opposition within the CPS, the Gulfport camp was opened in February 1945.[83] Men installed privies; conducted sanitation surveys; assisted in laboratory tests for hookworm infestation, venereal disease, and milk sanitation; and worked on other public health projects. An after-hours—non-CPS—project was devoted to the improvement of the African American North Gulfport school. A women's summer service unit in 1946 offered recreational and religious programs to black and white children in the community. A photo in the Mennonite Church USA archives from the Gulfport unit showed five white women teachers with twenty-nine African American boys and girls "enjoying a chocolate milk drink on Friday morning" at "Turkey Creek (colored) Bible School."

Melvin Gingerich, who started working on his authoritative Mennonite history of the CPS, *Service for Peace,* while teaching at Mennonite Bethel College, commented on the Gulfport controversy: "CPS too was not a perfect situation but under the present conditions it was the best possible witness . . . by carrying on a health program that serves both races equally and by doing small acts which quietly demonstrate one's beliefs in the brotherhood of man, much more can be

17. Mennonite Central Committee women's summer service, Gulfport, Mississippi. Women with children at "Turkey Creek (colored) Bible School." (Mennonite Church USA Historical Committee and Archives, Goshen, Indiana)

accomplished toward the solution of the problem than by taking a course that would prevent the camp opening in the south."[84]

The Gulfport controversy highlighted the different religious philosophies among the historic peace churches. The MCC's position was consistent with the Mennonite principle of nonresistance: recognize the existence of evil in the world, avoid conflict with government authorities, and witness to God through good works and individual acts of kindness. This belief stood in contrast with the philosophy of the Friends and others that evil in the world must be confronted through nonviolent resistance and even civil disobedience. These differences in philosophy would be seen when the COs were confronted by horrific conditions and brutality in the nation's mental hospitals and training schools.

The AFSC unit at the Cheltenham "School for Negro Juvenile Delinquents" would create a dilemma and an opportunity for the CPS and COs in 1943. On the one hand, Cheltenham was a segregated institution. Rothman and Ginsberg singled it out by name in their criticism of NSBRO's complacency about racial segregation. On the other hand, it would enable COs to put into practice their beliefs about racial equality. The caption on a photo of a Cheltenham CO and a young African American boy in the archives of the Swarthmore College Peace Collection described Cheltenham as an "interracial" unit. CO William Channel recalled that about half of the roughly twenty CPS men at Cheltenham were African American.[85]

According to Channel, Cheltenham had always been run by white southerners until recently when the superintendent had hired black staff because of wartime labor shortages. The African American staff lived and ate in separate quarters. COs were expected to abide by segregationist practices at Cheltenham: "Forced to eat in the kitchen, Wally Nelson, a black CO, transferred back to his previous camp to protest the segregation."[86] Nelson was a Methodist from St. Paul, Minnesota.

White COs approached Cheltenham's white superintendent, Vance Thomas, for permission to eat in what was called the "colored dining room." Not thinking that allowing it would create problems, the superintendent gave permission. Two of the regular African American staff then said to the COs, "We've decided that the COs have done enough for black staff members at Cheltenham, and it's time we did something for ourselves. So if you will guarantee that empty chairs will be there tomorrow morning, we're going to eat breakfast in the white dining room." The next day, black staff members had breakfast in the white dining room. Old-time white staff went directly to the superintendent, who called the white COs and said, "Get those fellows out of there. There's going to be bloodshed!"[87]

As often happened in the CPS, word of the Cheltenham situation spread throughout the camps and units. About fifty COs from the AFSC camp in

18. CPS man with boy at Unit no. 62, Cheltenham Training School for Negro Juvenile Delinquents, Cheltenham, Maryland. (Swarthmore College Peace Collection, Swarthmore, Pennsylvania)

Colesville, California, wrote the AFSC to denounce Cheltenham's racist practices.[88] COs at Cheltenham were ready to ask to be transferred back to their camps. NSBRO and the AFSC got involved in the situation. French thought that it would be a mistake for the COs to withdraw from Cheltenham and that they should use pacifist techniques to resolve the controversy: "It will be a major defeat if this isn't worked out on the basis of goodwill and understanding." Dr. Thomas, Cheltenham's superintendent, called French to say that he was going to ask the Selective Service to remove the CPS unit. French and other representatives of NSBRO and the AFSC went to Cheltenham that same day and got Thomas to agree to postpone asking for removal of the unit while a compromise could be worked out. French and Thomas spoke the next day. Thomas said that he had met with the CPS men and was pleased with their attitude, but that the "colored staff would be unwilling to consider any compromise." Three days later, two CPS men from Cheltenham visited French and told him that Thomas had called a special meeting of the board of managers and planned to discharge two African American staff members. On the next day, Thomas called French to tell him that the board had approved a resolution to make Cheltenham completely interracial in terms of eating, sleeping, and employment. French reflected in his diary: "If this goes through, it means a definite advance in racial relations in Maryland and the CPS men have played a real part in it."[89] This compromise was not the end of the story.

Local opposition to the integration of Cheltenham grew. One month after he had written about the advance in race relations in Maryland, French wrote in his diary:

> Vance Thomas came in from Cheltenham tonight and had dinner with us. He talked about the problems there and the difficulty he had in getting the men to understand the community attitude toward interracial living and eating. He said that the Grand Jury in Prince George County, who asked that all c.o.s be fired from the institution, had been instigated by a group of local people who had threatened to lynch all of the c.o.s and the Negro staff members if any interracial business was started. . . . He said he would move ahead just as fast as he could and get the interracial living and eating under way when local resentment became less acute.[90]

CO Channel was one of the CPS men called to testify at the grand jury investigation of Cheltenham: "And I went in, and as soon as I sat down, somebody in the back of the room jumped up and pointed their finger at me and said, 'Would you marry a nigger?' and before I could answer, another one jumped up and said, 'Do you have a sister? Would you have your sister marry a nigger?'"[91]

The Prince George's County Grand Jury asked that the CPS unit be withdrawn, but could find no basis for filing criminal charges in the situation.[92] The resolution of the board of managers to integrate Cheltenham School stood. Writing many years later, another CO at the unit, Stephen Angell, gave his recollection of the outcome of the COs' efforts: "At Cheltenham [Training School for Boys] we walked into a racially segregated institution. The CPS unit broke down the walls of segregation, got the racially biased white Superintendent fired and a black one hired. The black Superintendent left quite a bit to be desired. He was not a devotee of nonviolence."[93]

CPS men at Cheltenham ran recreational and educational programs and supervised cottages containing as many as fifty to sixty boys ages six to nineteen.[94]

A photo at the Swarthmore College Peace Collection shows a Cheltenham CO giving a lesson to an African American young man. Michael Schwartz, a deaf law professor, Ph.D., and disability studies scholar at Syracuse University, concluded that the young man was most likely deaf or otherwise hearing impaired. Schwartz, who was trained to communicate through speech and lipreading, was in the place of the black student many times while growing up. The lesson was consistent with the "oral method" of teaching deaf or hard-of-hearing students to communicate: "The figure on the blackboard is that of a side view of a face with a rectangular shape (like a cup) inside the mouth—the shape corresponds with a larger rectangular shape to the right of the face (just behind the teacher's arm), and notations 'e, I, i, u, o' alongside the sides of the shape correspond with vowels. The white man is underlining 'AH,' while holding the black man's chin, obviously trying to help him make the sound. The black man's mouth appears to be in the shape of 'Ah.'"[95]

There is irony in the photo. This location was a segregated training school for African American boys. Yet the young man was being trained in a mode of communication favored by paternalistic educators of deaf students from the late 1800s

19. CPS man teaching a deaf young man to speak at Unit no. 62, Cheltenham Training School for Negro Juvenile Delinquents, Cheltenham, Maryland. (Swarthmore College Peace Collection, Swarthmore, Pennsylvania)

until the 1970s and beyond.[96] The oral method of instruction was designed to make deaf people communicate like hearing people instead of relying on the method of communication—sign language—developed by deaf people themselves. Beginning in the 1970s, many deaf people began to reclaim their identity as a linguistic minority using sign as the natural method of communication.[97] In mid-twentieth-century America, the idea that deafness or disability could be a difference to be accepted, even celebrated, rather than a defect to be treated or cured would have been foreign to the most compassionate hearts and the most enlightened minds.

◆   ◆   ◆

Most northerners have prided themselves on being more racially tolerant than southerners. It is certainly true that the North has not practiced the extreme forms of segregation and violent racial oppression found in the South. Yet northern states and the federal government practiced racial segregation in the 1940s. The staffs at many mental hospitals and training schools in the North were segregated. Many COs learned this fact when they were assigned to the institutions.

At Byberry in Philadelphia, COs involved in forming a CPS union circulated a paper, "Facts and Policy on the Employment of Negroes as Attendants at Phila. State Hospital." Although Superintendent Charles Zeller felt he could not hire African Americans to work at the hospital as regular attendants, he was open to the assignment of African American COs there: "The attitude of the hospital administration toward the introduction of colored employees into the wards is favorable. Dr. Zeller has stated that all CPS men are eligible for assignment here, regardless of race or color. . . . However, in deference to the attitude of the regular employees, he feels he cannot hire negroes as attendants at the present time." The COs anticipated the problems that might arise with the assignment of an African American to the CPS unit:

> Although there seems to be a good possibility of having a negro assigned to this unit, he will still have to contend with the opposition of the regular attendants. If they themselves do not come to accept colored workers on the wards, no progress made will be permanent. The prejudice of the regular attendants will wear off as they are exposed to and become familiar with negro co-workers. . . . It may well happen, for instance, that any negro assigned here will have trouble adjusting to the wards. It is our business to insure in whatever way seems best that he is able to do a good job as an attendant.[98]

In one of the letters to his family, Byberry CO Warren Sawyer wrote that the first black CO arrived at the mental hospital on February 22, 1945: "Because of the institution's long-standing prejudice against hiring blacks, he may run into some flack. I hope not."[99] Interviewed in 2007, Sawyer remembered the black CO and did not recall any problems or incidents after he had arrived.

Thomas Green, a member of the Church of God in Christ from Detroit, was the first African American at the CPS unit at Cleveland State Hospital. The AFSC had opened a detached unit at Cleveland State in December 1942. Following an exposé of conditions and brutality at the institution, the unit was withdrawn in December 1943 at the insistence of the superintendent.[100] After the dismissal of that superintendent, his replacement, E. H. Crawfis, who had worked with a Mennonite unit at Lima, Ohio, invited the MCC to reopen a CPS unit at the mental hospital. The MCC unit was established at Cleveland State Hospital in April 1945.

Mennonite Paul Goering, who had served at a CPS unit at a mental hospital in Howard, Rhode Island, was appointed director of the MCC unit. Goering described the tension between the COs and the regular attendants who recalled the negative publicity brought about by the former AFSC unit: "We had to work very hard to establish a relationship with these employees. They were suspicious of us. Their antagonism was overt." He explained another controversial issue between the COs and the regular employees: "Another point of tension in the Cleveland unit, I need to mention this, was our unit introduced the first black conscientious objector into the hospital unit, Tom Green. I remember that. And this was the first black in at least a Mennonite hospital unit." The MCC headquarters in Akron, Pennsylvania, had asked Goering if he would accept a black CO in his unit. He said that he would and took the matter up with Superintendent Crawfis, who agreed to have the man at the hospital. Goering recalled what happened when Green arrived: "These state workers were from the South and highly prejudiced—not only about COs but about blacks. Tom was frightened, and we were all tense."[101]

Throughout the United States, the integration of eating areas offended racist sensitivities. Eating together is a preeminent social activity, with its own set of rituals, expectations, and rules. To "break bread together" is to acknowledge common humanity. Like the COs at Cheltenham, Goering challenged the segregation of dining rooms: "I took Tom into the dining hall. . . . This was the first time many of those employees ate in the same room as a black person and when some of us sat at the same table as the regular employees they would get up and leave, just with us white guys. And with Tom coming I didn't attempt to sit him at a table where there were state employees. That was a very tense meeting and also very exciting. Tom stayed and the unit stayed."[102] The staff of Cleveland State Hospital had been integrated. A photo of the men at the MCC unit at Cleveland at the Mennonite Church USA archives probably taken in 1946 includes two African Americans.

20. CPS men assigned to Mennonite Central Committee Unit no. 69, Cleveland State Hospital, Cleveland, Ohio. (Mennonite Church USA Historical Committee and Archives, Goshen, Indiana)

Mennonite CO Van Dyck commented on the significance of race to CPS men: "Second only to the issue of war and peace, the race problem was the social issue of greatest concern to COs in CPS; not unemployment or the plight of the poor, not divorce or juvenile delinquency, not crime or alcohol and drug abuse—it was racial oppression of blacks. This is not to suggest that all CPS men were free of race prejudice. There were many who were not inclined to shoulder the cause of blacks, even vocally, to say nothing of overtly challenging America's racist institutions."[103]

Throughout the CPS, NSBRO and the religious service committees did not always live up to their ideals about race, out of fear of generating public backlash, offending the Selective Service, or harming the program. The CPS itself was integrated, but there were few members of ethnic minority groups to begin with. Van Dyck never saw a black or Asian CO and described racial tolerance in the camps as "largely an abstraction."[104] Yet individual COs did work to further racial justice when given the opportunity. Most social change for the better starts with individual acts of conscience.

6

"A Working Compromise Between Church and State"

"The B.S.C. recognizes C.P.S. as a limited instrument that is inadequate for the achievement of all ends sought by pacifists," read the statement on the Civilian Public Service by the Brethren Service Committee. The statement continued: "We consider C.P.S. further as a working compromise between church and state—the church submitting under conscription to an alternative to military service, and the state recognizing conscience as a basis of exemption from military service."[1]

Of the major groups involved in the CPS, some compromised more than others. The AFSC was never satisfied with the Selective Service Act of 1940 or the Selective Service's administration of the CPS. In particular, the Friends were unsuccessful in having "absolutists" exempted from the conscription system. In 1945, it reiterated its opposition to conscription: "The participation of the American Friends Service Committee in the Civilian Public Service program does not imply its approval of conscription. We continue to believe that the entire war system, including its conscription of the lives and service of men, is morally wrong."[2] The AFSC favored voluntary national service for men conscientiously opposed to any form of conscription.

Beleaguered by criticism from COs and war resisters for its cooperation with the Selective Service, the AFSC would withdraw from the administration of the CPS in the spring of 1946, prior to the end of the program. As early as April 1943, the AFSC had considered withdrawing from the CPS.[3] The Friends would never again participate in an alternative service program for COs. At an AFSC board meeting on September 17, 1952, one Friend summarized the position of the Friends on the Korean War draft: "The Mennonite and Brethren attitude is different from that of the Friends. They are willing to work with any programs that will allow them to keep control of their own conscientious objectors, and they are willing to adhere to Selective Service regulations because of this. Our position is more of opposition for military purposes, and of unwillingness to be a party to the success of the conscription operation."[4] The Catholic CO organization, the ACCO, withdrew from the CPS and severed ties with NSBRO in October 1945. Arthur Sheehan of the ACCO wrote Paul Comly French to tell him that he believed the religious groups should no longer administer conscription.[5]

The Brethren regarded the CPS as a less-than-ideal compromise. For the BSC, the CPS was restricted by "congressional action, public opinion, pressure groups, Selective Service, and administrative agencies," but represented an improvement over the situation of COs during World War I—a position that was certainly true. The BSC recognized that the CPS was "not an institution of such intrinsic worth that we desire to perpetuate it indefinitely."[6] Although the BSC and men in its camps disagreed with and resisted many Selective Service policies, the Brethren stayed with the CPS until its end in March 1947.

Among the historic peace churches, the Mennonites were the most satisfied, or perhaps the least dissatisfied, with the administration of the CPS. The MCC did not resist government authority and was willing to cooperate with the Selective Service as long as members of the church did not have to perform military service or violate their consciences. One of the few times in which Mennonite COs bucked the CPS was when forty-five men at an MCC camp at Fort Collins, Colorado, refused a work assignment to thin beets.[7] Colonel Kosch of the Selective Service called Paul French of NSBRO to ask him what he proposed to do about the situation. French spoke with Orie Miller, who said that the men understood that the beets were to be used to make alcohol for military purposes. Miller asked French to tell Kosch that he was sorry, but the MCC would support the men. The MCC could move the camp, or, if this solution was not satisfactory, the men would all go to jail. When French called Kosch to tell him what Miller proposed, Kosch said that he had contacted the Soil Conservation Service, which had assured him that the beets would not be used for anything but human consumption. This promise satisfied Miller and the MCC.

Because of their backgrounds in farming, most Mennonites did not object to soil conservation, forest service, park service, or agricultural projects, although many found work in mental hospitals and training schools and public health projects to be a more meaningful form of witness to God. A survey of 634 Mennonite CPS men indicated that 71 percent thought that the work they did in the CPS was "generally significant."[8] Even the lack of pay for CPS men, which provoked strong opposition among other religious agencies and COs, did not create dissension among the MCC and Mennonites. From the beginning of the CPS, Mennonite leaders believed that the witness of the church would be stronger if men were not paid. At the time, Orie Miller said unequivocally that Mennonites "would gladly pay their share of the bill . . . even though every Mennonite farmer had to mortgage his farm."[9] In response to the question "Do you think that people in general consider CPS men more sincere because they work without pay?" 75 percent of 634 Mennonite CPS men answered "Yes."[10]

◆   ◆   ◆

NSBRO received more than its fair share of criticism from COs dissatisfied—usually with good reason—with the CPS. The organization consistently advocated for COs and their rights and interests: for pay, worker's compensation, dependency allowances, foreign relief work, and other matters important to COs. Yet NSBRO had no control over the Selective Service, the technical supervision agencies, or the church committees and other religious agencies. It was in the unenviable position of having to communicate Selective Service policies and decisions, and was often viewed as complicit in the conscription machine by individual COs, the War Resisters League, and the Fellowship of Reconciliation for not fighting them harder. At the same time, the church committees, especially the AFSC, sometimes undermined NSBRO's efforts by going directly to the Selective Service and government officials.

Paul Comly French, the executive secretary of NSBRO, had published an influential book, *We Won't Murder* (1940), in the lead-up to World War II. A sincere pacifist and Friend, he was committed to trying to resolve problems and issues through communication, compromise, and consensus and was as well suited as anyone to lead NSBRO during the stormy history of the CPS. French worked tirelessly in the impossible job of trying to satisfy everyone involved with the CPS— and it took its toll. On June 8, 1942, he wrote in his diary: "Went to the doctor's this morning and he told me that I had better start taking it easy if I didn't want to have a nervous breakdown. Felt terribly weak over the weekend."[11]

French was attuned to the mood of Congress and the public during the war and found it difficult to communicate to others how precarious the position of the COs was during World War II. Right after the Japanese bombing of Pearl Harbor— with three thousand American casualties—French reflected, "I guess that it means now that the honeymoon is over." When NSBRO became the subject of severe criticism by the War Resisters League, the Fellowship of Reconciliation, and COs dissatisfied with the Selective Service and faced disagreements among the church committees during the spring of 1943, French wrote, "I am getting more and more convinced that I should resign and let some of them come here and see the temper of Congress and Selective Service. They might find that it was not as easy as they now feel." On May 14, 1943, French submitted his resignation to Brethren M. R. "Bob" Zigler, chairman of NSBRO's Board of Directors: "I have reached the point where I feel inadequate to the job of being constantly in the middle between the agencies and the government. I think it is possible to take the pressure from one side or the other, but not both for so long." He later agreed to put his resignation on hold to deal with pressing problems with the CPS. Almost a year later, at a meeting on April 3, 1944, the NSBRO board asked French to withdraw his resignation.[12] French decided to stay with NSBRO until the end of the CPS.

On December 4, 1944, French's wife of twenty years, Marie, died of a heart condition. By the end of the month, French was back to working on CPS issues day and night. For a long time afterward, he wrote of feeling depressed and lonely, as he carried out his NSBRO responsibilities:

> Tonight I feel nearly worn out and close to exhaustion. Yesterday and today seem to have taken about the last of the physical, mental, and spiritual reserve I had left. I just feel drained out and am nearer ready to lay down the burden of life than I ever have before. There seems so little to live for without Marie. . . .
>
> I thought today that Marie was wiser and more understanding than I appreciated at the time when she said she did not want me to promise I would never re-marry. I think she had deeper insights than I had in the nature and oppressiveness of loneliness. I know that my love for her will last as long as life, yet it seems that a human being needs companionship to survive and maintain sanity. Loneliness is something that eats into your very soul. If I must remain here, and if I am to have any usefulness in the rest of my life, perhaps some day I will find a companion and a kindred spirit.[13]

Paul Comly French married Dorothy Felten on November 2, 1946. Around the same time, French started his new job as general manager of the international relief agency CARE, "with full power to operate the entire program."[14] Sometimes good things happen to good people—even after bad times.

◆   ◆   ◆

The Selective Service controlled the CPS, but it ended up compromising with NSBRO and the religious agencies on some positions. Although it limited the types of service projects in which COs could serve, it approved detached units in mental hospitals, training schools, farms and agricultural projects, guinea pig experiments, and public health—all of which were more meaningful to CPS men and the religious agencies than the original work camps. In 1943, it yielded to pressure from various groups and approved government-administered camps.

NSBRO and leaders of the service committees of the peace churches reported positive relations with General Hershey and, to a lesser extent, Colonel Kosch. Selective Service officials liked to present themselves as buffers between COs and hostile members of Congress, veterans' groups, and citizens. They went to great lengths to reassure Congress that they had weeded out slackers and to present a sympathetic, though patronizing, image of the average CO as a sheltered country bumpkin. At a Senate subcommittee hearing on August 19, 1942, Maj. J. T. Coatsworth, representing General Hershey, testified:

> [Many] of these boys have been confined in their early lives to such an extent, having been under the influence of their church and their elders, that they do not have worldly knowledge and experience as other people have; so instead of their being slackers they are the result of this rather isolated life.
>
> They have been brought up on farms; they haven't had radios, newspapers, automobiles, not the normal mixing with other people. They are the result of this type of life and influence rather than being slackers.[15]

At those same hearings, Colonel Kosch said:

> If a man buys an automobile, he is kicked out of the church. We have had cases of that, where these boys have bought automobiles and were kicked out of the church, and boards said they could not be conscientious objectors because they had left the church. They won't have radios in these places; they won't have telephones; they won't have electric lights. If they buy a farm that has electric lights, they tear them out. All they have in their places is their church papers. The ministers tell them what is going on in their church. . . .
>
> We feel that if we could get these youngsters out from the influence of these older people we could do something with them.[16]

General Hershey had an affinity for the Mennonites, but he and other Selective Service officials had enough dealings with NSBRO, the church committees, the War Resisters League, and the Fellowship of Reconciliation to know that the stereotype of the most conservative Mennonites and Amish applied to a small percentage of CPS men.

As Leslie Eisen and some COs argued, the Selective Service probably exaggerated public opposition to COs.[17] A public opinion poll conducted by the Office of Public Opinion Research in Princeton, New Jersey, in April 1945 found that although only 26 percent of persons pooled approved of conscientious objectors, 60.8 percent approved of pay for COs and 67.1 percent approved of federal aid to dependents of conscientious objectors.[18] Of course, on controversial social issues, government policy reflects not necessarily public opinion but rather the influences of powerful interest groups. During World War II, the American Legion and the Veterans of Foreign Wars had a strong influence on Congress.

Selective Service officials could be congenial and accommodating with NSBRO and the religious agencies. Yet when COs threatened to create unrest, draw negative public attention to the CPS, or disobey their orders, Hershey and the Selective Service did not hesitate to crack down on them and take harsh measures to try to keep them in line. This same tendency would be Hershey's downfall during the Vietnam War.

◆   ◆   ◆

Of the nearly 12,000 COs who entered the CPS, many were discharged from or left the program prior to completing their service: 1,566 were discharged because of a disability; 30 men died in the CPS; 518 were released for dependency, occupational, and other reasons; and 523 left their camps or units without permission, refused to work, or otherwise violated the terms of their service.[19] The latter were viewed as "delinquent," and most ended up in prison. Edward Burrows, who had registered for the draft at the urging of his family, decided to leave the CPS after serving at a Forest Service camp and public health unit: "What I was concerned about was the making of a stand against conscription, because I think conscription is evil."[20] After a long series of protests of the CPS while at the AFSC Powellsville, Maryland, and government Mancos, Colorado, work camps, Igal Roodenko, a member of the War Resisters League, went on a hunger and work strike in late October and early November 1943 and was arrested and sent to prison.[21] Another 905 men gave up their IV-E classification and entered the military. Some of these men had families and left the CPS because they could not provide for their dependents. Others changed their beliefs about war, especially as the horrors of Nazi Germany became known. S. Allen Bacon described the philosophical dilemma of many CPS men: "A good and respected friend came to decide to join the Army, leaving our CPS unit. This made me think hard about my own refusal to fight against Hitler's horrors."[22]

Of the remainder, 8,408 stayed in the CPS until systematic demobilization of the program. A small number of men forty-two years of age and older were discharged in April 1945 when the enlisted men in the army that old were discharged. After that time CPS discharges were based on a combination of length of service, age, and fatherhood of a dependent child.[23] The first mass discharges occurred in late 1945 and the winter and spring of 1946. The last discharges happened in March 1947.[24] Germany had surrendered in May 1945 and Japan in September of that year.

◆   ◆   ◆

As the CPS wore on, dissatisfaction with the program grew among COs. Many COs, if not a majority, would later value their time in the CPS and regard it as having provided an opportunity to demonstrate the sincerity of their convictions, to perform meaningful service, and to grow spiritually or intellectually. A large number of former CPS men would attend regular camp or unit reunions well into the 1990s. However, just about every CO had a complaint about the hardships of life in the CPS: the lack of pay and support for dependents and the rigid regulations of the Selective Service. Even many Mennonite COs, who were the most positive about the CPS, questioned why they could be assigned to detached dairy or agricultural units but not to do similar work on their family farms.

Men who did not come from the historic peace churches were among the least satisfied with the CPS. Some objected to what they saw as subtle—or not so subtle— proselytizing on the part of the AFSC, BSC, ACCO, and MCC, while others resented being under the authority of any religious agency. There also was a sentiment among some COs that NSBRO and the church committees had become administrative arms of the government and, hence, collaborators in the military conscription system. With the support of the War Resisters League, in particular, CO opposition to the CPS system and Selective Service policies became organized.

In the spring of 1943, COs planned the Chicago Conference on Social Action, "for men in Civilian Public Service and others who have filed form 47 or have refused to register" independently of NSBRO and the religious agencies. The sponsors of the conference described it as "indicative of serious discontent with C.P.S. as a pacifist program during wartime."[25] All of the members of the conference planning committee came from AFSC or BSC camps. The secretaries for the conference were Rex Corfman, a member of the United Brethren Church who was at the AFSC camp in Powellsville, Maryland, and Philip Isely, who had served at the BSC camp at Cascade Locks, Oregon, until February 1943.

At the Cascade Locks camp, Isely was known for his "continual, none-too-tactful criticism of project work."[26] He was a member of the Socialist Party and the War Resisters League.[27] The Forest Service superintendent of the camp moved him from one project to another until he refused to accept him for any kind of work: "Isely was then placed on camp overhead supplying wood to the various buildings on camp." After going on a furlough, Isely never returned. A Selective Service official had visited the camp shortly beforehand. The BSC camp director believed that the Forest Service and Selective Service had unjustly pushed Isely to walk out of camp.[28]

The conference planners invited General Hershey and representatives of NSBRO and the religious agencies to attend the April 12–18 conference "to participate in discussion of the problems and issues confronting all persons concerned with building a better functioning democracy."[29] General Hershey and Colonel Kosch of the Selective Service were strongly opposed to the Chicago Conference. French of NSBRO met with Kosch on March 30, 1943:

Talked with Colonel Kosch this afternoon and he said the General was very much disturbed about the Chicago meeting that some of the men were planning on their furlough time and that he was writing to me with instructions to cancel the furloughs for men involved in the Conference, pointing out to them that they were stepping into an area that was no concern of theirs. He said the General felt the whole c.o. position was under so much pressure now that it was seriously unwise to try to have that kind of meeting with all of the publicity that the boys would try to get in the Chicago papers.[30]

On the way out of the meeting with Kosch, French ran into Hershey. He told him that he thought canceling the furloughs of the men would be a mistake. Hershey told French that he might be right but that there could not be a more inopportune time to make a public issue of the CO program: "I gathered from what he said that if the men actually went, he wouldn't be too much disturbed but what he was really doing was going on record so that when the Chicago Tribune attacked him over it, he would be in the clear."[31]

Later that same day, Kosch called French and told him that the Selective Service was ordering cancellation of all furloughs at once. Kosch then made a cryptic comment: "He said he could give me no reason on the phone because it could not be discussed, but that it wasn't punitive and that it covered the army and navy and all of the armed services. Said something big was in the wind."[32] Furloughs for military men were never canceled, but Kosch's cryptic comment would add to the confusion surrounding Hershey's order.

That day Hershey sent a telegram to all camp directors canceling all furloughs for CPS men indefinitely: "Effective immediately and until further notice. No furlough or leave will be granted any assignees at your Conscientious Objector unit. Only exceptions will be made in case of emergencies. Refer to this office for proper approval. A copy of this is being furnished National Service Board."[33] Under Selective Service rules, furlough time could be earned at a rate of two and a half days per month of service for a maximum of thirty days per year. For men "absent without leave," a mandatory penalty of three days' forfeiture of furlough for every day AWOL was to be imposed. Continued AWOL of ten days or more or three separate periods of AWOL could result in disciplinary measures, including reclassification of a CO's status. The cancellation of furloughs would make it impossible for CPS men to attend the conference.

On March 31, Hershey sent another order to CPS camps: "You are informed that assignees in Civilian Public Service are at all times under the supervision and control of the Selective Service until discharged therefrom and their actions are subject to control of this headquarters. No assignee in Civilian Public Service

Camps will attend this meeting and no Directors of Civilian Public Service Camps will grant furloughs to assignees for the purpose of attending this meeting."[34] The Chicago Conference and Hershey's reaction created an uproar throughout the CPS. Just about every important person associated with the CPS became involved. French continued to try to talk Selective Service officials into withdrawing the orders and told them they were moving into an area of civil liberties and freedom of speech and assembly. Hershey and Kosch stood firm:

> Kosch said that if it meant a showdown with some of the men, he and the General were prepared for it. He said that they both felt that it was time that some of the men understood that a war was going on and that each man's individual desires were not of vital importance to the government. . . . He said that they both felt that the program would be better without some of the men who seemed unwilling to cooperate at any point and that if they walked out over this issue, they were ready to handle it.[35]

A. J. Muste of the Fellowship of Reconciliation and Evan W. Thomas of the War Resisters League distributed a statement on April 7 questioning the constitutionality and legality of an order restricting the civil liberties of CPS men by a major general of the army. Muste and Thomas urged support of CPS men who attended the conference and called upon NSBRO and the church committees to resist the order: "We trust that the Service Committees and N.S.B.R.O. will immediately make it clear to Selective Service that they will oppose to the utmost any penalization of men who are impelled to act."[36]

Both Muste and Thomas had been active in progressive causes for years. During World War I, Muste had become a pacifist after being exposed to Quaker philosophy.[37] In the 1920s and '30s, he became involved in revolutionary politics and the labor movement. In 1936, he abandoned Marxist-Leninist politics and returned to Christian pacifism. He served as executive secretary of the Fellowship of Reconciliation from 1940 to 1953 and was an opponent of conscription. Muste would become an early leader of the antiwar movement in the Vietnam era prior to his death in 1966.

Evan W. Thomas had gone to prison for his refusal to enter the military during World War I and later became a medical doctor specializing in the treatment of venereal diseases.[38] He joined the Fellowship of Reconciliation and the War Resisters League in the late 1930s and chaired the WRL during World War II. He was the brother of Norman Thomas, who was one of the founders of the American Civil Liberties Union and was a leader of the Socialist Party. He had been the Socialist Party's presidential candidate in 1940.

The WRL and FOR had joined NSBRO as consultative members soon after the establishment of the CPS. They had overlapping memberships. A. J. Muste served on the executive committee of the WRL, and Evan Thomas was a member of the FOR. Both the WRL and the FOR were frequent critics of NSBRO and the peace churches' administration of the CPS. They split over the issue of whether CPS camps should be run by the church committees or the government. Muste strongly believed that the church committees should run the camps, while Evans and other leaders of the WRL opposed NSBRO's "religious monopoly on CPS."[39] In 1943, the WRL withdrew as a consultative member of NSBRO, while the FOR continued its membership. Evans and some other members of the WRL resigned from the FOR over this issue. Among the WRL members joining Evans in resigning from the FOR was David Dellinger, who had become an outspoken critic of the church committees' involvement in the CPS.[40] Dellinger would go on to become a leader of the antiwar movement during the Vietnam era. He wrote the introduction to Philip Berrigan's autobiography, *Fighting the Lamb's War: Skirmishes with the American Empire.*[41]

The day after the Muste and Evans letter was sent, French and other members of NSBRO, including Paul Furnas of the AFSC and Bob Zigler of the Brethren, met with representatives of the National Committee on Conscientious Objectors (NCCO) of the American Civil Liberties Union. Roger Baldwin (the head of the ACLU), A. J. Muste, Norman Thomas, and others represented the NCCO.

The NCCO had been founded by the ACLU to provide legal advice and assistance to COs. A history written by an unnamed staff member of the Swarthmore College Peace Collection in December 1947 described the kinds of requests and cases that came to the NCCO:

> The most frequent requests were for: (1) information as to how to deal with draft boards which ignored the legal provisions for conscientious objections; (2) information as to the rights of men who had ceased cooperating with conscription; and (3) assistance in arranging paroles and jobs for imprisoned objectors. However, though these were the most frequent patterns, the NCCO records are rich with out-of-the-ordinary cases that explored new areas. (Here are a few random samples: A school board requests the resignation of a CO teacher; a man who has ceased to be a conscientious objector is rejected when he attempts to join the army and is confined in a CPS camp; a civilian CO arrested for a traffic violation is removed from a city jail to an army prison and declared to be inducted.)[42]

There was probably tension between NSBRO and the NCCO because two of the attorneys at the NCCO's Washington, D.C., office, R. Boland and George B. Reeves, had previously worked at NSBRO.[43] They had left NSBRO because they thought it had not adequately represented COs' concerns and had ignored the rights of secular pacifists. Reeves was at the April 8 meeting.

At the April 8 meeting, NSBRO and the NCCO discussed the representation of COs in prison or on parole and the constitutionality of the Selective Service system.[44] The NCCO was considering bringing test cases against the Selective Training and Service Act and Selective Service rules. The issue of the civil liberties of men planning the Chicago Conference came up. NSBRO members later felt that Norman Thomas had unfairly attacked French on this issue without knowing that he had already communicated his concerns to Colonel Kosch. Immediately after this three-hour meeting, Rex Corfman, one of the secretaries of the Chicago Conference, showed up. French, Baldwin, Muste, and Thomas advised him to postpone the meeting to provide an opportunity to try to resolve the problem with Hershey. Corfman said he could not make a commitment without discussing it with the conference planning committee.

French met again with General Hershey on April 9. Hershey informed him that furloughs were not a right but a privilege and that the Selective Service had the legal authority to cancel them. He also told French that he would be meeting with Baldwin and a group from the ACLU that evening and was prepared to tell them that "under the Act of Congress non-religious objectors had no place and had no right to be in camp."[45]

Then, Clarence Pickett had dinner at the White House and discussed the Chicago Conference and General Hershey's "attitude" with Mrs. Roosevelt: "He said the president was at the table and while he did not participate in the discussion, probably heard most of it."[46] Mrs. Roosevelt offered to meet with General Hershey to tell him that he had made a mistake in trying to cancel the conference. The executive committee of the AFSC decided it would be unwise to have Mrs. Roosevelt meet with Hershey, since it would probably antagonize the general further. French agreed with this assessment.

Paul Furnas of the AFSC urged the organizers to postpone the Chicago Conference while discussions could be held with Hershey. For Furnas, the controversy raised broader issues of the relationship between the Selective Service and the church service committees. Furnas, along with others, believed that the Selective Service had overstepped its bounds in issuing direct orders to the camps without going through the church committees. The controversy also brought to the surface a long-simmering problem within the CPS: the presence of men in camps administered by religious agencies who did not want to be there.

As was often the case when controversies arose within the CPS, men in AFSC camps made their opinions known on the Chicago Conference and Hershey's actions. Sixty-three men at the Friends camp at Big Flats, New York, called on the

AFSC to discontinue administration of CPS units if Hershey's order was not with-drawn.[47] Sixty-seven of the seventy-two men at the Powellsville, Maryland, camp pledged noncompliance with the order. Fourteen AFSC men and six BSC men from detached Fish and Wildlife Service units in Maryland wrote Paul Furnas of the AFSC to protest the Selective Service directive: "We urge the American Friends' Service Committee to refuse to accept this order. If the order is not withdrawn, we believe the time will have come for the American Friends' Service Committee to withdraw from administering conscription to Civilian Public Service."[48]

In mailings to CPS men, Chicago Conference secretaries Corfman and Isely took the position that NSBRO and the religious committees could not negotiate with the Selective Service on behalf of conference planners and suggested that they were more concerned about administrative protocol than protecting the civil liberties of CPS men.[49]

COs at the AFSC Oakland, Maryland, camp issued a statement expressing regret that a rift had been created over the Chicago Conference. They summarized the position of the conference organizers:

> 1. We have a clear-cut and fundamental violation of our civilian rights on which we must act at once.
> 2. Delay seems to be giving in to SS's power.
> 3. Negotiating evades the issue.

Then they turned to the AFSC position:

> 1. The Friends do not wish to make an issue out of this particular incident, but rather to take a stand on the broad general principles of freedom and democracy which are at stake.
> 2. In order to do this, time for discussion is important.
> 3. The Friends see this in a broad historical perspective involving (1) their unity with the other Peace Churches, (2) SS's curtailing of their autonomy leaving them little voice and just permitting them to pay the bills, (3) the future of their European relief work, and (4) the traditional patient Quaker approach to problems.

Although the Oakland group indicated that thirteen of seventeen of their members would take action if freedom of assembly was clearly the issue, they questioned whether the real reason for the ban on furloughs was because the Selective Service was contemplating changes in the CPS program—a rumor that had been circulating among COs. They presented their position: "After receiving today a specific request from the Friends for delay—in order to carry on discussion with

SS on the principles involved—we feel that going ahead with the Conference Monday divides the Pacifist stand on a minor point when we should be united on the broad general issue. This does not mean that we believe we should ask permission to hold the meeting."[50]

The organizers of the Chicago Conference, who had delayed the conference one week during all of the discussions and communications, decided not to postpone the meeting any longer. In a letter to Hershey dated April 15, 1943, Corfman and Isely rejected the Selective Service's authority to restrict the civil liberties of COs:

> It appears to us that if this order is allowed to stand, men in Civilian Public Service will have lost all civil liberties, and will, in effect, be under military control. But we cannot agree to that interpretation of the status of conscientious objectors. We feel that it is a violation of both the spirit and letter of the law, as well as a breach of contract with the religious agencies involved. Most important, we do not feel that by accepting Civilian Public Service we surrendered the fundamental rights to worship as we choose, to speak freely, and to freely assemble with men of goodwill.

The letter went on to communicate defiance of Hershey's order: "It is with these thoughts in mind that we are now writing to tell you that we feel called by conscience to attend the Chicago Conference on Social Action, which has been rescheduled to begin Monday, April 19 and run through Saturday, April 24."[51]

That same day, French wrote Corfman to express regret that the conference was going to be held: "I can't help but feel that real progress is not made on the basis of confronting people with ultimatums. Again I want to say how sorry I am that you feel impelled to push on without waiting until we have had an opportunity to have a full and frank discussion with General Hershey."[52]

The Chicago Conference on Social Action opened on April 19. The number of CPS men attending the conference is open to question: forty men from thirteen camps or detached units; thirty-three CPS men, along with twenty-two other registrants; or twenty-one CPS men.[53] The proceedings of the conference included minutes from a general meeting; reports from action committees on work, training, conscription, and prison; and two resolutions adopted by the participants.[54] One resolution expressed solidarity with Stanley Murphy and Louis Taylor, CPS "walk-outs" serving time at Danbury Prison in Connecticut, who were staging a hunger strike to protest war and conscription. Murphy and Taylor enjoyed strong support among WRL members who favored radical action to oppose conscription.[55] The other resolution concerned NSBRO's representation of CPS men:

> The Chicago Conference on Social Action expresses its deep concern over the serious rift between NSBRO and various groups of men in CPS. We recognize the major cause for this rift as one of contradictory and mutually exclusive functions within the Service Board—this agency must both administer the Selective Service program to the men in camp, and simultaneously represent the men before Selective Service. . . .
>
> The record of the NSBRO clearly indicates that the function of representation has been subordinated to that of administration. Despite continuous requests for participation in the deliberations of the Service Board, no more than a series of regional meetings had been arranged for. A national conference of CPS men had been postponed for over a year. When it became apparent that a conference would not be called by the administrative agencies, the Chicago Conference was independently planned by the men in camps.

The resolution went on to fault NSBRO for not working hard enough "in regard to racial segregation in the camp system, civil rights of the men, allowance for dependents, pay for work done, and liability compensation" and for ignoring the situation of COs in prison. It also described as "immoral and undemocratic" the imposition of a program on all pacifists by the "sole pacifist agency recognized by the government." The end of the resolution called on the Selective Service and other agencies to recognize the National Committee on Conscientious Objectors of the ACLU as the "representative agency" of concerned CPS men.[56]

The COs at the Chicago Conference were demanding direct representation with the Selective Service by an organization that was experienced in legal services and independent of NSBRO and the church committees administering the CPS. Hershey and other Selective Service officials wanted nothing to do with an organization representing the interests of COs and especially "political objectors."

On April 27, Furnas of the AFSC wrote to one of the men involved with the conference and expressed his frustration that it had gone forward against the best judgment of the AFSC. He reminded the man of the potential penalties for violating Hershey's order:

> What I meant was that the possibility of obtaining a *common agreement* as to the holding of the conference *was closed* when the conference was held against the will of Selective Service and against our best judgment as to the circumstances under which it should be held. . . .
>
> As to possible punishment for men attending the Conference; when the issue reached that stage we hoped that there would be no special action on the part of Selective Service and that all men would return to camp before the ten day period elapsed. As you know, absence after ten days, according to rule, automatically

places the matter in the hands of the Department of Justice. It seems reasonable to us to suppose that each man knew the regular rule of Selective Service in regard to furlough penalty for absence without leave and was not unprepared for its effect.[57]

The AFSC, MCC, and BSC imposed the required three-day ban for each day AWOL on the men who had attended the Chicago Conference. The ACCO left it to the camp director to decide whether to penalize the men.[58] At that time, the ACCO was administering only one training school unit, and it was struggling to stay afloat. French recommended that the service committees impose an additional penalty for a direct violation of Hershey's order in an attempt to placate the general. The BSC and MCC followed this recommendation.[59] Men at MCC camps and units had little interest in the conference, and many Mennonites believed that "no good could come of such a conference." The AFSC did not accept French's recommendation to impose the additional penalty. The Selective Service ordered that all leaves for men who attended the conference be denied and indicated that it would not approve the assignment of any of these men to detached units.[60] NSBRO declined to send this order. Eisen reported that the Brethren "refused to transmit to the camps a later order from Selective Service disciplining the men who had attended the conference in spite of the prohibition."[61] The Selective Service turned down assignments of the men to detached units for a year.[62] Conference secretary Corfman would later transfer to a detached unit at Byberry mental hospital in Philadelphia. On May 31, Hershey told French that he had decided not to prosecute the men who had attended the conference.[63]

Paul French received a visit from an FBI agent inquiring about the Chicago Conference on July 28:

> He was particularly interested in whether we had any communications indicating that organizations like the War Resisters and the F.O.R. had advised men to disobey General Hershey's order. He had a copy of the mimeographed letter signed by A. J. Muste and Evan Thomas and wanted additional material along that line. I had nothing in our files except that letter. He was particularly interested in Philip Isely and Rex Corfman. I explained to him that I was satisfied the men were sincere and felt they were making a determined stand for civil liberties although we had felt it was poor judgment to proceed with the conference until we had a chance to discuss the situation further with General Hershey.[64]

The controversy surrounding the Chicago Conference died out before long. NSBRO's 1945 *Four Year Report of Civilian Public Service* made it sound as though the controversy had never occurred: "Selective Service banned all CPS furlough on March 31, 1943; lifted the ban 22 days later; never explained the reason."[65]

The Chicago Conference marked the first widespread organized resistance to Selective Service policies within the CPS. It would not be the last.

◆   ◆   ◆

As soon as the historic peace churches agreed to administer and fund the CPS program in 1940, the Selective Service resisted efforts to have the government directly administer camps or units. NSBRO's French shared this opposition to government camps.[66] In September 1942, the board of NSBRO approved a memorandum, drafted by the Fellowship of Reconciliation, that expressed its reservations about government-administered camps but indicated that it would not actively oppose them:

> We are apprehensive of grave dangers if the Selective Service administration sets up at this time machinery . . . to operate Government-financed camps. It seems that the inevitable tendency will be for that agency to extend its control also over Civilian Public Service [i.e., church-administered camps], and to limit and perhaps completely to abolish such freedom as we have in Civilian Public Service. We, therefore, do not see our way clear in joining at this time in any steps for requesting Government-operated camps. . . . However, we do not stand in the way of others taking such measures as they deem right and proper.[67]

Over time, pressure built for the opening of government-administered camps. The AFSC had originally "agreed to accept all men assigned to it by Selective Service regardless of religious affiliation but reserved the right to return to the hands of the Selective Service Administration any man who in its opinion showed by his character, behaviour [sic], or attitude that he could not satisfactorily perform service under the direction of the Committee."[68] As a result, the AFSC wound up with a large majority of men in its camps who were not members of the Society of Friends. Many of these COs did not accept the Friends' beliefs and ways of doing things. According to the AFSC, "In 1943, the Committee asked that only men who expressed a desire to work under its administration be assigned to its projects." The BSC was also reluctant to have men in its camps who believed that the peace churches had become "agents of the government in enforcing the evils of conscription."[69]

At the same time, individual COs, the War Resisters League, and some religious bodies were pressing for government operation of camps as an alternative to administration by the AFSC, MCC, BSC, and ACCO. The Methodists had the fourth-largest number of men in the CPS. Methodist bishop G. Bromley Oxnam, who also served as chairman of a committee on COs of the Federal Council of

Churches of Christ in America, believed that the government should have to bear the expenses of COs in the CPS because it had drafted them, and he did not want to continue raising funds to support Methodists in camps run by agencies of other churches.[70] In June 1942, Oxnam told General Hershey that he no longer intended to pay for members of his church in CPS camps.[71]

On April 16, 1943, the board of NSBRO approved a memorandum to be sent to the Selective Service recommending that men who did not want to serve under the church committees be placed directly under government supervision.[72] It was certainly no coincidence that this action by the NSBRO board occurred in the midst of the controversy surrounding the Chicago Conference on Social Action. CPS men had gone off on their own in planning a conference independently of NSBRO and the church committees and had rejected requests to postpone the conference while NSBRO tried to negotiate an agreement with the Selective Service. The conference organizers had been critical of NSBRO and the church committees, and participants at the conference had passed a resolution demanding independence from NSBRO.

General Hershey had resisted the establishment of government camps. After the Chicago Conference, NSBRO and the church committees were united on the need for government camps:

> In the evening in Philadelphia, Paul Furnas, Orie Miller, Bob Zigler, and I spent three hours on the problems of Selective Service. It was finally agreed that I should tell General Hershey that many of our problems in the past resulted, in our opinion, from having men who did not want to be under religious controlled administration; that we felt with the opening of a government camp we would be able to operate on the basis of our original agreement with Clarence Dykstra in 1940, and that unless we could return to that agreement, it was our judgment that the Historic Peace Churches had better withdraw from the program. This is the first time in nearly a year that we have had complete agreement on an approach to Selective Service, and I think it should be useful in talking with the General to have him know that all the groups feel the same. . . . I have the feeling that if Hershey knows there is unanimity of opinion, we probably can work out the difficulties, although it may be we are coming close to the end of our experiment.[73]

General Hershey gave in and agreed to establish government camps, but both he and Colonel Kosch made it clear that they would decide on how these camps would be run. When French asked Kosch not to move anyone from a church committee camp to a government camp for disciplinary reasons for at least three months, Kosch flatly refused. He told French that he had just received additional inquiries from the president and the American Legion on how the CPS was being run and expected to be investigated by Congress: "He said that he felt that the Friends had failed to handle the problems that we had had, and he personally could see no valid reason for giving us additional time to work something out. He said he felt definitely that he was to be investigated by Congress and that he would like to make the decisions which resulted in an investigation and not be held responsible for something over which he seemed to have little control."[74]

The first government camp, announced in May 1943, was opened in Mancos, Colorado, in July 1943.[75] The second was a former MCC camp in La Pine, Oregon, that was taken over by the Selective Service in January 1944. Both of these camps were operated under the Bureau of Reclamation, in cooperation with the Camp Operations Division of the Selective Service. The third camp was opened in Germfask, Michigan, in May 1944 under the Fish and Wildlife Service, along with the Selective Service. By 1945, there were 152 men at Mancos, 121 at La Pine, and 95 at Germfask. In June 1945, the Germfask camp was moved to Minersville, California.[76] The Selective Service also had a unit of some 40 men working with the Coast and Geodetic Survey, mapping sections in the Far West.[77] In these units, the government paid for men's maintenance, medical and dental care, and clothing and provided an allowance of five dollars per month.[78]

When the government camps were announced by NSBRO and the AFSC in May 1943, Rex Corfman, secretary of the Chicago Conference, described it as a "small step forward."[79] Many COs saw the government camps as an opportunity to be free from the authority of the church committees. It also would enable them to express their opposition to the Selective Service and the conscription system more directly: "Many of the men who requested government camps are those who generally feel most strongly about the CPS system and conscription in general." Albert Keim and Grant Stoltzfus wrote: "The government camps also became the setting for those whose philosophy of conscientious objection gave high credence to resistance to war. The camps became arenas setting for action against conscription by imaginative noncooperation. Those who lacked sympathy for the alternative service philosophy of Civilian Public Service now had a way to put their convictions to work against Selective Service."[80]

For the Selective Service, government-administered camps would make it easier to deal with CPS men who created problems or consistently violated the rules. NSBRO reported: "Selective Service stated that it had no intention of setting up 'concentration camps,' that men in the government camps had the same general rights as men in the church camps. However, men have transferred from church camps to government camps against their will by Selective Service. The reasons given by Selective Service: disciplinary reasons, mental, physical observations."[81]

Bent Andresen had been a member of the War Resisters League and the Socialist Party in the 1930s. He entered the CPS in March 1944 and served at a BSC camp in Kane, Pennsylvania, and participated in a Cornell medical experiment. He then transferred to the government camp at Germfask: "The government camps were essentially for what they like to think of as troublemakers. There were people there who didn't belong there because somebody goofed in their understanding of what the guy was trying to say or do at some camp. But the ones I came to associate with and know best were the rebels."[82] After the Germfask camp closed in 1945, Andresen went to the government camp in Minersville, California. The United States dropped the atomic bomb on Hiroshima shortly afterward. He walked out of the camp in protest on August 10 and was sentenced to prison, where he spent seven months.

Because of self-selection and the tendency of the Selective Service to send troublemakers to the government camps, these camps ended up with "a variety of radicals, dissidents, agitators, and malingerers—as well as some less demonstrative COs who sincerely wanted to avoid dependency upon the churches."[83] Almost from the time they opened, the government camps experienced unrest and non-cooperation on the part of the COs.[84] Some men claimed real or feigned illnesses, hoping to obtain medical discharges, avoid work, or simply disrupt camp operations. Other COs adopted creative obstructionist tactics: "Perhaps the most imaginative tactic was the slowdown technique, carried to its logical extreme by a few COs. Technically, these men obeyed all work orders, but they refused to engage in any act of labor without a direct order from a supervisor. Waiting for instructions on how to pick up a hammer or hold a nail before driving it in required prodigious forethought and self-discipline."[85]

A *Time* magazine article on February 19, 1945, titled "The Tobacco Road Gang" described an open revolt against government authorities at the Germfask camp: "Selective Service officials were at their wit's end last week. The problem that vexed them: how to deal with a group of draft-age Americans who have refused to fight, who now decline to work, and spend most of their waking hours finding new and more ostentatious ways of thumbing their noses at all authority." The name "Tobacco Road Gang" had been taken from a 1932 novel about Depression-era southern sharecroppers written by Erskine Caldwell that had been turned into a popular Broadway play and a 1941 movie. The same name had been adopted by a rebellious group of COs in an AFSC camp described by H. Otto Dahlke.[86]

Time reported the frustration of the camp director: "Camp Director Norman V. Nelson, who described them as 'intellectuals,' said sadly that there was nothing he could do. Revolters gloried in their nom de guerre: the 'Tobacco Road Gang.' They feigned sickness, passively resisted all orders. Told to cut down a tree, a Tobacco

Roader would ask, 'How do I do it?' Told to take hold of the axe, he would ask, 'What do I do next?' Told to swing the axe, he would swing, cut out a small chip, inquire. 'Now what do I do?'"

The article went on to state that the COs smuggled liquor into their quarters, went AWOL, and "roamed the nearby towns, making ardent and often successful love to local girls." Citizens of one town "had one waylaid and thrashed a group of them." The COs were even reported to have threatened officials with violence. According to Mumford Sibley and Philip Jacob, many COs took exception to the *Time* article and held that it had exaggerated the facts.[87]

Within days of the publication of the *Time* article, Kosch ordered men at the Germfask camp restricted from visiting the village of Germfask. Then an editorial appeared in the *Post* (probably the *Washington Post*) criticizing Colonel Kosch for the situation at Germfask. The AFSC four-year report on the CPS referred to "isolated incidents surrounding the camp at Germfask, Michigan" under the topic "Public Relations."[88] This coverage was not the kind of publicity that the Selective Service or NSBRO wanted.

Although the COs at Germfask and the other government-administered camps have been widely described as unruly and rebellious, the Selective Service's administration of the camps invited discontent and dissent. In the fall of 1944, a controversy erupted over the government's handling of Don Charles DeVault, a Ph.D. in chemistry assigned to Germfask.[89] DeVault had claimed IV-E CO status in 1941. He was given a temporary deferment for teaching and research at Stanford University, but classified as I-A-O in 1942. He rejected induction into the army in January 1943 and was convicted and sentenced to prison in March of that year. In December, DeVault was paroled to the government-administered Mancos CPS camp.

At Mancos, DeVault and another CO there, Forrest Leever, began experimenting on their own time with methods to develop antibiotics with chemicals purchased by themselves and laboratory glassware donated by friends. In May, June, and July 1944, DeVault unsuccessfully appealed to his parole officer to be transferred to a research laboratory. He was then ordered to Germfask on July 27 and resumed laboratory work on his own time in August. In September, DeVault wrote General Hershey requesting an assignment doing chemical research. Replying on Hershey's behalf, Colonel Kosch told DeVault he could not be assigned that kind of work but would be considered later for assignment to a guinea pig experiment. The *Germfask Newsletter* described what happened next: "Sept. 27: DeVault tells Director Nelson: 'This reply means that I am done with this foolishness. Henceforth I shall be reporting for work on penicillin or related subjects.' Remains in camp at his chosen work. Oct. 17: Submits detailed report to Director Nelson of the scientific work he has completed. Oct. 27: Arrest blocks DeVault's work."[90]

When two COs at Germfask tried to call newspapers to report the incident, they were told by the local telephone operator that camp director Norman V. Nelson had asked her to stop all long distance calls from the camp. Later that day, the COs left the camp to call from a location in town. The operator told them that she would have to call the camp for permission to put through a call. When she called the camp, she reached one of the COs, who said it was fine for assignees to make long distance calls. The two COs reached the *Chicago Tribune* and told DeVault's story. The next day, Nelson announced that all COs would be confined to camp and that no long distance calls could be made from the camp phone. This was the same camp director who was quoted in *Time* as describing the Germfask COs as "intellectuals."

An article in the October 31 issue of the *Escanaba Daily Press*, a newspaper published in the Upper Peninsula of Michigan, summarized DeVault's story:

> Since September 27, DeVault has contended he should not waste his scientific skill in building duck ponds for the Fish & Wildlife Service. . . . Each morning when the trucks take the other men out to their pick and shovel work, he has remained in camp to carry on research with penicillin in the crude laboratory he has constructed in his barracks.
>
> Author of 10 research papers in the field of physical chemistry and holder of a Ph.D. degree, the young scientist stated before his arrest: "My case is no different from that of several thousand professionally trained men confined by Selective Service in labor camps when they are anxious to use their training in a way which benefits humanity." Conchies at Germfask say DeVault's case brings to a head the high-handed way in which Selective Service has wasted their skills at ditch-digging jobs.[91]

The *Washington Post* subsequently published an editorial questioning why the talents and abilities of COs were not used more effectively in the CPS.

DeVault announced to his friends that he would not fight his arrest and would plead "nolo contendere," or no contest, at his trial. NISBCO's 1996 *CPS Directory* indicated that DeVault left the CPS on October 27, 1944. After the war, DeVault conducted research and published in the areas of laser technology, biophysics, and quantum mechanical tunneling. He also was active in the civil rights movement as a member of the Congress of Racial Equality. DeVault died on November 26, 1990.[92]

For the Selective Service, it was not enough that COs were required to leave their homes and jobs to do work for no pay. Nor was the Selective Service committed to COs doing "work of national importance." What mattered most to the Selective Service was that men yielded to government authority and obeyed orders.

Men who questioned the authority of the government to begin with were bound to clash with the Selective Service. Paul French discussed DeVault's situation with Kosch and another Selective Service official on October 31: "Colonel Kosch was adamant in refusing to do anything for him. He said he had no sympathy at all with men who refuse to do the job assigned to them, regardless of the motivation and that he would have been willing to help DeVault work something out if he had not written an ultimatum saying what he would and would not do, to Colonel Kosch. It is the sort of approach that Colonel Kosch does not appreciate."[93]

The Germfask camp was closed in June 1945, and the Minersville camp opened the same month. The government camps continued to experience problems with COs. Ninety men at the Minersville camp went on strike in April 1945.[94] Twenty-eight men at the Mancos, Colorado, camp went on a hunger strike.[95] The AFSC withdrew from administration of the CPS in March 1946, and the government took over operation of the remaining AFSC camps and units. In April, fifty-five men at the Glendora, California, camp went on strike. By May 1946, there were eighty-one men on strike at Glendora, forty-one at Big Flats, New York, and two at Gatlinburg, Tennessee.[96]

Beginning with the April 1943 Chicago Conference and General Hershey's furlough ban, COs at AFSC and BSC units started urging the church committees to turn over administration of units to the government to protest the conscription system or Selective Service policies. In 1944 and 1945, COs at a Friends unit at Middletown State Hospital in Connecticut asked the AFSC to withdraw administration of the project. A statement issued by the Civilian Public Service Union summarized the situation at Middletown:

> The unit voted to ask the AFSC to withdraw its sponsorship of the unit in order that it might be sponsored directly by the state or Selective Service. The principal motive for this was a belief on the part of most of the men that it is wrong for a religious agency to administer conscription. An additional motivation circumstance was that in two consecutive years a majority of those in a poll of the men in Friends' CPS had voted that the AFSC withdraw from its administration, yet the AFSC had decided each time to renew its agreement with Selective Service and continue its administration.[97]

The AFSC accepted the position of men at Middletown and notified the Selective Service that it wanted to withdraw its administration of the unit.[98] It did not want to administer a unit if the men there did not want to be under the AFSC. The Selective Service declined to take over administration of the unit and stated that it would not accept administration of one Friends unit unless it was going to administer all of them. It indicated that it would close the unit and transfer any men who had voted against the withdrawal of the AFSC to any other Friends camp or unit. COs interpreted this statement to mean that those COs who were in favor of the AFSC's withdrawal would be "transferred to one of the remote government camps to do largely manual labor": "The conclusion seems inescapable that Selective Service's action is punitive—punishment, first, for acting on an opinion that church administration of conscription is wrong, and that there should be a mental hospital project under direct government administration without the involvement of a church agency."[99]

By June 1945, the Selective Service had taken over administration of the Middletown unit "temporarily." Selective Service officials had hoped that the MCC would take over the unit. Orie Miller was open to the idea but did not want to get involved in any controversy with the men at Middletown.[100] The unit remained open under government administration until it closed in September 1946.

An uprising over AFSC administration of the CPS camp at Elkton, Oregon, occurred in late 1944.[101] Men had been transferred to Elkton from Powellsville, Maryland, and Big Flats, New York, both of which had experienced unrest. A number of men at Elkton insisted that the AFSC withdraw from administering the camp. The AFSC maintained that the men should be persuaded or forced to transfer out of the Friends CPS. One CO in particular, Americo Chiarito, refused to work. The AFSC requested his transfer out of the unit, and the Selective Service approved it. Half of the men at the camp protested the transfer. Chiarito and six other men were arrested. NISBCO's 1996 directory of the CPS listed Chiarito as having entered the CPS on June 1, 1943. No date was given for his discharge, suggesting that he was treated as delinquent and did not fulfill his CPS commitment.

Although the AFSC withdrew from the CPS around March 1946, the BSC and MCC continued administering units and camps until September and December 1946, respectively. The BSC seriously considered withdrawing from the CPS in late 1945 and early 1946 and even polled COs at its units on the matter.[102] On August 9, 1945, COs at the BSC unit at Columbus State Hospital in Ohio passed a resolution urging the BSC to withdraw from the administration of a unit in Augusta, Maine, in support of the men there, "inasmuch as hospital officials are guilty of unfair treatment of CPS assignees and using those unpaid assignees in the place of available paid employees."[103] The Augusta unit remained open under BSC administration until May 1946.

If, as General Hershey had proclaimed, the CPS was an "experiment in democracy," government-administered camps represented a failed experiment. Yet the turmoil surrounding the government camps reflected the growing dissatisfaction of many COs with the entire CPS system.

◆　◆　◆

In 1944, COs at different camps and units banded together to create the CPS Union, sometimes referred to as the CPSU.[104] The CPS Union was not formed to oppose the CPS or conscription. As explained in a flyer, *You and the C.P.S.U.*, developed by COs at the AFSC camp at Powellsville, Maryland, "The Union is against a system that takes men from their homes and normal occupations, sets them to work at unaccustomed and unsuitable jobs, and gives them no pay. The Union is for total exemption in matters of conscience. Not that it expects to gain such a point in time of war. But there is also after the war; this is for the record." The union was intended to improve the pay, benefits, and working conditions and rights of CPS men: "The Union's primary objective is pay. Other aims are subsidiary. With the right to pay once granted, dependency allotments, workman's compensation and work commensurate with abilities follow logically."[105]

The first CPS Union local was established at the AFSC camp at Big Flats. The union's initial constitution was drafted by Howard Schomer, a Big Flats CO, and was modeled after the constitution of the International Ladies' Garment Workers' Union.[106] The ILGWU was a progressive and powerful union in the 1930s and '40s and enjoyed the support of Eleanor Roosevelt.[107] The union then spread to other CPS camps and units. On June 24, 1944, COs from eleven units met in New York to elect a temporary organizing committee of three CPS men, each of whom came from an AFSC unit.[108] A general executive board was subsequently elected and met in New York at the Labor Temple on October 14. Of the eleven men on the board, ten came from AFSC units and one had been discharged from the CPS.

According to Sibley and Jacob, approximately five hundred men in sixty-four camps paid the CPSU a twenty-five-cent initiation fee and monthly twenty-five-cent dues.[109] At Philadelphia State Hospital, or Byberry, alone, a financial record of CPSU Local no. 49, dated August 1944, listed seventy-eight men.[110] One month later, in September, seventy-six men at Byberry signed their names to the constitution of the local union.[111]

The CPS Union was dominated by men from AFSC units. When the Friends turned over administration of AFSC units to the government in early 1946, COs at some of the former AFSC camps, especially Big Flats, New York, and Glendora, California, remained active in the union. The CPS Union did not attract strong interest among more radical COs at government-established camps, although the War Resisters League supported the formation of a union.[112] The union endorsed negotiation as the tactic of choice and regarded strikes as a last resort. Germfask had a small local, but many men there viewed the CPSU as "too conservative."[113] Interest and participation in the CPS Union in Mennonite camps and units were negligible. In Brethren units, the union movement was weak, except for men in the guinea pig experiments at the University of Minnesota and the Columbus, Ohio, mental hospital unit.[114]

The most active man in the CPSU from a BSC unit was Max Kampelman, a Jewish CO from New York City. Kampelman had become active in the CPSU when he was serving at the AFSC Pownal, Maine, unit and was elected to the union's General Executive Board.[115] He remained active in the CPSU and continued to serve on the board after his transfer to Minnesota to serve as a guinea pig in the semi-starvation experiment. He also was a member of the War Resisters League and contributed articles to the newsletter the *Conscientious Objector,* which reflected WRL positions.[116] Kampelman renounced his pacifist views after the United States dropped the nuclear bomb on Hiroshima and became a staunch anticommunist after the war. Kampelman became a close legislative aide to Hubert Humphrey when Humphrey was elected to the U.S. Senate in 1948 and remained close to him during his years in the Senate and as vice president under President Lyndon Johnson. Kampelman subsequently became an arms negotiator in the Carter and Reagan administrations and was awarded the Presidential Medal of Freedom by President Bill Clinton in 1999.[117] For someone who started his adulthood as a con-scientious objector during the "Good War," served as an organizer for COs, and was a WRL member, Kampelman had an unexpected career.

Local no. 49 at Byberry mental hospital had one of the largest CPSU locals. Two of the initial eleven members of the General Executive Board in 1944 came from Byberry, and in May 1945, three out of twelve board members came from that AFSC unit.[118] Byberry was the largest CPS mental hospital or training school unit, with a peak population of approximately 135 COs in 1945. It would also be the center of COs' efforts to reform mental institutions. Like the CPSU in general and other locals, CPS no. 49 advocated for pay and benefits for COs. The local expressed a strong commitment to pacifist principles and mentioned improvement in patient care as one of its objectives. Its constitution, passed in September 1944, read:

> We are convinced that our individual concerns are not separate from the problems of those who work with us. Therefore, to create a readier implement for coopera-tion on problems in which we are all concerned, we join in a Union in CPS #49, making these our objectives:
>
> 1) to improve patient care by improving the working conditions of hospital employees;
>
> 2) to apply the pacifist method to labor-management problems;
>
> 3) to have a representative in dealing with the government, should AFSC relinquish or delegate this function;

4) to remain acquainted with C.P.S. camp problems and to join with the campers in solving them;

5) to help workers in other fields bring about the better society we both see as necessary;

6) and to create a lasting organization of the pacifists of this war.[119]

It was the CPS Union at Byberry that approached the superintendent to approve the assignment of African American COs at the mental hospital. Racial justice was a priority throughout the CPSU.

At Byberry, and probably at all units or camps with union locals, sentiments about and involvement in the union among COs varied widely. There was a small group of men who were active in the local and the CPSU. Most were too busy with other things to become involved in the union. A group of men was focusing on the problems of mental hospitals and training schools. Others were beginning to start new lives by going to school, getting married, or becoming active in Philadelphia groups. The CPS and hospital work had worn others down. An undated, unsigned handwritten letter addressed to the CPSU in the archives of the Swarthmore College Peace Collection located with other documents on Byberry's CPS Union communicated one CO's frustration: "While the men hang back from an active union under the excuse that so many of us are too involved in Philad. activities to take time or risk, it's still easily observable that it is the situation we are in that *drives* the men into non-hospital activities in order to compensate for CPS shit and hospital shit as well. How can I take interest in my work when it is only the more frustrating the better the job I try to do?" The writer went on to take a swipe at do-gooder pacifists and especially those COs trying to improve the plight of the inmates: "How ridiculous it appears for these pacifists to pour their frustration into every rat-hole in sight except the one inhabited by the rat. We all know where to point and at whom to snipe, but our foolish 'privileges' have successfully bought off the men into silence and such enlightened movements at the Mental Hygiene Program of CPS. What a laugh—any real mental hygiene study would show the boys that they need to face *their* own problems, not those of a few thousand unfortunate crazy people."[120]

A radically different sentiment was expressed by Paul Wilhelm, who had grown up Baptist and then joined the Society of Friends after entering the CPS. Wilhelm later served on the Philadelphia Human Rights Commission and was active in opposing racial discrimination in that city. For Wilhelm, the CPSU directed attention away from the pacifist mission:

I fear that by uniting myself with the practical objects of the union I may endanger my purpose in coming to CPS. . . . I am not unconscious of the hardships wrought by our present circumstances, but I think our purpose as pacifists will be better served by accepting these than by risking the misunderstanding of the non-pacifist "workers and populations" in an effort to overcome the circumstances by organization. To spend as much energy as would be required to achieve the union objectives on selfish ends would surely be to diminish the effectiveness of our protest against war.

Wilhelm described his purposes for joining the CPS:

> I wish to stress the fact that my coming to CPS was to give a service, to make a demonstration to all who would see—and I hoped that this group would be an ever expanding one, so that the effect of all of us who took this alternative to war would be spread widely upon the consciousness of the general public. . . . That we feel a responsibility to the larger society is evident in our willingness to compromise our repugnance to conscription in order to perform a constructive service in lieu of military service, our presence in CPS demonstrates our acceptance of the judgement of the larger society that we must somehow serve. Yet, to most of us this service is not enough; we wish not only to testify by this service that the majority is wrong in taking war to resolve its questions, we seek an alternative to war that will be acceptable by the majority of society.[121]

Former Byberry COs interviewed in 2007 only vaguely recalled the CPS Union or remembered nothing about it, even though their signatures were listed on the CPSU no. 49 Constitution and their names were on the financial report. Warren Sawyer and Neil Hartman had no recollection of the CPS Union and wondered aloud whether it was formed by COs at the government camps. Charles Lord and Leonard Stark had forgotten about the union and remembered it only after being sent a photo of a demonstration of Byberry COs demanding pay and a copy of the record of men who had paid the union dues.[122] Each of these men had clear memories of other aspects of the CPS and Byberry hospital.

The CPSU was never recognized by the Selective Service and, hence, played no formal role in the CPS. On November 30, Ralph Rudd and Willard Hetzel from the CPSU's General Executive Board met with Colonel Kosch of the Selective Service. Both Rudd and Hetzel had come from Byberry. Hetzel, an attorney, also was a key figure in the mental health reform movement initiated by Byberry COs. Paul Comly French had arranged the meeting between Kosch and the COs. Rudd and Hetzel reported that Kosch was friendly and listened patiently to them. However, he expressed his dislike of unions and pressure groups: "Kosch, whose opinions are reflected in many CPS policies, doesn't like unions which monopolize jobs in their industries, he said. He doesn't like racketeers that line their own pockets, not organizations that are out for their own interests, regardless of the interests and rights of others. In addition, he dislikes 'pressure,' at least from CPS men; when it's used to back an idea, the idea must be weak and unjust. Pressure is not needed anyhow, because he is 'always ready to listen to a just idea from any source.'"[123]

Regarding pay and dependents' allowances, Kosch told Rudd and Hetzel that these matters were up to Congress. When Rudd and Hetzel asked about matching individual jobs with men's talents, Kosch said that individual assignments would create too many public relations problems for the CPS. Toward the end of the meeting, Kosch told Rudd and Hetzel that the COs were too impatient and had to learn that, as a minority, they had to influence the majority through patient persuasion. Kosch asked to be placed on the mailing list for CPS publications.

The CPS Union's positions on pay, worker's compensation, dependent allowances, and the importance and relevance of COs' work assignments reflected long-standing complaints about the CPS. Most COs knew of these drawbacks when they entered the CPS or became aware of them shortly afterward. Although COs were willing to sign their names to position statements and even pay their union dues, it was difficult for union leaders to mobilize protests or mass actions on these issues. The Selective Service created a firestorm in early 1945 when it issued new rules regulating the lives of COs in their off-work hours.

In the detached units especially, many COs had attempted to restore a semblance of a normal life within the confines of their required CPS work. Mental hospitals and training schools tended to be located in or near cities or towns that could supply the required labor force to staff them. As CPS men transferred from remote camps, many of their wives followed them there and often found jobs at the institutions, which were also short of women employees. Others married women they met at women's service units sponsored by church committees or at religious or social events in the local community. Many COs at Byberry attended dances at the Quaker Whittier Hotel in Philadelphia and met women there. Neil Hartman referred to the Whittier as a "USO" for CPS men.[124] For unmarried women, young men at the time were hard to come by, Hartman recalled. Married COs tried to spend as much time with their wives as they could, and a number of couples lived together.

At the same time, COs started to take college courses or find paying jobs after working forty to sixty hours a week or more in their CPS units. Many COs who had subsisted on a small monthly maintenance fee jumped at the opportunity to make some money. Byberry CO Forrest Altman had a paying job at the private Friends Hospital, while Dick Ruddell worked as an optician in Philadelphia.[125] COs working at agricultural stations or on dairy farms sometimes worked for local farmers in their off-hours.

Veterans' groups, which seemed to welcome the opportunity to protest against the CPS any time they could, took exception to any "privileges" granted to COs. As early as 1943, the Veterans of Foreign Wars in New Jersey passed a resolution condemning "colonization" at the Veterans Administration Hospital Lyons, New Jersey, CPS unit.[126] The wives of five COs at Lyons had been hired by the hospital, and the married couples had been given housing on the hospital's grounds.

Until 1945, mental hospital and training school superintendents had implemented their own policies regarding off-duty work and living off grounds for COs. The Selective Service's provision that men should live on grounds was not always followed by the superintendents or enforced by the Selective Service. William A. Bryan, superintendent of Norwich State Hospital in Connecticut, issued a policy to Selective Service assignees on outside work on April 5, 1944: "The Hospital administration has no desire to impose unduly severe restrictions upon Selective Service assignees but the public relations of both hospital and the assignee group are too important to be disregarded."[127] The policy stated that no CO could work outside the hospital without approval of the superintendent; that the hours would be limited; that the work would be restricted to farmwork, employment in general or special hospitals, or employment in philanthropic organizations; and that no assignee would be permitted to work in any industrial or mercantile organization, including retail or wholesale establishments. Other superintendents paid little attention to men's activities outside of their hospital or training school work.

Always sensitive to public relations and believing that COs should not be able to lead normal lives in the CPS, the Selective Service attempted to impose new restrictions on COs' residence and off-work activities in early 1945. In 1944, Austin S. Imirie of the Selective Service had visited Middletown State Hospital in Connecticut after COs there had asked the AFSC to withdraw from administering the unit. Imirie learned that Roland Watts, the AFSC unit director, was living in town with his wife, which he viewed as contrary to the regulations, and ordered that Watts be transferred to the government work camp at Germfask. He then discovered that sixteen other men at Middletown were living with their wives at least part-time and concluded that this fact was owing to "a lax administration by the hospital authorities." He canceled the transfer order for Watts, but "laid down the law in no uncertain terms that no men were to live off hospital grounds except for their one free night a week."[128]

The Selective Service sent mental hospital and training school superintendents a questionnaire about COs' off-duty hours in late 1944. It asked questions such as "Are any conscientious objectors on duty in your hospital living off Institution grounds?" and "Are conscientious objectors assigned to your institution allowed to take outside employment?"[129] The superintendent at Augusta State Mental Hospital in Maine, Dr. Tyson, asked F. Nelson Underwood, the BSC director, to fill out the questionnaire. Underwood sent a letter to W. Harold Row, national director of the Brethren CPS, providing his answers to the questionnaire, which he attempted to keep "as short and simple as possible." The answers indicated that some COs were living off grounds at least several nights a week and that some had taken outside employment: "During the past year some half-dozen of the men have worked at a nearby lumber mill and at odd jobs mowing lawns, washing windows, etc." Other superintendents reported that it was commonplace for COs to live off grounds at their institutions.[130]

Colonel Kosch issued a directive limiting the conditions under which CPS men could be absent from their units and prohibiting them from holding outside jobs unless explicitly approved by the Selective Service in January 1945. The Selective Service held a meeting with representatives from NSBRO and the church committees and officials from mental hospitals and training schools in Pennsylvania, Connecticut, Maryland, Virginia, and New Jersey to discuss the directive.[131] The meeting was stormy at times. Kosch said that he had been receiving complaints from veterans' groups about CPS men at hospitals living off grounds with their wives: "He felt that the veteran groups would attack the whole program in Congress unless they were satisfied that the Selective Service System maintained some measure of control over the men in special service units. He expressed his belief that we had better accept his decision and inconvenience the hundred men involved rather than risk a general American Legion attack on any program for conscientious objectors." Paul French, along with Paul Furnas of the AFSC and Howard Row of the BSC, proposed that each institution work out arrangements for the men and that public relations be handled on that basis. Dr. Charles Zeller of Byberry was the only institutional official who supported French. Colonel Kosch refused to budge on his position. After the meeting, Kosch took everyone to the Army and Navy Club for lunch. French wrote, "I imagine that many of them would have been shocked to know who we were. The place was full of military people, with several generals and admirals in the group."[132] For NSBRO, it was probably for the best that radical COs did not learn about this lunch at the Army and Navy Club.

On February 23, Imirie of the Selective Service met with the superintendents of Ohio mental hospitals having CPS units and ordered them to implement the directive forbidding assignees to live or work outside the hospital immediately.[133] Also, in February, CPS Union no. 49 at Byberry issued an alert to all CPS camps and units warning that violations of the Selective Service directive could result in severe penalties:

Selective Service is issuing a new Administrative Instruction #4. . . . This states that Selective Service believes that the off-duty hours of the men in the hospitals and training schools should be used for recuperative purposes, and that superintendents should give permission for spare time work only after each individual case has been specifically approved by Selective Service headquarters. . . . It is reported that Colonel Kosch was asked whether three Philadelphia State Hospital assignees might continue their jobs as soda jerkers, and that he answered, "Absolutely not." The only reason reported to have been given was that at such a job they had too much contact with the general public. . . .

On the question of living off the grounds the conference of January 26 is reported to have resulted in a modification of the preliminary instructions so as to allow one to sleep away on both the night before and the night after his day off, instead of restricting him to twenty-four hours away from the institution. But steady residence outside is prohibited "unless there has been approved" by SSS headquarters "an arrangement which will permit the man to live in quarters provided adjacent to the Hospital or Institution. . . . "

For those who might disregard these instructions they say, "Assignees who are absent without permission from the Hospital or Institution, are considered to be absent without leave," and are subject to prosecution for violation of the draft law, maximum penalty for which is five year imprisonment or $10,000 fine, or both.[134]

At least some mental hospital and training school superintendents took the Selective Service's directive seriously. On March 23, 1945, Homer Rogers, acting manager of the Lyons, New Jersey, Veterans Hospital, who would be inclined to follow government rules, wrote a memo to the BSC unit director indicating that the Selective Service had approved the off-hour employment of nineteen COs working from six to twenty hours per week in "Agricultural," "Feed Store," "Dairy Industry," or "Truck Gardening." Rogers issued a stern message to the BSC director:

The Executive Officer, Camp Operations Division, Selective Service System, by letter, dated March 20, 1945, approved the continued employment of these men as indicated with the following proviso: "Approval is given for so long a period as employment does not interfere with their efficiency on the hospital job or as long as public relations are not involved. If adverse conditions arise under either of these headings, it is expected that you will immediately discontinue the employment."

The instructions of the Executive Officer, Camp Operations Division, Selective Service will be strictly adhered to, and you are requested to advise concerned assignees accordingly.[135]

NSBRO and the church committees had been caught off guard by the controversies surrounding outside employment and off-grounds living of COs at mental hospitals and training schools.[136] Yet they were unable to get the Selective Service to rescind the directive. In a letter to Nelson Underwood of the Augusta State Hospital unit, W. Harold Row of the BSC cautioned, "I do not believe we can afford to disregard Directive No. 4. Administratively, we must be quite fair with SSS regarding it. . . . I am not sure what penalties SSS would assess for a persistent violation of Directive No. 4. I would think it would mean at least a transfer to Germfask."[137]

COs, CPS units, and the CPS Union strongly opposed the Selective Service's action as an infringement on their civil liberties. In a letter to his family on February 5, 1945, Byberry CO Warren Sawyer wrote:

> SSS is getting ready to clamp down on privileges. No outside work, no living out three nights a week etc. CPS is getting organized to act in case such a move comes. At Pennhurst, a state training school, the CPS had to live off the grounds because the school did not have room or facilities to keep them on the grounds. SSS is trying to force them to live on the grounds. Living off the grounds enable men to be home with their wives every night. Paid employees also live outside the grounds. That is how it started. We get no dependency allotments which makes it absolutely necessary for some men to work extra to support wife and kids as much as is possible. . . . A CPS union was formed some time ago to act as a bargaining unit.[138]

The CPS Union distributed information about the Selective Service directive throughout the CPS and explained the options open to COs:

> Our analysis, in summary, is this:
> 1. Men opposed to the restrictions may comply with them and petition for exceptions;
> 2. They may comply but ask for transfer back to camp;
> 3. They may refuse to comply, voluntarily risking the legal or administrative penalties for noncompliance.[139]

Some CPS units reluctantly accepted the directive. The BSC director at Augusta State Hospital, Underwood, wrote in his administrative report that the directive hurt the unit's morale but that the men would go along with it: "The recent edict of Selective Service restricting the men's off-duty activities has not made the men any more happy. It is true that the reaction here has not been so violent as it was in some places,—in fact, the few men directly affected here have been inclined to acquiesce. But the general affect [sic] has been to contribute to a feeling of restlessness."[140]

At some AFSC and BSC units, COs met to decide on a united course of action. At a regular unit meeting at Byberry on February 21, members considered five positions: (1) do not comply because the Selective Service did not have the right to conscript men twenty-four hours a day; (2) comply and try to get changes made in the directive; (3) negotiate and do not comply until negotiations are completed; (4) do not comply and let it be known that the men would not comply; and (5) do not comply but do not make an issue of it. The men present at the meeting agreed that the unit should be polled on the matter. Out of 115 men polled, 65 answered a questionnaire about complying with the directive. Of these men, 36 expressed their hope that the unit would comply with the directive, while 21 indicated their desire that the unit would refuse to comply, risking legal penalties. Three asked that the unit take no action, and 5 gave no answer. The unit was unable to decide on what to do if an individual violated the directive.[141] The Byberry superintendent, Charles Zeller, subsequently asked the AFSC unit director, Bob Blanc, to assume administrative responsibility for observance of Directive 4.[142]

Members of the BSC unit at Columbus State Hospital unofficially voted overwhelmingly to take united action to oppose attempts by the Selective Service to regulate men in their off-duty hours.[143] COs at the Columbus unit consciously decided to ignore Directive 4. Eighteen out of 42 men at the unit broke the regulation, and more than 35 went on record as indicating an intent to do so, making themselves liable for punishment.[144]

The furor over the Selective Service's directive on outside employment and off-grounds residence dissipated as quickly as it had started. Selective Service officials readily approved exceptions to the rule and did not appear eager to crack down on COs who violated the directive.[145] The mental hospital and training school units at which the directive was aimed for the most part were not filled with "troublemakers" intent on bucking the Selective Service. Even the CPSU locals at these units did not advocate radical resistance to the Selective Service. For its part, the Selective Service had its problems with the government-administered camps. Directive 4 probably encouraged some superintendents and unit leaders to disapprove certain arrangements for COs, but it was just as likely that COs became more discrete about holding outside jobs or staying overnight with their wives.

◆　　◆　　◆

The Civilian Public Service can be viewed from different perspectives. It might be regarded as the government's—or social system's—way of handling a distinct minority in a manner that respected that minority's traditions while upholding its own social institutions, values, and norms. It could also be viewed as a site of social conflict between the military machine and those men opposed to government domination. It might even be seen as an attempt to subject dissenters to the authoritarian "gaze" of government officials, with some of the dissenters transgressing the government's rules.

Any understanding of the CPS is incomplete if it does not take into account the perspectives of the COs themselves. The CPS was not a single experience. Its meaning was constructed in multiple ways by the individuals involved. For some, the CPS provided an opportunity to demonstrate the depth and sincerity of their religious or philosophical beliefs. Others saw the CPS as representing an evil in society that must be actively opposed. Still others put their time in and tried to get by as well as they could.

Some COs found in the CPS a way to channel their moral convictions into a new social cause: the reform of America's system of caring for people with psychiatric and intellectual disabilities. They transferred their concern about their own situations to the plight of those individuals put away in mental hospitals and training schools. When they first volunteered for transfers to mental hospitals and training schools, the COs had no idea of the worlds they would be entering. What they found when they went to the institutions saddened and shocked most of them. The same sentiments that had led them to oppose war and violence caused them to pursue new and different ways of treating those individuals who had been rejected by society and their communities. Some called upon their pacifist beliefs in their individual treatment of patients—or inmates. Others attempted to organize a national reform movement. The movement started with exposés of specific institutions but soon moved to the national scene. These COs believed that they could make a difference.

PART TWO

"A Lasting Contribution in the Field"

I went over the mental hospital program with [Colonel Kosch] and the plans proposed by the men at Philadelphia State Hospital, and found him much interested and enthused with the idea. He agreed that it offered a very real chance to make a lasting contribution in the field.

—Diary of PAUL COMLY FRENCH, August 1, 1944

7

"Out of Sight, Out of Mind"

In her popular "My Day" column published in newspapers across the country on July 22, 1947, Eleanor Roosevelt, wife of deceased president Franklin Delano Roosevelt, gave a glowing endorsement of a recent book: "A book that everyone should read is 'Out of Sight, Out of Mind,' by Frank L. Wright, Jr." The book, which described conditions at state mental hospitals, had just been published by the newly formed National Mental Health Foundation. The foreword of *Out of Sight, Out of Mind* was written by former U.S. Supreme Court justice Owen J. Roberts, chairman of the National Mental Health Foundation: "Mr. Wright's forceful book cannot fail to shock us, to awaken us, to impel us to action. It is not pleasant reading, for it deals realistically with exceptionally unpleasant facts. Nevertheless, Americans should read it, for unless these facts are faced frankly, and the problem solved satisfactorily, many thousands of mentally handicapped persons will continue to be 'out of sight, out of mind.'"[1]

Out of Sight, Out of Mind was reportedly based on more than two thousand eyewitness reports of conditions and treatment at forty-six mental hospitals in the United States. The institutions themselves were not named. The states in which they were located were Connecticut, Delaware, Illinois, Indiana, Iowa, Maryland, Michigan, New Jersey, New York, Ohio, Pennsylvania, Rhode Island, Vermont, Virginia, Washington, and Wisconsin. The implication was clear. The conditions and treatment reported in the book had been found in institutions among the most progressive and wealthy states—not poor states in the South, as Mrs. Roosevelt herself had assumed when first shown photographs of one of the institutions.[2]

The majority of the book consisted of edited narrative accounts, typically starting with a quote from a mental health authority on how patients should be treated or an observer commenting on the state of affairs. Photos comparing some of the worst institutional scenes with some of the best were interspersed with the narratives. The juxtaposition of what should be with what was led the reader to draw the inescapable conclusion that things were terribly wrong in the nation's mental hospitals. The book contained sixty-three separate reports detailing horrendous conditions, brutality, and medical indifference. The first account was told from the perspective of the "first day on the job":

"To attendants: You perhaps more than anyone else, can help patients get well. You are with them constantly—days to the doctors' hours. The little things you do week by week, day by day, hour by hour, minute by minute, can make or break them. Of all the members of the hospital staff, you are closest to the patients. You can support the work of doctors and nurses, or cancel it. Yours is the important, cornerstone job in the hospital."

EDITH M. STERN

In The Attendants' Guide

Published by The Commonwealth Fund.

Picture, if you can, a ward where two hundred and forty mental patients are locked in one room from morning until night. No patient is ever permitted to leave the ward unless accompanied by an attendant.

Most of these patients are forty-five years old or more. They're vegetative. They eat, they sleep, they void. Then they eat, sleep, and void all over again. The only variation in this program is twice a week when someone shaves them and bathes them. Many of them can't dress themselves or help keep themselves decently covered. They never stand up when they can sit down. They never sit down when they can lie down. Most of them look as if they wouldn't even lie down if they could find a less demanding way of existing.

Now, into this atmosphere, inject a young boy in his early twenties. He gets no greeting, no introduction, no explanation. The door is opened and he is pushed into the ward. He finds a seat or stands in the corner. He looks around him and sees hopeless despondency. His ears are assaulted by the vocal discord of two hundred disordered minds. His nose—well, you can't *picture* that.

You're the attendant on the ward.[3]

The second report captured the labor problems experienced by mental hospitals:

"During the period of July 1, 1944, through June 30, 1945, the employment situation has remained critical, and has shown little or no improvement over the previous year. With 660 established positions, we have had an average of 193 vacancies for the year. Through the twelve months' period we employed 324 persons and 340 resigned. . . . "

—From the annual report of a large mid-western hospital.

"Eight Dismissed: Excessive Alcoholism"

"Hey, Joe! Did you hear that Nelson is back?"

"No! You can't mean it! Surely they wouldn't hire him *again!*"

But that's what they had done. Joe found out for sure when he went to take over his ward for the day shift. Even as he came near the door, he could tell that the night shift man hadn't changed many beds during the long twelve-hour shift. The odor was unbearable.

Inside, half the patients were up and half of them still in bed. A dozen or more were walking up and down the ward completely naked. Water and feces were all over the hall. And Big John, with a wet towel, was lording it over a cowering group of fellow patients in the dormitory.

Joe sighed, hitched up his pants, and took off his white coat as he strode into the office. There was Nelson, slouched in the chair, sound asleep.

"Come on. Get out! You're off duty—officially now." Nelson didn't stir. So Joe shook him and finally roused him enough to send him off duty. Joe had to go along most of the way, because Nelson couldn't get his key in the locks. He was that drunk.

Nelson had been employed at that hospital before—that's why Joe couldn't believe he was back. Nelson had been fired a few months earlier, and had worked at another hospital in the meantime. He had been dismissed from the other hospital because of bad eyesight.

With the help of a powerful magnifying glass, Nelson just managed to scratch out a night report that passed for writing. He admitted that he couldn't read the labels on medicine bottles—yet he was allowed to give hypodermic shots of morphine and other drugs to patients. At a distance of twenty feet, he couldn't recognize people he knew well.

Nelson was still employed at the hospital six months later when Joe gave up in disgust and left.[4]

Most of the accounts in *Out of Sight, Out of Mind* reported on conditions and treatment on men's wards at the institutions. However, some concerned women's wards. Women patients had it no better than men:

"Let me emphasize that none of the good hospitals use straight-jackets or other forms of mechanical restraint, except in rare cases; nor do they resort to sedative drugs and seclusion except as a last resort. . . . Force, which would excite and arouse even sane people, has given way to psychology and patient effort."
   —INNIS WEED JONES
   in *Scribner's*

"Hilda, if you open your mouth just once more, you'll go right into the 'strip' room. I'm sick and tired of your godawful talking and singing."

Hilda, of course, could no more stop talking and singing than a woman with a sprained ankle can stop limping. It was a symptom of her illness. But Mrs. Gladwyn, the attendant, slammed her magazine down on the desk and said, "By God, I'll show you."

She unlocked a small, barred room which was entirely empty except for a young girl who lay naked on a torn piece of blanket in the corner. Mrs. Gladwyn seized upon the nude girl by the hair and gave a sudden pull.

"Come on, Goon-child. It's the bench for you tonight. We've got a customer for your room."

The girl got nimbly to her feet and was led off without protest. Mrs. Gladwyn put a wristlet around the girl's wrist and tied her to a long wooden bench. The girl lay down on the bench to spend the night in the middle of the drafty ward hall.

Mrs. Gladwyn got a bath towel, wet it, rolled it, and sneaked up behind the singing, excited Hilda. Quickly, she whipped the towel around Hilda's neck, pulled it tight, and began to twist. "Now, me proud wench. To the 'strip' room." Punctuating her words with jerks and twists on the towel, she half pushed, half dragged Hilda to the room just emptied. Once in the room, she gave one final, tighter twist, and let Hilda fall to the floor unconscious.

Mrs. Gladwyn removed Hilda's single garment, took the piece of blanket from the room, slammed and locked the door.

"Now," she said, "I guess we'll have some peace and quiet around here for a while."[5]

Most of the accounts in the book depicted cruel, brutal, or indifferent treatment of patients by attendants, but there were reports of medical neglect as well:

"Careless medical practice should never be tolerated by the mental hospital administration. . . . Failure to investigate the somatic side of the problem is careless psychiatric practice."

—WILLIAM A. BRYAN, M.D.

"Aren't you going to remove the gallbladder?" asked the young doctor assisting at the operation.

"We'll just wipe it out and leave a drain in it. That's best," replied the senior surgeon who performed most of the operations at the state hospital.

The young doctor—McMasters by name—showed his amazement even through his operating mask. He knew that for at least twenty years it had been standard procedure to remove inflamed gallbladders. He knew that removal was the only thing to do in this case. But he also knew that his suggestions held no weight against the clumsy confidence of Dr. Spellman, the senior surgeon.

Still, he could not hold his tongue when he saw that Dr. Spellman was going to close the incision with just one row of wire sutures—it needed to have at least three different closures if it was to heal. "The peritoneum is ready for closing," Dr. McMasters suggested.

But Dr. Spellman disregarded the suggestion and quickly closed all of the layers of the abdominal wall with the single row of stitches. "Finished," he announced.

That night, the inevitable happened. A few stitches broke through the tissue, and the wound reopened. At three a.m., the night nurse found the patient with his intestines spilled out of the abdominal wall and the wound wide open. Knowing that such a catastrophe required immediate restitching, she called Dr. Spellman at his apartment on the grounds, and reported what had happened. Dr. Spellman gave directions that a heavy dressing be drawn tight with adhesive tape to hold the intestines in. "I'll stop in to see the patient in the morning at eight-thirty," he concluded, and hung up.

When Dr. Spellman "stopped in" at eight-thirty, the patient was dead.

Dr. McMasters and Dr. Spellman met again over the patient's open abdomen at the autopsy. Signs of negligence were plainly evident.

"Well, after all, what could you expect?" Dr. Spellman commented. "He was just a poor dope."

Dr. McMasters turned on his heel and left the room. He had heard it said before, but now he believed it. Some doctors, of being in the Hippocratic tradition, were most certainly in the "hypocritic" tradition.[6]

In some of the accounts, the writers attempted to describe what the patients must have felt. After quoting renowned psychiatrist Karl Menninger before a string of reports, *Out of Sight, Out of Mind* included the story of "Mr. Frazer" in which the writer put himself in the patient's shoes:

"Certain technical things help to create the desired atmosphere of confidence and reassurance in the hospital and assist in rebuilding mentally sick patients. There is always a degree of exhaustion, both physical and mental, which must be counter-balanced by external measures such as ultra-comfortable beds, attractive and well-ventilated rooms, easy access to toilet facilities, and appetizing, nourishing food."
—KARL A. MENNINGER, M.D.

Mr. Frazer lay on his bed telling himself that he must get up and go to the toilet, he must keep his bed dry, must try to get back on Ward 62. For three nights he had slept on Ward 70, but he had to get away from it. Only one sheet on his bed, coarse blankets which were dirty from many nights on other patients, the smell of urine and feces, men urinating on the radiators, rats and cockroaches—he must get back to Ward 62! The attendant had told him it was easy enough—just keep his bed dry for a week.

Yes, that was easy enough. At least, it had been during all of Mr. Frazer's last seventy-six years. But for the last month or so, it had been difficult. This cold weather, and sleeping in a dormitory with twenty other men, and being put to bed right after supper, and the distance—oh, the distance.

Mr. Frazer winced as he recalled that long journey from his back hall room on Ward 62 to the toilet. He remembered every detail of it. How he would awaken in the night, and start building up his courage. How he would finally throw back the covers and shudder as the cold air struck his body. How he would struggle out of bed and, clothed only in his light nightshirt, begin the long journey. . . .

If only he could have had a urinal near his bed. Or a robe to put on for the journey. Then he might never have undergone the ignominy of that first hot urinal bath, followed by many more, and now a bed in a room where all the patients wet their beds every night, where it was expected of them.

Suddenly the lights flashed on in the dormitory room where Mr. Frazer lay thinking. "All out for the toilet," called the attendant. He went along the closely packed beds and got each patient up in turn. "Whew, what a mess!" he muttered, as he routed out the patient next to Mr. Frazer. "Hey, Bill, take this one to the shower room for a scrubbing," he called to his patient-helper.

Mr. Frazer got out of bed and felt the sheets. They were dry. "Good boy," said the attendant. "Go on down and unload now." Mr. Frazer joined the parade of naked, misshapen old men. Some stopped in dark corners of the corridor along the way, but fifteen men crowded into the toilet to use the two stools and two lavatories.

On his way back to bed, Mr. Frazer noticed the attendant and his helper were hanging urine soaked sheets on the radiators to dry. "We haven't enough sheets for the first change tonight, Bill," the attendant was saying, "so I guess we'll be using these again in a couple of hours."

Mr. Frazer stifled a tendency toward nausea and went on to his dormitory. He had some trouble finding his bed, so he counted again—seventh bed from the door—but somebody was in it. He yanked the blanket down and struck the patient. "Get out of my bed," he hissed. The other patient hurried out and climbed into the next open bed.

Mr. Frazer looked down at his sheet, and the heart flowed out of him. Right in the middle of his sheet was a big blob of human excrement. He ripped off the sheet and threw it on the water-soaked floor. He climbed into bed between the uncovered mattress and the coarse blanket, determined to make his bed the filthiest in the whole dormitory.[7]

The last chapter of *Out of Sight, Out of Mind*, "Responsibility Is Ours," started with a summary of the themes in the reports: "Inadequacy, Ugliness, Crowding. Incompetence, Perversion, Frustration. Neglect, Idleness, Callousness. Abuse, Mistreatment, Oppression. These have been the principal characters in the drama of the preceding chapters. They have always dominated the center of the stage."[8]

The first part of this chapter was organized around questions that a skeptical reader might ask. "Is It True?" Wright quoted a congressman from a midwestern state who refused to believe that conditions at mental hospitals could be as bad as reported in the book: "It isn't true. It just isn't true!" Wright assured readers that

Out of Sight, Out of Mind was based on accurate firsthand reports signed by the observers: "Every person depicted is a real person; every place described is a real place; every recorded event actually occurred—and they all took place in mental hospitals in the United States within the last five years, 1942–46."[9]

"Is It Representative?" "We all wish this picture were *not* generally true," Wright wrote. "But the fact is that there is *no* hospital in *any* state where there is not room for improvement." To support the position that the conditions reported in the book were representative of all mental hospitals, Wright quoted a long list of statistics from an informal survey conducted of forty-five mental hospitals by the NMHF: "95% were overcrowded, some by as much as 50%; patients of all kinds were thrown together on one ward in many of these hospitals"; "95% indicated that attendants, who have most contact with patients, often violated rules of good treatment and care."[10]

Wright also assured readers that the incidents in the book had occurred in some of the most progressive states. Those readers who might believe that only the worst conditions and incidents were depicted in the book were informed: "(Some of the most flagrant examples of mistreatment were omitted because of the impossibility of making them seem plausible. Could anyone believe that a doctor would resort to Jew-baiting a poor refugee, offer to assist in suicide, or force a sick man to take an ice cold shower? Or could anyone believe that hospital patients would be forced to sleep on a wet tile floor with no mattress or covering but a piece of rubber sheeting? Only seeing is believing such things.)"[11]

"Can It Just Be the War?" Wright challenged a widely claimed assertion that labor shortages and wartime controls on goods were responsible for the conditions reported in *Out of Sight, Out of Mind*. Shortages and limitations had been increased by the war, but evidence could be presented that conditions were woefully inadequate prior to the war.

"So What? Does It Matter?" Wright quoted the head of a prominent women's club at which a speaker had just made a presentation on institutions: "Well, I suppose it really doesn't matter. After all, the patients are crazy, aren't they? They don't know what's happening to them, do they?"[12] This perspective represented one of the greatest challenges facing the National Mental Health Foundation: convincing people that the mentally ill were human beings who differed from other people only by degree: "We are like the old Quaker who had been crossed by the members of his Meeting. He said to his wife: 'Everyone in the world seems queer except thee and me, and sometimes, even thee seems a little queer.' He would have uttered a profound truth if he had included himself among those who are a little queer."[13]

"Why Bother? Isn't It a Hopeless Cause?" To counter the belief that the mentally ill were incurable, Wright rattled off a list of effective and promising medical treatments: "Fever treatment, controlled 'shock' therapy, psychoanalysis, brain surgery, drug therapy, directed occupational therapy and activity therapies—all these have been highly developed and have proven themselves to be aids in the 'cure' of previously incurable cases. Many other methods are being used today with increasing success—vitamin treatment, group re-education, drug-induced semi-consciousness and low-temperature sleep, among others."[14]

"Why Worry? Is It Really Important?" It was important. According to the U.S. surgeon general, mental illness was America's number-one health problem.

"It Couldn't Happen to Me!" Yes, it could: "No one can be certain that he is safe from the specter of mental illness. It lays its hand on rich and poor, high and low, young and old, men and women, intelligent and ignorant. No class or creed, no race or clan is beyond its reach."[15]

The second part of the last chapter of *Out of Sight, Out of Mind* addressed what could be done. The answers: "Let's Learn More," "Let's Give More," "Let's Influence More." The book concluded by exhorting readers that it was *their* responsibility to do something about the plight of people confined to the nation's mental hospitals: "You are on trial before the bar of justice for gross neglect and indifference. You cannot plead irresponsibility, saying that you did not know. The only valid plea that you can enter is that you are working hard to see to it that such things shall never happen again."[16]

The appendixes of *Out of Sight, Out of Mind* were almost as important as any of the reports in the book. They included a list of sixty-six prominent religious, civic, political, business, educational, medical, and labor leaders who served on the Board of Directors or as professional advisers or national sponsors of the National Mental Health Foundation. The board included such notable Americans as Roger Baldwin, executive director of the American Civil Liberties Union; Mary McLeod Bethune, president of the National Council of Negro Women and founder of Bethune-Cookman College; Mrs. William H. Biester Jr., past national president of the American Legion Auxiliary and editor of the *Legion Auxiliary Magazine*; Mrs. LaFell Dickenson, president of the General Federation of Women's Clubs; Mordecai W. Johnson, the first African American president of Howard University; Rufus Jones, professor emeritus at Haverford College; Orie O. Miller, secretary-treasurer of the Mennonite Central Committee; Arthur E. Morgan, past president of Antioch College and former head of the Tennessee Valley Authority; Clarence E. Pickett, executive secretary of the American Friends Service Committee; Owen J. Roberts, former U.S. Supreme Court justice; Mary Jane Ward, novelist and author of *The Snake Pit*; and M. R. Zigler, executive director of the Brethren Service Committee.

The foundation could point to an impressive list of medical, psychiatric, and legal advisers, including Robert Felix, head of the Mental Hygiene Division of the

U.S. Public Health Service; Karl Menninger, one of the most influential and widely known psychiatrists in the mid-twentieth century; and William Draper Lewis, a legal expert. The advisers also included Charles A. Zeller, who had recently been appointed director of the Michigan Department of Mental Health after serving as superintendent of Philadelphia State Hospital, Byberry.

There was a long list of national figures willing to lend their names as sponsors of the National Mental Health Foundation: wives of presidents (Eleanor Roosevelt and Bess Truman); members of Congress (Senator Claude Pepper, Representative Helen Graham Douglas, Representative Percy Priest); the U.S. surgeon general (Thomas Parran); a powerful labor leader (Walter Reuther of the United Auto Workers); a leading publisher (Henry Luce, founder of *Time* magazine); a well-known theologian (Reinhold Niebuhr) and religious leaders (Henry Emerson Fosdick, pastor of the Riverside Church in New York City, and Daniel Poling, editor of the *Christian Century*); a heralded author (Pearl Buck); a major actress (Helen Hayes); philanthropists and business leaders (Mrs. Louis Gimbel of Gimbel's department store, Anne Morgan, and Lessing Rosenwald of Sears, Roebuck, and Company); college and seminary presidents (Henry P. Van Dusen of Union Theological Seminary and Felix Morley of Haverford College); psychiatrists (Daniel Blain of the American Psychiatric Association, Adolf Meyer, and Gregory Zilboorg); a widely published criminologist (Sheldon Glueck); and a renowned physicist who had led a team working on the atomic bomb (J. R. Oppenheimer), among others.

The appendixes of *Out of Sight, Out of Mind* also contained a description of the National Mental Health Foundation by Harold Barton, executive secretary: "The National Mental Health Foundation is an outgrowth of concern on the part of citizens who, shocked and chagrined by what they have learned about institutions for the mentally ill and mentally deficient, have themselves set about to learn more, serve more, give more, and influence more—to the end that the atrocities which daily occur in mental hospitals may be speedily reduced."[17]

The citizens to whom Barton referred were COs who served at state mental hospitals and training schools in the Civilian Public Service. *Out of Sight, Out of Mind* made only fleeting references to COs in Wright's preface and one page in the last chapter of the book. In fact, Wright was still a CO when he did the bulk of the writing of the book. He had served as an attendant at a Mennonite Central Committee mental hospital unit at Marlboro, New Jersey, before being assigned to the Mental Hygiene Program of the Civilian Public Service, a detached unit formed by Byberry COs and approved by the Selective Service. By the time the book was published, Wright had been discharged from the CPS and had returned to a job at the YMCA in Baltimore.[18]

The origin of the National Mental Health Foundation could be traced back three years to the founding of the Mental Hygiene Program of the CPS in 1944. The history of the foundation ended three years after the publication of *Out of Sight, Out of Mind* in 1950. The story behind the rise and fall of the National Mental Health Foundation will come shortly. *Out of Sight, Out of Mind* deserves analysis in and of itself.

◆   ◆   ◆

Out of Sight, Out of Mind was an artfully created document. It represented years of careful planning. First, repeated appeals were made to CPS mental hospital and training school units asking COs to record their observations at the institutions. Instructions were even given on how the reports should be written. Then the reports were carefully cataloged and filed. Wright was selected to write the book because he had demonstrated his skill at writing with a previous handbook. He did not merely sit down one day and decide how to write the book on his own. The design and organization of the book had been the subjects of numerous discussions among the leaders of the Mental Hygiene Program of the CPS.

As sociologist Laurel Richardson noted, all forms of writing share "common rhetorical devices such as metaphor, imagery, invocations to authority, and appeals to audience."[19] Both "objective" writing—whether scientific writing, nonfiction, or journalistic reporting—and fiction use narrative, or rhetorical devices, to persuade readers to interpret events in a certain way, to arrive at certain conclusions, or to experience certain emotional reactions.

Out of Sight, Out of Mind was written and organized in a way to convince readers of its authenticity and credibility. Throughout the book, readers were reminded that it was based on factual firsthand eyewitness reports. The inside cover of the book even read: "A graphic picture of present-day institutional care of the mentally ill in America, based on more than two thousand eye-witness reports." Whether two thousand reports were really collected is unclear, and many of the ones that were collected bear little resemblance to the accounts in the book. Wright's preface and the concluding chapter repeatedly told readers that the book reported factual observations. COs were mentioned in the book simply because readers would have wanted to know who wrote the accounts in the book. A *Life* magazine article published the previous year had used some of the reports and attributed them to COs.[20]

Wright was a talented editor, and the authors of the narratives were compelling writers. The "firsthand eyewitness" reports showed signs of literary license in making the authors' points. Some of the dialogue was melodramatic. When Mrs. Gladwyn in Hilda's story said, "Now, me proud wench. To the 'strip' room," it sounds like a line from a late 1930s or early '40s movie or novel. Feelings and motives were attributed to the characters in the narratives. The story of Mr. Frazer's trip to the toilet was personal and empathetic. It even had the ring of truth. Yet the story was not told by Mr. Frazer. It was told by someone who was trying to imagine what Mr. Frazer might have felt. In the narratives, opinion was casually interjected into the reporting. When the author of Hilda's story wrote, "Hilda, of course, could no more stop talking and singing than a woman with a sprained ankle can stop limping," an opinion was being offered about the nature of mental illness. The narratives in *Out of Sight, Out of Mind* were designed to convey an understanding of what the institutions were like. The narratives were at times more realistic than real.

The National Mental Health Foundation also tried to establish the authenticity of *Out of Sight, Out of Mind* by including quotes from authorities before the narratives. By quoting published reports as well as authors and medical authorities such as Karl Menninger, Wright and others at the national foundation attempted to convince the reader that the conditions or incidents reported in the book were, in fact, out of line with accepted practice.

The concluding chapter of the book was as skillfully done as the narratives contained in the previous chapters. That chapter both anticipated the skeptical reactions readers might have to the narratives and provided specific actions they could take to change the conditions and problems reported in the book. Anyone working for social reform must convince people of the need for and the possibility of reform. If problems are perceived as too massive for anyone to do anything about, then no one will be likely to try to solve them.

Wright also cited statistics in the concluding chapter to persuade readers that the narratives in *Out of Sight, Out of Mind* were accurate and representative. As Cecelia Tichi wrote in her analysis of investigative writers exposing the excesses of industrial capitalism, "Numerical and chronological facts appear to be neutral and incontestable, but they are overtly malleable in serving strategic purposes, as writers, politicians, scientists, and accountants know well."[21] By citing statistics, Wright tried to convey that the problems identified at mental hospitals were beyond dispute and objectively verifiable. An appeal to statistics is an especially effective narrative device.

The leaders of the national foundation not only had to demonstrate the authenticity of the narratives in *Out of Sight, Out of Mind*. They also had to establish the credibility of the foundation itself and faced two major challenges in this regard. First, the foundation was founded by conscientious objectors not long after the end of the "Good War." Although the resentment of, even bitterness toward, conscientious objectors had lessened somewhat after the war had been won, COs were still viewed as people who did not come to the defense of their country at a time of pressing need. One way to establish the credibility of the foundation was to show that major public figures supported its work. No less a figure than a former Supreme Court justice had agreed to serve as chairman of the foundation and to write a foreword to *Out of Sight, Out of Mind.* The Board of Directors and national sponsors included persons whose names would be familiar to practically anyone in America.

The Board of Directors necessarily included leaders of the service committees of the historic peace churches—Rufus Jones, Orie Miller, Clarence Pickett, and M. R. Zigler. The AFSC, MCC, and BSC had not only sponsored the CPS but also contributed funds to the Mental Hygiene Program of the CPS while the National Mental Health Foundation was being formed. It was not enough to have the endorsements of the historic peace churches. The foundation needed the support of leaders whose patriotism and sense of duty to the nation could not be questioned. Who could question the judgment of the widow of the president who had won the war in Europe and the wife of the president who had ended the war against Japan—or members of Congress, the physicist who led the team to develop the nuclear bomb, the surgeon general, and many other board members and national sponsors?

Especially in the formative years of the national foundation, the leaders worked tirelessly to get prominent Americans to lend their names to their reform efforts. The leaders of the peace churches and Eleanor Roosevelt, in particular, were instrumental in introducing the young COs to other public figures. It often seemed as though the names meant more than anything else. Most of the original members of the Board of Directors would not be active in the foundation. A large majority of the national sponsors neither knew anything about mental health nor became involved in the foundation.

Second, at least as challenging for the credibility of the foundation, young "laymen" lacked the psychiatric and professional expertise to lead a national reform movement. The fields of mental health and mental deficiency were the provinces of professionals and psychiatrists, in particular. Harold Barton, the executive director, was about thirty-one years of age when *Out of Sight, Out of Mind* was published. None of the founders of the NMHF had any professional training or background in mental health or mental deficiency.

To be a credible organization, the National Mental Health Foundation needed to be able to demonstrate that it operated under the guidance of trained psychiatrists and professionals. So the professional advisers were critical to the success—even the existence—of the foundation. National figures would have been unlikely to have their names associated with the foundation unless it could demonstrate that it had close ties with the professions. The Mental Hygiene Program of the CPS, which formed the basis for the foundation, would never have been approved by the Selective Service had its leaders not been willing to have their activities subjected to psychiatric oversight.

During the existence of the national foundation, there was tension between the foundation's former CO leaders and the psychiatric establishment. Most psychiatrists viewed exposés as unseemly and worried that negative public attention to mental hospitals could damage the standing of the profession. They also were loath to cede any influence or control over their professional territory to a group of unpredictable laypersons. It was only the support of Byberry superintendent, and then Michigan mental health director, Charles Zeller and psychiatrists such as Karl Menninger who were trying to reform psychiatry themselves that made the foundation possible.

The former COs distrusted the psychiatric profession and believed that only a movement led by laypersons could bring about the necessary reforms. They also had no confidence in another major organization that had been established by another layperson—a former mental patient himself—almost forty years earlier: the National Committee for Mental Hygiene.

8

"A Mind That Found Itself"

Throughout its brief history, the National Mental Health Foundation, which had been founded by young COs, had an ambivalent relationship with the well-established and respectable National Committee for Mental Hygiene. On the one hand, the COs' Mental Hygiene Program of the Civilian Public Service, the predecessor to the national foundation, depended on the sponsorship of the National Committee and the support of its medical director, George Stevenson. Without this sponsorship and support, it is doubtful whether the Selective Service would have approved the establishment of the Mental Hygiene Program. On the other hand, the leaders of the MHP and then the national foundation viewed the National Committee as too cautious and too cozy with the psychiatric establishment and questioned its ability to bring about the necessary reforms in state institutions. It would also compete with the National Committee in fund-raising. Ironically, the National Committee had itself been founded as a reform organization by Clifford Beers.

In 1908, Beers published his autobiographical account of three years in Connecticut mental hospitals, *A Mind That Found Itself*. Beers was born in Connecticut in 1876. He received his high school diploma and entered Yale University in 1894. That same year, his older brother was stricken with what was thought to be epilepsy and subsequently died in 1900. Beers reported experiencing attacks of nervousness and anxiety at the time, but graduated from Yale University in 1897. He then held jobs as a clerk in the office of collector of taxes in New Haven and at a life insurance company in New York City. Then, in June 1900, believing that he was destined to become epileptic like his brother, Beers unsuccessfully attempted suicide by jumping out of the fourth floor of his family's home. After treatment at a general hospital for broken bones in his feet and a sprained spine, his mental condition deteriorated and his family placed him at the first of two private institutions. He was later committed to the Connecticut Hospital for the Insane. Beers recounted the brutal and harsh treatment he received at the three mental hospitals. He was placed in a straitjacket for long stretches of time and was routinely beaten by attendants.

Beers was released from Connecticut Hospital in 1903 and committed himself to writing a book about his experiences. He reflected on the kind of book he wanted to write: "'Uncle Tom's Cabin,' I continued, 'had a very decided effect on the question of slavery of the Negro race. Why cannot a book be written which will free the helpless slaves of all creeds and colors confined to-day in the asylums and sanitariums throughout the world? That is, free them from unnecessary abuses to which they are now subjected.'"[1]

From the outset, Beers sought not just to tell his story but to lead a reform movement. As he wrote in an epilogue to *A Mind That Found Itself* published in a later edition of the book:

> As I have noted in the preceding pages, this book was neither conceived nor written merely as an entertaining story; it was intended to serve as the opening gun in a permanent campaign for improvement in the care and treatment of mental sufferers, and the prevention, whenever possible, of mental illness itself. It was not conceived as an end in itself, but rather as the beginning—the first step—of a movement calculated to organize public opinion, scientific knowledge, and a humane application of that knowledge, into a unified force directed toward the attainment of the goal in view. I had abounding faith in the possibilities of such a movement.[2]

Prior to publishing *A Mind That Found Itself,* Beers circulated his manuscript to prominent psychologists, physicians, and civic leaders and obtained their endorsements not just of his book but of his plans for a national movement as well. Psychologist, philosopher, and author William James wrote a letter to Beers that was quoted at the beginning of the book: "You have handled a difficult theme with great skill, and produced a narrative of absorbing interest to scientist as well as layman. It reads like fiction, but it is not fiction; and this I state emphatically, knowing how prone the uninitiated are to doubt the truthfulness of descriptions of abnormal mental processes."[3] When the book was finally published, it received widespread attention and rave reviews in the popular press. In medical and psychiatric publications, reviews of the book were generally favorable, but not uncritical. Even some of Beers's supporters were bothered by the sensationalistic portrayal of mental hospitals in the press.[4]

In 1908, Beers convened a small group of supporters (thirteen, including his father and brother) to form the Connecticut Society for Mental Hygiene. The phrase "mental hygiene" had been suggested by Adolf Meyer, a leading psychiatrist at the time and early supporter of Beers. Throughout the rest of his life, Beers would have a stormy relationship with Meyer, who thought that his plans were too grandiose and questioned whether a layperson should play a prominent role in a mental hygiene movement.[5] Against Meyer's advice, the National Committee for Mental Hygiene was founded by twelve charter members one year later. The objectives of the national society were described in a 1912 pamphlet:

> To work for the protection of the mental health of the public; to help raise the standard of care for those in danger of developing mental disorder or actually insane; to promote the study of mental disorders in all their forms and relations and to disseminate knowledge concerning their causes, treatment and prevention; to obtain from every source reliable data regarding conditions and methods of dealing with mental disorders; to enlist the aid of the Federal Government so far as may seem desirable; to coordinate existing agencies and help organize in each state in the Union an allied, but independent, Society for Mental Hygiene, similar to the existing Connecticut Society for Mental Hygiene.[6]

Beers envisioned the National Committee to be an auxiliary organization to the psychiatric profession. As C. E. A. Winslow wrote in a supplement describing the origins of the mental hygiene movement published in a later edition of Beers's book, "The Mental Hygiene Movement, then, bears the same relation to psychiatry that the public health movement, of which it forms a part, bears to medicine in general. It is an organized community response to a recognized community need; and it lays its prime emphasis on the detection and control of those incipient maladjustments with which the physician *qua* physician never comes into contact, unless specific community machinery and far-flung educational facilities are provided for the purpose."[7]

Until 1912, Beers paid for most expenses associated with the National Committee through borrowed money. Then late in 1911, he received donations of fifty thousand dollars for the National Committee and five thousand to pay off debts and for his personal use from Henry Phipps.[8] The committee hired Dr. William Stanton, who later became its first medical director. One of Stanton's initial tasks was to conduct visits to asylums and other institutions during which he documented the widespread presence of brutality and substandard conditions reported by Beers.[9] Stanton subsequently conducted a national survey of mental hygiene facilities in the country.

Upon the entry of the United States into World War I, the federal government created a division of neurology and psychiatry in the Office of the Surgeon General. The office turned over responsibility for organizing this division to the National Committee.[10] The division was involved in screening recruits for fitness for military service based on mental conditions and preparing for the treatment of soldiers for mental diseases.

By 1918, Beers had founded the International Committee on Mental Hygiene. When the first International Congress on Mental Hygiene was held in Washington,

D.C., in 1930, there were mental hygiene societies in twenty-five countries.[11] Beers established the American Foundation for Mental Hygiene to fund mental hygiene activities in 1928.[12]

◆   ◆   ◆

In histories of people with psychiatric and developmental disabilities in America, Beers's name has often been paired with that of another dedicated reformer a half century earlier: Dorothea Dix. Dix's exposés of poorhouses and jails in the 1840s and '50s and her famous memorials, like Beers's *Mind That Found Itself*, have been reported in any serious history of asylums or mental disabilities. She was described as a "fiery, world-famous standard-bearer in a unique cause," an "indefatigable investigator," and a "dynamic force."[13] Major histories of psychiatry and mental illness in America described Dix's crusade in their introductions.[14] Dix has also been mentioned in many school history texts alongside abolitionists, women's rights advocates, and other social reformers during her era.[15] Dix addressed legislatures and Congress in an era in which women seldom, if ever, spoke in public forums. Her first major address before a state legislature was made five years before the first women's rights convention in Seneca Falls, New York, led by Susan B. Anthony, Elizabeth Cady Stanton, Matilda Joselyn Gage, and others.

Dorothea Dix's crusade against the squalid conditions and harsh treatment of idiotic and insane people in jails and poorhouses in the 1840s and '50s captured national attention and placed her as one of the leading reformers in the years leading up to the Civil War. Over one three-year period in the 1840s, Dix traveled an estimated ten thousand miles throughout the United States exposing conditions in town and county homes for the poor and dependent.[16] During this time, the care of poor and needy people was almost exclusively the responsibility of local governments. Although some towns offered "outdoor relief"—direct assistance to people in need—the poorhouse, jail, or almshouse was the most common way of providing public assistance.

Dix's journey started in 1841 when she visited the East Cambridge jail in Massachusetts.[17] A retired schoolteacher, Dix was approached by a young theological student who had been assigned to provide Sunday-school instruction to women at the jail and wanted Dix's advice. Dix immediately volunteered to take over the task. When she visited the jail the next Sunday, she was shocked by what she saw: filth, lack of heat, signs of brutality, and neglect. Especially troubling to Dix was the presence of insane people locked in cells.

Over the next two years, Dix toured almshouses and jails throughout the Commonwealth, documenting conditions that paralleled what she had seen at East Cambridge. Based on her notes, she presented her observations in a memorial to the legislature, which she addressed in 1843 through the efforts of Dr. Samuel Gridley Howe, a member of the legislature, social reformer, and pioneer in the development of institutions for blind and idiotic people. Dix pleaded, "I come to present the strong claims of suffering humanity. I come to place before the Legislature of Massachusetts the condition of the miserable, the desolate, the outcast. I come as the advocate of helpless, forgotten, insane and idiotic men and women. . . . I proceed gentlemen, briefly to call your attention to the *present* state of insane persons confined within this Commonwealth, in *cages, closets, cellars, stalls, pens! Chained, naked, beaten with rods,* and *lashed* into obedience."[18]

Dix's memorial was controversial in Massachusetts, and she was accused by local officials in Massachusetts newspapers of inaccuracies, distortion, and slander. A letter to the editor of one newspaper read:

> An article published in the Boston Mercantile Journal a few weeks since and copied into the Gazette & Courier this week, extracted from a Memorial to the Legislature by Miss Dix is a most slanderous reflection upon the Overseers of the poor, and the inhabitants of the town of Shelburne. We have not seen Miss Dix's Memorial, and therefore do not know her object or motive, or what she expects to accomplish in presenting and publishing it, with the bare-faced falsehoods, false impressions, and false statements, as she has done in the case of the insane pauper in this town.[19]

Dix also had her supporters, however, including prominent national figures. In addition to Howe, Horace Mann, a champion for public education, and Charles Sumner, later a U.S. senator, founder of the Republican Party, and abolitionist, provided strong support to Dix. In his own letter to a newspaper's editor, Sumner wrote:

> It appears from an examination of the memorial that there are twelve alms-houses, which are particularly described by Miss Dix, as the scenes of painful wretchedness. . . . In the course of last autumn, in company with Dr. Howe, I visited the alms-houses in four of these towns. . . .
>
> I have read over carefully the account of the visit to the four alms-houses last mentioned and for the sake of humanity, I am sorry to be obliged to add that it accords almost literally with the condition of things at the time of my own visit. . . . The correctness with which Miss Dix has described these four alms-houses, which I have seen, leads me to place entire confidence in her description of the other eight.[20]

The legislature subsequently approved an appropriation for the enlargement of Worcester State Hospital to accommodate the insane.

Dix then took her crusade to other states. As in the case of Massachusetts, she toured poorhouses and then reported her findings to anyone who would listen. According to Robert C. Scheerenberger, Dix addressed the legislatures of New York, New Jersey, Pennsylvania, Kentucky, Tennessee, North Carolina, Mississippi, and Maryland between 1844 and 1852. Albert Deutsch reported that she was instrumental in having New Jersey's legislature approve the establishment of the state hospital at Trenton.[21]

For Dix, there was only one solution to the wretched conditions in the poorhouses: the creation of separate mental hospitals or asylums. She had no confidence in the possiblity of reforming the poorhouses and was a staunch opponent of outdoor relief and family care.[22]

Although Dix was an advocate for the establishment of state institutions, she believed that the federal government bore responsibility for financing the states' efforts. In 1850, she gave another stirring memorial, this time before the Congress of the United States:

> I have myself seen *more than nine thousand idiots, epileptics, and insane, in these United States, destitute of appropriate care and protection;* and of this vast and most miserable company sought out in *jails,* in *poor-houses,* and in *private dwellings,* there have been hundreds, nay, thousands, bound with galling chains, bowed beneath fetters and heavy iron balls, attached to drag chains, lacerated with ropes, scourged with rods, and terrified beneath storms of profane execrations and cruel blows; now subject to gibes, and scorn, and torturing tricks—now abandoned to the most loathsome necessities, or subject to the vilest and most astounding violations. These are strong terms, but language fails to convey the astounding truths.[23]

Dix proposed that the federal government grant public land to the states that could be sold to fund mental hospitals or asylums: "I ask for the thirty States of the Union 5,000,000 acres of land, of the many hundreds of millions of public lands, appropriated in such manner as shall assure the greatest benefits to all who are in circumstances of extreme necessity, and who, through the providence of God, *are wards of the nation,* claimants on the sympathy and care of the public, through the miseries and disqualifications brought upon them by the sorest afflictions with which humanity can be visited."[24]

The idea that people with psychiatric and developmental disabilities were "wards of the nation"—the responsibility of the federal government—was a radical notion in the mid-1800s. It would not be until the mid- to late 1940s that the U.S. Congress would fund the National Institute of Mental Health to support research and training and the 1960s and '70s that the federal government would allocate significant funding for services for people with intellectual or psychiatric disabilities.

After six years of advocating for the land-grant bill, Dix was successful in convincing both houses of Congress to pass what became known as the "12,225,000 Acre Bill" (10,000,000 acres for the insane and 2,225,000 acres for deaf-mutes). To Dix's tremendous disappointment, President Franklin Pierce vetoed the act and characterized it as unwarranted federal intrusion on state affairs:

> I readily and, I trust, feelingly acknowledge the duty incumbent on us all as men and citizens, and as among the highest and holiest of our duties, to provide for those who, in the mysterious order of Providence, are subject to want and to disease of body and mind; but I can not find any authority in the Constitution for making the Federal Government the great almoner of public charity throughout the United States. To do so would, in my judgment, be contrary to the letter and spirit of the Constitution and subversive of the whole theory upon which the Union of these States is founded.[25]

During the Civil War, Dix served as the head of women nurses for the Union army. After the war, she resumed her efforts on behalf of the insane. According to Deutsch, Dix was distressed to find many of the same conditions that she had documented many years earlier, even in some of the asylums founded as a result of her efforts.[26]

Although Dix failed to have the federal government fund care of the indigent insane and idiotic, her efforts, together with the help of the emerging professional class in insanity and idiocy, ultimately led states to take over responsibility for caring for people with mental illness and mental retardation by establishing specialized hospitals and asylums. By 1860, twenty-eight of the thirty-three states had established public insane asylums. Deutsch reported that Dix was personally responsible for the founding or enlargement of thirty-two mental hospitals in the United States and abroad.[27] The first state institution for the feebleminded was opened in Massachusetts in 1848, and by 1890, fourteen states had established such asylums.[28] Dix died in 1887 at what she called her "first-born child," the New Jersey State Hospital at Trenton.[29]

Dix's exposés of poorhouses and efforts to create state asylums have been heralded as signaling a new day in America's treatment of people with intellectual and psychiatric disabilities.[30] In a supplement to Beers's *Mind That Found Itself* published in 1956, Dr. C. E. A. Winslow wrote, "A notable reform in the field of institutional care was initiated in this country by Dorothea Dix, and no less than thirty-two new institutions were established for the insane as a result." Yet, as historian David J. Rothman poignantly asked, "Was an organization that would eventually turn into a snake pit a necessary step forward for mankind?"[31]

Progress has been a powerful narrative in the care of people with psychiatric and intellectual disabilities in society.[32] The belief in the steady improvement of institutions owing to more enlightened views and the accumulation of scientific knowledge has been dominant since at least the mid-1800s. When Clifford Beers died in 1943, his obituary published in the National Committee's journal, *Mental Hygiene*, referred to institutional problems in the past tense.[33] Then came *Out of Sight, Out of Mind*, published by a new group composed of former COs.

◆　◆　◆

From the founding of the National Committee, Beers cultivated relationships with medical professionals and psychiatrists. They embraced his cause—the creation of a national movement—and he worked hard to obtain their approval and support. In a later edition of *A Mind That Found Itself*, the epilogue reprinted correspondence and communications from others. Beers proudly quoted from an address by Dr. Lewellys F. Barker, who had served as a president of the committee and had praised the initiative of a layman, Clifford W. Beers, for creating "the impulse to arouse public opinion in favor of a definite plan for mental hygiene."[34]

Beers next quoted a 1916 letter from Walter Fernald, superintendent of the Massachusetts School for the Feeble-Minded and a recognized leader in mental deficiency. Fernald singled out the National Committee for involving physicians knowledgeable about mental deficiency and for avoiding "propaganda" in favor of "dependable data":

> It has been my privilege to witness and, in various ways, to participate in the growth of the now widespread movement in behalf of the mentally defective. At first this was a slow growth, but during the past ten years—and especially during the past five—it has been one of the most striking social developments of the day. Many individuals, groups and forces have contributed to this fortunate result. The National Committee for Mental Hygiene felt the force of this movement within one year of the time it began its active work in 1912 and wisely began then to bring into its membership physicians who had special knowledge. As in all new fields—when pioneer work is done by many unrelated groups and by zealous individuals—there was great danger that propaganda might outrun dependable data and that unwise plans, policies and laws relating to State care of the mentally defective might be hastily adopted in many States. This danger, however, has been averted, and I believe that The National Committee for Mental Hygiene and its affiliated State Societies are destined to continue to influence,

along wise and effective lines, the management of all phases of the great problem of mental deficiency.[35]

Except for Beers, laypeople never played a prominent role in the National Committee. Beers devoted his energies to building the organization and obtaining funding for the committee. He left it to medical professionals to direct the work of the National Committee.[36] In 1917, the president and one of two vice presidents of the committee were doctors. Of seven members of the executive committee, five were doctors. Two out of three executive officers were medical doctors; Beers was the secretary. The National Committee's journal, *Mental Hygiene,* which was established in 1917, listed seven M.D.'s and one Ph.D. on its editorial board. By 1939, the president and two out of three vice presidents of the committee were medical doctors.[37] Six out of eight members of the executive committee were physicians. Although Beers responded sympathetically to other current or former mental patients who contacted him, he saw no role for these persons in the committee. He rejected outright proposals to organize former mental patients themselves.[38]

Over time, the priorities of the National Committee steadily shifted away from mental hospitals. Beers remained concerned about the treatment of mental patients. The committee's medical director, Thomas Salmon, published a scathing report on the treatment of the insane in a county poor farm at which inmates were kept in cages in the inaugural issue of *Mental Hygiene* in January 1917.[39] However, in the 1920s and '30s, the committee paid little attention to conditions in mental hospitals and asylums. Rather, the National Committee focused on prevention, education, and social work. When the committee did devote attention to mental hospitals in the 1930s, it was at the urging and with the financial support of the Rockefeller Foundation, which had become a benefactor of the committee. Even then, the committee focused on developing hospital standards and conducting professionally acceptable surveys. Meyer and many other physicians associated with the committee abhorred exposés and scandals.[40]

Soon after the founding of the National Committee for Mental Hygiene it found itself aligned with a darker mission. In the later part of the 1800s and the first part of the 1900s, the eugenics movement was strong in America.[41] Eugenics represented a social theory and program of social action designed to halt the spread of alleged defective genes presumably responsible for growing social problems in society. Feeblemindedness and insanity were regarded as hereditary conditions that caused crime, delinquency, sexual immorality, poverty, and other social ills. Leading physicians, psychologists, and civic leaders subscribed to eugenics notions and advocated for the prevention of insanity and especially feeblemindedness through sterilization, restrictive marriage laws, and segregation.

Many of those individuals influential in the National Committee were proponents of eugenics. Beers approvingly quoted an address by Dr. Lewellys F. Barker, who had served as president of the committee, in the epilogue to *A Mind That Found Itself* published in a later edition of the book: "The general problems of mental hygiene become obvious; broadly conceived, they consist, first, in providing for the birth of children with good brains, denying, as far as possible, the privilege of parenthood to the manifestly unfit who are almost certain to transmit bad nervous systems to their offspring—that is to say, the problem of eugenics; and second, in supplying all individuals, from the moment of fusion of the parental germ-cells onward, and whether ancestrally well begun or not, with the environment best suited for the welfare of their mentality."[42]

Walter Fernald, who was the superintendent of the Massachusetts School for the Feeble-Minded and had praised the National Committee in a 1916 letter published in Beers's epilogue, was a member of the editorial board of *Mental Hygiene* when it was first published in 1917. As late as 1912, Fernald had characterized the feebleminded as a "parasitic, predatory class" and wrote, "Every feebleminded person, especially the high-grade imbecile, is a potential criminal, needed expression of his criminal tendencies. The unrecognized imbecile is a most dangerous element in the community. . . . It has been truly said that feeblemindedness is the mother of crime, pauperism and degeneracy. It is certain that the feebleminded constitute one of the great social and economic burdens of modern times."[43]

Beers himself never took a position on eugenics and many other social and political issues of his times, but the National Committee was amenable to preventative actions aimed at the insane and especially the mentally defective.[44] In 1912, the committee passed a resolution urging Congress to enact legislation requiring mental examinations of entering immigrants and favored efforts to limit reproduction by mental defectives. The National Committee's quarterly magazine, *Mental Hygiene,* often published articles advocating eugenics measures, and eugenics was a frequent topic in addresses at meetings of societies associated with the committee. In a 1917 article published in the inaugural issue of *Mental Hygiene,* Beers matter-of-factly listed the titles of addresses at mental hygiene meetings in recent years, including "Practical Eugenics," "Segregation of the Feeble-Minded," "Feeblemindedness and Crime," "Relation of Insanity to Criminality," and "Heredity in Relation to Insanity and Eugenics."[45] As late as 1945, the Canadian National Committee for Mental Hygiene, which had been founded with the help of Beers in 1918,[46] created an uproar when it issued a report endorsing "sterilization in connection with physically attractive moron girls prior to discharge from residential school [for mental defectives]."[47] The head of the Canadian National Committee at the time, C. M. Hincks, was named as the author of the report mentioned in the

Time article. Hincks had stepped down as medical director of Beers's National Committee in 1939.[48]

The National Committee's interest in prevention went hand in hand with its attention to the "problem" of the mentally deficient or feebleminded. Fernald's involvement in the committee reflected Beers's commitment to extending the committee's influence beyond the mentally ill. Beers wrote in 1917, "In striving to help the insane and conserve mental health, the National Committee soon found itself called upon to help also the mentally deficient, the epileptic, the inebriate—in fact all of the mentally abnormal groups." He went on to specify the groups that would be "benefited" by organized work in mental hygiene: "The two chief groups are the insane, of whom over two hundred thousand are already in institutions and tens of thousands still outside of them, and the mentally deficient or, as they are more commonly called, the feeble-minded, of whom only a few thousands are as yet cared for in institutions while uncounted thousands are still at liberty, a menace oftentimes to the communities in which they live."[49] Beers's characterization of the feebleminded as a "menace" paralleled the views of Walter Fernald, Henry Goddard, and other leaders of the American Association for the Study of the Feeble-Minded who favored eugenics measures during the era.[50] A movement inspired by *Uncle Tom's Cabin* and designed to free asylum inmates from "unnecessary abuses to which they are now subjected" had taken a strange turn.

During the 1920s and '30s, Beers and the National Committee continued to receive public and professional acclaim. Beers received an honorary degree from Yale University, his alma mater, in 1922, the Cross of the Knight of the Legion of Honor from the French government in 1932, and the Gold Medal of the National Institute of Social Sciences in 1933. At the eightieth meeting of the American Psychiatric Association, he was elected an honorary member of the association, one of the few laypeople ever admitted to membership.[51] Beers and the National Committee were lauded in *Time* magazine articles in 1923, 1927, 1928, 1929, 1930, and 1933.[52] The May 15, 1933, article, titled "Mind Triumphant," read: "Insane asylums 25 years ago were mostly custodial institutions. Mr. Beers's National Committee for Mental Hygiene has converted most of them into hospitals for scientific treatment."

Meanwhile, the National Committee experienced organizational and financial problems from its founding until Beers left the organization. Alan Gregg of the Rockefeller Foundation, the National Committee's longtime benefactor, announced that the foundation would terminate its grants for operations and mental hospital services to the committee in early 1939. Norman Dain quoted a confidential Rockefeller Foundation report: "Despite repeated warnings the Committee remained dependent on the Foundation and continued to suffer from this status of a dependent intermediate set-up. Behind this unsatisfactory record lay

such factors as the depression, the doubtful judgments and temperamental incon-
sistency of some of its executive personnel, the inherent difficulties of the mental
hygiene field as such, and a gradually evident lack of sober and solid policy within
the organization."[53]

In 1939, George Stevenson was appointed medical director, the chief executive officer, of the National Committee, with Beers's support.[54] Stevenson had
served as director of the National Committee's Division of Community Clinics.
He would remain as medical director for as long as the National Committee for
Mental Hygiene existed in name.

Beers retired as secretary of the National Committee shortly after the appointment of Stevenson as medical director when he experienced a reported relapse of
his mental illness. An announcement in *Mental Hygiene* read:

> At a meeting of the Board of Directors of the National Committee for Mental
> Hygiene held on June 1, Clifford W. Beers requested that his resignation as Secre-
> tary of the Committee be accepted. . . .
>
> The board immediately elected Mr. Beers the Honorary Secretary of the
> National Committee for Mental Hygiene. In accepting his resignation as Secre-
> tary, the board by resolution recorded the recognition and profound appreciation
> of the board and of the National Committee for the notable and unique services
> of Mr. Beers as the founder of the mental-hygiene movement and of the National
> Committee, and of his stimulating and devoted work as Secretary of the Commit-
> tee for more than thirty years.[55]

Beers spent his final years at Butler Hospital in Providence, Rhode Island,
where he was described as "seclusive, passive, indecisive, and often close to tears."
He died there on July 9, 1943, at the age of sixty-seven. The causes were listed as
"Terminal bronchopneumonia, Cerebral thrombosis," along with "Arteriosclerotic
cardiovascular-renal disease."[56] An obituary by C. M. Hincks, head of the Canadian National Committee, was published in *Mental Hygiene:*

> When Clifford Beers began his work, American psychiatry had not achieved the
> status that it enjoys to-day. It was hampered by many handicaps. Public mental
> institutions, which employed the great majority of men engaged in the psychiat-
> ric field, were inadequately financed and, for the most part, were organized for
> custodial care, with scant arrangements for active therapy. . . . The general public
> was apathetic to this unfortunate situation and there was little incentive to psy-
> chiatry to transform asylums into creditable hospitals, to convass [sic] possibilities
> for prevention, or to embark upon programs to improve the mental health of all
> sections of the population.[57]

This obituary was published almost four years prior to the release of *Out of Sight, Out of Mind*.

◆   ◆   ◆

In 1946, the year the National Mental Health Foundation was established, there were 445,561 patients in state mental hospitals, an increase of 28,246 patients over 1941, the first year of America's involvement in World War II. An additional 48,235 psychiatric patients were housed at veterans' hospitals and 23,150 at county and city hospitals. Also in 1946, there were 113,475 patients in public institutions for mental defectives and epileptics, an increase of 13,831 patients since 1941.[58]

In the years prior to the war, both the National Committee and the Public Health Service had conducted surveys of state hospitals. In 1934, the National Committee published a report, *State Hospitals in the Depression: A Survey of the Effects of the Economic Crisis on the Operation of Institutions for the Mentally Ill in the United States*. The survey, which was conducted by committee staff with an advisory committee composed of twelve medical doctors, was sent to hospital superintendents "to obtain from them an account of their experience during these difficult times and secure their judgment as to how budgets may best be maintained in the face of the present necessity for retrenchment." Out of 181 mental hospitals in the states, 104 responded to the survey. The survey found that the number of mental patients in state hospitals had steadily increased from 272,252 in 1929 (225.6 per 100,000 of the general population) to 318,948 in 1933 (254.8 per 100,000 of the general population).[59] Not much else could be gleaned from this survey.

The Public Health Service's report was titled *A Study of Public Mental Hospitals in the United States, 1937–39*. The report was conducted under the auspices of the Mental Hospital Survey Committee, which was composed of fifteen medical doctors, in cooperation with eight participating agencies, including the Public Health Service, National Committee for Mental Hygiene, American Psychiatric Association, and American Medical Association. The survey reported hospitalization rates for various patients in 1938: mental disease, 447,321; mental deficiency, 94,284; epilepsy, 21,026; and others, 6,634. The *average daily population* in state hospitals for mental disease was 376,787. The survey also reported a per capita maintenance expenditure for all state hospitals for mental disease of $291.27, or about 80 cents a day.[60] Per capita expenditures varied widely from region to region, with the New England and Middle Atlantic states spending by far the most on patients. The District of Columbia ($669.64), Wisconsin ($481.89), Massachusetts ($423.34), and New York ($406.74) had the highest per capita expenditures. Kentucky ($130.14), Mississippi ($148.52), Virginia ($155.77), and North Carolina ($169.26) had the lowest.

The Public Health Service report also contained a description of facilities and programs at institutions in the various states. The survey staff had visited 149 institutions and obtained information on 33 more. Occasionally, the report commented on conditions: "Wards for disturbed patients in the older buildings were rather bleak and bare"; "The better institutions have fine assembly halls." *Mental Hygiene* contained a one-paragraph description of the report in an announcement published in 1942: "The Chapter on 'Contrasts' is particularly enlightening and should move state authorities and the general public to consider seriously how the present unsatisfactory situation can be improved." That same year, the journal contained a review of the report in the "Book Reviews" section by William A. Bryan of Norwich State Hospital in Connecticut. Bryan summarized the "on the one hand, on the other hand" tone of the report: "The picture drawn of American hospital psychiatry is encouraging in that some states have made notable progress toward higher standards. But as yet there is no standard that prevails throughout the country." Bryan concluded that the report was fair: "One is impressed by the fairness of the report. While there is no attempt to minimize the situation or gloss over the worst spots, the authors have not humiliated individual institutions which, in many cases, are what they are through no fault of those in charge."[61]

The report did contain enough fodder for journalistic critics of mental hospitals. In articles in *Reader's Digest*, condensed from *Survey Graphic*, and *PM*, a New York newspaper, journalists Edith Stern and Albert Deutsch latched onto the report to condemn institutional abuse and neglect. *Mental Hygiene*'s "Notes and Comments" section contained a brief announcement on how Stern and Deutsch had stimulated public interest in mental hospitals. The announcement painted a far more favorable picture of institutions than either Stern or Deutsch had: "Both stories gave an illuminated and constructive analysis of the situation, based on the findings of institutional surveys conducted during the past four years by the United States Public Health Service and The National Committee for Mental Hygiene, showing where mental hospitals were doing good work and where, more often, for lack of adequate funds, facilities, and personnel, they were reduced to little better than custodial asylums."[62]

In the 1940s, the National Committee played a less direct role in surveys of state mental hospitals. The committee's 1946 *Annual Report* summarized the state of the surveys:

The years of close cooperation between the National Committee and the United States Public Health Service are bearing fruit. More and more states are requesting the Service to make a survey of their institutions for the mentally ill. In the past, such surveys were conducted by the National Committee in cooperation

with eight leading medical and lay organizations, and while they are not primarily conducted by the Service, the reports come to us for review and recommendation before being submitted to the states. In this way we are kept abreast of
conditions in the mental hygiene field.[63]

A footnote added that Dr. Samuel Hamilton, who served as director of the Division of Mental Hospitals for the National Committee without compensation, had
taken over the surveys for the Public Health Service.

The National Committee and Public Health Service reports were based largely
on reports of hospital superintendents and did not always give a clear picture of
conditions at the institutions or what life was like for the patients. They were written in a style unlikely to offend the psychiatric establishment or superintendents
of state mental hospitals or training schools. Samuel Hamilton had directed the
1936–39 survey on behalf of the Mental Hospital Survey Committee before moving
on to the Public Health Service. After his death in 1951, *Mental Hygiene* published
an obituary written by Edith M. Stern: "Sam Hamilton had critics, among the most
vehement some of my colleagues in journalism. His mild, understated reports and
recommendations, they allege, held up rather than helped progress in mental hospitals. There is no denying that the surveys are circumlocutious [*sic*]. Indeed, I once
parodied them with 'It is thought that the patients would be more comfortable
were they not sleeping three in a bed.' . . . His function was not that of a policeman,
but of an advisor; he went into institutions, not by warrant, but by invitation."[64]

The Brethren Historical Library and Archives contains a one-page report of
two mental hospitals in Maine, filed along with documents from Augusta State
Hospital. The report, which stated that it had been sent out by the National Committee for Mental Hygiene, painted a positive picture of the institutions, although
it identified deficiencies:

> Conditions in the state hospitals at Augusta and Bangor are, in general, good, and
> the care and treatment of patients on a high level. A survey of these institutions
> made in the spring of 1940, however, revealed defects and a few directions in
> which improvements might be made.
>
> Most important were the shortages of doctors and nurses as measured by the
> standards set by the American Psychiatric Association, which require ratios of 1
> physician to 150 patients, and 1 nurse or attendant to 8 patients. The proportion
> of the personnel to patients at Augusta were 1 assistant physician to 318 patients,
> and 1 nurse or attendant to 10 patients; and at Bangor 1 assistant physician to 231
> patients, and 1 attendant to 10 patients.
>
> The lack of a sufficient number of physicians and nurses accounts largely
> for inadequacies of care and treatment along some lines. . . . The upkeep of the

hospitals and provisions for treatment are otherwise generally good, though some laboratory work could be strengthened by providing adequate personnel.

There is also weakness in admission procedures which should be strengthened by amending the commitment law.[65]

◆   ◆   ◆

Another report published independently in 1934, which barely saw the light of day, provided a more meaningful view of institutions than the National Committee's, Mental Hospital Survey Committee's, and Public Health Service's surveys.[66] In 1930, the American Medical Association commissioned its Council of Medical Education and Hospitals to conduct an intensive study of mental hospitals and training schools. The study included a six-page questionnaire sent to the superintendent of each institution and personal visits by physicians to 600 of the 631 institutions in the study. Dr. John Maurice Grimes directed the study, with the assistance of three other physicians and a statistician.

The study was controversial before it even started. According to Grimes, "A small group of men, located in the East but nationally known, protested that the American Medical Association was entering territory sacred to another organization, and that it would be more proper for the American Psychiatric Association to make, or at any rate to direct the contemplated study." An advisory committee on mental hygiene established by the American Medical Association was sympathetic to this position. Grimes continued with the study and submitted a draft report to the secretary of the Council of Medical Education and Hospitals in 1933, who rejected the report. A revised version of the draft report was then submitted to the council's subcommittee on hospitals, which reviewed the report and recommended that it be accepted by the full council. The council accepted the report. Grimes reported what happened next: "Three weeks later the secretary of the Council informed me that financial considerations made it necessary to discontinue my services. I replied that if funds were low I was prepared to work without salary until salary payments could be resumed; this offer was refused."[67] The secretary subsequently published a ten-page report, with appendixes, based exclusively on the questionnaire results. None of the information from the visits made to the 600 hospitals was included in this report.

Undaunted by the actions of the council, Grimes decided to publish the report on his own. "It is unfortunate," he wrote, "that this report cannot be published in the name and by the authority of the American Medical Association, and cannot be given the wide publicity and distribution that it might have had through that great organization."[68] *Institutional Care of Mental Patients in the United States*, which was published by Grimes in 1934, was 138 pages long, excluding a detailed preface reviewing the history of the report.

Grimes included a dedication at the beginning of the book:

TO THE MENTALLY ILL

Misunderstood, unwanted, neglected, ridiculed, maligned, thwarted, abused; often curable, but not often cured; whose heroism through years of suffering never inspired a poet; whose loneliness in delusion wakes contempt instead of compassion; whose death-in-life goes on for decades in indescribable hopelessness; whose rapidly increasing numbers carry the hint that, tomorrow, we ourselves may be among the stricken—to these most numerous and most pitiable of all human sufferers, this story is most sympathetically

INSCRIBED

It is a story full of unwelcome facts—a story many would like to suppress. It is being published and distributed by the author, after his wish to tell the story without distortion cost him his economic position. . . . The author has endeavored to make the narrative easy to read and understand—but his primary effort has not been to please; it has been to tell the story as it is.[69]

Institutional Care of Mental Patients in the United States contained vivid accounts of the deficiencies of mental hospitals and training schools. Grimes argued, in fact, that no one familiar with institutions for the mentally ill "can honestly refer to them as a group of hospitals." He reported that overcrowding at state institutions for the mentally ill was "an almost universal characteristic" and that "barred windows and locked doors are the rule." Staff members, especially attendants, were few in number, inadequately trained, and insufficiently paid to attract "intelligent, energetic individuals." State schools for the mentally deficient were little better than institutions for the mentally ill: "The school enrolls only a small per cent of the institution's total population, even as the hospital actually treats a small per cent of the total number of its patients, but in the case of either hospital or school, an accommodation is made and the name applied to the entire institution." Grimes criticized the commitment of "higher grade, educable" children who "need an environment vastly different from the one into which they come when institutionalized," although he expressed a less benign view toward "lower grade, uneducable children," whom he characterized as an "unredeemable residue of human worthlessness."[70]

Citing reforms initiated by Dorothea Dix in the mid–nineteenth century and Clifford Beers, Grimes called for a new era of reform:

Institutions for mental patients in the United States have passed through two periods of major improvement during the past century. The first period was initiated through the efforts of Dorothea Dix; the second was started by Mr. Clifford

Beers. Neither of these two individuals was in any way associated with the medical profession, and, although the American Medical Association came into existence long before the start of the first period, it apparently had very little to do with either of these two moves to improvement. Another period of major improvement in institutions for mental patients is due.[71]

In a section titled "An Afterthought," Grimes disputed the widely held notion that more money and new legislation would fix the problems of the institutions. Rather, he advocated for the "concentration of the medical staffs on the problem of de-institutionalization, with the definite aim of paroling all parolable patients." The concept of deinstitutionalization would not become popular in the fields of psychiatric and intellectual disabilities until the period from the late 1950s to the '70s. Grimes concluded the book with a call for change that would be echoed by the National Mental Health Foundation thirteen years later in *Out of Sight, Out of Mind*:

> It is easy to cry "Impossible!" and just as easy to answer that it has not been tried. It is easy to protest that these patients are dangerous and cannot be given privileges and responsibilities with safety; such a protest kept the insane bound with chains for generations. It is easy to contend that the cost of such changes is prohibitive; but it is delay in making them that is expensive and the changes will more than pay for themselves from the beginning. It is always easy to find excuses for resisting change; but change is the most irresistible, the most inevitable thing in life.[72]

◆　◆　◆

Clifford Beers was not unaware of problems in mental hospitals in the 1930s. Complaints about institutional conditions frequently were made to the National Committee. Yet Beers believed that progress was being made and that any complaints should be taken up with the mental hospitals or state officials. In 1934, the same year that Grimes published his book, Beers rejected a critical article on mental hospitals, "Ten Centuries in an Insane Asylum," for publication in *Mental Hygiene* because relatives of patients "would or might assume that conditions in *all* mental hospitals" were bad.[73]

From Beers's retirement in 1939 until 1946, the National Committee paid scant attention to institutional conditions, which had not been good throughout the Depression and certainly had deteriorated during the war. From 1939 through 1945, not one of the approximately forty articles published each year in the committee's journal focused on institutional conditions or the treatment of patients. One article, "Life in Our Mental Hospitals: Its Meaning for the

Individual," written by Samuel Hamilton of the Public Health Service, discussed mental hospitals in general terms but referred to conditions only in passing and in understated terms: "And what shall we say of overcrowding? It disrupts all hospital programs. Sometimes it is the reason and more often the excuse for the practice of constant repression. If any one starts to go about, he is told to sit down, because there is little space and he may clash with someone else"; "There should be room enough so that patients will not be in too much discomfort or their health imperiled by too close contact with one another." When institutions were mentioned in *Mental Hygiene*, it was usually in articles with titles such as "The Utilization of the State Hospital in the Training of Psychiatrists," "The Mentally Deficient Child in the Residential School," "Improving Protestant Worship in Mental Hospitals," "Mental-Hospital Newspapers," and "Public Relationships of the Mental Hospital."[74]

The National Committee's annual reports did occasionally refer to conditions in mental hospitals. In a rare mention of institutional conditions in *Mental Hygiene*, the news feature of the journal, "Notes and Comments," summarized the National Committee's *Annual Report* in October 1941. The report had expressed concern that standards of care and treatment in mental hospitals would be lowered by war conditions and reviewed the results of a recent survey: "The depression has put in its deadly work, and standards of care in many institutions have fallen far below the requirements of modern psychiatric practice, in some cases to such a point as to suggest a revision to the conditions of the old insane-asylum era. A primitive neglect of elementary human needs and decencies characterizes many of them." The column cited overcrowding, poor sanitation, badly fed and clothed patients, and staff shortages at mental hospitals and added: "It is not the doctors who are to blame, the report explains, so much as legislative inaction and public indifference and apathy."[75]

A vague hint of problems at mental hospitals came in brief references to staff shortages in medical director George Stevenson's 1942 and 1943 annual reviews of the National Committee's work published in *Mental Hygiene*. In the report on 1942, Stevenson wrote, "We have brought it to the attention of a large number of mental hospitals that attendant personnel may be recruited from civilian-service camps for conscientious objectors. Many hospitals have made application for such personnel and received them. In some cases the wives of such men are able to be employed on salary as attendants, whereas the husband receives only a small allowance."[76]

Stevenson's report on 1943 stated that the shortages of psychiatrists and psychiatric social workers had made it impossible for the National Committee to help fill vacancies at community clinics and again referred to attendants in the mental hospitals: "The paucity of attendants in our mental hospitals has been only slightly relieved by the allocation of conscientious objectors to these institutions."[77]

The National Committee's *Annual Report* for 1944 provided a candid assessment of conditions in state mental hospitals. Three pages of the forty-seven-page report were devoted to mental hospital conditions. The section started out with quotes from George Stevenson's testimony before congressional committees. The first quote was from a hearing of the Senate Subcommittee on Wartime Health and Education of the Committee on Education and Labor: "The situation of the psychiatric casualty and the rejectee highlights the conditions of our mental hospitals. In some states these facilities still are excellent, although everywhere some deterioration has occurred during the war, but in other states there is no place, no, not excluding our jails and the third degree, in which the rights of the human being are so seriously violated as in some of our mental hospitals." Then, in testimony before the House Subcommittee to Investigate Aid to the Physically Handicapped, Stevenson forcefully stated, "Man's inhumanity to man is nowhere so evident as in our mental hospitals." Stevenson's testimony placed the blame for hospital conditions squarely on the shoulders of the public: "All too frequently the public is content to delegate its conscience to the officials in order that it may wash its hands of matters which it should make its concern." The National Committee's 1944 *Annual Report* also quoted extensively from an address by Dr. Frank Tallman, Ohio's commissioner of mental diseases, presented at the November annual meeting of the National Committee: "Poor physical facilities have resulted in a denial of timely, efficient treatment to many and the herding of people together in an inhuman manner. . . . The professional and nursing staff are too few and badly trained." Finally, the report included a quote from Hamilton of the National Committee's Division of Mental Hospitals and the Public Health Service. After referring to the shortage of psychiatrically trained professionals at mental hospitals, Hamilton said, "A state that thinks so little of its physicians that it does not give them an opportunity to live comfortably has no right to expect that it will get the services of very able men for any length of time."[78]

Although the annual reports and other major events were usually summarized in the "Notes and Comments" feature in *Mental Hygiene,* and it was commonplace for major addresses at the annual meeting to be reprinted in the journal, no mention of Stevenson's congressional testimony or Tillman's and Hamilton's addresses was made in *Mental Hygiene.*

From the beginning of 1941 to the end of 1945, *Mental Hygiene,* the publication organ of the National Committee, published more than thirty-two hundred pages of articles, notes and comments, and book reviews. Fewer than six pages contained references to problems in state mental hospitals: brief, understated comments about overcrowding or labor shortages by Hamilton or Stevenson in three articles in 1942, 1943, and 1944; two short mentions in "Notes and Comments" and one book review related to the 1936–39 U.S. Public Health Service report in 1941 and 1942; a brief description of the NCMH's annual report in 1941; and a "Note and Comment" on a New York state commission in 1943.

The National Committee and other professionally dominated organizations were not yet willing to take public positions and aggressive actions against the widespread abuses and neglect at state institutions. This reluctance partially reflected a belief that the problems at institutions should be addressed by the psychiatric establishment and, occasionally, by the government bodies that funded mental hospitals and training schools—and not in the public arena and especially not in the media. It also reflected deeply held assumptions about the nature of the problems themselves. The assumptions could be seen in the narratives told by leaders in psychiatry and mental hygiene, which differed in subtle but important ways from the assumptions of reformers outside of these fields.

The narrative told by psychiatrists and mental hygiene leaders went something like the following: "There are excellent mental hospitals and substandard, even terrible, institutions. Superintendents and psychiatrists are doing the best they can under difficult circumstances and especially with the shortages caused by the war. Public apathy and indifference are at the heart of the problem. The public needs to convince legislatures to give superintendents and psychiatrists the resources and tools they need to practice their professions and provide the highest-quality care to patients. Superintendents and psychiatrists can solve the problems found at institutions." The narrative told by the COs associated with the founding of the National Mental Health Foundation and contained in *Out of Sight, Out of Mind* was very different: "Mental hospitals are a national disgrace, despite occasional examples of positive treatment and sincere concern. Superintendents and psychiatrists have sometimes been complicit in abusive and neglectful conditions and in keeping mental hospitals out of sight and out of mind. The public needs to be aroused to moral indignation at the treatment of mental patients in America. An informed citizenry and involved laypersons can solve the problems found at institutions." These narratives, and the actions implied by them, would clash throughout the history of the national foundation.

It was not until 1946 that the National Committee, along with the American Psychiatric Association, began to respond directly to the abuses and squalid conditions at state institutions exposed by current or former COs. *Time* magazine, which had heralded the National Committee for its reform efforts in the 1920s and '30s, described the address by writer Edith Stern at the "conservative" National Committee's annual meeting in 1946:

"Patients are beaten up and murdered by attendants. . . . [They] are starved. . . . [They live in] antiquated, unsanitary buildings [amid] filth, vermin and over-crowding. . . . Care of the mentally ill is a national disgrace."

This description of U.S. mental hospitals last week came from no muckraker but from a speaker before the sober, conservative National Committee for Mental Hygiene. Mental health officials, gathered in Manhattan at the committee's annual meeting, agreed with this indictment by Mrs. Edith M. Stern, a writer on psychiatric problems.[79]

The conditions described by Stern had been documented by COs at state mental hospitals and training schools and reported by magazine and newspaper writers working closely with the COs. The exposé, long considered unseemly and irresponsible by the psychiatric and mental hygiene establishments, had become an effective tool of the COs in bringing public attention to the nation's treatment of people with psychiatric and intellectual disabilities. Established organizations had no choice but to acknowledge publicly the problems of institutions and to take actions to do something about them.

9

"They Asked for a Hard Job"

Frank Olmstead was fieldwork director of the War Resisters League and a frequent critic of the Civilian Public Service, the National Service Board for Religious Objectors, and the church committees administering camps and units. He had visited many CPS work camps and written a critical report in November 1942 describing the dissatisfaction of CPS men and questioning the meaningfulness of the work at the camps.[1] Olmstead then spent several weeks visiting mental hospital units to see if the work there was more significant. He spent a week working as an attendant at the first institution he visited and wrote an article that was published in *Fellowship* in November 1943 based on his time there.[2]

On Olmstead's first day at the mental hospital, he was given a quick tour of the incontinent building and then led into a locked ward: "First there was the odor. Outdoors it had been decidedly disagreeable; inside the front door it had become nauseating, but when we stepped into that room the unadulterated stench was overpowering." Two attendants were on the ward. One of the attendants told Olmstead that the institution was short-staffed and asked him if he would mind being left alone in charge for a while. Right after the two attendants left, Olmstead reflected on the scene in front of him: "I have been in storms at sea, in train wrecks, and in Moscow during the Bolshevik revolution, but I have never had quite the feeling that I had when I turned from that locked door to face three hundred insane incontinents."[3] Olmstead went on to describe observations during his time at the mental hospital that were similar to the assertions later published in *Out of Sight, Out of Mind:* mass nudity, filth, and herding. He wrote about the pacifist techniques used by the COs, contrasting them with how regular attendants treated the patients under their charge, and speculated on whether they would make a lasting difference at the institutions. The title of Olmstead's article was "They Asked for a Hard Job."

◆　◆　◆

Soon after the establishment of the first CPS mental hospital unit by the American Friends Service Committee at Williamsburg, Virginia, in June 1942, mental hospital units were opened by the Mennonite Central Committee at Staunton, Virginia; Brethren Service Committee at Sykesville, Maryland; and the AFSC at Philadelphia in August.[4] Before the end of the CPS, there would be forty-three units at state mental hospitals and one mental health unit at a veterans' hospital at Lyons, New Jersey. Most of these units were administered by the MCC, AFSC, or BSC, although the Disciples of Christ, the Evangelical and Reformed Church, and the Methodist Commission on World Peace would also administer one each. The first CPS unit at a training school for people with intellectual disabilities— the "mentally defective," "feebleminded," or "mentally deficient"—was opened by the MCC at Vineland, New Jersey, in April 1943. Eventually, there were four-teen CPS units at state training schools for the feebleminded, in addition to Vine-land, a private institution. The AFSC administered five, the MCC five, and the BSC three, with the Association of Catholic Conscientious Objectors and the American Baptist Home Mission Society administering one each. Throughout the CPS, the phrases *mental hospital program* and *mental hospital units* generally referred to units at both mental hospitals and training schools.

The idea of CPS mental hospital units came from COs at two AFSC Forest Service camps in Massachusetts who wanted to do more socially significant work. They approached the secretary of a local YMCA, who put them in contact with the superintendent of Gardner State Hospital in Massachusetts. The super-intendent brought the idea of having a CPS unit at the mental hospital to the state mental health commissioner. After the commissioner and the Selective Service had approved the idea, the AFSC agreed to open a unit in April 1942. Shortly

21. CPS Unit no. 49, Philadelphia State Hospital (Byberry), Philadelphia, Pennsylvania. (Swarthmore College Peace Collection, Swarthmore, Pennsylvania)

22. CPS Unit no. 69, Cleveland State Hospital, Cleveland, Ohio. (Mennonite Church USA Historical Committee and Archives, Goshen, Illinois)

before the unit was opened, the Massachusetts American Legion learned about it and condemned the assignment of COs at the mental hospital as "un-American."[5] The unit was canceled. Massachusetts would be the only New England state that did not have a mental hospital or training school unit during the CPS. A proposed mental hospital unit in Elgin, Illinois, the headquarters of the Brethren Church, suffered the same fate as the one at Gardner when the American Legion there protested the establishment of a CO unit.[6] At the Veterans Administration Hospital at Lyons, New Jersey, potential opposition by the American Legion was anticipated, and its approval was sought and gained prior to the opening of a BSC unit there.[7]

After the opening of the first mental hospital units, word of the program spread among mental hospital and training school superintendents who were facing critical staff shortages during the war. Superintendents or state officials typically requested CPS units from the church committees or NSBRO. After a church committee was selected to administer the unit, NSBRO requested Selective Service approval. In addition to not approving the proposed Gardner and Elgin units, the Selective Service denied requests for CO units to work with "mentally deficient children" at Manchester, New Hampshire; Richmond, Virginia; Providence, Rhode Island; Elwyn, Pennsylvania; and Southbury, Connecticut.[8]

Even after the opening of the mental hospital and other special service units, CPS men were required to spend a minimum of ninety days in work camps. After that period of time, they could apply for transfers to detached units. The church committees and then NSBRO initially approved transfers, with the Selective Service making final decisions.

Announcements of openings at mental hospitals and training schools were sent to CPS camps. Some superintendents tried to recruit COs directly. In July 1943, Dr. E. L. Hooper, superintendent of Dayton State Hospital, wrote Vernon Stinebaugh, assistant director and educational director of the BSC camp in Walhalla, Michigan, informing him that his hospital had just been approved for a CPS unit. Hooper said that he had requested ten men and briefly described his institution: "I may say that the Dayton State Hospital is caring for approximately 1800 mental patients, is located in a beautiful setting within the corporate limits of Dayton and we fear no contradiction in saying that it compares favorably with the other institutions of this and other states."[9] In some cases, superintendents even visited work camps to attract and interview CPS men. For example, Dr. J. Berkeley Gordon, superintendent of Marlboro State Hospital in New Jersey, visited CPS camps to recruit men.[10] Dr. Charles Zeller of Byberry went personally to the AFSC camp at Coshocton, Ohio, to recruit the first group of COs who would work at the institution.[11]

Especially after the units had been in operation for a while, camp administrators representing the church committees often developed descriptions of the units and working and living conditions there. One fancy brochure titled *25 Men Needed at Lyons* was used to recruit COs to the veterans' hospital unit administered by the BSC in New Jersey. The brochure described the unit and was candid in describing the living and working conditions: "The hospital administration has now decided to house all men in the attendants' building, four men to a room, using double-deckers. Selective Service has approved this. There has been considerable objection on the part of some men, but the majority are willing to accept the crowded conditions. The building is modern, fireproof and newly renovated, and despite the inconvenience should result in great unity of the group."[12]

F. Nelson Underwood, assistant director of the BSC unit in Augusta, Maine, wrote a detailed five-page paper, "Information for Men in CPS Camps Concerning the CPS Unit, Augusta State Hospital, Augusta, Maine." The paper started with a description of Augusta, Maine, and the state hospital's superintendent, Dr. Forrest C. Tyson: "Dr. Tyson is not a C.O., but he has no aversion to conscientious objectors as such. He has here a job that needs to be done, a task that cannot wait, and he is ready to use anyone who is ready and able to do it."[13] The paper went on to describe CPS men's living conditions, including lodging and opportunities for work for wives, working conditions (hours and time off), the kinds of work ("this work is often hard and dirty") and types of jobs, openings for women, maintenance and allowance, compensation and medical care, vacations and leaves, education and recreation, and transportation to Augusta.

CPS men with specific qualities were sometimes recruited for the training schools and mental hospitals. Ralph Delk, the assistant director at Mansfield State Training School, sent a letter to the BSC on the "type of man for replacement at Mansfield." The letter described the qualifications the training school's chief supervisor was looking for:

> A mature man at least 24 or 25 years of age, and one who can handle men. They would prefer a man of good physical build—approximately 6 feet tall and one who would weigh around 180 lbs. The supervisors are asking for this type of man as they want to place him in the Boys' Custodial Building where discipline problems are the greatest. They feel a man of large build has a psychological advantage over a small man in discipline. The boys in BCB, as the building is commonly called, are mainly morons and trouble makers here. The building also houses epileptics, who by nature are of a disposition to be hard to discipline at times. This man should also be willing to follow the orders and instructions of the doctors, supervisors and charge attendants without too many questions asked. He should be able to cooperate well in most all situations.[14]

This wording was used verbatim in "Memo #564 Replacement Needed at Mansfield," with the preface "Following is information forwarded us by the Unit Leader," in an announcement prepared by the BSC.[15]

CPS men also learned about mental hospital and training school units through word of mouth and newsletters written by men in the units. Harold (Hal) Barton recalled how he wound up at Byberry: "I recall reading an issue of the Unit# 49, Philadelphia State Hospital, paper in which the statement was made by one of the CPS-men that if additional help had been available 'George would not have died last night.' The thrust of my aspirations was to be life-giving and not-taking and I believe it was that phrase that caused me to request assignment to the hospital 'where the need was greatest,' then considered to be either Philadelphia State Hospital [Byberry] or the Williamsburg State Hospital [Virginia]."[16]

COs had various motivations for applying for transfers to mental hospitals and training schools. Some, like Hal Barton, felt that they could address a pressing human need by working at an institution. Others found work at the camps to be meaningless or boring and wanted to be involved in more socially significant work. Quaker Warren Sawyer recalled being at the Buck Creek National Park Service camp in North Carolina: "I was extremely frustrated there. I preferred to be working with people." Still other men applied to transfer to mental hospitals or training schools for reasons unrelated to work at those units. Men's families could move to the cities or towns where the institutions were located, and many wives could easily find employment there. Some units offered foreign relief training in the off hours, which attracted some men to these units. Mennonite Edwin Schrag admitted that he had been scared of mental hospitals, but transferred to the Hudson River State Hospital unit in Poughkeepsie because it offered relief training to CPS men. Similarly, Charles Lord wanted to be a "human guinea pig" in jaundice experiments at the University of Pennsylvania in Philadelphia, and "working at Byberry came along with that." For men who had worked at camps in remote rural areas, the training school and mental hospital units would also enable them to return to living a semblance of a normal life. John Hostetler, a Mennonite, had entered the CPS from West Liberty, Ohio, and had worked at Soil Conservation Service camps in Wells Tannery, Pennsylvania, and Downey, Idaho. Transferring to the Greystone Park mental hospital in New Jersey represented "one step back into society again to live." John Bartholomew, who entered the CPS as a Methodist and later became a Quaker, had accumulated a number of college credits prior to being sent to CPS camps in Kane, Pennsylvania, and Elkton, Oregon. He wanted to transfer to Byberry "to get back into civilization" and to obtain some experience and eventually pursue his education. For some men, relieving the church committees from having to pay for their expenses in the work camps was a consideration in transferring to the hospital units.[17]

Quite apart from the nature of the work itself, the detached special service units differed from the work camps in one major way: payment of the expenses for CPS men and overhead. In the work camps, the church committees paid approximately $30–$35 per month for room, board, and maintenance of the men, including a fee of $1.50–$3.50 for men's personal expenses. The mental hospitals and training schools paid all of these expenses, in addition to the administrative costs of the church committees for the units. The monthly personal maintenance fee was initially $2.50 per month and later increased to $10–$15 per month. Out of this latter sum, men at some institutions were expected to pay for their standard white uniforms. The difference between the normal payment for institutional staff and the costs for the CPS men and unit administration was eventually turned over to the U.S. Treasury.

Mental hospitals and training schools were expected to pay for men's medical care and emergency dental care, expenses that the church committees paid for in the work camps. Some even covered worker's compensation. The Selective Service's controversial 1945 directive prohibiting off-grounds living of men at mental hospitals and training schools also ordered the institutions to pay for the men's medical and dental care. Colonel Kosch believed that some institutions were shirking their responsibilities by sending men physically unable to do the work back to the camps.[18]

By April 1, 1944, there were 1,863 men serving in CPS hospital units, including 115 in general hospitals.[19] Mental hospital and training school units had between 15 and 95 COs, with Greystone Park State Hospital in New Jersey and Norristown and Philadelphia (Byberry) state hospitals in Pennsylvania having the highest number, 95 men. The population of men in CPS mental hospital and training school units grew throughout 1944 and reached its peak in 1945.[20] Byberry would eventually have approximately 135 COs working there. In September 1945, there were more than 1,000 men in MCC mental hospital and training school units alone, and by the end of 1945, 1,500 men had served in these Mennonite units.[21]

The religious composition of men in CPS mental hospital units paralleled the makeup of the work camps: MCC units had mostly Mennonites, BSC units were typically split between Brethren and non-Brethren, and AFSC units had a minority of Friends. In March 1944, the MCC Mount Pleasant unit in Iowa had 25 men, 23 of whom were Mennonite.[22] Of the 106 CPS men assigned to the MCC unit at Western State Hospital in Virginia over the course of its history, 98 were Mennonite or Old Order Amish, and 2 were Hutterite Brethren, who came under the MCC.[23] The BSC unit at Marion, Virginia, had 37 men as of February 1945; 13 of

23. CPS men assigned to CPS Unit no. 51, Western State Hospital, Fort Steilacoom, Washington. (Brethren Historical Library and Archives, Elgin, Illinois)

them were listed as Brethren and 6 as affiliated German Baptists.[24] At the BSC unit at Mansfield State Training School, 21 of 30 men were Brethren. Of 100 men identified as having been at the AFSC Byberry unit around August 1944, 22 were Friends, while 28 were Methodists and 18 had no denomination listed in the 1996 NISBCO *CPS Directory*.[25]

Most men assigned to the mental hospital and training school units served as attendants and worked directly on the wards with patients, although some also worked as cooks, lab technicians, farm supervisors, therapists, social workers, teachers, physicians, psychologists, engineers, and in other roles. At the MCC units at Mount Pleasant State Hospital and Cleveland State Hospital in 1945, 29

24. CPS man in bedroom at CPS Unit no. 69, Cleveland State Hospital, Cleveland, Ohio. (Mennonite Church USA Historical Committee and Archives, Goshen, Illinois)

out of 33 and 30 out of 45 COs worked as attendants, respectively.[26] At the BSC unit in Marion, Virginia, in 1945, 23 of the 37 men worked as attendants, while 19 of the 30 men at the BSC Mansfield unit were attendants.[27] The MCC unit Tiffin State Institute in Ohio was an exception to other CPS units in that none of the 20 men there worked as attendants.[28] All of them did maintenance or farmwork at the institution. The COs who worked as attendants were the ones who did the really hard jobs.

◆   ◆   ◆

The mental hospital and training school units were administered by an institutional superintendent, who reported to the Selective Service regarding the CPS men, and an assistant director or unit leader, who was responsible to the church committee sponsoring the unit. The superintendent had authority over the men's work, and the assistant director ostensibly was in charge of the men's educational and religious experiences and their off-duty hours.

As in the case of the work camps, the detached units were granted "overhead" positions—men relieved of normal work responsibilities to coordinate the units on behalf of the church committees. All mental hospitals and training schools had a unit assistant director who reported to the MCC, AFSC, BSC, or other church committee; filed reports; acted as a liaison with the institution's superintendent; and oversaw the unit's activities. The larger units typically had an educational director as well. The educational and religious activities in the hospital units were fewer in number and less intensive than in the work camps. The cities and towns in which the institutions were located offered more diversions and opportunities than the areas in which the work camps were located. Many men were married and wanted to spend as much time as they could with their wives and families. The work schedules at the institutions often were not conducive to holding unitwide meetings and activities. Men did not always work the same hours and usually were assigned to different shifts and days of the week to ensure full-time coverage of the wards.

Many mental hospital and training school units published newsletters and yearbooks. In MCC units, the educational director was supposed to oversee the publication of periodicals.[29] Newsletters had titles such as *Release* (Cherokee State Hospital in Iowa), *Penn Points* (Pennhurst State Training School in Pennsylvania), *White Coat* (Eastern Shore State Hospital in Maryland), *This Week* (Lyons Veterans Administration Hospital in New Jersey), *Scribe* (Connecticut State Hospital in Middletown), and the *Dope Sheet* (Philadelphia State Hospital).[30] The newsletters contained announcements of unit activities and community events, articles on topics ranging from pacifism to mental illness or mental deficiency, descriptions of the wards, and other news and informational items. One tongue-in-cheek item in the *Dope Sheet* asked men not to borrow other people's property without permission: "SINCE IT IS STILL THE afsc and not the Communists who are administering C.P.S., we really ought to observe the rules of private property within our unit. Everyone, almost, realizes what this means when he suddenly finds a favorite hat or coat or typewriter or . . . borrowed at the wrong time."[31] Yearbooks were popular in MCC units: *P.R.N.* (Marlboro State Hospital in New Jersey), *Files* (Norristown State Hospital in Pennsylvania), *The Seagull* (Howard State Hospital in Rhode Island), and *Ypsi* (Ypsilanti State Hospital in Michigan). The yearbooks, which were as long as eighty pages, contained a history and background of the unit and often photos and profiles of the men currently on the unit as well as "alumni."[32] The yearbooks resembled a typical high school yearbook.

The institutional superintendents had far greater authority over CPS men than the technical supervisors in the work camps. In the work camps, work schedules were fairly well established by policy, although the technical supervisors had the authority to require men to work additional hours in exceptional circumstances, such as fighting forest fires, flood control, and emergency farm labor. Mental hospital and training school superintendents set the number of hours the men worked, and some expected COs to work long hours, without any form of compensation. Since COs were expected to live on the grounds, they were under the constant scrutiny of the superintendents and other officials. For its part, the Selective Service gave mental hospital and training school superintendents greater authority than the technical superintendents in the work camps. When the Selective Service issued its directive on off-grounds living and outside jobs in early 1945, it expected superintendents to enforce it.

Superintendents varied greatly in the degree to which they exercised authority and control over the lives of the CPS men. Reform-minded superintendents such as Charles Zeller at Byberry, John Ross at Poughkeepsie (Hudson River State Hospital), and E. H. Crawfis at Cleveland State Hospital, when the unit was under the MCC, seemed to appreciate the sincerity and commitment of the COs and their nonviolent handling of patients and gave them relatively free rein in their off-duty hours. Ross was accused of favoring COs when he fired four regular attendants accused of abuse by some COs at the hospital, which was probably true. Zeller left it to the CO assistant director to handle many Selective Service directives issued to superintendents. Crawfis let MCC assistant director Paul L. Goering supervise the CPS men and put Goering's desk in the same office as the regular supervisor.[33] Goering did not concern himself with COs' off-duty hours, which was apparently satisfactory to Crawfis.

Other superintendents tended to run their institutions with an iron fist and kept COs under tight control. Dr. C. C. Atherton was the superintendent of Southern Wisconsin Colony and Training School, which housed an MCC unit. According to the assistant director, Arthur Weaver, COs were frequently called into Atherton's office for discipline. Two men were punished with a loss of seven days' furlough for visiting in their quarters while they were off duty. Weaver explained what happened on another occasion:

> The Superintendent visited a ward without advance notice and found one of the fellows sitting in a chair. The patients were in bed and the work was completed for the night. The CPS man, not knowing who the visitor was, did not rise to his feet when the charge attendant stood up. The Superintendent ordered the fellow to his feet with a command to rise in the presence of his superior officer. The fellow then explained that in his two months of service in the institution he had never been given the opportunity to see or meet his "superior officer" and therefore did not know who his superior officer was. The scolding that followed was tempered by this fact but the incident was illustrative of the relationship which existed between the Superintendent and the members of the unit throughout the entire history of the unit.[34]

At Marlboro State Hospital, Superintendent J. Berkeley Gordon was a former navy man and accustomed to running a tight ship. The assistant director of the MCC unit, Loris Habegger, dealt with Gordon in a deferential and diplomatic manner:

> I disagreed with him once, and when I disagreed I wondered whether I would last there because any regular employee who disagreed with him was out now, and if possible, one minute before now. But he had . . . given me an order to take out one of, two of our men. I asked him for the privilege of expressing my view of the situation, for his evaluation. I assured him he was my superior and I recognized it. But I said I would like to present my viewpoint. And he said, "Okay, you may do so." So I presented it, and I said, "It's your decision. I will carry out your order without further question." And he looked at me a little bit, and then he said, "Do it your way." . . . I have high regard for him, although I was unhappy with some of his hot-handed ways with patients and so forth.[35]

Dr. Neil A. Dayton was superintendent of Mansfield State Training School in Connecticut at which the BSC had a CPS unit. In a yearbook written by men at the unit, Dayton wrote an open letter: "To say that your service at Mansfield was worth while is putting it inadequately. You made a very valuable contribution to the training and welfare of our patients at the Mansfield Training School at a time when it was urgently needed."[36]

Dayton weathered a storm as superintendent at Mansfield.[37] He had been appointed superintendent in 1941 and shortly afterward began to clash with James Purcell, the business manager, who had run the day-to-day operations of the training school between the resignation of the previous superintendent and Dayton's appointment. Then Dayton brought in Florence Nichols from Massachusetts to serve as superintendent of nurses. This assignment infuriated other employees, who found Nichols's manner to be "offensive, discourteous, and insulting." In August 1944, Purcell and other staff at the institution sent a letter to the governor complaining about Dayton. At some point in the controversy, Dayton relieved Nichols from her position and acknowledged that her appointment had been a mistake. Nichols then joined the group complaining about Dayton.

In November 1944, Governor Raymond Baldwin of Connecticut and Justice Allyn Brown, president of Mansfield's Board of Trustees, initiated an inquiry into the complaints about Dayton. Six days of hearings were held at the governor's office and Mansfield between that November and the following January. Many of the staff dissatisfied with Dayton testified, as did Dayton and one of his supporters. A declaration of loyalty to Dayton signed by ninety-six employees was submitted. In a report released in March 1945, Governor Baldwin and Justice Brown concluded that although Dayton had made mistakes in his administration, he was an effective superintendent and should continue in this role. They also recommended to the board that Purcell, Nichols, and two other employees be dismissed. These four employees protested the action and accused Dayton of incompetence.

The Mansfield controversy was widely reported in Connecticut newspapers, including the *Hartford Times* and the *Sunday Herald*. The COs had supported Dr. Dayton, and, to the great relief of Ralph Delk, the unit's assistant director, the CPS unit had not come up in the newspapers. Then, as often happened when controversies erupted at institutions having CPS units, the "conchies" were dragged into the Mansfield dispute. The four employees to be dismissed lodged a series of specific charges against Dayton that were reported in the *Sunday Herald*. "Love among a pair of inmates blossomed in the kitchen of Dr. Dayton's home," the employees charged, and the female inmate's head was shaved, in accord with "standard procedure." The employees further charged that Dayton had accorded preference to some thirty COs assigned to Mansfield and that he was "unduly impressed" by their educational backgrounds compared with regular attendants, lowering the morale at the training school. Delk's wife, who worked at the institution, was singled out by the protesting employees: "Mrs. Delk, wife of the supposed leader of the conchies, was employed as attendant until she walked off the floor of a ward, leaving 90 patients to themselves."[38] They argued that she should have been dismissed immediately but was rewarded by being given a job as a teacher at a much higher rate of pay.

Delk copied the newspaper article and sent it to NSBRO and the BSC. He was furious with the criticism of his wife and explained that she had been ill one day and left the ward in the charge of a nurse. He admitted that the situation had taken its toll on the unit: "I hope you can see the kind of situation we are up against here. Believe me we are on 'the front lines' here. Some of us need some relief so that we can calm our nerves a little. The tension and pressure is terrific."[39] The controversy appeared to peter out on its own, but it had obviously taken its toll on Delk, along with other events.

Dr. Dayton was reported as showing favoritism toward the COs, and the CPS unit had stood behind him during the inquiry and public controversy at Mansfield. Yet the dictatorial style Dayton was accused of by the disgruntled employees characterized his relations with the CPS unit. Dayton exercised tight control over the unit and often treated Delk like a subservient schoolboy or underling. He routinely sent Delk memos chastising him and giving him orders. On one occasion, he sent Delk a memo advising him on how he should conduct his work as assistant director:

> I think it would be a good plan for you to make a sharp division in the work that you do for us and the necessary paper work that you have in connection with your position as Assistant Director of the Mansfield Unit . . .
>
> As far as possible, I would discourage the boys coming in for a chat during business hours. If there is some definite item of business that has to be attended to, this is a different matter, but I think in the main I would talk to the men when you see them during the evenings at the Home. . . . After all, the young men of your group are being trained for a future life of usefulness and we do not want them to get any wrong ideas of what the world is going to expect of them in the line of work.[40]

Dayton routinely turned down reasonable requests from Delk. When the BSC unit wanted to publish a newsletter, like other camps and units, Dayton refused to let them use the institution's supplies: "I have made inquiries of allowing the C.P.S. unit at Mansfield to use supplies furnished by the institution for the publishing of a weekly or monthly paper. The answer is that this should not be allowed because of the fact that all of the employees of our institution would not be served by such a publication."[41]

In late December 1944, Delk asked Dayton for permission to send the unit's educational director, Kenneth Hetrick, to attend a planning committee meeting at Vineland Training School in New Jersey for a training school conference scheduled for February. The conference was being sponsored by the Mental Hygiene Program of the CPS for representatives of CPS units, superintendents, and church committee representatives.[42] By this time, the Mental Hygiene Program had been approved by the Selective Service. One day of the conference would include presentations by training school superintendents and leaders in mental deficiency, including James Lewald and Edgar Doll. Materials describing the conference indicated that CPS men would have to attend on vacation or leave time and that their travel should be financed by their church committees. Dayton told Delk that he would need permission from both the BSC and the Selective Service for Hetrick to attend the planning meeting: "I have no authority to release any man from the camp unless the conference has not only been approved by your central body but by the Selective Service. In the future, will you please see that this is obtained before any travel is arranged." The training school conference was held February 23–24, a Friday and Saturday, 1945.[43] Among the fifty-seven attendees from CPS units, church committees, and state offices was a representative from the Mansfield unit, but not Hetrick, the educational director.

Superintendent Dayton's attempts to control CPS men went even further. Several Mansfield COs wrote short stories on work at the institution for the *Reporter*, which was published by NSBRO.[44] Delk sent the stories to NSBRO and showed copies to Dayton to "use as he sees fit." The next day, Delk wrote NSBRO again, asking that drafts of the stories be submitted for Dayton's review prior to publication: "He is concerned about the use of some of the words some of the boys used. For instance: Holsopple used the term 'straight jacket.' Wolfe used 'Pandemonium Hall' and Coulson spoke of giving keys to patients. We do not have 'straight jackets' here of the type often thought of. Ours is a very modified form. Neither does the institution recommend giving keys to the patients."[45]

Each of the stories written by the men was benign and described their work with the "feebleminded." Ross H. Coulson discussed the daily schedule for boys on his ward and his technique in dealing with them: "I have also trusted the boys. Given them keys which would give them means of escape, etc. I have taken them on walks and let them run loose." Ralph S. Wolfe's "Work in Pandemonium Hall" contained his reflections on working at an institution: "Work of this kind is closely related with juvenile delinquency. It has opened to me the whole world of institutions, their purpose and service to society—a whole world within a world that I never realized existed." Donald G. Holsopple described how attendants dealt with patients who attack others: "That usually takes the form of putting the patient in a straight-jacket, or a restraining sheet." He concluded his brief story by writing, "Yes, in fact, I rather like my work here at Mansfield."

The assistant directors at CPS hospital units communicated confidentially with their respective church committees on a regular basis. They prepared frequent reports on the units, addressing relations with superintendents and staff, unit morale, public relations, and any problems experienced within the unit. Representatives of the church committees gave them guidance on running the units and advised them on how to handle difficult situations. Assistant directors and the units themselves communicated with each other on CPS matters. CPS union locals and the Mental Hygiene Program of the CPS also sent assistant directors confidential memos and reports. Many of the letters sent by the Mental Hygiene Program were marked "Confidential: For CPS Men Only."

In September 1943, Delk learned that all of his mail was being opened by personnel at Mansfield and objected to Superintendent Dayton: "I received a personal letter from a friend in another C.P.S. Unit and it was opened and stamped and possibly read before I had the pleasure. That irritates me just a little." Delk asked, "Please let all my personal mail come to me" and also suggested that opened letters be put back into their envelopes so he would know who had sent them. Dayton responded in a tone similar to his other communications with Delk: "I think you are now getting acquainted with what it means to be occupying an official position as Assistant Director of the unit: all mail coming to the Institution is considered as official." Dayton recommended that Delk tell his friends to write "personal" on the outside of envelopes and said that this mail would be sent along without being opened. He told Delk he had a "good point" in preserving envelopes.[46] In his response to Delk, Dayton made it clear that he considered any mail regarding the institution or Delk's role as an assistant director of a CPS unit to be the official business of the institution.

For the church committees, the CPS program had an explicit educational and religious mission. CPS men were accepted into AFSC, BSC, MCC, and other church-sponsored committees not merely to perform jobs—some meaningful and some not—but to confirm their commitment to religious principles or pacifist beliefs. Outside speakers appeared regularly at CPS camps and units. Colonel Kosch testified at Senate subcommittee hearings in August 1942 that the Selective Service could not say no to speakers selected by the church committees to address men at the camps.[47] Mansfield's Dayton and other hospital superintendents claimed the right to be informed of, or even to approve or disapprove of, speakers at mental hospital or training school units. In January 1945, Dayton chastised Delk for not notifying him about a speaker coming to Mansfield: "I have your mimeographed notice of the activities of the Unit during the month of January. You will recall some time ago that I made a specific request that I know of all who are coming to the school. I do not recall of [sic] receiving any notification of the visit of Dr. R. C. Baldwin."[48] Dayton had received the notice of upcoming events and actives, just like everyone else.

A newspaper article on March 22, 1944, reported on an uproar at the Lynchburg Colony in Virginia over a speaker at the CPS unit there.[49] The speaker was Perry Saito, described in the article as an "American-born Japanese and racial secretary of the fellowship of reconciliation." Saito had met with twelve members of the CPS unit in a building housing the COs. H. Minor Davis, a member of the state hospital board, had learned about the meeting and had visited the hospital to investigate. Davis requested a written report on the meeting from Dr. A. D. Hutton, acting superintendent of the colony. Hutton was quoted in the article as saying a meeting like this one would "never occur again as long as I am here." "I am as innocent as a lamb," Hutton added. "Neither I nor any of the officials here had any idea that such a meeting was taking place." According to Hutton, the unit's assistant director, D. K. Christiansberry, had expressed regret that he had not consulted with the superintendent prior to the meeting.

Superintendents at state mental hospitals and training schools were used to having control over everything that occurred on the institutions' grounds. Some treated COs at their institutions accordingly, and some assistant directors of CPS units accepted this fact. What a number of superintendents would learn was that they could not always control COs at their institutions.

In the midst of the controversy surrounding the Mansfield dismissals and the charges of preferential treated accorded the "conchies" there, Delk wanted to step down as assistant director of the CPS units. Ross Coulson was elected to succeed him. Coulson declined the position and said that he could not perform the duties of an assistant director for two reasons. One reason was that he could not carry out Selective Service regulations and "unjust demands." The other reason involved the treatment of people at Mansfield: "I can't conscientiously ask others to perform duties which I know are damaging to the patients' welfare and to the physical and mental health of the attendant. I am referring to the necessity of using unwholesome techniques of fear and physical force as means of keeping the patient disciplined. Both techniques are a natural outgrowth of the anomalous standards for decorum, 'keeping the patients quiet and sitting on chairs.'"[50] Coulson was saying that he could not, in good conscience, administer a CPS unit at a training school at which commonly accepted routines and practices hurt the people the institution was ostensibly designed to help. The "problem" at Mansfield and other institutions was not that superintendents often acted in an authoritarian and arbitrary manner toward other administrators, staff, and COs. The problem was the institution itself. More and more COs came to accept this view, and some acted on this perspective.

◆   ◆   ◆

Relations between the COs, as conscientious objectors, and the others at the institutions and the people in the communities in which the institutions were located had their ups and downs. The superintendents of the mental hospitals and training schools had requested the COs and were generally tolerant of the COs' beliefs. Some were concerned about public relations and did not want anything to happen that would stir up opposition to the COs. Prior to the establishment of the MCC unit at Mount Pleasant State Hospital, John M. Mosemann visited the institution and reported on the superintendent's attitude: "The Superintendent takes a very cautious attitude regarding any possible public reaction to the presence of conscientious objectors in the state institution." At Augusta State Hospital, the superintendent, Forrest C. Tyson, accepted the COs but wanted to make sure that they did not try to get others to accept their beliefs: "Dr. Tyson is not a C.O., but he has no aversion to conscientious objectors as such. . . . Because the employees of the Hospital are responsible to the taxpayers of the State of Maine, and because the patients dare not be unduly disturbed or excited, Dr. Tyson wants no propagandizing of any kind, either among the patients or employees."[51]

The initial reactions of other staff at the mental hospitals and training schools ranged from indifference to hostility. Many attendants and other employees did not agree with or even understand the views of the COs but were willing to work with them. A description of the American Baptist Home Mission Society unit at Eastern Shore State Hospital read: "Other employees are not in sympathy with the conscientious objector's stand, but they are cooperative and friendly." A report from the assistant director of the BSC unit at Norwich State Hospital indicated that relations with other staff and the community were quite good: "The relations with other employees and with the community have been very good at Norwich. Of course there are many who are bitter and can not hide the fact, but it is surprising how well accepted we are. A man who can earn respect through his work and behavior under normal conditions will have no trouble at the hospital."[52]

Some staff at the institutions wanted nothing to do with the COs. At Augusta State Hospital, relations between the COs and regular employees were generally good, but an incident occurred with a drunken worker at the institution: "Thomas has been working in the kitchen temporarily; and some weeks ago one of the painters came in at noon, rather drunk, and proceeded to make a nuisance of himself. Among other things, he objected to being served at the counter by a CO. . . . [T]his man had worked here over twenty years; and his 'gang,' the painters, the engineers, etc. have entertained some antipathy towards the C.O.'s from the beginning it seems."[53]

Warren Sawyer had a "little set" with two attendants about COs soon after he arrived at Byberry. Later, he had problems with a regular employee when he worked briefly on a farm detail:

> The farm boss absolutely hates us. He thinks we are cowards and yellowbellies. He has a son over seas and I can see why that would make him feel that way. I have tried to do my work well and see if I couldn't make friends with him so that he might have the chance to understand us a little better. After I had worked on the farm three weeks he ceased to give his orders to me. He had them passed thru his assistant. . . . [T]o-day, the boss told another farm attendant not to talk to me because I am a Co and un American.[54]

Sawyer recalled that when the COs first came to Byberry, Superintendent Zeller was afraid for their safety and posted a guard around their cottages.[55]

When controversies arose at the hospitals or training schools or COs reported substandard conditions or incidents of abuse by regular attendants, relations with other employees soured quickly, as happened at Cleveland State Hospital, Mount Pleasant State Hospital, Hudson River State Hospital, and elsewhere. The COs were sometimes able to restore positive relations and sometimes not.

At a small number of institutions, some patients challenged the conscientious objectors or even ridiculed them, although they might have been put up to it by hostile employees. At Vineland Training School, COs on the MCC unit had some problems being accepted by the patients: "At first we experienced some very definite opposition from the children. This situation was aggravated by propaganda purposefully distributed by certain employees." A history of the MCC unit at Eastern State Hospital in Virginia described what happened when COs first arrived at the institution: "Soon a crowd of patients and on-lookers had gathered to see the new curiosities. We heard remarks of, 'slackers,' 'draft dodger,' 'yellow bellies,' and from one of the wards, 'I just dare you to come up on this ward and work you conscientious objector, you! Do you object to work too?'"[56] Any resentment of or opposition to the COs by patients dissipated almost as soon as they started working at the mental hospitals and training schools.

Community relations for the CPS mental hospital units were generally good. Many local churches of various faiths invited the COs to their services, and local ministers occasionally visited the units. Every now and then, an incident occurred involving community members and COs. At Southern Wisconsin Colony and Training School in Union Grove, the director of the MCC unit did not exactly receive an open-arms welcome from a prominent local citizen: "Early in the history of the unit, the director, John Ewert, was called to the private office of the banker of Union Grove and told that the people of Union Grove did not like CO's and did not want to see them on the streets and even suggested that the irritated citizens might resort to a neck-tie party." Neil Hartman recalled taking a bus to and from Byberry: "Since we were young it was obvious we were COs. People behind us would talk about seeing the yellow streak down our backs. A couple times we got off the bus and other people got off and stepped on our heels which was very irritating." Most people in Philadelphia were tolerant, remembered Ward Miles, but "you had to watch out for some bus drivers who might come over the curb to try to hit you."[57]

COs were invariably drawn into any public controversy surrounding an institution and blamed by anyone who had a grievance of any kind. State and local chapters of the American Legion and Veterans of Foreign Wars were always looking for evidence that COs were being coddled, as in the case of men who lived with their wives, and tried to arouse public indignation whenever they could.

◆　　◆　　◆

The mental hospitals and training schools operated as self-contained communities, with their own powerhouses, kitchens, laundries, farms and dairies, administrative offices, and medical facilities and laboratories as well as residential buildings and therapeutic, recreational, or educational facilities. Mount Pleasant State Hospital in Iowa was typical of the institutions: "The institution generates it's [sic] own power, has it's own bakery, a laundry, a carpenter shop, paint shop, machine shop, fire department, telephone system, greenhouse, gardens, and farms." The concept of "total institutions," developed by sociologist Erving Goffman to describe a broad range of seemingly different types of organizations, captured the essence of the state hospitals and schools: "A total institution may be defined as a place of residence and work where a large number of like-situated individuals, cut off from the wider society for an appreciable period of time, together lead an enclosed, formally administered round of life."[58] Self-reliant and isolated, total institutions developed their own routines and rhythms of life. Both staff and patients could be said to be "institutionalized."

The institutions at which CPS units were established varied greatly in size. Byberry, or Philadelphia State Hospital, was one of the largest, if not the largest, with approximately 6,100 patients.[59] Eastern Shore State Hospital in Maryland, with 500 patients, and Vineland Training School, with 550 patients, were among the smallest. Most mental hospitals and training schools ranged in size from around 1,000 to roughly 5,000 patients: for example, Mount Pleasant State Hospital (1,600), Hudson River State Hospital (more than 5,000), Ypsilanti State Hospital (3,300), and Norwich State Hospital (2,400).[60]

CPS men were required by the Selective Service to live on the grounds of the mental hospitals and training schools, although exceptions were granted and some men broke the rules, with or without the knowledge of assistant directors and superintendents. It was not uncommon for non-CPS hospital and training school staff to live at the institutions. Superintendents usually had their own, often lavish, houses complete with patient domestic workers. Physicians and nurses often had their own residences. So did attendants. Free or cut-rate room and board arrangements were offered to attendants to offset low wages, generally ranging between fifty and one hundred dollars per month. Staff residences were separated by gender, with separate buildings for men and women employees.

Most COs were housed in staff residences or converted patient buildings or cottages. The living quarters were usually a step up from the generally old, drafty, and cold barracks at CPS work camps. Men at Hudson River State Hospital, Norwich State Hospital, Mansfield State Training School, Eastern Shore State Hospital, Harrisburg State Hospital, and other institutions lived in single or double rooms. Accommodations at the Poughkeepsie unit were quite good: "The quarters of the men are perhaps the best in C.P.S., the men living in the comparatively new Male Home, a residents [sic] for male employees. Over fifty per cent of the residents in this home are now composed of C.P.S. men. Each man has an individual, modern, well-equipped room with an individual lavoratory [sic], shaving mirror and medicine cabinet." Edwin Schrag recalled that CPS men even received maid service from patients at the Poughkeepsie unit.[61]

At other mental hospitals and training schools men lived in dormitories or a combination of single or double rooms and dormitories.[62] The CPS unit at Tiffin State Institute in Ohio was given two cottages that had space for sleeping quarters, a kitchen, a dining room, a reading room, and an enclosed porch.[63] At Byberry, the CPS men lived in dormitories in former patient cottages. Men slept in bunk beds, pushed closely together with about eighteen inches between them.[64] A separate cramped room was set aside for lockers containing their personal possessions. Photos at the Swarthmore College Peace Collection confirm the cramped quarters at Byberry.[65]

Institutions that had residences for staff or CPS men usually also provided at least some housing for married COs whose wives worked there (Augusta, Byberry, Cleveland, Eastern Shore, Ypsilanti, and others). When housing was offered to married couples, it was usually, but not always, located in separate residences or women's staff housing.

At some institutions, housing for the COs was woefully inadequate. During the first year of operation of the CPS unit at Southern Wisconsin Colony and Training School, many men and even some of their wives had quarters on patient wards.[66] Late in the second year, a frame cottage was built to house ten married couples and eleven single men. When nineteen CPS men arrived at Western State Hospital in Staunton, Virginia, in August 1942, there was no housing for them. Men slept on the wards on which they worked. Emory Layman, one of the COs in the unit, described his first night at the institution:

> My room was used as the attendant's office for supplies and patients' medicines. It was a long, narrow room with two beds and one window. A whiskey patient who worked on the ward had the other bed at the window. I had no privacy at all and there was practically no place to put any of my belongings except for a very crude wardrobe; therefore I didn't unpack. . . .
>
> I shall never forget that first night. The door to my room was to be left open to the ward so the night attendant could come in for supplies, etc. I found the patients very annoying—most of them being locked, of course—but their noise carried to my room all too easily. My bed was next to an old built-in open wardrobe, where old suits of patients were stored, with only a curtain for a door. Soon after I was settled in bed the rats began to stir, one running over my pillow. I was wondering whether to go to sleep and not mind the rats or to get up, when I felt a few bits [sic] and then it dawned on me that there were bed-bugs at hand. I got out of bed and dressed. The night attendant didn't know what to do so I sat up with him until the night watchman came through the ward at two or three o'clock in the morning. He put me in a room that had a mattress on the floor, but there were no bed-bugs and I finally got a little sleep. That was my first day.[67]

After seven months, a CO house was built on the grounds of Western, and ten men moved their beds there.

CPS men ate their meals at employee cafeterias, sometimes among themselves and sometimes with other staff, depending on the degree to which they had been accepted. Food was described as being from poor to good. Meals usually did not include fresh fruit and vegetables, were lacking in variety, and were starchy. At their best, meals were described as "institutional."[68] During the first year of the CPS unit at least, the food at Western State Hospital in Virginia was probably the worst. Clarence Kreider kept a record of meals in his diary. Breakfast each day consisted of bread, oatmeal, and gravy. The menu for the first five days of January 1943 was offered as an example of the meals served the men:

Lunch—Canned beans, canned tomatoes.

Dinner—Cheese, tomatoes, cold red meat.

Lunch—Potatoe [sic] hash, apples.

Dinner—Meat, apples.

Lunch—Beans, prunes.

Dinner—Red meat, sour pears.

Lunch—Potatoes, apples.

Dinner—Meat, apples.

Lunch—Soup, beets.

Dinner—Meat, cabbage salad.

Bread was included with each meal.[69]

CPS men working as attendants were assigned exclusively to male buildings and wards. The mental hospitals and training schools were separated by gender. Men and women—or boys and girls, if the institution held minors—lived in separate buildings, which were staffed by members of the same gender. At most institutions, one could draw an imaginary line down the middle for men's and women's buildings. This segregation reflected a long-standing institutional practice of separating men and women to prevent the possibility of sexual relations.[70] The only buildings or wards not separated by gender were wards for ill people at some institutions.

Mental hospitals maintained different male and female buildings for different "types" of patients or for different purposes. The buildings might have had official names such as male or female "Infirmary Ward," "Disturbed Ward," "Receiving Ward," "Convalescent Ward," "Continued Care," and "Physically Ill Ward."[71] Names commonly used by institutional staff and CPS men to refer to buildings included Admissions; Incontinents or "Untidy" Patients; Violent or Dangerous Patients or Punishment Wards; Senile Patients; Worker Patients; Infirmaries, including nonambulatory patients confined to bed; and sometimes Alcoholics and Tubercular Patients. It was not unusual for people with different conditions to be mixed in together, however.

Training schools usually had separate wards for "high grades" and "low grades"—or "morons," "imbeciles," and "idiots"—and children and adults, as well as males and females. Southern Wisconsin Colony and Training School had wards for "small morons, imbeciles age 8 to 16," "large morons, workers," "babies, sick, crippled, small imbeciles and idiots," and "large morons, large idiots, and punishment cases," with separate wards for males and females.[72] A single building housed male and female tubercular patients.

Each building or ward at the institutions had a "charge attendant" and sometimes an "assistant charge attendant." The charge attendant was usually called the "charge," and this title was used at institutions well into the 1970s.[73] As the name implied, the charge supervised the ward and directed the work of other attendants. Some CPS men eventually served as charges, especially when wards or buildings were staffed mostly or solely by CPS men.

Working hours at CPS mental hospital and training school units varied widely. Men assigned to work as cooks, lab technicians, farm foremen, and similar positions usually worked eight hours per day, five, five and a half, or six days per week. For CPS men working as attendants, schedules and work hours depended on the individual mental hospital or training school. At Hudson River State Hospital at Poughkeepsie, men worked regular hours during the day. The Poughkeepsie unit was established as a foreign relief training unit, and men took classes on their off hours. So the men worked as attendants eight hours a day, six days a week, or forty-eight hours per week. CPS men at Mount Pleasant State Hospital also worked a regular schedule of fifty-seven hours per week, from 6:00 A.M. until 7:00 P.M., with two and a half hours off for meals and breaks, six days a week, with the seventh day and every fifth Sunday off.[74]

At most institutions, men worked eight- to twelve-hour shifts six or seven days a week. Men often rotated shifts. At Southern Wisconsin Colony and Training School, men worked eight-hour shifts starting at 7:00 A.M., 3:00 P.M., and 11:00 P.M. The work schedule at Mansfield Training School was more complicated. COs

25. CPS man pouring drinks for patients during a meal, CPS Unit no. 63, State Hospital, Marlboro, New Jersey. (Mennonite Church USA Historical Committee and Archives, Goshen, Indiana)

worked fifty-four hours per week on different shifts. The day schedule called for attendants to work three "long" days from 6:00 A.M. to 7:12 P.M. and then two "short" days from 7:00 A.M. to 5:30 P.M., with two days off. The night schedule had men working five consecutive days from 7:12 P.M. to 6:00 A.M., with two free days. Eastern Shore State Hospital COs worked sixty-three hours per week in 1944 and fifty hours per week in 1945. At Norwich State Hospital and Ypsilanti State Hospital, men worked fifty-four hours per week. COs at Augusta State Hospital worked sixty hours per week.[75]

COs worked excessively long hours at some institutions. During the first year of the MCC unit at Western State Hospital in Virginia, men worked seventy-five to eighty-four hours per week, although the hours were reduced to sixty and then fifty-four per week in later years.[76] In 1945, COs at an AFSC unit at Eastern State Hospital at Williamsburg, Virginia, rebelled against a seventy-nine-hour work-week imposed by the superintendent, Dr. Barrett. Five men refused to work, and four new arrivals "went out and got drunk and were not there to handle their wards." Colonel Dunkle and A. S. Imirie from the Selective Service went to Williamsburg to start prosecution of the men refusing to work. Anytime COs complained about working conditions or hours, Colonel Kosch and other Selective

26. CPS men taking patients for a walk, CPS Unit no. 69, Cleveland State Hospital, Cleveland, Ohio. (Mennonite Church USA Historical Committee and Archives, Goshen, Indiana)

Service officials liked to talk about soldiers who faced harsh conditions on the battlefield. Paul French of NSBRO and Paul Furnas of the AFSC became involved in the controversy and supported the COs. Negotiations between French, Furnas, and Selective Service officials went on for weeks. French acted as a liaison between the Selective Service and the AFSC, communicating positions back and forth. He met with Kosch, Imirie, and Dunkle of the Selective Service and tried to work out a compromise. The Selective Service officials proposed sending more men to Williamsburg to ease the labor shortage. On November 3, Dr. Barrett asked the men to continue to work a seventy-nine-hour week until new men arrived, at which time the workweek would be reduced to seventy-two hours.[77] The COs refused, and Furnas of the AFSC supported their position. He also refused to send more men to Williamsburg until the matter was resolved.

In an attempt to break the stalemate, Colonel Kosch said he would call Dr. Barrett and tell him that COs were not to work more than sixty hours weekly. Furnas responded that he would not ask additional men to go to Williamsburg until there was a definite commitment not to make men work more than sixty hours a week. He insisted that Kosch put his directive to Barrett in writing. Kosch, in turn, said he would put the directive in writing after additional men went to Williamsburg. The situation was deteriorating into a "You go first," "No, you go first" impasse. French

27. CPS men with patients on benches, CPS Unit no. 69, Cleveland State Hospital, Cleveland, Ohio. (Mennonite Church USA Historical Committee and Archives, Goshen, Indiana)

became concerned that the Selective Service would take over the Williamsburg unit and another AFSC unit at Gatlinburg, Tennessee, and then order men from Gatlinburg to go to Williamsburg. COs would refuse to go, and prosecutions would result.[78] Finally, Kosch offered to give a letter to the AFSC and NSBRO saying that he would write Barrett about the hours after the men arrived. Kosch wrote a draft of this letter, but Furnas objected to his use of the word *direct* in the letter because he felt that the Selective Service had no right to give orders to the AFSC. Furnas showed French a draft response to Kosch that French was sure would antagonize the colonel. French tried to explain to Furnas that Kosch was simply accustomed to using the term *direct* and was requesting the AFSC to send the men. French helped draft a different letter to Kosch that he thought would be more palatable. The controversy apparently ended there. It was yet another brush fire Paul French tried to put out.

◆   ◆   ◆

The vast majority of CPS men knew next to nothing about mental hospitals and training schools before arriving at the institutions. The institutions themselves usually did little to help them adjust to their new jobs. Men often received nothing more than a welcome or a quick tour of the building or unit to which they had been assigned. One of the original group of COs assigned to Southern Wisconsin Colony and Training School explained, "We were given a key and commanded to report at a certain ward building. No instructions of any kind were given in advance. Months later we received the hospital rules. We learned by making mistakes and being corrected in militant fashion. We took advise [sic] from patients and occasionally a word from a charge attendant whose methods we were not always willing to take. It is not exaggerated to say we lived in fear."[79]

COs at the MCC unit at Virginia's Western State Hospital had bad living quarters, bad food, bad working conditions—and no orientation or training—when they arrived in August 1942. Emory Layman wrote, "The day we arrived we were placed on various jobs over the institution within an hour after our arrival. Most of us going on wards, my lot being an untidy one. . . . No instruction was given on how to handle the mental patients or what to expect or who to contact in case we wanted advise [sic]."[80]

Shortly after the CPS unit at Augusta State Hospital had been opened in April 1943, F. Nelson Underwood, the assistant director, reported that the superintendent believed that he did not have sufficient staff to offer training to the twenty-five COs there: "Dr. Tyson states that his staff is too small at present to conduct a course in psychiatry for our men."[81]

In September 1943, A. S. Imirie of the Selective Service wrote mental hospital and training school superintendents to inform them of the importance of providing an orientation and training to CPS men: "Since they have chosen the hospital units voluntarily, most of the men want to do their work as effectively as possible. This has made orientation or job-training a matter of special interest and importance to the men, to the hospital authorities, to the religious agencies and to Selective Service officials." Imirie explained that representatives of the Selective Service, the religious agencies, NSBRO, and the U.S. Public Health Service, including Dr. Samuel Hamilton, had met in August to discuss training programs for CPS men: "It was the decision of the group that all men should receive a minimum orientation course as soon as they enter hospital work."[82]

Even after Imirie's letter, training for CPS men at mental hospitals and training schools was spotty, at best. Harry Van Dyck wrote about coming to Hawthornden State Hospital in Macedonia, Ohio, in November 1943: "Hawthornden was strictly an on-the-job training enterprise. I spent my first day observing Jim and Dole, the CO attendants who worked the day shift on Cottage Four, go through the morning routine. This brief apprenticeship was the extent of my job orientation. I soaked up what I could about hospital policies plus some do's and don't's of ward work."[83]

Ralph Delk described the training offered to employees at Mansfield State Training School as of August 1945: "Training here consists of the supervisor giving a new attendant his keys and telling him to keep his eyes open and keep things clean and the patients well taken care of—see that they have clothes on and don't get rough with them. From there on the program is one of 'learn by experience' and if something is done wrong the attendant catches 'hell.' After so much hell some of them leave."[84]

Norwich State Hospital initiated a Program of Attendant Instruction for Conscientious Objectors in August 1943. The training program involved a three-month course taught by the superintendent, clinical director, director of nursing, assistant director of nursing in charge of education, director of psychological laboratories, and head occupational therapist. The written curriculum for the course noted that members of the hospital staff had faculty appointments at Yale University, Wesleyan University, and the University of Connecticut. COs received 60 hours of "theoretical work" on topics such as the etiology of psychiatric disorders and the social problems associated with mental illness and 588 hours of "practical work" on men's wards and in clinical services. Yet by October 16, 1943, the assistant director at Norwich reported that training was no longer being provided to new CPS arrivals: "The first group of men to arrive were given training in the work of an attendant, but the recent scattered arrivals have had no such training. An effort is being made to get the men included in some of the training given to student nurses. The hospital has a reputation for its educational standards, but it is limited at present by the personnel shortage. Much can be learned through experience."[85]

At Byberry, some training was offered to the COs, but not necessarily when they first arrived at the mental hospital. Hal Barton recalled in a September 5, 1966, account his time at Byberry:

> I came to the mental hospital about as ignorant of the whole field of mental illness as anyone could be. It was over a month before I received an orientation or training course planned by the hospital for new employees. All CPS-men took the course but it was not unusual for regular employees to avoid the training for many months or sometimes years. . . . The attitudes and methods used had to be gleaned from fellow-CPSers who had already had a few months of ward experience or from regular attendants. Sometimes the attitudes and methods of the two groups seemed at opposite poles and this was a bit confusing for the newcomer.[86]

Paul Wilhelm was another Byberry CO. He described his first job at the institution:

> My first job at Byberry was with no introduction and no training whatever. I was told to report to a building. When I got there, I was the only attendant. The nurse brought me into this dayroom with about 325 epileptics with these instructions: "These men, when they're about to have a seizure, become very combative, and here's a pillow and a tongue depressor wrapped in adhesive tape. If you can possibly get this between their teeth, and if you can possibly get a pillow under them, when they have a seizure, to keep them from hurting themselves, do it." And she gave me these and pushed me through the door and locked the door behind me.[87]

Wilhelm eventually took an attendants' class at Byberry. His notes are included in manuscript collections at the Swarthmore College Peace Collection.[88] The class covered mental hygiene and various techniques used with the mentally ill, including "continuous baths" and "standard wet pack." A printed handout on mental hygiene, with "Dr. Frignito" handwritten at the top, listed "three important aspects of mental hygiene":

> 1. Attempt to secure as far as possible through eugenics and otherwise, of satisfactory intellectual and temperamental endowments for all persons.
> 2. Consists in securing such adjustments in life that would best fit the physical, educational, vocational, social, sexual make-up of an individual.
> 3. Prevention of mental disorder.

The MCC unit at Poughkeepsie was developed specifically for men interested in receiving foreign relief training in the off hours. Dr. John Ross, the superintendent of Hudson River State Hospital, was an enthusiastic supporter of the educational goals of the unit and made accommodations for men to be able to receive relief training during the evening.[89] Dr. Ross and another physician at the mental hospital offered evening lectures on "mental hygiene and psychiatry."[90] The lectures had titles such as "Mental Hygiene from the Standpoint of Prevention," "Old and New Ideas about Insanity," "Nervousness: Its Causes and Prevention," "Child Psychiatry," and "Historical Review of Psychiatry."

The mental hospitals and training schools did not always offer training to CPS men, and even when they did, the training often came after the men had started their work at the institutions. More important, it was difficult to see how any of the training that was provided would help the COs in their jobs on the wards. Theories about mental illness and the need for prevention of insanity and mental deficiency had little, if anything, to do with the realities of the mental hospitals and training schools. Even information about current therapies and treatment approaches would be almost impossible to apply at the institutions. As Hal Barton explained, "We were presented with the latest insights into the nature, the care, the treatment of mental illness. Our instruction was on a high and idealistic level. The contrast between the ideal and the practical day-to-day ward situation was so striking as to be upsetting to say the least."[91] When COs started the Mental Hygiene Program of the CPS, practical training for attendants would be a major priority.

◆   ◆   ◆

No amount of training could have prepared the COs for what most would see, hear, and smell when they first stepped onto the wards of the mental hospitals and training schools. Conditions on the wards stood in stark contrast to the stately exteriors of the buildings and manicured grounds of the institutions. COs often were shocked and depressed by the wards. Paul L. Goering recalled his first impression of Howard State Hospital in Rhode Island: "My initial reaction was one of shock. I didn't realize and couldn't believe that these conditions would exist in our country." John Bartholomew remembered his reaction to Byberry: "I was very depressed at first to think that the government treated human beings like that." Charles Lord felt a similar way when he first showed up at Byberry: "The buildings looked good. When I got inside I was shocked." Many years later, the stench of some of the buildings stood out in the minds of some Byberry COs.[92]

The institutions were terribly overcrowded and understaffed. Most had many more patients than their official capacities, and these capacities would have made them overcrowded by today's standards for residential facilities. Mount Pleasant

State Hospital had a capacity of 1,100 patients but housed 1,600; Southern Wisconsin Colony and Training School was built to house 545 patients but had 800; Hudson River State Hospital had a certified capacity of 4,131 patients and held more than 5,000.[93] These statistics do not adequately capture the degree of overcrowding on some of the wards at the institutions. At Byberry, more than 300 patients in some of the buildings spent their days in rooms approximately forty feet by seventy feet, whereas at Mansfield State Training School, as many as 105 to 110 patients were crowded into rooms thirty feet by twenty-five feet.[94]

The mental hospitals and training schools had severe labor shortages. Hudson River State Hospital had more than 250 attendant vacancies alone.[95] To care for 1,600 patients, Mount Pleasant had 66 attendants, compared to a normal complement of 125.[96] Byberry had 110 vacancies out of 179 positions for male attendants and 1 paid attendant on duty each shift for 144 patients at the 6,100 patient mental hospital.[97] Even after COs arrived at the institutions, wards were extremely short-staffed: often 1 attendant for 105 to 110 patients at Mansfield.[98] Soon after

28. Photograph of patients in A Building, Philadelphia State Hospital (Byberry), Philadelphia, Pennsylvania. Used in prospectus for the National Mental Health Foundation. (Swarthmore College Peace Collection, Swarthmore, Pennsylvania)

COs started working at Byberry, there were usually 1 to 3–4 attendants for more than 350 patients in the "violent" building.[99] When the CPS unit was at its peak in number of COs, there were usually 6–7 attendants during the early day shift and 5 attendants on the 2:00 P.M. to 11:00 P.M. shift in that building.[100]

The institutions, and wards within individual institutions, were not all the same. Some, such as Howard State Hospital in Rhode Island, had relatively modern facilities, whereas others, such as Cleveland State Hospital, were old and run-down.[101] At mental hospitals, the "incontinent" and "violent" wards had the worst living and working conditions: overcrowding, lack of activities, insufficient supplies, and injuries to patients and attendants. The "low-grade" or "custodial" wards at training schools were similar. Hospital admission wards, infirmaries, and wards for worker patients were smaller and more pleasant for both patients and attendants. The same was true of many "high-grade" or "moron" wards at training schools. School-aged children on the moron wards generally received some form of education, although it could be as little as an hour a day.[102]

The attendants' jobs were primarily custodial in nature and involved keeping the wards clean and orderly and the patients from injuring themselves or others. A description of one building at Hudson River State Hospital provided a candid appraisal of the COs' efforts: "Our efforts were concentrated on giving better and kinder treatment to the patients and to keep the ward as clean as possible under the circumstances." The description did not try to hide the COs' frustration: "I'm sure we all chafed under this necessity of giving only custodial care and we were all keenly aware of the improvements that could be instituted with more attendant help, more supplies and better facilities." An information sheet on Augusta State Hospital described the attendants' work: "This work is often hard and even dirty and is seldom glamorous. There is much of changing of soiled clothing and bedding, and bathing and shaving and feeding of persons who are likely to be revolting at first sight." The COs' work was similar at Mount Pleasant State Hospital: "A day's work usually consists of filling out reports, escorting Doctors and Supervisors on their rounds of the wards, seeing that the patients are properly dressed and fed, passing out medications, supervising ward housekeeping, and maintaining discipline and order on the ward."[103]

One of the more unexpected tasks CO attendants performed at some institutions was preparing dead bodies for the morgue. Warren Sawyer had been at Byberry less than a month when he had his first experience with a dead body: "Last night I learned how to wrap a body in preparing it for the morgue. It seemed like quite a repulsive job at first but after I got up my nerve to touch the body and close the eyes and mouth it was not so bad." When he was recovering from an injury in the infirmary at Byberry, Hal Barton was asked by a doctor to "pack" a dead body: "The Doctor on the ward requested that I 'pack' the body for the morgue. I had no concept of the procedure but following such instructions as he could give (he was a fine old, Doctor—too old in his senility, who had returned to practice under wartime shortages), I did the best I could."[104]

Most attendants had little time to provide any kind of therapy, training, or even recreation to patients. A group of COs at Howard State Hospital who called themselves the "Committee for Improvement of Patient Care" described conditions on the wards: "On wards, for instance, where 250 patients are cared for by three or four, often two, day attendants, and one night attendant, it is easy to visualize the breakdown of routine which must inevitably occur. . . . The few attendants whose duty it is to care for these patients cannot possibly give individual attention to 250 patients." Hal Barton characterized the attendant's job at Byberry: "The routines of housekeeping, feeding and medication for the patients took almost all we could give to the job. The hours were long and the work sufficiently exhausting, physically and mentally, that during these first few months there seemed little time for anything but the ward duty, eating and sleeping."[105] A small number of attendants assisted in providing shock therapy to the few patients who received it at some mental hospitals. Byberry and other mental hospitals had hydrotherapy rooms in which patients were immersed in warm water or placed in cold packs and restrained in tubs to calm them down. The equipment was often in disrepair, and staff shortages made it difficult to offer hydrotherapy to more than a handful of patients.

The conditions at some mental hospitals and training schools were worse than others, but none had good conditions. Paul L. Goering was a CO at the MCC unit at Howard, Rhode Island, before moving to Cleveland State Hospital to become assistant director of the MCC unit there. Cleveland had a reputation of being one of the worst mental hospitals, and Howard was probably one of the better ones. Both were depressing. Goering described Howard:

> They were modern buildings with modern equipment. The concepts of treatment were not very modern. They certainly didn't have the staff to carry them out. So there seemed to be very little treatment. It was custodial care. This was the depressing thing. . . . We were not encouraged and in some cases not allowed to take initiatives to do things for the patients. The charge man where I worked lined the chairs up around the perimeter of the room and wanted it quiet. . . . He didn't like it when I brought a radio in and got patients to sing. He said, "You're stirring them up. Don't do that." Of course, I'd do it when he was off, when he was away and he didn't like it that I'd do those things.

Goering had the following to say about Cleveland State Hospital: "In Cleveland, the physical setting was very poor. . . . There was nothing modern about it. We were fighting cockroaches, and cleanliness was a thing. And filth. We had incontinent patients. . . . But I have to say the boredom and the feeling of oppression and depression was very overwhelming. You'd have to struggle as a worker not to succumb to all of this yourself."[106]

Conditions at Byberry were thoroughly documented by COs at the AFSC unit there. Even before the collection of stories for *Out of Sight, Out of Mind*, men recorded their observations and experiences in reports, diaries, and letters. Photos secretly taken by CO Charles Lord at Byberry would appear in *Life* magazine and newspapers.

Byberry was an awful place and had been that way for years. It had been run by the City of Philadelphia as the Philadelphia Hospital for Mental Diseases. Throughout the 1930s, it had been investigated by numerous panels and commissions. In 1938, it was turned over to the Commonwealth of Pennsylvania and officially named Philadelphia State Hospital. With severe staff shortages during World War II, it was no better—and had probably become worse—by the early to mid-1940s.

A and B Buildings on the men's side of Byberry were the worst at the institution, and many COs worked there. At times, they were staffed exclusively by COs. Both buildings housed roughly 325 to 350 patients, although it was not always clear how many patients lived there. An anonymous report dated June 20, 1944, illustrated the confusion regarding how many patients lived in B Building:

> The bed count for two [*sic*] night has not been satisfactory. Seemingly there were not enough empties which would mean that these empties subtracted from the known number of beds would give the census. But one night it gave more which couldn't be traced. One bed was found taken apart and one broken and in the hall, but when Hall counted the beds he got 351 instead of 350. . . . The thing is that we have no census book to check against. In counting the number of cards in trying to ascertain the number of men we only [have] 341 rather than 345, but we have nothing to check them against to see who is missing.[107]

A Building was known as the building for incontinents ("incontinents are patients who do not control their excretory functions"): "Of the 350 patients in 'A' Building, about 250 are classed as this type. One result is to make the building a dirty place. You can expect to see feces in wards, or the dining hall at any time. . . . Naturally also, the incontinent's beds are soiled night after night, the day room floor is dirtied, and despite constant efforts and improvements, a certain aroma lingers in the atmosphere."[108]

Patients slept in large dormitories in A Building. Fifty to 80 patients were confined to a "sick ward" in one of the basement dormitories. This ward was a dark, damp "dungeon" containing a mixture of ill patients:

> In this room, mixed in with the other patients, are twenty-three active tuberculosis patients. . . . Living in the damp, sunless climate, forced to walk barefoot over clammy cement floors whenever they go to the toilet, kept in bed for month

29. Patients in bathroom in A Building, Philadelphia State Hospital (Byberry), Philadelphia, Pennsylvania. (Swarthmore College Peace Collection, Swarthmore, Pennsylvania)

after month when most of them are perfectly capable of moving about and exercising—it seems a forlorn hope that any of these T.B. cases will ultimately survive. Among the other patients in the ward are several with jaundice and nine who are on weak notice. Some of the latter, though young men, are truly pitiful human skeletons, suffering from a diarrhea so virulent that their bowels seem almost to retch.[109]

Leg ulcers from lying in feces and urine were common among the patients living in this dormitory.[110]

Most of the patients spent their days in a large forty-by-seventy-foot barren dayroom. The dayroom sometimes had a couple of wooden benches. Most of the patients were forced to lie or sit on the floor or walk aimlessly around the room. Clothing, bed linens, and cleaning materials were in short supply in A Building. Most patients were usually naked. On cold winter nights, many patients slept on rubber mattresses, with only a sheet to cover them. Sometimes there were not enough sheets to go around.

Patients who could walk had their meals by going through a "food line" where they ate walking, with about five minutes to eat.[111] At one point, patients in A Building went months without even spoons with which to eat: "The patients grab the spaghetti in their hands and jam it down their gullets."[112]

Head lice and especially crab lice were commonplace among A Building patients. On August 23, 1943, attendants found 35 cases among the dayroom patients.[113] The patients' heads were shaved on a regular basis.

To care for the patients in A Building, there were sometimes as few as 2 attendants on duty during the day. Occasionally, an attendant worked alone.

B Building was the "violent" ward at Byberry. It also was used as a "punishment" ward for patients who tried to escape from the institution, got into fights with other patients, or had "sex irregularities."[114] The ward had one large dayroom for patients, a small hydrotherapy room with tubs for 6 or so patients when the equipment was working and enough attendants were present, and a "restraint" room where 15 to 30 patients were kept tied or strapped in bed. These latter patients were even fed in bed. In 1944, 2 to 4 attendants were usually on duty during the day shift ending at 2:00 P.M., with fewer staff during other hours.[115] The number of attendants had increased by 1945, when additional COs had been sent to Byberry.

B Building, like A and other buildings at Byberry, was often in disrepair. On March 22, 1944, Warren Sawyer wrote home:

Things here continue to go to pieces. The ceiling of the violent ward came down on Monday. Large pieces of plaster dropped leaving a gaping holl [sic] about 3 feet

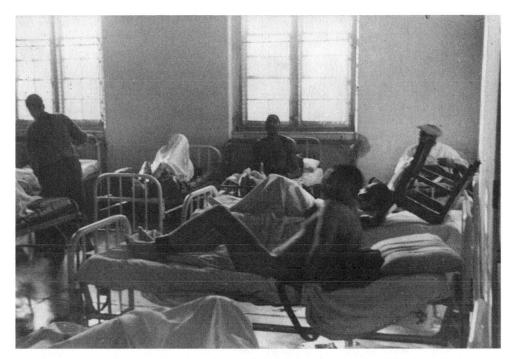

30. Patients strapped to beds in B Building, Philadelphia State Hospital (Byberry), Philadelphia, Pennsylvania. (Swarthmore College Peace Collection, Swarthmore, Pennsylvania)

square. From down stairs one can look up through the beans [*sic*] on the second floor right up to the roof. The roof leaks and of course can now reach the first floor without stopping off at the second floor. . . . Plaster in A Bldg. has come off to a much greater degree. The water in the bathroom comes through the roof in shower. In C Bldg., the epileptic building, the floor is so bad that patients can pull the boards out of the floor. When it rains the water that comes in from leaks in the roof washes two floors.

Sawyer continued to describe the run-down conditions at B Building and Byberry in general:

The roofs continue to leak, patients continue to escape, doors have to be nailed and boarded shut because maintenance doesn't find time to repair the locks, rows of lights are out in buildings (especially nice in the violent ward on a black out night with only one attendant on by himself), patients just miss death from fallen plaster, attendants continue to wash out sheets and hang them on radiators to dry . . . drains and toilets stay plugged and overflow before maintenance gets around to unplug them and the patients continue to live in condemned buildings.[116]

"Violent" was an apt description for B Building. Gangs formed in B Building, and fights were common. In his letters home, Warren Sawyer referred to the "gore story" of the week, and many of the stories came from B Building: "Two weeks ago a patient was killed in B. Bldg. by another patient when he was struck over the head with a broom handle."[117] Sawyer referred to B as the "death house":

> This new accident happened on Sunday 9/3/44. It was in B Building "the death house." Due to the shortage of cuffs and straps and restraint locks that has prevailed in B building for some time one of the patients was able to get himself loose. He is a very dangerous fellow. He only had one cuff and strap on and he got out. He had a spoon that had been broken off and the end was sharpened almost to a knife edge. After he was loose he went to another patient and jabbed him in the side of the neck on top of his shoulder and drove the spoon down about one inch deep, just missing the jugular vein. Nobody saw the accident but another patient told on the patient that did it. The attendant was in the toilet at the time. Pressure was applied to stop the bleeding and a suture was applied. 2½ hours later the patient victim collapsed at dinner and vomited. . . . He was transferred to the infirmary where blood plasma was injected and he was given glucose. It took a long time to get the intravenous apparatus going because of the three that were on hand, one was rotten, one cooked and melted in the sterilizer and the third was dirty and clogged. Imagine only having three for a hospital the size of this one. . . . The patient came very close to dying.[118]

It was not unusual for patients in B Building to have weapons. Years later, John Bartholomew recalled a patient in B Building who continued to free himself from being strapped in bed. The patient had cut the straps with a piece of a razor blade hidden in his anus. Sawyer wrote home about a weapons search in B Building at the time: "This week in B Building, the slaughterhouse pen, a complete search was made of the building for knives and razors etc. Such articles were found in beds, inside mattresses, razor blades hidden in anises (don't know about that spelling) pieces of blades hidden in mouths, a hack saw hidden in a mattress and a couple of knives. These weapons are found everywhere."[119]

B Building was chronically short in the supply of clothes, linens, and cleaning materials. The shortage of restraining cuffs and sheets was a common complaint among the CO attendants. Warren Sawyer kept a careful list of maintenance supplies and clothing requisitioned and received at B Building during 1945. Of thirty-six categories of maintenance items, the building received only four (shaving soap, cleaner, radiator brushes, toilet bowl brushes) of the number or amounts requested. Fifteen gallons of DDT were requested, none received; 48 cuffs and 48 straps requested, 24 of each received; 5 gallons of Lysol requested, none received; 240 mop heads requested, 8 received; and 1,225 pounds of detergent requested, 150 pounds received. The situation was similar for requisitioned clothing: 900 pairs of shoes requested, 566 pairs received; 499 pairs of underpants requested, 3 pairs received; 1,433 undershirts requested, 30 received; 1,530 pairs of pants requested, 345 pairs received; 1,176 shirts requested, 170 received; and 475 blankets requested, 302 received. The building received the requested number of sheets (493), jackets (4), sneakers (30), and some other items.[120]

B Building was a difficult place at which to work. COs were frequently injured by patients: "Three of our fellows have had tough times of it in B Bldg. One man got all scratched up in the face and arms"; "A couple of our men have received some good stiff blows this past week from various patients"; "One of the new men came in yesterday with a big bandage wrapped around his head and his glasses smashed to nothing. One of the patients took a leg off his bed and knocked him over the head with it."[121] Hal Barton was hospitalized after being injured by a patient in B Building:

> I was thrown over the head of a 230-pound ex-Commando-trainee who had "broke" in training. My only chance to prevent the toss was a direct hit to the face of the patient. This I could have done easily, but the patient was a paranoid. . . . I permitted myself to be thrown, hit on the lower extreme of the backbone, and flashed out. When I came to, my right leg was completely paralyzed. A circle of patients stood warily at a distance not wanting to get embroiled. I managed to stand up only to be approached by the paranoid patient swinging heavily at me again. I stepped back with the left foot, drug the right one, and the blow glanced off my chest. Seeing that I was not inclined to attack him, the patient withdrew. Moments later two other CPS-men returned from lunch and I gave them what little help I could in carrying out the orders for hydro-therapy for the aggressive patient, then went to the infirmary for a stay.

According to Barton, most COs could last only three or four weeks working in B Building. William March had been a charge at B Building but had to transfer to another building after he started having nightmares about the building.[122]

A and B Buildings were known as the worst buildings at Byberry, but it was not as though living and working conditions in the other buildings were good. CO Thurston Griggs wrote a report on two of the smaller men's wards, 2W and F Hydro, on February 4, 1946. The first ward was an "incontinent 48 bed ward of helpless and confused patients": "Often patients lie in unchanged beds for as long as 4 to 6 hours. Patients in restraints are rarely given a chance to toilet themselves."[123]

The beds were pushed so closely together that a soiled linen cart or wheelchair could not move between them. One, or at most 2, attendants worked on the ward, and it was sometimes left unattended when attendants left for meals.

F Hydro was a ward for 20 patients. It was located in a cellar, and the floor did not meet the wall: "In the space between, trash is thrown, urine is voided and cockroaches and mice traffic." John Bartholomew recalled using hydrotherapy at F Hydro: "We would soak sheets in ice water all night and then in the morning we would wrap up the patients in the cold sheets and in five or six hours their body heat would warm them up. In the meantime, that was supposed to calm them down." Leonard Stark also worked at F Hydro: "There were two kinds of tubs. One had warm water. Patients would lie there for three hours. The other had cold packs. Three cold sheets were wrapped around them. Just their toes and heads stuck out."[124] Like the ones in B Building, some of the patients in F Hydro were violent. Bartholomew remembered breaking up fights often. While working at F Hydro, Stark was surprised by a patient wielding a sharpened knife who cut him in the arm down to the bone. The wound became infected, and he was hospitalized at a general hospital for two weeks. When Stark returned to work at Byberry, he was assigned to A Building but became sick every time he went there. After seeing a psychiatrist, he was reassigned to work on the dairy farm at Byberry.

Their work as attendants was stressful to many of the COs. The conditions at the institutions were often depressing and shocking. The brutality of many of the regular attendants was just as bad, if not worse.

10

"Bughousers" and "Conchies"

Mental hospitals and training schools had been short-staffed on the wards prior to the war, but faced critical staff shortages once the war started. Many young men working as attendants were drafted into the military. Of those men who were not drafted, many, both men and women, took higher-paying jobs in industry and agriculture, which faced labor shortages of their own. Attendants' pay was low, roughly $50 to $120 per month, with the costs of room and board often deducted.[1] The attendants who remained were older men and women who had worked at the institutions for a long period of time and did not want to switch jobs or were unfit to be drafted or hired for other positions. Ralph Delk characterized the quality of attendants at Mansfield State Training School: "Attendants (except CPS personnel) are largely uneducated, poorly equipped people. They can find no other employment now at which they can remain long. Neither do they remain long here. . . . Present day attendants are sometimes described as 'anybody who can handle keys and walk and talk.' Some are able to take temperatures and read a thermometer! These are real finds!!"[2]

As Ward Miles noted, in discussing the attendants at Byberry, "There's always good and bad." Some regular attendants tried to do a conscientious job, although their attitudes and methods might have seemed backward and harsh to the COs. Byberry COs Arthur Stevenson and Michael Marsh recalled an exceptional charge attendant in A Building: "'A' Building's charge attendant's approach to care of the patients has served as a constant example of how they should be treated; he is a most unusual man."[3] Other attendants were outcasts themselves.

"Bughouse" was a name sometimes used to refer to mental hospitals, and attendants were often called "bughousers."[4] Some of them were transients and "drifters" who went from one institution to another, having been fired or simply wanting a change of scenery. David Patrick Lee, a self-identified bughouser, described the lifestyle: "When they got tired of one bughouse they moved on to another, sometimes staying just long enough to pick up one paycheck. There was always a help shortage and it made it easy to get a job. So when you got in 'a jam' in one place you moved to another. In this way many bughousers managed to work in almost every institution in the country." Alex Sareyan reported that some bughousers bragged that they had worked at as many as one hundred different institutions. Loris Habegger recalled that most regular attendants at Marlboro State Hospital were undependable and irresponsible: "Many were floaters going from one hospital to another."[5] Staff housing at the institutions made it easier for attendants to move from one to another.

A number of the regular attendants were known to be alcoholics or problem drinkers, who either showed up drunk on the job or skipped work altogether. Charles Lord described attendants at Byberry: "A lot of them were problem drinkers and had problems with drunkenness. . . . They just wouldn't show up for work." Paul L. Goering remembered a charge at Howard State Hospital: "My charge attendant at Rhode Island was an alcoholic and was abusive to patients." In a letter home on December 5, 1945, Warren Sawyer wrote, "The drunks in the attendants home have been having a wonderful time dragging each other around for the past two weeks. Several have been out of work for these past two weeks on really tight binges." Many years later, Sawyer characterized attendants at Byberry: "A lot of those guys were drunks, went from one institution to another. They'd come back again to Byberry after a session elsewhere."[6]

"Bughouser" was not simply a name. It represented a way of thinking about and acting toward patients. William Ludlow, who worked at the AFSC unit at Eastern State Hospital in Williamsburg, described the perspective: "Violence was what was recommended by the old bughouse attendant who told us, 'The first thing you do when they come in is you beat them up, and you won't have trouble with them.'" Even when the term *bughouser* was not used, it accurately captured the institutional culture. Lee, the bughouser, said it best: "It must be understood that the bughouser was no more than a product of our mental hospital system. A product of the bughouse." He concluded his article with these words: "Patients were made to mind, they weren't allowed to escape and cause mischief, they seldom succeeded in killing each other or anyone else, and the public didn't need to worry. What more could you want?"[7]

Harsh treatment and brutality were commonplace at many mental hospitals and training schools and offended the pacifist sensibilities of many COs. COs would expose abuses at mental hospitals at Poughkeepsie, Williamsburg, Cleveland, and elsewhere that would result in major public scandals. COs at Southern Wisconsin Colony and Training School became involved in a less public investigation. One of the COs at Southern Wisconsin testified before a state welfare board on an attendant's fatal beating of a patient: "This threatened a PR problem for a time, but the regular employee was discharged and the situation was forgotten."[8]

COs at Byberry documented abuse by regular attendants. Much of the abuse occurred in B Building, the violent ward, but it happened in other buildings as well. Warren Sawyer described one attendant's rough handling of patients in the infirmary: "I work with a CPS man right now. Before, I had a young fellow who was as cruel to patients as if they were just sticks of wood. Patients with broken hips or arms or paralyzed men he would yank around from one side of the bed to the other like a sack of meal. Last night he was put in another building. I hope he stays there."[9]

31. Pipe used by regular (non-CPS) attendants to control or punish patients at Philadelphia State Hospital (Byberry), Philadelphia, Pennsylvania. (Swarthmore College Peace Collection, Swarthmore, Pennsylvania)

Especially in B Building, regular attendants sometimes used clubs or a hose filled with buckshot to control difficult patients. The attendants took care not to be seen clubbing or beating patients: "Two of the regular attendants have expressed themselves about being very careful when they use weapons or fists upon patients—very careful *not to be seen*." The ward charge was one of the attendants who routinely beat patients:

> Just today I observed something which is quite common: a patient who had been entertained by visitors and had evidently made a "break" for the door in an effort to escape. The regular Charge man brought him into the day room and as soon as the doors were closed, swung broadly and with full force, striking the patient open-handed on both sides of the face, 3 hard blows in all. I've seen a very much bewildered and uncooperative, but unassaultive, patient brought in from the yard by the same Charge and [patient helper], slump to the floor weeping violently and with blood streaming from his nose and red marks all over his body from slapping and pounding.[10]

Regular attendants often used patient "trustees" or "enforcers" to control other patients. Floyd Greenleaf reported, "Patients often used to handle other patients when there are not enough attendants to do it. Patients cannot understand the reasons for a disturbed patients actions, therefor [*sic*] often get angry and hurt the patient." Similarly, Hal Barton described a patient worker who was especially brutal with other patients: "A common sight in the building is to see regular attendant _____ or patient [name] walking about the building with a heavy stick with which to 'club' the patients into obedience. . . . Patient [name] . . . has been seen on two occasions to strike quite viciously with the stick and five or more patients have reported and shown evidence of real abuse with the weapon at the hands of [patient]."[11]

Some of the regular attendants may have been sadistic, but it would be too easy to blame their brutality and rough treatment of patients solely on personality factors. Especially given the terrible overcrowding and chronic understaffing of the wards, the attendant's job was difficult and stressful. Violence was one way of trying to maintain control and order on the wards. Pacifist COs would struggle to come up with different ways.

◆   ◆   ◆

The work at mental hospitals and training schools challenged the pacifist beliefs of many COs. Men who believed that war was immoral would be likely to renounce the use of force or violence in their dealings with other human beings.

Most subscribed to principles of nonresistance or nonviolent resistance in the face of conflict. Mennonites, in particular, took the biblical teachings "Turn the other cheek" and "Resist not evil" literally.

For many COs, work at the institutions represented an important form of "witness" in which they would alleviate human suffering and put their religious principles to the test. In a study of the COs at the time, sociologists L. E. Maechtle and H. Gerth described the perspectives of many COs: "Most C.O.'s . . . emphasize the position that their mental hospital experience is an opportunity to test their pacifism in practice and to demonstrate to themselves and to others the sincerity and practicality of their beliefs in nonresistance and nonviolent coercion."[12]

A summary of the experiences of the MCC unit at Hudson River State Hospital captured the sentiments of many religious COs:

> Our biggest job on work project was to be the "Christian conscience" against the use of brutal force and sadistic measures in the treatment of mental patients. Our witness, as a group of Christian attendants, for another philosophy and method of dealing with mentally ill patients, was, to my thinking, an even greater contribution than the supplying of help in a critical labor shortage. The fact that we willingly worked on the deteriorated and disturbed wards and did our task well was indeed significant. But the more significant contribution was our demonstration

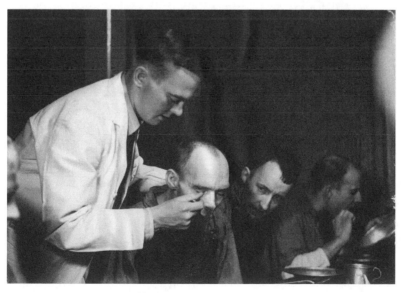

32. CPS man feeding patient, CPS Unit no. 51, Western State Hospital, Fort Steilacoom, Washington. (Brethren Historical Library and Archives, Elgin, Illinois)

that, even when dealing with a group of people who were mentally incompetent, the philosophy of love practiced in all human relations, was both practical and achieved the best results.[13]

Work on the wards of the institutions created a tension between the convictions of many COs and the demands of the job. Some patients attacked others, including attendants, tried to hurt themselves, refused to do what was asked of them, or attempted to escape. Attempts to reason with patients might not prevent them from harming themselves or others or disrupting ward routines. Force or coercion was the easiest way of dealing with difficult patients, especially considering the overcrowding and understaffing on the wards.

"Absolutists"—COs whose beliefs prevented them from using any form of coercion or force—were ill-suited for work as institutional attendants and probably did not last long on the wards. Those COs who stayed working on the wards searched for a way to justify imposing their will on others physically. Maechtle and Gerth noted that Mennonites, in particular, had to rationalize actions that ran counter to the principle of nonresistance: "They recognize that they need to use some form of restraint and coercion in handling mental patients—such as forcibly undressing a man who has a mania for clothing, dressing another who has a 'nakedness' mania, sitting on a man while he is being shaven or medically treated, or subduing another whose violent behavior endangers his own life and the lives of other patients."[14]

Many COs eventually came to a position that distinguished between unacceptable violence, on the one hand, and acceptable force or nonviolent coercion, on the other.[15] The line between violence and force or coercion was not always clear, and COs often discussed or debated the difference between the two.[16] As Paul A. Wilhelm noted, "We had interminable arguments all through CPS." A report on the MCC unit at the Southern Wisconsin Colony and Training School described the "problem of ward discipline": "The problem of ward discipline constantly faced the group and was never solved completely to the satisfaction of the unit members but as the group became thoroughly acquainted with the staff and patients and made their personal adjustments, opportunities rose in which improvements on the old methods of beatings could be made."[17]

The construct of force was generally thought of as using the minimal amount of physical effort necessary to maintain control of the wards or restrain patients from doing things that could harm themselves or others. It was to be used only with respect for patients and concern for their welfare, and never as punishment. Ludlow contrasted force with the violence used by the bughouse attendant: "Force was restraining, but with concern and respect for the person you were restraining."

Warren Sawyer described what he saw as the COs' contribution: "One of our biggest contributions at Byberry and other institutions was that we developed a trust of the patients toward us. They knew they wouldn't be beaten. They would be treated humanly . . . a matter of restraining patients as opposed to beating them." Bill March was a CO charge attendant at Byberry who replaced a non-CO charge who used a rubber hose filled with buckshot to control patients: "When I replaced him the patients learned very quickly that my use of physical force was an effort to protect the patients from hurting each other—not to hurt them."[18]

Second-miler was a term used to describe COs who gave all of their effort at CPS work camps as a demonstration of their sincerity.[19] At the mental hospitals and training schools, some COs went the "second mile" in attempting to put their religious, pacifist, or humanitarian beliefs into practice. They went to great lengths to avoid the use of force. When Hal Barton was attacked by the "230-pound ex-Commando trainee" at Byberry's B Building, he did not use force to defend himself, although he might have been able to avoid being injured: "We were taught in training that we had the right—even duty—of self-defense. But we were also taught that what these patients needed most was to come to a realization that someone cared, that not everyone was out to 'get him.'"[20]

Loris Habegger, a Mennonite who was the assistant director of the MCC unit at Marlboro State Hospital, illustrated the perspective of some of the COs who went the "second mile" to avoid violence and force. Habegger would use force to restrain patients on occasion. He recalled an incident when one patient assaulted another: "I was the only attendant on the ward and I tried the full nelson on the man to control him, but in no way beat him or bruised him. And I do not feel that is misusing our Mennonite principles. Here was a man who had to be helped to control himself and to protect others."[21]

On some occasions, Habegger handled potentially explosive situations in a calm and gentle way that avoided the use of force. He explained how he dealt with one man who was threatening to throw a dinner tray at him:

> These were people, and they're people even when they're mentally ill. There was a young man who had a good set of fists on him. . . . I went in to get his tray, and he threatened to throw it at me. And I said to him, "Well, this is your room. I'd like the tray to wash it, but I'm not going to come into your room. You have a right to say who can come in or stay out. It's your room, not mine. . . . If you won't let me in, will you bring me your tray so we can wash it?" . . . He didn't let me come in but he brought me his tray. It didn't work in every case, but it's amazing how people want to be treated as people, even when they're suffering from disorientation.

Another time, when he was working on X-rays, Habegger gently coaxed a woman patient afraid of X-rays into having one:

> There was a lady who would become very violent, and we were doing X-rays. . . . So I went up to her and I said, "Ma'am, I know you are a lady and you don't want to be pushed around by men. You have every right to say, 'Keep your paws off me,' and I respect you for it. I would like to have your chest X-rayed and I'll go up to the chest X-ray machine and I'll show you how I would like you to stand. . . . I will never push you. I won't put my hand on you." And we did a few more, and then I came to her, and I said, "Now it's your turn. Will you go?" And she walked up to the X-ray machine and stood there. She was frightened, but she did so with no argument.[22]

Not all COs were as gentle as Habegger in handling patients, and some found it difficult to maintain their patience with them. Their jobs could be nerve-racking. Mansfield's assistant director, Ralph Delk, wondered about his own "mental condition" and admitted acting in "unchristian and intolerant" ways toward patients. At Hudson River State Hospital, J. Willard Linscheid described the frustrations of COs in one building: "Although we were told repeatedly that our handling of patients was much better than that of the former attendants, the frustrations encountered gave rise to fits of temper which at times resulted in unnecessarily rough language and rough handling of patients. This loss of control grew more frequent as the time on the ward grew longer." It also was natural for some COs to react forcefully, even violently, when caught off-guard by patients. Paul Wilhelm recalled being attacked by a patient at Byberry: "Another patient had syphilis in the maximum degree and was very combative, and they put him in my ward. I came in one time and found him in complete restraints, and when I took him his food, I let him out, and he grabbed my testicles, and I automatically cauliflowered his ear! And then we all felt so badly about it that all the shifts on the ward concentrated on him, and in four months we had him out."[23]

COs at Byberry generally tried to avoid using force and overt violence, but there were differences of opinion about the appropriateness of various approaches to the patients. A Byberry CO reported that one of his fellow objectors in B Building struck a patient: "[CO name] one of our own struck Abe [last name] also a very difficult problem child. Abes [sic] head hit the wall. Result a nose bleed." The CO explained: "[CO name] and [CO name] and Idiagree [sic] on method somewhat. Bobs name did not appear on the sheet of attendants schedules. He has been fired from Building B because it is not under control. No one seems to be able to really define control seems to be a matter of principle. [Last name] also said Bobs pacifist techniques were to [sic] much in evidence. I wonder how long I will last."[24]

The distinction between force and violence, as explained by most COs, would have ruled out any form of physical punishment or intimidation. Yet some COs regularly used measures that went beyond restraining patients to keep them from immediate harm to themselves or others. NSBRO's Paul Comly French was distressed to learn that some COs at Cheltenham were using corporal punishment on the boys: "Read a letter from one of the men at Cheltenham which certainly indicates that men should have some understanding of the non-violent techniques before being assigned to mental hospitals or to reformatories. He said that a number of the men were using corporal punishment on the Negro boys and that is in line with what Eli Wismer said about Sykesville. Certainly if we can't demonstrate that we are capable of solving problems without force, we have no right to ask the country to exempt us from military service."[25]

Corporal punishment and intimidation were not things COs sought to hide from others. In stories written for NSBRO's *Reporter* in 1943, Mansfield COs Ralph S. Wolfe and Donald G. Holsopple described the methods they used with patients. Wolfe believed that pacifist methods were inadequate in dealing with patients: "Unfortunately, ideal pacifist methods are not adequate to meet the situations immediately for such a large number. These patients over a period of time have been accustomed to discipline through force. Consequently, fear must still play an important part in dealing with them." Holsopple believed that pacifist methods worked in most, but not all, situations: "I would say for the most part, pacifism is quite successful in the handling of these patients. It must be realized that there are times when a paddling is the only way to bring results, but those times are few."[26] Mansfield's superintendent, Dr. Neil Dayton, read these stories and took exception to some of the things the COs wrote.[27] He did not appear to object to these statements.

COs by and large rejected the "bughouse" culture of the old-time attendants with its gratuitous violence. The training schools and mental hospitals themselves prohibited beatings of patients and the use of clubs and other weapons to control them. Yet the institutions sanctioned practices that would be seen as abusive, dehumanizing, or exploitative today. For the most part, COs did not question the broader institutional culture.

Physical restraints—cuffs, straps, and straitjackets—were widely used to control patients at the institutions, especially on the violent wards. Patients might be placed in restraints for hours, days, weeks, or longer. Even where straitjackets or other restraints were not used, such as at Hawthornden State Hospital, difficult patients were locked in barren isolation cells or "strong rooms."[28] Many COs tried to avoid placing patients in restraints or isolation and freed them when they thought it might be safe to do so, but did not view restraining patients, often in uncomfortable or painful positions, or locking them in isolation cells as inherently wrong. The use of restraints or isolation was not seen as incompatible with pacifist methods. A frequent complaint among COs at Byberry's B Building was that the institution did not supply them with a sufficient number of cuffs and straps.

Institutions cultivated certain ways of thinking about and rationalizing the treatment of patients. Patients who were ostensibly committed to institutions for "treatment" were seldom provided any form of treatment or even personal and individual attention. If they became violent, disturbed, or unruly, it was acceptable to limit their freedom and movement, even when it was recognized that more humane approaches could have been used if only sufficient staff and resources were available. Further, patients' behaviors were taken out of context. Most COs found the wards to be stressful, noisy, and distracting, and some lost their composure just working there during their shifts. Patients lived there all of the time. In addition, they had been stripped of their possessions; their personal appearances; their relationships and roles; their sense of privacy, security, and control over their bodies; and their regular routines—in short, their social "selves" or identities.[29] A review of the admission process on the women's side at Byberry casually described women's initiation into the institution:

> The reception ward is quiet until two large cars draw up before the door and the patients from the General Hospital are let out. Then, quite suddenly, the silence is broken by singing, screaming, and threatening voices mingled with crying and questioning in frightened tones. The ride in the big car, the dread of the "unknown," even the restraining paraphernalia that prevents the violent patients from doing harm to themselves and others—these things inevitably provoke outbursts as the cars are unloaded. . . .
>
> At last we are alone with the new group. Each talks about herself and her being there, according to her own state of illness. They know they are at a mental hospital, but not *why*. It is always a mistake, and somebody will come tomorrow to take them home. . . .
>
> Our first procedure is to remove all pieces of personal property. These are put away for safe keeping. The next step is the disrobing, weighing and measuring. This is not done, of course, without comment and some resistance. Only tact and patience help. We gather the clothes of each patient in a sheet and attach a list. Clothes are cleaned and kept in a special place until the patient is discharged. As soon as possible each new patient is bathed and dressed in hospital clothes—neat, figured cotton dresses. By noon they are back in their chairs, the more disturbed ones in bed, and ready for dinner.[30]

Patient behaviors that were defined in terms of individual pathology were often a reaction to the nature of the institutions themselves. The institutions created or fostered some of the very behaviors that were defined as symptomatic of some underlying mental disturbance and used to justify harsh and coercive measures. In the institutional culture, it was not morally problematic to do things to patients that would not otherwise be done to human beings, save those individuals convicted of crimes through a court of law. COs, or at least many of them, were part of this culture. It was not as though they could have or should have let mayhem reign on the wards of the mental hospitals and training schools. It was that moral human beings often could not see the immorality of a system in which coercive methods were the only ones available.

The institutions long depended on peonage, that is, unpaid labor of patients, and would continue to do so well into the 1970s, although it had been officially prohibited by that time.[31] This practice too was not usually questioned. Like other attendants, the COs relied on patients to do most of the work at the mental hospitals and training schools. A bulletin used to recruit COs to Augusta State Hospital, "Information for Men in CPS Camps," explained what men could expect: "The more capable patients are used in helping to care for the wards and even aiding in the care of the more helpless; thus the ability to direct the work of the more able patients is of great value. Also, some of the patients are taken out in crews to work on the grounds and farm."[32]

Patient workers often did the most unpleasant and dirtiest jobs at the institutions. At Norwich State Hospital, COs had patients do most of the physical work: "There are some rather filthy situations to meet, and it is no place for a weak stomach. However, patient helpers do most of the heavy and dirty work." Patient workers took care of incontinents at Mansfield State Training School: "Of the five or six hundred boys here, I should say that 150 of them would come near the incontinent stage. However, the attendant does not have to clean up such patients as there are what we call worker patients to take care of them."[33]

A common rationalization for the use of patient workers was that it gave capable patients something to do rather than being idle all of the time. An overview of Byberry's A Building rationalized using patients to do the dirty work: "The building's greatest debt, however, is to the forty worker patients who do most of the actual nasty drudgery needed that the life of the place may continue. These patients, better adjusted than the others, have as their chief reward just this—they are kept busy, and so may be helped to a cure. Their material gain is tobacco to smoke and occasional candy."[34]

Patient workers even shaved patients in A Building: "Removal of feces marks on the walls is supervised by attendants, as is cleaning the day room floor. Worker patients again, do the major part of the job, as they do when the patients are shaved once a week." Warren Sawyer gave a vivid picture of the shaving routine:

33. CPS man directing patient worker, CPS Unit no. 63, State Hospital, Marlboro, New Jersey. (Mennonite Church USA Historical Committee and Archives, Goshen, Indiana)

On Fridays each gets a shave. Boy that is a job. Patients have to shave patients. Some of them look as if they have been slaughtered they are bleeding in so many places. Other patients do a good job shaving. No wonder they hate to be shaved. . . . It stings and burns to have the soap get in the cuts. The next week it is worse because you have the scabs to contend with and so they are reopened. Some get badly cut because they can't sit still and it takes four men to shave one fellow as it did with me the other day. It is not an easy or pleasant job and I don't blame them for not liking to be shaved. And some of those beards are plenty tough and mixed in with caked feces.[35]

The mental hospitals and training schools could not have operated without patient labor. So the use of unpaid patient labor was largely taken for granted by COs and non-COs alike. Unpaid COs, many of whom were advocating to be paid, usually did not see the irony in using unpaid patients to do the institutions' dirty work. Every once in a while, some COs did see the unfairness of situations involving patient workers. Warren Sawyer commented on the use of a patient to help ease the critical labor shortage in the women's buildings at Byberry: "The situation was once on the female side that one attendant had to care for two buildings. That meant that a patient had to be given keys in order to watch 350 patients. I know, because I was talking to the patient that had to do it. She said that she was worn out and that she got nothing but yelling at all day from the nurse who never seemed satisfied with her work. That was the thanks she got. No remuneration."[36]

The Mental Hygiene Program of the CPS—and then the National Mental Health Foundation after the CPS ended—would devote considerable attention to the attendants' work. Distinguishing between acceptable force and unacceptable violence would be one of its first priorities, and it would eventually consider the use of restraints and unpaid patient labor.

◆   ◆   ◆

During World War II, the country rallied around the war effort. Women could not serve in combat but found other ways to support the armed services. Many women volunteered to serve in the Army Nurses Corps or joined the Women's Army Auxiliary Corps, which later become the Women's Army Corps (WAC). Approximately 150,000 women eventually served as clerks, lab technicians, secretaries, air controllers, cryptographers, mail handlers, and in similar roles in the WAC.[37] On the home front, many housewives carefully rationed goods and supplies and raised "victory gardens," and some left their homes to support the war more directly. "Rosie the Riveter" was perhaps the most enduring image of women's contributions to America during World War II. The fictional Rosie was depicted in posters, magazine covers, postage stamps, and a popular song to recruit women into the labor force and especially war industries.[38] "Soldiers without guns" read one poster showing a Rosie-type worker and two other women. During World War II, approximately 18 million American women worked in war plants.[39] Between 1940 and 1945, female employment jumped by 460 percent in war industries.[40] Even if they could not join their husbands, brothers, and male relatives and neighbors in combat, women could support the effort by helping to build the weapons of war.

Unlike their male counterparts, pacifist women did not have a way of publicly bearing witness against the war.[41] Women were not drafted during World War

II, although proposals were made to do so along with a general labor draft.[42] So women could not officially be "conscientious objectors." The CPS itself was totally dominated by men. Not a single woman served on NSBRO's eleven-member Board of Directors.[43] Of the roughly seventy members of the AFSC, about a dozen were women. The BSC had one woman among its fifteen members, and the twenty-one-member MCC had no women. As Rachel Waetner Goossen noted, the "Civilian Public Service, created by the federal government and administered by historical peace churches, reflected the gender ideology of the era."[44]

As CPS men moved from the work camps to the mental hospitals and training schools, many women followed them. First wives and later members of women's service units would perform the same kinds of work and endure similar conditions as the men.

By mid-1943, a significant number of men at many mental hospital units were married. At the largest BSC units, for example, fifteen out of twenty-four COs were married at Lyons Veterans Administration Hospital, thirteen of thirty-nine at Fairfield State Hospital, eleven of twenty-eight at Mansfield Training School, and nine of nineteen at Lynchburg Training School as of June 30, 1943. As the CPS wore on, more and more COs got married, either to women friends with whom they had been reunited or to women they met in the areas in which the institutions were located. In a July 1945 letter, Warren Sawyer wrote about the latest marriage at Byberry: "Yesterday another fellow in the unit got married to a girl from the Frankford YWCA who is a Pacifist and Socialist. . . . Soon this will be a unit for married men only."[45] Of the forty-six men who had served at Mansfield as of July 1946, at least twenty had been married.[46] In May 1945, seventeen of the forty men were married at the MCC unit at Harrisburg State Hospital.[47] Of the twenty-five COs who had arrived at Southern Wisconsin Colony and Training School by January 1944, twelve were married. Twenty-seven of the thirty-three COs at Mount Pleasant State Hospital were married as of July 17, 1945.[48]

Labor shortages in the women's buildings at mental hospitals and training schools were at least as critical as in the men's buildings. At Eastern State Hospital in Williamsburg, Virginia, there were fifteen women attendants to care for twelve hundred women's patients day and night.[49] The superintendent at Ohio's Hawthornden State Hospital was so desperate for women staff that he hired a contingent from the state prison for women at Marysville, Ohio.[50] The staffing situation on the women's side of Byberry was much worse than on the men's side. Sometimes there were not enough women attendants to cover each of the buildings.[51] Arthur Stevenson and Michael Marsh described the situation: "Ideas that the attendants on the male side were working under stringent conditions were rudely shaken when we realized the situation that existed on the female side. In one two story building, housing 243 patients, there has not been more than one female attendant on duty at any one time. A semi-violent ward of over 250 patients has two attendants on the first shift, one on the second, and one on the third."[52]

Most mental hospital and training school superintendents were eager to employ the wives of the COs. Superintendent Adolph Soucek at Mount Pleasant State Hospital was initially reluctant to hire wives before the CPS unit had been accepted at the institution, but started hiring them before long.[53] Eventually, nineteen worked at the hospital or in the nearby town of Mount Pleasant. Twenty wives of CPS men worked at Mansfield from March 1943 to July 1946. The same number of CO wives worked at Norwich State Hospital in 1945.[54] At Marion and Augusta state hospitals, six and five CO wives worked at the institutions in 1945 and 1944, respectively. According to Goossen, fifty-eight CO wives worked at Marlboro State Hospital during the CPS.[55]

The wives of COs held similar positions as the men at the institutions. Many worked as attendants in women's buildings, but they also had jobs in the laundry, kitchen or dining service, business office, and elsewhere. Wives were paid the same as regular employees. At Augusta State Hospital, they received $12 to $14 per week, plus room and board, for work on the wards and in the laundry and the dining service. Norwich State Hospital paid a starting annual salary of $1,080, minus $316 for room, food, and laundry. Goossen reported that wives who worked as attendants and lived with their husbands were paid an average of $80 per month.[56]

For CO wives, working at the institutions provided opportunities to earn some money and to be close to their husbands. Many of the institutions also provided housing to married couples so that they could live together. For other women, work at mental hospitals would have a deeper meaning.

As young Mennonite, Brethren, and Quaker men were conscripted into the CPS and assigned to special service projects, some young women from the peace churches looked for ways in which they could perform humanitarian service. The ill-fated CPS foreign relief training program, which was blocked by Congress in 1943, also had caught the attention of some young women who had wanted to join men in alleviating the suffering in war-torn areas overseas. The mental hospitals, where so many men were serving, provided an alternative for women wishing to demonstrate their commitment to pacifist beliefs and service to others.

In August 1943, a group of women met at the Mennonite Goshen College in Indiana to form a women's conscientious objector society, the "COGs," for "CO girls." Among the purposes of the group were "to give expression to and to develop convictions on peace and war," "to assume our responsibility in supporting the stand taken by the young men," and "to relieve human need because that work is consistent with our stand as Christians." Similarly, women who had participated in a foreign relief training program at the Brethren Manchester College in Indiana developed recommendations for the inclusion of women in the CPS, at the suggestion of M. R. Zigler of the BSC.[57]

In Philadelphia, Byberry COs were well known at Friends meetings and participated in Quaker educational and social activities. Especially since some of them had wives working at the mental hospital, it was natural for the AFSC to sponsor a women's unit there. Superintendent Charles Zeller was a strong supporter of the CPS mental hospital program and was interested in recruiting women through the AFSC to address the critical staff shortage on the women's side of the institution. In March 1943, AFSC officials and Byberry staff planned for the establishment of a women's service unit.[58] The unit was opened that June with eight women. In October 1943, Ruth Dingman, a psychiatric nurse, was appointed executive director of the AFSC-CPS Women's Service in Mental Hospitals. Dingman would later become active in the Mental Hygiene Program of the CPS. According to Goossen, the AFSC was the only one of the three peace church service committees to appoint a woman administrator of women's service. Two years after the establishment of the Byberry unit, an AFSC women's unit was opened at New Jersey State Hospital in Trenton.[59]

Between 1944 and 1946, the MCC opened women's summer service units at Hudson River State Hospital, Cleveland State Hospital, Ypsilanti State Hospital, Howard State Hospital, Norristown State Hospital, and Wernersville State Hospital. A BSC women's unit was established at Elgin State Hospital in Illinois in 1944.[60] This mental hospital is the same one at which M. R. Zigler was unsuccessful in opening a CPS unit at the start of the mental hospital program because of the opposition of the American Legion.

From June 1943 to October 1944, twenty-nine women worked at the Byberry unit.[61] Five of the women were married to Byberry COs, and at least three others would marry Byberry men. Eight were Friends, and others were Methodist, Episcopalian, Lutheran, or members of other religions. The women included college students, teachers, and secretaries. Some, especially students, had worked for only a summer. Others had been on the unit for a year and a half. Several had started working at Byberry before the women's unit had been formed.

Women were recruited to the unit through AFSC pamphlets and announcements as well as word of mouth: "Desire to give constructive service where there is urgent need, and interest in practical psychological and sociological factors in our entering the Women's Service in Mental Hospitals. Through representatives from or pamphlets issued by the American Friends Service Committee, or through members of the CPS units we learned of this opportunity." Lois (Holloway) Barton's

34. Women's Ward, Philadelphia State Hospital (Byberry), Philadelphia, Pennsylvania. (Swarthmore College Peace Collection, Swarthmore, Pennsylvania)

cousin Walter Kirk was a CO at Byberry and sent her copies of the unit paper when she was a social work student at Schauffer College in Ohio.[62] A note in one of the papers caught her eye and interested her in the women's unit that her cousin had told her about: "George wouldn't have died last night if you'd been here to help." It was the same note that had drawn her eventual husband, Hal Barton, to apply for a transfer to Byberry.

The women worked as attendants and were paid $66.50 per month, plus room and board and laundry, for a fifty-four-hour workweek. They lived in the Female Attendants' Home along with regular employees. The women's experience with training was similar to the COs on the men's side of the institution. Classes on mental illness and therapies were offered, but not before women starting working on the wards. Alice Calder, who later married CO Ward Miles, characterized the orientation provided by a nurse as "useless" and remembered a session in which she was taught how to fold clothes and give sponge baths. Lois Barton recalled, "We had no real preparation for our work as attendants."[63]

An official description of the unit painted a challenging but orderly picture of work on the wards: "To be an attendant in a mental hospital, especially in days of personnel shortage, is to be a combination nurse, housekeeper, watchman, companion, and general handy-man. The actual duties vary depending on whether one works on a building for senile, worker, incontinent or overactive patients or in the infirmary where the physically ill are cared for, but the general routine is the same." The description went through the daily work of getting patients up, dressed, and toileted; feeding the patients; supervising the cleaning of the ward by patient workers; keeping an eye out for "accidents, fights and runaways"; and putting the patients to bed at the end of the day. The difficulty of the work seemed understated: "Any spare time which the attendant may have (and there is little of that if, as sometimes happens, she is alone with 200 or more patients) may be spent in talking with the patients, getting to know and understand them better and in that way learning the best methods of handling each case."[64] Official photos of women on the wards make the work seem serene and uneventful: a woman attendant sitting at a desk at the end of a walkway between rows of beds in a clean and orderly dormitory, an individual woman attendant letting a patient into a locked ward, that same woman attendant standing in a clean and tidy hydrotherapy room.

For the women in the service unit, the work at Byberry was difficult, and the conditions were depressing. Alice Calder Miles's first impression of Byberry was that it was "overwhelming."[65] She worked for a time on the elderly senile ward, which was not considered one of the worst at the institution. There was no treatment. She remembered a woman patient from another ward who spent all day washing incontinent patients. Every once in a while, the worker patient would throw open a window and scream. It was "sad." Like some of the COs, she had to prepare dead bodies for the morgue. She recalled one occasion in which a doctor came in the ward, looked at a patient, and declared her dead from ten feet away.

Lois Barton worked on different wards at Byberry. Years later, memories of various wards stood out. In the infirmary she was helping to bathe a bedfast patient who had "something between her legs that on a man might have been distorted testicles." She recalled, "The nurse told me it was a prolapsed uterus, but nothing was done to remedy the situation." The hydro ward had twenty-five to thirty patients. Most were strapped to a bench or in their beds. When the ward became chaotic or violence broke out, the nurse would shut herself in an office and call burly male guards, who would come to the ward to restore order. An older woman in one ward was strapped to a bench and given a bedpan. After urinating in the bedpan, she would drink the urine. A fifteen-year-old girl would get her hands on cigarettes and a light and then burn restrained patients on their arms or legs. Lois Barton could not remember any therapeutic things done on the wards: "I have more of a sense of 'riding herd' on the imprisoned humans."[66]

Just as Byberry was stressful for the COs, it took its toll on members of the women's service unit. Warren Sawyer wrote home at the time, "No wonder that three girls cracked up from the unit and had to leave. One of the girls is in the hospital down town now for a complete rest. A fourth one left not long ago. We fellows have it easy compared to the girls."[67]

Some members of the women's service unit at Byberry worked with the Mental Hygiene Program of the CPS and helped produce its magazine, the *Attendant.*[68] They would also write some of the narratives that formed the basis for the National Mental Health Foundation's *Out of Sight, Out of Mind.*[69]

The MCC women's units were operated as summer units for college women. These units were organized very differently than the AFSC women's service unit at Byberry. The young women were supervised closely. Activities were tightly scheduled. Work was coordinated with educational, religious, and social events.

Goossen estimated that three hundred college women served at mental hospital units from 1943 to 1946.[70] Howard, Rhode Island, had a summer service unit of twenty-five women in 1944 and fifteen women and three men in 1946. Ypsilanti State Hospital had women's summer service units of thirty-six women in 1944 and fifteen women in 1945. At Cleveland State Hospital, eighteen women were

35. Mennonite women's summer service unit, CPS Unit no. 85, Howard, Rhode Island. (Mennonite Church USA Historical Committee and Archives, Goshen, Indiana)

recruited from Mennonite colleges to work in the infirmary in the summer of 1945. In 1946, twenty-two college women worked at the mental hospital. The MCC assigned a woman director and a male educational director for the summer unit. The woman director in 1945 was the registrar at Bethel College. In the summer of 1945, twenty-nine women were assigned to an MCC unit at Hudson River State Hospital in Poughkeepsie, New York.[71]

Edna Ramseyer, who had been the leader of the Howard women's unit the previous summer, was the director of the Poughkeepsie unit. She had worked with AFSC volunteers and refugee children in Spain and taught at the Mennonite Bluffton College. In the summer of 1943, she went to Goshen College to teach nutrition at the ill-fated foreign relief training program. Ramseyer had advocated for women to become involved with the CPS and was the inspiration behind the founding of the COGs.[72]

Of the twenty-nine women at the Poughkeepsie summer unit, twenty-seven were Mennonites, including twelve Old Mennonites and ten General Conference Mennonites, and two were Methodists.[73] Their ages ranged from eighteen to thirty-one; most were nineteen to twenty-two years of age. The majority of the women were college students, although a small number were grade school teachers. The women's schools included Goshen, Bethel, Bluffton, Messiah Bible, and Tabor colleges; Hesston Junior College; and Eastern Mennonite School. Two of the women had served at the Ypsilanti women's unit the previous summer, and one had been at the Howard, Rhode Island, unit.

The Poughkeepsie CPS unit had been established as a relief training unit for COs in their off-duty hours.[74] The women's unit was designed for women interested in relief training. The unit had a tight schedule. Women generally worked on the wards from 9:00 A.M. to 5:00 P.M., although they were sometimes called upon to fill in on other shifts. In the evenings, relief training was offered on Mondays, Bible classes were held Tuesdays, choir practice followed by church service occurred on Wednesdays, mental hygiene classes were offered on Thursdays, and vesper services were held on Sundays. Friday evenings were free, and there was organized recreation on Saturday evenings. COs and the women participated in most of the activities together. The women also had group devotion at 10:00 P.M. five nights of the week. Groups of the women took organized excursions to New York City, Vassar College, Lake Mohawk, Washington, D.C., the Catskill Mountains, and Hyde Park. Speakers also visited to meet with the women and the COs. A highlight of the summer for many women was when Eleanor Roosevelt visited to speak to the men's and women's units. This visit would become important in a public controversy involving the CPS men.

The women arrived at Poughkeepsie at a tense time. That May, the Hudson River State Hospital superintendent, Dr. John Ross, had fired four regular attendants after COs had accused them of abusing patients. A public controversy had erupted, with the American Legion in the middle, and had continued throughout that summer. The CPS assistant director, Bert Smucker, briefed the women on the controversy on the first evening most of them arrived and warned them that they might be viewed with suspicion. Later that evening the women met to come up with COG standards for working and living at the institution. The standards included: "Speak a greeting to any and everyone on the hospital campus, in the corridors, on the wards, and in the cafeteria"; "Be willing to do any kind of task, regardless of how menial or filthy"; "Be willing to mingle and eat with others in the dining room"; "Discuss first with your ward attendants any concerns you may have about unsatisfactory conditions"; and "Be at any time ready to give witness to what you believe."[75] The women resolved to follow a distinctively Mennonite way of dealing with the other employees.

Many of the regular women employees were standoffish toward the women when they first started working on the wards: "These women attendants decided to be very cold in their reception of the girls, to be very brief in responding to the girls' questions, and to give them as little help as possible in acquainting the girls with the work." The women kept following their COG standards, and after several weeks some of the regular attendants became convinced of their sincerity and started to act friendly to them: "The attendants expressed regret for their ugly reception of the girls working with them, and one attendant broke down and wept."[76] Several of the regular attendants explained that they thought the young women had come to the institution to spy on them and to create the same kind of trouble that COs had created on the male side of the institution. Despite the breakthrough with some attendants, there were others who remained cold toward the young women. One young woman reported that a charge always seemed to look for "something to find fault with": "I hate to have to ask her about anything; she is so critical and cross."[77]

Although the young women tried to be humble, friendly, and helpful with the regular attendants, it was not always easy for them to accept the ways of the regular attendants. Swearing and obscene language bothered them, although the cursing decreased over time. One of the women was surprised that regular employees did not say grace before meals: "At our tables the nurses and attendants never say any grace before beginning a meal. What attitude should one take toward that? It doesn't seem right to eat a meal without giving thanks for it." Another woman drew the line at getting cigarettes for a charge: "I'm afraid that the charge didn't appreciate the fact that I refused to go to the store to get cigarettes for her, although I tried to be as polite about it as possible."[78]

The young women did practically any and every kind of work on the wards: dressing, bathing, and feeding patients; cleaning floors and tables; escorting patients to appointments; supervising patient workers; giving haircuts and cutting toenails; sorting laundry; making beds; taking temperatures and pulses; filling out reports; and other parts of the daily routine. Some of the young women were frustrated at not being able to do more to help the patients. The culture of the institution emphasized custodial care and little else. One young woman commented, "The charge is very hard to work with. While she is friendly the ward is very disorganized and she put a wet blanket on any improvement one tried to make." Another wanted to take patients out of their straitjackets: "I'd like to be able to let patients out of camisoles, give them harmless things to do, take them for walks, etc. which just seems to be too much trouble for the attendants. I wasn't able to do much along that line."[79]

For many of the young women, the experience at Hudson River State Hospital confirmed their commitment to Mennonite principles: nonresistance and Christian love. Some also developed a deeper understanding of human nature and humanity. One young woman even discovered what would much later be described as the "social construction of humanness"—the idea that the social meaning of a person is not inherent in the qualities or characteristics of that person but dependent upon how others "construct" or define that person.[80] She reflected on the humanity of one of the "worst emaciated cases" on her ward: "The husband and cousin of one of our worst emaciated cases came today. We fixed the woman up and brought in the visitors. The husband kissed his wife— and when they parted his eyes were red. He watched her as I took her away with such a sorrowful look. To us, the woman was a poor creature, with no personality, no character—to them she was a person with a past. She was the most important person in the whole world to the[m], while we hardly knew she existed except to administer food and clothing."[81]

The women in the Poughkeepsie unit, along with the COs, developed a solidarity and sense of fellowship. This feeling was probably aided by the suspicion and hostility of some of the regular attendants on both the male and the female sides of the institution. In their work as attendants, the Mennonite women from different conferences and the Methodists did not differ much from each other. There were clear distinctions when it came to social lives, however. At least some of the women bemoaned the modern attitude of some of the other women and the CPS men: "I regret that the social life tends to take too modern a trend: folk games, square dancing, social dancing. Why can't Mennonite groups be considerate of all members instead of only the progressive ones?" Another said, "Many did not lead the simple lifestyle—attending movies, openly, frequently, etc."[82]

In discussing the women's service units, Goossen pointed to an underlying tension: "Throughout the war a creative tension existed between the COGs, who wanted to address human need as conscientious objectors in their own right, and church leaders, who utilized them to raise the esprit de corps of male conscientious objectors."[83] Clearly, some of the COs at Hudson River State Hospital did not have religious communion on their minds when they interacted with the members of the women's unit. As one woman noted, "CPS men are subject to so many temptations." For their part, most of the women were college age and like some people making the transition to adulthood anywhere—Mennonite or not: "Too many are not vitally enough interested in the real objective of the unit—adventure and social contacts with the CPS men motivates them."[84] The unit director, Edna Ramseyer, had consciously selected some women to be on the unit who had shown "some maladjustments in an area of their Christian and social living" in the hope that mental hospital work would be a "corrective measure."[85]

Whether MCC leaders viewed COGs in terms of increasing the "esprit de corps" of CPS men, it was clear that the women had a positive effect on the men where the summer service units were located. A history of the Hudson River State Hospital unit described the unit after the end of the summer: "The glamour of the summer had worn off; the women had gone; studies were getting to be an old thing; the men found out that novelty was being replace [sic] by routine." Melvin Gingerich referred to the improvement of the morale among CPS men at the Howard and Ypsilanti units when women's service units were established there.[86]

During the CPS, women generally played supportive roles to men, if they played any roles at all. When COs at Byberry established the Mental Hygiene Program of the CPS and then the National Mental Health Foundation, women would play a more prominent part.

◆　◆　◆

Toward the end of the CPS, Colonel Kosch of the Selective Service wrote mental hospital and training school superintendents, requesting reports on their CPS units: "While we have statistical summaries of man-days used and work accomplished we do not have an evaluation of the program based on the experiences and observations of the people directly connected with the units. What we would like is a frank and candid statement covering defects in organization or administration as well as the value of the work performed."[87] Of those superintendents who chose to write reports and whose reports are maintained in MCC, AFSC, and BSC archives, most were positive about the CPS and the COs.[88] E. H. Crawfis, superintendent of Cleveland State Hospital, wrote, "We believe that the C.P.S. Unit has been very worthwhile here at the hospital in the matter of assistance to our ward personnel." Arthur Noyes of Norristown State Hospital in Pennsylvania gave a similar assessment: "Almost without exception these men recognized the serious handicaps and contributed their services to the best of their ability." From Spring Grove State Hospital in Maryland, Silas W. Weltmer wrote, "During the operation of the unit forty-four men have worked in the hospital, and, as a group and individually, their service has been uniformly efficient and entirely satisfactory." R. E. Bushong from Lima State Hospital in Ohio had the following to say: "With practically no exceptions the men have been diligent, compatible, conscientious and well-behaved."[89]

Superintendents who were negative about the COs seemed to object to their general attitudes and pacifist beliefs. The Selective Service published a monograph containing the anonymous comments of superintendents about the COs in 1950.[90] One superintendent wrote, "In my opinion, Selective Service would have accomplished more by declaring these so-called conscientious objectors unfit for military service because of mental disorders and let it go at that. It is my further opinion that they are a group of men who are anarchistic in their thinking and general plan of living, and by and large are the most selfish group of men I have ever had dealings with." Another stated, "Personally, I feel that the C.O.'s are selfish and uncooperative. They resented working under rules and regulations. They were critical of the work of others. I feel that the problem of conscientious objectors, in general, when not founded on a recognized religious basis, in time of war should result in disenfranchisement. Not even the United States, as powerful as it is, can stand when its citizens remain divided and uncooperative, when threatened with danger of extinction from the outside world."[91]

In terms of their own positions, some superintendents had reasons for being unhappy with the COs. Some COs would create public uproars at the institutions to which they were assigned.

11

"The Exposé as a Progressive Tool"

The origins of *Out of Sight, Out of Mind* can be traced to the beginning of special service units at mental hospitals and training schools. Many COs were shocked by institutional conditions and dismayed by the treatment of patients. They told others about what they had observed at the institutions. Some went public with charges of squalid conditions and widespread abuse and would become embroiled in major controversies. By the time Civilian Public Service men had started organizing and editing narratives for *Out of Sight, Out of Mind,* the exposé had become a finely honed tool in the COs' hands.

COs at AFSC units were more likely to initiate exposés of institutions and to plan campaigns to reform institutional conditions than their counterparts elsewhere. Protests of all kinds were more common at American Friends Service Committee camps and units than the sections of the other church committees. No major exposés occurred at Brethren mental hospital and training school units. The public controversy surrounding Superintendent Neil Dayton at Mansfield State Training School, where a Brethren Service Committee unit was located, did not relate to institutional conditions, and COs there were only tangentially involved. Mennonites would find themselves in the middle of controversies at the institutions at which they served, but their involvement in public flare-ups was unintentional. Mennonite principles emphasized nonresistance, Christian love, and personal service, not confrontations with the state. Although not all COs would feel comfortable leading exposés of institutions, practically all units submitted observations and reports that would be used by the Mental Hygiene Program of the CPS.

◆　◆　◆

The first CPS mental hospital unit administered by the AFSC at Eastern State Hospital in Williamsburg, Virginia, had been open about a year when COs brought about a public investigation of the institution.[1] Founded in the late 1700s, the Williamsburg institution was the first public "lunatic asylum" in the United States.[2] Since arriving at the institution beginning in June 1942, many COs had been concerned about conditions at the mental hospital and the treatment of patients there. An article in the *Catholic Worker* on March 22, 1943, quoted from a letter by one of the CPS men there: "The low wages paid the attendants insured that in general only those who could not find work elsewhere worked here, and sympathetic treatment of the patients came close to being the exception rather than the rule. Not infrequently, we have seen patients treated with cruelty and brutality. Friction between us and some of these has caused many of us to seriously consider returning to camp at times."[3]

One of the COs at Williamsburg made friends with a non-CO, Marshall E. Suther Jr., who had worked at the hospital while awaiting induction into the military. Suther resigned from the hospital around late June 1943. He had a friend who was familiar with Eastern State Hospital and knew about conditions there. His friend introduced him to a lawyer who also was aware of problems at the institution. A group of COs met with Suther, his friend, and the lawyer and gave them specific information on the mental hospital. A meeting was arranged between Suther and Virginia governor Colgate Darden. Following that meeting, the governor had the state hospital commissioner, Dr. H. C. Henry, meet with Suther. Henry decided that the state hospital board should hear Suther's reports. Hearing what Suther had to say, the board launched an official investigation.

Colonel Kosch of the Selective Service became aware of the COs' charges against the institution. Right before hearings were held, he called Paul Comly French to inform him about the situation: "Colonel Kosch called me this morning and said the boys at the Williamsburg Hospital had asked the government of Virginia to investigate it on administrative structure and on the grounds that it was highly inefficient." Suspicious of CO troublemakers who threatened to bring negative public attention on the CPS, Kosch said that if the charges were unfounded he would send the COs to a government camp: "He said if their charges didn't stand up, he thought he might close the unit and send the men to Mancos. I think they are making a mistake in continuing to think of Mancos as a punitive center and a place to send all the boys that they don't like."[4] The stakes were high for the CPS men.

The state hospital board held hearings from July 29 to August 4. Suther, who had been inducted into the Marine Corps by that time, submitted a forty-three-page brief detailing charges that had also been given to the governor and the commissioner. At least four of the COs testified at the hearing, and as many as sixteen of the thirty-three COs in the AFSC unit testified or furnished information contained in the brief submitted by Suther. One CO, Hubert Taylor, a law graduate from Temple University, testified that he had been working in a ward for violent patients who were caged, and he had not been told what to do in case of a fire.

Another CO described how some patients on the ward on which he worked were forced to sleep on a urine-soaked floor and did not have blankets to keep themselves warm. Yet another reported the following incident:

> Some of the patients eat in a basement dining room, commonly called the hole. I helped supervise feeding the patients the first morning I was there. As the patients finished their meal and began returning to the ward, one lagged behind to pick up clothing. The charge attendant became highly irritated, slapped the patient and knocked him down. He then bent over and slapped him again. Next he lifted the patient's leg by his ankle and kicked him several times in the seat of his pants. The patient begged him to stop and finally the attendant let him go with the admonition—"that'll teach you to move the next time I speak to you."[5]

Others testified at the hearings as well. One woman who had worked as an attendant at Eastern for three months testified that she had observed another attendant abusing a patient. After the complaints were heard at the hearings, mental hospital officials were given the opportunity to respond. The main "rebuttal witness" was Dr. I. S. Ziass, clinical director of Eastern State Hospital, who denied the charges against the institution.

Dr. George W. Brown was the superintendent of the mental hospital. Seventy-four years of age, he had been Eastern's director for thirty-two years. Brown was represented at the hearings by attorney Ashton Dovell, the former Speaker of the Virginia House of Delegates. Dovell tried to impugn the testimony of the COs by arguing that they had not worked at the institution a sufficient length of time to be capable of passing judgment on the operation of the mental hospital. In addition, four of the COs admitted that they had used physical violence on the patients.

At the hearings, Western State Hospital in Staunton, Virginia, came up briefly. Wilma Virginia Clark, secretary to the registrar at the College of William and Mary, testified that her brother had been mistreated at that institution as well as at Eastern. Shortly after the hearings, the state hospital board invited the Reverend W. Carroll Brooke to testify on Western State Hospital at one of its regular meetings. Brooke had heard complaints about the hospital from men at the MCC unit there. According to a history of the unit, "The coming of the C.P.S. men with their Christian emphasis and testimony of existing conditions tended to supply the missing link for definite evidence against the hospital management. The greater part of evidence against the hospital was brought by the Rev. W. Carroll Brooke, Staunton Episcopal minister. Rev. Brooke referred to the CPS Unit and in particular to Landis Martin, Unit Leader, for a good part of his testimony."[6] At the state board meeting, Brooke said that the hospital needed more funds and that the superintendent, who was seventy-seven years old and had been superintendent for thirty-seven years, should be replaced.

Other stories appeared in Virginia papers in August 1943 that were not favorable to mental hospitals in the state.[7] On August 23, a story appeared about a nineteen-year-old woman who had been arraigned on charges of being a fugitive from Eastern State Hospital. The young woman described the hospital food as "garbage" and said that she received no medicine or medical care while at the institution. She said she would rather spend a year in jail than be returned to the mental hospital. Then, on August 26, a story in a Marion, Virginia, newspaper reported that an attendant at Southwestern State Hospital, Lane Kilby, had been indicted for manslaughter in the death of a patient at the institution. The indictment alleged that Kilby had struck the patient several times and then kicked him in the stomach. An autopsy concluded that the patient had died of peritonitis resulting from an irregular perforation of his small intestines.

On August 21, Superintendent Brown at Williamsburg launched what one newspaper called a "counter-attack" against the COs. In a written statement, he accused the COs of mistreating patients and argued that they had not proved their charges against other attendants or the mental hospital. He said that the investigation had not given adequate attention to the hospital's defense. Charges of neglect, he maintained, referred to neglect on the part of the COs, which violated institutional policy: "Perhaps the most rigid and inviolable of this hospital's regulations is the one referring to the handling of patients. Any mistreatment of patients, or even suspicion of such mistreatment, is followed by immediate dismissal of the attendant and in some instances even persecution by law."[8] Brown called for the immediate removal of the CPS unit at Eastern State Hospital.

Released with Brown's statement was a resolution of Peninsula Post no. 39 of the American Legion, condemning the COs: "We call upon the administration of the Eastern State hospital to rid itself of these men at once, and in the event this cannot be promptly done that they be placed under military discipline so long as they remain with the hospital."[9] The Legionnaires said the COs should be replaced at the mental hospital by wounded veterans of the current war. This idea was perhaps the most novel solution to the problem of staff shortages at mental hospitals proposed during World War II. Post no. 39 indicated that it would present its resolution to the state convention of the American Legion opening the next day.

Two days later, H. C. Henry, head of the state hospital system, issued a clear rebuke to Superintendent Brown. In a letter released to the press on August 23, Henry expressed his disagreement with Brown on the need for COs at the mental hospital and reminded him that his position ran counter to his "previous attitude." He also took exception to Brown's complaints about the investigation: "My recollection is that you were allowed all the time you desired, and after the testimony was closed on the early morning of August 4, the chairman asked whether there was any more testimony to be presented on whether anyone else present desired to testify. I feel certain the board, even now, will hear any further testimony you may wish to offer. In fact, the investigation has continued since we were in Williamsburg, and has not been concluded yet."[10]

The chairman of the state hospital board, state senator Morton G. Goode, expressed his surprise at Brown's statement. Both he and Governor Darden also sent telegrams to the American Legion, stating that it would be unwise to remove the COs from Eastern State Hospital and that doing so would "unnecessarily cripple our hospitals during this dire emergency." On August 24, American Legion Post 39 withdrew its resolution calling for the removal of COs at Eastern State Hospital and their replacement by wounded soldiers. "Legion Steers Clear of Fight on Hospital" read the headline of an Associated Press article.[11]

Then, on August 30, a petition signed by 112 workers at Eastern State Hospital was submitted to the governor and the state hospital board. The signers claimed that they represented 94 percent of the staff at the mental hospital. The petition asked for the immediate removal of the COs who had testified at the hearings and the gradual removal of the remaining COs within a month. It explained why it had been submitted: "Firstly, in the interest of greater harmony, efficiency and a sincere desire for the better welfare of the patients at Eastern State hospital, and, secondly, as a testimony to our loyalty, respect and complete agreement with Dr. Brown's opinion."[12]

The state hospital board issued a report on its investigation on September 9. It immediately dismissed Superintendents Brown of Eastern State Hospital and J. S. DeJarnette of Western State Hospital. Brown was offered a position as a consulting physician at Eastern, and DeJarnette was allowed to remain in charge of the "DeJarnette sanitarium." The board's report had kind words to say about DeJarnette: "The considered care of the patients at Western State Hospital has been the major purpose of his life." The report added, "However, the Western State hospital has grown to an institution of more than 2,300 patients, the largest institution in the state of Virginia. The magnitude of its operation is appalling. Dr. DeJarnette is a man of action and tries to direct most of the details in connection with his hospital. At his age he should not be required to do so, nor allowed to undertake to do so."

The state hospital board acknowledged the thirty-two years of service of Dr. Brown, but stated that he was "indifferent in cooperation and apparently uninterested in the plans for improvement and progress which the board and the commissioner's office for some time have been endeavoring to carry into effect." The board's report said, "The cumulative effect of all of the evidence, together with Dr. Brown's attitude leads to but one conclusion: namely, that the Eastern State hospital under the present management is not capable of making any improvement." Brown's defiance contributed to his dismissal, and it is unclear whether he could have saved his job if he had handled the investigation differently.

The report's findings indicated that charges of cruelty at Eastern had been denied and that no case of gross cruelty had been proven. However, four of the complaining witnesses, COs, had admitted using physical violence against patients. The board recommended their removal and the dismissal of the night supervisor, "who has a very imperfect understanding of his responsibilities . . . and is in no way qualified to hold an important supervisory position."[13] It also indicated that charges against an assistant physician and nurse supervisor be inquired into by the next superintendent. The board's report made a number of additional recommendations for the operation of the state's mental hospitals and colonies for the feebleminded, including the Petersburg colony for Negro feebleminded. One recommendation called for shorter working hours for doctors, nurses, and attendants. This suggestion would later prove to be ironic when COs refused to work seventy-six-hour workweeks at Williamsburg, and the Selective Service, NSBRO, and the AFSC would become involved in the controversy.

Dr. DeJarnette accepted his dismissal in stride: "Dr. DeJarnette, 77, said he supposed he was getting too old for the duties." Dr. Brown initially withheld comment on his dismissal but later assailed the state hospital board's actions. In a statement released on September 16, he reviewed his accomplishments during thirty-two years as superintendent and charged that the board's report was full of inaccuracies.[14] He accused the board of ignoring the "conscientious objector problem" and alleged that the public had been misled about the facts of the situation.

On October 6, the state hospital board recommended to Governor Darden a major increase in the state's budget for mental institutions for capital improvements and the addition of medical, nursing, and attendant staff.[15] Years later, COs at the mental hospitals in Virginia would report problems there.

Regardless of whether the COs' actions resulted in any lasting improvements at Virginia's mental hospitals and colonies for the feebleminded, they brought widespread public attention to institutional conditions and abuses and succeeded in having "old-school" superintendents dismissed from Eastern and Western state hospitals. Four COs at Eastern were singled out for removal after admitting to harsh, even violent, treatment of patients, but the AFSC unit survived.

The COs at the AFSC unit at Eastern used tactics that would be refined by COs at other institutions and then perfected by the Mental Hygiene Program of the CPS and the National Mental Health Foundation: carefully document conditions and abuses and find non-COs to support the charges. The COs at the MCC unit at Western reported their experiences to a non-Mennonite minister, who, in turn, made the charges public. It is not a coincidence that COs at AFSC and MCC units responded differently to what they found at the institutions. It reflected different worldviews on how to respond to evils in the world and especially evils committed by the state.

Eastern State Hospital at Williamsburg was the first institution exposed by COs. Next would come Cleveland State Hospital.

◆   ◆   ◆

An AFSC unit was opened at Cleveland State Hospital in December 1942. The Cleveland institution had been established in 1855, and many of its buildings had been built in the 1800s.[16] In 1945, it held twenty-eight hundred patients, six hundred more than its official capacity.

The CO unit had rocky relationships with the hospital's administration almost from the start. By March 1943, two of the COs had been given "severe workhouse sentences and fines" and dismissed from service at the hospital for violating a "blackout ordinance," and the superintendent, Dr. Hans P. Lee, had refused a request from the unit to reconsider his harsh punishment. According to the AFSC assistant director, Leland Bullen, the COs had been given an attractive picture of work at the institution prior to going there, but arrangements for the men were terribly inadequate. Men had to be in by "an-as-yet-undefined bedtime" every night, were provided no instruction prior to starting their jobs, and would not be given sick time until they had worked at the institution for six months. Further, the mental hospital staff members put in charge of the COs were far from friendly or welcoming: "Dr. Lee has delegated our supervision to subordinates who have been hostile from the first."[17]

Robert Cox arrived at Cleveland State Hospital from the AFSC work camp at Big Flats, New York, on June 18, 1943. He and Willard Hetzel were replacements for the two disciplined COs. Cox's first assignment at the institution was in Ward B, the violent ward, and he continued to work there throughout his time at Cleveland State except for occasions when he filled in on other short-staffed wards. Prior to coming to the hospital, Cox was aware of problems between the regular employees and the COs. Once he got to the institution, he learned of the reasons for the difficult relations: "It was evident that most of the difficulty was a result of the conscientious objectors reporting each case of maltreatment suffered by the patients at the hands of other attendants, as instructed in the Department of Welfare's instruction booklet. The natural result was that many regular attendants distrusted the C.P.S. men and they lost faith in the hospital administration

when they saw nothing was done to change the attitude and action of the attendants toward the patients but rather they, the conscientious objectors, were put to
work elsewhere in the hospital." Cox observed the first of many incidents of abuse
within his first week at the mental hospital:

> The first mistreatment of patients I was to witness occurred as I was attending
> the patients on their way to Chapel on the first Sunday of my work. As the men
> approached the Chapel one patient was ordered to "shut up" by Robert Adams, a
> regular attendant, who immediately supported his command with two blows on
> the back of the patient's head with a closed hand. This later proved to be a very
> minor incident but remains symbolic of the continual "Damn it, do as I tell you, or
> else" attitude expressed toward the patients by the majority of the hospital staff.[18]

Cox would observe many worse incidents of abuse during his relatively brief
time at the institution. One of the most abusive attendants was a charge, Hayden
Blake, who mistreated patients himself or had a worker patient do the dirty work
for him: "Upon returning a patient, who had caused trouble in the patient's dining
room, to ward E, he was kicked in the groin by Hayden Blake, charge attendant
on ward E. Blake was known to frequently have a sore, swollen hand from hitting
the patients although he had a large negro patient called 'Eckles' who was usually
used to forcibly disciplining the patients on ward E."[19] Cox discussed mistreatment at the mental hospital with the chief male supervisor, Leslie Mugford, during two lengthy conversations. Mugford said he was aware of the mistreatment
but felt he could not dismiss abusive employees because he could not find replacements for them.[20]

COs reported many instances of abuse to hospital authorities. The institution's
superintendent, Dr. Lee, was perplexing to the COs. Not only would he refuse to
do anything about abusive attendants, but he also retained a CO who was unsuitable for work at the mental hospital. This CO had admitted to the superintendent
that he was hot-tempered and that he had beaten a patient. He made two requests
to return to a work camp. Lee refused to allow him to transfer.

Eventually, COs took their complaints about the treatment of patients at Cleveland State Hospital to Rev. Dr. Dores R. Sharpe, executive director of the Cleveland
Baptist Association, and Walter Lerch, a reporter for the *Cleveland Press*.[21] Lerch
ran with the story. In October 1943, the first of what would become a long series
of articles, features, and editorials condemning abuses at the institution was published in the *Press*. For his part, Sharpe made sure that conditions stayed in the
public eye and were not swept under the rug by public officials. The exposé would
go on for more than two years and would eventually reach the national media.

Incidents concerning the mental hospital in November would lend credibility to the COs' charges. In early November, a warrant was issued for the arrest of attendant Hayden Blake by a municipal court. COs had reported Blake for abusing patients to administrators on at least three occasions. The warrant was issued for Blake's arrest after a complaint was filed, supported by sworn affidavits, by the son of a sixty-year-old partially blind patient whom Blake had allegedly beaten and kicked. When police attempted to arrest Blake at the mental hospital on November 4, he was nowhere to be found. Hospital officials, who had been informed about the warrant, said that he had left the hospital. CO Bob Cox saw Hayden speaking with the male supervisor Mugford an hour and a half after the police had left. A little more than two weeks later, another patient wandered away from the hospital, threw himself in front of a train, and was killed.[22]

Shortly after the first stories about Cleveland State Hospital appeared, the state welfare director, Herbert Mooney, announced that he would investigate charges against the hospital. In an editorial on October 30, the *Cleveland Press* called for an independent investigation of the mental hospital. Immediately afterward, a group of three hundred Protestant ministers associated with the Cleveland Ministerial Association endorsed an investigation of the institution by a committee of persons unrelated to the control of the state hospitals. Then, in the second week of November, Mooney and Lee responded to the complaints about the mental hospital. In a written report, Mooney stated that the stories on the mental hospital were "gross exaggerations": "These printed charges resulted apparently from unreliable sources. The department feels very deeply that as a result of the sensationalism associated with the story, not only was the entire staff of the hospital placed in a cloud of suspicion in the public mind, but unnecessary anxiety was created among relatives and friends of patients." Mooney also said that Dr. Lee took issue with how he had been quoted in the paper. Here was the quote: "Yes, we have beatings. But now, during the war, we have to employ anyone who is willing to work here and we can't get the best. We know some of the attendants are rough with patients and beat them. When this happens and we have proof, we fire them. But we can't accept the word of a patient. They will call us murderers at any time. The word of several patients is better. But evidence from a sane witness is best of all." Sharpe criticized the state report as a whitewash and reiterated demands for an independent investigation of the institution.[23]

On November 10, Superintendent Lee moved to immediately dismiss COs on the AFSC unit whom he said "make trouble." These COs included two men who were prepared to testify against the fugitive attendant Hayden Blake. The following day, the *Cleveland Press* published a strong editorial condemning Lee's actions: "Dr. Lee should be removed."[24] Dr. George Stevenson, medical director of the National Committee for Mental Hygiene, was at a meeting in Cleveland at the time and said to the paper that COs had been among the most reliable employees at the mental hospitals at which they were placed and that he was surprised they were to be dismissed from Cleveland State Hospital.[25] Lee then asked the Selective Service to close the entire CPS unit. Both the Selective Service and the AFSC agreed to pull out from Cleveland State. The AFSC stated that mutual distrust between the administration and the COs made it best to move the men.[26] The CPS unit closed on November 30, 1943. It would not be the end of the COs' involvement with Cleveland State Hospital.

Responding to publicity surrounding Cleveland State Hospital, Governor John W. Bricker created the Committee on the Mental Health Program to study Ohio's system on December 23, 1943.[27] Hal Griswold, an attorney and former state welfare director, was appointed to chair the committee.

The men from the Cleveland unit were dispersed to different camps and units. Bob Cox and Will Hetzel were transferred to Byberry. Others went to Middletown State Hospital, Iowa State Hospital, and elsewhere. Justin Reese, who had been sent to a work camp at Gatlinburg, Tennessee, wondered if he was being blacklisted for his role in the exposé of Cleveland State Hospital.[28]

Shortly after the removal of the Cleveland CPS unit, Reese started working on a report of the COs' observations at the state hospital. He wrote other former members of the unit and asked them to send him accounts of their experiences. Then when they sent him something he needled them to add details. He wanted to write a thorough and specific report. Both Bob Cox and his wife, Martha, who had worked on the women's side of the institution while Cox was there, sent narratives to Reese. Reese's plan was to have Sharpe release the report to the public: "I'm going to Cleveland the first week in March and dump the stuff probably in Dr. Sharpe's lap and let him present it to the committee under proper auspices. At least that's what I think will happen. We have the idea down here that it will be far better to have the report sponsored by men like Sharpe than to be submitted unsponsored. Sharpe doesn't know this yet, but I'm writing him later to tell him how he can make another magnificent contribution."[29]

Reese's report was completed in late February or early March. It was a five-page single-spaced report with a three-page "Resume of Attendants' Activities" attached. The report started with a strong condemnation of the administration of Cleveland State Hospital, which was often referred to as Newburgh: "It is impossible in an institution where patient abuse is as widespread as it is at Newburgh for the authorities not to be aware of its existence. Moreover, the authorities in this institution had been made aware of this." The first part of the report described one abuse after another, including incidents that had resulted in the deaths of patients.

Then it reviewed the lack of treatment for patients, the deteriorated physical plant, and the poor conditions: "The daily routine for most patients is a hell of empty monotony."[30] The attached "résumé" went through a list of seventeen attendants, both men and women, and described incidents in which they had been observed abusing patients.

On March 7, 1944, Sharpe sent Reese's report to the chairman of the governor's special committee, Griswold, and the state welfare director, Mooney. The headline of the *Cleveland Press* story written by Walter Lerch read: "Church Leader Cites Brutality to Mentally Ill: Dr. Sharpe's Report Says State Hospital Conditions Worse." In the story, Sharpe said that the COs' claims had been corroborated by patients' relatives who had come forward and by evidence he had gathered personally. Reese was quoted in the article as saying that "brutality, neglect and calloused indifference are widespread." The article noted that Superintendent Lee was not available for comment. An editorial in the *Press* that same day urged Governor Bricker's committee to conduct a full investigation of Dr. Sharpe's charges.[31]

Less than a week later, Sharpe released a second report on food and food handling at Cleveland State Hospital. The headline to a *Cleveland Press* article on this report was: "Claims Mentally Ill Undernourished: Charges Filed by Church Federation President." This thirteen-page report had been written by Donald Knoke, a former CO at the institution. Food at the institution was described as overly starchy and lacking in quality and variety. Little meat was served to patients, and when it was, it was usually "mouldy [sic] wieners, partially-spoiled fish and very old salt pork."[32] Rats and cockroaches infested food preparation areas.

Justin Reese received an early release from the CPS, on April 16, 1944. He continued to work with Sharpe on the ongoing investigations and exposés of Cleveland State Hospital. Reese was hired by the National Committee for Mental Hygiene and later appointed executive secretary of the Citizens Mental Health Committee by reform-minded governor Luther Youngdahl of Minnesota.[33] He later held positions in Indiana, New Jersey, and Connecticut.

Hans Lee held on as superintendent of Cleveland State Hospital until July 1944. He resigned his position and asked to be appointed to a medical or psychiatric position somewhere else in the state hospital system. His resignation coincided with the resignation of a staff physician at the institution, Luisa Kerschbaumer, who had just accepted a position in St. Louis. Upon leaving the mental hospital, Kerschbaumer leveled a series of charges against Lee and the institution itself. She had encountered difficulties obtaining medications and sterilized medical supplies and said that the staff shortage at the institution was serious. She frequently found wards without attendants and patients put in charge of other patients. Worse for Dr. Lee, Dr. Kerschbaumer alleged that the superintendent had threatened to fire her if she made public comments about mistreatment at the mental hospital. When she told him she was leaving, he asked her "to be 'loyal' to him and go out quietly without saying anything."[34] At Sharpe's urging, Dr. Kerschbaumer delayed her departure to St. Louis to present her story to Hal Griswold, the chairman of the state hospital commission.

Dr. Lee's dismissal or resignation was probably a foregone conclusion. Dr. Frank Tallman had been recruited from Michigan to assume the new post of commissioner of mental diseases for Ohio.[35] Tallman was known as a reformer. He officially started this position on August 1. Lee was replaced as superintendent of Cleveland State Hospital by Dr. E. H. Crawfis, who had held a position at Lima State Hospital for the Criminally Insane.

On November 20, 1944, Hal Griswold submitted to Governor Bricker a fifty-four-page report, *Report of the Governor's Committee on the Mental Health Program in Ohio.* The report did not address abuses at Cleveland State Hospital but did contain far-reaching recommendations for Ohio's mental health system: a $36,710,000 construction program for the mentally ill, the epileptic, the mentally deficient, and others; a major upgrading of the staffing at institutions; and an expansion of outpatient and community programs. By this time, Bricker was on his way out of office. He had been Wendell Wilkie's running mate in the unsuccessful presidential campaign against Roosevelt, and had not run for reelection as governor of Ohio. He was succeeded as governor by Frank J. Lausche, who had pledged to do something about Ohio's mental hospitals.[36]

Then, in early 1945, an event occurred that would thrust Cleveland State Hospital into the national spotlight. In the Court of Common Pleas, Criminal Branch, County of Cuyahoga, State of Ohio, a grand jury was formed during the January–May term to investigate the institution. The person appointed to serve as foreman of the fifteen-member grand jury was none other than Rev. Dr. Dores R. Sharpe. The grand jury called approximately seventy-five witnesses to testify and examined additional evidence. Many of the witnesses had been COs at the CPS unit at the mental hospital. Bob Cox was one of the COs who received a subpoena to appear at the grand jury and testified on March 9, 1945.[37] He was questioned about the treatment of patients, food at the hospital, and the actions of administrators when informed about abuses. The grand jury did not receive statements from patients themselves because their statements were not accepted in a court of law.[38]

At the end of March, the grand jury handed down indictments of three former attendants at Cleveland State Hospital who had fled the institution, including Hayden Blake, and issued an eight-page single-spaced report that indicted the institution itself. The grand jury condemned the hospital in harsh words: "The Grand

Jury is shocked beyond words that a so-called civilized society would allow fellow human beings to be mistreated as they are at Cleveland State Hospital especially since these helpless people have no one to speak or act for them except the society whose wards they are. If society fails them, they indeed are they of all men most miserable. And society has failed them. No enlightened community dare tolerate the conditions that exist in our Cleveland State Hospital." The grand jury's report reviewed brutality and assaults, the suspicious deaths of patients, weapons used on patients, and the use of violent patients for "strong-arm" purposes. It faulted the previous administration for dismissing the COs "for no other reason than that they carried out the rules and regulations of the institution" and characterized attendants as "misfits and riffraff." The grand jury made a series of recommendations for the hospital, including the "retirement" of male supervisor Leslie Mugford and other staff. It concluded its report with these words:

> We indict the uncivilized social system in which the first instance has enabled such an intolerable and barbaric practice to fasten itself upon the people and which in the second instance permits it to continue.
>
> We are told these inhuman conditions have long existed. If this be so, we indict all those who have abetted—or even tolerated—such foul treatment of these unfortunate ill, even as history will indict us if we fail to redress this ancient and inexcusable wrong.
>
> The Grand Jury condemns the whole sociopolitical system that today allows this unholy thing to exist in our State of Ohio. The responsibility is widespread and it must be met. . . . All must, moreover, share in the responsibility for instituting immediate redress of this long-standing and terrible injustice.[39]

Judge Samuel H. Silbert accepted the grand jury's report and thanked members for their service and courage. In concluding his remarks to the grand jury, he said, "A condition has been tolerated here which smacks of Nazi concentration camps."[40] He would not be the last to make the comparison between American institutions and Nazi concentration camps.

The grand jury's recommendations for Cleveland State Hospital were not binding on state officials. It had no authority over public agencies. However, a grand jury's findings and conclusions carried special weight with the public. Reports by conscientious objectors who had avoided military service or stories by investigative journalists or "muckrakers" could be dismissed. It was harder to question the credibility of a panel with subpoena powers appointed by a court of law. In the spring of 1946, Albert Deutsch and Albert Maisel would publish scathing exposés of state mental hospitals in *PM* newspaper and *Life* magazine with information provided by the Mental Hygiene Program of the CPS. Both would quote extensively from the grand jury's report and use its words to demonstrate the horrors of institutions. A story and editorial in the *Cleveland Press* on May 4, 1946, reported on the *Life* article and lauded the efforts of reporter Walter Lerch: "Mr. Lerch's persevering investigations set in motion a crusade which was joined by Dr. D. R. Sharpe, executive secretary of the Cleveland Baptist Association, and finally awakened the conscience of the entire state."[41] It all started with a group of COs.

The newly appointed commissioner of mental diseases, Tallman, and Cleveland State Hospital superintendent Crawfis were committed to reform. Crawfis had overseen a Mennonite Central Committee unit at the Lima institution and had been pleased with the work of the COs there. He discussed the possibility of reestablishing a CPS unit with the state's Welfare Department and then the MCC. In a "History of CPS Unit #69," Crawfis provided background on the initial AFSC unit at the institution: "This group did not seem to adjust well in the hospital and there was constant friction between members of the unit and regular employees. Finally, as a result of this difficulty the group was withdrawn in December 1943." Crawfis wanted Mennonites: "Because of familiarity with Mennonite Groups, who had made a satisfactory adjustment in hospitals we desired such a group and Selective Service was agreeable to such an arrangement."[42]

On April 18, 1945, an MCC unit was opened at Cleveland State Hospital.[43] After careful consideration by Crawfis and the MCC, Paul L. Goering from the MCC unit at Howard, Rhode Island, was selected to be assistant director of the unit. During the time the unit was open, forty-five COs served at Cleveland State Hospital, in addition to forty women on summer service units in 1945 and '46.

Although Superintendent Crawfis had met with regular employees to explain why he was inviting COs back to the institution, there was a great deal of tension with these employees when the COs arrived. As assistant director, Goering had been briefed on the experience of the AFSC unit at the institution and knew what to expect: "The main challenge as unit leader was to re-establish the second unit in a setting where one had previously been closed out, removed, and had attracted considerable notoriety and publicity." He described the tension between the COs and the regular employees: "They were very suspicious of us. Their antagonism was overt . . . They assumed we would be carrying notebooks and writing down episodes of abuse that we saw." The other attendants would not sit with the COs during meals. Goering recalled a visit to the unit by Colonel Kosch and other Selective Service officials. The regular employees were "amazed" and "irate" to see men in military uniform eating with the COs. Some COs were only vaguely aware of the history of the AFSC unit but felt the hostility from other employees nevertheless.[44]

Even after all of the publicity and the grand jury investigation, the mental hospital continued to have problems with attendants. Vernon Rocke reported that patients cowered when COs came near them when the unit first arrived and described the nature of regular attendants hired by the institution: "The hospital has to depend on parolled [sic] prisoners, drunkards, and drifters to too great an extent, as a supply from which to draw their attendants. This is evidenced by a personnel turnover at this hospital of over 100% every ten months." Leonard Boehs recalled seeing attendants beat patients with a strap or bare hands during his time at the MCC unit.[45]

The Mennonite CPS men were assigned to the Male Infirmary and given full responsibility for the care of the 365 "infirm and untidy" patients there.[46] A CO supervisor was put in charge of the entire building, which included a ward for tubercular patients. As the closing of the unit approached in March 1946, the COs were spread throughout the institution to minimize disruptions to any single building. Most of the women on the summer service units were assigned to Pellow Building, the Female Infirmary.

Assistant director Goering and other COs had confidence in Dr. Crawfis and his commitment to improving the mental hospital. Vernon Rocke, who served as supervisor of the Male Infirmary for a period of time, commented, "Dr. Crawfis is constantly seeking information from CPS men which will help him improve conditions within the hospital."[47] When COs complained to Dr. Crawfis about the quality of meals served to patients, he assigned a CO to the kitchen over the protests of the dietician, who quit her job within two weeks. This confidence in Superintendent Crawfis led Goering to run afoul of the Reverend Dores R. Sharpe.

Sharpe expected the MCC unit to keep him informed of conditions at the institution, as COs on the AFSC unit had done. Goering felt that he could bring any problem to Dr. Crawfis and was loyal to him. He believed that he did not need to go outside of the institution to resolve anything that came up. When Sharpe failed to receive reports from Goering, he complained directly to MCC headquarters in Akron, Pennsylvania. An official from the MCC went to Cleveland to chastise Goering:

> I had not maintained contact with Dr. Sharpe, the Baptist minister, the head of the Baptist Federation of Cleveland who had been very interested in the hospital and who helped the previous unit expose the conditions there. I was introduced to him when I came, and he let me know that he wanted information on conditions in the hospital and he was my ally and he was very concerned about the hospital and wanted me to keep him informed. Well, I was not, I had not training and didn't know where to go for help in maneuvering and relating to him and

being loyal to Dr. Crawfis who was making an honest effort to reverse, to change conditions. And I had an open door to him. I could see the superintendent at any time that I wanted to. And I simply wasn't sophisticated enough to give, to follow up my contacts with Dr. Sharpe. . . . I sensed no problem, that is, that would lead to an exposé because the superintendent was working. In retrospect, I saw that I mishandled it. I should have kept Dr. Sharpe informed. . . . He wanted to know what had happened. He thought I was selling out.[48]

Dr. Crawfis had wanted an MCC unit for a reason. Mennonites were more inclined than other COs to work through official lines of authority. Dr. Sharpe, the unofficial watchdog of Cleveland State Hospital, would not accept being left out in the cold.

Sharpe, who had become president of the newly formed Ohio Mental Health Association, was honored at a luncheon on June 6, 1946, for his efforts in reforming Ohio's mental hospitals. Louis B. Seltzer, editor of the *Cleveland Press*, served as toastmaster. Testimonials were given by Governor Lausche and Justin Reese of the National Committee for Mental Hygiene as well as former COs at the AFSC unit and civic leaders and public officials. Sharpe responded to the testimonials: "Dr. Sharpe, in response to the testimonials, emphasized that the real testimony was that there was an aroused citizenry and urged that they continue to keep themselves informed regarding the problem of mental health. He warned that reform was only begun and that in reality much needed to be done. Dr. Sharpe further stated that due credit should go to the C.P.S. unit which was responsible for bringing out authentic information."[49] Nine members of the MCC unit were sure to attend the luncheon.

The MCC unit closed in August 1946.

Journalist Albert Deutsch published an exposé of Cleveland State Hospital in April 1946 as part of his "Shame of the States" series in the newspaper *PM*. He was impressed by the openness of the "frank and earnest" thirty-five-year-old superintendent, Ewing H. Crawfis. Crawfis candidly told Deutsch: "We have all we can do right now to turn this into a decent custodial institution. We haven't even started to give these patients adequate medical care." Deutsch also interviewed Governor Lausche for his story. The governor told him about his three-million-dollar program to build new mental health facilities in Ohio but said that he did not think that he could get the legislature to approve increases for staff wages at the current time. In a 1948 book based on his newspaper series, Deutsch commented on some of the events that had occurred in the months following the original publication of his exposés. He described a recent incident at Cleveland State Hospital in which three patients were scalded to death by another patient on a ward guarded by an ex-patient attendant. Then he added: "Not long ago Dr. Frank Tallman resigned as Ohio's State Mental Hygiene Commissioner in despair; he had tried hard but unsuccessfully to bring about fundamental reforms in the state hospital system."[50]

◆ ◆ ◆

Mennonites at an MCC unit at Mount Pleasant State Hospital in Iowa found themselves in the middle of an awkward controversy surrounding an exposé of the institution in 1944. The unit had opened in August 1943 on the recommendation of John Mosemann of the MCC, who had visited the institution to examine facilities, working conditions, and arrangements on January 13, 1943.[51] Mosemann had noted at the time that the superintendent, Dr. Adolph Soucek, was cautious about public reactions to the presence of COs at the mental hospital but that Colonel McLean of the Selective Service had obtained a commitment from the American Legion and local unions that they would not agitate against a CPS unit.

On August 1, 1944, Earl Leinbach, assistant director of the CPS unit, sent an urgent telegram to Albert Gaeddert at the MCC headquarters in Akron, Pennsylvania: "NEWSPAPER ARTICLE HAS CAUSED SERIOUS TROUBLE IMMEDIATE ASSISTANCE IMPERITIVE [SIC] SUGGEST TELEPHONE CALL." This telegram was followed almost immediately by a second one from Leinbach to Gaeddert: "DES MOINES REGISTER ARTICLE WRITTEN BY METHODIST MINISTER AFTER LISTENING TO SOME OF OUR GROUP COMPLAIN HAD CREATED A REAL PROBLEM WITH HOSPITAL ADMINISTRATION AND REGULAR EMPLOYEES. MAY OR MAY NOT BE SERIOUS. LETTER FOLLOWS. REUTER HERE WEDNESDAY. BEECHY HERE THURSDAY." Gaeddert responded by telegram the same day: "DEPENDING ON YOU TO CARRY THINGS THROUGH WITH BEECHY AND REUTER. IF YOU FEEL FURTHER HELP NECESSARY NOTIFY US. AWAITING DETAILS. CALL D.J. FISHER, KALONA IF NECESSARY."[52]

In early July, a conference was held at Iowa Wesleyan College, which was located not far from the mental hospital. On the afternoon of July 6, several attendees at the conference paid a visit to Mount Pleasant State Hospital to meet with members of the CPS unit. Leinbach was on furlough at the time. They met with ten COs and two of their wives. The visiting group was curious about the work and conditions at the hospital. Some members of the CPS group gave them an earful:

> There were a number of individuals in the group of C.P.S. present, who were very free in talking and were very ready to denounce the hospital; including hospital doctors, regular employees, care of patients, and other vital subjects. They did such an effective job of painting a black picture of the hospital that the ministers were immediately up-in-arms and wanted to do something about the conditions. They immediately wanted to fill the papers with articles exposing these

conditions. They were warned that—they must not do it! It was explained that it would be very bad for us and would not solve the problem.[53]

Nothing happened for several weeks. Then, on July 31, the *Des Moines Register* published a letter to the editor by one of the ministers who had visited the CPS unit, L. L. Dunnington, pastor of the First Methodist Church of Iowa City. Dunnington launched a scathing attack on the mental hospital: "Something is radically wrong at Mount Pleasant State Hospital." He explained that he, Dr. Kirby Page of LeHabra, California, and Dr. Carroll Hildebrand, professor of philosophy at DePew University, had met with a group of Mennonite COs at the institution: "These Mennonite young people are clean, fine looking, outstanding Americans." Dunnington said that the COs had given the visitors information about Mount Pleasant, and he proceeded to make a series of charges against the institution. The charges could have been made about the vast majority of the mental hospitals or training schools to which COs had been assigned: No instruction was given to the COs prior to working on the wards. Doctors were poorly trained and did some "strange things." The buildings were acceptable and the grounds beautiful, but patients were not getting adequate care. The regular employees were poorly paid and were "undesirable and incompetent." According to Dunnington, "One of the Mennonite helpers said that he removed one of the help only recently who was so drunk that he had passed out completely."[54]

As soon as Dunnington's letter appeared, it created problems for the COs: "It has created a very tense situation with the regular employees, with whom we have enjoyed very good relations so far. The hospital administration is also very much in the air about it."[55] Leinbach maintained close contact with Albert Gaeddert of the MCC. Dick Reuter of NSBRO visited the MCC unit on August 2, and Ralph Beechy, MCC central states regional director, had a regular visit scheduled for the next day.

Superintendent Soucek was indignant about the charges, and he and the hospital's board wanted the COs to issue a statement refuting Dunnington's letter. Soucek drafted a statement for the COs: "Rev. Dunnington is using us for purposes of sensationalism against our will, by misrepresenting isolated, informal statements of fragmentary information, and by crediting to our group certain statements which none of us ever made, he is presenting to the public a false picture of conditions at the Mt. Pleasant State Hospital." Leinbach did not want to criticize Dunnington, especially in the press. Reuter of NSBRO told the unit that he thought that it was not their place to make such a statement.[56]

The COs disputed some of the statements made by Dunnington but thought that his charges were largely true. What bothered them was that he chose to publish his statements in a newspaper: "Half of our group seem to more or less agree with the article but of course do not approve the fact that it was published." Leinbach himself did not feel comfortable challenging the mental hospital or raising a public stink: "I for myself have always tried to uphold the institution and work with it in its understaffed and handicapped condition. . . . While I do not feel that conditions here are ideal, I am not sure that I would care to challenge the conditions and condemn them."[57]

The unit desperately wanted to mend fences with the administration and the regular employees. They decided to issue an apology. On August 3, Leinbach sent a letter to the Board of Control of State Institutions: "We authorized no such statements; they were made against our will and wishes and we regret the publication of such articles. We wish to assure you that the publications do not reflect the feelings of our unit. We have enjoyed and appreciated the co-operation of the Hospital Administration and employees, and their willingness to help us adjust to our new jobs of serving the patients at Mt. Pleasant."[58]

The following day, the thirty or so members of the CPS unit sent a letter addressed to all hospital employees. At the beginning, it stated, "We wish to show you our deepest concerns and regrets." The last paragraph of the letter read: "May we again assure you that the unit is truly, most appreciative for the kind and tolerant attitude manifested by both the administration and the employees, in this recent disturbance. It is our sincere concern that we may in return for your kindness, in our daily work and fellowship, be of greater service in cooperating with you in serving the patients of this Hospital."[59]

The weeks following the publication of Dunnington's charges saw a spate of pro and con letters to the editor and editorials in local papers. On August 2, a newspaper in Davenport, Iowa, published an editorial, "Caring for Our Insane": "Dr. Dunnington is not the first to complain of these conditions. It is an old story which should be rectified by the board of control." The Board of Control responded to Dunnington's charges in a letter published in the *Des Moines Register* on August 4. The board said it had investigated all of Dunnington's claims and interviewed five COs and two of their wives. It either refuted the charges or explained that problems had been caused by the war: "May we say, also, this hospital has given three psychiatrists to the war effort, all of whom are in active service at this time." Dunnington had inflicted "irreparable injury" on the institution, caused "heartache in the homes of 1500 patients," "erected a barrier between the decent, loyal, hard working employees of the institution and the conscientious objectors," and insulted "women employees who are giving husbands and sons to the war effort." The letter concluded: "Last, but not least, he has brought disrepute on an institution of this state, erected and maintained for the humanitarian purpose of caring for those most to be pitied in all the world—the mentally ill." An editorial in the *Iowa City Press-Citizen* on August 7 stated that conditions at all of the state mental hospitals had been bad for many years and suggested that the public should demand change. In the *Des Moines Register* on August 8, Rev. Alton Koch, pastor of Faith Lutheran Church, wrote a letter defending the institution based on his experiences with the administration, employees, and patients, whereas F. E. Weitz gave a political perspective on the controversy: "The insane, in the eyes of the Marxian Socialist Labor party are human beings, many the victims of circumstances beyond their control."[60]

By mid-August, the controversy had died down. Robert Kreider of the MCC had visited Mount Pleasant and "had quite a talk with Superintendent Soucek." The COs' apology to hospital staff had apparently smoothed things over: "I would say that our relations with the regular employees are as good or better than they were before."[61]

The Reverend L. L. Dunnington again made news on November 26, 1944, when he called upon the governor-elect, Robert Blue, to order an investigation of the "bad conditions that exist in our state mental hospitals." This time Dunnington urged a complete overhaul of the state's insanity hospitals and institutions for the feebleminded. He argued that the asylums kept many patients who did not belong there and that almost half could be returned to normal life and society if they had proper treatment. It would take a while for Dunnington's ideas on the care of the mentally ill to become popular. MCC assistant director Leinbach forwarded the article to the MCC and NSBRO: "It does not seem at the present time as though the article should involve us. Dr. Soucek takes the article very calmly, even joking with me about it."[62]

In the midst of the controversy surrounding Dunnington's charges against Mount Pleasant State Hospital, Earl Leinbach expressed regret over the actions of men in his unit: "We feel that we have made a very serious mistake in talking and griping to the extent that has been our custom in the past. A number of us at least are accepting this situation as a challenge to show our sincerity and our willingness to do the best work in this situation which may have a few minor faults, but none of such a serious nature." Leinbach exemplified the attitude of "Resist not evil" held by many Mennonites. He would not challenge the conditions under which patients lived and COs worked. Leinbach was succeeded as assistant director by Howard Mishler. In a description of the unit, Mishler said that the COs had "witnessed to a better life," but was candid in describing the feelings of men in the unit: "Long hours, excessive criticism, open resentment, and a continual lack of appreciation on the part of the Hospital administration, has had a wearing effect upon some of the men."[63]

The MCC unit at Mount Pleasant closed in September 1946.

◆   ◆   ◆

Dr. John Ross, superintendent of Hudson River State Hospital in Poughkeepsie, New York, had come from the State Mental Hospital at Howard, Rhode Island, where he had held the same position. He had worked with an MCC unit at Howard and had been pleased with the performance of the men: "I don't know what we would have done without them. I only wish we could get a lot more of them."[64] Ross was eager to have COs at Hudson River and approved adjustments in their work schedules so that they could participate in foreign relief training in their off-duty hours.

An MCC unit opened at the roughly five thousand–patient institution in April 1945. It took about a month for a controversy to erupt over attendants' treatment of patients.[65] The COs were assigned to different buildings at the institution. One of these was Ryan Hall, the building for disturbed and violent patients. Both Superintendent Ross and the supervisor of male employees had anticipated potential problems between the COs and regular employees at Ryan Hall: "According to advance notices from both the Superintendent and the Supervisor of Male Employees, Ryan Hall had possibilities of being a 'hot spot' as far as relations between state employees and CPS men were concerned, both as regards the CO position of the 'intruders' and in terms of patient care, with perhaps a little difficulty with labor unionism."[66]

Regular attendants at Ryan Hall were brutal and cruel to patients: "hitting them, tapping their penis's with their keys."[67] COs went to the administration to report abuse. Edwin Schrag recalled what happened:

> There was on one ward, especially, the disturbed ward, the violent ward, they sometimes called it, there was quite a bit of abuse of patients. The regular employees there were, you might call them, sadists. They would torment the patients and get a big kick out of it. So some of us decided . . . we're going to talk to the authorities about this. Two of the fellows got pretty brave and, first, they went to our camp director. . . . They went to the personnel director. . . . He said, "This is going to the top," Dr. Ross, the Superintendent of the hospital. So they went and this is exactly what Dr. Ross had been waiting for. . . . He knew this mistreatment of patients had been going on, but somehow he could never catch anybody. . . . He called us in. There were four of us on that ward, and we had to give him our story.[68]

Told of abuse at his institution by credible informants, Superintendent Ross took decisive action. He fired four attendants accused of brutality by the COs. One of the fired attendants was a veteran of World War I, and one had served in World War II. Three of the attendants were members of a union.

The dismissal of the four attendants was reported in the newspaper the next day: "Boy, the next day there was a big full-blown story in the Poughkeepsie paper: 'Employees discharged on the word of the COs.'"[69] Over the next several months, there were at least seventeen newspaper stories involving the COs or the fired attendants in the papers.[70] The American Legion and labor groups jumped into the controversy. They demanded trials for the fired attendants, and the American Legion chapter said it was going to ask local legislators to conduct a thorough investigation of how the mental hospital treated the COs. It charged that Superintendent Ross had coddled the COs, giving them special privileges, and wanted the unit dismissed. An editorial in the *Poughkeepsie New Yorker* endorsed trials for the fired attendants and an investigation of the COs.[71] Poughkeepsie was a mile or two away from the state hospital, and for a while COs avoided going into the city. Then an event occurred that swayed public opinion to the side of the COs.

On the evening of July 9, Eleanor Roosevelt visited the CPS unit and women's summer service unit at the mental hospital. It was not Mrs. Roosevelt's first visit to a CPS mental hospital unit. She had previously met with Loris Habegger, assistant director of the MCC unit at Marlboro State Hospital, during a visit to the institution with a friend of hers who was a member of the hospital's board. Habegger recalled that she was gracious and wanted to know whether COs would be willing to do hospital service among the wounded from the war. He told her that he would personally but that he could not speak for other COs.[72]

Mrs. Roosevelt and her secretary came to the Hudson River State Hospital units to discuss foreign relief training at the invitation of Edna Ramseyer, the women's summer service director, and perhaps Bert Smucker, assistant director of the CPS unit.[73] She had a special interest in foreign relief and had supported the training program at Quaker, Mennonite, and Brethren colleges for COs that had been blocked by Congress. During the visit, Mrs. Roosevelt discussed the mental hospital with the COs and the COGs, as they were known, and she had an opportunity to speak with Superintendent Ross. Edwin Schrag recalled, "She was quite sympathetic to our cause."[74] The men and the women who met with Mrs. Roosevelt were in awe of her. Schrag also remembered that as soon as Mrs. Roosevelt left, one of the women rushed over to the teacup she had been drinking from and drank what was left.

Writing in her nationally syndicated "My Day" column on July 11, Mrs. Roosevelt expressed her support for the COs at Hudson River State Hospital. The headline of the front-page story on her column in the *Poughkeepsie New Yorker* read: "Mrs. Roosevelt Told COs Raised HRSH Standards." The lead-in to Mrs. Roosevelt's column in the Poughkeepsie paper stated, "She said the superintendent had told her that COs had been of 'tremendous help' in disclosing certain practices which existed at the hospital and about which he could never get any real evidence." In her column, Mrs. Roosevelt described the important work COs were doing at mental hospitals. By coincidence or not, right next to the front-page story in the *Poughkeepsie New Yorker* was a photo showing a heralded World War II general and Mrs. Roosevelt at a grave: "General Dwight D. Eisenhower places a wreath upon the grave of the late President Franklin D. Roosevelt at Hyde Park, N.Y., July 10, as Mrs. Roosevelt looks on."[75]

In an editorial on the following Sunday, the *Poughkeepsie New Yorker* took a much more sympathetic position on the COs than it had previously. It repeated the conclusions of Mrs. Roosevelt and then added: "The local public is familiar with the fact that recently several attendants at the hospital were discharged on accusations of manhandling patients laid with the superintendent by the COs. In light of this experience, the public cannot help but draw the conclusion that Dr. Ross had believed misuse of patients had existed for some time but had not corrected conditions because he had been unable to obtain evidence against the paid employes [sic]." The paper went on to say that the charges against the fired employees had not yet been proven and wondered aloud why Superintendent Ross had not been able to prove his suspicions previously. The editorial concluded by expressing concern about the future of the state hospital after the COs left: "We can only hope that in consideration for the CO's, hospital employees and, above all, the patients themselves, that services rendered this far by these temporary employes [sic] have corrected to a large degree the conditions which Dr. Ross said existed and which he has been unable to remedy. But lest the public take undue comfort in this thought, it must be remembered that Dr. Ross was quoted further by Mrs. Roosevelt as having said if the CO's could stay longer, 'they would probably improve the standards even more.'"[76]

The COs testified in civil hearings against the fired attendants, and the dismissals stood. The public controversy dissipated. One of the CPS men, Ralph S. Lehman, would later reflect, "It soon became apparent to the hospital employees, and particularly to those with whom we worked, that we were sincere in our convictions against the type of treatment these patients were receiving, and also that we would be firm in our attempt to improve the situation. The hospital and civil service hearings gave us further opportunity to state our convictions against the use of inhumane methods and our faith in a philosophy of kind, humane treatment and concern for each individual patient."[77]

The "Ryan Hall incident," as it was called, convinced many men on the Hudson River State Hospital unit of the need to challenge abusive practices and substandard conditions. In his orientation to the members of the women's summer service unit, Bert Smucker told the women that the COs had decided "hereafter" to discuss problems with the charge on a ward before going to the superintendent, but if doing so did not resolve things, they would go to Dr. Ross. He added, "If no solution would be forthcoming it would be permissible to consult each of the next higher persons in responsible positions until there would be some definite plan to improve a condition." J. Willard Linscheid was more forceful in stating how institutional conditions should be confronted: "I think we were all fired with a desire to expose mental hospital conditions to the general public in the hope that such an exposé would lead to action toward the improvement of such institutions."[78] "Resist not evil" was falling by the wayside.

The CPS unit closed in April 1946, one year after it had opened.

For his part, Superintendent Ross demonstrated that it might be a good idea for institutional officials to take immediate actions when abuses and problems were brought to their attention. Had Brown at Williamsburg and Lee at Cleveland acted in the same manner, they might have lasted longer in their positions.

◆　◆　◆

Philadelphia State Hospital, Byberry, was the birthplace of the national movement to reform state mental hospitals and training schools through the Mental Hygiene Program of the CPS and then the National Mental Health Foundation. For years, COs at Byberry collected reports of abuses and conditions at state mental hospitals and training schools by CPS men and others. In soliciting information, Byberry COs assured others that institutions and individuals would not be named in any reports. They wanted to protect persons providing the information and to avoid the witch hunts that sometimes accompanied exposés of institutions and deflected attention away from the need for states to allocate more funds for institutions. Byberry superintendent Charles Zeller was an adviser to and strong supporter of the reform-minded COs and cautioned against individual exposés.[79] Protecting the names of institutions would later cause a rift among the COs when Albert Maisel was planning his *Life* magazine exposé of mental hospitals.

As the CPS was coming to an end in the late winter and spring of 1946, conditions at Byberry itself would be exposed in newspapers and *Life*. Byberry COs mounted a campaign to pressure the Commonwealth of Pennsylvania to allocate more money to the state's institutions. The campaign was led by COs who were not directly involved in the national reform movement. Warren Sawyer was discharged from the CPS on January 14, 1946, and continued working at Byberry as a paid employee to make some money while waiting to serve on a Brethren "cattle boat" to Europe. Sawyer had not been directly involved in the Mental Hygiene Program of the CPS. In a letter home, he explained the COs' plans for Byberry:

> We are working on a carefully laid out plan to blow this place open in two months. Several of us are gathering information from various sources for publicity in city newspapers. We are working along with the Hopetown Association which is made up of relatives of patients. . . . We have newspapers cooperating with us and things are moving ahead. This is being kept quiet as far as the administration knows. . . . We hope to make it good enough so that Harrisburg will be pressured enough so that by the time the next legislature meets they will be acutely aware of conditions and vote sums for improvements in bldgs. and facilities, and wages for attendants. . . . If we COs do nothing about this place to improve it our stay here has been to no avail and we have accomplished nothing. Two other fellows and I are heading up this thing to launch the campaign and gather material.[80]

Superintendent Zeller had been close with the CPS men who started the Mental Hygiene Program but was not well known by the other COs. He had a reputation of being personable and committed but unable to do much about the conditions at Byberry. By early 1946, Zeller had announced that he would be leaving Byberry to accept the position of director of Michigan's newly formed Department of Mental Health. The superintendent of Norristown State Hospital, which was located not far from Philadelphia, also had announced his retirement. Letters to the editor about the two superintendents had appeared in the Philadelphia papers.[81]

At the same time, COs were moving ahead with plans to exposé Byberry. Charles Lord had been secretly taking photos of A and B Buildings that would later be published in *Life, PM,* and Mental Hygiene Program of the CPS and National Mental Health Foundation materials, including *Out of Sight, Out of Mind.*[82] A patient in B Building had seen Lord taking pictures of patients tied in bed and had told a doctor about it but refused to give the doctor Lord's name: "I suppose Dr. Zeller will hear about it." The COs started to suspect that the administration might know about their plans to expose Byberry: "We wonder if some of the nurses and doctors are suspicion [sic] something because various things are said once in a while. I wondered once because some repairs seemed to get done faster than they have for a long time. Supplies have suddenly started to come in better than they have for three years. The clinical director Dr. Peatick made rounds in all the buildings the other day so we wonder if they don't smell something."[83]

On Sunday, February 10, the front page of the *Philadelphia Record* contained a story on Byberry's B Building. Superintendent Zeller had met a reporter at the hospital the previous day, and she had been given a tour of B Building. The story's headline read: "Head of Byberry Says B Still Is Disgrace: Dank, Overcrowded

Building Gets Dregs of Mental Cases." It started out with a candid appraisal of B Building by Zeller:

> When Dr. Charles A. Zeller quits the superintendency of Philadelphia State Hospital (Byberry) about March 1, among the serious problems he leaves for his successor is the dank, overcrowded B Building.
>
> "It's a disgrace," said Dr. Zeller, "but there is little I have been able to do about it." . . .
>
> Flanked by two guards and the psychiatrist on duty this reporter went through every part of B Building where 318 dangerous mental cases are crowded into a dilapidated structure with a normal capacity of 100 patients. Until recently 350 patients were kept in this building.

The reporter explained that all of the "guards" on duty during the day were COs and that the institution was dangerously understaffed. She took readers through her tour of the building: the dayroom with 170 patients and chairs or benches for only 80, the disturbed ward with 28 men strapped to their beds, the dormitory in the "damp, dark and dirty" cellar. Asked why he had resigned from Byberry, Zeller said that Michigan had "inaugurated a modern program to take care of the mentally ill far in advance of Pennsylvania's system." He also stated that the capacity of Byberry needed to be expanded by tearing down old buildings and constructing new ones: "'There's a criminal potential in every mental case,' Dr. Zeller warned, 'And there are thousands waiting for admission who should be committed.'"[84] It was perhaps not the best way to improve public attitudes about mental illness.

Immediately following the publication of the story, COs wrote letters to the editorial page of the newspaper, and one wrote letters for relatives of patients visiting the hospital to sign. Two of the letters were published on February 12.

On February 14, S. M. R. O'Hara, secretary of Pennsylvania's Department of Welfare, came to Byberry to inspect B Building. She was critical of the COs: "As a result of the article in the Record and the letters about this place, Miss O'Hara of the Welfare Dept of Pa. came down on Thursday for an 'inspection' of B Building. She passed some snide remarks such as this one to one of our men: 'You fellows seem to have more time to write letters to the papers than you do to clean the floor.' What brought that on was the fact that a patient in restraint had urinated on the floor just prior to her entry to the ward."[85]

No longer a CO, Warren Sawyer sent O'Hara a strongly worded letter that took exception to her demeanor during her visit:

> In regard to your visit here to the hospital you made it quite plain to one of the men on "B" Building that you did not like the work that the CO's of the Civilian

Public Service Unit 49 were doing, because you saw some urine on the floor. (For one year we have been cleaning the floors with bath towels since we have been unable to get mop-heads.) I am sorry that you have such feelings. Dr. Zeller does not apparently agree with you on the matter of how well we have done our job, for the state, for four years with no pay. . . .

Your apparent disgust with the job we have done to date does not equal our disgust for the filth, distasteful job, red tape and working with no equipment that this "hole" has offered since we came in August 1942. . . .

Something must be done and can be done.[86]

Things died down at Byberry, but only temporarily. After Zeller had stepped down as superintendent, Byberry was visited by writer Albert Deutsch, who was following in the footsteps of *Life* writer Albert Maisel. Members of the Mental Hygiene Program of the CPS had been in communication with Deutsch about mental hospital conditions at least since the summer of 1945.[87] Deutsch came to Byberry to review Mental Hygiene Program files on institutions and to visit the mental hospital. He was given free rein to tour Byberry by the new superintendent, Eugene Sielke, and CO Charles Lord served as his photographer.

On April 17 and 18, Deutsch published a series of articles on Byberry in *PM*. They appeared a week before his exposé of Cleveland State Hospital. The top of the front page of *PM* on April 17 read, in large, bold letters: "Byberry Horror Camp." A headline on one of the stories inside the paper was: "Mental Patients Rot in Philadelphia's 'Bedlam.'" Near the beginning of one of the stories on April 17, Deutsch explained how he was able to visit the mental hospital: "I am able to present this picture documentary story of a typical state hospital because Byberry happens to have an enlightened head with a conscience, and because of the co-operation of a group of humanely intelligent young conscientious objectors assigned as attendants here under a special Selective Service program." Deutsch's stories provided descriptions and photographs of the squalor at Byberry—the lack of treatment, filth, restraints, overcrowding—and accounts of attendants' brutality based on diaries of the COs. Deutsch did not mince words in a story on April 18: "Byberry, along with too many of our state hospitals, can be compared only to Buchenwald and Belsen in its contempt for human dignity and human needs."[88]

Fewer than three weeks after Deutsch's exposé, Maisel would publish his own exposé of conditions and brutality at state mental hospitals in *Life*, "Bedlam, 1946: Most U.S. Mental Hospitals Are a Shame and Disgrace."[89] Maisel's story carried photographs of patients at Byberry with the captions "Idleness," "Nakedness," and "Crowding." The *Philadelphia Record* carried an article on mental hospitals on May 9, three days after the publication of the *Life* article. The headline of the article was: "Convicts Fare Better than Insane: CO's Seeking to Ease Lives of Mental Patients."[90]

The publication of Deutsch's and Maisel's exposés provoked a strong reaction from Pennsylvania public officials. Republican governor Edward Martin released a two-page letter criticizing Deutsch's articles as "prejudicial" and stating, "Your concern over the operation of the Philadelphia State Hospital would be justified if the impression conveyed by these articles were correct. Briefly, that impression seems to be that Philadelphia State Hospital is operated without consideration for the needs of patients and without effort to correct substandard care and treatment in the hospital. Such impression is not correct."[91]

The governor attached a six-page report critiquing Deutsch's articles by public welfare director O'Hara. O'Hara faulted Deutsch for not making a "calm presentment of facts" and failing to acknowledge the "corrections" made at Byberry since Pennsylvania had taken over operation from the City of Philadelphia in 1938. She went on to accuse Deutsch of favoring a federal takeover of state institutions, although he had said no such thing: "I am constrained to believe that Mr. Deutsch intends to aide a certain group in the United States to centralize the operation of all agencies of government in Washington, and to give a central agency the power to control the well-being of 130,000,000 persons residing in every state in the Union. This is a new variety of Fascism."[92]

O'Hara took aim at the National Mental Health Foundation, which had just been established by former Byberry COs. Both Maisel and Deutsch had mentioned COs as sources in their stories, and the *Philadelphia Record* had highlighted their activities. O'Hara charged that the national foundation had provided a distorted picture of Byberry.[93] She wrote the foundation to dispute its account of conditions at the institution. On May 20, Hal Barton replied on the foundation's behalf. He started by presenting the foundation's perspective on the roots of the problems at state mental hospitals:

> We have received repeated assurances from persons in all positions in the mental health field that the greatest block to expanding and improving the facilities for caring for the mentally ill has been the lack of public support for necessary appropriations. Few states have had ample provisions for securing enough trained attendants, nurses, and doctors. Over and over again the appropriations requested by Superintendents or by State Departments concerned with mental health have been denied.
>
> We feel that if citizens know the effects of their neglect and lack of support for these facilities, that if they knew some of the basic problems of care for the mentally ill, and if they knew what was being accomplished in our better hospitals, then they would no longer withhold the support and assistance that State agencies need in order to do an adequate job of care and treatment.

Barton proceeded to ask O'Hara a long series of rhetorical questions about Byberry: "Is it not true that much brutality continues to be meted out to patients on the wards of Philadelphia State Hospital? Is it not true that a great many of the attendants could be classified as 'undesirable' and that much remains to be done within the power of the commonwealth to accomplish?" He referred to a May 6 letter from former superintendent Zeller saying that he felt his hands had been tied by a lack of a sufficient appropriation for attendant salaries. Barton then disputed several questions of fact about Byberry included in a May 1 letter from O'Hara to the governor. The letter concluded, "May I respectfully ask that you forward us a copy of the plans of your Department for remedying the present difficult personnel situation and indicate the manner in which we may be of greatest help in supporting your efforts to achieve a humane standard of care and an enlightened standard of treatment for the mentally ill."[94]

Marvin Weisbord described what happened next in the controversy: "As the public outcry mounted, Governor Martin made a well-publicized tour of Byberry with state legislators. One asked how chewing tobacco came to be splattered so high up the wall in A building and was told that what he saw was feces thrown by the inmates. Later Miss O'Hara, to save face, came out with her own report on mental hospitals, because 'it is fitting that the fullest information by made available to the people, for full free, and public discussion.'"[95] According to Weisbord, Pennsylvania allocated eighty million dollars for new mental hospital construction the following year.

The Byberry superintendents, first Zeller and then Sielke, were unscathed by the exposés of the institution. Public officials who acknowledged the failings of institutions almost always fared better in the public eye than the ones who tried to deny problems or shift the focus to the individuals who called attention to abuses and substandard conditions.

The AFSC unit at Byberry officially closed in October 1946. Some of the Byberry COs carried on their work to reform state institutions after the end of the CPS.

◆　◆　◆

Training schools for the mentally defective or feebleminded by and large escaped the public scrutiny received by mental hospitals at the hands of COs. None of the major exposés brought about by COs involved a training school. *Life* and *Out of Sight, Out of Mind* made no mention of conditions at the nation's institutions for people with intellectual disabilities. Albert Deutsch's "Shame of the States" series included a story on one training school, Letchworth Village in New York, but a CPS unit had not been located there. If the 445,561 patients in the nation's mental hospitals were "out of sight, out of mind," then what could be said about the 113,979 people in state training schools?[96]

About one-quarter—fourteen out of fifty-nine—CPS "mental hospital units" were located at training schools, although these units tended to have fewer COs than the mental hospitals.[97] The narratives collected by the Mental Hygiene Program of the CPS, which were used for *Out of Sight, Out of Mind* and shown to Maisel and Deutsch, included reports of conditions at Mansfield, Lynchburg, Union Grove, Stockley, Pennhurst, Pownel, Laurel, Skillman, and Woodbine training schools.[98] Len Edelstein of the Mental Hygiene Program visited the Pennhurst institution in Pennsylvania in 1945 and reported that it was similar to Byberry: "At Pennhurst I found conditions rather similar to those at Byberry—namely lovely grounds, nice 'façade,' but very old wooden buildings, dimly lighted and often pervaded with strong odors. The boys, crammed into day rooms—fed poor looking food on metal trays, are often worked 12 hours per day, 7 days a week—if they have sufficient brawn or mental ability."[99] One of the COs at Pennhurst, Anthony Leeds, later recalled working at Pennhurst:

> I went for a miserable 20 months to a concentration camp called Pennhurst State School for Mental Defectives, in Spring City, PA. The patients most likely to get training and get better and go into a real world of work somehow were found to have "broken a rule" so they were sent to U-Cottage, a slave house where they were beaten, had arms tied to steam pipes, and made to provide all the major labor of the institution. The Director, an alcoholic, and the Comptroller were in cahoots, many of the charge attendants in the cottages were drunks and even more of the assistant attendants were "rum-bums."[100]

Pennhurst would receive public notoriety in the late 1970s and early '80s when it became subject to first a major class-action lawsuit, *Halderman v. Pennhurst State School and Hospital*, and then a U.S. Supreme Court case involving abuses and injuries to a Pennhurst resident, Nicholas Romeo, in *Romeo v. Youngberg*.[101] Pennsylvania eventually closed Pennhurst in 1988. NSBRO's *Reporter* published an article, "Training Schools and CPS," by CO Stephen Angell in July 1944. The article reflected common stereotypes about people with intellectual disabilities and repeated language that seems dehumanizing by today's standards. COs referred to patients of all ages as "children" and distinguished between "low grades" and "high grades." The introduction of the article read: "No new problem is mental deficiency. Mental deficiency, feeble mindedness has been known in all civilizations; still remains one of the great causes of pauperism, delinquency, crime. But concern for the care of the feeble minded is relatively new."[102] Angell explained that the training schools were terribly overcrowded and understaffed and described some of the work of COs at the institutions.

The constructs of "mental hygiene" and "mental health" were broad enough to include mental deficiency or feeblemindedness. The National Committee for Mental Hygiene directed attention to feeblemindedness soon after its establishment, although its focus was usually on prevention by limiting reproduction. The Mental Hygiene Program of the CPS and then the National Mental Health Foundation held some conferences and meetings on training schools and distributed a handful of publications on mental deficiency, but people with intellectual disabilities were not a high priority and were lost in the emphasis on mental hospitals and psychiatric disabilities. Training school superintendents were almost always medical doctors or psychiatrists, but mental deficiency was not a major concern of the medical and psychiatric professions.

The care and treatment of the mentally deficient had been left to the American Association on Mental Deficiency (AAMD). The AAMD had been founded by a small group of asylum superintendents as the Association of Medical Officers of American Institutions for Idiotic and Feeble-Minded Persons in 1876 after the American Association of Medical Officers American Institutions for the Insane had limited membership to insane asylum superintendents. The association's name was later changed to the American Association for the Study of the Feeble-Minded and then to AAMD.[103] It became the American Association on Mental Retardation in the 1970s and is named the American Association on Intellectual and Developmental Disabilities today. Up until the late 1940s, the AAMD's leadership and journal, the *American Journal of Mental Deficiency*, were dominated by physicians.

The National Committee for Mental Hygiene and the American Psychiatric Association ignored or downplayed problems at institutions throughout the early to mid-1940s. With the exposés brought about by COs and the formation of the National Mental Health Foundation, which would keep a spotlight on mental hospital conditions, both the National Committee and the APA would initiate their own reform efforts beginning in 1946. The AAMD would not direct serious attention to institutional abuses, overcrowding, and understaffing until decades later. Between 1944 and 1947, the *American Journal of Mental Deficiency* did not publish a single article on problems at state training schools.[104]

The major exposés brought about by the COs—those men lasting for a period of time—had certain elements in common: a group of people knowledgeable about problems and willing to bring them to the attention of others, one or more writers or reporters interested in the stories, and civic and community leaders outraged by the problems and willing to support those individuals who brought them to light. Decisive or rash actions by one or more public officials added to the news-worthiness of the stories and kept them alive. For whatever reason, these elements never came together at the state training schools. It was not because the problems at the training schools were unknown to COs.

Channing B. Richardson had been a CO at the AFSC unit at Pennhurst State Training School and was discharged from the CPS in December 1945. Shortly after-ward, he published an article, "A Hundred Thousand Defectives," in the *Christian Century*. The beginning of Richardson's article repeated faulty beliefs about feeb-lemindedness and heredity and did not exactly paint a flattering picture of people with intellectual disabilities: "When one learns that approximately 80 per cent of our defectives inherited their luck, one gets a glimpse of a huge future problem. The immediate background of the present problem is familiar to social workers—poverty, low home and family standards, delinquency, ignorance and sickness. A drag on his schoolmates, a joke for the cruel and a threat to his community, the defective committed to a state institution by court or agency receives little better than custodial care to the end of his days."

Richardson's story was written in a straightforward, "factual" narrative style. He described the ideal type of environment for defectives in which they would be "secure against dangers, protected from illness and guarded against reproducing his kind" and be provided with psychometric testing, recreation, and work pro-grams. Then he explained the problems that prevented the realization of the ideal. Some problems were personal-psychological and reflected "patient attitudes and actions, personality traits of varying individuals." Other problems were institu-tional. Here he gave a bleak account of the nature of institutions: "A catalogue of specific blockages on the road to reform would include interdepartmental rivalry, favoritism, tradition, boondoggling, buck-passing, incompetence, fear of supervi-sors and the future, lack of knowledge and pride in the work, shortsightedness and concern with appearances."[105] Low wages and poor working conditions for employees and penny-pinching by state officials were major problems at institu-tions, wrote Richardson. Nowhere in the article was Pennhurst named.

CO Gordon Zahn was the initial assistant director at the first and only Asso-ciation of Catholic Conscientious Objectors mental hospital or training school unit at Rosewood Training School in Maryland. The unit was opened in May 1943 and taken over by the government when the ACCO withdrew from the CPS. It officially closed in July 1946. Shortly after his discharge from the CPS in April 1946, Zahn wrote a blistering letter to the institution's Board of Visitors, criticizing the treat-ment of residents at Rosewood. Residents, he charged, were "subject to capricious, careless, and unjust disciplinary actions."[106] Recreational programs and facilities were lacking. Residents were required to work long hours with little time off.

Starting in July 1946, Zahn wrote a series of articles on Rosewood in the *Catholic Worker*. The first article was "State School Unnatural, Maltreats Children": "It is a recognized crime against morality for parents to neglect or mistreat children they have brought into the world. Yet how far greater a crime is it for Society to take these same children into its custody and then proceed to continue their neglect and, in addition, subject them to an unnatural life pattern dominated by fear and denial. It is such a pattern we witnessed as conscientious objectors assigned to duty at the Rosewood Training School for mentally subnormal children in Maryland." Zahn placed responsibility for Rosewood squarely on the shoulders of the professional staff and Board of Visitors. The staff, he said, "have chosen to stagnate and protect a situation that places them in the rather ignoble position of waxing fat upon the neglect of their helpless and inarticulate charges." He accused the board of "whitewashing this unholy state of affairs through a near-criminal disinterest and inactivity."

Zahn's second article was titled "Slaves or Patients?" In this article, Zahn charged that "children" at Rosewood performed virtually all of the work involved in the operation of the institution and were forced to work long hours, often from 5:30 A.M. to 7:00 P.M. The title of the final article in the series was taken from Dante: "Abandon Hope." This article reviewed the various ways in which Rosewood failed its residents and concluded: "The people of Maryland have the right and the Christian duty to demand full investigations to learn who is accountable for this situation. Only if they act can there be hope that Rosewood may yet become a thoroughfare of promise."

The *Baltimore Sun* subsequently published a series of articles on Rosewood and other Maryland institutions describing inadequate care and filthy conditions.[107] The series sparked a flurry of investigations and reports initiated by a judge in Baltimore County, Maryland's governor, the Maryland Psychiatric Society, and the state legislature. An anonymous comment in the *American Journal of Psychiatry* concluded that the *Baltimore Sun* had exaggerated problems at Rosewood and elsewhere and that any deficiencies were owing to overcrowding and understaffing beyond the control of the administrators of the institutions.

It was unusual for state training schools to become the subjects of public exposés in the 1940s. Training schools differed from mental hospitals in an important way. Conditions at mental hospitals aroused public outrage because of the nature of mental illness: "It could happen to anyone." This thought was a frequent theme in exposés of the mental hospitals. Beliefs about mental deficiency were different. Since it was assumed that most mental deficiency was handed down from one generation to the next in the lower classes, political and civic leaders were less inclined to identify with those individuals in the state training schools. The mental defective was the "other." Beginning in the late 1940s and extending into the 1960s, the construct of mental deficiency, or mental retardation, became radically redefined by parents and others. Conditions at state institutions for people with intellectual disabilities would command public attention and spark outrage in the 1960s and '70s.

◆   ◆   ◆

"The Exposé as a Progressive Tool" was the title of an article written by Albert Deutsch for the mental health community. Deutsch had gotten his start in the field of mental illness when he published a popular history of the treatment of the mentally ill in the United States in 1937, with the support of Clifford Beers and the American Foundation for Mental Hygiene.[108] Deutsch's book *The Mentally Ill in America: A History of Their Care and Treatment from Colonial Times* was well researched and thorough. It gave him credibility in mental hygiene and mental health that would last until his death.[109]

In 1941, Deutsch became a reporter for *PM*, a left-leaning New York City newspaper with a national circulation. He would become a leading "muckraker" of the 1940s, in the tradition of early-twentieth-century writers Jacob Riis *(How the Other Half Lives)*, Upton Sinclair *(The Jungle)*, Lincoln Steffens *(The Shame of the Cities)*, and Ida Tarbell *(The History of the Standard Oil Company)*. The muckrakers exposed public malfeasance through factual presentation designed to stir civic action.[110] In a review of a book on Jacob Riis, Deutsch himself characterized muckrakers as "journalists who not only investigated and exposed evil social, economic, and political conditions, but insisted on having them changed." Deutsch would become controversial with certain public figures, such as Pennsylvania's public welfare director, S. M. R. O'Hara, but he enjoyed the respect of emerging leaders in psychiatry and mental health in the late 1940s.[111] He shared many of the goals of the psychiatric and mental health professions: increased funding for research, training, and public hospitals and programs.

Deutsch's first exposé of mental hospitals was published in *PM* in 1941 based on surveys of the U.S. Public Health Service. Then, in 1944, he published a series of exposés on mistreatment in American veterans' hospitals. His exposés helped bring about a congressional investigation and resulted in a contempt citation from Congress when he refused to provide the names of Veterans Administration physicians who had supplied him with information to the House World War Veterans Legislation Committee. The contempt citation was rescinded after a flurry of newspaper editorials condemning an assault on freedom of the press. Deutsch reported what happened next: "I was called back to resume my testimony—without being asked again to name my confidential sources—and I experienced the satisfaction of seeing the old guard in the Veterans Administration deposed by the President, and the VA medical program drastically reorganized under General Omar Bradley."[112]

For his exposés on mental hospitals in *PM* in 1944 and '47, Deutsch visited about forty institutions across the country, in addition to relying on reports of the COs, the Ohio grand jury investigation of Cleveland State Hospital, and other documentary materials.[113] In 1948, he published a collection of these newspaper exposés in a book titled *The Shame of the States*. The use of *shame* in the title reflected his affinity with earlier muckrakers. Deutsch published a revised edition of *The Mentally Ill in America* in 1949. This edition included a discussion of mental hospital conditions during World War II: "In some of the wards there were scenes that rivaled the horrors of the Nazi concentration camps."[114] Deutsch must have felt strongly about including this comparison. It was accompanied by a footnote: "The Editorial Committee interprets this as figurative language rather than a literal comparison." Deutsch continued his muckraking in the 1950s. He published a 1950 book on juvenile delinquency, *Our Rejected Children*, and a 1955 book on law enforcement problems, *The Trouble with Cops*. In 1960, Deutsch was selected editor in chief of an ambitious project for an encyclopedia of mental health. He died in 1961, two years prior to the publication of the six-volume encyclopedia.[115]

In "The Exposé as a Progressive Tool," Deutsch reviewed the history of exposés of asylums and mental hospitals in the United States, from Dorothea Dix to Nelly Bly to Clifford Beers. He distinguished between different types of exposés. A common type was the "nine-day sensation" that instilled a sense of horror among the public but seldom had a lasting impact. The more effective type represented a long-term campaign to change conditions. Deutsch noted that recent years had witnessed "a sustained and widespread barrage of exposés of the mental-hospital system" and that the rash of recent exposés "was largely stimulated by a group of young conscientious objectors who had been assigned to mental-hospital ward duty in lieu of military service." He characterized the recent exposés: "The exposés of this period, in the main, have differed radically from the routine 'asylum horror' exposé of former times. They are infused with greater understanding of fundamental factors. They have more sense, less sentimentalism. They rarely concentrate on personal scapegoats. Many put the blame where it rightly belongs—on callous state executives, penny-pinching legislatures, and an apathetic and ill-informed public. Invariably, they have concluded with generally sound programs for improving the 'discreditable conditions.'"[116]

12

"They Were Fighting Everybody"

Harold Barton. Born: 1916. Original denomination: Baptist. Drafted from: Eugene, Oregon. Entered CPS: 3/11/43. Left CPS: 5/27/46. CPS Units: Forest Service, Coleville, CA, AFSC; Mental Hospital, Byberry, AFSC.

Leonard Edelstein. Born: 1915. Original denomination: Jewish. Drafted from: Germantown, PA. Entered CPS: 11/15/42. Left CPS: 4/24/46. Units: Forest Service, Gorham, NH, AFSC; Forest Service, Campton, NH, AFSC; Mental Hospital, Byberry, AFSC.

Willard Hetzel. Born: 1912. Original denomination: Methodist. Drafted from: Toledo, OH. Entered CPS: 10/15/42. Left CPS: 4/15/46. Units: Soil Conservation Service, Big Flats, NY, AFSC; Mental Hospital, Cleveland, OH, AFSC; Mental Hospital, Byberry, AFSC.

Philip Steer. Born: 1919. Original denomination: Methodist. Drafted from: Chester, PA. Entered CPS: 3/10/42. Left CPS: 1/22/46. Units: Soil Conservation Service, Coshocton, OH, AFSC; Mental Hospital, Byberry, AFSC.

Four Byberry COs created a national movement to reform state mental hospitals and training schools and forced established organizations, including the National Committee for Mental Hygiene and the American Psychiatric Association, to take actions to address the plight of people languishing at America's institutions.[1] Len Edelstein and Phil Steer were from upstate New York and had received undergraduate degrees from Syracuse University. Edelstein went on to receive a law degree from Harvard University and to work for the FBI for a brief period of time. After the war, he changed his name to Cornell to avoid discrimination against Jewish people. Like Edelstein, Will Hetzel was a lawyer. Hal Barton had been a mining engineer before the CPS.

In 1968, Marvin R. Weisbord published *Some Form of Peace,* a book documenting five stories of the work of the American Friends Service Committee. One chapter told the story of four COs at an AFSC unit at Philadelphia State Hospital who started the Mental Hygiene Program of the Civilian Public Service and then the National Mental Health Foundation. The title of this chapter was "Out of Sight,

36. Founders of the Mental Hygiene Program of the Civilian Public Service and the National Mental Health Foundation *(from left):* Philip Steer, Leonard Edelstein, Willard Hetzel, and Harold Barton. (Swarthmore College Peace Collection, Swarthmore, Pennsylvania)

Out of Mind." Weisbord's account was based on interviews with the men involved as well as a detailed narrative written by Hal Barton. To avoid misinterpretations, Weisbord sent a draft of his chapter to at least some of the men for comments and corrections. Interviewed many years later about the COs, Weisbord said, "They were fighting everybody."[2]

◆   ◆   ◆

Like many other COs at state institutions, Edelstein, Barton, Hetzel, and Steer were appalled by conditions at Byberry. Hetzel had come to Byberry from Cleveland State Hospital, where he had given an account of abuses he had observed to Justin Reese for the report provided to the Reverend Dores R. Sharpe and released to state officials and the public. At Byberry, he was working in the powerhouse. Steer had barely lasted a month on the wards before transferring to a clerical job at the institution. Edelstein started a recreational program for patients in his off-duty hours to help ease their boredom. Barton was working in the violent building, B.

It was during one of the frequent "bull sessions" in one of the cottages for CPS men that the idea of a mental hygiene program emerged.[3] Barton and Edelstein agreed that it was not enough to do their best for patients while they were working at the mental hospital. They wanted to make a lasting change. Barton kept a diary of his impressions while at Byberry. On February 2, 1944, he wrote, "We're not thinking enuf as a group and sharing experiences relative to a plan and method in the future: are we going to stress 'leadership' or simple back-wearying toil in service. Don't they go together? . . . We're not thinking creatively enough in the realm of contacts with patients and regular attendants." Edelstein and Barton started to discuss ideas on how they could have an impact on all mental hospitals. An exchange of information among COs at the various institutions might help. Barton, who had been ready to go to the newspapers to expose Byberry, wanted to do something to confront hospital conditions more directly. He and Edelstein came up with the idea of collecting reports of conditions at all of the mental hospital units for a "Summary Statement."[4] Then they got Steer and other CPS men and women in the AFSC service unit at Byberry interested in working with them on the emerging project.

At a meeting of AFSC mental hospital and training school personnel directors in March 1944, Edelstein raised the idea of having the Byberry unit take responsibility for coordinating activities and communications among the various units. The personnel directors expressed support for his proposal.[5]

Edelstein approached Byberry superintendent Charles Zeller about the COs' ideas.[6] More than most superintendents, Zeller had welcomed and supported the CPS men and was aware that mental hospital conditions needed to change. He approved the creation of a mental hygiene program as long as the COs agreed that they would not try to expose individual mental hospitals or officials. He offered to make an office available to the COs where they could work during their off-duty hours. Zeller would be instrumental in putting the COs in contact with reform-minded psychiatrists and mental hygiene leaders. Paul Furnas of the AFSC agreed to provide a monthly eighty-dollar stipend: ten dollars for expenses associated with a summary and seventy dollars for a newsletter.[7]

The Mental Hygiene Program of the CPS was established in May 1944. Edelstein was the coordinator of the program, an ambiguous role that would later create misunderstandings. Steer took responsibility for publications and specifically for an interunit newsletter, whereas Barton was responsible for preparing a "Summary Statement of Conditions" at mental hospitals and training schools. Hetzel would join the program sometime afterward.

On May 8, Edelstein wrote the assistant directors of all CPS mental hospital and training school units announcing the establishment of the program. His letter included a description of the program's objectives: "That we who have been assigned to work in mental hospitals and training schools for mental deficients apprise ourselves of the service that we may render; that we may better perform that service by an exchange of knowledge regarding our mutual concerns; and that we as a united group may leave behind us when we return to private pursuits a contribution to the field of mental hygiene that will be concrete and enduring."[8]

Edelstein's letter included a summary of the two phases of the program. The first phase was a monthly interunit publication for "sharing ideas, attitudes and methods of work that seem useful in the care of the mentally ill and mentally deficient."[9] A description of this phase indicated that communications should be sent to Phil Steer and requested suggestions for the name of the publication, ideas for symposia and materials, and the names of persons who should receive the publication. The second phase of the program was the preparation of the "Summary Statement of Conditions" that would be released after the war:

> We expect to bring about an improvement in the treatment of mental patients only if we clearly understand the organization and dynamics of the institutions in which we work. A proper understanding will be obtained only by a use of the scientific approach, a gathering of facts, an objective scrutiny of conditions, and a careful study of actions and reactions on the part of both patients and staff. . . . Already we know that there are insufficient facilities, lack of individual care and treatment, public misunderstandings of hospital problems, and in some cases actual abusive practices. When, however, we have gathered a sufficient amount of evidence, we will have the bases for concrete methods of action to overcome the abuses and to promote better remedial and custodial care.[10]

The description of the "Summary Statement" stressed that information would be confidential and would not reveal names: "It is not the intent to 'smear' anyone, nor to use the specific revelations as the basis for action against individuals." In a subsequent report to CPS units, Hal Barton indicated that the statement would include an analysis of laws governing mental institutions and issued "a call for legal talent."[11] Then, in July, Barton responded to "specific problems, questions and criticisms" about the plans for the "Summary Statement." One CPS man suggested that the Mental Hygiene Program should secure the sponsorship of some organization such as the National Committee for Mental Hygiene to help collect information about the hospitals. Barton responded that the National Committee had offered assistance to the program but that the program should avoid official sponsorship by any such organization: "There are definite advantages in maintaining our independence. Sponsorship might to some extent influence our objectiveness, or commit us to some prearranged policy thus limiting our usefulness."[12]

By June, a rough organization of the Mental Hygiene Program had been formed.[13] Steer would lead the Publication Committee, with the help of CO Tom Leonard and Jane Terhune, a member of the AFSC women's service unit at Byberry.

Barton headed up the Summary Statement Committee on which COs Don Riggs, Abe Siegel, Arthur Stevenson, and Tom Riggs served, along with Margaret Riggs from the women's service unit. A diagram of the organization showed the membership of the committees in two columns, with Edelstein as coordinator in the middle. Bernard Lemann, Ward Miles, and Warren Sawyer had also helped prepare an initial outline of the "Summary Statement."

The "Summary Statement" would become *Out of Sight, Out of Mind,* compiled by Frank Wright. It would be published three years after the initial call for reports from COs.

The first issue of the MHP's interunit publication, the *Attendant,* was published in June 1944. This issue featured an article by George S. Stevenson, medical director of the National Committee, called "The Mental Hygiene Movement," and included these articles as well: "Self Control and Objectivity," "Pennhurst Profile," and "Doctors Are People." Stevenson's article briefly reviewed the history of the NCMH and concluded with a ringing endorsement of the MHP:

> The Mental Hygiene Program of the Civilian Public Service can be an invaluable aid in meeting this emergency, but promises even greater benefits through the fact that hundreds of men after the war will through first-hand experience be acquainted with the problems and the needs. The conscientious objector is bound at the present time to suffer from the attitude accompanying a united forceful effort to win the war. I think of this group of a few thousand men as an army of vigilantes who in this society of ours carry the function of preserving and securing peace. The loss of a few thousand men from our armed forces is a small price for a country to pay to have within it an intelligent group directed year in and year out toward those elements that tend to preserve international good-will and directed against those elements that would destroy it. If we can add to this value that it is potentially a nucleus of informed citizenry directed against violence in the handling of the mentally ill and aimed at the reduction of conflict in the minds of the mentally disturbed, the price paid will be even more justified.[14]

This inaugural issue of the *Attendant* was a resounding success. It was the first time anyone had paid serious attention to the lowly attendants who performed the day-to-day work at mental hospitals and training schools. Words of appreciation and congratulations poured in to the Mental Hygiene Program.[15] Eleanor Roosevelt sent the MHP a note: "I know of your work and think it good." Paul Comly French of the National Service Board for Religious Objectors wrote, "In discussing the hospital program with Colonel Kosch and Mr. Imirie yesterday, both spoke highly of *The Attendant,* and said they felt it would serve an extremely useful purpose."[16]

THE ATTENDANT

THIS ISSUE:
Symposium — Self Control and Objectivity
Pennhurst Profile
Doctors Are People

VOL. I, No. I
JUNE, 1944

THE MENTAL HYGIENE MOVEMENT
By George S. Stevenson, M. D.

Dr. Stevenson is medical director of the National Committee for Mental Hygiene, 1790 Broadway, New York, N. Y.

•

The National Committee for Mental Hygiene was founded by Clifford W. Beers in 1909. This sounds like a very definite statement of a beginning. But all of the humanitarian movements have had a much subtler beginning than that and the mental hygiene movement is no exception.

There was a time in our western European culture when mental illness was interpreted in terms of demoniacal possession. There seemed to be no other way of explaining the fact that a person with the same bodily form as a loved one, the same tone of voice, the same language and the same knowledge as existed in the past was in spirit quite changed. This could be explained by the idea that a new spirit, a demon, had entered into the body in place of the original spirit and that this was no longer the father, or mother, or brother, or sister, or friend, but a demon in disguise. It is understandable that cruel measures should be employed to give the devil punishment for having done so foul a deed. It is equally understandable that the mentally ill should be avoided and that they should be looked upon with some degree of fear, horror or loathing.

When the time came that this attitude could be sufficiently mollified for curiosity to replace fear and horror, a distinct advance had been made. Today we are apt to think it pretty terrible that the mentally ill could be visited as one now visits the zoo, but we probably had to go through such a stage of dangerous curiosity as a preliminary to scientific study. Through greater familiarity with the mentally ill, Pinel came to understand that the cruel restraints, then the vogue, were unnecessary and he did much to demonstrate the validity of his viewpoint, but the idea that the mentally ill were not quite on the same level as other human beings prevailed and crusades have been necessary from time to time to overcome that attitude.

In the middle of the last century Dorothea Dix found that the public had not grown to the point of fully utilizing the recommendations of Pinel, and that much neglect as well as downright cruelty and unnecessary restraint still characterized the handling of the mentally ill. Her crusade, too, was ahead of its time.

When it is realized that up to 1900 psychiatry was practically unknown as a specialty of medicine, it will be understood how much ahead of her time she really was. Prior to 1900 there were only about four psychiatric out-patient clinics in the whole country and these were established under other than psychiatric auspices. With the opening of the twentieth century the development of psychiatry appeared in no uncertain terms. Taking the out-patient clinic as an indicator of this progress we have the startling figures that in the first five years of the twentieth century three new clinics appeared and five more in the next half decade. From 1910 to 1915, twenty-three additional clinics were opened and in the next five years sixty-one more.

It is, therefore, evident that Clifford W. Beers came on the scene with a tide that was ready for his contribution. His book A Mind That Found Itself, written after several years as a patient in a mental hospital, resulted in the organization of the Connecticut Society for Mental Hygiene in 1908 and the National Committee for Mental Hygiene in 1909. Already several medical schools had conceived of good (for those days) psychiatric departments, and university facilities conceived along the lines of the best hospital practice

(*Continued on Page 6*)

A Publication of Civilian Public Service Units in Mental Hospitals and Training Schools

37. *The Attendant* (Mental Hygiene Program of the Civilian Public Service). (Mennonite Church USA Historical Committee and Archives, Goshen, Indiana)

The publication was so successful that the MHP leaders decided in August to orient the publication to all attendants working at institutions, not just COs.

It was not a coincidence that an article by Stevenson was featured in the first issue of the *Attendant*. Almost from the start, the leaders of the Mental Hygiene Program had believed that to have credibility, and even to be permitted to continue their work, they needed to have the support of respected medical and psychiatric leaders. The care of the mentally ill and the administration of mental hospitals and training schools fell under the province of the medical profession. Their work would be challenged unless they could demonstrate that they had the blessings of leaders of that profession. Before long, they had assembled a group of four well-respected advisers, Stevenson from the NCMH, Byberry superintendent Zeller, Samuel Hamilton of the U.S. Public Health Service, and Earl Bond of Pennsylvania Hospital.

On July 31, Zeller sent a letter introducing the MHP of the CPS to superintendents of all of the mental hospitals and training schools to which COs had been assigned: "I am confident that the program is well directed toward helping the institutions for which the men are working. I can also attest to the integrity of these men and have been assured that the results of their effort will be achieved through consultation with professional persons and will not divulge either the sources of material or names of individuals and institutions." Zeller explained that he, Bond, Hamilton, and Stevenson had agreed to serve as advisers to the program and would ensure that materials prepared by the MHP would be "of value to those working in the psychiatric field" and would not be "of a type which will be construed as exploiting Civilian Public Service or indicting or exposing any institution."[17] He concluded by welcoming the reactions and suggestions of superintendents to the program. The letter actually had been drafted by Edelstein.

Two months after the publication of the inaugural issue of the *Attendant*, the Mental Hygiene Program started the *Exchange Service* as a vehicle for sharing information and ideas among CPS units.[18] In contrast to the *Attendant*, the mimeographed *Exchange Service* was not circulated outside of CPS mental hospital and training school units. It often contained candid and confidential information. Unlike the *Attendant* and other MHP publications, prior review and approval by professional advisers were not required for the *Exchange Service*.

Sometime around the summer, Hetzel joined the MHP. He would take responsibility for a third phase of the program, the preparation of legal materials with an emphasis on outdated state commitment laws through which mentally ill persons could be railroaded into institutions. The reform of commitment laws had been neglected by psychiatric and mental hygiene groups. As early as March 1941, Roger Baldwin of the American Civil Liberties Union had contacted the National Committee to obtain information on commitment laws. Medical director Stevenson had attempted to steer Baldwin away from adopting a civil liberties approach to commitment. He explained that the concerns surrounding commitment were complex and involved "conflicting issues." In cases in which mentally sick persons might need prompt hospitalization and custody for protection against suicide and homicide, Stevenson wrote, it was best for the patient "when the legal procedure is reduced to a minimum." When it came to individuals who were not a danger to themselves or others but were not mentally healthy, decisions should be placed in the hands of psychiatrists: "The usual theories surrounding criminal procedure are not applicable, I mean such things as 'reasonable doubt' and more dependence has to be placed on professional judgment."[19]

Later, in August 1944, the ACLU approached the American Psychiatric Association to offer cooperation in studies of commitment laws. Clifford Forster, staff counsel of the ACLU, who had written the APA, received a curt response from Dr. Winfred Overholser, the APA's secretary-treasurer: "The Association looks upon laws relating to the admission of patients to mental hospitals as affecting intimately the welfare of persons suffering from mental disease, and in general I think it is safe to say that members of the Association would favor fewer legal restrictions regarding admissions rather than the reverse."[20] Overholser told Forster that he would be glad to bring his letter to the attention of the chairman of the Committee on the Legal Aspects of Psychiatry, Dr. Paul L. Schroeder. Schroeder was serving in the U.S. Army at the time. Hetzel and the MHP would have a different perspective on commitment laws than the National Committee and the APA. Together with the ACLU, they would seek to expand legal protections for people committed to mental hospitals or facing commitment.

Hetzel would join Edelstein, Barton, and Steer on a four-member "Central Committee" of the MHP. They would serve as the governing structure of the MHP until its end in 1946 and the formation of the National Mental Health Foundation.

It did not take long for the COs to run afoul of some psychiatrists. The second issue of the *Attendant* featured an article by Ruth Dingman, R.N., director of the AFSC's women's service unit in mental hospitals, and included a symposium, "The Use of Force."[21] The symposium dealt with a question that had plagued COs at state mental hospitals and training schools: how could violent or disturbed patients be handled in a nonviolent way? The symposium stressed kindness and respect, but also acknowledged that there were situations that arose on institutional wards in which some kind of intervention was necessary to protect patients from themselves or others. It contained descriptions, with illustrations, of a variety of holds (for example, "arm hold," "half nelson and arm lock," and "full nelson"). The symposium created a stir. Some psychiatrists claimed that the holds advocated in the symposium could be dangerous. Samuel Hamilton of the U.S. Public Health Service, one of the MHP's advisers, was especially disturbed by the symposium and believed that it demonstrated the risk of allowing laypersons to prescribe techniques to be used for the mentally ill.[22] Privately, the leaders of the MHP were delighted that the symposium had generated interest in and discussion of a long-neglected issue at institutions. The September issue of the *Attendant* contained another symposium on the use of force that published reactions to the initial contributions.

The initial enthusiasm of some of the COs involved in organizing the Mental Hygiene Program soon turned to pessimism and doubt. Hal Barton started feeling the strain of "double duty," working full-time on the ward and then off-duty work on the MHP, and questioned whether the program would have any long-term impact. Will Hetzel had similar feelings. Both Barton and Hetzel were ready to give up. Then Len Edelstein came up with a novel idea: get the Selective Service to approve the formation of a detached unit to allow Edelstein, Barton, Hetzel, and Steer to work full-time on the MHP.[23] Barton and Hetzel were skeptical about whether the Selective Service would approve the plan, but told him to go ahead and try.

Edelstein spoke with Paul Furnas of the AFSC and Paul Comly French of NSBRO about his idea.[24] Both supported it, but they knew that they would need to have Zeller's support for the Selective Service to go along with the proposal. Zeller was a bit unsure about the establishment of an MHP detached unit, but Furnas met privately with him about it in August and Zeller seemed willing to endorse it. The church committees and NSBRO met with the program's leaders to discuss the plan. Barton was still unsure about committing himself but told French in a private conversation that he would stay with the program if full-time service were approved. From August to October, numerous discussions were held involving the MHP leaders, NSBRO, Zeller, the AFSC and other church committees, the National Committee, and the Selective Service.

Effective October 27, 1944, Barton, Steer, Hetzel, and Edelstein were assigned to work full-time on the Mental Hygiene Program. That same day, sixty-three persons met at the Hotel Sylvania in Philadelphia to discuss the future of the CPS mental hospital program. Participants included six state officials; fifteen hospital superintendents; twenty CPS assistant directors; the Central Committee of the MHP; MHP advisers George Stevenson and Earl Bond; representatives of NSBRO, the AFSC, the BSC, and the MCC; and Colonel Kosch and Austin Imirie of the Selective Service. In the minutes of the meeting, Dr. Bond was quoted as describing the MHP as "a chance that comes once in a lifetime to raise the standards of attendant's work in mental hospitals."[25]

A complex plan for a detached Mental Hygiene Program unit had been worked out. The men were assigned to a Fish and Wildlife Service unit at Bowie, Maryland, for administrative purposes, although it meant little more than a unit name on their CPS ID cards. Zeller continued to provide the men with room and board and office space at Byberry. The AFSC, BSC, and MCC agreed to allocate funds for program expenses. The church agencies would provide a total of $1,364.73 in 1944, $11,696.82 in 1945, and $11,619.66 in 1946.[26] NSBRO and the AFSC covered the men's monthly maintenance fees. A final issue to be ironed out related to technical supervision of the men's work. George Stevenson of the National Committee agreed to assume this responsibility, subject to approval by the NCMH's board. It took a number of months for details to be finalized.

Stevenson wrote the MHP around February 15, 1945, to specify the conditions under which the National Committee would supervise the program. He started by explaining that the COs would need to accept restrictions imposed by the National Committee: "One cannot have the full freedom of an individual without carrying the full responsibility. If this responsibility is divided with or incorporated into that of others, as would be the case in operating under the egis [*sic*] of the National Committee for Mental Hygiene, limitations have necessarily to exist." Stevenson proceeded to confirm that the National Committee would not incur any financial obligations for the MHP. Then he stated his requirements: "I must be kept informed of all activities. This will be best accomplished by monthly reports of activities, achievements and problems. *The report must be made to me as Medical Director* and any reports that are to be distributed must be channeled out for general use in this way." On April 9, Stevenson wrote the MHP to confirm that the Selective Service had approved the arrangement. He quoted from a letter from Austin Imirie of the Selective Service regarding "Leonard Gerald Edelstein, Philip Riegel Steer, Willard Charles Hetzel, and Harold Edwin Logan Barton": "From now on the control and reporting for these men is your responsibility."[27]

Throughout the history of the MHP, Stevenson was a strong supporter of the group. He gave the program the freedom to pursue its objectives and never interfered with its activities. Years later, the organizers of the MHP would express their appreciation of and respect for Stevenson.[28] The Selective Service never would have approved the detached unit if an organization like the National Committee and medical leaders such as Stevenson had not been willing to sponsor it. At the same time, the COs considered the National Committee to be too cautious and unwilling to confront the problems at institutions.

The Mental Hygiene Program's brochure listed the National Committee for Mental Hygiene as a sponsor of the program and six men as advisers. Bond, Hamilton, Stevenson, and Zeller stayed on as advisers. Dr. James Lewald, superintendent of the District Training School in Laurel, Maryland, was added to demonstrate the program's interest in mental deficiency as well as mental illness, and William Draper Lewis, director of the American Law Institute, was included as a legal adviser.

◆   ◆   ◆

With the four COs working full-time, and then some, the MHP flourished throughout 1945 and into 1946. Edelstein continued to serve as coordinator of the program and worked on public relations and the administration of the overall program. Barton was the chairman of the Education Division; Hetzel, chairman of the Legal Division; and Steer, editor of the *Attendant*. Zeller permitted two male Byberry patients to work for the MHP as clerks and secretaries.[29] Around July 1945, Zeller also approved the assignment of Herb Stoddard, a Byberry CPS man, to the MHP on a half-time basis. Stoddard had been volunteering as treasurer of the MHP on his free time. The Central Committee identified COs at forty-two mental hospitals and sixteen training schools to serve as program representatives and board members of the *Attendant*.[30]

After the establishment of the MHP as a detached unit, NSBRO, the church committees, and the Selective Service continued to be pleased with the program. The MHP brought positive attention to the CPS at a time when CPS camps and units were organizing unions and rebelling against the Selective Service, NSBRO, and some of the church committees. By the summer of 1945, the Central Committee was confident that the Selective Service would approve the assignment of additional men to the MHP and wrote units inviting men to apply for work at the program.[31] Thirteen applications were received. Paul French lobbied the Selective Service to approve the assignment of additional men to the MHP. In late fall, the Selective Service approved the transfer of seven men to the program: Frank Wright, John Steer, Stephen Thiermann, Grant Stoltzfus, George Thorman, Harmon Wilkinson, and Herbert Stoddard.[32] Except for Stoddard, all of the new men came from units other than Byberry. Stoltzfus and Steer had come from training schools; the rest of the men had been at mental hospitals. The new men were to live at a house on Spruce Street in Philadelphia. When Barton wrote NSBRO's French to ask if the men could live in their own places, French warned him that Colonel Kosch would probably cancel their assignments if they did not live at the Spruce Street location.[33] They were still in the CPS, and the Selective Service did not want men to live on their own.

Freed of their work at Byberry, the members of the Central Committee traveled to other CPS units to build interest in the MHP.[34] From January 29 to February 6, 1945, Barton visited five institutions in the Northeast. That spring, he took a trip to visit CPS units and camps in Ohio, Colorado, Utah, California, Oregon, Washington, Montana, and Iowa, with stops at the Menninger Clinic in Kansas and the BSC headquarters in Illinois. Steer traveled to CPS units in Maine in June. Barton and Hetzel met with CPS men in Lyons, New Jersey, in August. Hetzel made a trip to the Midwest in the fall of that year. Edelstein traveled frequently to meet with representatives of other organizations.

Under Steer's editorship, the *Attendant* continued to receive acclaim and gave the MHP national visibility. The eight- to twelve-page magazine carried stories,

38. *The Psychiatric Aide* (National Mental Health Foundation). (Mennonite Church USA Historical Committee and Archives, Goshen, Indiana)

commentaries, letters, and cartoons featuring mental patients and attendants. In January 1946, the magazine was renamed the *Psychiatric Aid* (and later the *Psychiatric Aide*), reflecting the MHP's goal to upgrade the status of direct-care staff. By February of that year, the magazine had a paid circulation of 1,446.[35] That number would double by the following October.

The *CPS Attendant Handbook* was finalized in April.[36] The thirty-three-page mimeographed handbook was edited by Barton, with contributions by men at other CPS units. It included four parts: "A Look Backward" (for example, "Birth of a Science"), "The Patient and You" ("Patients Are People—Sick People"), "Common Types of Mental Illness" ("General Paresis and Cerebral Syphilis"), and "Sources of Further Information and Study." The *Handbook on Restraint* was drafted in late 1945.[37] The MHP also developed public education pamphlets, including *One Out of Twenty*, on mental illness; *Forgotten Children*, on mental deficiency; and *Concerning the Least of These*, on idiocy.[38] Reprints of articles written by others and directories of state mental hygiene associations were distributed by the MHP as well. Barton continued to edit the interunit *Exchange Service*, one-page flyers based on reports of men at the various mental hospital and training school units. For example, one *Exchange Service* on training schools included excerpts of letters on topics titled "A Mixed Ward" ("low grades and nearly normal patients on the same wards"), "Camisole and Sedative Pack," "Slapping 'Behind Scenes,'" and "Recreation."

Hetzel and the MHP prepared model laws and legal digests and worked with both the American Bar Association and the American Civil Liberties Union. By February 1946, legal surveys of eighteen states had been completed.[39]

Barton continued working on the "Summary Statement." He developed "Fact Finder" questionnaires to solicit information from COs and institutional staff about all aspects of the operation of institutions: restraints, personnel policies and hiring, laundry, nutrition, the handling of tuberculosis patients, and others. For narratives, Barton gave detailed instructions: "STATE ONLY FACTS; ACTUALLY WITNESSED; DESCRIBE THEM VIVIDLY AND ACCURATELY WITH CORROBORATION GIVEN WHEN NECESSARY; RECOMMENDATIONS ESPECIALLY DENOTED AS SUCH; AND THE WHOLE STATEMENT CERTIFIED TO BE TRUE." A four-page single-spaced paper gave good and bad examples of descriptive, factual writing. Other notices sent to CPS units requested copies of photographs of the institutions and news clippings related to them. As the end of the CPS neared in early 1946, Barton and the MHP gave a final push for COs to submit materials. One document, "Ways and Means of Increasing Participation in Mental Hygiene Program of CPS," listed ten methods to encourage CPS men to learn about the MHP and collect information for the "Summary Statement," including "Be a Reporter," "Be a Recorder," and "Group Meeting." For new men, the document advised, "Any new men who come to the unit should be oriented to MHP. 'Of course, now that you're at this hospital (or training school) unit, you'll be sending materials to the MHP.'" An accompanying figure, "Participation in MHP," listed all of the mental hospital and training school units and charted the number of fact finders returned, narratives received, supplementary materials submitted, and attendant articles published.[40] COs at the Byberry, Greystone, Lyons, and Fairfield units each had submitted more than 50 materials. Those COs at three units, Rosewood, Cambridge, and Buckley, had submitted none. A total of 335 fact-finder questionnaires and 449 narratives had been received by the MHP.

Barton was receiving materials almost daily. Overwhelmed by the narratives he was getting, Barton typed a one-page summary of reports received on one day: "All in the Day's Mail—Things That Need Not Be." He listed abuses at five institutions submitted by COs: "The wet towel is used quite often in strangling a patient into submission"; "73 patients on the ward . . . 24 in cuff restraint." At the bottom of the page, Barton wrote: "THESE AND THOUSANDS OF SIMILAR NAZI-AMERICAN ATROCITIES ARE BEING COMMITTED EVERY DAY IN OUR PUBLIC INSTITUTIONS. AND . . . WHAT ARE *YOU* DOING ABOUT IT? WHY NOT TRAIN *FIRST* IN AMERICA FOR THE FOUR FREEDOMS?"[41]

Phil Steer was generally quiet and went about his job of publishing the *Attendant*. He sent a strongly worded note to the other members of the Central Committee, expressing concern that Barton's summary might get into the wrong hands. "My God! I hope this has not gone out yet!" wrote Steer. He continued:

> We have a terrific opportunity to win a mighty battle against mistreatment and kindred evils thru the summary statement. Let's not tempt enemy aggression against us before we are ready for him. . . . There is a time for telling the story, but it is not yet. . . . Let's work like dogs to collect and organize available information. Then, with plenty of ammunition . . . let's plan a strategy. Then when the time is right, let's start our war! But why invite unnecessary trouble by making big noises and loading our guns with confetti like this? You're right: I'm excited. This thing scares me half to death.[42]

This incident revealed the true nature of the Mental Hygiene Program. Steer was correct. Premature release of some of the information the MHP was getting and a revelation of how the members of the MHP thought about the institutions could threaten the entire program. Edelstein, Barton, Hetzel, and Steer had carefully framed the MHP as an educational program working hand in hand with the psychiatric and mental hygiene establishments. They had accepted the sponsorship of the National Committee, which was dominated by medical professionals, and shied away from actions that might embarrass psychiatrists and institutional officials. The MHP's brochure described the "Summary Statement" as a cooperative effort with institutional superintendents and professionals: "A statement of conditions, based upon the experiences of C.P.S. men working in mental hospitals, prepared in cooperation with and under the guidance of hospital superintendents and other professional persons in the field. 'Fact-finder' forms will be used, in part, to collect material for the statement. It is felt that discussion centered around the 'fact-finders' will prove helpful in an understanding of institutional procedures." This description was included in NSBRO's *Four Year Report of Civilian Public Service*.[43]

From the start, what the four COs had in mind for the "Summary Statement" was not a report on improving institutional procedures prepared under the supervision of superintendents and professionals or a survey comparable to ones that had been conducted by the National Committee and then the Public Health Service under Hamilton. It was intended to be a hard-hitting exposé of the nation's treatment of people in institutions. Hetzel, Barton, Steer, and Edelstein knew that it would be controversial among many superintendents and professionals. The release of the statement was planned for after the war because they would then be free from the CPS and the control of the Selective Service. Hetzel had been at Cleveland State Hospital when COs went to *Cleveland Press* reporter Walter Lerch and the Reverend Dores R. Sharpe with complaints about abuses at the institution. The Selective Service and the AFSC had agreed to close the unit, and the four COs knew that their detached unit could be closed if they offended public officials.

Less than a month after Steer's emotional rebuke of Barton's premature paper, Edelstein, Barton, Hetzel, and Steer would reveal their plans in a confidential letter sent to CPS mental hospital and training school units.

◆   ◆   ◆

On August 8, 1945, Edelstein, Barton, Hetzel, and Steer sent all CPS mental hospital and training school units a "Special Release" titled "MHP on the Move." The release was marked "For CPS Circulation Only," and the first sentence read: "This is a confidential report." The release laid out the COs' strategy for the Mental Hygiene Program. It would take on not individual institutions but the entire institutional system:

> STRATEGY—Rather than attempt exposés of individual institutions, which flare up sensationally and then are forgotten in a week or two leaving complicated administrative issues and sore spots often as injurious as the original problems, we plan to disclose to the public the *inherent weaknesses* of all the institutions we now serve—those that stem from deep-rooted social causes—as representing the weaknesses of the whole institutional system. . . .
>
> [W]e think it much smarter to *prepare now*—to gather as much materials showing institutional conditions and needs as possible—to get from each of you the day-by-day eyewitness accounts of general conditions; physical abuses, poor servings of food, crude, unkind personnel who have been inadequately trained, poorly paid, and stifled in possibilities for promotion—in short to get all evidence

which bears on the treatment of the patients in as specific form as possible that we can eliminate false general opinions which can not be substantiated. We also desire information describing activities or departments of the institution which give model or ideal methods of care, treatment, or personnel relationships. Then, when ready, this material will be presented without names of persons or places, unless prior approval is secured, to the public in the form of an appealing, colorful story of the mental institutions of America as we have observed them.[44]

The COs' plan did not stop at a national exposé of institutions. The report on institutions would kick off the establishment of a permanent mental hygiene program. Ironically, Edelstein, Barton, Hetzel, and Steer pointed to the founding of the National Committee as an example: "It can certainly serve to introduce to the public the permanent MHP in much the way as Clifford Beers' book describing his ill-treatment in only 3 institutions laid the basis for the National Committee for Mental Hygiene." Without mentioning the NCMH by name, they suggested that it had failed to address the needs of those patients in institutions: "At present there is not one national organization that focuses primarily on the needs of patients in mental institutions and bolstering the sagging attendant position."[45]

In the following months, the four COs concentrated on drumming up support for a permanent national organization and exploring sources of funding for their efforts. Len Edelstein played the central role in making contact with civic leaders and public figures. Through its relationship with the AFSC, the MHP was well positioned to be introduced to key persons. Clarence Pickett and Rufus Jones of the AFSC arranged for Edelstein and others to meet with prominent Philadelphia citizens. In addition, Edelstein had written a thirty-two-page paper titled "We Are Accountable: A View of Mental Institutions for the Pendle Hill Publications Committee."[46] Pendle Hill was a well-known Friends adult education and meeting center located outside of Philadelphia.[47] Edelstein received an award for his paper, and it was published as a Pendle Hill pamphlet. Mrs. Curtis Bok, wife of a Pennsylvania Supreme Court justice, purchased hundreds of copies of Edelstein's paper and sent them to friends, asking them for their help.[48]

Clarence Pickett arranged a meeting between Edelstein and Barton and Eleanor Roosevelt in September 1945. Roosevelt had written favorably about the Hudson River State Hospital COs in her "My Day" column. Edelstein and Barton brought photos of Byberry secretly taken by Charles Lord to the meeting. Weisbord described what happened when they showed Roosevelt Lord's photos:

Mrs. Roosevelt was appalled. "But surely these are exaggerations," she said. "They were taken in Mississippi or Georgia, weren't they? I've seen such things in the

South. But wouldn't it be unfair to publicize these generally? It would upset the families of other mental patients."

"Mrs. Roosevelt," said Hal Barton, "these pictures were made within ninety miles of here, at a hospital in one of our wealthiest northern states."[49]

Mrs. Roosevelt immediately pledged her support of the program. Edelstein sent her MHP literature and asked her to write a letter of invitation to prominent Americans. On October 31, she wrote the following letter to seventeen persons, including the secretary of commerce, the surgeon general, labor leader Walter Reuther, William Paley of CBS, and Robert McLean of the Associated Press: "A short time ago I saw Leonard Edelstein and Harold Barton of the Mental Hygiene Program. I am enclosing some of the literature which they sent me. As you know the care in our mental hospitals has always been poor and during the war this group has raised the standards. These young men wish to do a more permanent job and I am very interested in having them succeed. I hope very much, if it is possible, that you will see them or write to them if you are interested." Surgeon General Thomas Parran wrote Mrs. Roosevelt back, saying that he has asked Dr. Robert Felix, chief of the Mental Hygiene Division of the U.S. Public Health Service, to speak with Edelstein and Barton.[50] The MHP had already been in contact with Felix.

Edelstein met again with Mrs. Roosevelt in November to discuss ways in which she could support the Mental Hygiene Program's efforts. In December, the MHP sent a "Special Emergency Release" to all CPS hospital units: "Recent developments have shown that we must obtain as soon as possible a large supply of pictures showing conditions within our institutions. In a recent conversation with Mrs. Roosevelt, a handful of pictures impressed her more than all the words we had. If you have pictures, either negatives or prints, or if you know of some that are available, please contact us immediately."[51] Members of the MHP could not contain their glee at gaining the support of Eleanor Roosevelt. Mrs. Roosevelt would later assist the MHP in 1946 and '47.

Edelstein and the others used a "snowball" technique to line up supporters of their program: having prominent figures introduce them to other prominent figures. Arthur Morgan, former head of the Tennessee Valley Authority and past president of Antioch College, was instrumental in helping them gain support.[52] Rufus Jones and Dr. Earl Bond approached former U.S. Supreme Court justice Owen J. Roberts on the MHP's behalf. Author Pearl Buck, who happened to have a daughter with intellectual disabilities, had seen the *Attendant* and knew NSBRO's French. She would introduce members of the MHP to other people.

Gaining the support of prominent public figures was one thing; obtaining the cooperation of the psychiatric and mental hygiene professions in establishing a new organization was another. The MHP's formal and informal psychiatric advisers had mixed feelings about the COs going off on their own.[53] The National Committee's Stevenson was willing to go along with the formation of a new organization and told Barton: "Do what you have *got* to do to get done what you *want* to do."[54] Robert Felix thought that the problems facing mental health were big enough that it could use all of the help it could get. Hamilton was less than enthusiastic about the idea, especially if the MHP planned on publicizing institutional conditions. Through his Public Health surveys of institutions, he had taken a cautious, understated approach and did not want to embarrass institutional superintendents.

Edelstein and Barton attended an informal meeting in New York City with eighteen to twenty officers of the National Committee and psychiatrists to discuss the establishment of a permanent program.[55] The meeting went on six hours and covered Edelstein and Barton's public education and training goals for the Mental Hygiene Program. The professionals in the room split into three groups. One group believed, like Hamilton, that publicity could do more harm than good. Others questioned whether laypersons should be involved in leading a public education and training effort. A third group thought the job needed to be done and that the men should do it if they were willing to do so. By the end of the meeting, Edelstein and Barton resolved to go ahead with the program, even if unanimous support from the professional community would be lacking.

In November 1945, members of the Central Committee of the MHP reviewed their commitments to the program.[56] When the program had become a detached unit under the sponsorship of the National Committee, the men had pledged to stay with it an additional two to three years. However, they had never made a commitment in writing, and there were different understandings of what they had pledged. Much depended on the future of the CPS. The war had ended, but mass demobilization of the CPS had not occurred. The American Legion and other groups opposed speedy discharges from the CPS. The men suspected that the CPS would be over by the following spring, though. The general sentiment was that the four men would stay on with the MHP if the program could pay at least some of their living expenses. Fund-raising would become important.

The January 1946 issue of the *Psychiatric Aid,* the new name of the *Attendant,* announced that the Mental Hygiene Program of the Civilian Public Service had become the National Mental Health Program. The February issue corrected the new name. Because of Pennsylvania law, the program could not incorporate under that new name. Instead, the program would be called the National Mental Health Foundation.[57] This name was certified as available and registered with the Commonwealth of Pennsylvania on February 11. An application for corporate charter was filed on February 21, and a charter was granted on April 26. According to the charter, Hetzel, Barton, Edelstein, and Steer would serve as directors of the national foundation, effective May 1, until "the election of their successors." The CPS was winding down but not yet over in the spring of 1946. On April 3, the Central Committee met to formalize the transition from the MHP of the CPS to the NMHF. An agreement was signed by Barton, Hetzel, Steer, and Edelstein and approved by Stevenson: "Since the activities of the National Mental Health Foundation are consistent with the expressed purposes of the Mental Hygiene Program of Civilian Public Service, the Central Committee has agreed to continue to loan services of assigned personnel to the Foundation."[58]

The formation of the National Mental Health Foundation was publicly announced on May 6. The headline of an article in the *Philadelphia Inquirer* read: "Drive Opens to Assist Mentally Ill: Health Unit Asks Higher Standards." The first sentence of the article stated, "A countrywide campaign to aid in the treatment and care of more than 8,000,000 Americans suffering from mental diseases and another 2,000,000 persons who are mental defectives has been instituted by the National Mental Health Foundation under the leadership of former United States Supreme Court Justice Owen J. Roberts, national chairman."[59] The story was picked up by the Associated Press and printed in the *New York Times*, the *New York Post, PM,* the *Baltimore Sun,* and other newspapers.[60] On the same day the formation of the national foundation was announced, Albert Maisel's article "Bedlam, 1946: U.S. Mental Hospitals Are a Shame and Disgrace" was published in *Life.*

◆   ◆   ◆

Maisel's *Life* magazine article was a stunning indictment of the treatment of mental patients in America's institutions. It started with a description of Philadelphia State Hospital: "In Philadelphia the sovereign Commonwealth of Pennsylvania maintains a dilapidated, overcrowded, undermanned mental 'hospital' known as Byberry." Maisel went on to characterize Byberry as representative of mental hospitals across the nation. Beatings, and even murder, occurred at institutions. Patients often were fed a starvation diet, jam-packed into crowded firetraps, and denied any form of treatment or therapy. Many spent their time in bodily restraints: "Thousands spend their days—often for weeks at a stretch—locked in devices euphemistically called 'restraints': thick leather handcuffs, great canvas camisoles, 'muffs,' 'mitts,' wristlets, locks and straps and restraining sheets."[61] Maisel described abuses at one institution after another: Byberry; Cleveland State; Massillon, Ohio; Nevada, Missouri; Hastings, Nebraska; Fairfield, Connecticut; and mental hospitals in New York, Pennsylvania, Iowa, New Mexico, Utah, and elsewhere. Characteristic of *Life* magazine, Maisel's article was a photo essay. The article featured stark photographs depicting overcrowding, neglect, restraint, useless work, nakedness, overcrowding, forced labor, idleness, and despair at Cleveland State, Byberry, and elsewhere. To dispute the notion that the horrors were "the best that can be done for the insane," Maisel pointed out that some states had managed to avoid overcrowding and some hospitals provided therapy to their patients and had eliminated beatings.

Maisel explained that he had visited a dozen institutions personally but that his charges against the institutions were "far too serious to be based solely upon the observations of any single investigator." He cited findings of investigating commissions and covered Walter Lerch's *Cleveland Press* exposé and the Reverend Dores Sharpe's grand jury investigation. In addition, he had access to hundreds of reports from mental hospitals in twenty states and quoted widely from them in his article:

> There is now available for the first time a reliable body of data covering nearly one third of all the state hospitals in 20 states from Washington to Virginia, from Maine to Utah. A by-product of the war's aggravation of the long-existing personnel shortage, this data represents the collated reports of more than 3,000 conscientious objectors who, under Selective Service, volunteered for assignment as mental hospital attendants. The majority are still in service and, with Selective Service approval, these serious young Methodists, Quakers, Mennonites and Brethren have been filling out questionnaires and writing "narratives" for use in the preparation of instructional materials for mental-hospital workers.[62]

The war had been over for less than a year, and patriotic fervor continued to run deep in the nation. *Life* had given extensive coverage to World War II and had published graphic photographs of the ravages of war. To many people, the COs had failed to come to the defense of their country. Maisel anticipated and countered tendencies to dismiss reports of mental hospital conditions by a group of COs: "One may differ, as I do, with the views that led these young men to take up a difficult and unpopular position against service on the armed forces. But one cannot help but recognize their honesty and sincerity in reporting upon the conditions they found in the hospitals to which they were assigned."[63]

Maisel concluded his article with a call for reform. He urged leaders and common citizens "to put an end to concentration camps that masquerade as hospitals and to make cure rather than incarceration the goal of their mental institutions."[64]

Two months after the publication of Maisel's *Life* article, *Reader's Digest* published a condensed version of the article, minus the photographs. The article ran in the July 1946 issue of the magazine and was titled "The Shame of Our Mental Hospitals."[65]

In the 1940s, magazines like *Life* and *Reader's Digest* were influential in shaping popular opinion. Together with radio, the theater and movies, fiction and nonfiction books, and newspapers, national magazines served as major sources of information on current events, popular culture, and national trends. There was no television, let alone cable, with its multitude of choices. There was no Internet, no Web sites, listservs, blogs, chat rooms, e-mail, Webcasts, or instant messaging. An article in *Life* or *Reader's Digest* in the 1940s would have many, many times the impact of a magazine article today.

Life, in particular, held a special place in American culture. Started by Henry Luce in 1936, the magazine targeted a popular audience.[66] By the late 1940s, *Life* reached 21 percent of the population over ten years of age, roughly 22.5 million people.[67] It had an extremely high "pass-along" rate, with a copy of each issue read by as many as fourteen to seventeen persons in the late 1930s. *Life* could be found in waiting rooms, barbershops, and beauty parlors across the country. Its extensive use of photographs made the magazine interesting and easy to skim. A casual reader could have perused the gripping photographs in "Bedlam, 1946" and gotten the message that something was terribly wrong at America's mental hospitals. As James L. Baughman noted, "*Life's* reliance on visual imagery undoubtedly gave it greater influence than its audience size alone indicated. A single photograph in *Life* may have, in some instances, moved many more Americans than a stream of dreary, formula-driven newspaper stories and the fatuous generalities—often nothing more than background noise—of radio commentators."[68]

The publisher and editors of *Life* sought to represent American ideals and values—"nationalism, capitalism, and classlessness, a sense of confidence, optimism, and exceptionalism, and the sure belief that the American way was the way of the world."[69] *Life* articles and advertisements—Coca-Cola, Maytag, Whitman's, Maxwell House, Goodyear, Mobilgas, Gillette, Scot Tissue, Windex, French's, and many others—communicated a distinctly American way of life. To be condemned in a *Life* magazine article would have been akin to being called un-American.

The idea of approaching a national magazine to publish reports collected by the Mental Hygiene Program of the CPS and the NMHF came from one of the foundation's supporters.[70] A book might reach a few thousand readers; an article in a national magazine could reach millions. This supporter arranged a meeting between Len Edelstein and one of the editors of *Reader's Digest*. Edelstein showed the editor the same photographs that had appalled Eleanor Roosevelt. Like Roosevelt, the editor was hooked by the squalid scenes of Byberry's A and B Buildings. Meanwhile, Albert Maisel, who had published an exposé of Veterans Administration mental hospitals, had spoken with *Life* editors about doing a similar story on state mental hospitals. The *Reader's Digest* editor put Edelstein in contact with Maisel. *Life* would publish Maisel's article, and *Reader's Digest* would reprint it.

Maisel visited the NMHF, which had moved from Byberry to a former Friends school located in West Philadelphia. Years later, he described the visit: "'I recall,' Maisel said, 'coming to a hectically busy office in a basement a few blocks from the University of Pennsylvania and being welcomed by about a dozen young men and women. I spent an entire day—and later many more days—while we all sat around a big table, drank barrels of coffee, and they competed with each other in contending that the hospital each had served in was really the worst of the lot.'" Maisel paid Hal Barton's secretary to help him go through the questionnaires and narratives that had been collected for the "Summary Statement."[71] He also contracted with Charles Lord to use his photographs of Byberry and to take additional pictures. Members of the national foundation put Maisel in touch with other current or former COs and others who could guide him on tours of institutions and give him information. Justin Reese, who had been instrumental in collecting reports of abuses at Cleveland State Hospital, accompanied Maisel on visits to Ohio institutions, and the Reverend Dores R. Sharpe provided information about the grand jury investigation of Cleveland State.

The pending *Life* article created the first serious disagreement within the national foundation. The magazine wanted Maisel's article to name names. An exposé of unidentified mental hospitals would hardly have been an exposé at all. Yet Barton, Edelstein, Hetzel, and Steer had made repeated assurances to CPS men and others that the names of individuals and institutions in any narratives or questionnaires would be treated as confidential. A letter from Byberry superintendent Zeller to institutional superintendents, which had been drafted by Edelstein, made a similar guarantee. A draft of Maisel's article included the names of mental hospitals contained in the reports of CPS men in the foundation's files. Barton estimated that it had twenty-three violations of the commitment to conceal individual names.[72] Maisel claimed that *Life* would not publish his article without the names. Barton and other members of the national foundation insisted that the names be removed from the article in accord with how the "Summary Statement" had been represented to numerous people. Edelstein took the position that the names could be used if the permission of the people who had submitted the reports was obtained. For Edelstein, the opportunity to bring national attention to conditions at state institutions was too great to pass up. At a meeting between Maisel and members of the foundation, Edelstein proposed contacting the CPS men. Maisel was satisfied with this arrangement. NMHF members were divided. Barton and some of the other men believed that publication of the names of institutions could jeopardize their entire program. Barton had to leave for a conference in New York City. When he returned to the foundation, he was chagrined to learn that Edelstein and Steer had been calling CPS men for permission to use the names of institutions in their reports. He found the letter that had been sent by Zeller to superintendents, and Edelstein was forced to agree that assurances had been made that individual names would never be used. So Maisel was contacted and told that the names of institutions included in the reports collected by the program could not be used.

Life published Maisel's article without the specific names of institutions in the reports. Maisel had visited a dozen institutions himself and had access to the Cleveland State Hospital grand jury report and other documents. He had plenty of mental hospital names to use in his article. When he cited incidents in the national foundation's reports, he referred to the state in which the institution was located. The article was filled with references to reports from an Iowa, Pennsylvania, New Jersey, and so on state hospital. Anyone wanting to know the identities of the institutions could have narrowed them down to a small handful of mental hospitals at which COs had served. The controversy over the anonymity of institutions would not be the last serious disagreement within the foundation.

NMHF members hoped that the *Life* article would be published in the fall of 1946, which would have given the Central Committee time to build up the organization of the foundation. Until all of the members of the Central Committee were discharged from the CPS and out from under the control of the Selective Service, the foundation was an organization in name only. Hetzel and Edelstein were not discharged from the CPS until April. Barton was discharged on May 27 and was subject to Selective Service control when the *Life* article was published. Had publicity related to COs displeased the Selective Service, it could have sent men to government camps or even postponed their discharges. When the article was scheduled for publication in May, the foundation's members had to scramble to plan for publicity for the program. The public announcement of the NMHF was carefully timed to coincide with Maisel's article. Justice Roberts was named national chairman of the foundation before it had an external board of directors.

For Maisel, publication of his *Life* article probably came weeks too late. The founders of the Mental Hygiene Program had been in contact with Albert Deutsch on publicizing institutional conditions at least since July 1945.[73] When the possibility that *Life* or *Reader's Digest* might publish an exposé of mental hospitals first arose, the names of Deutsch and Maisel came up. Both had written about conditions at Veterans Administration hospitals. *Life* selected Maisel to write the article, but Deutsch was planning his own exposé in *PM*.

Although Maisel's *Life* article reported on conditions at institutions across the country, Byberry and Cleveland State received the most attention. His most dramatic photographs had been taken at these two institutions. Deutsch's exposés of Cleveland State and Byberry appeared in *PM* in April, weeks before the publication of Maisel's article. Deutsch had visited Byberry and reviewed the foundation's files after Maisel had been there. He received a tour of Byberry from the new superintendent, Eugene Sielke, and asked Charles Lord to see the pictures he had taken at the institution on his own and under contract with Maisel. He then asked Lord if he could use his photographs. Lord gave him permission, but only if Deutsch promised not to publish them before Maisel's article appeared. Deutsch gave his promise. Days later, *PM* published Deutsch's exposé of Byberry, along with Lord's photos. Deutsch had scooped Maisel. Maisel was livid. He called Lord, and Lord recalled that "the phone line was burning."[74] Many years later, Lord, a kind person reluctant to say anything negative about anyone, said that Deutsch had lied to him.

Despite controversies surrounding Maisel's article, and even uncertainty about whether it would ever be published, it did draw national attention to the plight of mental patients languishing in America's institutions. It also gave the fledgling National Mental Health Foundation, which had been founded by a group of young COs who had the idea that they could shine a public spotlight on conditions at state institutions, instant credibility. Even Colonel Kosch of the Selective Service believed that the story in *Life* was a "very useful article" and that the work of the men assigned to the Mental Hygiene Program would "improve the mental hospital situation."[75] After the *Life* article, neither institutional conditions nor the organization established by the COs could be ignored in the fields of psychiatry and mental hygiene.

13

"Mental Hospitals
Are Again under Fire"

The mid- to late 1940s was a difficult time for state institutions. They were barraged by a series of exposés and attacks. COs, literally outsiders to mental hygiene and psychiatry, brought public attention to conditions at individual institutions and eventually to the entire institutional system. The *Life* magazine and *PM* exposés of 1946 were followed by the publication of Frank Wright's *Out of Sight, Out of Mind* in 1947.

Albert Deutsch was not only a muckraker but a keen reporter on the history of mental illness and mental deficiency as well. Deutsch credited the National Mental Health Foundation with starting a "new crusade" to reform state mental hospitals. Like Maisel in his *Life* article, he introduced the NMHF by dissociating himself with the pacifist views of COs: "Much as we might disagree with the attitudes of the conscientious objectors who refused to bear arms or otherwise participate in World War II in defense of their imperiled country, we must admit that large numbers of them acquitted themselves most creditably in various types of humanitarian service." He explained how the COs were appalled by the conditions they found, documented their observations, and then created the National Mental Health Foundation: "This group has worked up a file of reports from scores of mental hospitals that prove conclusively that brutality and neglect are by no means rare. This file constitutes a damning indictment of our institutional treatment of the mentally sick." Deutsch singled out individual leaders of the national foundation for their enthusiasm in organizing citizens and psychiatrists, sending out information, and publishing "a lively little periodical called *The Psychiatric Aide*."[1]

The COs led the most organized efforts to draw attention to conditions at state mental hospitals in the mid- to late 1940s, but they were not alone in exposing institutions. In his *PM* series and subsequent book, *The Shame of the States*, Deutsch wrote about not only Byberry and Cleveland State Hospital but a broad range of state and city institutions at which COs had not served: Manhattan, Rockland

State, Pilgrim, and Brooklyn State Hospitals in New York; Letchworth Village, a "village for the feebleminded" in New York; Bellevue Psychiatric Hospital in New York; Detroit Receiving Hospital in Michigan; Napa State Hospital in California; and Milledgeville State Hospital in Georgia. Conditions at the institutions were depressingly familiar: terrible understaffing and overcrowding; infectious diseases, vermin, and parasites; injuries and abuses; and restraints. Only Brooklyn and buildings set aside for a U.S. Army hospital at Pilgrim were offering therapy to any but a handful of patients. *Time* reviewed Deutsch's *Shame of the States* book in a December 20, 1948, article with the title "Herded Like Cattle."[2]

Deutsch was merely one of a number of journalists who published in-depth exposés of institutions in the mid-1940s. In *The Shame of the States*, he rattled off the names of investigative reporters who had "enlisted in a long-range crusade to civilize the state mental hospital system":

> Walter Lerch of the *Cleveland Daily Press*, who has crusaded tirelessly for decent state hospitals in Ohio.
> Peter Lisagor of the *Chicago Daily News*, who has done an outstanding job on the state hospitals of Illinois.
> Al Ostrow of the *San Francisco News*, whose series on California's mental hospitals of his state were reprinted and widely distributed by his paper as a public service.
> Mike Gorman of the *Daily Oklahoman* of Tulsa, whose series on the mental hospitals of his state were likewise reprinted under the title, "Let There Be Light."
> Marge Whitmore, who graphically portrayed Hawaii's Shame in 1947, L. D. Parlin of the *St. Paul (Minneapolis) Dispatch*, and others who are taking up the torch in many other parts of the country to cast light on the darkest recesses of institutional life. To this journalistic fellowship, one must add Albert Q. Maisel, whose picture story on America's Bedlams in *Life* magazine in 1946 attracted wide attention.[3]

Like Deutsch, Mike Gorman remained active in the field of mental health after the publication of his exposé. He would later head up a new national mental health organization in the 1950s. Gorman did not set out to expose Oklahoma's institutions. He had become a reporter in 1945 after his discharge from the army. In 1946, his publisher at Oklahoma City's *Daily Oklahoman* asked him to investigate complaints the paper had received about one of the state's institutions in Norman. Gorman visited the mental hospital and was given a tour by its superintendent. He gave his first impressions of the institution:

> We started out at Hope Hall, the general receiving building. When the guard unlocked the big iron door and let us into the first ward, an awful stench hit me

in the face. There was not one fan, and the temperature was 95 degrees in the shade.

Walking down the center of the ward I saw a patient climbing over the end of his bed to get to the floor. Rather odd, I thought, until I saw that the beds were jammed so closely together that it was the only way a patient could move about.

The next two hours were a series of spine shattering shocks: patients writhing and groveling, even on toilet floors; constant moanings and screamings; seclusion cells where patients, seen through peephole slits in the iron doors, thrashed about naked; and everywhere dirt and filth.[4]

When Gorman met with his publisher the next morning, he asked him if he could do a series on Oklahoma's state hospitals. The publisher gave him the go-ahead, and Gorman proceeded to visit the other state institutions, along with George Tapscott, a former combat photographer in Italy and Germany. All of the institutions were terrible, but one stood out in Gorman's mind: "At Taft, mental hospital for Negroes, I witnessed the most galling thing I had seen on the entire tour: little children, adult mental defectives, epileptics, schizophrenics and tubuculars [*sic*], all mixed in the same wards."[5]

The first article in Gorman's series was titled "Misery Rules in State Shadowland." The *Daily Oklahoman* would eventually publish two hundred news stories and sixty editorials on state mental hospitals and mental illness. The series sparked civic indignation at the treatment of people at Oklahoma's mental hospitals, and groups ranging from the State Federation of Women's Clubs to the American Business Club joined in calls for reform. The state legislature held hearings on the institutions, and some legislators went on tours of the mental hospitals to get a firsthand look at conditions. Former Cleveland State Hospital CO and National Committee for Mental Hygiene fieldworker Justin Reese made a weeklong visit to Oklahoma to meet with citizen groups and to explain that reform was possible if the legislature would allocate sufficient funds for the institutions. Despite initial resistance, the legislature doubled appropriations for the mental hospitals and passed a "model" mental health bill reforming state commitment laws. Reporter Gorman helped found the Oklahoma Committee for Mental Hygiene and raised thousands of dollars to support its operations. Oklahoma's story was told by Gorman in a *Reader's Digest* article titled "Oklahoma Attacks Its Snake Pits" in September 1948.

Institutions were under siege in newspapers and magazines across the country. That was not all. They would be exposed by fiction and nonfiction writers, and one book would be made into a widely acclaimed motion picture.

In 1947, a self-described alcoholic writing under the pseudonym Harold Maine published his autobiography, *If a Man Be Mad*. Maine had been committed to a mental hospital for alcoholism as a teenager and later worked as an attendant at a private mental hospital and then a Veterans Administration hospital. His autobiography recounted his experiences as both a patient and an attendant. Compared with Clifford Beers's *Mind That Found Itself*, Maine's account was both more insightful into the nature of institutions and less grandiose about his plans to change mental hospitals. He was at his best when describing the "bughouser" culture of institutional attendants: keep wards quiet and orderly, do not leave marks when "disciplining" patients, protect institutions from public scrutiny, and insulate doctors from any knowledge of violence or abuse. Maine even told the story of a bughouser attendant at a mental hospital in Washington who quickly moved on to another institution when COs showed up there.

Maine considered going to a newspaper to furnish information for an exposé but decided against this course of action. It would not get at the nature of the institutional system, he believed:

> If I supplied one of these specialists on a large metropolitan paper with material for an exposé, the material might be used for political purposes, or at best would have to be restricted to "facts" that were minor symptoms of a huge malignancy. Those "facts" would always be the names of attendants who had beaten patients. The reasons these attendants were brought to such unnatural acts would be lost. The truth would remain unaltered. Attendants would still be forced to beat patients in order that an outmoded and inhuman institution system could survive. A public that didn't want the responsibility of paying for decent care for the patients would also be involved if the truth were known.[6]

Maine's autobiography received a sympathetic review in *Time* shortly after its publication. The message of *If a Man Be Mad* was crystal-clear to the reviewer: "He finally blamed the universal system of neglect less on attendants than on a public so indifferent that it would allow hospitals to be dark closets for storing the mental wreckage of modern civilization. When he quit his attendant's job to write a book, Maine was plenty mad—but not in a medical sense."[7] After Maine's autobiography was published, it was heavily promoted by the national foundation.

Mary Jane Ward's novel *The Snake Pit* was published in 1946. Ward's book told the story of Virginia Cunningham, a woman placed at Juniper Hill, a state mental hospital. The book was based on Ward's own experiences as a mental patient at Rockland State Hospital in New York, one of the institutions described in Deutsch's *Shame of the States*. "Long ago," wrote Ward in the novel, "they lowered insane persons into snake pits; they thought that an experience that might drive a sane person out of his wits might send an insane person back into sanity."[8] A "snake pit" was a fitting metaphor for Cunningham's—and Ward's—experiences at a mental hospital. Shocked by the numbing regimentation, lack of privacy, indignities, and absurdities of institutional life, Cunningham gradually regained her sanity and was reunited with her loyal husband, Robert.

The Snake Pit received rave reviews when it was published, although it "caused a mild stir in psychiatric circles," as noted in a *Time* article ironically published the same day that Maisel's *Life* article appeared.[9] The book portrayed the dark side of mental hospitals, but certainly not the darkest side. The brutality, stench, mass use of restraints, and nakedness so widely reported in accounts of institutions were absent from the book.

A movie based on Ward's novel was released in 1948. The movie was directed by Anatole Litvak and starred Olivia de Havilland in the role of Virginia Cunningham. It received even higher acclaim than the book. On December 20, 1948, *Time* published a cover story on the movie: "Hollywood, certainly not the sanest community on earth, has managed to turn out an excellent movie about insanity. The Snake Pit (20th Century Fox), starring Olivia de Havilland, is not a great work of cinematic art. It is, like the frightening scream from Miss de Havilland which rattles its sound track, an honest, accurate and dramatically powerful echo of certain ugly facts of modern life. It does what Hollywood has rarely done before: look harsh reality in the eye."[10]

The Snake Pit received a large number of motion picture awards. In 1949, the movie received an Oscar for "Best Sound, Recording." It was nominated for a "Best Picture" Oscar. De Havilland was nominated for "Best Actress," Litvak for "Best Director," the screen writers for "Best Writing, Screen."

The movie captured the flavor of institutional life described in Ward's novel. *Time's* review stated: "The large, hidden population of the mentally ill lives amid squalor, dirt and creeping fear, in the solitary confinement of the sick mind and behind the walls of the world's indifference." Former CO Justin Reese was a consultant on the movie.[11] Yet the plot of *The Snake Pit* was different in the book and the movie in a subtle but important way. The book was about the fog of mental illness and callous treatment of the mentally ill. The movie depicted these things but shifted the focus to the cause and cure of mental illness. A key figure in the movie was psychiatrist Dr. Kik, who remained in the background throughout most of the book. The film version of Kik helped Virginia discover the roots of her mental illness in her overbearing parents and subconscious guilt over the death of her father. Through psychoanalysis, Kik brought Virginia to her cure. A photograph of Sigmund Freud hanging on a wall appeared in scenes in the movie.

Director Litvak was a strong believer in psychoanalysis, and Virginia's case history "was worked out in close collaboration with three prominent psychiatrists."[12] In the postwar era, psychiatry was in transition, with influence shifting from institutional psychiatry to psychodynamic therapy. Institutional custodialism represented the old way of doing things; psychoanalysis was the new way. The release of *The Snake Pit* represented a partial victory for mental hospital reformers, but the critique of institutions was liable to be overshadowed by the triumph of psychoanalysis. After the publication of her book, Mary Jane Ward joined the Board of Directors of the National Mental Health Foundation.

By the second half of the 1940s, the institutions were no longer out of sight, out of mind. Their evils and shortcomings had been exposed in newspapers, national magazines, popular literature, and a major film. Leaders in mental hygiene and psychiatry would respond—finally.

◆   ◆   ◆

"The National Committee for Mental Hygiene," wrote Samuel Hamilton in 1943, "is a quiet organization, ordinarily not creating many ripples in public life, but on occasion it has gathered a volume of popular support for some humane measure that has been a surprise to practical men."[13] For years, the National Committee had focused on research and training as well as the establishment of community clinics. It had lobbied for years, along with others, for an increased role of the federal government in these areas and was eventually successful when President Truman signed into law the National Mental Health Act in July 1946. The act authorized the establishment of the National Mental Health Institute, which would become a major federal funding source for psychiatric training and research. When it came to the institutions, however, the National Committee paid scant attention and never did anything to create "ripples in public life."

Dr. Edith G. G. Graff was one of the fiery organizers of a little-known group called the Starry Cross, which was dedicated to "more humane institutional care." The Starry Cross rejected the often-made claim that all of the problems of mental hospitals were owing to public indifference and laid blame squarely on the shoulders of psychiatrists and "the Mental Hygiene Body." In a January 15, 1945, article in the *Churchman*, Graff explained her frustration with the National Committee's refusal to confront mental hospital conditions. She had urged the National Committee to release the findings of its survey of state institutions conducted in the late 1930s: "I think that having these reports printed and circulated in very large numbers would do a great deal toward educating the public, though I have more to say than is what in those reports. I was told in a letter from the National Committee for Mental Hygiene that they 'do not want any sensational exposure.'"[14]

Deutsch had closely followed the National Committee for more than a decade, starting when he published *The Mentally Ill in America* in 1937, with the support of Clifford Beers. In his 1948 book, *The Shame of the States,* Deutsch gave a candid appraisal of the NCMH. He started by reviewing its founding: "Improvement of mental hospital conditions was one of the main aims of the National Committee for Mental Hygiene when it was founded forty years ago by the late Clifford W. Beers. . . . He was determined to build a reform movement, and started it off with a remarkable crusading book—The Mind That Found Itself." After its establishment, something had gone terribly wrong with the National Committee, according to Deutsch: "Somehow the movement never obtained adequate financial support. In time it became dominated largely by institutional heads who suspected and resented public revelations of bad conditions in mental hospitals. The original will to reform was gradually paralyzed by conservative leadership and entanglements with hospital heads who felt their status and security might be upset by public exposures. Thus a potentially powerful organ for betterment was transformed into what was, in effect, a cloak for evils and abuses."[15]

Deutsch was heartened by a recent editorial in *Mental Hygiene* by the National Committee's medical director, George Stevenson, that seemed to indicate that the organization had "at last thrown off the false loyalties that held it in thrall." The July 1946 issue of *Mental Hygiene* led off with Stevenson's editorial, "Attacks on Mental Hospitals," which was published without an author's name. "Mental hospitals are again under fire," the editorial started. This time, Stevenson noted, "They are an attack on a system rather than on the administration of a specific institution." The editorial's tone was different from the occasional "there are good institutions and there are bad institutions" article or notice previously published in the journal. Stevenson seemed to suggest that there were merely different kinds of bad institutions: "The current attacks recognize that a system enmeshes in itself at best administrators who see the ills, want to do better, but find themselves blocked at every turn by the system itself. At worst, the system attracts those whose talents and ideals are so dwarfed that their shortcomings can persist undetected and unchallenged in a set of hidden and isolated routines."[16]

Stevenson maintained that the public got what it wanted in the mental hospitals: "cheap and isolated enough not to be an unpleasant reminder of guilty negligence." He pointed out, though, that recent exposés had recognized that the incrimination of specific individuals would not change a broken system and had prevented the public from looking for scapegoats when problems were brought to light. The National Mental Health Foundation's, and especially Hal Barton's, commitment to focus on the institutional system rather than on individual mental hospitals or officials had won over Stevenson. Toward the end of his editorial, Stevenson made a striking charge. Administrators who sought to hide the deficiencies of their institutions or even failed to make the public aware of them were part of the problem: "Recent articles recognize, nevertheless, that the administrator who has done his best with what he is given may be an accessory to the crime by failing to keep the public informed of its neglect." He called upon administrators to keep the public informed, even if the public resented it and tried to replace them with a "more malleable soul."[17]

Stevenson's editorial represented a major departure from the posture of the National Committee in its recent history. During the first half of the decade of the 1940s, the National Committee's house organ, *Mental Hygiene,* had almost nothing to say about the conditions at the nation's institutions. The second half of the decade would be different. Starting with Stevenson's editorial, *Mental Hygiene* would frequently publish articles critical of institutions and contain notices of awards given by the National Committee to some of those individuals involved in exposing institutions. Of course, the institutions themselves had not changed. What had changed was that the failures of institutions were in public view.

The National Committee's 1946 *Annual Report* seemed to acknowledge that it had become complacent about conditions at mental hospitals. It briefly reviewed its mission when it was founded by Clifford Beers: "When The National Committee for Mental Hygiene was founded, its 'chief concern' was 'to humanize the care of the insane'; to eradicate the abuses, brutalities, and neglect from which the mentally sick have traditionally suffered; to hospitalize 'asylums,' to extend treatment facilities, and raise standards of care; in short, to secure for the mentally ill the same standards of medical attention as that generally accorded to the physically ill." The report made exaggerated claims about the success of the National Committee in reforming mental hospitals: "The improvement brought about in mental institutions shone as a bright page in the annals of American welfare work; the sickening neglect and the cruel abuse of helpless inmates was largely eliminated, and institutional facilities were greatly extended and improved."[18] Circumstances had halted the progress being made, and the National Committee committed itself to returning to its original mission:

> But the greater part of all this progress in mental hospitals had taken place before the National Committee had passed its twenty-fifth birthday. Shortly after that, the depression depleted appropriations for state hospitals almost to the vanishing point; then came World War II, which drained hospitals of administrative and attendant manpower. Today the result of these two cataclysms is plain to be seen. The deliberations of the National Committee ended, therefore, on a sober note. The National Committee resolved that once again (in the words of its Founder) "its chief concern was to humanize the care of the insane." All our services, it was decided, were to be concentrated on the improvement of mental hospital

conditions with the exception of those divisions committed to the furtherance of the establishment of community and child guidance clinics or engaged in research and rehabilitation.[19]

The National Committee would wage a campaign to inform the public about the facts about mental hospitals: "Not until the demand of the public for better state hospitals is so insistent that widespread action is taken will The National Committee for Mental Hygiene feel that it is adequately carrying out the purpose of its founder."[20]

Mental Hygiene no longer shied away from articles critical of mental hospitals. Writer Edith Stern published a 1947 article, "Mental Hospitals, 1946," based on her paper presented at the annual meeting of the National Committee, an organization that *Time* had described as "sober, conservative" in an article reporting on Stern's address.[21] Stern questioned the effectiveness of exposés but acknowledged that the problems of mental hospitals had become common knowledge: "Recently the man in the street has had every opportunity to learn about the appalling conditions in our state hospitals. He can hardly pick up a magazine without finding one or more articles on the subject. Whenever he is bored with the newspapers for lack of titillating horror stories about concentration camps, he can turn to them for equally horrific stories about conditions in mental hospitals. Thousands upon thousands of lady patrons of rental libraries are intimately acquainted with daily life in a mental hospital because they have read *The Snake Pit*."[22]

Several months later, Dr. Frank Fremont-Smith, vice president of the National Committee and director of the Medical Division of the Josiah Macy Jr. Foundation, published an article titled "New Opportunities for the Improvement of Mental Hospitals." Like Stern, Fremont-Smith noted the influence of the press in drawing attention to mental hospital conditions: "The press has awakened us from our lethargy—a rude awakening, perhaps, but the rudeness of the awakening is often in proportion to the depth of somnolence." Stern and Fremont-Smith pointed to lack of funds and public indifference as the underlying causes of the problems at mental hospitals. Both called on superintendents to open their institutions to public scrutiny. Fremont-Smith wrote, "Instead of evasive and defensive action, let us take the offensive and lead the battle. Let each superintendent, within the limitations of his particular situation, boldly and progressively inform his community of those basic needs of his patients for which he is now unable to provide."[23]

One year after his editorial on attacks on mental hospitals, in July 1948, Stevenson published another article in *Mental Hygiene* deploring conditions at mental hospitals and calling for citizen action to put pressure on state legislatures.[24] For

Stevenson, citizens were immature and unwilling to become involved in demands for change.

In 1944, the National Committee started providing Lasker Awards for out-standing service in mental hygiene. The one-thousand-dollar award was funded by the Albert and Mary Lasker Foundation. The foundation had established Lasker Awards to honor contributions in medicine. Separate awards were made by the National Committee for Mental Hygiene, the American Public Health Association, and the Planned Parenthood Federation.[25] William Menninger was the first recipient of the National Committee's award. The 1946 award was split. One-half of the award was made to Dr. W. Horsley Gantt, head of the Pavlovian Laboratory at Johns Hopkins University. The second half of the award was given to Dr. Dores Sharpe and Walter Lerch "for an outstanding contribution to the advancement and improvement of public mental hospitals." The citation for the award read: "In 1943 a group of religious objectors who were serving as attendants at the Cleveland State Hospital protested the outrageous treatment of patients in that institution. To Mr. Walter Lerch, of the *Cleveland Press*, this was a challenge to employ his skill and his medium for the enlightenment of the public. To Dr. D.R. Sharpe, of the Cleveland Baptist Association, it was an imperative call to arouse the public conscience." Albert Deutsch was given a certificate of honorable mention: "No newspaper writer is more clearly identified with the field of mental hygiene than is Albert Deutsch."[26]

Lerch, Sharpe, and Deutsch were not the last reformers or muckrakers to be honored by the National Committee. A special Lasker Award for Public Information Leading to Public Action in Mental Health was presented to Mike Gorman in 1947 for his series in the *Daily Oklahoman*. Al Ostrow of the *San Francisco News* and then Deutsch in 1950 were recipients of this award. It was not in the nature of National Committee officials to plot exposés of institutions, but they had learned that it was better to acknowledge mental hospital abuses than to remain silent.

◆ ◆ ◆

Like the National Committee for Mental Hygiene, the American Psychiatric Association joined calls for the reform of mental hospitals in 1946. The previous year, the APA had approved the Standards for Psychiatric Hospitals and Out-Patient Clinics developed by its ten-member Committee on Psychiatric Standards and Policies.[27] For mental hospitals, the standards called for the establishment of special units and departments for different types of patients along with minimum ratios of psychiatrists, graduate nurses, professionals, and attendants for the various types of units. For psychiatrists, the ratios ranged from 1 psychiatrist for every 25 to 200 patients. For attendants, the ratio was 1 for every 6 to 8 patients. The APA recognized that the standards could not be achieved within a short time and set a goal of ten years for meeting them.

The APA's annual convention was held in May 1946, the same month in which Maisel's *Life* article was published. Deutsch characterized the convention as "startling and heartening": "The century-old organization broke with a long-standing tradition of timidity and institutional isolationism and went on record urging every state mental hospital superintendent to take the lead in exposing to public view any bad conditions that prevail."[28] The APA issued the following statement to the public at the convention: "The APA called on its entire membership, including state mental hospital superintendents, to call forcefully to the attention of the public and their legislatures all of the shortcomings and deficiencies in state hospitals, and to demand the assistance and backing necessary to maintain mental hospitals as hospitals in fact as well as name."[29] The APA's policy-making council also endorsed a series of resolutions proposed by its Committee on Standards and Policies, including one calling for the development of an inspection and rating system for state mental hospitals.[30] That committee stated in a 1946 resolution: "The American public will not consider psychiatry as a legitimate scientific branch of medicine as long as mental patients are treated in institutions with a cost of a minimum 65 cents per capita per day and a maximum cost of $2 per capita per day."[31]

Deutsch contended that the APA had long been silent on the problems of mental hospitals and had even attempted to whitewash institutional conditions: "Whatever criticisms it made were mainly 'in the family' and in closed door sessions." It set good minimum standards, Deutsch maintained, but had done nothing to enforce them. Deutsch's characterization of the APA and generalizations about mental hospital conditions were disputed in a book review of *The Shame of the States* published by William L. Russell in the *American Journal of Psychiatry* in 1950.[32]

In his presidential address at the annual meeting of the APA in Chicago in May 1946, Karl M. Bowman acknowledged the attacks on mental hospitals in newspapers and magazines. According to Deutsch, Bowman "surprised many of his listeners, and amused some" when he claimed that psychiatrists had been speaking out against mental hospital conditions for years. Bowman said:

> Recently we have seen a whole series of attacks on our state hospitals in newspapers and magazines. Like most such attacks there has been a basis for claims that there were many unsatisfactory conditions in our state hospitals. It is a little distressing to many of us, however, to find that things which we have all been saying for years are suddenly produced by outsiders as startling discoveries and as evidence of something being wrong. It is also important to point out that these

investigations of state hospitals have been made at a time when the state hospitals were suffering from conditions imposed by the war.[33]

Bowman rattled off the major complaints about state mental hospitals and offered a defense of psychiatrists for each. Mental patients were inadequately housed, and the state hospitals were overcrowded: "We have been saying all this for years." The mental hospitals were understaffed: "Again our answer is that we have been saying this for years." Salaries of institutional staff were inadequate, and working conditions for those staff were poor: "You have all heard such statements made many times by our members. This is nothing new." Abuse of patients occurred at the state hospitals: "Here we should point out that for the past five years our state hospitals have been operating under war conditions. . . . Under such conditions our state hospitals have been working under enormous handicaps and it is not surprising that at times abuses have crept in."[34] Psychiatrists were not to blame for the problems of state hospitals, according to Bowman. An apathetic public and political corruption were.

Despite the spirited defenses of psychiatry by Bowman and others, the APA was forced to take some kind of action about mental hospital conditions. The same year as the 1946 convention the APA sponsored the establishment of the Psychiatric Foundation as a fund-raising arm.[35] Promoted by APA executive assistant Austin Davies, the Psychiatric Foundation was intended to support a rating system for state mental hospitals as well as research and educational efforts. The initial Board of Directors of the Psychiatric Foundation included prominent philanthropists and business leaders, including Harold Elley, chemical director of E. I. DuPont de Nemours and Company; Joseph Mackey, president of the Mergenthaler Linotype Corporation; John B. Hawley, president of Hawley Inventions and other corporations; Robert M. Hillas, vice president of United Carbide and Carbon; Burton F. Peek, president of Deere and Company; and Pierre S. DuPont III of E. I. DuPont de Nemours and Company.[36] The Psychiatric Foundation awarded a grant of $1,140 to the APA for a mental hospital inspection system in 1947.[37] In 1949, the foundation's grant to the APA totaled $35,136. The foundation was incorporated as an independent organization, but functioned as an "appendage of the APA."[38] Austin Davies served as both executive director of the foundation and executive assistant of the APA.

The post–World War II era was a transitional period for the APA and psychiatry in general. The year 1946 stands out as especially significant. As late as 1940, the APA was dominated by institutional psychiatrists; two-thirds of its members worked at public mental hospitals. The organization was insular and concerned itself with the operation of institutions. A broad reform movement arose within the APA in 1946. Right before the start of the 1946 convention, fifteen psychiatrists led by William Menninger met to discuss the reform of psychiatry. Out of this meeting came the Group for the Advancement of Psychiatry (GAP), founded to change the APA from within. GAP, whose members generally came from the ranks of psychoanalytic and psychodynamic psychiatrists, believed that psychiatry should devote itself to solving social problems and preventing mental illness. GAP members, noted Gerald N. Grob, "tended to be far removed from the daily activities of those psychiatrists employed in state mental hospitals."[39] Within the next year or two, GAP members dominated the leadership of the APA. William Menninger was elected president of the APA in 1947.

GAP was controversial within the APA and brought to the fore differences in philosophies and priorities. According to Grob, GAP polarized the APA and almost led to its demise. Some GAP critics within the APA believed that a minority was trying to take over the entire organization. Outgoing APA president Samuel Hamilton, the U.S. Public Health Service psychiatrist, National Committee associate, and adviser to the Mental Hygiene Program of the CPS, commented on GAP in his 1947 presidential address. Hamilton was more welcoming to GAP than many APA members, but warned that it should not attempt to speak for the association: "Those of us who are distributively minded welcome the new Group. It includes many of our best minds and our jobs will soon be done better by those who are 20 years younger than we. We enjoy their enthusiasm and expect great things of them. We urge them not to use their machinery by which their opinion shall be given out as the opinion of the Association."[40]

As APA president, Menninger strongly supported the appointment of a full-time administrative officer to strengthen the association.[41] Despite the resistance of some GAP opponents who feared that appointing an administrative officer would take control away from the APA membership, the APA's council appointed Dr. Daniel Blain, former chief of neuropsychiatric services at the Veterans Administration, medical director in early 1948. Blain had been one of the original members of GAP.

Under Blain, the reform of mental hospitals became a priority. The APA started publishing a monthly newsletter in August 1948. The newsletter included announcements of APA activities as well as events sponsored by the National Committee for Mental Hygiene, the National Mental Health Foundation, and other organizations. The September 1949 issue contained news clippings from stories on the APA's inspections of mental hospitals.[42] Stories in the *New York Times* on July 24 and July 30 reported that half of the states had requested inspections from the APA's Central Inspection Board.

In April 1949, the APA held its first Mental Hospital Institute in Philadelphia. The objective of the institute, which was organized by Blain and the APA's

Committee on Hospital Standards, was "to reveal the best techniques evolved by hospital officials in the United States and Canada for alleviating the effects on the treatment and care of mental hospital patients of personnel shortages, overcrowding, out-of-date facilities, and related difficulties."[43] The institute addressed mental hospital problems in four areas: administrative problems, community aid problems, personnel problems, and clinical problems.[44] Blain, William Menninger, the National Committee's George Stevenson, and other physicians gave addresses at the institute. In a close vote, Stevenson had been selected president-elect of the APA in 1948. Program consultants for the institute included both medical doctors and laypersons, including Paul Harris of the National Mental Health Foundation. Following the institute, the APA published its proceedings in a two hundred–page volume titled *Better Care in Mental Hospitals*. A description of the proceedings published in the APA's September newsletter invoked the name of Deutsch's exposés: "The volume makes available for the first time a comprehensive picture of how the hospital superintendents and their co-workers view 'the shame of the States' and what can be done about it."[45]

By the mid-1950s, the focus of the APA had shifted away from mental hospitals toward prevention and community psychiatry. GAP and other reformers within the APA were successful in having their philosophy accepted by a majority of psychiatrists. By 1957, approximately 17 percent of psychiatrists worked in state mental hospitals or Veterans Administration hospitals. The rest worked in private practice or community settings. As Grob pointed out, "The APA, as an organization, slowly disengaged itself from public mental hospitals—the same institutions that had brought the association into existence."[46]

◆   ◆   ◆

In late 1947, Walter Starnes was selected as the first recipient of the annual National Mental Health Foundation Psychiatric Aide of the Year Award by a prestigious panel of judges that included Albert Deutsch, Mary Jane Ward, and Robert Felix of the Mental Hygiene Division of the U.S. Public Service, among others.[47] The five-hundred-dollar award was established in the spring of 1947 "to focus attention on the important role played by psychiatric aides and attendants in the care of the mentally ill; to help gain prestige and dignity for those engaged in this profession; and to encourage the promotion of higher standards of on-the-ward care."[48]

Throughout its history, the National Mental Health Foundation was committed to improving the pay and training of institutional attendants and elevating the attendant's role to the status of a profession. The *Attendant* and then the *Psychiatric Aide* provided a forum for the discussion of the attendant's job and responsibilities and for sharing information on national and statewide trends regarding frontline workers at institutions. The magazine carried stories supporting the professional licensing of attendants and included debates on the pros and cons of the unionization of attendants. The Psychiatric Aide of the Year Award was a strategy for focusing professional and public attention on the importance of attendants in patients' care. Stories on award recipients would be published in newspapers across the country as well as *Time* and *Newsweek* magazines.[49] In the spring of 1950, the national foundation announced that it had established an award for Aide to the Mentally Retarded to complement the Psychiatric Aide of the Year Award. The first recipient of the new award was Eileen Bunyan, who worked at the Children's Colony at Monson State Hospital in Massachusetts.[50]

Starnes, the recipient of the inaugural Psychiatric Aide of the Year Award in 1947, was African American. He had been "born of humble Negro parents, in Topeka, Kansas, on December 12, 1905." Prior to his enlistment in the Army Transportation Corps in 1942, he had worked as a waiter, bellhop, and elevator operator. He became an attendant in April 1946 after his discharge from the military. Recognized by his superiors for his "outstanding administrative ability," Starnes was assigned as charge attendant on three separate wards "where previously poor morale and disorganization had prevailed": "Although Mr. Starnes is colored and has many white aides under his supervision, at no time has dissension, disagreement or racial feeling entered into the working relationship."[51]

The institution at which Starnes worked was the Winter Veterans Administration Hospital in Topeka, Kansas, which was closely connected with the Menninger Foundation.[52] Karl Menninger, who served as manager of the hospital, expressed his appreciation of the national foundation for recognizing the contributions of undervalued institutional attendants:

> The National Mental Health Foundation, in initiating its yearly award for the outstanding psychiatric aide, is calling the attention of the public to a group of people whose service is rendered far away from the public eye and whose excellence can only be judged as one judges the excellence of one's friends. The psychiatric aide is, in the last analysis, the friend and companion of the mentally ill. By day and by night he is our ambassador to the "normal" world. . . . Many will commend the National Mental Health Foundation for initiating this contest and in this we heartily join. That this honor has been given one of our aides is one of the most gratifying things that has ever happened to us at Winter Veterans Administration Hospital.[53]

The Menninger brothers, Karl and William, were among the most influential figures in psychiatry in the twentieth century. Dr. C. K. Menninger had established the Menninger Clinic, along with his son Karl, in 1919 to advance the practice in psychiatry and medicine. By the 1930s, Karl had become a nationally known psychiatrist with the publication of his book *The Human Mind*. In 1941, C. K., Karl, and William Menninger established the Menninger Foundation in Topeka. William rose to prominence during World War II for his efforts in reorganizing the delivery of mental health services in the army in his role as chief consultant in neuropsychiatry in the Office of the Surgeon General.[54]

In the postwar era, both Karl and William Menninger were involved in the reform of psychiatry and the APA. Karl was instrumental in the APA's Special Committee on Reorganization, and William was the driving force behind the Group for the Advancement of Psychiatry.[55] William's election as president of the APA in 1947 solidified his stature in psychiatry. He appeared on the cover of *Time* on October 25, 1948, and was described as psychiatry's "salesman" and leader of what *Time* called the "Young Turks" of GAP.[56]

Unlike many psychiatrists, neither Karl nor William Menninger shied away from aligning themselves with lay reformers, even muckrakers, in mental health. Although initially reluctant to do so, Karl wrote an introduction to Deutsch's *Shame of the States*.[57] Menninger characterized Deutsch as "a scientifically trained student and recorder of social conditions" and said that the writer "has probably done more than anyone else to keep before the American people the abuses that are perpetrated in their name in public psychiatric hospitals." He acknowledged "the incompetents among us," but argued that most mental hospital administrators had "done the best they could with inadequate help from the public." Menninger even gave a plug to *Out of Sight, Out of Mind* and described the leaders of the national foundation as "earnest, honest, dedicated men and women."[58] He shared the foundation's goal of obtaining professional recognition for attendants and commented favorably on an August 1950 report in the *Psychiatric Aide* on attendants at Moose Lake State Hospital in Minnesota who had passed a resolution urging state registration of trained attendants: "I was very greatly impressed by this statement of the goals of the psychiatric aides for professional recognition."[59] William, or "Dr. Will" as he was often called, served as an unofficial adviser to the national foundation and strongly supported its efforts to improve attendant training.[60] He was critical of the National Committee.[61] During a visit by Hal Barton to the Menninger Foundation, Dr. Will told Barton that the National Mental Health Foundation had been a more effective organization than the National Committee: "He emphatically (off-the-record, of course) said that NMHF had done more in 3 yrs. than NCMH had done in 30 and that someone ought to tell 'our bunch' (NMHF) just that!"[62]

In 1946, the Menningers established a model training program for psychiatrists, the Menninger School of Psychiatry, at Winter VA Hospital in Topeka. During its first year of operation, the school accepted 108 medical doctors for psychiatric training.[63] At the same time, the Menningers believed that attendant training was essential. Karl said, "My feeling is, however, that one cannot train physicians in psychiatry adequately or properly unless one at the same time trains the psychologists, the nurses, attendants and everyone else who works with those physicians in the proper care and treatment of the psychiatric patient."[64] By 1946, Dr. Karl, as he was commonly called, was planning a training school for attendants.

It was not a coincidence that Walter Starnes, the first recipient of the national foundation's Psychiatric Aide of the Year Award, was an attendant at Winter VA Hospital. The Menningers had established its School of Psychiatry at the hospital and recognized the importance of the attendant's role in patient care. The Winter hospital had established a committee to nominate one of its attendants for the award. That the nominating committee selected an African American who had worked as an attendant for a bit over a year may or may not have been a coincidence. The nominating statement read, "In this hospital where white aides outnumber Negro aides perhaps 10-1 and in which we have many persons of southern birth and rearing, this Negro man was selected and his selection met with universal approval."[65] Whether intentional or not, the nomination and selection of an African American for a national attendant award at a time when the staffs of many mental institutions were segregated sent a message that it was time for the institutions to change.

The National Mental Health Foundation and former COs worked with the Menninger Foundation in establishing a training program for attendants. At Winter VA Hospital, a group of attendants came up with the idea of a training program for attendants.[66] One of the leaders of this group was Paul Harris, who later moved to the national foundation and replaced Phil Steer as managing editor of the *Psychiatric Aide* in October 1947.[67] The attendants at Winter VA Hospital conducted a rough survey of mental hospitals nationally and concluded that an aide training program that would adequately prepare attendants to provide more than custodial care did not exist. Karl Menninger discussed the group's idea for a training program with Alan Gregg, medical director of the Rockefeller Foundation. Gregg met with the attendant group in August 1947. The group proposed the establishment of a training program to license aides, but both Menninger and Gregg thought that further study of the need for a program was necessary.[68] The Rockefeller awarded a grant of fifty-five hundred dollars for the study to the Menninger Foundation that ran from January 1 to July 1, 1948.

The Menninger project was titled the Psychiatric Aide Education Research Project. It was directed by Dr. Bernard Hall, and Ward Miles served as executive assistant. Miles, a Friend, had been a CO at Byberry, in addition to participating as a human guinea pig in jaundice medical experiments at the University of

Pennsylvania.[69] At Byberry, he had worked at the notorious B Building, the violent ward at the institution, and had witnessed the abuse and dehumanization of mental patients firsthand. He would later become a physician specializing in family practice in a medical group serving people in Washington and Idaho. His wife, Alice Calder Miles, had been a member of the AFSC women's service unit at Byberry.

The Psychiatric Aide Education Research Project drew on information and materials from the National Mental Health Foundation.[70] A report on the project cited a national foundation study that found that the mean wage of attendants nationally was one hundred dollars for a fifty-hour week.[71] Resources identified through the project included an annotated bibliography of articles in the *Attendant* and *Psychiatric Aide,* Wright's *Out of Sight, Out of Mind,* and the *Handbook for Psychiatric Aides* as well as individual articles by national foundation staff. The project used a large number of consultants. Members of the project consulted personally with forty-four persons, both professionals and laypersons. Only eighteen of the consultants were medical doctors. The consultants included Albert Deutsch; Harold Maine, former mental patient, attendant, and author of *If a Man Be Mad;* and members of the NMHF Hal Barton, Paul Harris, Will Hetzel, and Dick Hunter. In May 1948, four members of the Menninger group, including Hall and Miles, traveled to Philadelphia for a three-day meeting with the national foundation.[72]

The Menninger aide project was less a research study than a curriculum development project. Its final report recommended plans of instruction and a well-rounded set of curriculum units. The proposed curriculum addressed topics ranging from the history of psychiatry, general nursing techniques, psychiatric nursing, and first aid to English composition and an introduction to literature, sociological factors and the patient, the legal aspects of psychiatry, and public speaking. Both didactic lectures and clinical experiences were recommended. The final report included an exhibit called the "Administration and Estimated Cost for Proposed School for Psychiatric Aides."

The Menninger Foundation proposed that the Rockefeller Foundation fund an experimental school for psychiatric aides based on the Psychiatric Aide Education Research Project report in July 1948. The Rockefeller Foundation postponed action on the proposal until January 1949.[73] In the meantime, a plan for the Menninger Foundation to join with Winter VA Hospital in operating an aide education program hit a snag. The director of nursing services for the Veterans Administration told representatives of the Menninger Foundation that the VA would not endorse an experimental program for the training of aides until it had established a psychiatric training program for nurses. The move to professionalize attendants was controversial among some nurses and others who feared that licensed or certified attendants would infringe upon the professional status of nursing. In a visit to the Menninger Clinic in May 1945, Hal Barton had encountered resistance to the Mental Hygiene Program's promotion of training for attendants from a Mrs. Lowney, a nursing supervisor who had come from a mental hospital at Greystone Park, New Jersey. Barton reported, "She questioned our right to act in the field of attendant education; believed that this was solely the responsibility of the nursing profession. Her feeling is that the attendant should always and only be under the supervision of nursing staffs."[74] Several years later, Paul Harris of the national foundation met with Lela Anderson, nursing consultant to the APA, to discuss the foundation's activities. Anderson told Harris that she personally supported the foundation's plans for attendant or psychiatric aide training but that she could not publicly associate herself with these plans as long as she remained at the APA. There was opposition to the professionalization of aides among nursing groups and some members of the U.S. Public Health Service:

> Went to N.Y. last Friday to see Lela Anderson, at her request. She is all for our activities and hopes for psychiatric aides, subscribes 110% to our broadest concepts of his potential role. . . . She cannot ethically or diplomatically afford to have her name used with some of these ultra progressive concepts as long as she is still A.P.A. connected—all of which is personally understandable. Most important was her revelation that professional nursing and that segment of the U.S.P.H.S. is on the move nationally to check the development of P.A.'s as an independent group. She feels it vital that we give immediate study to stimulating establishment of a National Examining Board for P.A.'s to be made up of representatives of 6 or 7 special classifications, only one of which would be the nursing group.[75]

As late as 1955, the council of the APA considered attendants as falling under the control of the nursing profession and opposed any requirements for attendant qualifications and training. It issued a position statement on psychiatric aides in November of that year: "The American Psychiatric Association considers that the training and development of psychiatric aides as technical specialists within the nursing services of mental hospitals is most auspicious for the advancement of treatment and care of the mentally ill, but considers that the formulation of legislation to govern the qualifications, training standards, and practices of psychiatric aides should be deferred until this area within the general field of nursing has been more fully defined."[76]

With plans to collaborate in an aide training program with Winter VA Hospital blocked, the Menninger Foundation turned to Topeka State Hospital. In early 1949, Kansas state hospitals had come under public scrutiny, and the state legislature had appropriated funds for the Topeka institution to become a center of psychiatric education.[77] William and Karl Menninger themselves had lobbied the governor and legislators to increase funding for the state's mental hospitals.[78] Topeka State Hospital agreed to collaborate with the Menninger Foundation in sponsoring an aide training program. In April 1949, representatives of the Menninger Foundation and Topeka State Hospital met with a member of the Rockefeller Foundation to discuss the proposed experimental aide training school.[79] The Rockefeller Foundation agreed to fund the proposal and awarded a $70,500 grant to support the school under Karl Menninger's direction.

The Psychiatric Aide School was opened in October 1949. Between 1949 and 1952, eighty-five men and women were trained at the school. The program of study lasted one year and included clinical ward training and classes. The training followed the curriculum proposed in the Psychiatric Aide Education Research Project report. No fees were charged for the training program, and students were paid by the state hospital. They received $143 per month during the first six months of training and $157 during the last six. Housing was not provided to the students: "He would not live on the hospital grounds because of the conviction that he should assume responsibility as a member of the local community and not lead a cloistered life within the institution."[80]

The Psychiatric Aide School developed an official patch and established a Creed for Psychiatric Aides:

> I dedicate my life to the companionship of the men and women of broken spirit. With humility, I accept the patient as my sacred trust. His behavior is mine to understand and to accept without personal insult or judgment. I will befriend the patient against his illness.
>
> My weapon is myself; my sword—my smile; my voice—needed strength. Where there is fear I will be reassurance, where there is despair I will be hope. Kindness will be my talisman and I will not tolerate brutality or neglect. My respected fellow workers shall be my pilots.
>
> Faithful to my trust, may my reward be an ever greater appreciation of the blessedness of giving.[81]

A final report on the Psychiatric Aide School, published as part of the Menninger Clinic Monograph Series, singled out World War II COs and then the National Mental Health Foundation for drawing attention to the need to improve the quality of care provided by attendants:

> Since World War II more has been done to improve the quality of care rendered by attendants than in any equal period of history. One of the first steps forward

was taken by the young men who in their work in the Civilian Public Service Units in mental hospitals were demonstrating the value of capable attendants. Several of these men published in June 1944, as part of the Units' mental hygiene program, the first issue of *The Attendant*. This monthly magazine was intended to be a source of practical suggestions for the worker on the mental hospital ward; it accomplished this purpose in the nineteen issues published.

A milestone was reached on January 1, 1946, when several of these same young men launched the National Mental Health Foundation. Under the capable leadership of Leonard Edelstein and Harold Barton this organization sought "to encourage better training for hospital and training school workers, to secure the adoption in every state of progressive mental health legislation, and to educate the public to the needs and problems of individuals with mental handicaps." They fostered the recognition and training for attendants and published for them handbooks, and a monthly magazine, *The Psychiatric Aide*, originally known as *The Attendant*. The work of the staff of this service-dedicated Foundation commands the attention of the historian of psychiatry.[82]

In the late 1940s, the National Mental Health Foundation and the Menninger Foundation would join with the National Committee for Mental Hygiene and the Psychiatric Foundation in discussions of forming a federation to conduct joint fund-raising. Plans for the federation would fall through. The Menninger Foundation would continue on and move to Houston, Texas, as the Menninger Clinic in 2003.[83] In contrast, the years of the national foundation were numbered.

14

"Another Growing Pain"

The spring of 1946 should have been an exciting, even heady time for the founders of the National Mental Health Foundation. What had started as an off-duty project by a small handful of Byberry COs had evolved into a formidable national reform movement. *Life* magazine and *PM* newspaper had featured stories based on the reports painstakingly collected from COs and others working at mental hospitals and training schools, and other national and local media had published stories announcing the formation of the NMHF. The *Attendant* and then the *Psychiatric Aide* had received national recognition, and the COs assigned to the Mental Hygiene Program of the Civilian Public Service had published or drafted handbooks, pamphlets, and other educational materials that could be distributed by the newly established foundation. *Out of Sight, Out of Mind* was close to being finalized and ready for national release. The now former COs had gained the cooperation, if not active support, of prominent, reform-minded psychiatrists and mental hygiene leaders. National figures, including the wife of the recently deceased president and a former U.S. Supreme Court justice, had agreed to lend their names to the national foundation and to enlist the support of other civic lead ers and well-known personalities. What should have been a time of celebration for the foundation was filled with internal turmoil and uncertainty about its future.

The controversy between Barton and Edelstein over the use of names in Maisel's *Life* story was the first open rift within the NMHF, but tensions had been building for quite some time. When the COs were part of the Civilian Public Service, the personal lives of the men were not easy. They were not paid for their work and were under the thumb of the Selective Service and the control of the National Committee for Mental Hygiene. However, the Mental Hygiene Program could operate as a loosely run grassroots group, and its expenses were underwritten by the American Friends Service Committee, Mennonite Central Committee, and Brethren Service Committee, with contributed space and resources from Byberry superintendent Charles Zeller. The move from being a detached CPS unit to an incorporated foundation placed new demands on the group. With the discharge of the men from Selective Service control and the pending end of the CPS, the church committees would no longer fund the program's expenses. Just as important, after years of going without pay, the former COs needed to start earning a living and to carry on with their lives. At least two of the founders of the Mental Hygiene Program, Edelstein and Barton, were married and ready to raise families. Not only would the four founders of the program need to be paid, but so would other members of the staff if the foundation were to fulfill its aspirations. The program could no longer rely on the unpaid work of other COs and volunteers. Fund-raising and spending priorities would become critically important issues for the new foundation. Further, an independent foundation, with an as yet unnamed board of directors, would need to be organized differently than a CPS unit run by a central committee. The national foundation faced the same challenges as any other grassroots movement that becomes formalized.

Len Edelstein had the title of coordinator of the MHP, while Barton, Hetzel, and Steer headed different divisions. Barton was responsible for education and the "Summary Statement," Hetzel directed the Legal Division, and Steer was editor of the *Attendant* and then the *Psychiatric Aid*. Edelstein handled external relations for the program and then the national foundation. He drummed up support for the program among influential public figures, took responsibility for fund-raising, and handled relations with the media. He was the primary contact with *Life*'s Maisel. Edelstein's 1945 Pendle Hill pamphlet, *We Are Accountable: A View of Mental Institutions,* had caught the attention of prominent Friends and others.

Edelstein was known as sophisticated, forceful, and personable.[1] He especially impressed many of the civic leaders with whom he came into contact. Mrs. Curtis Bok, the wife of a Pennsylvania Supreme Court justice, described him as "the prototype of a young man who could attract older people to his mission—never sentimental, but hard-hitting and reliable," whereas author Pearl Buck characterized him as "one of the finest young men we have met."[2]

Edelstein's title of coordinator of the Mental Hygiene Program was ambiguous. The program was run by the Central Committee composed of Barton, Hetzel, and Steer as well as Edelstein. The Central Committee operated democratically, or as Hetzel put it: "We usually don't vote but follow that delightful Quaker custom of the 'sense of the meeting.'" As early as fall 1945, tensions had arisen among members of the Central Committee regarding who could speak for the program and what communications had to be approved by all members of the committee. In October, Edelstein sent a memo to Barton, Hetzel, and Steer in reference to "complaints of sending out material before cleared by other members of staff."[3] He started by saying that he had received complaints regarding two statements he had recently sent out without obtaining clearance from other members of the Central Committee. One statement was an article for the Fellowship of Reconciliation's newsletter that Edelstein said had to be sent right away to avoid missing a publication deadline. The other was a letter Edelstein had written to Roy Kepler, a CO at the government CPS camp at Minersville, California. The previous summer the Germfask newsletter, which was published by radical COs who had led strikes at government camps, had attacked the Mental Hygiene Program. Edelstein had drafted a response to the newsletter, but at the urging of Barton and with the agreement of Hetzel and Steer, Edelstein's letter was not sent. With the knowledge, but not necessarily agreement, of the other three men, Barton subsequently sent a short note to the publishers of the Germfask newsletter urging them to get accurate information before they attacked anyone in the future. The Germfask newsletter then published a retraction of sorts. In his letter to Kepler, Edelstein expressed appreciation for "the sense of real fairness" on the part of the Germfask newsletter and explained the purposes of the MHP. He did not show this letter to the other men before sending it. In his memo to Barton, Steer, and Hetzel, Edelstein complained that Barton often sent out material without having it checked by others or gave it to them only after it had been finalized. He questioned the need for all of the men to "start picking word for word" the letters of each man. Then Edelstein raised an additional issue "before I get the steam all out": "It is very disturbing to receive letters addressed to me—already answered by one of the other members of the staff." The memo concluded, "This is not intended as a personal blast—but it is a release of a few things that have piled up and disturbed me lately."[4]

Hetzel responded in writing to Edelstein in a memo addressed to "Brothers." He suggested that communications regarding the Mental Hygiene Program's policies should be cleared by the entire committee, but that other materials should be able to be sent out by individual members on their own: "Official communications to the world, or part of it, outside CPS, involving a first statement of any policy should be cleared—unless substance thereof has been formally approved. But individual utterances, letters, speeches, articles, etc. need not be in my opinion, unless we wish to lose our identity as members of a group and be completely swallowed by the group. The latter I'm not willing to do."

Hetzel advocated for participatory decision making, with room for individual men to use their own judgment when it came to communications and actions: "*Argument* if O.K., but any group *pressure* on such scores is *verboten* as far as I'm concerned, and if not, I'm out paddling my own canoe." Hetzel concluded his memo on a conciliatory note: "I feel extremely cordial to everyone concerned and believe that these disagreements that grow out of widely varying temperaments will contribute to a well balanced and effective program, providing we maintain our identity and try to help each other, counsel and advise when we are able, and avoid being irritated by each other's idiosyncracies."[5]

Any group of people who work closely together and care passionately about their common work is likely to experience tensions and disagreements at times. Of the four men who founded the Mental Hygiene Program and the National Mental Health Foundation, Phil Steer was the quietest and had the least-distinctive personality. Interviewed many years later, many former Byberry COs had clear memories of Edelstein, Barton, and Hetzel, each of whom was usually described as "impressive," but could scarcely remember Steer.[6] Steer seems to have been the kind of person who did not argue his position unless he had a strong opinion about something. On December 13, 1945, Steer sent a memo to Edelstein, with copies to Barton and Hetzel, regarding a planned conference of mental health groups. Edelstein had left the National Committee off the invitation list. Members of the MHP and NMHF had, at best, mixed feelings about the National Committee. On the one hand, they respected Stevenson and appreciated his support and sponsorship of their program. On the other hand, they believed that the National Committee was too dominated by psychiatrists and professionals, was too timid in the face of the problems surrounding mental hospitals, and had lost its bearings. Steer strongly objected to the exclusion of the National Committee: "I feel rather strongly that the forthcoming joint conference on mental health strategy should include all national groups and organizations whose primary interests are in mental health problems. I think I see why you don't want to invite the National Committee for Mental Hygiene. They are bigger and better established than we are, and might conceivably monopolize the affair. But I don't think this is likely to happen. . . . This probably needs more discussion on the part of us all."[7]

Whatever differences of opinion existed among the four founders of the Mental Hygiene Program were brought to the fore when the national foundation was established, with the need for independent funding and an organizational structure for an incorporated entity. The incorporation papers for the foundation listed Barton, Edelstein, Hetzel, and Steer as members of the Board of Directors until their successors could be named. Yet there were misunderstandings or disagreements regarding the priorities and structure of the national foundation among the four founders. Edelstein had a dramatically different perspective on the needs of the organization than Barton, Hetzel, and Steer.

For Edelstein, the most pressing priority was to promote the national foundation publicly in order to put it on a firm financial footing with the ending of support from the church committees.[8] The organization's resources should be devoted to this priority, Edelstein maintained. For example, around the time of the publication of the *Life* article, Edelstein arranged for the placement of advertisements on the national foundation in Philadelphia and New York newspapers. Although he had arranged for some of the supporters of the foundation to underwrite the costs of the ads, these supporters failed to cover the costs, and the ads ended up being a drain on the organization's scarce resources, according to Barton. Similarly, Edelstein committed about two thousand dollars for the publication of a prospectus to raise funds for the foundation. Barton, Hetzel, and Steer recognized the importance of promotion and fund-raising, but placed equal emphasis on educational and legal projects. The three of them had a heated disagreement with Edelstein over paying one thousand of the three thousand dollars the foundation had in reserve for the printing of *The Handbook for Psychiatric Aides*. The handbook was printed despite Edelstein's objections. Edelstein also was frustrated with Barton for not taking time away from his educational activities to have his picture taken along with the other founders and Justice Owen Roberts for a story in the magazine *Philadelphia*.

There was a deeper area of disagreement within the national foundation. The Central Committee of the Mental Hygiene Program had been succeeded by an Executive Council composed of Barton, Edelstein, Hetzel, and Steer when the national foundation was formed. The MHP had functioned more or less democratically, and members of the newly formed national foundation wanted to continue this mode of operation. Even "associates," members of the foundation apart from the Executive Council and clerical staff, wanted to play a role in policy making. After a meeting of the associates on June 10, 1946, the associates sent a memo to the Executive Council summarizing their conclusions: "That the basic philosophy of the Foundation should be striving toward the use of democratic process in every function; there should be reasonable balance of authority between the executive committee, associates, and secretarial associates; there should be no reason for the associates to act as a prod to the executive council."[9] The associates noted that "this philosophy is not being applied as well as it might" and recommended improved communication and greater participation in policy making.

The members of the Executive Council agreed, in principle, on the importance of participatory decision making within the foundation. All members of the foundation should have had a say in setting its priorities and deciding on policies. Yet Edelstein disagreed with Barton, Hetzel, and Steer on how the foundation should operate. His title had been changed from coordinator to executive secretary when the foundation was established. He believed that this title carried with it the responsibility and authority for overseeing the overall program of the foundation and the power to implement policies established by the Board of Directors and Executive Council. From his perspective, it was critical to the future of the foundation for it to have an executive director coordinating the activities of the various programs within the organization: "I submit to you again that the Foundation is in need of an Executive Secretary *in fact* as well as principle; that the organization will fall apart at the hinges unless concerns of reasonable importance are focused to the Executive Secretary and he is given the necessary power to execute the policy established by the Board of Directors, and more immediately by the Executive committee." Without having such an executive director, maintained Edelstein, the national foundation ran the risk of "establishing 4 separate programs loosely held together."[10] He pointed to examples in which other members of the Executive Council had taken actions on major issues without his involvement.

For Barton, Hetzel, and Steer, Len, as executive director, was merely one of four leaders of the foundation, with no more or less authority than the others. Within the Executive Council, at least, they wanted to maintain the nonhierarchical structure of the Mental Hygiene Program. There might be disagreements or miscommunications among the four men at times, but they could be worked out as long as each man respected the judgment of the others in performing their respective roles. Steer edited the *Psychiatric Aid*, Hetzel led the Legal Division, Barton directed the Educational Division, and Edelstein was the public face of the organization and handled relations with potential donors and supporters. As Edelstein expressed it, Hetzel, Barton, and Steer viewed the executive secretary as "a mere figure-head or a glorified spokesman to the public."[11]

Edelstein acknowledged that he had failed to persuade the other men to accept his position and informed the others that he had no alternative but to resign from the foundation. He ended his letter of resignation on a gracious note: "You know that my heart will be with you in your continuing efforts whatever will be the course of my future endeavors; and that it has been a genuinely rich experience to know each of you and work to this point in developing efforts that began so humbly. I hope that my departure will be considered just 'another growing pain' which will bring with it a depth of organizational maturity and that you will meet the future with even greater strength."[12]

Edelstein announced his intention to go on vacation from June 21 until July 12 and then continue with the national foundation until August 15 or leave earlier if the other three men desired him to do so. When he returned, the four members of the Executive Council attempted to work out an arrangement that would be satisfactory to all.[13] Edelstein proposed that he step down as executive director but be placed in charge of a division on fund-raising. The council voted to accept this suggestion, but the disagreements ran too deep for there to be any reconciliation. Barton, Hetzel, and Steer finally accepted Edelstein's resignation, and he left the foundation. As Barton later explained, "Len's approach would not harmonize with that of the balance of the Council and of the other CPS associates on the staff. Clearly it came to a point of 1 resignation or 3 on the Council."[14]

The problem of leading and managing an incorporated, externally funded organization while working within democratic principles would continue to plague the National Mental Health Foundation. Hal Barton recognized the problem in an account of the resignation of Len Edelstein: "We crave a balance between centralized, one-man authority and the democratic deliberations of the staff."[15] Barton succeeded Edelstein as executive director of the national foundation. Throughout his tenure, he would attempt to run the foundation democratically, treating Hetzel and Steer, in particular, as equals in deciding on the course of the organization. This organizational style would lead one member of the staff involved in fundraising, Richard Mitchell, to resign from the foundation. Mitchell had been on the staff when Edelstein resigned and had agreed with him on the need for a strong executive director. In a September 1948 memo, he explained his position:

> Basically I agreed with Len Edelstein, that Exec. Council should not have the power to veto the decisions of the Executive Secretary. The executive secretary should have had the freedom of action for making major policy decisions, certainly with full discussion and expression of opinion by the executive staff. . . .
>
> I believe that while in some areas the Foundation was accomplishing real progress, internally, it was marked by lack of organization and an opportunism that directed the program on impulse and not on plan. The need for some means of evaluating the abilities of the various members of the executive staff was long over due, and no serious efforts were being made to cope with this.[16]

The dispute over leadership of the foundation and the resignation of Edelstein occurred before the organization had even selected a Board of Directors. The existence of a board with the authority over all of the national foundation's operations would eventually complicate decision making within the organization. Over time, control of the foundation would shift from the idealistic COs who established the organization, and those individuals who joined it later, to board members who did not necessarily understand the vision on which it was founded.

◆   ◆   ◆

One of Barton's first priorities as executive director was to put together the Board of Directors of the National Mental Health Foundation. The foundation had enlisted the support of a group of prominent Americans to serve as national sponsors, but most of these persons played little more than a figurehead role. Like the Mental Hygiene Program before it, it had also recruited professional experts to be advisers to the organization. Stevenson and Hamilton declined to be formal advisers to the national foundation, citing potential conflicts with their positions in other organizations. Stevenson continued to be the medical director of the National Committee, and Hamilton had been elected president of the American Psychiatric Association. The initial list of advisers included Lauretta Bender, M.D., professor of psychiatry at New York University; Earl Bond, M.D., administrative director of the Institute of the Pennsylvania Hospital; Robert Felix, M.D., general chief of the Mental Hygiene Division of the U.S. Public Health Service; James Lewald, M.D., superintendent of the District Training School in Laurel, Maryland; Karl Menninger, M.D., manager of Winter Veterans Administration Hospital in Topeka, Kansas; Elizabeth Ross, a psychiatric social worker; Charles Zeller, M.D., director of the Michigan Department of Mental Health; and William Draper Lewis, director of the American Law Institute.[17] The advisers would consult with the foundation on professional matters and lend credibility to a mental health organization run by laypersons, but would not be involved in the operation of the foundation or assist it in fund-raising, an activity critical to its future. The Board of Directors would oversee the operation of the national foundation and be depended upon to raise money.

It was natural for leaders of the church committees to continue their involvement with the work of the now former COs and serve as members of the foundation's board. Clarence Pickett, Rufus Jones, and Louis Schneider of the AFSC, Orie Miller of the MCC, and M. R. Zigler of the BSC were initial members of the national foundation's Board of Directors. The Reverend Dores Sharpe, the minister who had led the grand jury investigation of the Cleveland State Hospital, and Mary Jane Ward, author of *The Snake Pit*, had brought public attention to conditions at mental hospitals and were likely candidates to serve on the board. Both accepted invitations to do so. Former Supreme Court justice Owen Roberts had already agreed to be listed as chairman of the foundation, although he did not feel that he could organize a fund-raising campaign for the organization.[18] Roger Baldwin of the American Civil Liberties Union shared the foundation's Legal Division's interest in reforming commitment laws and was willing to serve on the organization's board. When the Board of Directors was being formed, Baldwin gave Barton candid advice on the kind of people who should be invited to serve: "Your board is now representative of liberal and religious interests but not of people who are particularly conversant with this field. There must be many ex-members of public commissions dealing with the mentally ill, and lawyers who have handled cases, who could be suitable for your board."[19]

The leaders of the foundation wanted a board that could not only give them guidance and technical advice but also help them raise funds. They looked to their previous contacts to recruit board members who had ties to the philanthropic world. Clarence Pickett and other members of the AFSC could help them make connections with prominent Philadelphians. Eleanor Roosevelt agreed to host two meetings in New York City between members of the foundation and political, civic, and business leaders in September 1946 and wrote letters of introduction on behalf of the foundation.[20] Roosevelt would continue to assist the foundation in fund-raising at least through 1947.

The first board meeting of the national foundation was held on October 11, 1946, and presided over by Owen Roberts.[21] Eight members of the board attended the meeting, and Roberts was elected chairman and pro tem president. The board members in attendance voted to appoint nineteen persons to serve two- to three-year terms on the board. The interim directors of the foundation, Barton, Hetzel, and Steer, offered their resignations from the board. The members of the Executive Council, now three men with Edelstein's resignation, were appointed ex officio nonvoting members of the board.

The resignations of Barton, Hetzel, and Steer as interim directors and the appointment of an external Board of Directors marked an important transition in what had been started as a grassroots movement led by laypersons. The founders of the Mental Hygiene Program and then the National Mental Health Foundation had been adamant about the need for layperson control. At the initial board meeting, Barton informed members that "the National Mental Health Foundation has been from its beginning a layman's organization seeking professional advice." Barton, Edelstein, Hetzel, and Steer had wanted to avoid what they saw as the downfall of the National Committee in becoming dominated by medical professionals. Their public comments about the National Committee were muted and downplayed their disapproval of that organization. As Barton reviewed the history of the foundation for the board at its first meeting, he stated, "We constantly kept in mind the fact that our organization was the only organization working at the institutional level and though we recognized that our major contribution might be produced there, nothing could be accomplished until the public understood the situation."[22] A prospectus developed to raise funds for the foundation stated:

> There is no national organization today devoting primary efforts to public education in the field of mental health. Little more than $9,000 was expended in public education efforts during the past year by the two leading national organizations in the field of mental health. (The National Committee for Mental Hygiene—the American Psychiatric Association.)
>
> This is not an attempt to discredit these organizations, for both serve a very essential role in the field of mental health and their contributions, particularly in the realm of research, have been deeply significant. . . . At most the combined

efforts of these groups is inadequate and strongly indicate the need for a full-fledged program. In addition, it should be stated that the organizations mentioned are directed primarily by professional persons and the educational material prepared by them is not usually written for the man in the street.[23]

Privately, the leaders of the national foundation were more critical of the National Committee and the APA. Barton later recalled: "We did not feel that existing organizations interested in mental health were sufficiently grass-roots and community-organization minded enough to attract the broad and inter-disciplinary support that would be needed for real advances in the field. The only way we could see around the frustration was to commit ourselves for an extended stay with the work." In a note to Barton on the organization of the foundation on September 19, 1946, Hetzel commented on the need to "prevent our becoming a replica of the Nat'l Committee."[24]

Barton, Hetzel, and Steer felt strongly enough about lay control of the foundation that they inserted a clause in the organization's bylaws excluding medical doctors and nurses from serving on its Board of Directors: "Qualifications. Any member, provided that he or she is not a physician or registered nurse may be nominated and elected as a director."[25] Two days before the first meeting of the board, the Executive Council composed of the three men amended the bylaws to be more restrictive by excluding public mental health officials: "Qualifications. Any person, provided he or she is not a physician or registered nurse or engaged as an executive or administrative officer in relation to a public department, authority, agency or institution concerned with care and treatment of the mentally disordered, may be nominated and elected as a director."[26]

The foundation's board had its own idea about the participation of medical personnel. It revised the Executive Council's bylaws in October and January. The final bylaws approved by the board made an exception to the exclusion of medical professionals by requiring the appointment of "one psychiatrist as nominated and elected by the professional advisors."[27] Earl Bond was the psychiatrist appointed to the Board of Directors. It would not be the last time the board would move in a direction that was different from what the founders had in mind when they started the organization.

In the fall of 1946, the foundation faced a more pressing issue than the membership of a psychiatrist on its board: finances.

◆　◆　◆

With the end of the CPS, the national foundation needed to raise funds to support the operation of the organization. Unpaid COs became staff members who had to be paid. Money was needed to pay for the costs of publications and other activities. Fortunately, the Race Street meeting of the Society of Friends provided a building for the foundation's offices at 1520 Race Street in Philadelphia for a period of two years, rent free.[28]

By October 1946, the staff of the foundation numbered ten Executive Council members and associates, in addition to five secretaries and clerical staff.[29] Included among the associates were former COs Herbert Stoddard, treasurer; Alex Sareyan, public relations associate; William Kenney, acting director of the Educational Division; Richard Hunter, Educational Division associate; Stephen Thiermann, Legal Division associate; and Richard Mitchell, acting director of the Promotion Division. The national foundation had even hired a staff psychiatrist, Dallas Pratt, in May 1946 "for day to day on-the-spot consultation by various Divisions and for active participation in certain projects which required professional psychiatric assistance." Pratt understood his place in an organization run by laypersons:

> I ought to add a few words on how it feels to be a psychiatrist on the staff of an organization which was organized by laymen, largely for laymen, speaking and writing laymen's language, and with (up to the present) an exclusively lay Board of Directors. . . . I have never been conscious of any serious disagreement or friction, despite the fact that many of them have worked in hospitals as attendants where the attendant-physician relationship was extremely poor.
>
> The reason for the smoothness of our association comes, I am sure, from the fact that the N.M.H.F. has essentially a patient-centered program. . . . [A]ll members of the staff, including myself, have consistently tried to set our faces towards goals which are *patient-centered*, and here I think there is only one point of view.[30]

At its first meeting, the board was confronted with a fiscal crisis surrounding the national foundation.[31] Steer pointed out that the organization had been "amassing an increasing deficit," and Barton explained that the foundation was $7,000 "in the red." Justice Roberts told the board at its inaugural meeting: "The Board should not let the program die." Clarence Pickett "expressed the opinion that the staff should not be reduced as this would 'cripple' the organization." The board appointed a finance committee to explore ideas for fund-raising. Barton continued to appeal to Eleanor Roosevelt for help in fund-raising and sent her a financial statement indicating that the foundation had a deficit of $8,544.88 at the end of 1946.[32]

The foundation's financial situation was probably even more dire than explained to the board. The organization had a budget surplus of $247 as of July 31, 1946.[33] The church committees had provided $9,220 to the foundation up until the end of July, and their contributions were scheduled to end in August. Once funding from the church committees ended, the organization immediately faced problems meeting its expenses. The foundation's budget called for the executive secretary and directors of the divisions to be paid annual salaries of $3,600 and associates $3,200. Their actual salaries were $150 per month, a figure that equaled $1,800 per year. By the end of the year, no staff member had been paid more than $175 per month.[34] Even then, some of the senior members of the staff had to skip their paychecks so that the clerical staff could be paid. In January 1947, Hal Barton reflected on the financial status of the organization and his own situation:

> As I left home this morning Lois reminded me that she had *one* car token and 2 cents left. I had two one-dollar bills and some loose change and our bank account was practically at the same point. Along with five or six other ex-CPS'ers on the staff, I'd "skipped" receiving the last pay check in order that sufficient funds would be available to pay clerical help. This pattern has been repeated many times in the past few months and up to the present there has been little but such situations to look forward to—unless we had been willing to give up and curtail even token activities on what seemed to be very essential projects if we were to be ready for the work which should be done in 1947. We have been fortunate to retain the nucleus of our old "MHP" crew. Several were very close to leaving—of necessity rather than because of choice—at the first of the year. Had we not been able to hope for better things and provide for a living wage to begin Jan. 1, we might have lost part of the "old faithfuls." Only yesterday some were in desparate [*sic*] need of advances; some of the clerical staff were getting uneasy about their job security and no funds were on hand. But we have never wanted to give up and retrench— and our Board Executive Committee had indicated that they didn't want us to curtail. . . . A short summary might read, "the situation was tight"![35]

Bill Kenney of the Educational Division would later refer to the late summer and fall of 1946 as "the dark and gloomy days" when it seemed that the foundation "would not be able to meet the next payroll." By November, the foundation had been forced to lay off some staff, and remaining members had been diverted from research and the production of new materials to sales of literature and services. Financial problems were taking a toll on Barton and the other staff. On November 16, a discouraged Barton wrote, "Our failures of the past year weigh heavily upon us and we are challenged by the work yet undone. Looking ahead, we feel that it is 'now or never' to overcome the handicaps of insufficient secretarial help and to become the efficient, productive unit we once were before salaries and expanded activities made fund-raising a first essential."[36]

Financial problems continued to plague the foundation in 1947 and 1948. The board approved an annual budget of $172,750 for 1947.[37] Early in 1947, the financial picture was looking better. The Rockefeller Foundation and the Carnegie Corporation of New York had given the foundation a combined grant of $50,000 for 1947 and pledged to make another $50,000 grant for 1948 if the organization could raise an additional $90,000 by February of that year.[38] By late March 1947, the Board of Independent Aid in New York had given the foundation $2,500 and a "Philadelphia Campaign" launched by the board had brought in $2,000, including a $1,000 gift from Justice Roberts.[39] The MCC had even contributed $250 to support the organization, although the CPS had ended.

By the fall of 1947, the foundation still was experiencing serious financial problems. "Our need for current operating funds continues to be urgent," wrote Barton.[40] Sales of materials and memberships in the national foundation, at $1 per year, lagged, and the foundation could not attract additional large grants or gifts. The staff was reduced from a high of thirty-two to twenty members, and the printing of some materials was delayed. The board approved the hiring of a financial consultant, John Rich, and the firm of Oram and Rich would later be contracted with to assist in direct mail campaigns and other fund-raising.[41] Income from all sources totaled $107,450 for 1947, far short of the $172,750 originally budgeted by the board.[42] At the beginning of 1948, the deficit was $5,669.[43]

In 1948, the national foundation failed to receive the $50,000 Rockefeller and Carnegie grant because it did not meet the deadline for raising the additional $90,000 in funds. Even so, its income for that year was $106,944, including $84,296 in grants and contributions ranging in size from $1 to $3,000.[44] Staff continued to face hardships throughout the year. In a strongly worded memorandum to the Board of Directors and "certain Advisors and Friends" in May, Will Hetzel summarized the situation confronting the staff: "They must be paid a suitable financial compensation for services and time rendered. The days of *sacrificial* giving of time, skills, and emotional energy to planning, organization, research, and administration must quickly end." Hetzel went on to describe the problems facing the staff: "There is to date no provision for retirement annuities for staff. No deductions from pay or other provision is made for qualifications under federal or state social security for any member of staff. . . . No provision whatever is made for medical or nursing services to staff or families. Neither is there any insurance to cover injuries or disability incurred in the course of employment. The inadequate salary has sometimes gone unpaid at least in part with several months delay."[45]

When the national foundation was established, its founders envisioned a large national organization, with field offices spread throughout the country. The projected annual budget contained in the original prospectus for the foundation was $412,400, a huge sum of money in 1946.[46] Its income never reached more than a bit over a quarter of that amount. The organization struggled to keep up with staff salaries and program expenses. Its continued financial problems, combined with a gradual loss of its unique identity, would eventually lead to the demise of the National Mental Health Foundation.

◆   ◆   ◆

Despite its financial problems and the seemingly endless staff time and energy devoted to fund-raising, the national foundation completed a number of successful projects and received public visibility and acclaim between 1946 and 1950. *Out of Sight, Out of Mind* was released in mid-1947 and received the glowing endorsement by Eleanor Roosevelt in her "My Day" column. By September, one thousand copies of the book had been sold.[47] Paid subscriptions to the *Psychiatric Aid*, later renamed the *Psychiatric Aide,* continued to climb, and its annual "Psychiatric Aide of the Year Award" was reported in national newsmagazines and newspapers across the country.[48] As stated in the foundation's *Annual Report* for 1949, "Of all the efforts made by the Foundation in this direction, the most widely publicized has been its annual Psychiatric Aide of the Year award."[49]

The Educational Division continued to prepare and sell handbooks, reprints, information packets, pamphlets, and booklets. The *Handbook for Psychiatric Aides* sold fourteen thousand copies between 1946 and early 1949, then in its fourth printing.[50] Materials presented information about mental illness and mental deficiency as well as mental hospitals and training schools. Booklets included *About the Feebleminded, Your Child Is Slow, Forgotten Children,* and *Some Special Problems of Children* on mental handicaps or feeblemindedness and *One Out of Ten, From Folly to Fetters to Freedom: The Story of the Mentally Ill, Mental Health Is a Family Affair,* and *Toward Mental Health* on mental illness and mental hospitals. One pamphlet, *Here's Where Your Money Goes,* illustrated how national spending on mental illness fell far behind spending on tuberculosis, infantile paralysis, and cancer. Two booklets, *What to Look for in a Mental Hospital* and *What to Look for in a State Training School for the Feebleminded,* were laypersons' guides to visiting, observing, and asking questions about institutions. The national foundation's fourth *Annual Report* indicated that as many as three hundred thousand copies of some booklets had been sold.[51]

Under Will Hetzel, the Legal Division prepared digests of state mental health laws and reviews on topics such as public laws and practices on the administration of mental hospitals and commitment laws and practices.[52] Hetzel, along with C. Lloyd Bailey of the Friends Committee on National Legislation, prepared a detailed brief, *The Mental Health Laws of Ohio*, jointly planned by the national foundation and the National Committee for Mental Hygiene.[53] The brief contained a preface by the Reverend Dores Sharpe and a foreword by George Stevenson. The foundation's 1948 *Annual Report* indicated that a grant of $16,120 was expected from the U.S. Public Health Service under the National Mental Health Act for a study of "Public Laws and Practices Pertaining to the Administration of Mental Institutions in the United States," but the 1949 *Annual Report* made no mention of it.[54]

The national foundation waged several notable public education campaigns. Between 1947 and 1950, the foundation prepared three radio series, *For These We Speak, The Tenth Man,* and *Hi, Neighbor,* that aired in as many as 450 cities.[55] The dramas were prepared under the direction of Alex Sareyan, who held various titles with the foundation, including promotion manager and special services director. Sareyan had been a CO at Middletown State Hospital in Connecticut and joined the foundation in April 1946. The programs were narrated or contained introductions by well-known celebrities or public figures, including Eleanor Roosevelt, Helen Hayes, Mary Jane Ward, and Eddie Albert. The first series, *For These We Speak,* contained eight fifteen-minute dramas that cost $7,325 to produce, including staff and promotion costs, and aired as public service programs.[56] Program 5 of the first series, which had Mary Jane Ward as a guest speaker, was titled "Hats Off to Sarge!": "Sarge McCarthy: Charge Attendant (placid and easygoing on the surface, is actually deeply interested in the welfare of his patients. Speech has tones of Irish brogue)." Another hourlong documentary, *Mind in the Shadow,* starring actor Eddie Albert, was broadcast by CBS on February 2 and February 20, 1949. The program started with this dramatic introduction taken directly from Sharpe's grand jury investigation of Cleveland State Hospital: "This Grand Jury is shocked beyond words that a so-called civilized society would allow fellow humans to be mistreated as they are at our State Mental Hospitals. It would be a prison for the well; it is hell for the sick. We indict the uncivilized social system which has enabled such an intolerable and barbaric practice to fasten itself upon the people. MUSIC"[57]

In 1949, the U.S. Junior Chamber of Commerce (JCs) sponsored a national Mental Health Week with the advice and support of the foundation.[58] The JCs sent out a package of information nationally that included materials from the foundation. The foundation used this occasion to convince Barry Bingham, president of the *Louisville Courier Journal* and the American Newspaper Publishers Association, to write newspaper editors across the country encouraging them to use nonstigmatizing language in their stories about mental illness. Bingham's March 2, 1949, letter asked editors to help improve public understanding of mental illness and suggested specific language they should use in their stories:

> Would you please be willing to help in the cure of sick people by the simple power of words? This letter is to suggest how you can do just that. I have been asked to write it by the National Mental Health Foundation. It is a request for help from you—not for money, but a still more vital contribution to public understanding of the problems of mental illness.
>
> With the widespread attention now being given to the care of patients in mental hospitals and with the approaching National Mental Health Week to be sponsored by the Junior Chamber of Commerce beginning April 24, your newspaper will have occasion to write numerous stories on the subject of America's number one health problem—MENTAL HEALTH. . . .
>
> You can perform a great service in promoting the cause of mental health by helping to take the stigma out of mental illness. You can do this by discarding from the vocabulary of your paper any possible archaic and stigmatizing expressions, and substituting others. Three that I would especially like to urge are PATIENT in place of INMATE; MENTAL ILLNESS in place of INSANITY or LUNACY; MENTAL HOSPITAL instead of INSANE ASYLUM.

According to Sareyan, Bingham received almost a thousand replies to his letter, and many newspapers adopted his recommended language in their style manuals.[59]

In 1949, a group of mental health and psychiatric organizations joined together to sponsor the Mental Health Week in cooperation with the JCs. Alex Sareyan of the national foundation served as executive director of the Mental Health Week Planning Committee, which also included representatives of the National Committee, APA, National Institute of Mental Health, and State Charities Aide Association. For Mental Health Week, NBC produced two half-hour radio dramas, and CBS aired a one-hour documentary.[60] Fox Movietown News prepared a thirty-second newsreel on mental health to be shown in theaters across the country.

In a relatively short period of time, the national foundation had gained national recognition and had attracted at least as much publicity as well-established organizations such as the National Committee and the APA. On July 26, 1948, President Harry S. Truman wrote Justice Owen Roberts a letter expressing his "profound gratitude" for the work of the National Mental Health Foundation. "If we are to improve the quality of our mental institutions," the letter read, "we must have public understanding and support." The letter concluded: "I want to commend you for your own fine work and urge you and the National Mental Health Foundation to carry forward the splendid program you have started so vigorously."[61]

◆   ◆   ◆

The year 1948 would be a pivotal time for the national foundation. It would be marked by the transition from a staff to a board-controlled organization and the resignation of one of its founders and key leaders. By the end of the year, events set in motion a process that would lead to the demise of the organization.

Mrs. Percy (Margaret) C. Madeira became acting chairman of the foundation in January 1948, and would later become chairman. Madeira previously had worked for the Pennsylvania Department of Welfare and served as the director of the Pennsylvania Citizens Association for Health and Welfare.[62] An article in the *Philadelphia Evening Bulletin* in October 1948 characterized her as a well-known Philadelphian.[63] Madeira had dealt with the national foundation prior to joining the board. In the fall of 1946, she had worked with representatives of the foundation on the establishment of a department of mental health in Pennsylvania. At a luncheon of the Mental Hygiene Division of Public Charities on November 6, Madeira, a Mr. Wolfe, and a representative of the foundation were asked to serve on a committee to develop a plan for a department of mental health. Will Hetzel took the place of the foundation's representative on the committee when he left for a trip to the Midwest. Then, on December 7, 1946, that same representative reported that Mrs. Madeira had called him. She was surprised by a disagreement between her and the national foundation. Madeira and the staff of the foundation apparently did not see eye to eye on some matters: "Mrs. Madeira called me and in the course of our conversation asked what I thought of her legislative proposal which had been drawn and referred to Mr. Hetzel. I said it was my impression we did not agree fully with it, particularly the administrative board. This comment apparently surprised her, and she suggested a conference with us and Dr. Bond on Dec. 19. Dr. Bond, I believe, was unable to attend and Mrs. Madeira called here. Mr. Hetzel and Mr. Barton talked with her. No further record."[64]

After the appointment of Mrs. Madeira, Justice Owen Roberts continued to serve as honorary president of the foundation, a title that aptly described his role in the organization. Roberts had presided over meetings and events but was not actively involved in the day-to-day operations of the foundation. Madeira was a different kind of board chair. She was hands-on. Richard Hunter would later write about her: "The time and attention that she devoted to matters of program, organization, and financial support were far beyond what any organization might reasonably expect even from its most devoted volunteer." The foundation's *Third Annual Report* was more specific in describing how Madeira strengthened the board's leadership of the organization:

> When NMHF was organized almost three years ago, it was virtually a "staff" organization. It was recognized, however, that the lack of strong board support would be a decided handicap. The first Board was soon organized and its members were all extremely sympathetic toward the work of the organization, but

39. Harold Barton, Mrs. Percy (Margaret) Madeira, and Willard Hetzel
of the National Mental Health Foundation. (Swarthmore College Peace
Collection, Swarthmore, Pennsylvania)

most of them were obligated in so many ways that they could not do all that
needed to be done. With the coming of Mrs. Percy C. Madeira, Jr. to the Board
in January, 1948, the situation was vastly changed. Mrs. Madeira worked untir-
ingly on all problems brought before her. She was in the office almost daily. Most
important, she was able to reach and interest strong and influential persons who
have joined our Board and are lifting from the staff the responsibilities which
more properly rest with the Board. During 1948, there were 10 meetings of the
Board or its Executive Committee.[65]

The foundation's Board of Directors met on March 19, 1948, under Madeira's
direction.[66] The agenda for the meeting was jam-packed, and decisions were made
that would alter the course of the organization. Of seven new persons appointed or
nominated to the board at its meeting, all were from the Philadelphia area. Under
Madeira, the size of the board would grow and be dominated by members from
the Philadelphia area, none of whom had played a prominent role in the history of
the Mental Hygiene Program or the national foundation. According to the October
28, 1948, article in the *Philadelphia Evening Bulletin*, seventeen of the twenty-eight
members of the board were Philadelphians. Many of the original national figures
remained on the board, but most seldom, if ever, attended meetings. At its March

meeting, the board established a temporary Executive Committee composed of eight members, each a Philadelphian. The board voted that the Executive Committee should meet monthly, an action that made it difficult for members from outside of Philadelphia to be actively involved. Before long, the Executive Committee, led by Madeira, would play an increasingly influential role in the operation of the foundation. Madeira announced at the March meeting that she had invited three members of the board to serve on a program evaluation committee and would be naming members of a staff evaluation committee. The establishment of program and staff evaluation committees strengthened the board's oversight of and control over the foundation and its staff.

At the March meeting, the board passed a resolution approving the national foundation's membership in a federation of mental health groups: "Resolved that the National Mental Health Foundation join with other non-profit organizations in the field of mental health on a national scale to form a council to be known as the American Federation for Mental Health." The federation had grown out of repeated, and often contentious, meetings between the National Mental Health Foundation, the National Committee for Mental Hygiene, the Psychiatric Foundation, and the Menninger Foundation. The first meeting had been called on May 16, 1947, by Dr. Frank Fremont-Smith, vice president of the National Committee and director of the Josiah Macy Jr. Foundation.[67] Each of the organizations had sought to capitalize on the increased public attention to mental hospitals and mental health by stepping up their fund-raising efforts. The organizations often went to the same foundations and other sources of financial support and found it difficult to explain how their efforts differed from the others. The May meeting started with each of the organizations explaining its mission. According to Dr. Leo Bartemaier, the Psychiatric Foundation was devoted to raising money to carry out the directives of the APA and, specifically, a survey and rating of state mental hospitals. The Menninger Foundation was engaged in psychiatric research and training, explained William Menninger. Representing the national foundation, William Kenney reviewed the organization's programs of public education and improvement of mental hospitals. George Stevenson of the National Committee said that the committee's activities focused on preservation of mental health and prevention of mental disorders and encompassed the entire field. By the end of the meeting, agreement had been reached that the organizations should continue to meet to discuss the possibility of joint fund-raising campaigns.

The foundation's board gave its first approval of the concept of a federation of mental health groups in June 1947: "The Board of Directors approves the general policy of federation with the Psychiatric Foundation, the Menninger Foundation, and the National Committee for Mental Hygiene for the primary purpose of creating a formal and continuing channel for the exchange of organizational objectives and activities, and for the coordination and prevention of duplication in the work of the various organizations operating on a national level in the field of mental health. The plan of working toward a combined fund-raising effort is approved."[68] By September 1947, a poll of the Executive Committee of the national foundation indicated strong support for the formation of a federation of national mental health organizations and authorized its representatives at meetings among the groups, including Hal Barton and Earl Bond, to make binding commitments on behalf of the foundation.[69] The Executive Committee confirmed its approval of federation at a meeting on October 31.[70] The four organizations met on November 12 to report on their boards' actions on the federation.[71] The meeting was chaired by Fremont-Smith, representing the Macy Foundation. Barton, Bond, and Dallas Pratt, staff psychiatrist, represented the national foundation. Stevenson reported that the National Committee's board had approved further exploration of a federation, and William Menninger said that his foundation's board had voted in favor of incorporation of the federation. Fremont-Smith read a letter from the National Mental Health Foundation that stated that its board had approved the principle of federation. The Psychiatric Foundation, which was represented by Bartemeier, Dr. Mesrop Tarumianz, and Austin Davies, was a stumbling block at the meeting.

The board of the Psychiatric Foundation had disapproved participation in a federation and had expressed opposition to joint fund-raising. Bartemeier and Tarumianz said that they personally supported collaboration, and Tarumianz stated that he thought that the board might approve joint fund-raising if specific proposals were presented to it. As discussion continued, it became clear that members of the Psychiatric Foundation's board had reservations about some of the other collaborators. Some shared the skepticism of many psychiatrists about the National Mental Health Foundation: "[Tarumianz] stated that the National Mental Health Foundation was not wholly acceptable to certain of the Board members. He feared that the former group might deviate from the principles which other mental health organizations had accepted for many years. It was also felt that the National Mental Health Foundation was identified with pacifists and might be committed to a policy of not defending the country in time of war."[72]

The national foundation was not the only organization about which some members of the Psychiatric Foundation had concerns. The Menninger Foundation was also viewed with suspicion: "[Tarumianz] went on to say there was some question as to the inclusion of the Menninger Foundation." Menninger offered to withdraw from discussions about the federation if the Menninger Foundation's participation would "prejudice joint action," but representatives of the other organizations expressed the desire that Menninger continue to be involved.

As the meeting continued, the National Committee, the National Mental Health Foundation, and the Menninger Foundation wanted to draft articles of incorporation and bylaws for the federation. The representatives of the Psychiatric Foundation said that they could not participate in this activity without the approval of their board. Austin Davies of the Psychiatric Foundation then stated that he was personally opposed to a federation because he thought that it could more easily raise money on its own. At the end of this discussion, Davies made a proposal that caught others off-guard and was immediately dismissed: "Mr. Davies stated that since joint fund-raising was a major objection, a merger rather than a federation might be the solution. The Chairman said that this would be technically too difficult."[73]

Before the meeting ended, the group agreed to adopt the name "'Federation for Mental Health' (a national council of voluntary, non-profit organizations)" and to invite Dr. Alan Gregg of the Rockefeller Foundation to accept chairmanship of the federation once specifics had been worked out among the cooperating organizations. Gregg was familiar with all of the organizations, and Rockefeller Foundation funding had been sought by each of the groups. The meeting ended with a commitment to meet again in January and with a statement by three of the groups: "Representatives of the Menninger Foundation, the National Committee for Mental Hygiene and the National Mental Health Foundation expressed themselves in favor of going ahead with the federation,—if necessary, without the Psychiatric Foundation."

The reticence of the Psychiatric Foundation to join together with the National Mental Health Foundation and the Menninger Foundation was not surprising. Many psychiatrists were suspicious of an organization founded by laypersons and former COs who had exposed mental hospitals and embarrassed the psychiatric profession. When he was an executive assistant at the APA, Austin Davies had tried to prevent the Rockefeller Foundation from funding the national foundation and had characterized the group as "a fly-by-night and irresponsible organization . . . whose program will encroach too much on the field of medicine or be too limited to be any good."[74] Menninger's attempt to reform the APA through the Group for Advancement of Psychiatry had alienated many psychiatrists and created a rift within the APA itself.

Representatives of the four organizations met in March 1948 in Washington, D.C., to discuss the purposes of the federation and outline the steps that needed to be taken for incorporation.[75] Madeira, Barton, and Pratt represented the national foundation at this meeting. The purposes of the federation were stated in general terms and emphasized "cooperative association" and "information and understanding about the work of the agencies." The name was changed to the American Federation for Mental Health at the meeting.

On May 21, 1948, the four organizations met again to discuss incorporation.[76] The meeting was held in Washington, D.C., in conjunction with the annual meeting of the APA. The boards of the Menninger Foundation, the National Committee, and the national foundation had approved incorporation. The Psychiatric Foundation's board had voted against joining an incorporated federation, but its representatives indicated that it might reconsider its decision on June 10. Representatives of the other three organizations decided to move forward with the federation. They would set conditions under which other organizations could join later. The representatives of the Psychiatric Foundation were permitted to sit in on the meeting as observers. Stevenson of the National Committee and Mildred Law of the Menninger Foundation proposed articles of incorporation for the federation, and a resolution was passed to forward these articles to legal counsel to prepare a draft for the boards of the three organizations. In another resolution, Barton was elected to be secretary-treasurer for "the American Federation for Mental Health (A Council of Voluntary, Non-Profit Organizations)."

Hal Barton reported at the meeting that the National Mental Health Foundation, the National Committee for Mental Hygiene, and the Menninger Foundation had sent an application to the Proctor and Gamble Company to be selected as the beneficiaries of a fund-raising campaign through the popular *Truth or Consequences* radio program emceed by Ralph Edwards. *Truth or Consequences* had previously raised $1.5 million for the American Heart Association, and Edwards had expressed an interest in the field of mental health.[77] Listeners of the radio program were invited to mail in their guesses about the identities of a mystery couple, along with a contribution to the designated charity.[78] Proceeds from the program, projected at $1 million, would be shared by the three groups. This venture would represent the first joint fund-raising effort by the three organizations. The funds would go a long way toward resolving the foundation's long-standing financial problems.

Leaders of the three organizations were thrilled to be selected as beneficiaries of *Truth or Consequences* later in 1948, but proceeds from the program turned out to be far lower than anyone anticipated. A federal agency had ruled that the program could not require donations from people sending in their guesses, and the mystery couple was identified relatively early on. By November 18, *Truth or Consequences* had raised only $4,000, a figure that shocked the program's producers: "NBC's promotion department was shocked (says Alex) when it learned the $4,000 figure, so it's rather obvious that the contest is not doing as well as in previous instances."[79] Nearly a month later, on December 17, when the mental health campaign was coming to an end, the radio program had raised only $56,000.[80] *Truth or Consequences* ended up raising less than one-tenth of the amount that was originally anticipated.[81] A 1949 report indicated that the National Committee and the national foundation had been awarded $22,250 and $20,000 grants, respectively, from the *Truth or Consequences* program and that $75,000 remained to be allocated. A committee composed of Alan Gregg of the Rockefeller Foundation, Charles Dollard of the Carnegie Corporation, and a Mr. Reed of the National Information Bureau had been formed to make allocations from the *Truth or Consequences* funds.[82] Funding from the program helped but did not solve the national foundation's chronic shortage of funds.

The Psychiatric Foundation continued to stay on the margins of the American Federation for Mental Health. An apparent breakthrough occurred in a meeting between Barton and Hunter of the national foundation and Dr. Harold Elley, president of the Psychiatric Foundation and vice president of the DuPont corporation, and W. F. Murphy, assistant director of the foundation, on August 13.[83] In a memorandum to his board, Barton reported on the meeting and reviewed the relationship between the Psychiatric Foundation and the American Federation. Austin Davies, executive director of the Psychiatric Foundation, had been a roadblock to participation of the foundation in a federation:

> Our first contact with representatives of the P.F. was with Mr. Austin Davies, Executive Director, who disclaimed any interest in the "mental hygiene movement" or in any public education or publicity on mental health. At that time it was suggested that the N.M.H.F. merge with the P.F. and continue only its work on attendant training. Strong emphasis was given by Mr. Davies to the fact that any work carried out under the P.F. would be solely controlled by psychiatrists. . . . In other words, great stress was given to a monopoly on direction by psychiatrists.

Barton went on to explain that in all discussions of the American Federation, Davies and other representatives of the Psychiatric Foundation "have presented viewpoints that would call for the merger of all organizations under the wing of the Psychiatric Foundation." This was unacceptable to representatives of the other three organizations. Elley and Murphy had a different point of view than Davies and others at the Psychiatric Foundation. Elley "expressed complete agreement with the need for a greatly expanded program of public education and community action to meet mental health needs," and Murphy said that "a united front can be presented." Murphy added that some potential large donors to the Psychiatric Foundation had indicated that they would make contributions to it only if it coordinated its work with the American Federation. Elley and Murphy believed that they could convince the board of the Psychiatric Foundation to join the American Federation. Barton concluded on a hopeful note: "If the attitude of Mr. Murphy and Dr. Elley is representative of the Board of the P.F., then the last barrier to a nation-wide effort combining all forces in the mental health field would seem to be removed." Yet at a meeting between Barton, Madeira, and Pratt and the Psychiatric Foundation on September 15, representatives of the Psychiatric Foundation once more proposed that it be recognized as the national fund-raising agency of the mental health field.[84] Barton, Madeira, and Pratt expressed their unanimous opposition to the proposal. There was internal disagreement within the Psychiatric Foundation.

Hal Barton announced his resignation from the National Mental Health Foundation, effective November 1, at a board meeting on September 28, 1948.[85] Together with Len Edelstein, Barton had been a guiding force behind the formation of the Mental Hygiene Program and the national foundation. Since Edelstein's resignation in August 1946, he had been the foundation's most visible leader. Barton cited "personal reasons" and the importance of returning to his "own chosen profession" as a mining engineer for his resignation. The board accepted Barton's resignation "with great regret." Madeira informed the board that she had approached Richard Hunter to act as executive secretary on an interim basis. Hunter was not at the meeting, although Barton, Hetzel, Steer, Pratt, and Sareyan were. The board's Executive Committee formally appointed Hunter as acting executive secretary at its meeting on October 18.[86]

Barton did not elaborate on the reasons for his resignation. It seemed to have come suddenly. Like other members of the foundation's staff, he had endured more than two years of low pay and late paychecks while trying to raise a family. The organization's financial future had never looked brighter. The National Mental Health Foundation, the National Committee, and the Menninger Foundation were on the verge of establishing the American Federation as a fund-raising vehicle, and Barton had agreed to serve as secretary-treasurer the previous May. The upcoming *Truth or Consequences* campaign was expected to bring in significant funds for the foundation. In contrast with Len Edelstein's resignation, there did not seem to be strife between Barton and other long-standing members of the staff. A cryptic item appeared on the agenda of a meeting of the Executive Committee of the board dated April 23, 1948: "Approval of sum ($10,000) for a salary for a new top executive to push for extensions of organization and program."[87]

One thing was clear: control of the foundation was slipping from the grasp of the people who had founded it and nurtured its growth. Even before Barton's departure at the end of October, events would move the national foundation in a dramatically new direction.

◆   ◆   ◆

In early October 1948, three members of the National Committee for Mental Hygiene's board approached the board of the national foundation with a surprising proposal: formal merger of the two organizations.[88] Throughout the discussions of the American Federation for Mental Health, a merger of the participating organizations had never been seriously considered. The idea had been dismissed. At the March 19 board meeting, Madeira and Barton reported, "The federation would be a coordinating body and not a merger and would serve as a clearing house for the exchange of information, joint planning and for fund-raising."[89] The founders of the national foundation had remained skeptical of the National Committee and believed that it was too conservative and dominated by medical professionals.

From October 1948 and into the early months of 1949, the foundation's Board of Directors and its Executive Committee would take a step closer to accepting this proposal at each of their respective meetings. At an Executive Committee meeting on October 18, three issues were discussed: "1. Joint Fund-raising Campaign," "2. Federation," and "3. Merger."[90] Fremont-Smith, vice president of the National Committee and director of the Macy Foundation, had approached Madeira and Barton about the national foundation's participation in a joint fund-raising campaign along with other organizations. This idea had been under discussion for quite some time, and it was not controversial. The American Federation had been established as a legal entity, but bylaws had not been approved by any of the three participating organizations. The board of the National Committee had put further action on the federation on hold, in large part because it wanted to explore the possibility of a merger. At the October 8 meeting of the American Federation, representatives of the organizations decided to have "an objective study made of the agencies in the mental health field in order to determine by what means a unified cooperative effort could best be made."[91] The momentum for establishing the American Federation as a viable organization had been lost.

Notes prepared for the October 18 Executive Committee meeting described the posture of the National Committee: "The National Committee for Mental Hygiene is now very eager to bring about merger, more than generous in acknowledgement of past shortcomings, apparently willing to bring into being a *new* organization in which the values of both would be preserved." Speaking on behalf of the National Committee, Fremont-Smith, who had been the driving force behind bringing the national mental health groups together, had asked the national foundation to appoint two members of its board to the National Committee's board and for Madeira to serve on the National Committee's nominating committee. Madeira's initial reaction was that she and the board and staff of the foundation were too busy to put much time into the National Committee and merger: "Mrs. Madeira's feeling is that her hands are already too full; both she, Richard Hunter and Harold Barton feel that while merger is possible, right now we have too much to do to give time to it; that it is too important a step to take in haste." The notes for the Executive Committee did not indicate an author. Barton almost always included his name at the top of documents he prepared for the board or added an "HB" at the end.

The initially cautious "too important a step to take in haste" stance on merger by Madeira turned to a posture of "full-steam ahead" by November. Hal Barton returned to his hometown of Eugene, Oregon, in November but remained deeply committed to and interested in the foundation. He exchanged letters frequently with Hetzel, Steer, and Hunter after leaving the organization. On December 30, he wrote both Hetzel and Steer. "I've been fairly starved for news," wrote Barton to Steer. To Hetzel, he wrote, "I do want to hear from you—dirt and all. In fact I'm starved for dirt." Reports Barton received from Hetzel, Steer, and Hunter were not encouraging. On November 11, Hunter wrote, "Things are really moving along, but I'm not always sure where they are going."[92] Steer was open to a merger, but thought that it should be done slowly and cautiously:

> Mrs. Madeira is going all out these days for merger with NCMH. Some of us are counseling caution, but she hasn't seen the point yet. She seems to feel that if we don't do it right away, we may miss forever the glorious opportunity. I think she feels that our strength is likely to decline in the future as the strength of NCMH increases. Her attitude seems to be one almost of desperation. Needless to say, some of us who favor the idea of merger want to be convinced that it is the thing to do, and that its consummation would not impede general progress in the field (of the sort this Foundation has been spearheading) before any decisive steps are taken.[93]

Hetzel was even more alarmed by how things were going and worried that the Board might work out an agreement with the National Committee without involving the staff:

> We attended an Executive Committee meeting of the Board yesterday. Mrs. Madeira and Mr. Wolfe seemed to feel that a merger is greatly to be desired. My contention, and I believe the general opinion of the staff, is to the effect that merger should not be considered until we have explored by means of a joint committee of the staffs of the two organizations the ways in which merger would benefit the mental health movement generally as distinguished from the progress we might make separately or upon some other cooperative arrangement such as the Federation.
>
> I am greatly disturbed that we have lost the initiative apparently for developing federation. This paves the way of course for the National Committee making propositions (to our Board) which I believe are entirely out of line with our major

objectives and basic principles of operation. I do not see how we can needle the National Committee, for example, or any other organization if we are merged with it. We would be in about the same position, it seems to me, that we are in today with respect to our own Board. If you ask me, it is one "H" of a position.[94]

Barton was deeply skeptical about whether a merger between the national foundation and the National Committee would work. The differences between the two groups were too vast. "As far as I'm concerned," he wrote Steer in December, "NMHF and NCMH never did come to grips with essential differences while I was around—we just couldn't get the NCMH people to do it!" Barton continued to believe that a federation, not a merger, was the way to go. On his way from Philadelphia to Eugene, he stopped by the Menninger Foundation to meet with "Dr. Will" and Mildred Law. Menninger told him that the foundation had been a much more effective organization than the National Committee and that a merger would work only "if NMHF retained complete control of operations." Both Menninger and Law agreed that the American Federation should be preserved, even if it included only the National Mental Health Foundation and the Menninger Foundation. Barton advised Hunter to continue to work with the Menninger Foundation on the federation: "Inasmuch as the last action of NCMH was against proceeding with Federation, unless you receive other word, it might be simpler all around to proceed with the meeting with only NMHF and MF represented."[95]

The Executive Committee of the national foundation's board met on November 23.[96] The merger was a major subject of discussion. A disagreement emerged between the staff and some of the board members. Madeira reported that the National Committee had appointed three of its board members to discuss a merger with a similar committee of the NMHF. She stated that "it would be extremely unwise not to have our representatives meet with the committee of the National Committee." Hunter suggested that members of the respective boards should not meet to discuss a merger without staff members present: "It was the feeling of Mr. Hunter that if three of our Board members were to meet with three Board members of the National Committee, such a meeting would get no further than generalities. He reported that discussion among staff members had led to the decision that any committee from the two organizations should include staff members who would be in a position to deal with the specific problems which would be included in merger and who would be able to turn the meeting into working sessions." One of the board members, Mrs. McClean, said that Hunter's approach was too negative. Another board member felt the same way: "Mr. Wolf[e] agreed and said he felt we were handling the subject too delicately; that it is not so complicated as it appears." Wolfe added, "The two committees should meet and get a general outline of the views of both groups as to how the merger could be accomplished." Little over one month after the idea of a merger had been raised with the Executive Committee, the discussion was already shifting to *how* a merger could be brought about.

Hetzel expressed the same opinion he had stated in his November 24 letter to Barton. The national foundation and the National Committee were fundamentally different organizations: "Mr. Hetzel stated that it was the opinion of the staff that the increase in interest and benefits accruing to all organizations is due to a large degree to the program and the needling done by this organization. He also indicated that the methods and principles of the two organizations involved in the merger discussion are different and that there is just as much need today for the activities of the Foundation as there were on the day the organization was started." Brandon Berringer of the board sidestepped Hetzel's position and recommended that "our staff take the initiative in outlining what we think ought to be the type of organization resulting from merger." The Executive Committee then voted to authorize Mrs. Madeira to appoint a committee including "at least one staff member" to meet with the National Committee to discuss a merger.

Throughout discussions of a merger, the board of the foundation never struggled with the basic question raised by Hetzel: were the principles and approaches of the two organizations compatible? The founders of the Mental Hygiene Program and then the National Mental Health Foundation—Hal Barton, Len Edelstein, Will Hetzel, and Phil Steer—had answered this question years earlier. Their principles and approaches were different from the National Committee's. Hence, a new organization was necessary. Edelstein was long gone by the time the merger was proposed. Nothing in Barton's or Hetzel's experiences with the National Committee had changed their original opinions. Steer was open to the idea of a merger, but wanted to make sure that the work of the foundation would carry on. Most members of the board in late 1948 did not seem to understand the history of the national foundation or appreciate the philosophy of its founders and its unique role in leading established organizations to devote attention to the conditions in America's mental hospitals and training schools. In its vote to include "at least one staff member" on the committee to meet with the National Committee, the board finessed the concerns expressed by staff members while appearing to be sympathetic to their point of view. It did not even seriously consider the position taken by one of the national foundation's founders. The Board of Directors, not the staff, would make decisions about a merger.

The first meeting between representatives of the organizations to discuss the merger was held on December 10.[97] Madeira and two staff members, Hunter and Pratt, represented the foundation. The National Committee was represented by

Fremont-Smith and two other board members as well as a staff member, a Mrs. Ginsburg. Dr. Elley and Mrs. Brooks of the Psychiatric Foundation also showed up at the meeting. General agreement was reached on four points at the meeting:

(1). In the process of merger each of the merging organizations would lose its operating identity so far as the public was concerned.

(2). That the board of the new organization would be predominantly lay.

(3). That the president of the new organization would not be drawn from the officers, board or staff of any of the merging organizations.

(4). That the top administrator would be a person qualified to administer the organization on a full time, paid basis and that he would not be drawn from the officers, board or staff of any of the merging organizations. (It was understood as a part of the foregoing statement that the administrator might be a medical person but if he were, that would be incidental inasmuch as it was felt by the majority of those present at the meeting that administrative and organization skills would be of primary importance.)

Ginsburg of the National Committee disagreed with the majority of people present at the meeting on the last point. She strongly believed that the top administrator of the new organization should be a medical person. Representatives of the staffs of the national foundation and the National Committee subsequently met on December 17 to attempt to iron out "misunderstandings." Hunter, Pratt, and Sareyan represented the foundation. Hetzel and Steer did not attend the meeting. Neither founder of the foundation would be centrally involved in discussions about the merger. George Stevenson, Ginsburg, and two other staff members represented the National Committee at the December 17 meeting. The National Committee's staff supported Ginsburg's position on medical leadership: "They supported Mrs. Ginsburg in the belief that the top executive should nevertheless be a psychiatrist. They expressed a fear, which is not without justification, that some types of lay leadership might lead to an emphasis on promotion and fund-raising to the exclusion of program." The foundation's representatives continued to be skeptical of placing administration of the organization under the control of a medical professional: "We, too, have been aware of certain risks such as the possibility of placing the future organization in the hands of leaders who are overly cautious and conservative though extremely well-qualified in the field of psychiatry."[98] The question of medical leadership would be a contentious issue throughout negotiations on the merger.

The National Committee's original merger proposal to the foundation's board involved only the two organizations. The national foundation's representatives were surprised by the participation of Psychiatric Foundation board members at the December 10 meeting: "Arrangements for their attendance had been made by officers of the National Committee at Dr. Elley's request, without consultation from us." Elley had previously been unsuccessful in getting the Psychiatric Foundation to join the American Federation for Mental Health. On December 14, Hunter met with Elley to discuss the national foundation's concerns about the Psychiatric Foundation: "Mr. Hunter discussed with Dr. Elley certain misgivings we have concerning the Psychiatric Foundation, particularly in regard to the conservative professional members of the board."[99] Several days later, Hunter wrote Barton to inform him of this latest development: "There are now three parties to the discussion. The third party is the, shall we say, 'left wing' of the Psychiatric Foundation represented by Dr. Elley. He, as you probably know, is much closer to our point of view than to the National Committee's point of view and in a conference with Elley in Wilmington on this last Tuesday he told me that he felt that his point of view, while it would not be unanimously supported, represents the majority in the Psychiatric Foundation."[100]

Barton wrote Hunter back to communicate his reservations about the Psychiatric Foundation. He had more misgivings about that organization than he did about the National Committee, and continued to believe that federation, not merger, was the best option:

> On the surface I'd quite agree that the NMHF point of view most nearly coincides with Dr. Elley's, etc. But underneath it all I can't help but think that the NCMH is a much more liberal and progressive group than Elley's! I know that most of the good things about the NCMH are atrophied because of little or no use, but I think they are there. The one big danger with that group is, of course, the heavy hand of the medical group which would of its own might and power (and without lay help!) run the universe. I believe Elley's group represents another point of view which would do the same, namely the a-socially-minded industrial group. Holding such views, I can't help but lean to Federation—even yet.[101]

Representatives of the three organizations continued meeting about a merger in 1949. At a meeting on January 12, a committee composed of one staff member from each organization was formed to formulate a merger plan. Richard Hunter represented the national foundation in these discussions. The committee started holding weekly meetings: "Staff relations have been most cordial and on the whole it appears that the staffs of the organizations considering merger might be quite compatible."[102] At the same time, the National Committee and the National Mental Health Foundation proposed to the *Truth or Consequences* Allocations Committee that a study be conducted of mental health organizations.

On February 11, the national foundation issued its *Third Annual Report.* By that time, the staff of the foundation was down to eight professional positions: Richard Hunter, executive secretary; Dallas Pratt, staff psychiatrist; Emerson Green, business manager; Philip Steer, finance associate; Willard Hetzel, legal director; Alex Sareyan, promotion manager; Roy Simon, education associate; and Paul Harris III, education associate. The *Third Annual Report*'s tone was different from previous descriptions of the national foundation, which stressed its uniqueness in the field of mental health:

> During 1948 it became more and more apparent to the leading national and local agencies that some way must be found through which all who are working toward the same ends can be drawn together into a coordinated effort. The answers were not all found in 1949, but progress was made.
>
> Neither the National Committee for Mental Hygiene nor the National Mental Health Foundation have the organizational strength or the breadth of program at this time to be prepared to lead a mental health movement alone. In view of the special strengths of each, much time has been spent in attempting to coordinate the efforts of both without the loss of the unique qualities of either.[103]

Will Hetzel had taken a leave of absence to study for the Pennsylvania bar exam starting January 1, but continued to be involved with the foundation "to have my voice and also try to keep the organization going along the lines which seem to me to be right and which will eventually make it possible for staff to do the best possible job." Madeira was frequently in the office, even though she wanted to step down as chairman of the foundation. Hetzel hoped that she would come to understand how the foundation had always operated: "Mrs. Madeira is around the office a great deal and is working faithfully and earnestly and in many respects is doing a good job. I believe she is getting a better appreciation of the kind of relationship that we feel should exist between board and staff. Whether or not she is willing to accept that type of organizational structure, I am not sure."

Hetzel continued to be skeptical of the National Committee for Mental Hygiene and the Psychiatric Foundation and worried that the board was moving too quickly toward a merger:

> I've been somewhat discouraged by the tendency on the part of some of the board members to favor an early merger with the National Committee for Mental Hygiene. It seems to me to be very important that we firmly establish ourselves as a citizens' organization with a broad membership represented by vote, either directly or through representatives in the national organization, and that we develop our program much more significantly before we let that program be

frozen along lines on which it might be frozen by a merger with a group which is still as professional as the National Committee is. I think staff is much more cautious about the possibility of merger than is our board. For my money it seems that the work you did along the lines of federation was much more to the point and in the end would be a more effective means of bringing about actual merger along sound lines.[104]

Richard—Dick—Hunter had a different perspective on merger than Hetzel. During the CPS, Hunter, a Methodist, had served at an MCC unit at Marlboro State Hospital in New Jersey. He had not been one of the founders of the Mental Hygiene Program and the foundation who had felt strongly about the need to establish a new and totally independent organization. As early as December 1948, he seemed to believe that a merger was inevitable and directed his time and energy to working out the details. He followed up on Madeira's and the board's desires, and "acting" was soon removed from his title as executive secretary. Hunter did not share Barton's and Hetzel's concerns about the National Committee and the Psychiatric Foundation and felt that those organizations were coming around to the national foundation's philosophy. In a letter to Barton on January 21, he wrote, "I think, on the whole, we are moving cautiously enough and that whatever comes out of it in the end should be pretty sound."[105] Hunter and Hetzel meant different things by the word *cautious*. For Hunter, planning for the merger was proceeding cautiously. For Hetzel, the board was not cautious enough in entertaining the idea of a merger.

In March, Barton wrote Hunter to express his dismay that the American Psychiatric Association and the Psychiatric Foundation were receiving publicity for the Junior Chamber of Commerce's Mental Health Month campaign. He felt that other groups were co-opting the national foundation and taking credit for its work:

> I'm a bit perturbed by the fact that the JC's are depending upon the APA for the designation of local cooperating committees. . . .
>
> I was a bit perturbed, too, to note that in the guides sent out with the Menninger recording "Meet your Mind," which is tremendously popular in some circles out this way, the Psychiatric Foundation got the big plug!!! . . . [T]here is plenty of evidence out here that the Psychiatric Foundation and the APA and the NCMH are making considerable inroads through back doors—through agencies not connected with the mental health assn such as school principals, public health agencies, and now the JC's!!!! Watch it a bit or you'll be out-flanked by those capitalizing on NMHF's publicity but adverse to its basic goals.[106]

Hunter sought to reassure Barton that there was no need to worry about the Psychiatric Foundation and the National Committee:

The Psychiatric Foundation is doing nothing about expanding its activities and I am sure that its influence cannot be very strong. Most of the attention of Dr. Elley and Mr. Murphy is now directed toward the possibility of merger of NCMH and NMHF. There is not doubt that NCMH has gained considerable strength with the addition of people such as Nina Ridenour and Marian McBee. Their influence is being felt, but it is also good to note at the same time that the new persons in the national committee seem to be very much inclined toward our approach to things in many respects.

Hunter also reiterated his belief that the board was taking a cautious approach toward the merger:

We do not yet know what is going to happen on the subject of merger. It continues to be explored. There is a great deal to be said for it, if it is brought about on the right set of terms. It is gratifying to know that our Board has a rather cautious attitude. The members feel that on the whole a really good single organization would be better than multiple organizations, but they are also convinced that the approach of NMHF must definitely be part of any new agency, and they are also convinced that the merged body must not be professionally dominated.[107]

Hunter devoted his time to the merger throughout 1949. The work of the foundation, and especially the Educational Division, suffered as a result, and Hunter could not even keep up with monthly reports to the board.[108] The American Federation for Mental Health, the joint fund-raising venture of the National Mental Health Foundation, the National Committee for Mental Hygiene, and the Menninger Foundation, all but died in 1949. Mildred Law of the Menninger Foundation wrote Barton in March, "The Federation, I am afraid, is hibernating and whether it will ever take a new lease on life is something I do not know the answer to. I have heard from Mr. Hunter, I believe, only once since the meeting in September."[109]

Mrs. Madeira stepped down as chairman of the national foundation on July 17, but agreed to serve as vice chairman, along with Alexander Cassatt and Giles Zimmerman of the board.[110] She continued to play a dominant role on the board.

A Mental Health Study and Planning Committee was established in 1949 to consider the establishment of a new national mental health association. The committee, which issued its report on August 12, was composed of three "public members" and two members, with one alternate, from the boards of the National Committee, the national foundation, and the Psychiatric Foundation.[111] The foundation's representatives were Mrs. Percy C. Madeira and Morris Wolf, with Brandon Berringer as the alternate. None of these persons had been on the foundation's board when it was founded or been involved directly or indirectly with the CPS.

The committee concluded that there was "no conflict between the programs of the three sponsoring agencies" and unanimously recommended the establishment of a single citizens' mental health organization. The report of the committee listed for general "objects" of the new organization: improvement of the mental health of persons of all ages, prevention of mental and nervous disorders, better care and treatment of the mentally ill, and better training and supervision of the mentally deficient. It also specified the organization of the new association: the selection of four incorporators from each of the three organizations, the formation of a board of directors composed of these twelve persons and three additional persons from the general public, and the appointment of an executive director and a medical director responsible to the executive.

The Board of Directors of the foundation met in September 1949 to consider the Mental Health and Planning Committee's report.[112] Six members of the foundation's staff attended the meeting. Three of them, Howard Curry, Leon Ehrlich, and George Vyverberg, had joined the staff since January. None of them had been members of the CPS during the war. Hunter reported that the board of the National Committee had voted to accept the report and that the Psychiatric Foundation was polling its board by mail. He said that the staff had carefully gone over the report and had prepared a memorandum "suggesting certain preferences which might be of value to the incorporators." Hetzel spoke against accepting the report and argued that changes proposed by the staff should be made before the board accepted it. He said that the report did not ensure that the new organization would be controlled by citizens and that a provision in it would permit a medical director, but not other staff, to have direct access to the board. "The National Mental Health Foundation," said Hetzel, "has always taken the position that lay participation will best be stimulated by lay leadership." The staff had reiterated this position in a report to the board's Program Evaluation Committee in November 1948: "The National Mental Health Foundation has deep respect for professional guidance, but it has carefully guarded its character as a lay organization."[113] Dr. Frederick Allen of the board took an opposite position and stated that a medical professional should be in charge of the organization. Madeira, Hunter, and others said that nothing in the report precluded a medical professional from serving as executive director. The board voted eleven to one to accept the report, with Allen dissenting.

During the first half of 1950, the board and its Executive Committee continued discussions of the structure of the new organization. At the Executive Committee's February meeting, the deliberations of the interim board of the new organization were discussed.[114] Representatives of the foundation and the National Committee on the interim board disagreed about provisions regarding the position of medical director and membership on the board in the bylaws. The Executive Committee also reviewed the search for an executive director of the new organization. The salary for this position had been set at a maximum of thirty thousand dollars per year, a huge sum in view of what foundation staff had been paid.

Hetzel again raised concerns about the structure of the new organization at the board's Executive Committee meeting in March 1950: "Mr. Hetzel expressed considerable concern over the membership structure, feeling that it would place too much control in the hands of a few people who would not necessary be representative." The minutes of the meeting included a single sentence in response to Hetzel's concern: "While this concern may be worthy of consideration, it was pointed out that there are certain practical problems involved in setting up an organization which make it impossible to function according to strictly democratic forms."[115] The national foundation had been founded on democratic principles, however imperfectly it adhered to them. The new organization would not follow the same principles.

The foundation's *Annual Report* for 1949, which was released in April 1950, announced that a merger appeared to be imminent: "Paradoxically, during what is clearly a period of ascendancy for the National Mental Health Foundation, we foresee the possible end of our existence as an independent organization. So that there may be a greater movement, we have developed, with two other agencies, a plan for consolidation. . . . It now appears that the incorporation of the National Association for Mental Health is imminent."[116]

At the Board of Directors meeting on May 23, 1950, Hunter announced that Willard Hetzel had resigned as director of the foundation's Legal Division.[117] No further mention of Hetzel was made in the meeting minutes.

The fate of the foundation was sealed at its annual meeting of members on July 25, 1950.[118] A resolution was introduced approving the consolidation of the National Mental Health Foundation with the National Committee for Mental Hygiene and the Psychiatric Foundation to form the National Association for Mental Health, Inc. Thirty ballots were distributed at the meeting: twenty-six voted in favor, three voted in opposition, and one abstained. The meeting had been called to order at three o'clock and was adjourned a half hour later.

In organization and in spirit, the National Mental Health Foundation died in 1950.

◆   ◆   ◆

The October 1950 issue of *Mental Hygiene* announced the establishment of the National Association for Mental Health.[119] The front of the journal listed the new name of the organization: "The National Association for Mental Health, Inc., The

Voluntary Promotional Agency of the Mental Hygiene Movement, Founded by Clifford W. Beers." The journal would continue to be published as *Mental Hygiene* at least through the 1960s and '70s and would list "The Voluntary Promotional Agency of the Mental Hygiene Movement, Founded by Clifford W. Beers" under the organization's name until the latter part of the 1950s. The identity of the new organization would be the same as the former National Committee.

Mental Hygiene listed twenty-two members of the Board of Directors of the NAMH. Four members had come from the National Mental Health Foundation: Mrs. Percy C. Madeira, Brandon Berringer, Alexander J. Cassatt, and Morris Wolf. Arthur Bunker, formerly of the National Committee, served as chairman, and Elley from the Psychiatric Foundation and Madeira were vice chairmen. Four members of the board were M.D.'s. By 1951, the board had twenty-five members, including six M.D.'s. In 1952, it had grown to forty members, twelve of whom were M.D.'s. Oren Root, an attorney who had represented the interim board during consolidation talks, was the full-time president of the NAMH. Dr. George Stevenson was both a member of the board and the medical director, the same title he had held at the National Committee. Stevenson had this title until 1954, when he was named national and international consultant.[120]

Stevenson published an editorial on the formation of the new National Association in the October 1950 issue of *Mental Hygiene*. As Stevenson described it, the national association was an outgrowth of the movement started by Clifford Beers:

> I worked for many years at the side of Clifford Beers. I am sure that he would have been not a little disturbed by the efforts of the last two years to effect such a merger, for it meant the overshadowing of an organization about which his whole life was entwined. But I am equally confident that his practical sense and his belief in his goals would lead him to understand and to welcome the strengthening of his "baby," as he called the mental-hygiene movement, to meet the challenges of its second fifty years. . . .
>
> The goals of the National Association for Mental Health are the goals of the mental-hygiene movement—the promotion of mental health, the prevention of mental and nervous disorders, the improved care and treatment of the mentally ill, and the special training and supervision of the mentally deficient.[121]

Stevenson briefly commented on the qualities that each of the founding organizations brought to the national association. The qualities of the organizations were the qualities of Clifford Beers, claimed Stevenson. The National Committee was Beers's "formal creature" and reflected a "concern for the mentally sick that could tolerate no injustice to them." The National Mental Health Foundation possessed Beers's sense of impatience with slow progress and "sprang from first-hand experience in our mental hospitals, the experience of a few men as war-time attendants." The Psychiatric Foundation "burst forth" in the professional ranks and was "convinced that money could be raised for the broad purposes for which Clifford Beers worked, and this effort was spearheaded by the rating of mental hospitals."[122]

The headquarters of the national association was located in New York City, the home of the National Committee. At least five former members of the national foundation moved to the new organization: Paul Harris, Dick Hunter, Alex Sareyan, Roy Simon, and Phil Steer. Harris became director of the Psychiatric Aide Section of the national association. Hunter spent his career with the NAMH or its affiliates. For Hunter, the persistent financial problems of the National Mental Health Foundation had necessitated the merger with the other organizations. It had no choice, in his opinion, and he had no regrets about the merger.[123] Mrs. Percy C. Madeira died suddenly not long after the merger, and Hunter wrote her obituary in *Mental Hygiene* in July 1951: "She was among the first to recognize the need for the consolidation that brought The National Mental Health Foundation, The National Committee for Mental Hygiene, and the Psychiatric Foundation together into one united organization—The National Association for Mental Health." Sareyan directed public relations for the national association and coordinated activities for the National Mental Health Week.[124] He left the national association in 1953 and cofounded the Mental Health Materials Center, which assisted other nonprofit agencies in preparing publications and educational materials. In 1994, Sareyan published *The Turning Point: How Persons of Conscience Brought about Major Change in the Care of America's Mentally Ill.* Roy Simon served as editor of the *Psychiatric Aide* for a brief period of time after the establishment of the NAMH. Phil Steer was the only one of the four founders of the national foundation to make the move to the new organization. Marvin Weisbord, who interviewed Steer and the other three men for his 1968 book, *Some Form of Peace,* reported that Steer stayed with the national association "for some years" after the merger.[125] If Steer had any opinions about the events leading up to the merger and the structure of the new organization, they were not recorded in any of the minutes of Board of Directors or Executive Committee meetings. Steer was present at meetings at which Hetzel had expressed his strong reservations about the merger.

Hetzel became executive director of a group called Democratic Rights after leaving the national foundation. One of the members of the Board of Directors of this organization was none other than former U.S. Supreme Court justice Owen Roberts. Hetzel became even more critical of the new organization after it had actually been established. In a letter to Hal Barton, he wrote, "I'm too pushed for time at the moment to go into details about the new Assoc. for Mental Health—but from everything I can pick up, things are a real mess, with a lot of stuffed shirts trying to do something they know nothing about. Old Nat'l Committee was better than what they have now."[126] Hetzel's distrust of the NAMH was so strong that he did not want records of the Mental Hygiene Program of the CPS falling into the hands of that organization and filed a legal notice demanding custody on behalf of Barton and himself on February 16, 1951:

> It has come to my attention that the successor to the National Mental Health Foundation proposes to take into custody the records, files, correspondence, reports, surveys and other papers of THE MENTAL HYGIENE PROGRAM OF THE CIVILIAN PUBLIC SERVICE, an unincorporated association composed of four individuals. Of these four individuals, two, Harold Barton and Willard Hetzel were entrusted with custody and protection of said papers, records, etc. . . .
>
> Because of facts that have just come to my attention it has become my duty to make formal request that said files, papers, correspondence, reports, surveys and papers be preserved intact at 1520 Race Street and that I be notified of a suitable, appropriate and time convenient to you when I may take the same into my personal custody on behalf of the members of the association known as The Mental Hygiene Program of the CPS and more particularly on behalf of Harold Barton and myself (Hetzel) who were specifically entrusted with the responsibility of protecting and preserving the same.[127]

The new national association had little of the missionary zeal that had characterized the National Mental Health Foundation and the Mental Hygiene Program of the Civilian Public Service before it.[128] Almost from the start, it lacked an identification with the COs who had organized the MHP and the national foundation to shed a public spotlight on the conditions at state mental hospitals and training schools. It would not take long for the national association to discontinue the efforts that its founders were most proud of and had brought the national foundation the most attention. The February 1952 issue of the *Psychiatric Aide* announced that the Psychiatric Aide of the Year Award would no longer be sponsored. This award had brought publicity in national newsmagazines and newspapers across the country. It not only focused attention on the attendants selected for the awards but raised awareness of the need for changes in mental hospitals as well. For example, the April 29, 1949, issue of *Time* carried a story on Roland Brand, an attendant at the Milwaukee County Asylum who had been named the 1948 recipient of the award by the national foundation. The title of the article was "Where Are the Straight-jackets?" Brand had been given the award for taking restraints off of disturbed patients on a 70-bed dormitory and 124-person ward at the institution. The *Time* article quoted Brand as saying the patients were happier and acted better after the restraints were removed.[129] The editor of the *Psychiatric Aide* in 1952, Roy Simon, explained that although an increasing number of mental hospitals had partici- pated in the award program—ninety in 1950—the program had been discontin- ued because of criticisms: "There have been some criticisms, however, especially from those who refused to participate in the program because they felt that it was not possible to select one person in the nation who merited an award more than all others. They felt that this was particularly questionable since it was impossible for the judges to make personal on-the-spot observations of candidates."[130] In place of the annual Psychiatric Aide of the Year Award, the NAMH would encourage mental hospitals to select their most outstanding aides, in cooperation with local mental health and other groups. The NAMH would honor each of these attend- ants with a Certificate of Achievement.

Then, in March 1952, without prior notice, editor Simon informed subscribers that the March edition would be the last issue of the *Psychiatric Aide:* "We regret the necessity for informing you that publication of THE PSYCHIATRIC AIDE will be discontinued after this issue. Refunds to cover the unfilled portions of current subscriptions will be mailed during the current month to all active subscribers." In "An Open Letter to Our Readers," NAMH president Oren Root explained why the *Psychiatric Aide* would be discontinued. "I am very sorry," wrote Root, "that my first opportunity to address the readers of THE PSYCHIATRIC AIDE should come about as a result of the discontinuance of the magazine." Root continued: "The discontinuance of THE PSYCHIATRIC AIDE is part of a reorganization and stream- lining of our operations which, we hope, will ultimately result in more effective service to the mental health field. The first year since the consolidation of the three national mental health organizations has not been easy, but we feel that we have made progress."[131] He assured readers that the NAMH would continue to work in the area of psychiatric aide education, but said that there were too many questions about the effectiveness of the publication. Its circulation was too low—around thirty-five hundred—and attempts to obtain suggestions for improving the maga- zine had been unsuccessful, argued Root. He expressed his deep regret that editor Roy Simon, who had come to the NAMH from the national foundation, would be leaving the organization.

The discontinuation of the *Psychiatric Aide* symbolized the estrangement of the NAMH from the roots of the National Mental Health Foundation. The *Attendant* was what had first brought recognition and credibility to the four men who had founded the Mental Hygiene Program and then the national foundation. It had led the Selective Service to approve the CPS program, without which there would never have been a national foundation. Bringing information and training to attendants had been central to the identity of the MHP and the national foundation. The COs had been attendants themselves, and this experience had led them to believe that true reform depended on persons outside of the medical profession.

Under Hetzel's leadership, the reform of state mental hospital commitment laws had been a priority of the Mental Hygiene Program and the national foundation. Neither the National Committee for Mental Hygiene nor the American Psychiatric Association had expressed an interest in this topic when approached by the ACLU in 1941 and 1944.[132] Both organizations had taken the position that the less legal intrusion into this area of professional judgment, the better. Hetzel wrote Roger Baldwin, head of the ACLU and an inactive board member of the national foundation, on April 17, 1950, informing him of his decision to leave the organization. Baldwin replied that he was distressed that Hetzel was leaving the foundation and expressed his hope that Hetzel's work would be used to prepare a model statute for state legislatures. In late 1953, Baldwin wrote the director of the NAMH, Robert Heininger, to inquire about the status of the association's efforts in state laws on commitments and releases. George Stevenson replied to Baldwin on Heininger's behalf on January 6, but Baldwin was dissatisfied with Stevenson's response: "You will recollect that the Marshall Trust gave a substantial grant to the old Foundation for this study. It may well be that the Trust would be interested to contribute more if a definite project were to put up to it concerning effective steps for fair admission and release legislation and practices." Later in 1954, Baldwin again wrote Stevenson inquiring about the NAMH's activities on commitment and release: "That perennial subject of state laws in relation to commitments and releases from mental institutions prompts me to ask whether there is any progress or any moves toward inducing something like uniformity among the states." Stevenson responded that he did not know of any current progress regarding commitments and releases. A frustrated Baldwin shot back: "Your reply of October 4 does not quite give me the information I wanted. You will recollect that some years ago I secured an appropriation through which the Association or one of its predecessors made extensive study of state laws with a view to urging amendments in accordance with uniform national standards. The study was not quite complete but we were told it would be and that the Association would adopt standards which could be used in each of the states requiring revision."[133]

Stevenson then gave Baldwin a report explaining that the original project of the national foundation had been overly ambitious and that the NAMH had scaled back and reformulated it in 1951 as a study of state administrative practices for mental hospitals:

> The National Mental Health Foundation set up a rather ambitious goal of developing, first of all, a comprehensive model mental health law for the states. It was

not appreciated how difficult a task this would be so that I advised that they limit themselves in the beginning to the accumulation of existing laws. Even this proved to be more of a task than had been anticipated because of the reluctance to formulate this material in brief form and to utilize conscientious objectors in each of the states to do the job for that state.

The project had to be trimmed down to practical proportions and to that end it was re-formulated about 1951 to make a study of the forces that make for good or poor state administration of mental hospitals.[134]

Shortly before leaving the national foundation, Hetzel had given a report to the board on the activities of the Legal Division.[135] The report, written almost four years after the end of the CPS, highlighted the national foundation's study of state commitment laws and practices. The NAMH gave up on the project soon after it was established. The priorities of the NAMH were not the same as they had been for the National Mental Health Foundation.

The NAMH floundered after the merger of the three organizations. Nina Ridenour, who had joined the NAMH from the National Committee, gave a candid account of the association's early years: "Integrating the points of view of three organizations as diverse as these was not a simple matter, and for several years the new organization labored under severe merger pains." A decade after its establishment, there was not agreement among the NAMH's leaders on how it should be organized: "In the years since the merger, the National Association for Mental Health has placed much emphasis on public relations, fund-raising, and the organization of state and local associations, and it has taken on a structure entirely different from that of its predecessors, although there is not yet agreement as to exactly what the structure ought to be."[136]

It did not take long for some of those persons who had exposed institutions in the mid-1940s to express their disillusionment, if not disgust, with the NAMH for abandoning the mental hospitals. In 1953, Albert Deutsch criticized the association and state mental health societies for their "vapid discussions of positive values" and failure to address the problems of mental hospitals: "I do feel so concerned about this tendency in many of these [mental health] societies to drop the mental hospitals, to write them off as if nothing could be done about them anyway, and go off into uncharted seas in very many respects in areas in which we know little or nothing, and areas which are being adequately covered by other types of organizations."[137] Three years later, Deutsch published an article in *Mental Hygiene* repeating his criticisms of mental health associations. He welcomed the establishment of the NAMH, but questioned its effectiveness: "The mental health movement in America, in spite of chronic financial difficulties, has shown renewed vigor in recent years, especially since the great reorganization of the National Association for Mental Health. But it still suffers sadly from lack of clear direction and stable leadership." "Disgraceful and remediable" conditions in most public mental hospital were being ignored: "I see, in too many states, a virtual abandonment of mental hospital patients by societies especially entrusted with the task of mobilizing public support for improved institutional conditions. . . . It remains a capital irony that the traditional neglect of hospitalized mental patients is too often supplemented by neglect on the part of groups supposedly dedicated to better care and treatment."[138]

Mike Gorman, the reporter who had led the exposé of Oklahoma's institutions in the *Daily Oklahoman* and subsequently wrote the article "Oklahoma Attacks Its Snake Pits" in *Reader's Digest,* was an even harsher critic of the NAMH. In 1953, Gorman became executive director of the National Mental Health Committee, which had been founded in 1951 by Mary Lasker.[139] The Albert and Mary Lasker Foundation had funded the annual service awards given by the National Committee for Mental Hygiene. Like others, Lasker had grown disillusioned with the National Committee and then the NAMH for their ineffectiveness and especially for their failure to influence public policy. Gorman was an effective lobbyist and a hard-hitting commentator.[140]

Gorman's 1956 book, *Every Other Bed,* contained a scathing attack on the NAMH. He faulted the organization for failing to lobby Congress for increased funding for mental health and to support state mental health societies. Commenting on the NAMH's lack of action on a key research construction bill before Congress, he wrote, "The National Association for Mental Health, the senior citizens' organization in the field, followed its usual dynamic policy of doing absolutely nothing. Afraid that some congressmen might bite them—an unwarranted fear, since congressmen prefer good, vigorous beef—the leaders of the NAMH sat knitting and tatting in their custodial hayloft at 1790 Broadway in New York City while a few of us burned up down in Washington." Gorman questioned whether the NAMH stood for *anything:* "It is really most difficult to portray the negativism of the 'new' National Association for Mental Health. The name implies that it takes a stand for mental health. As to mental illness, it has never taken a clear-cut position one way or another. Like Calvin Coolidge's minister, who was against sin, I believe the NAMH is against both sin and mental illness, but I have little evidence to go on."[141]

Gorman traced the problems of the NAMH to the National Committee for Mental Hygiene. He briefly reviewed the history of the merger of the National Committee, the National Mental Health Foundation, and the Psychiatric Foundation and concluded: "In 1950, the three organizations amalgamated into the present

National Association for Mental Health. However, the dreary bureaucrats of the old National Committee for Mental Hygiene continued to hold the balance of power. The young firebrands of the National Mental Health Foundation, many of whom had taken staff positions with the new organization, soon found themselves gasping for air amid the encircling smog of the hayloft at 1790 Broadway. Most of them left for greener and more lively pastures."[142]

The dissatisfaction with the NAMH led to the creation of the National Mental Health Committee, another organization competing for the national spotlight and public support in mental health. Ironically, it was what the merger of the three organizations that formed the NAMH was designed to eliminate. Despite its reported effectiveness in lobbying, the National Mental Health Committee never became a grassroots citizens' organization and remained the "personal instrument" of Mary Lasker, Mike Gorman, and Florence Mahoney, the wife of an affluent business leader.[143] It too eventually faded from public view.

The National Association for Mental Health was a radically different organization from the National Mental Health Foundation. It had abandoned the philosophy, principles, and priorities that had characterized the foundation and lacked the passion and zeal felt by those persons who had established it. Almost from the start, it turned attention away from the problems that plagued state institutions and pursued a more cautious agenda compatible with the psychiatric establishment. State mental hospitals and training schools would once more become out of sight and out of mind.

15

"Scandal Results in Real Reforms"

The November 12, 1951, issue of *Life* magazine published another article by Albert Q. Maisel on state mental hospitals. This time the news was positive: "Scandal Results in Real Reforms." Maisel reviewed the exposés of the mid-1940s and argued that they had made a concrete difference: "Five years ago shock and revulsion swept the country as one reporter after another dug up evidence proving that most of the public mental hospitals of the U.S. were little more than filthy, brutish concentration camps. Newspapers, magazines (LIFE, May 6, 1946), books and movies backed the exposures with demands for reform. Such crusades have been seen before in the U.S., but all too often they have quickly run down, leaving things pretty much as they were before. This time it was different."[1]

Maisel reported that many states had increased funds for mental hospital renovation and construction and additional physicians, professionals, and attendants. Spending for mental hospitals had increased 100 percent. The number of mental hospital employees had risen from 79,740 to more than 100,000. More important than increased spending, argued Maisel, had been a shift in philosophy at many mental hospitals. They were moving from a custodial philosophy to one that emphasized intensive care. More and more patients were being treated and then released from mental hospitals. Maisel cited the work of the Menninger brothers and the Menninger Foundation's psychiatrist training program as exemplifying this new emphasis on treatment and therapy.

Characteristic of *Life* articles, Maisel's story was accompanied by a dozen photos. The most dramatic of them were before and after photos of institutional wards. The beginning of the article juxtaposed a photo of Byberry's A Building published in 1946 with one taken at the same building in 1951. The 1946 photo showed a corner of a dayroom filled with roughly thirty men, almost all naked and sitting on the floor or wandering around the room. The room had no chairs or benches. Puddles covered the floor. This photo was captioned: "1946: Nakedness and Idleness." The 1951 photo showed about twenty men in the same corner of the dayroom. Now all of the men were clothed. The room had more than enough chairs for the men, and it also had a bench and a table. Most of the men were looking toward a distant part of the room. This caption read: "1951: Chairs and a TV Show to Watch."

Maisel highlighted the significant strides that individual states and mental hospitals had made in improving patient care. Minnesota governor Luther W. Youngdahl was singled out for his commitment to reform. During a visit to one of his state's mental hospitals, Youngdahl was appalled by the conditions he observed and committed himself to improving the state's care of mental patients. He established the Governor's Citizens Mental Health Committee and appointed Justin Reese to direct it.[2] Reese was one of the COs at Cleveland State Hospital who had exposed conditions at that institution. After the Civilian Public Service, he worked for the National Committee for Mental Hygiene and then became director of the Minnesota Mental Health Society. On the Governor's Committee, Reese helped draw public attention to the need for changes at Minnesota's mental hospitals.

Youngdahl advocated for the state legislature to increase funding for mental hospitals. He was successful in doubling funding for the operation of the state hospitals and obtaining an appropriation of twenty-eight million dollars for hospital repair and construction. He established a new position of commissioner of mental health for the state, and the person appointed to this role led a campaign to dramatically reduce the use of restraining devices at the state hospitals. Maisel's article ended with a photo of Governor Youngdahl setting a torch to a pile of straitjackets and restraining devices outside of one of the state hospitals. In December 1949, the National Mental Health Foundation hosted a dinner in Youngdahl's honor in Philadelphia.[3] Maisel acknowledged that most state mental hospitals were still overcrowded and that only a small handful met the staffing standards of the American Psychiatric Association. He concluded, however, that two-thirds of the nations 207 mental hospitals had made substantial progress during the previous five years.

The exposés of the mid-1940s led many states to increase appropriations for mental health and to pass new mental health laws. Reforms were launched in California, Indiana, Kansas, Minnesota, Pennsylvania, and other states.[4] In 1949, the national governors' conference directed its Council of State Governments to conduct a study of the care and treatment of the mentally ill.[5] The council issued a comprehensive report, *The Mental Hospital Programs of the Forty-eight States,* in 1950 and completed a report on mental health training and research in 1953. Frank Bane, the executive director of the council, published an article titled "The Governors' Study on Mental Hospitals" in the January 1951 issue of *Mental Hygiene* in which he stated that mental hospitals were overcrowded and poorly staffed and that more funding was need for them: "Money is needed, large amounts of money."[6] At a meeting in 1954, the Governors' Conference on Mental Health endorsed a ten-point program calling for increases in spending for mental health, expanded research and training, and new community mental health services.[7]

Despite the widespread public attention given to mental hospitals and increased funding for mental health in the 1940s and early '50s, conditions remained bleak at state institutions. Maisel's claim that real reforms had occurred were overstated. Deutsch concluded in 1954 that mental hospitals continued to have the same problems documented years earlier. He quoted from a recent address by APA president Kenneth Appel: "Conditions in our public mental hospitals are shocking, monstrous, and horrible. The majority of hospitals do not give treatment. They give custody—poor at that."[8]

Public attention gradually turned away from the state institutions. Psychiatry and mental health focused on treatment in community clinics and centers and prevention programs. The populations of state mental hospitals peaked at 558,922 in 1955 and declined steadily after that year.[9] State institutions for people with intellectual disabilities reached their peak twelve years later—194,650 in 1967—before they started their steady decline.[10]

In the 1960s and '70s, the institutions would be confronted with a new wave of public attacks. In contrast to the exposés of the 1940s, these new attacks would call into question the legitimacy of the institutions themselves.

◆   ◆   ◆

The National Mental Health Foundation was committed to the reform of state institutions: improving the training, pay, and status of attendants; obtaining higher appropriations for the operation of hospitals and training schools; eliminating understaffing and overcrowding; reforming the procedures leading to the commitment of patients to mental hospitals; increasing the number and quality of psychiatrists and other professionals; and other measures that would lead to the humane and therapeutic treatment of patients. Most other reformers of the era shared the same goal. The concluding chapter of Deutsch's *Shame of the States* was titled "Toward the Ideal State Mental Hospital." Deutsch described his "dream" of a mental hospital that had a maximum of one thousand patients and was located near a large population center, was furnished with enough funds, treated patients with dignity and respect, utilized modern forms of therapy, was adequately staffed, and relegated straitjackets and restraints to its Museum of Antiquities. Many harmless mental patients, in Deutsch's dream, would be placed in families and satellite colonies "under close supervision from the mother institution."[11]

The most forward-looking reformers of the late 1940s and early '50s did not envision a society in which state institutions would be unnecessary. Some psychiatrists and mental health leaders placed more emphasis on the expansion of community services than did the leaders of the national foundation, but they did not believe that mental hospitals could be eliminated. George Stevenson of the National Committee for Mental Hygiene and then the National Association for Mental Health advocated for a more community-centered approach in mental health. Prior to becoming medical director of the National Committee, he had worked in the area of child-guidance clinics. In 1947, he published an article in the *New York Times Magazine*, "Needed: A Plan for the Mentally Ill," in which he proposed that mental hospitals be an "adjunct service" to a community system of services.[12] At a meeting of the American Federation for Mental Health in May 1948, Stevenson described the National Committee's plans for an experiment on "a completely reorganized public service for the mentally ill, centering in the community rather than in the mental hospitals."[13] For Stevenson and others, public mental hospitals should have served as centers for short-term treatment for persons requiring intensive care and long-term care for those individuals for whom a cure would be unlikely.

The 1960s and '70s brought not only a new wave of exposés of state institutions but also a radical critique of those same institutions as well. The new attacks came from people both inside and outside of the fields of mental health and mental retardation, and they would appear in professional and public forums. A small but influential group of psychiatrists led by Thomas Szasz and R. D. Laing started publishing devastating critiques of psychiatry in the 1960s.[14] Szasz's work, in particular, received widespread visibility, and he continued to receive publicity and acclaim—or condemnation—well after the turn of the century. He argued that mental illness was a myth, metaphor, and ideology, not an objective medical condition. The title of one of his best-known books was *The Myth of Mental Illness*. Szasz's 1970 book, *The Manufacture of Madness*, made the comparison between mental illness and witchcraft: "The concept of mental illness is analogous to that of witchcraft. In the fifteenth century, men believed that some persons were witches, and that some acts were due to witchcraft. In the twentieth century, men believe that some people are insane, and that some acts are due to mental illness."[15]

For Szasz, psychiatrists served as instruments of social control of persons who did not conform to society's rules or expectations. He leveled his harshest criticisms on "institutional psychiatry": "psychiatric interventions imposed on persons by others."[16] Involuntary mental hospitalization exemplified institutional psychiatry. In an especially provocative commentary in *Medical Opinion and Review* published in 1968, Szasz went so far as to characterize the involuntary commitment of persons to mental hospitals as a crime akin to slavery. Psychiatry legitimated the oppression of a group of persons in the name of helping them: "In this therapeutic-meliorist view of society, the ill form a special class of 'victims' who must, both for their own good and for the interests of the community, be 'helped'—coercively and against their will, if necessary—by the healthy; and among the healthy, especially by physicians, who are 'scientifically' qualified to be their masters. This perspective developed first and has advanced in psychiatry, where the oppression of 'insane patients' by 'sane physicians' is by now a social custom hallowed by legal and medical tradition."[17] Szasz's commentary was accompanied by photographs of mental hospitals reminiscent of the National Mental Health Foundation's *Out of Sight, Out of Mind:* poorly dressed or barely clothed patients sitting on benches, huddled on the floor, or milling around barren wards; patient workers in dark and dank work areas; and restrained, shackled, and straitjacketed patients.

The critique of psychiatry by Szasz and others within the profession was joined by sociologists and anthropologists who viewed people with mental illness and other disabilities as targets of societal processes of labeling people as outsiders. Labeling theory focused attention on social and cultural aspects of social deviance.[18] Deviance was not a quality inherent in any act or state of being. It was a label placed on certain persons by society: *"Social groups create deviance by making rules whose infraction constitutes deviance,* and by applying those rules to particular people and labeling them as outsiders. From this point of view, deviance is *not* a quality of the act the person commits, but rather a consequence of the application by others of rules and sanctions to an 'offender.' The deviant is one to whom that label has successfully been applied; deviant behavior is behavior that people so label."[19]

In *Being Mentally Ill: A Sociological Theory,* Thomas J. Scheff applied labeling theory directly to the study of people with mental illness in society. Scheff proposed labeling theory as an alternative to the medical model of mental illness in which that construct was defined exclusively in terms of individual pathology. Mental illness was a cultural concept through and through. Who was or was not labeled mentally ill reflected complex social processes. People broke societal rules for a variety of reasons, ranging from organic factors or stress to volitional acts of innovation or defiance. Of all of those individuals breaking the rules, some fitted cultural stereotypes of mental disorder and were defined as mentally ill. Once defined as mentally ill, these people were cast into a deviant social role in which they were rewarded for playing the role and punished for attempting to play conventional roles. Labeling became self-fulfilling, and labeled people were likely to become trapped in a social role.

The most well-known and widely read sociological critic of institutions was Erving Goffman. Goffman was not a labeling theorist per se, although much of his work resonated with those persons identified with that branch of sociology. He characterized his own theoretical framework as dramaturgy and used the metaphor of the theater to characterize human social interaction.[20] For Goffman, human beings were like actors in a play, carefully managing the impressions of the audience. His books *Asylums: Essays on the Social Situation of Mental Patients and Other Inmates* and *Stigma: Notes on the Management of Spoiled Identity* were especially influential in shaping the thinking of persons in mental health and the broader field of disability. The idea that mental illness and related conditions could be stigmatizing was certainly not new. The National Mental Health Foundation attempted to counter the stigma surrounding mental illness in the 1940s. Goffman's *Stigma* presented a sophisticated and complex notion of stigma. Stigma was not merely an abstract concept represented by societal attitudes and reflected in language such as insanity and lunacy. It manifested itself in face-to-face interactions between social actors attempting to influence each other's impressions: "Stigma involves not so much a set of concrete individuals who can be separated into two piles, the stigmatized and the normal, as a pervasive two-role social process in which every individual participates in both roles. The normal and the stigmatized are not persons but rather perspectives."[21]

Asylums was a devastating critique of institutions. The study was based on a yearlong field research project conducted at St. Elizabeth's mental hospital in Washington, D.C., supplemented by other sociological and anthropological studies, first-person accounts, and literature. Goffman coined the phrase "total institutions" to refer to a broad range of seemingly disparate social organizations including mental hospitals, prisons, concentration camps, military boot camps, and others: "A total institution may be defined as a place of residence and work where a large number of like-situated individuals, cut off from the wider society for an appreciable period of time, together lead an enclosed, formally administered round of life." Total institutions congregated and segregated certain groups of people and subjected them to round-the-clock formal authority. Goffman went beyond the official goals and ideologies of total institutions to examine how they actually operated: "Many total institutions, most of the time, seem to function merely as storage dumps for inmates, but, as previously suggested, they usually present themselves to the public as rational organizations designed consciously, through and through, as effective machines for producing a few officially avowed and officially approved ends."[22]

Goffman's major concern in writing *Asylums* was to develop "a sociological version of the structure of the self." Total institutions stripped patients, inmates, or residents of their typical social selves or identities: their roles, personal appearances, individual ways of presenting their identities, reputations, and sense of personal space and privacy. In response, inmates developed routines and rounds of life designed to counter the effects of having been stripped of their identities.

Behavior or ways of thinking that might appear bizarre or pathological when viewed out of context became reasonable and rational when examined in light of the nature of institutions: "Any group of persons—prisoners, primitives, pilots, or patients—develop a life of their own that becomes meaningful, reasonable, and normal once you get close to it."[23]

Based on Goffman's analysis of total institutions, a mental hospital might have been more or less crowded, had more or fewer physicians, attendants, and professional staff, or been characterized by brutal or humane staff practices, but it would still be a total institution, with the characteristics of that type of social organization. From this perspective, mental hospitals could not truly have been reformed. The "ideal" mental hospital would have been a contradiction in terms. Goffman himself could not envision a modern society without mental hospitals: "Mental hospitals are not found in our society because supervisors, psychiatrists, and attendants want jobs; mental hospitals are found because there is a market for them. If all the mental hospitals in a given region were emptied and closed down today, tomorrow relatives, police, and judges would raise a clamor for new ones; and these true clients of the mental hospital would demand an institution to satisfy their needs." Although Goffman could not foresee an end to the commitment of people to mental hospitals, his work fueled a growing antipsychiatry and anti-institution movement in the 1960s and '70s.[24]

Around the same time that Szasz and Goffman starting publishing their critiques of psychiatry and mental hospitals, Michel Foucault published his *Madness and Civilization: A History of Insanity in the Age of Reason* in French.[25] Foucault traced how madness had been conceptualized in Western cultures and challenged the notion that the medical construct of mental illness was a sign of progress. Rather, the medicalization of madness represented a new form of authoritarian control over those persons who did not conform to conventional morality. *Madness and Civilization* was translated into English in 1965, but it did not attract the same attention in mental health in the United States in the 1960s as the writings of Szasz, Goffman, and others. Foucault's writings would become extremely influential in American academic circles in the 1980s and '90s.

Just as Mary Jane Ward's novel *The Snake Pit* was popular in the 1940s, *One Flew over the Cuckoo's Nest* by Ken Kesey received widespread public attention in the 1960s. Balancing pathos with humor, Kesey blurred the line between sanity and insanity and depicted mental hospitals as stifling independent thinking and individual spirit. The novel resonated with the antiauthoritarian mood of the 1960s. The mental hospital was a metaphor for societal structures designed to enforce conformity. *One Flew over the Cuckoo's Nest* was released as a movie starring Jack Nicholson in 1975. The movie was enormously popular and received five Academy Awards, including Best Picture. Both the novel and the movie were important in shaping popular opinion about mental hospitals. In his book defending psychiatric science, Edward Shorter noted, "The works of Foucault, Szasz, and Goffman were influential among university elites, cultivating a rage against mental hospitals and the whole psychiatric enterprise. Yet the book that did the most to inflame the public imagination against psychiatry was a novel written by Ken Kesey."[26]

Frederick Wiseman's all-too-realistic documentary *Titicut Follies*, released in 1967, painted a far more depressing picture of mental institutions than Kesey's novel or any sociological study of institutions.[27] Filmed at an institution for the criminally insane in Massachusetts, the documentary captured the dehumanization and absurdity of life at mental hospitals. It depicted degrading treatment, violations of privacy and bodily space, taunting, and professional incompetence. Even staff or volunteer efforts to treat inmates nicely came across as patronizing, dismissive, or even cruel. Wiseman's documentary received widespread acclaim, despite the fact that it was banned from being shown in Massachusetts by a court on the grounds that it violated patients' privacy.

The critiques of mental hospitals, labeling, and psychiatry in the 1960s would later be used by civil libertarians and the emerging "psychiatric survivor" movement to oppose involuntary institutional commitment, electric shock therapy, and forced drugging.[28] Yet in mental health, these critiques were never fully embraced by the vast majority of professionals in the field. The community mental health center movement led by mental health professionals and psychologists was probably more influential in shaping mental health policy in the 1960s and '70s.[29] The situation would be different in the field of mental retardation in which some of the harshest critics of institutions came from within the profession and translated sociological concepts into a new philosophy of caring for people with intellectual disabilities.

◆　◆　◆

State training schools for mental defectives were an afterthought in the exposés and reform efforts of the 1940s. Except for Deutsch's discussion of Letchworth Village in *The Shame of the States*, anyone following the exposés of institutions would not have known that the training schools shared the conditions and problems of the mental hospitals.[30] The National Mental Health Foundation and the National Committee for Mental Hygiene, as well as their successor, the National Association for Mental Health, included prevention and care of mental defectives in their mission statements, but devoted scant attention to the training schools. The national foundation published some pamphlets on the topics of mental deficiency and training schools and made Training School Aide of the Year Awards for a brief period of time. It did little else. Ironically, one of the foundation's few direct efforts in mental deficiency involved a state school whose name would become synonymous with "snake pit" in the 1970s, Willowbrook.[31] At the request of the recently formed Association for the Help of Retarded Children in New York City, Dr. Dallas Pratt of the foundation met with Veterans Administration and New York State Department of Mental Hygiene officials to advocate for the return of Willowbrook to a state school after it had been turned over to the VA as a general hospital during the war.[32]

The year 1950 was a critical time in the history of intellectual disability in America. That year, parents representing ninety organizations in sixteen states met in Minneapolis to found the National Association of Parents and Friends of Mentally Retarded Children.[33] That organization would soon be renamed the National Association for Retarded Children and is the Arc of the United States today. The same year, Pearl Buck published her book *The Child Who Never Grew*, about her daughter who had mental retardation. Within several years, other books and articles on parents' experiences were published, including *Angel Unaware* by Dale Evans Rogers.[34] Because mental deficiency was assumed to be largely hereditary, the stigma associated with intellectual disabilities had rubbed off on family members. This situation was slowly changing as parents stepped forward to discuss their situations and their children's needs.

The 1960s was an era of hope for families of people with mental retardation. At the urging of his sister Eunice Kennedy Shriver, President John F. Kennedy established the President's Panel on Mental Retardation in late 1961.[35] The next year, the Kennedy family revealed that the president had another sister with mental retardation living at a private institution in Wisconsin. Eunice Shriver became the champion of families of people with mental retardation and worked to inform the public that retarded children could be helped. In 1963, Congress passed the Mental Retardation Facilities and Community Mental Health Centers Construction Act to provide funding for mental retardation and mental health.[36] In a message to Congress in February 1963, Kennedy urged Congress to act on his recommendations "to bestow the full benefits of our society on those who suffer from mental disabilities." The president called on Congress to fund a program of prevention, expansion of community services, and research on mental retardation. He commented on the training schools, "State institutions for the mentally retarded are badly underfinanced, understaffed, and overcrowded. The standard of care is in most instances so grossly deficient as to shock the conscience of all who see them."[37] Kennedy announced a national goal of reducing by hundreds of thousands the number of people in mental hospitals and training schools. After

40. Men's Ward, State Institution for People with Mental Retardation. (Burton Blatt and Fred Kaplan, *Christmas in Purgatory*, 1966; Center on Human Policy, Syracuse University)

the act was passed, states used the new federal funds to build or remodel institutions for people with mental retardation.[38]

Before long, professionals in the field of mental retardation itself led an attack on institutions.[39] The attack started with a widely publicized exposé. "There is hell on earth," wrote Burton Blatt, "and in America there is a special inferno. We were visitors there during Christmas, 1965." Blatt, then a professor at Boston University, had followed the controversy surrounding Senator Robert Kennedy's unannounced visits to New York's Willowbrook and Rome state schools for people with

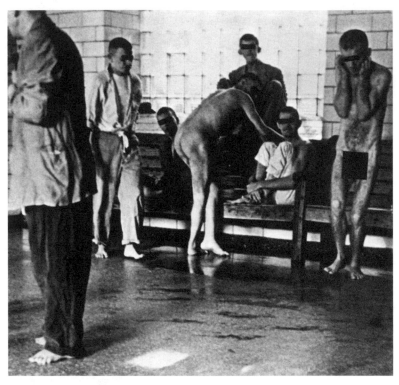

41. Men's Ward, State Institution for People with Mental Retardation. (Burton Blatt and Fred Kaplan, *Christmas in Purgatory*, 1966; Center on Human Policy, Syracuse University)

mental retardation in the fall of 1965. Kennedy publicly denounced the shocking conditions at the institutions. In response, public officials and supporters of Governor Nelson Rockefeller accused Kennedy of painting a misleading picture of conditions at the institutions based on superficial tours. Blatt was aware that Kennedy had accurately portrayed the nature of conditions found at institutions throughout the country: "In fact, we know personally of few institutions for the mentally retarded in the United States completely free of dirt and filth, odors, naked patients groveling in their own feces, children in locked cells, horribly crowded dormitories, and understaffed and wrongly staffed facilities."[40]

With the aid of a friend, photographer Fred Kaplan, Blatt decided to expose institutional conditions on his own. He arranged for visits to four large state institutions in the Northeast at which Kaplan secretly took pictures of conditions on "back wards" with a camera secured to his belt. Blatt and Kaplan then visited Connecticut's Seaside Regional Center, a small, relatively new facility, where Kaplan openly took pictures of brightly lit wards, well-dressed residents, decorated dormitories, and educational programs.

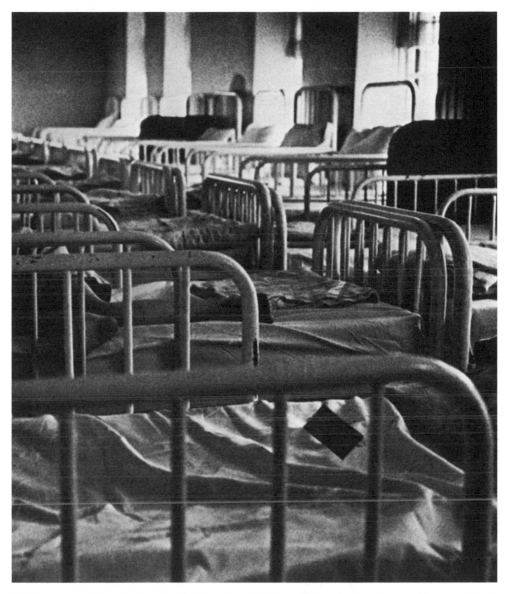

42. Dormitory, State Institution for People with Mental Retardation. (Burton Blatt and Fred Kaplan, *Christmas in Purgatory*, 1966; Center on Human Policy, Syracuse University)

Blatt and Kaplan's photographic exposé, *Christmas in Purgatory,* was published in 1966. The book depicted horribly overcrowded wards, naked and half-clothed residents, and barren dormitories and dayrooms. The second part of the book showed the relatively positive scenes from Seaside. The conclusion was inescapable: people with mental retardation, even those individuals with the most severe disabilities, did not have to live in institutional squalor. The back cover of *Christmas in*

43. Young man tied to a bench, State Institution for People with Mental Retardation. (Burton Blatt and Fred Kaplan, *Christmas in Purgatory*, 1966; Center on Human Policy, Syracuse University)

Purgatory included testimonials to its importance from Senator Edward Kennedy, Michigan governor George Romney, and Minnesota governor Karl Rolvaag, in addition to professional experts.

One year later, Blatt, together with senior editor Charles Mangel, published a version of the exposé in *Look* magazine. The article began: "These children do not have to be locked up in human warehouses. Yet, to our shame, this is where we put them—in back wards, without compassion, without even basic care. A Connecticut experiment proves that we have an alternative."[41] Blatt later reported that the article prompted more than three hundred letters sent to *Look*, Seaside, or Blatt himself.[42] Not one was critical of Blatt's exposé. The year the *Look* article was published, 1967, also represented the year in which state institutions for people with mental retardation reached their peak population of 194,650.[43] The number has declined every year since.

In 1967, Blatt was invited to give a keynote address at a special session of the Massachusetts legislature convened at one of the state schools. He reviewed his

44. Men's Ward, State Institution for People with Mental Retardation. (Burton Blatt, Andrejs Ozolins, and Joe McNally, *The Family Papers: A Return to Purgatory,* 1979; Center on Human Policy, Syracuse University)

findings in *Christmas in Purgatory* and urged the commonwealth to develop a "network of small, community-centered residential facilities."[44]

Blatt's *Christmas in Purgatory* and *Look* article not only received widespread public and media exposure but captured professional attention as well. Although critics would later argue that Blatt's and other photographic exposés did not accurately characterize all institutions, professionals in the field of mental retardation were at least openly receptive to Blatt's efforts.[45] In 1968, Blatt published an article based on *Christmas in Purgatory* in *Mental Retardation,* a journal of the American Association on Mental Deficiency.[46] In 1974, Blatt received the Humanitarian Award from the AAMD and was elected to serve as its president in 1976.[47]

When he first exposed the institutions, Blatt advocated for institutional reform and the humane treatment of residents. By the mid-1970s, if not earlier, he had given up hope that the institutions could be reformed. In 1979, Blatt, with two junior colleagues, published a follow-up photographic exposé, *The Family Papers: A Return to Purgatory,* based on visits to the original institutions, other institutions, and community settings. The institutions were smaller and cleaner, and the residents were better dressed, but the pictures in *The Family Papers* depicted idleness, loneliness, and neglect. In the introduction, Blatt wrote, "As you will see, everything has changed during the last decade. As you will see, nothing has changed." *The Family Papers* concluded:

> A decade or so ago, we went to five state institutions for the mentally retarded, the purpose then not as clear as the purpose for our return last year. Then, we found little to give us hope but we were reluctant to admit that the concept of "institution" is hopeless. Today, we find much to give us hope, but we are now unable to see a way to save the institutions. Ten years ago, with the exception of the Seaside Regional Center, every institution we saw was terrible. We convinced ourselves that by making them smaller, providing more resources, developing ways to insure proper inspection and accountability, by working at improving things, we could make good institutions out of bad institutions. The subsequent years and this most recent round of visits convince us that those were foolish ideas. We must evacuate the institutions for the mentally retarded.[48]

The field of mental retardation was ripe for the publication of *Christmas in Purgatory* in the 1960s. Parents were clamoring for change, and professionals were starting to question long-standing practices in the field.

From the 1800s until the latter half of the 1900s, the field of mental retardation was dominated by physicians and then psychologists. What is now the American

45. Young woman restrained in a wheelchair, State Institution for People with Mental Retardation. (Burton Blatt, Andrejs Ozolins, and Joe McNally, *The Family Papers: A Return to Purgatory*, 1979; Center on Human Policy, Syracuse University)

Association on Intellectual and Developmental Disabilities was established in 1876 as the Association of Medical Officers of Institutions for Idiotic and Feeble-Minded Persons. Philosophies and concepts reflected medical perspectives: medical causes and treatment. Beginning in the early 1900s, psychological perspectives started to become more prominent and placed an emphasis on psychological treatment and psychometrics and testing. By the mid-twentieth century, psychologists and educators dominated the professional organization, which was then called the American Association on Mental Deficiency.[49] In the 1960s and early '70s, sociological concepts came to the fore.

Influenced by Goffman and the labeling theorists in sociology, sociologists and anthropologists started to examine mental retardation as a social and cultural phenomenon.[50] In contrast to the field of mental health, a sociological understanding of mental retardation was translated into a clearly articulated philosophy of caring and treatment.

In 1969, the President's Committee on Mental Retardation (PCMR) published an influential book, *Changing Patterns in Residential Services for the Mentally Retarded*.[51] Established by President John F. Kennedy as the President's Panel on Mental Retardation in 1961, the PCMR intended *Changing Patterns* to serve as a resource in formulating recommendations on residential care to the president and the nation. The book included invited contributions from American and international leaders, including two chapters by Blatt based on *Christmas in Purgatory*.[52]

Changing Patterns contained two chapters by Bengt Nirje, then executive director of the Swedish Association for Retarded Children. In the first chapter, "A Scandinavian Visitor Looks at U.S. Institutions," Nirje described his observations during visits to institutions in several states. As Nirje explained, his observations were similar to what Blatt and Kaplan had shown in *Christmas in Purgatory*. He did, however, take exception to the use of the word *purgatory* in Blatt and Kaplan's book. To Nirje, *hell* more accurately characterized the institutions. Nirje's second chapter, "The Normalization Principle and Its Human Management Implications," was more important. He started the chapter by explaining, "In an earlier section of this book I have described some observations and reactions upon visiting public institutions in the United States. I will now attempt to describe the theoretical perspective from which my reactions to my observations stem. My entire approach to the management of the retarded, and deviant persons generally, is based on the 'normalization' principle."[53]

The concept of normalization was developed in Scandinavia and incorporated into a 1959 Danish law governing services for people with mental retardation.[54] Until Nirje's *Changing Patterns* chapter, it had not been systematically stated and explained.[55] Nirje provided the following definition: "The normalization principle means making available to the mentally retarded patterns and conditions of everyday life which are as close to possible to the norms and patterns of the mainstream of society."[56] He then gave eight implications of normalization (for example, normal rhythm of day and normal routine of life).

In the introduction to *Changing Patterns*, Robert B. Kugel wrote regarding the normalization principle: "This construct has never been fully presented in the American mental retardation literature, but it is of such power and universality as to provide a potential basis for legal and service structures anywhere. Indeed, the editors of this book view the normalization principle as perhaps the single most important concept that has emerged in this compendium." Gunnar Dybwad, the past executive director of the National Association for Retarded Children, was more straightforward in the conclusion to the book: "Without a doubt, as far as the future of residential (as well as many other) services is concerned, the concept of normalization presented in Nirje's chapter has emerged as the most important one in this book."[57]

Various contributors to *Changing Patterns* approached mental retardation from the perspective of the sociology of deviance. Dybwad described normalization as a sociological concept: "The normalization principle draws together a number of other lines of thought on social role, role perception, deviancy, and stigma that had their origin in sociology and social psychology." Wolf Wolfensberger's history of the origin and nature of institutions started with a review of the historical "role perceptions" of retarded persons (for example, as sick, as a subhuman organism, as a menace) and explained: "Social scientists in the recent past have elaborated a concept of great importance to the understanding of the behavior and management of retarded persons. The concept is that of 'deviance.' A person can be defined as deviant if he is perceived as being significantly different from others in some overt aspect, and if this difference is negatively valued. An overt and negatively valued characteristic is called a 'stigma.'"[58]

Lloyd Dunn, who was a critic of much of special education, used language to describe institutions that could have come from labeling theorists in sociology in his contribution in *Changing Patterns:* "Frequently, they have been operated on the medical model which views mental retardation as a disease, and has an emphasis on labeling and determining etiology; and once one has viewed mental retardation as a disease and affixed the label to an individual, one has a built-in, self-fulfilling prophecy."[59]

Three years after *Changing Patterns*, Wolfensberger published another influential and widely read book, *The Principle of Normalization in Human Services.* In this book, Wolfensberger elaborated on the dimensions of normalization and offered a reformulated definition: "Utilization of means which are as culturally normative as possible, in order to establish and/or maintain personal behaviors and characteristics which are as culturally normative as possible."[60] In 1974, Blatt, then the chair of the Division of Special Education and Rehabilitation at Syracuse University, recruited Wolfensberger to Syracuse, where he established a training institute to promote normalization and later "social role valorization," a refined version of the principle.[61]

The principle of normalization represented a direct challenge to the existence of institutions. Both Nirje and Wolfensberger were explicit that the principle applied to all people with mental retardation, including those individuals with the most profound disabilities. It would be difficult for an institution to meet the standards for normal living articulated by Nirje and Wolfensberger in their formulations.

Throughout the 1970s and beyond, attacks on state institutions escalated. In contrast to earlier decades, the attacks were made not only in the media but in federal courts as well. In 1975, the U.S. Supreme Court handed down a unanimous decision regarding to rights of Kenneth Donaldson, a man involuntarily committed to a Florida mental hospital. Writing for the Court, Justice Stewart stated, "A State cannot constitutionally confine without more a nondangerous individual who is capable of surviving safely in freedom by himself or with the help of willing and responsible family members or friends."[62] No longer could states legally warehouse mental patients who did not pose a danger to others and who could survive in the community on their own or with the help of others.

Lawsuits filed against institutions for people with mental retardation sought to establish far-reaching rights for institutional residents. The first case to receive widespread national attention was the *Wyatt* case brought against the Partlow Institution in Alabama. In the *Wyatt* case, federal district judge Frank Johnson characterized Partlow as a "warehousing institution" and commented on the "atrocities" that "occur daily": "A few of the atrocious incidents cited at the hearing in this case include the following: (a) a resident was scalded to death by hydrant water; (b) a resident was restrained in a straight jacket for nine years in order to prevent hand and finger sucking; (c) a resident was inappropriately confined in seclusion for a period of years; and (d) a resident died from the insertion by another resident of a running water hose into his rectum." Judge Johnson, who was the federal judge who ordered Governor George Wallace to integrate the University of Alabama in the 1960s, ruled that the state had to comply with forty-nine "minimum constitutional standards for adequate habilitation of the mentally retarded" in its operation of Partlow.[63]

Willowbrook State School in Staten Island, New York, was the next state institution to be cast into the public spotlight. Following a series of articles in the *Staten Island Advance* describing substandard conditions at Willowbrook, reporter Geraldo Rivera made an unannounced visit to Willowbrook on January 6, 1972. Footage depicting overcrowded and dehumanizing conditions was shown on that evening's 6:00 news. National and local media then covered the story, and the *New York Times* declared Willowbrook a "tragedy" and "disgrace" in an editorial.[64] Shortly after his visit to Willowbrook, Rivera exposed conditions at Letchworth Village State School, north of New York City. Letchworth Village had been the one institution for people with mental retardation exposed by Albert Deutsch many years earlier. Approximately two months after Rivera's initial exposé, parents of Willowbrook residents filed suit against the institution in federal court. The case was assigned to district judge Orin Judd. Like Judge Johnson in the *Wyatt* case, Judge Judd was appalled by conditions at the institution: "Testimony of ten parents, plus affidavits of others, showed failure to protect the physical safety of their children and deterioration rather than improvement after they were placed in Willowbrook State School. The loss of an eye, the breaking of teeth, the loss of part of an ear bitten off by another resident, and frequent bruises and scalp wounds were typical of the testimony. During eight months of 1972, there were over 1,300 reported incidents of injury, patient assaults, and patient fights."[65]

Judge Judd ordered the state to implement immediate emergency steps to address conditions at Willowbrook, pending a final order. When elected governor of New York in 1975, High Carey, who had made Willowbrook a campaign issue, entered into a settlement with the plaintiffs to resolve the case. After Judge Judd's death in 1976 and his replacement by Judge John Bartels, implementation of the settlement was characterized by stormy relations between the state and a review panel appointed to monitor the state's actions.

Both the *Wyatt* and the Willowbrook cases resulted in significant deinstitutionalization, and both institutions were eventually closed. However, the Pennhurst case in Pennsylvania was the first major case filed with the explicit aim of closing the institution. The attorneys for the plaintiffs in this case found a receptive judge in Judge Raymond Broderick. Broderick found that Pennhurst shared the many inadequacies and abuses of other institutions. He went further, however, in ruling that the institution was inconsistent with the principle of normalization: "Since the early 1960's there has been a distinct humanistic renaissance, replete with the acceptance of the theory of normalization for the habilitation of the retarded. . . . The basic tenet of normalization is that a person responds according to the way he or she is treated. . . . The environment at Pennhurst is not conducive to normalization." Broderick ordered the state to close Pennhurst and move all of its residents to suitable arrangements in the community. Although the U.S. Supreme Court did not uphold Broderick's order on two separate occasions, Pennhurst nevertheless closed in 1988.[66]

The reform efforts of the 1960s and '70s occupy a central place in the history of intellectual disabilities. The works of leading reformers not only are mentioned in histories but continue to be read today. The American Association on Mental Retardation published monographs in 1999 based on Blatt's writings and Dybwad's speeches.[67] Wolfensberger continued to publish articles well after the turn of the century, and two edited volumes of his work have been published.[68]

In 2000, the National Historical Trust on Mental Retardation, a consortium of seven organizations, including the American Association on Mental Retardation (AAMR), Arc of the U.S., and President's Committee on Mental Retardation, issued a list, "Significant Contributions of the 20th Century," at a ceremony held at the AAMR's annual meeting. Among the thirty-five honorees were Burton Blatt; Gunnar Dybwad and his wife, Rosemary; Wolf Wolfensberger; Geraldo Rivera; Bernard Carabello (a former Willowbrook resident featured in Rivera's exposé); Robert Perske (a contributor to Wolfensberger's 1972 normalization book); Judge Bartels (the judge in the Willowbrook case after Judd died); Judge Broderick (Pennhurst); Judge Johnson *(Wyatt)*; and "class members" of lawsuits against institutions.

❖ ❖ ❖

Many of those individuals associated with the Mental Hygiene Program of the CPS and the National Mental Health Foundation believed that the exposés of the 1940s had changed the institutions for good. Maisel concluded that the exposés had resulted in real reforms. Former CO and national foundation staff member Alex Sareyan's book was titled *The Turning Point: How Persons of Conscience Brought about Major Change in the Care of America's Mentally Ill.* In the foreword to Sareyan's book, former CO Robert Krieder wrote, "The Turning Point is a celebration of how a few people—considered by some to be politically marginal—can profoundly effect change in the grim, gray institutions of our society."[69] In 1948, Deutsch believed that a new day had dawned in the field of mental health. By 1954, Deutsch was critical of mental health associations for not doing more about conditions at state hospitals but was nevertheless optimistic that lasting change was on the horizon.

In the 1960s and '70s, the institutions were exposed once more. The criticisms of the institutions often related to the nature of institutions themselves. For many critics, no institution could be a good institution, and this perspective was radically different from the perspectives of the 1940s-era reformers. Yet the exposés also revealed shocking conditions and practices that were not so different from what was reported in *Out of Sight, Out of Mind.* Blatt's photos and Wiseman's documentary depicted scenes that could have been shown in Maisel's *Life* article or Deutsch's *Shame of the States.*

Perhaps the institutions had changed between the 1940s and the '60s, but then what is change? A dayroom of 100 or 150 half-naked people is probably better than one of 250 or 300 naked people. A room with some benches and chairs and a television is probably better than one with none of these things. A ward staffed by three or four attendants is probably better than one staffed by one or two. A punch or a slap is probably better than being beaten with a pipe or a rubber hose filled with buckshot. None of this improvement, though, should be confused with real change in how some of the most vulnerable people in our society are treated.

Conclusion

All history is told from a point of view. As Laurel Richardson argued, any form of knowledge is "partial and situated." What we know about the world necessarily reflects the information we have at our disposal as well as our own social situations and past experiences. Richardson wrote, "There is no view from 'nowhere,' the authorless text. There is no view from 'everywhere,' except for God. There is only a view from 'somewhere,' an embodied, historically and culturally situated speaker."[1] To say that knowledge is partial and situated is not to claim that all versions of history are equally valid. They are not. Some versions of history—or constructions of reality, for that matter—are closer to the actual state of affairs than others. The problem is that we can never totally separate the knower from what is known or the history from the teller of history.

My interest in the history of World War II conscientious objectors who exposed state institutions reflects my personal and professional biography. I came of age, literally and figuratively, in the Vietnam era, and that shaped my views on war and peace. I was antiwar and thought of myself as a pacifist, although if pressed on the matter, I would have been forced to admit that I thought differently about Vietnam than I did about World War II. The idea of refusing to fight the war against Nazi Germany and the country that launched the attack on Pearl Harbor was foreign to me. I did not understand pacifism.

In my second year of graduate school in sociology, I made a three-day visit to Rome State School for people with mental retardation as part of a summer workshop that was taught through the Center on Human Policy at Syracuse University and initially designed by Burton Blatt. Rome was an awful place. I ended up studying a "back ward" for seventy-three "severely and profoundly retarded, ambulatory, young adult males" for approximately a year. What I observed firsthand differed only in degree from what was reported in Frank L. Wright's *Out of Sight, Out of Mind*, Albert Maisel's "Bedlam, 1946" article in *Life*, and Albert Deutsch's "Shame of the States" series in *PM*. I later visited other state schools and wrote my dissertation on attendants' work at state institutions, with a focus on the abuse of residents.[2] Even before finishing my dissertation, I became involved in exposés of institutions and eventually became active in the deinstitutionalization movement. Today, my interest in the academic area of disability studies reflects my first experiences trying to understand how society can dehumanize, marginalize, and systematically discriminate against people with real or presumed intellectual, mental, or physical differences.

In graduate school, I learned about Dorothea Dix and Clifford Beers and tended to view them as reformers whose efforts amounted to little lasting change. After all, the institutions seemed to be pretty bad in the early to mid-1970s. I had the opportunity to study with or attend lectures and workshops by leading reformers of the 1960s and '70s, including Burton Blatt, Gunnar Dybwad, Thomas Szasz, and Wolf Wolfensberger. I was convinced that I was about to be part of history: the first organized and sustained reform movement against the abuses of institutions in the modern era. I never heard about the Mental Hygiene Program of the Civilian Public Service or the National Mental Health Foundation. I vaguely recall seeing copies of photos from Maisel's 1946 *Life* magazine exposé in the 1980s, but probably viewed this exposé as one of those short-term sensations that has occurred every once in a while in American history.[3]

Relatively recent histories of mental health and mental retardation in America mention the World War II COs at state institutions only in passing, if at all. Edward Shorter's *History of Psychiatry* mentioned the COs in a single sentence of a 327-page book. Gerald N. Grob's *From Asylums to Community* paid a bit more attention to the COs, but discussed them mainly in the context of the formation of the National Association for Mental Health. James W. Trent's history of mental retardation in America, *Inventing the Feeble Mind*, devoted several pages to the COs and the National Mental Health Foundation. The most comprehensive accounts of the World War II COs and their legacy since the 1960s have been books written by former COs and published or distributed by religious groups.[4]

The World War II COs did not have the impact on state institutions hoped for by those persons who were directly involved. Yet much can be learned from their efforts nevertheless.

◆   ◆   ◆

Like many college students in the late 1960s, I was opposed to the Vietnam War and had decided that I would refuse to enter the military if drafted. I received a student deferment from the draft when I first entered college. Not long afterward, the draft lottery was put into place. In the lottery, young men were drafted according to where their birthdays came up in a random selection process. Men with low numbers were almost sure to be drafted. Those men with high numbers could breathe free. My birthday came out at 324 in the lottery for the year in which I was born. It was all but impossible for me to be drafted. I was never forced to demonstrate the depth and sincerity of my opposition to the war.

For many people in the 1960s and early '70s, it was difficult to separate opposition to war, in general, from opposition to the Vietnam War, in particular. For many conscientious objectors and antiwar activists, Vietnam was an unjust war involving the oppression of a nationalistic movement struggling to free a country from a long history of colonialism. Vietnam seemed to pose no threat to the United States. Further, the killing of innocent civilians, the destruction of entire villages, and the deforestation of the countryside were increasingly reported in the media as the war wore on. Vietnam helped turn young men into conscientious objectors and pacifists. John O'Brien performed alternative service at a small psychiatric unit affiliated with a medical school as a Vietnam CO. He would later become one of the creators of "person-centered planning," a nonprofessional approach for planning for positive community experiences for people with disabilities. O'Brien, a Catholic, reflected on becoming a CO during Vietnam: "Conscientious objection to the Vietnam War was, I imagine, considerably different from conscientious objection to World War II in ways that made my experience far easier than World War II COs. The Vietnam War was far more socially paralyzing and so I was choosing a way to express opposition many felt." O'Brien also wrote: "As a student of philosophy and theology convinced that nonviolence was ethically imperative in a post-Hiroshima world and that the Vietnam War was, in any case, an unjust war, my claim on conscientious objector status was complex." Don Forrest had been raised as an Episcopalian and "saw no conflict between serving in the military in the defense of country and living an ethically grounded life." During his high school and college years, he became increasingly involved in the civil rights movement. This involvement exposed him to activists, including former members of the military, who were opposed to the Vietnam War. When Forrest was drafted, he applied for CO status. After initially being turned down, he successfully appealed his draft board's decision. He reflected on his decision to become a CO: "It was clear someone had been lying to us big time when it came to race and justice, and it didn't take much to see that the same folks who had been shoveling it at us about race were the same people who were shipping us off to war." Steven Mcfayden-Ketchum, another Vietnam CO, gave his reason for avoiding military service: "I was raised southern Baptist and took the thou shalt not kill idea by heart. still do. Just didn't remain a Christian and by the time I was dealing with the draft I had decided that killing was wrong on humanitarian grounds except when defending. Vietnam was not an act of defense."[5]

The sentiments of O'Brien, Forrest, and Mcfayden-Ketchum reflected my own thinking about the Vietnam War at the time. The Vietnam War was downright unjust. Yet I never considered becoming a conscientious objector. If I were drafted, my plan was to go to prison or move to Canada. All war struck me as tragic and wrong, but somewhere in the back of my mind, I thought that there were circumstances under which war could be justified. Although I never remember being taught the "just war" theory, I probably believed in some version of it. It never occurred to me that World War II had been an unjust war.

◆　◆　◆

In various discussions and debates surrounding conscientious objection during World War II, many rationales were put forward to support this position. The most compelling rationale was that it was inherently wrong to kill other human beings, whether this belief was based on religious or humanistic grounds. Persuasive, though not as compelling, was the position that war and violence only beget more war and violence. This point is undoubtedly true, but even if most people or nations give up killing, it does not mean that all will. Some will not. Allowing a holocaust to occur every once in a while would be an extraordinarily high price to pay for reducing the occurrence of war. One of the least-compelling rationales for becoming a conscientious objector during World War II was that the past actions of the United States and its allies had brought the war upon themselves. Although it could be argued that the humiliation of Germany after World War I and Western imperialism and colonialism in Asia contributed to the start of World War II, it was impossible to turn back the hands of time. The situation of the early 1940s was what it was. Nazi Germany was invading other countries and murdering innocent citizens, and Japan was killing and raping its neighbors in Asia, let alone bombing Pearl Harbor. Past mistakes cannot justify doing nothing to confront evil or to defend a society in the present.

If the concept of a just war is valid, World War II came closer than most to fitting the description. After all, relatively large numbers of men from the historic peace churches accepted military service. Perhaps Studs Terkel and Ken Burns were right to refer to World War II as a good or necessary war. Maybe Tom Brokaw was correct to characterize those individuals who served in the military or supported the war in other ways as the greatest generation. Millions of Americans made enormous sacrifices during the war. More than four hundred thousand members of the military were killed.[6]

Even if World War II can be said to have been a just war, the COs should be respected for their acts of conscience. Any decent society must honor the beliefs of those citizens who refuse to harm other human beings, regardless of the basis of those beliefs. It would be obscene to force conscientious objectors to participate in any aspect of the military machine. Further, any society benefits from having members opposed to violence. Most societies seem to have too many people willing to harm other people or go to war on shaky grounds.

Given the perceived threat of Germany and Japan during World War II, it should not be surprising that the conscientious objector position was not a popular one. To a certain extent, this dislike undoubtedly reflected a misunderstanding of the positions of the majority of COs. It probably also represented misplaced hostility on the part of certain organizations and public officials. Groups like the American Legion and Veterans of Foreign Wars tried to stir public sentiment against COs in communities across the country. The Civilian Public Service was a favorite target, although only twelve thousand men participated in the CPS during the war. This small number of men hardly jeopardized the war effort or warranted the constant attacks by veterans' groups. Organized opposition to COs during the war said more about the opponents than about the COs or the war. Social groups often seek to build their identities and strengthen their solidarity by expressing their indignation at outsiders who do not share their belief systems.[7]

It is not unreasonable for a society to require public service in times of national crisis. World War II was a time of national crisis. The question is not whether people should be required to contribute to society when the society is under threat, but how they can contribute to the society. The experience of World War II was that just about all Americans could contribute to the society in some way. Most of the jobs performed by men in the CPS were not jobs that freed others to participate in the military. They were jobs that would not otherwise have been done. Pacifists who do not believe in any form of conscription or required service can always engage in civil disobedience or nonviolent resistance as a matter of conscience. These forms of protest were perfected during the 1960s with the civil rights movement and Vietnam War protests.

Americans who join the military to fight wars are generally thought of as acting out of a sense of duty to the country. Duty can be an important virtue. So can a sense of ethical or moral conscience. When these virtues conflict, conscience must trump duty. It is one of the things that distinguishes just societies from unjust ones. Nazi Germany and Japan expected their young men to act out of a sense of duty without regard to the morality of their governments and their actions.

◆　◆　◆

The Civilian Public Service during World War II was an imperfect or even fundamentally flawed institution from the vantage point of many, if not most, pacifists and conscientious objectors. The National Service Board for Religious Objectors and the church committees all too often did the bidding of the Selective Service. CPS men were not paid for their work or offered benefits and allowances for dependents. Much of the work was meaningless, and both Congress and the Selective Service limited the ways in which COs could contribute to humanity. The Selective Service restricted the freedoms and liberties of CPS men. The church committees did not do everything they could to challenge racism and social injustice in the CPS and society at large.

As imperfect as the CPS was, it would be difficult to imagine a better alternative for conscientious objectors in the context of World War II. It was a vast improvement over the treatment of COs during World War I, when they were forced to enter the military or face prison. Neither the president nor members of Congress had a sympathetic view toward COs. Especially after the bombing of Pearl Harbor, patriotism ran deep in the country, and it was a brand of patriotism that demanded military action and sacrifice in the name of war. Most members of the public did not appreciate pacifism. The historic peace churches were small, and their religious beliefs were not widely understood. To the extent that the Society of Friends, the Mennonites, and the Brethren were known, they were viewed as a bit peculiar. The beliefs of COs who came from traditional religions such as the Methodists and Catholics were foreign to their own churches. In many communities, groups such as the American Legion were eager to whip up public sentiment against "slackers," "cowards," and "yellow bellies" who refused to come to their nation's defense in a time of war.

For Gen. Lewis Hershey and Col. Lewis Kosch of the Selective Service, the assignment of COs to remote work camps cosponsored by government agencies and the church committees was a good solution to the "problem" posed by conscientious objectors. The COs would be out of public view, and the church committees would pay most of the costs of supporting them. Hershey and Kosch grudgingly approved service in detached units and later the establishment of government camps. They could be punitive in dealing with defiant or nonconformist CPS men, but they were probably correct in fearing a political and public backlash if they were seen as coddling COs.

Paul Comly French of NSBRO had the most realistic view of the CPS of anyone associated with the Friends, Brethren, and Mennonites or other pacifist groups. He had a finger on the nation's pulse and was keenly aware of the fragility of the arrangement between the Selective Service and the peace churches. On various occasions, French fretted that the government was going to shut down the CPS or at least close out the church committees from the program.

The rift between NSBRO and the church committees, on the one hand, and the War Resisters League and other radical pacifists, on the other, was understandable. The representatives of the church committees who cooperated in establishing the CPS wanted to find a way for the members of their churches to be able to avoid serving in the military or being sent to prison. The CPS was the best solution they could negotiate with the government. Once the CPS was established, the church committees voluntarily accepted men from other religions into their programs and paid for their upkeep. The American Friends Service Committee opposed conscription, but this opposition was not its primary goal. The War Resisters League was committed to fighting the conscription system itself and challenging the government's authority to force men into either military or civilian service. Its leaders did not worry about offending Selective Service officials or jeopardizing the CPS program. That the various pacifist groups got along and worked together at all was remarkable. After 1946, the American Friends Service Committee would never again cooperate with the Selective Service. The Mennonite Central Committee and Brethren Service Committee continued to do so.

For all of its flaws, the CPS facilitated organized action on the part of COs. Strikes and calculated resistance were easier to pull off when COs were concentrated at camps and units. After the official end of the CPS in 1947, the Selective Service would never again try to establish such a complex program. General Hershey, in particular, opposed the resurrection of the CPS. During the Korean and Vietnam wars, COs found individual public service placements, with or without the assistance of church or pacifist agencies. The designation I-W, "Worker in Alternative Service," was created as a public service program for COs.[8] Men with the I-W designation worked at mental hospitals, educational institutions, and general hospitals; as milk testers or human guinea pigs; or in other social welfare programs, subject to the approval of their draft boards. Gil Goering, a Mennonite from Kansas, turned eighteen in 1945 and just missed being drafted during World War II. He was subsequently drafted during the Korean War and served as an orderly at a hospital in Denver, where he was paid a regular salary and found his own place to live. Goering contrasted his experience with the experiences of his brothers who had served in the CPS: "We didn't have that cohesive feeling. We had a loose organization. We got together every once in a while, but I rarely saw any of the other people." Similarly, James Juhnke, a professor of history at the Mennonite Bethel College in Kansas, commented, "The scattering of forces in the I-W program is quite dramatic when compared to the concentration of energies in the CPS camps."[9]

The structure of the CPS made possible the organized efforts of COs who sought to reform state mental hospitals and training schools. The establishment of units containing 15 to 135 men, many of whom were idealistic and religiously motivated, at overcrowded, understaffed, and abusive institutions invited attempts to do something about the conditions at those institutions. Had the COs been dispersed individually throughout institutions, there probably never would have been the Mental Hygiene Program or the National Mental Health Foundation.

◆ ◆ ◆

The accomplishments of the National Mental Health Foundation were nothing short of remarkable. Established by four young COs who had no formal training or expertise in mental health, the foundation helped to focus national attention on the squalid conditions and brutality at state institutions. It enjoyed the support of political figures, civic leaders, and celebrities, and it forced both states and established mental health organizations to acknowledge the widespread problems at institutions and to initiate their own reform efforts. Yet roughly four years after the formation of the national foundation, it ceased to exist as an independent entity, and by the time of its merger with the National Committee for Mental Hygiene and the Psychiatric Foundation, three of its four founders had left the organization.

Merger killed the national foundation in spirit as well as name. It lost its identity and its missionary zeal, and its major activities were all but abandoned. Going back to the days of the Mental Hygiene Program of the CPS, the founders of the foundation had three broad priorities: educating the public about conditions at institutions, improving the training and elevating the status of attendants, and reforming mental hospital commitment laws. None of these items was a priority of the newly formed National Association for Mental Health. The abrupt cancellation of the *Psychiatric Aide* in March 1952, less than two years after the formation of the NAMH, symbolized the death of the spirit of the National Mental Health Foundation. The *Psychiatric Aide,* which was first named the *Attendant* and then the *Psychiatric Aid,* brought the Mental Hygiene Program to the attention of public figures and professional leaders and established the identity of that program and later the national foundation.

The National Association for Mental Health became a remodeled version of the National Committee for Mental Hygiene. This situation was not necessarily bad, but the NAMH had little to do with what the National Mental Health Foundation had stood for. It would be difficult to identify how the NAMH of, say, 1955 would have been different had not the national foundation been involved with its formation.

The National Committee and the Psychiatric Foundation, which had been established as the fund-raising arm of the American Psychiatric Association, did not set out to destroy the National Mental Health Foundation. The national foundation was an attractive merger partner to the other organizations. For a young organization, it had gotten an incredible amount of national publicity, could list many prominent Americans among its supporters and sponsors, and continued to come up with highly visible public education and media campaigns. It also was a competitor with the other two groups for foundation and corporate funding. For the National Committee, in particular, an affiliation with the national foundation could help refurbish its image as a staid, conservative upholder of the status quo, as held by Albert Deutsch and others. Merging with the national foundation was not without its drawbacks. The foundation had readily engaged in exposés of institutions, which were viewed as unseemly by many mental hygiene and psychiatric leaders, questioned medical authority, and had a lingering identification with COs who had refused to defend their country during the war. The advantages outweighed the disadvantages, however.

If not the intent of the National Committee and the Psychiatric Foundation in courting the national foundation, the effect of the merger was to co-opt the mission and purpose of the National Mental Health Foundation. The Mental Hygiene Program and then the national foundation had spearheaded reform efforts in mental health at a time when established organizations had turned their backs on the widespread problems at state institutions. After the exposés led by the foundation and other outsiders in mental health, neither the National Committee nor the American Psychiatric Association could afford to ignore the institutions any longer. The leaders of the National Committee all but acknowledged that they had lost sight of the abuses of institutions. The Psychiatric Foundation was formed by the APA to raise funds to support its surveys of mental hospitals. Leaders of the APA and the National Committee might have resented the publicity brought about by the national foundation and the organization's refusal to bow to medical professionals, but they did not attempt to defend the institutions. They could express general support for the national foundation's goals to improve public education and increase funding for mental health as well. All of these issues led the board of the national foundation and its last executive secretary, Dick Hunter, to believe that they could bring the National Committee and the Psychiatric Foundation along to the foundation's way of seeing and doing things. Once the organizations merged, however, it was the national foundation's identity and priorities that were lost. The problems of the state mental hospitals and training schools—the driving force behind the formation of the national foundation—were forgotten or ignored once more. Reform movements can be co-opted by being absorbed into organizations that do not share a passion about the need for reform.

On the national foundation's end, the merger with the National Committee and the Psychiatric Foundation was driven by the board. The national foundation's initial board was composed of many national figures who had been involved in various social or religious causes. Board members supported the staff's efforts and did not attempt to steer the organization. Over time, the composition of the board changed dramatically. National leaders were gradually replaced by Philadelphia philanthropic and business leaders. As chairman of the board, Mrs. Madeira became more and more involved in the activities of the foundation. Control of the organization steadily shifted from the staff to the board. The greater the control of the board, the further away from the original mission and structure of the organization the foundation moved.

From November to December 1948, Madeira's and the board's position on merger with other organizations underwent a radical change. In November, Madeira put off any serious discussion of merger. By December, the board started discussing how a merger could be accomplished. Madeira and other board members came to believe that a merger was the only way to ensure the survival of the national foundation. Dick Hunter became resigned to this point of view as well. Hal Barton and Will Hetzel believed that a federation of the National Mental Health Foundation, the National Committee, the Menninger Foundation, and perhaps the Psychiatric Foundation to engage in joint fund-raising was the way to go. A federation with other organizations would enable the national foundation to raise money without sacrificing its identity and autonomy. By late 1948, however, Barton had left the foundation, and Hetzel would have less and less influence with the board over time.

Most members of the board of the national foundation in 1948 and 1949 had little or no experience with the horror of institutions. They had not been associated with the foundation when it had been established and did not share the missionary zeal and passion of its founders. For the board, a merger offered the opportunity for the organization to become part of a bigger and more financially secure organization. Since board members did not fully understand or appreciate the identity of the foundation, as conceived by its founders, sacrificing that identity was not a concern. In the name of saving the organization, the board killed it.

◆   ◆   ◆

The National Mental Health Foundation might have been doomed from the start. With the end of the CPS, the organization faced severe financial challenges. The service committees of the peace churches no longer made significant financial contributions to the program, and the men's maintenance expenses were no longer paid. After years of going without a salary, former COs needed incomes. Many were ready to start their families. Insufficient funding might have made it impossible for the national foundation to endure over time.

The national foundation's chances of survival might have been better had its leaders stayed closer to the structure of the program from which it emerged. When it first received attention from mental hygiene and psychiatric leaders and public figures such as Eleanor Roosevelt and Pearl Buck, the Mental Hygiene Program was composed of four energetic, hardworking, and committed young men. It was small, grassroots, and focused on specific, if ambitious, goals. The national foundation was envisioned as a different type of organization. It was conceived of as a large national organization, with field offices across the country. The original prospectus for the national foundation projected an annual budget of $412,400, a figure comparable to more than $4.7 million in 2007.[10] The foundation never came close to having a budget this large, but it was not unusual for the organization to have budgets projected at close to $200,000 per year. What the founders of the national foundation seemed to have wanted to create was a more progressive, less professionally dominated version of the National Committee for Mental Hygiene. Had they been more modest in their aims, building the organization's activities around the three or four original men, the national foundation would have needed less money and would not have been forced to engage in constant fund-raising.

In contrast to the Mental Hygiene Program, the national foundation lacked a constituency. During the CPS, COs at state mental hospitals and training schools formed a base of support for the Mental Hygiene Program. They submitted reports on conditions at state institutions, attended meetings called by the program, and publicized the program's work. After the end of the CPS, the national foundation was not relevant to most former COs. Attendants never became a primary constituency of the foundation. The organization sought to improve the training and pay of attendants and to elevate their status to the rank of a profession. Referring to attendants as psychiatric aides communicated these goals. For the foundation, professionalizing attendants was a means to an end—improving patient care— but not an end itself. It could not represent attendants' interests, as unions eventually did in most states. Further, until the pay, training, and status of attendants were improved, it was unlikely for those individuals working as attendants to be interested in any kind of reform movement.

The national foundation never actively courted what would have been its natural constituency: former patients and family members of people with intellectual and psychiatric disabilities. It developed some educational materials for family members but never made any attempt to organize family groups or to reach out to former patients. As early as the 1930s, groups of former patients were being organized. A group of former patients from the Hastings Hillside Hospital in New York called the Wender Welfare League was founded in 1934. The preamble of the group's constitution read: "The purpose of the Wender Welfare League shall be to promote the welfare of the Hastings Hillside Hospital; to aid in the continuance and extension of the humane work for the relief and care of mental illness; to assist those who were formerly patients in the hospital or who, having had members of their immediate families as patients, have a common basis for joining in a movement to promote mental health."[11] In 1937, Recovery, a self-help group of former mental patients, was founded by Dr. Abraham Law of Chicago.[12] By the late 1940s and early '50s, families of people with intellectual disabilities were organizing their own groups across the country. It is difficult for reform groups to last if they do not directly involve those individuals who are intended to benefit from any reforms and the intended beneficiaries are capable of expressing their own points of view.

◆   ◆   ◆

As soon as the National Mental Health Foundation merged with the National Committee for Mental Hygiene and the Psychiatric Foundation, it started fading from professional memory. When it is mentioned at all in histories, it is usually in relation to the founding of the National Association for Mental Health. The accomplishments of the national foundation have been largely ignored. This point is especially striking because of the parallels between the reform efforts led by the foundation and those attempts of later eras.

The leaders of the national foundation came up with ideas that would emerge much later during the second half of the twentieth century and into the twenty-first. Both their exposés and the critiques and exposés of the 1960s and '70s were designed to uncover systemic problems in the nation's care of people with mental disabilities. The Mental Hygiene Program and then the national foundation collected reports from dozens of states and then used them to indict not individual institutions or officials but a pattern of abuse. Critiques of total institutions and psychiatry in the 1960s and '70s were not focused on individual malfeasance; they were focused on the very nature of institutions and psychiatry. In *Christmas in Purgatory*, Blatt chose not to name the institutions at which horrific conditions were found, both because it could have jeopardized administrators who had cooperated with him and because it could have left the impression that the widespread problems of institutions were characteristic of only a handful.

The national foundation was a lay organization, and its founders believed that only a movement led by nonprofessionals could bring about the necessary reforms. Major reforms in mental health and mental retardation in the 1960s and '70s built on the ideas of some psychiatrists and professionals but were spearheaded by nonprofessionals. People with disabilities and family members organized to challenge traditional practices and the authority of professional decision making. Independent living, disability rights, self-advocacy, and psychiatric survivor groups sprang up in the late 1960s and the '70s and remain strong today. Through its legal program, the national foundation sought to establish the legal rights of people committed to mental institutions. Beginning in the 1960s, public interest lawyers filed legal challenges to institutions in cases across the country.

The National Mental Health Foundation was the first group to attempt to professionalize the attendant role. The idea went nowhere for many years. Today, however, there is a movement to confer professional status on direct support workers in mental health and developmental disabilities, complete with a code of ethics, a credentialing system, and training programs. With the support of the Research and Training Center on Community Living at the University of Minnesota, a National Alliance for Direct Support Professionals has been formed. The Minnesota center also has developed a Web-based direct support professional training program called the College of Direct Support.[13]

Although many of the ideas of leaders of the national foundation emerged later in mental health and developmental disabilities, the new versions of these ideas cannot be traced to that organization. The ideas were rediscovered and not inherited or passed down over time to be refined by a new generation of reformers. After the merger that created the National Association for Mental Health, the ideas from the national foundation faded away, just as the institutions once more became out of sight and out of mind.

The reforms initiated by the national foundation failed to have a lasting impact on the fields of mental health and developmental disabilities. This failure partially reflected the co-optation of the organization's mission and priorities by other organizations. It also reflected the fact that the foundation never developed an alternative framework for caring for people with mental disabilities. The foundation stood for creating better institutions, with increased funding and additional and better-paid and trained staff. Its founders never questioned institutionalization itself. They were not suspicious of psychiatrists because they rejected psychiatry. In fact, they promoted psychiatric therapies. Their skepticism about psychiatrists was based on their belief that the psychiatric profession could not be counted upon to police itself.

It was not until the 1960s and '70s, when alternative theoretical frameworks and concepts emerged, that the legitimacy of institutions was questioned. Psychiatrist Thomas Szasz and the labeling theorists in sociology challenged medical authority and described psychiatry as a vehicle for stifling nonconformity. Erving Goffman and others argued that institutions functioned as storage dumps for people who were unwanted by society. Professionals and advocates in the field of mental retardation, in particular, translated critiques of labeling and institutionalization into a new philosophy of caring for people so defined. The concept of normalization and its offshoots, including social-role valorization and person-centered planning, shifted attention from the deficits of people with disabilities to the role in which they were placed in society.[14]

The development and refinement of new concepts for understanding disability in society coincided with and encouraged the emergence of disability rights movements in the late 1960s and the '70s. The independent living, psychiatric survivor, and self-advocacy movements rejected both institutions and the so-called medical model in which disability was viewed as a deficit to be ameliorated or cured rather than a difference to be accepted, accommodated, and even celebrated.[15]

What has become the interdisciplinary field of disability studies has its origins in disability rights movements and an understanding of disability as a social and cultural phenomenon.[16] Disability studies rejects the medicalization of disability, just as theorists in the 1960s and '70s questioned medical definitions of mental illness and mental retardation. As Simi Linton wrote:

> The medicalization of disability casts human variation as deviance from the norm, as pathological condition, as defect, and significantly, as an individual burden and personal tragedy. Society, in agreeing to assign medical meaning to *disability*, colludes to keep the issue within the purview of the medical establishment, to keep it a personal matter and "treat" the condition and the person with the condition rather than "treating" the social processes and policies that constrict disabled person's lives. The disability studies' and disability rights movement's position is critical of the domination of the medical definition and views it as a major stumbling block to the reinterpretation of *disability* as a political category and to the social changes that could follow such a shift.[17]

◆　◆　◆

It is difficult to point to any enduring effects of the efforts of the National Mental Health Foundation. It probably brought about some improvements in conditions at institutions as states increased funding for new construction and additional staffing, but any improvements did not fundamentally alter the nature of the institutions themselves. The widespread attention the national foundation brought to mental hospitals strengthened the position of psychiatrists such as the Menningers and the Group for the Advancement of Psychiatry who were seeking to reform psychiatry from within. Ironically, the reformers in psychiatry helped to shift attention away from the mental hospitals, which were the focus of the foundation's own reform efforts.

The most tangible outcome of the CPS mental hospital program was the establishment of Mennonite Mental Health Services after the end of World War II.[18] The experiences of Mennonite COs at state mental hospitals and training schools led the Mennonite Central Committee to explore the development of its own private mental hospitals. In contrast to the national foundation, the leaders of the MCC were not optimistic about the possibility of reforming large state institutions. For the MCC, state mental hospitals had inherent limitations and administrative problems. The solution to the widespread problems found at state institutions was the creation of small, privately operated mental hospitals founded on the Christian principle of love.

The Mental Health Section of the MCC was established in 1947 and was later renamed Mennonite Mental Health Services in 1952.[19] Between 1949 and 1954, three Mennonite mental hospitals built for between twenty-three and forty patients were opened.[20] The first was Brook Lane Farm in Leitersburg, Maryland, followed by Kings View Homes in Reedley, California, and Prairie View in Newton, Kansas. Although the hospitals were planned for Mennonites, they accepted non-Mennonites after they were opened. Several additional private hospitals, including Oaklawn in Elkhart, Indiana, were subsequently opened by the Mennonites in the United States and Canada. Mennonite Mental Health Services played a significant role in the community mental health center movement of the late 1950s and '60s. Prairie View, Kings View, and Oaklawn received national recognition as model community mental health centers in the mid-1960s.[21] Kings View eventually took over the administration of community services for people with psychiatric and developmental disabilities in a number of California counties.[22]

The National Mental Health Foundation and Mennonite Mental Health Services represented different approaches to dealing with evils in the world. The founders of the foundation were not members of the Society of Friends, but they were influenced by the Friends' philosophy of actively confronting social injustices, especially when committed by the government. Mennonite Mental Health Services reflected the Mennonite philosophy of countering societal evils by engaging in personal acts of love and caring. Neither philosophy is better than the other. Both are needed in society.

The young COs who exposed the abuses at the nation's institutions and went on to lead a national reform movement did not, in fact, make lasting changes in the care of people with psychiatric and intellectual disabilities in America. That is not the point of their story. The point is that they tried to make a difference. Acts of conscience in the name of benefiting humanity are always good and never bad or even neutral. Acts of conscience are inherently worthy and deserving of praise. Those people who commit acts of conscience need to be remembered and honored.

APPENDIXES

NOTES

BIBLIOGRAPHY

INDEX

Appendix A

Advent Christian	3
Apostolic Christian Church	3
Assemblies of God	32
Associated Bible Students	36
Baptist, Northern	178
Baptist, Southern	45
Catholic, Roman	149
Christadelphians	127
Christian and Missionary Alliance	5
Christian Scientist	14
Christ's Church of the Golden Rule	3
Church of the Brethren	1353
Church of Christ	199
Church of the First Born	11
Church of God of Abrahamic Faith	13
Church of God of Apostolic Faith	4
Church of God in Christ	12
Church of God, Guthrie, Okla.	5
Church of God, Holiness	6
Church of God, Indiana	43
Church of God and Saints of Christ	12
Church of God, Seventh Day	21
Church of God, Tennessee (two bodies)	7
Church of God (several bodies)	33
Church of Jesus Christ, Sullivan, Ind.	15
Circle Mission (Father Devine)	10
Community Churches	12
Congregational Christian	209
Disciples of Christ	78
Dunkard Brethren	30
Doukhobor (Peaceful Progressive Society)	3
Episcopal	88

Essenes	5
Ethical Culture, Society of	3
Evangelical	50
Evangelical Mission Covenant (Swedish)	11
Evangelical and Reformed	101
Evangelistic Mission	3
Faith Tabernacle	18
Fire Baptized Holiness	3
First Century Gospel	28
First Divine Association in America, Inc.	16
Followers of Jesus Christ	4
Free Holiness	3
Free Methodist	6
Free Pentecostal Church of God	4
Friends, Society of	951
Full Gospel Conference of the World, Inc.	4
Full Gospel Mission	3
German Baptist Brethren	157
German Baptist Convention of N.A.	4
Immanuel Missionary Association	13
Interdenominational	16
Jehovah's Witnesses	409
Jennings Chapel	9
Jewish	60
Lemurian Fellowship	9
Lutheran (nine synods)	108
Mennonites	4665
Methodist	673
Missionary Church Association	8
Mormons (Church of Jesus Christ of Latter Day Saints)	10
National Baptist Convention, USA, Inc.	5
National Church of Positive Christianity	5
Nazarene, Church of the	23
New Age Church	3
Old German Baptist	7
Pentecostal Assemblies of the World	3
People's Church	3
Pilgrim Holiness	3
Plymouth Brethren	12
Presbyterian, U.S.	5
Presbyterian, USA	192
Reformed Church in America (Dutch)	15
Rogerine Quakers (Pentecostal Friends)	3
Russian Molokan (Christian Spiritual Jumpers)	76
Seventh Day Adventist	17

Seventh Day Baptist	3
Theosophists	14
Twentieth Century Bible School	5
Unitarians	44
Union Church (Berea, Ky.)	4
United Brethren	27
United Presbyterian	12
Unity	3
War Resisters League	46
Wesleyan Methodist	8

Source: National Interreligious Service Board for Conscientious Objectors, *1996 Directory of the Civilian Public Service.*

Appendix B

Karl Menninger, M.D., Manager, Winter General Hospital, Topeka, Kansas
Mrs. Elizabeth Ross, Psychiatric Social Worker
Charles A. Zeller, M.D., Director, Department of Mental Health, State of Michigan

NATIONAL SPONSORS

Chairman, Owen J. Roberts
Daniel Blain, M.D.
Pearl Buck
Mrs. LaFell Dickinson
Helen Gahagan Douglas
Dorothy Canfield Fisher
Dr. Harry Emerson Fosdick
Mrs. Louis Gimbel
Sheldon Glueck
William Green
Helen Hayes
Rev. John Haynes Holmes
Rufus M. Jones
Bishop W. A. Lawrence
Henry R. Luce
Thomas Mann
Adolf Meyer
Anne Morgan
Arthur Morgan
Felix Morley
Reinhold Niebuhr
J. R. Oppenheimer
Thomas Parran
James G. Patton
Claude Pepper
Clarence E. Pickett
Daniel A. Poling
Percy Priest
Walter P. Reuther
Mrs. Franklin D. Roosevelt
Lessing J. Rosenwald
Mrs. Harry S. Truman
Dr. Henry P. Van Dusen
Richard Walsh
Gregory Zilboorg

Appendix C

AMERICAN FRIENDS SERVICE COMMITTEE

Unit 41: Eastern State Hospital, Williamsburg, Virginia
Unit 49: Philadelphia State Hospital, Philadelphia, Pennsylvania
Unit 69: Cleveland State Hospital, Cleveland, Ohio
Unit 75: Eastern State Hospital, Medical Lake, Washington
Unit 81: Connecticut State Hospital, Middletown, Connecticut
Unit 83: Warren State Hospital, Warren, Pennsylvania
Unit 84: Concord State Hospital, Concord, New Hampshire
Unit 87: Brattleboro Retreat, Brattleboro, Vermont

BRETHREN SERVICE COMMITTEE

Unit 47: Springfield State Hospital, Sykesville, Maryland
Unit 51: Western State Hospital, Fort Steilacoom, Washington
Unit 68: Norwich State Hospital, Norwich, Connecticut
Unit 70: Dayton State Hospital, Dayton, Ohio
Unit 73: Columbus State Hospital, Columbus, Ohio
Unit 74: Eastern Shore State Hospital, Cambridge, Maryland
Unit 80: Veterans Administration Hospital, Lyons, New Jersey
Unit 82: Fairfield State Hospital, Fairfield, Connecticut
Unit 88: August State Hospital, Augusta, Maine
Unit 109: Southwestern State Hospital, Marion, Virginia

MENNONITE CENTRAL COMMITTEE

Unit 44: Western State Hospital, Staunton, Virginia
Unit 58: Delaware State Hospital, Farmhurst, Virginia
Unit 63: Marlboro State Hospital, Marlboro, New Jersey
Unit 66: Norristown State Hospital, Norristown, Pennsylvania
Unit 69: Cleveland State Hospital, Cleveland, Ohio
Unit 71: Lima State Hospital, Lima, Ohio
Unit 72: Hawthornden State Hospital, Macedonia, Ohio
Unit 77: Greystone State Park Hospital, Greystone Park, New Jersey

Unit 78: Colorado Psychopathic Hospital, Denver, Colorado
Unit 79: Provo State Hospital, Provo, Utah
Unit 85: Rhode Island State Hospital, Howard, Rhode Island
Unit 86: Mt. Pleasant State Hospital, Mt. Pleasant, Iowa
Unit 90: Ypsilanti State Hospital, Ypsilanti, Michigan
Unit 93: Harrisburg State Hospital, Harrisburg, Pennsylvania
Unit 110: Allentown State Hospital, Allentown, Pennsylvania
Unit 118: Wernersville State Hospital, Wernersville, Pennsylvania
Unit 120: Kalamazoo State Hospital, Kalamazoo, Michigan
Unit 143: Spring Grove State Hospital, Catonsville, Michigan
Unit 144: Hudson River State Hospital, Poughkeepsie, New York
Unit 147: Tiffin State Hospital, Tiffin, Ohio
Unit 150: Livermore Veterans Hospital, Livermore, California
Unit 151: Roseburg Veterans Hospital, Roseburg, Oregon

DISCIPLES OF CHRIST

Unit 139: Logansport State Hospital, Logansport, Louisiana

EVANGELICAL AND REFORMED CHURCH

Unit 137: Independence State Hospital, Independence, Iowa

METHODIST COMMISSION ON WORLD PEACE

Unit 131: Cherokee State Hospital, Cherokee, Iowa

Appendix D

AMERICAN FRIENDS SERVICE COMMITTEE

Unit 119: State Training School, New Lisbon, New Jersey
Unit 124: Delaware State Colony, Stockley, Delaware
Unit 129: Pennhurst State Training School, Spring City, Pennsylvania
Unit 130: Maine State Training School, Pownal, Maine
Unit 132: District Training School, Laurel, Maryland

BRETHREN SERVICE COMMITTEE

Unit 91: Mansfield State Training School, Mansfield, Connecticut
Unit 95: Western State Custodial School, Buckley, Washington
Unit 105: Lynchburg State Colony, Colony, Virginia

MENNONITE CENTRAL COMMITTEE

Unit 92: Vineland Training School, Vineland, New Jersey
Unit 117: Exeter State Training School, Lafayette, Rhode Island
Unit 123: Southern Wisconsin Colony, Union Grove, Wisconsin
Unit 127: American Fork State Training School, American Fork, Utah
Unit 142: Woodbine Colony for the Feebleminded, Woodbine, New Jersey

AMERICAN BAPTIST HOME MISSION SOCIETY

Unit 136: State Home for Epileptics, Skillman, New Jersey

ASSOCIATION OF CATHOLIC CONSCIENTIOUS OBJECTORS

Unit 102: Rosewood State Training School, Owings Mills, Maryland

Notes

1. "Work of National Importance under Civilian Direction"

1. Gary B. Nash, *American Odyssey: The United States in the 20th Century,* 498.

2. Thomas V. Dibacco, Lorna C. Mason, and Christian G. Appy, *History of the United States,* 2:407–8.

3. Leslie Eisen, *Pathways of Peace: A History of the Civilian Public Service Program Administered by the Brethren Service Committee,* 31–33; Melvin Gingerich, *Service for Peace: A History of the Mennonite Civilian Public Service,* 5–13; Mulford Q. Sibley and Philip E. Jacob, *Conscription of Conscience: The American State and the Conscientious Objector, 1940–1947,* 11. Eisen, Gingerich, and Sibley and Jacob had firsthand knowledge of conscientious objectors during World War II and wrote their books soon after the end of the war. Eisen and Gingerich focused specifically on the experiences of members of the Church of the Brethren and the Mennonites, respectively. Sibley and Jacob devoted more attention to members of other religions as well as nonreligious objectors during the war. Each of these books was based on primary source documents and included appendixes containing copies of laws or Executive Orders, memoranda, and statements by church committees.

4. Quoted in Albert N. Keim and Grant M. Stoltzfus, *The Politics of Conscience: The Historic Peace Churches and America at War, 1917–1955,* 35–36.

5. Gingerich, *Service for Peace,* 25.

6. *Congressional Record,* 66th Cong., 1st sess., 3063–66, reprinted in Lillian Schlissel, ed., *Conscience in America: A Documentary History of Conscientious Objection in America, 1757–1967,* 162.

7. Quoted in Eisen, *Pathways of Peace,* 23.

8. Quoted in Gingerich, *Service for Peace,* 10.

9. Ibid.

10. Sibley and Jacob, *Conscription of Conscience,* 14, 16.

11. Keim and Stoltzfus, *Politics of Conscience,* 54.

12. Reprinted in Sibley and Jacob, *Conscription of Conscience,* 485.

13. Keim and Stoltzfus, *Politics of Conscience,* 77.

14. Eisen, *Pathways of Peace,* 35.

15. Keim and Stoltzfus, *Politics of Conscience,* 77.

16. Gingerich, *Service for Peace,* 41.

17. NSBRO, *Congress Looks at the Conscientious Objector.* This publication reprinted excerpts of testimony presented before and submitted to U.S. Senate and House hearings on conscientious objectors.

18. Ibid., 8, 22, 25.

19. Ibid., 4.

20. Ibid., 28.

21. Ibid., 24.

22. Ibid., 10.

23. Ibid.

24. Gingerich, *Service for Peace,* 52–61; Keim and Stoltzfus, *Politics of Conscience,* 94–95.

25. George Q. Flynn, *Lewis B. Hershey: Mr. Selective Service,* 69.

26. Keim and Stoltzfus, *Politics of Conscience,* 104.

27. Ibid.

28. Selective Training and Service Act of 1940, Section 5[g], reprinted in Sibley and Jacob, *Conscription of Conscience,* 487.

29. Diary of Paul Comly French, October 2, 1940, CDGA, SCPC. See also Gingerich, *Service for Peace,* 56.

30. Diary of French, October 2, 1940, SCPC.

31. Keim and Stoltzfus, *Politics of Conscience,* 10.

32. Diary of French, October 5, 1940, SCPC.

33. M. R. Zigler in Heather T. Frazier and John O'Sullivan, *"We Have Just Begun Not to Fight": An Oral History of Conscientious Objectors in Civilian Public Service During World War II,* 8. Frazier and O'Sullivan's book contains the verbatim accounts of former conscientious objectors and others involved in the Civilian Public Service based on interviews.

34. Paul Comly French, *Four Year Report of Civilian Public Service, May 15, 1941 to March 1, 1945,* 12.

35. Ibid., 12–13.

36. Gingerich, *Service for Peace,* 56–57.

37. Flynn, *Lewis B. Hershey,* 75.

38. Rachel Waetner Goossen, *Woman Against the Good War: Conscientious Objection and Gender on the American Home Front, 1941–1947,* 107.

39. Diary of French, October 2, 1940, SCPC.

40. AFSC, *The Experience of the American Friends Service Committee in the Civilian Public Service under the Selective Training and Service Act of 1940, 1941–1945,* 5; Gingerich, *Service for Peace,* 58.

41. Reprinted in Sibley and Jacob, *Conscription of Conscience,* 494–95.

42. Reprinted in ibid., 496.

2. "Religious Training and Belief"

1. Flynn, *Lewis B. Hershey,* 76.

2. Sibley and Jacob, *Conscription of Conscience,* 83.

3. The Selective Service and NSBRO gave different figures on the number of men in the Civilian Public Service: 11,500 (Selective Service) versus 11,996 (NSBRO) (ibid., 83, 168).

4. Albert N. Keim, *The CPS Story: An Illustrated History of the Civilian Public Service,* 8.

5. *United States v. Seeger,* 380 U.S. 163.

6. *Time,* January 25, 1971.

7. Philip Berrigan with Fred A. Wilcox, *Fighting the Lamb's War: Skirmishes with the American Empire,* 79, 93–108.

8. Ibid., 105.

9. Gordon Zahn, "The Great Catholic Upheaval," *Saturday Review,* September 11, 1971, Gordon Zahn, CDGA, SCPC.

10. Gordon Zahn, *Conscientious Objection: Catholic Perspectives*, 3–4.

11. Dorothy Day, *On Pilgrimage: The Sixties*, 359–60; Berrigan with Wilcox, *Fighting the Lamb's War*, 96.

12. Jerry and Carol Berrigan, interview, June 2007.

13. Berrigan with Wilcox, *Fighting the Lamb's War*, 92.

14. Frazier and O'Sullivan, *"We Have Just Begun,"* 247.

15. Studs Terkel, *"The Good War": An Oral History of World War Two*, vi, 15; *The War*, directed and produced by Ken Burns and Lynn Novick, a production of Florentine Films and WETA-TV, 2007.

16. Tom Brokaw, *The Greatest Generation*, xix.

17. For the history of the Mennonites, see Harold S. Bender, "Mennonite Origins and the Mennonites of Europe," http://www.bibleviews.com/menno heritage.html; James C. Juhnke, "Anabaptist/Mennonite History," http://raven.bethelks.edu/services/mla/guide/; and Dale R. Schrag, John D. Thiesen, and David A. Haury, "Anabaptist/Mennonite History: Sixteenth-Century Anabaptist Roots," http://www.bethelks.edu/services/mla/guide/. See also Gingerich, *Service for Peace*.

18. Harold S. Bender, foreword to *Service for Peace*, by Gingerich, v; Zigler in Frazier and O'Sullivan, *"We Have Just Begun,"* 7; "Civilian Public Service, Camp no. 86, Mt. Pleasant State Hospital, Statistical Report of All Men in Camp on March 15, 1944," IX-13-1, MCA.

19. Joseph Yoder, "Witness," *Menno-Hof Newsletter* 16, no. 4 (Fall 2006): 1.

20. In addition to the sources on Mennonite history, see Sibley and Jacob, *Conscription of Conscience*, 20–21.

21. Reprinted in Gingerich, *Service for Peace*, 447–48.

22. Orie Miller, Henry A. Fast, and Elmer Ediger, interview by James C. Juhnke, November 11, 1969, 940.5316 #67, MLA.

23. NSBRO, *Congress*, 72, 73.

24. Juhnke, "Anabaptist/Mennonite History," 3.

25. Diary of French, October 22, 1940, SCPC.

26. Eli J. Bontrager, introduction to *The Story of the Amish in Civilian Public Service with Directory*, edited by David Wagler and Roman Rader, 5–6.

27. G. Richard Culp, *The Minority Report: A Behind-the-Scenes Story of Civilian Public Service*, 12–17.

28. Ibid., 153–54.

29. Wilbert Kropf quoted in ibid., ix; G. Richard Culp, "A Summary of the Mental Hygiene Program of CPS 144," 1945, IX-12-1, MCA.

30. For the history of the Church of the Brethren, see Carl D. Bowman, *Brethren Society: The Cultural Transformation of a Peculiar People*; Eisen, *Pathways of Peace*; and Ken Shaffer and Kendra Flory, "Brief History of the Church of the Brethren," http://www.reformedreader.org/history/cobhistory.htm.

31. Zigler in Frazier and O'Sullivan, *"We Have Just Begun,"* 7.

32. Keim and Stoltzfus, *Politics of Conscience*, 22; Church of the Brethren quoted in Eisen, *Pathways of Peace*, 23.

33. Sibley and Jacob, *Conscription of Conscience*, 22.

34. Church of the Brethren quoted in Eisen, *Pathways of Peace*, 25; Bowman, *Brethren Society*, 350.

35. NSBRO, *Congress*, 81.

36. Eisen, *Pathways of Peace*, 38–39.

37. For the history of the Society of Friends, see David Murray-Rust, "Quakers in Brief," http://people.cryst.bbk.ac.uk/~ubcg09q/dmr/; and Allen Smith, "The Renewal Movement: The Peace

Testimony and Modern Quakerism," http://www.quaker.org/renewal.html. For a description of some Friends' beliefs and practices, see Ursula M. Franklin, *The Ursula Franklin Reader: Pacifism as a Map;* Sibley and Jacob, *Conscription of Conscience;* and Swarthmore College Friends Historical Library, "Glossary."

38. Zigler in Frazier and O'Sullivan, *"We Have Just Begun,"* 7.

39. Lorna C. Mason, William Jay Jacobs, and Robert P. Ludlum, *History of the United States,* 1:135.

40. Michelle Swenarchuk, introduction to *Franklin Reader,* by Franklin, 31.

41. Franklin, *Franklin Reader,* 47.

42. Sibley and Jacob, *Conscription of Conscience,* 23.

43. NSBRO, *Congress,* 25.

44. Sibley and Jacob, *Conscription of Conscience,* 24.

45. "Fighting Friends," July 20, 1942, 2, *Time* Magazine Archives.

46. AFSC, *Experience of the American Friends Service Committee,* 7. See also AFSC, *An Introduction to Friends Civilian Public Service,* 92.

47. Gingerich, *Service for Peace,* 476.

48. NSBRO, *Congress,* 87.

49. Ibid., 86, 89.

50. Gordon C. Zahn, *Another Part of the War: The Camp Simon Story,* 141; Anne Klejment, "The Radical Origins of Catholic Pacifism," http://www.catholicworker.com/klejment.htm.

51. Zahn, *Another Part of the War,* 36.

52. Zigler placed the number at 130 (in Frazier and O'Sullivan, *"We Have Just Begun,"* 9); Frazier and O'Sullivan estimated 200 (xviii).

53. Sibley and Jacob, *Conscription of Conscience,* 57.

54. Keim, *CPS Story,* 90.

55. Reprinted in Sibley and Jacob, *Conscription of Conscience,* 488–92.

56. Jack Allen, interview, January 2007; Neil Hartman, interview, January 2007; Zahn, *Another Part of the War,* 5–6; Flynn, *Lewis B. Hershey,* 129.

57. Sibley and Jacob, *Conscription of Conscience,* 168.

58. Stuart Palmer, interview, January 2007; Uriah Mast in Frazier and O'Sullivan, *"We Have Just Begun,"* 41–42; John Hostetler, interview by Joseph Miller, December 22, 1977, 940.5316 #78, MLA.

59. Gordon C. Zahn, *A Descriptive Study of the Social Backgrounds of Conscientious Objectors in Civilian Public Service During World War II: Abstract of a Dissertation.* This "abstract" was a single-spaced twenty-six-page summary of the major findings and conclusions of Zahn's dissertation (Catholic Univ. of America, 1953).

60. See H. Otto Dahlke, "Values and Group Behavior in Two Camps for Conscientious Objectors"; and Lowell E. Maechtle and H. H. Gerth, "Conscientious Objectors as Mental Hospital Attendants."

61. Zahn, *Descriptive Study,* 22.

62. See, for example, Talcott Parsons, *The Social System.*

63. Bowman, *Brethren Society,* 350, 351.

64. Ivan Amstutz in Frazier and O'Sullivan, *"We Have Just Begun,"* 67; Paul Frank Webb, "Mennonite Conscientious Objectors and the Civilian Public Service Camps of World War II," 67; Hostetler, interview by Miller, December 22, 1977, MLA.

65. Gingerich, *Service for Peace,* 90.

66. Loris Habegger, interview by Keith Sprunger, August 13, 1974, 940.5316 #15, MLA; Marvin Wasser, interview by Mark Kroeker, November 29, 1989, 940.5316 #206, MLA.

67. Bowman, *Brethren Society*, 422; A. Smith, "Renewal Movement," 3; Diary of French, October 24, 1945, SCPC.

68. Culp, *Minority Report*, 37.

69. Warren Sawyer, Letters, October 25, 1942.

70. Harold Barton to Marvin Weisbord, August 10, 1965, 1, Harold Barton Manuscript Collections, CDGA, SCPC; Everett Bartholomew, interview, January 2007.

71. Sibley and Jacob, *Conscription of Conscience*, 514.

72. Samuel Burgess, written statement provided January 2007.

73. Zigler in Frazier and O'Sullivan, *"We Have Just Begun,"* 11.

74. E. Bartholomew, interview, January 2007.

75. Sibley and Jacob, *Conscription of Conscience*, 36–40.

76. Stephen Cary in Frazier and O'Sullivan, *"We Have Just Begun,"* 23.

77. J. Benjamin Stalvey in ibid., 221.

78. Scott H. Bennett, *Radical Pacifism: The War Resisters League and Gandhian Nonviolence in America, 1915–1963*.

79. Nathaniel Hoffman in *"We Have Just Begun,"* by Frazier and O'Sullivan, 80.

80. "Lives: Leonard Cornell," *San Francisco Chronicle*, June 11, 2006, http://www.02138mag.com/tribe/lives/341.html; Leonard Edelstein quoted in Paul A. Wilhelm, *Civilian Public Servants: A Report on 210 World War II Conscientious Objectors*, 17.

81. Zahn, *Descriptive Study*, 22–26.

82. Hoffman in *"We Have Just Begun,"* by Frazier and O'Sullivan, 81; Edward Burrows in ibid., 129.

83. Sibley and Jacob, *Conscription of Conscience*, 34–35.

84. French, *Four Year Report*, 14.

85. Sibley and Jacob, *Conscription of Conscience*, 35–36.

86. French, *Four Year Report*, 14.

87. AFSC, *Experience of the American Friends Service Committee*, 30; "By the Numbers," May 1, 1943, *Time* Magazine Archives; Keim, *CPS Story*, 82; NISBCO, *1996 Directory of Civilian Public Service*; CPS no. 84 Members, New Hampshire State Hospital, no. 1 of 69, DG 002, File 44c, SCPC.

88. Zahn, *Another Part of the War*, 109–13.

3. "An Experiment in Democracy"

1. Keim and Stoltzfus, *Politics of Conscience*, 118; Sibley and Jacob, *Conscription of Conscience*, 123.

2. Zigler in *"We Have Just Begun,"* by Frazier and O'Sullivan, 6.

3. Flynn, *Lewis B. Hershey*, 126.

4. Habegger, interview by Sprunger, August 13, 1974, MLA.

5. Keim and Stoltzfus, *Politics of Conscience*, 101.

6. NSBRO, *Congress*, 39.

7. Ibid., 53–62.

8. Ibid., 38.

9. Gingerich, *Service for Peace*, 64–65.

10. Flynn, *Lewis B. Hershey*, 236–37.

11. "Lewis Blaine Hershey, General, United States Army," Arlington National Cemetery Web site, http://www.arlingtoncemetery.net/hershey.htm.

12. Flynn, *Lewis B. Hershey*, 128.

13. See, for example, Lewis F. Kosch to Col. H. R. Foster, September 26, 1945, Reel 31, BHLA.

14. French, *Four Year Report*, 4.

15. Reprinted in NISBCO, *1996 Directory*, xv–xxi.

16. Gingerich, *Service for Peace*, 63–69.

17. Eisen, *Pathways of Peace*, 435.

18. NISBCO, *1996 Directory*, xxviii; Sibley and Jacob, *Conscription of Conscience*, 497.

19. NISBCO, *1996 Directory*, xxii–xxviii.

20. Mennonite Central Committee Executive Committee, September 16, 1943, reprinted in Gingerich, *Service for Peace*, 449.

21. AFSC, *Introduction*, 93.

22. Diary of French, April 16, July 28, 1943, SCPC.

23. Ibid., April 27, May 31, June 1, 1943.

24. Ibid., March 9 (quote), April 19, 1943.

25. Eisen, *Pathways of Peace*, 436.

26. Sibley and Jacob, *Conscription of Conscience*, 326.

27. Gingerich, *Service for Peace*, 476.

28. French, *Four Year Report*, 4.

29. Zahn, *Another Part of the War*, 44; Dwight Larrowe to Miss E. S. Brinton, July 22, 1942, Association of Catholic Conscientious Objectors, CDGA, SCPC; Diary of French, February 24, 1943, SCPC.

30. Reprinted in MCC, CPS, *MCC*CPS: Camp Director's Manual*.

31. AFSC, *Experience of the American Friends Service Committee*, 6, 21.

32. Eisen, *Pathways of Peace*, 50.

33. Gingerich, *Service for Peace*, 85.

34. Ibid., 364.

35. Keim, *CPS Story*, 30.

36. Keim and Stoltzfus, *Politics of Conscience*, 119.

37. "Statement of Policy, Camp Operations Division of the Selective Service," 1942, reprinted in Sibley and Jacob, *Conscription of Conscience*, 508–13.

4. "A Significant Epoch in Your Life"

1. W. Harold Row to Dear Friend, May 15, 1944, Reel 16, BHLA.

2. NISBCO, *1996 Directory*, xxii.

3. Wagler and Rader, *Story of the Amish*, 28–33.

4. Gingerich, *Service for Peace*, 117–18.

5. Ibid., 139–47.

6. "Parachutes for Pacifists," January 25, 1943, *Time* Magazine Archives.

7. Sibley and Jacob, *Conscription of Conscience*, 12–27.

8. Gingerich, *Service for Peace*, 453–59.

9. Kenneth Keeton and Don Elton Smith, "History of CPS #21," 16, August 1945, Reel 16, BHLA.

10. AFSC, *Experience of the American Friends Service Committee*, 12, 16.

11. Keeton and Smith, "CPS #21," 16.

12. NSBRO, *Congress*, 36.

13. Ibid., 44.

14. French, *Four Year Report*, 3.

15. Ibid., 9.

16. AFSC, *Experience of the American Friends Service Committee*, 18, 19.

17. Eisen, *Pathways of Peace*, 108–9.

18. Goossen, *Women Against the Good War*, 79.

19. Gingerich, *Service for Peace*, 376–77.

20. Eisen, *Pathways of Peace*, 177.

21. Gingerich, *Service for Peace*, 377.

22. Aden Horst, "CPS Camp #4, Grottoes, Virginia," in *Our CPS Stories: Prairie Street Mennonite Church in Civilian Public Service, 1941–1946*, edited by Dorsa J. Mishler et al., 32.

23. Reprinted in MCC, CPS, *Camp Director's Manual*.

24. MCC, CPS, *Instruction Manual on Camp Records, Financing, and Procedures* and *MCC*CPS: Educational Director's Manual*.

25. MCC, CPS, *MCC*CPS: Educational Director's Manual*, 13; Gingerich, *Service for Peace*, 325.

26. Gingerich, *Service for Peace*, 325.

27. Don Elton Smith, "Development of Techniques of Administration in CPS #21," November 1944, Reel 16, BHLA.

28. Zahn, *Descriptive Study*, 10.

29. Adrian E. Gory and David C. McClelland, "Characteristics of Conscientious Objectors in World War II," 248; Paul L. Goering, interview by Kurt Goering, December 26, 1975, 940.5316 #47, MLA.

30. MCC, CPS, *Educational Director's Manual*, 1.

31. P. Goering, interview by K. Goering, December 26, 1975, MLA.

32. Culp, *Minority Report*, ix.

33. Bontrager, introduction to *Story of the Amish*, edited by Wagler and Rader, 5–6.

34. Gingerich, *Service for Peace*, 407.

35. Bontrager, introduction to *Story of the Amish*, edited by Wagler and Rader, 6.

36. Gingerich, *Service for Peace*, 407.

37. Ibid., 407; Wasser, interview by Kroeker, November 29, 1989, MLA.

38. Laban Peachley, interview by Joseph Miller, April 4, 1978, 940.5316 #82, MLA.

39. Edwin J. Schrag, interview by Tim E. Schrag, September 13, 1974, 940.5316 #17, MLA; Aden Horst in *Our CPS Stories*, edited by Mishler et al., 33; P. Goering, interview by K. Goering, December 26, 1975, MLA.

40. Diary of French, July 29, 1943, SCPC.

41. Dahlke, "Values and Group Behavior," 23.

42. Ibid., 25.

43. Ibid., 26.

44. Diary of French, October 28, 1941, SCPC.

45. Zahn, *Descriptive Study*, 9; Gory and McClelland, "Characteristics," 248; AFSC, *Projects and Incentives: A Study of the Work Projects and the Incentives for Work in the Civilian Public Service Camps and Units under the Administration of the American Friends Service Committee*, 5; Hartman, interview, January 2007; E. Bartholomew, interview, January 2007.

46. AFSC, *Experience of the American Friends Service Committee*, 13.

47. W. Harold Row to Dear Friend, May 15, 1944, Reel 16, BHLA.

48. Zahn, *Descriptive Study*, 11.

49. Gory and McClelland, "Characteristics," 248.

50. Eisen, *Pathways of Peace*, 411–13.

51. D. E. Smith, "Techniques of Administration," 2, 3.

52. Ibid., 3, 8.

53. Ibid., 16.

54. Quoted in Zahn, *Another Part of the War*, 146.

55. Ibid., 102–35.

56. Dahlke, "Values and Group Behavior," 26; Hartman, interview, January 2007; Charles Lord, interview, February 2007.

5. "Detached Units"

1. French, *Four Year Report*, 7.

2. Ibid.

3. AFSC, *Experience of the American Friends Service Committee*, 50.

4. Gingerich, *Service for Peace*, 305, 306.

5. French, *Four Year Report*, 7.

6. Gingerich, *Service for Peace*, 307.

7. Diary of French, May 14, 1943, SCPC.

8. NSBRO, *Congress*, 66. NSBRO reprinted the articles in the appendix of its *Congress Looks at the Conscientious Objector*, 1943.

9. Ibid., 95.

10. Ibid., 95–96.

11. Ibid., 66.

12. Ibid.

13. Gingerich, *Service for Peace*, 307–8.

14. "Kill Scheme of Mrs. F. D. R. for Objectors," *Chicago Tribune Press*, July 8, 1943, Reel 34, BHLA. As in the case of many newspaper and magazine articles maintained in archives, publication information on this article was incomplete. The article on microfilm in the BHLA did not contain a page number.

15. French, *Four Year Report*, 7.

16. Ibid.

17. *Marine Bull Pen*, April 12, 1946, 1, Reel 31, BHLA. The *Marine Bull Pen* was a newsletter published for "seagoing cowboys" by the Brethren Service Committee in Elgin, Illinois. "Seagoing cowboys" referred to men who rode on church-sponsored "cattle boats" to deliver livestock and supplies to war-ravaged areas of Europe after the war. Many of the seagoing cowboys were former members of the CPS.

18. Warren Sawyer, interview, January 2007; Hartman, interview, January 2007; Wasser, interview by Kroeker, November 29, 1989, MLA; E. Schrag, interview by T. Schrag, September 13, 1974, MLA; Richard Ruddell, interview, April 2007; Harold Wik, "A Brief Sketch of the Life and Views of H. T. Wik," April 24, 1997, Harold Wik Papers.

19. AFSC, *Experience of the American Friends Service Committee*, 14.

20. Quoted in Keim and Stoltzfus, *Politics of Conscience*, 118.

21. NSBRO, *Congress*, 118.

22. Ibid., 43.

23. Reprinted in AFSC, *Experience of the American Friends Service Committee*, 41.

24. NISBCO, *1996 Directory*, xxii–xvi.

25. Gingerich, *Service for Peace*, 253.

26. Ibid., 265.

27. Reprinted in AFSC, *Experience of the American Friends Service Committee*, 28.

28. Zigler in Frazier and O'Sullivan, *"We Have Just Begun,"* 11 (brackets in original).

29. Bob Barnes to Dear Friends, January 15, 1943, CPS no. 62, Box 6, SCPC.

30. Medical experiments were also conducted on British conscientious objectors. See Kenneth Mellanby, *Human Guinea Pigs*. 31. AFSC, *Experience of the American Friends Service Committee*, 9.

32. Sibley and Jacob, *Conscription of Conscience*, 9.

33. AFSC, *Experience of the American Friends Service Committee*, 9; Sibley and Jacob, *Conscription of Conscience*, 143.

34. Todd Tucker, *The Great Starvation Experiment: The Heroic Men Who Starved So That Millions Could Live*, 112, 161. Unless otherwise indicated, the information about the Minnesota experiment in this section came from Tucker.

35. Paul J. Furness to Directors and Unit Leaders, n.d.; W. Harold Row to Directors and Unit Leaders, n.d., Reel 39, BHLA.

36. "Procedure on Securing Men for Nutritional Rehabilitation, Semi-starvation, and Nutritional Rehabilitation Project," ibid. This was a one-page typed paper with handwritten notations.

37. *Will We Know How to Feed Europe When the Time Comes?* September 1943, ibid.; Gingerich, *Service for Peace*, 270–72.

38. Ward Miles, Hartman, Sawyer, Lord, Ruddell, and W. Forrest Altman, interviews, January–April 2007; Caryl Marsh, wife of Michael Marsh, interview, February 2007. Warren Sawyer's experiences were also described in his letters. Neil Hartman provided a copy of the journal article by the researchers and newspaper clippings on their activities.

39. John R. Neefe et al., "Hepatitis Due to the Injection of Homologous Blood Products in Human Volunteers."

40. Ibid., 851.

41. John R. Neefe et al., "Inactivation of the Virus of Infectious Hepatitis in Drinking Water."

42. Hartman, interview, January 2007.

43. Lord, interview, February 2007; Sawyer, Letters, November 29, 1943.

44. C. Everett Koop, M.D., Curriculum Vitae, July 1981, National Library of Medicine, http://profiles.nlm.nih.gov/QB/B/C/D/R/_qqbcdr.pdf; Hartman, interview, January 2007.

45. Sawyer, interview, January 2007; W. Miles, interview, February 2007; E. Bartholomew, interview, January 2007; Hartman, interview, January 2007.

46. Hartman, interview, January 2007; Sawyer, Letters, October 1–2, 1943.

47. Sawyer, Letters, February 28, 1944.

48. "Men Starve in Minnesota: Conscientious Objectors Volunteer for Strict Hunger Tests to Study Europe's Food Problem," *Life*, July 30, 1945, 43–46; Alex Sareyan, *The Turning Point: How Persons of Conscience Brought about Major Change in the Care of America's Mentally Ill*, 13.

49. Sareyan, Turning Point, 13; Neil Hartman Papers; Warren Sawyer Papers.

50. Tucker, *Great Starvation Experiment*, 188–91.

51. B. Leyendecker and F. Klapp, "Human Hepatitis Experiments in the 2d World War," translated from *Z. Gesamte Hyg.* 35, no. 12: 756–60, http://www.ncbi.nlm.nih.gov/sites/.

52. Adil E. Shamoo and David B. Resnick, *Responsible Conduct of Research*, 197.

53. David J. Rothman and Sheila M. Rothman, *The Willowbrook Wars: A Decade of Struggle for Social Justice*, 257–71; Shamoo and Resnick, *Responsible Conduct of Research*, 187.

54. 45 *Code of Federal Regulations* 46.

55. Tucker, *Great Starvation Experiment*, 70–71.

56. Interview, January 2007.

57. AFSC, *Experience of the American Friends Service Committee*, 31–34.

58. "Selective Service Special Form for Conscientious Objectors" (DSS Form 47), "Conscientious Objector Report" (DSS Form 48), reprinted in MCC, CPS, *Camp Director's Manual*.

59. Ibid.; NSBRO, "Personnel Record," reprinted in ibid.

60. Stalvey in Frazier and O'Sullivan, *"We Have Just Begun,"* 221; CPS Photographs, Photo 10-5, BHLA.

61. Terkel, *"The Good War,"* 32.

62. Eisen, *Pathways of Peace*, 472–73.

63. Keeton, "Race Relations in BCPS," December 8, 1944, Reel 25, BHLA.

64. Eisen, *Pathways of Peace*, 151–54.

65. Harry R. Van Dyck, *Exercise of Conscience: A WW II Objector Remembers*, 209.

66. "New England Fellowship of Reconciliation Fall Conference, November 9–11, 1945, Theme: 'The Pacifist Task in the Post-war World,'" Reel 3, BHLA.

67. Richard Kluger, *Simple Justice*.

68. Van Dyck, *Exercise of Conscience*, 211.

69. D. E. Smith, "Techniques of Administration," 15 (see chap. 4, n. 27).

70. Bennett, *Radical Pacifism*, 106.

71. Gingerich, *Service for Peace*, 254.

72. Van Dyck, *Exercise of Conscience*, 213; Gingerich, *Service for Peace*, 254.

73. Gingerich, *Service for Peace*; Van Dyck, *Exercise of Conscience*, 214.

74. Van Dyck, *Exercise of Conscience*, 214–15.

75. Gingerich, *Service for Peace*, 254.

76. Van Dyck, *Exercise of Conscience*, 215.

77. Gingerich, *Service for Peace*, 255.

78. Sibley and Jacob, *Conscription of Conscience*, 158–59.

79. Quoted in Wilhelm, *Civilian Public Servants*, 15 (brackets in original).

80. Gingerich, *Service for Peace*, 258–63.

81. Quoted in ibid., 259.

82. Sanford Rothman and Max Ginsberg, "History of CPS #21: Analysis and Criticism of the Handling of the Conscientious Objector in World War II," 1, 10, September 1945, Reel 16, BHLA.

83. Gingerich, *Service for Peace*, 260.

84. Ibid., 259–60.

85. Rothman and Ginsberg, "History of CPS #21," 10; William Channel in Frazier and O'Sullivan, *"We Have Just Begun,"* 160.

86. Channel in Frazier and O'Sullivan, *"We Have Just Begun,"* 156–57; Bennett, *Radical Pacifism*, 107.

87. Channel in Frazier and O'Sullivan, *"We Have Just Begun,"* 160.

88. Bennett, *Radical Pacifism*, 170.

89. Diary of French, March 20, 22, 23, 26, 27, 1943, SCPC.

90. Ibid., April 27, 1943.

91. Channel in Frazier and O'Sullivan, *"We Have Just Begun,"* 161.

92. *Conscientious Objector* 5, no. 5 (May 1943): 1, SCPC.

93. Quoted in Wilhelm, *Civilian Public Servants,* 15 (brackets in original).

94. Channel in Frazier and O'Sullivan, *"We Have Just Begun,"* 157.

95. Michael Schwartz, e-mail, May 5, 2007.

96. Douglas C. Baynton, *Forbidden Signs: American Culture and the Campaign Against Sign Language.*

97. Simi Linton, *Claiming Disability: Knowledge and Identity.*

98. "CPSU Facts and Policy on Employment of Negroes as Attendants at Phila. State Hospital," n.d., DG 008, Box 6, SCPC.

99. Sawyer, Letters, February 22, 1945.

100. See Chapter 11 for a detailed description of the events surrounding the removal of the AFSC unit from Cleveland State Hospital and the subsequent establishment of an MCC unit.

101. P. Goering, interview by K. Goering, December 26, 1975, MLA.

102. Marjorie L. DeVault, *Feeding the Family: The Social Organization of Caring as Gendered Work;* P. Goering, interview by K. Goering, December 26, 1975, MLA.

103. Van Dyck, *Exercise of Conscience,* 212.

104. Ibid.

6. "A Working Compromise Between Church and State"

1. Eisen, *Pathways of Peace,* 471.

2. AFSC, *Experience of the American Friends Service Committee,* 7.

3. Diary of French, April 7, 1943, SCPC.

4. Keim and Stoltzfus, *Politics of Conscience,* 143–44.

5. Sibley and Jacob, *Conscription of Conscience,* 322–33; Diary of French, October 31, 1945, SCPC.

6. Eisen, *Pathways of Peace,* 471, 473.

7. Diary of French, May 13, 1943, SCPC.

8. Gingerich, *Service for Peace,* 478.

9. Keim and Stoltzfus, *Politics of Conscience,* 113.

10. Gingerich, *Service for Peace,* 480.

11. Diary of French, June 8, 1942, SCPC.

12. Ibid., December 8, 1941, May 11, 14, 1943, April 3, 1944.

13. Ibid., April 1, 1945.

14. Ibid., October 18, 1946.

15. NSBRO, *Congress,* 39.

16. Ibid., 43.

17. Eisen, *Pathways of Peace;* Rothman and Ginsberg, "History of CPS #21."

18. Eisen, *Pathways of Peace,* 467.

19. Sibley and Jacob, *Conscription of Conscience,* 239.

20. Burrows in Frazier and O'Sullivan, *"We Have Just Begun,"* 131.

21. Bennett, *Radical Pacifism,* 108–13.

22. Quoted in Wilhelm, *Civilian Public Servants,* 15.

23. Gingerich, *Service for Peace,* 385.

24. Eisen, *Pathways of Peace,* 378.

25. Sibley and Jacob, *Conscription of Conscience,* 264.

26. D. E. Smith, "Techniques of Administration," 15 (see chap. 4, n. 27).

27. Bennett, *Radical Pacifism,* 105.

28. D. E. Smith, "Techniques of Administration," 16.

29. Rex Corfman and Philip Isely to Maj. Gen. Lewis B. Hershey, April 15, 1943, Reel 23, BHLA.

30. Diary of French, March 30, 1943, SCPC.

31. Ibid.

32. Ibid.

33. Hershey to Neil A. Dayton, March 30, 1943, copy of telegram, Reel 36, BHLA.

34. A. J. Muste and Evan W. Thomas, "Personal Memorandum on General Hershey's Order Affecting Chicago Conference," April 7, 1943, Reel 23, ibid.

35. Diary of French, April 3, 1943, SCPC.

36. Muste and Thomas, "Personal Memorandum."

37. A. J. Muste Memorial Institute, "A. J. Muste Biographical Background," http://www.ajmuste.org/ajmbio.htm.

38. Bennett, *Radical Pacifism,* 37–40.

39. Ibid., 82–83.

40. Ibid., 82; *Conscientious Objector* 5, no. 1 (May 1943): 2, SCPC.

41. David Dellinger, introduction to *Fighting the Lamb's War,* by Berrigan with Wilcox, vi–vii.

42. "American Civil Liberties Union: National Committee on Conscientious Objection," December 1947, DG 002, SCPC, 3.

43. Bennett, *Radical Pacifism,* 104–5.

44. Diary of French, April 8, 1943, SCPC.

45. Ibid., April 9, 1943.

46. Ibid., April 14, 1943.

47. Sibley and Jacob, *Conscription of Conscience,* 265.

48. Members from Brethren camps and members from Friends camps to Paul Furnas, April 5, 1943, Reel 23, BHLA.

49. Philip Isely and Rex Corfman, "To All Men in C.P.S.," April 7, 1943; Isely and Corfman, "To Men of Social Action," April 12, 1943, ibid.

50. Civilian Public Service Camp no. 89, Oakland, Md., "Statement of Principles and Position," n.d., ibid.

51. Corfman and Isely to Hershey.

52. Diary of French, April 15, 1943, SCPC.

53. Sibley and Jacob, *Conscription of Conscience,* 266; "33 Campers Defy SS Ban to Attend Chicago Meeting: Conference Is First Entirely Run by Men; One CO Plucked from Train en Route by FBI," *Conscientious Objector* 5, no. 5 (May 1943): 1, SCPC; Bob Zigler, cited in Diary of French, April 21, 1943, SCPC.

54. Chicago Conference on Social Action, "Proceedings," April 19–25, 1943, Reel 23, BHLA.

55. Bennett, *Radical Pacifism,* 88–94.

56. "Resolutions: The NSBRO and NCCO," in ibid.

57. Paul Furnas quoted in Rex Corfman, "Memorandum to Social Action Groups," May 11, 1943, 2, Reel 23, BHLA.

58. Corfman, "Memorandum," 3.

59. Sibley and Jacob, *Conscription of Conscience,* 267.

60. Ibid., 265, 268.

61. Eisen, *Pathways of Peace,* 386.

62. Sibley and Jacob, *Conscription of Conscience,* 268.

63. Diary of French, May 31, 1943, SCPC.

64. Ibid., July 28, 1943.

65. French, *Four Year Report,* 2.

66. Diary of French, March 10, 1942, SCPC; Sibley and Jacob, *Conscription of Conscience,* 243.

67. Quoted in Eisen, *Pathways of Peace,* 381 (brackets in original).

68. AFSC, *Experience of the American Friends Service Committee,* 6.

69. Eisen, *Pathways of Peace,* 381.

70. Ibid., 380; Zigler in Frazier and O'Sullivan, *"We Have Just Begun,"* 15–16.

71. Diary of French, June 8, 1942, SCPC.

72. Ibid., April 16, 1943; Eisen, *Pathways of Peace,* 382; Sibley and Jacob, *Conscription of Conscience,* 246.

73. Diary of French, May 19, 1943, SCPC.

74. Ibid., May 31, 1943.

75. French, *Four Year Report,* 2.

76. Eisen, *Pathways of Peace,* 382.

77. French, *Four Year Report,* 2.

78. Rothman and Ginsberg, "History of CPS #21," 6.

79. Rex Corfman, "Government Camps," *Social Action News,* May 24, 1943, 12, Reel 23, BHLA.

80. French, *Four Year Report,* 2; Keim and Stoltzfus, *Politics of Conscience,* 124.

81. French, *Four Year Report,* 2.

82. Bent Andresen in Frazier and O'Sullivan, *"We Have Just Begun,"* 111–26, quote on 117.

83. Van Dyck, *Exercise of Conscience,* 139.

84. Gingerich, *Service for Peace,* 387.

85. Van Dyck, *Exercise of Conscience,* 141.

86. Dahlke, "Values and Group Behavior," 30.

87. Sibley and Jacob, *Conscription of Conscience,* 253.

88. Diary of French, February 22, 23, 1945, SCPC; French, *Four Year Report,* 2.

89. CPS Union, "Special Bulletin of Friends of Civilian Public Service: Penicillin Research Blocked by Chemist's Arrest," November 7, 1944, DG 008, Camp 49, SCPC.

90. Quoted in ibid., 2.

91. Quoted in ibid., 1.

92. Michael Seibert, "Obituary," *Photosynthesis Research* 28, no. 3 (1991): 95–98.

93. Diary of French, October 31, 1944, SCPC.

94. Ibid., April 25, 1946.

95. Sibley and Jacob, *Conscription of Conscience,* 271.

96. Diary of French, April 26, May 6, 1946, SCPC.

97. CPSU, "The Issues at Middletown," May 15, 1945, 1, Reel 31, BHLA.

98. Diary of French, March 6, 7, 1945, SCPC; CPSU, "The Issues at Middletown," 1.

99. CPSU, "The Issues at Middletown," 1.

100. Diary of French, June 28, February 20, 27, 1945, SCPC.

101. Sibley and Jacob, *Conscription of Conscience,* 273–74.

102. F. Nelson Underwood to Harold Row, September 24, 1945, Reel 3; BSC, "The Future of the Brethren Civilian Public Service," Reel 36, BHLA. "The Future of the Brethren Civilian Public Service" was a survey of men in BSC camps about whether the BSC should continue to administer CPS units.

A copy was found at the BHLA along with documents concerning the BSC unit at Mansfield Training School in Connecticut. Summary results indicating that eight men believed that the BSC should withdraw from the CPS and eight that it should stay were handwritten on the form. A handwritten note also stated: "Results mailed to Elgin 3/4/46." Much of the growing unrest among men in CPS units in late 1945 and 1946 was owing to the fact that World War II had ended in September 1945.

103. Forest W. Shively, "Resolution Adopted by Meeting of CPS Unit No. 73," August 9, 1945, Reel 3, BHLA.

104. Sibley and Jacob, *Conscription of Conscience,* 269.

105. CPS Camp no. 52, Powellsville, Maryland, *You and the C.P.S.U.,* DG 008, Unit 49, SCPC.

106. "History of the CPS Union," *CPSU Newsletter,* October 5, 1944, 1, Reel 31, BHLA.

107. Allida Black et al., "International Ladies' Garment Workers' Union," Eleanor Roosevelt National Historic Site, 2003, http://www.nps.gov/archive/elro/glossary/ilgwu.htm.

108. "History of the CPS Union," 1.

109. Sibley and Jacob, *Conscription of Conscience,* 270.

110. "Financial Record of CPS #49 Local, CPSU, August 1944–," DG 008, Camp 49, SCPC.

111. "Constitution of the Union in C.P.S. #49," ibid.

112. Bennett, *Radical Pacifism,* 107.

113. "History of the CPS Union," 3.

114. Eisen, *Pathways of Peace,* 413.

115. "History of the CPS Union," 1.

116. Max Kampelman, "Democratic Front," *Conscientious Objector* 4, no. 8 (August 1942): 7. See also Bennett, *Radical Pacifism,* 76.

117. Tucker, *Great Starvation Experiment,* 218–19.

118. "History of the CPS Union," 1. The names and CPS units of members of the General Executive Board were listed on a letter from Ralph Rudd to "Members of and Nominees to the GEB," May 18, 1945, Reel 39, BHLA.

119. "Constitution of the Union in C.P.S. #49."

120. Undated, unsigned letter, DG 008, Camp 49, SCPC.

121. Paul Wilhelm, "Some Thoughts on the C.P.S. Union . . . ," n.d., 1–2, Wilhelm, Jayne Tuttle and Paul A., Collected Papers, CDGA, Box 3, SCPC.

122. Sawyer, interview, January 2007; Hartman, interview, January 2007; Lord, interview, February 2007; Leonard Stark, interview, February 2007.

123. "Col. Kosch Neutral to CPS Union," *CPSU Newsletter,* December 1944, 2, Reel 31, BHLA.

124. Hartman, interview, January 2007.

125. Altman, interview, February 2007; Ruddell, interview, April 2007.

126. "Convention Would Delay Vote on State Constitution Changes" (subheading, heading unintelligible on microfilm), *New York Times,* June 17, 1943; "Veterans Hit 'Colonization': Say Five 'Conscientious Objectors' Live with Wives at Lyons," *Newark Call,* June 17, 1943; "Oust Objectors from Facility: Session at Newark Asserts Preference Is Shown 23 Hired by Lyons Hospital," *New York Herald Tribune,* June 17, 1943. Copies of articles found in Reel 34, BHLA.

127. William A. Bryan, "Norwich State Hospital, Hospital Policy Concerning Employment Outside Hospital for Selective Service Assignees," April 5, 1944, Reel 36, BHLA.

128. Richard Reuter to Dick Lion, January 23, 1945, Reel 31, ibid.

129. Underwood to Row, January 4, 1945, Reel 3, ibid.

130. Reuter to Lion, January 23, 1945, Reel 31, ibid.

131. CPS Union Action Committee to All CPS Camps and Units, February 4, 1945, Reel 3, ibid.

132. Diary of French, January 26, 1945, SCPC.

133. CPS Unit no. 73 to All CPS Hospital Units, February 24, 1945, Reel 3, BHLA.

134. CPS Union Action Committee to All CPS Camps and Units, February 4, 1945, ibid.

135. Homer Rogers to Assistant Director, CPS Unit no. 80, March 23, 1945, Reel 31, ibid.

136. Reuter to Lion, March 23, 1945, ibid.

137. Row to Underwood, February 19, 1945, Reel 3, ibid.

138. Sawyer, Letters, February 5, 1945.

139. Ralph Rudd and Tom Leonard to CPS Camps and Units, February 4, 1945, Reel 3, BHLA.

140. Underwood to Row, "Administrative Report," February 3, 1945, 1, ibid.

141. Minutes of Unit Meeting, February 21, 28, 1945, Ward Miles Papers.

142. Council Minutes, March 12, 1945, ibid.

143. Forest W. Shively to CPS Men, February 13, 1945, Reel 3, BHLA.

144. CPS Unit no. 73, Columbus State Hospital, to CPS Hospital Units, February 24, 1945, ibid.

145. Diary of French, February 20, 27, 1945, SCPC.

7. "Out of Sight, Out of Mind"

1. Eleanor Roosevelt, "My Day," July 22, 1947, http://www.gwu.edu/~erpapers/myday/; Owen J. Roberts, foreword to *Out of Sight, Out of Mind*, by Frank L. Wright Jr., 7. I am grateful to Graham Warder and Laurie Block of Straight Ahead Pictures and the Disability History Museum (http://www.disabilitymuseum.org) for first bringing *Out of Sight, Out of Mind* to my attention. Permission to quote from *Out of Sight, Out of Mind* has been granted by Mental Health America (http://www.mentalhealthamerica.net).

2. Marvin R. Weisbord, *Some Form of Peace: True Stories of the American Friends Service Committee at Home and Abroad*, 44.

3. Wright, *Out of Sight,* 19–20.

4. Ibid., 23–24.

5. Ibid., 104–5.

6. Ibid., 71–72.

7. Ibid., 49–51.

8. Ibid., 123.

9. Ibid., 124.

10. Ibid., 127–28.

11. Ibid., 129.

12. Ibid., 133.

13. Ibid., 134.

14. Ibid., 135.

15. Ibid., 138.

16. Ibid., 151.

17. Harold Barton, "The National Mental Health Foundation," in ibid., 155.

18. Frank L. Wright, interview by Keith Sprunger and John D. Waltner, May 7, 1972, 940.5316 #4b, MLA.

19. Laurel Richardson, *Writing Strategies: Reaching Diverse Audiences*, 15.

20. Albert Q. Maisel, "Bedlam, 1946: Most U.S. Mental Hospitals Are a Shame and a Disgrace."

21. Cecelia Tichi, *Exposés and Excess: Muckraking in America, 1900/2000*, 91.

8. "A Mind That Found Itself"

1. Clifford W. Beers, *A Mind That Found Itself: An Autobiography*, 217–18.

2. Ibid., 255.

3. Quoted in ibid., xiii.

4. Norman Dain, *Clifford W. Beers: Advocate for the Insane*, 94, 92.

5. Ibid., 142–43.

6. Albert Deutsch, *The Mentally Ill in America: A History of Their Care and Treatment from Colonial Times*, 314–15.

7. C. E. A. Winslow, "The Mental Hygiene Movement (1908–33) and Its Founder," 305.

8. Dain, *Clifford W. Beers*, 158.

9. Nina Ridenour, "The Mental Health Movement," 1093.

10. Deutsch, *Mentally Ill*, 317.

11. Ridenour, "The Mental Health Movement," 1099.

12. Deutsch, *Mentally Ill*, 329.

13. Ibid., 159; Philip M. Ferguson, *Abandoned to Their Fate: Social Policy and Practice Toward Severely Retarded People in America, 1820–1920*, 22; Richard C. Scheerenberger, *A History of Mental Retardation: A Quarter Century of Promise*, 105.

14. Gerald N. Grob, *Mental Illness and American Society, 1875–1940*, 4; Gerald N. Grob, *The Mad among Us: A History of the Care of America's Mentally Ill*, 1; Edward Shorter, *A History of Psychiatry: From the Era of the Asylum to the Age of Prozac*, 4.

15. See, for example, Mason, Jacobs, and Ludlum, *History of the United States*, 1:412.

16. Deutsch, *Mentally Ill*, 173.

17. Ibid., 158–69.

18. Dorothea L. Dix, "Memorial to the Legislature of Massachusetts, 1843," 6.

19. "Dix Accused of Slander," *Franklin Democrat*, February 14, 1843, http://www.disability museum.org/lib/docs/895.htm, Disability History Museum, http://www.disabilitymuseum.org.

20. "Charles Sumner Supports Dix," *Boston Courier*, February 25, 1843, http://www.disability museum.org/lib/docs/755.htm, Disability History Museum, http://www.disabilitymuseum.org.

21. Scheerenberger, *History of Mental Retardation*, 105–6; Deutsch, *Mentally Ill*, 171.

22. Deutsch, *Mentally Ill*, 171; Ferguson, *Abandoned to Their Fate*, 23.

23. Dorothea L. Dix, *Memorial of Miss D. L. Dix to the Senate and House of Representatives of the United States*, 5.

24. Dix, "Senate and House of Representatives," 20.

25. Franklin Pierce, "Franklin Pierce Veto," May 3, 1854, 2 http://www.disabilitymuseum.org/lib/docs/682.htm, Disability History Museum, http://www.disabilitymuseum.org.

26. Deutsch, *Mentally Ill*, 183.

27. Ibid., 184.

28. Stanley P. Davies, *The Mentally Retarded in America*, 22.

29. Deutsch, *Mentally Ill*, 185.

30. Scheerenberger, *History of Mental Retardation*, 107.

31. Winslow, "Mental Hygiene Movement," 304; David J. Rothman, *The Discovery of the Asylum: Social Order and Disorder in the New Republic,* xiv–xv.

32. Scot Danforth, "On What Basis Hope? Modern Progress and Postmodern Possibilities."

33. C. M. Hincks, "Clifford Whittingham Beers."

34. Quoted in Beers, *Mind That Found Itself,* 282.

35. Quoted in ibid., 283–84.

36. Dain, *Clifford W. Beers,* 290.

37. "The National Committee for Mental Hygiene," *Mental Hygiene* 1, no. 1 (1917); "The National Committee for Mental Hygiene," *Mental Hygiene* 1, no. 1 (1939).

38. Dain, *Clifford W. Beers,* 289–90.

39. Thomas W. Salmon, "Insane in a County Poor Farm."

40. Dain, *Clifford W. Beers,* 289, 308, 289–90.

41. Martin S. Pernick, *The Black Stork: Eugenics and the Death of "Defective" Babies in American Medicine and Motion Pictures since 1915;* J. David Smith, *Minds Made Feeble: The Myth and Legacy of the Kallikaks;* Steven J. Taylor and Stanford J. Searl, "Disability in America: A History of Policies and Trends"; James W. Trent, *Inventing the Feeble Mind: A History of Mental Retardation in the United States.*

42. Quoted in Beers, *Mind That Found Itself,* 282.

43. Quoted in Wolf Wolfensberger, *The Origin and Nature of Our Institutional Models,* 35–36.

44. Dain, *Clifford W. Beers,* 167, 185.

45. Clifford W. Beers, "Organized Work in Mental Hygiene," 84–85.

46. Dain, *Clifford W. Beers,* 190.

47. "Sterilization Cry," December 17, 1945, *Time* Magazine Archives (brackets in original).

48. Dain, *Clifford W. Beers,* 314.

49. Beers, "Organized Work," 81.

50. Trent, *Inventing the Feeble Mind,* 131–83.

51. Winslow, "Mental Hygiene Movement," 317–18, 322.

52. "Mental Hygiene," November 19, 1923; "Mental Hygiene," November 21, 1927; "Mental Hygiene," November 19, 1928; "Mental Hygiene," November 25, 1929; "Mental Hygiene," May 19, 1930; "Mind Triumphant," May 15, 1933, *Time* Magazine Archives.

53. Dain, *Clifford W. Beers,* 311.

54. "Notes and Comments: Dr. George Stevenson Appointed Medical Director of the National Committee for Mental Hygiene," *Mental Hygiene* 23, no. 2 (1939): 314–18; Dain, *Clifford W. Beers,* 315–16.

55. "Notes and Comments: Clifford W. Beers Appointed Honorary Secretary of the National Committee," *Mental Hygiene* 23, no. 3 (1939): 505.

56. Dain, *Clifford W. Beers,* 320, 322.

57. Hincks, "Clifford Whittingham Beers," 654–55.

58. U.S. Bureau of the Census, *Patients in Mental Hospitals, 1946,* 11, 35.

59. Paul O. Komora, Mary Augusta Clark, and Ralph A. Pierson, *State Hospitals in the Depression: A Survey of the Effects of the Economic Crisis on the Operation of Institutions for the Mentally Ill in the United States,* 7, 19.

60. Samuel W. Hamilton et al., *A Study of the Public Mental Hospitals of the United States, 1937–39,* Supplement no. 164 to the Public Health Reports, 25, 82.

61. Ibid., 20; "New Publications," *Mental Hygiene* 26, no. 1 (1942): 160; William A. Bryan, review of *A Study of the Public Mental Hospitals of the United States, 1937–39,* by Hamilton et al., *Mental Hygiene* 26, no. 3 (1942): 469–70.

62. "Notes and Comments: Findings in State-Hospital Surveys Provoke Wide Public Interest," *Mental Hygiene* 25, no. 4 (1941): 683.

63. National Committee for Mental Hygiene, *Annual Report, 1946,* 22, MC#001, Box 1057, Folder 14, ACLU Records.

64. Edith M. Stern, "Samuel Warren Hamilton, *Mental Hygiene* 35, no. 4 (1951): 634–35.

65. National Committee for Mental Hygiene, "Maine," Reel 3, BHLA.

66. This section is based on a self-published book, John Maurice Grimes's *Institutional Care of Mental Patients in the United States,* and Grob, *Mental Illness and American Society,* 273–78. I would to thank Wolf Wolfensberger for loaning me his copy of the report, along with his own commentary. According to a two-page summary of this book written by Wolfensberger, he obtained his copy from the former New York State Department of Mental Hygiene. The book apparently received little public attention. It is significant because it demonstrated that conditions at public institutions were woefully inadequate, even abusive and dehumanizing, years before the outbreak of World War II and showed that the American Medical Association and the American Psychiatric Association not only ignored but attempted to suppress the release of unfavorable information about institutions.

67. Grimes, *Institutional Care,* viii, xi.

68. Ibid., xiv.

69. Ibid., iii.

70. Ibid., 9, 17, 21, 31, 46, 48.

71. Ibid., 111.

72. Ibid., 113, 117.

73. Dain, *Clifford W. Beers,* 294–97 (quote on 297).

74. Samuel W. Hamilton, "Life in Our Mental Hospitals: Its Meaning for the Individual," *Mental Hygiene* 27, no. 1 (1943): 8, 9; H. O. Colomb, "The Utilization of the State Hospital in the Training of Psychiatrists," *Mental Hygiene* 24, no. 3 (1940): 390–412; Harry V. Bice and Charlotte E. Graves, "The Mentally Deficient Child in the Residential School," *Mental Hygiene* 25, no. 3 (1941): 392–401; Seward Hiltner, "Improving Protestant Worship in Mental Hospitals," *Mental Hygiene* 26, no. 4 (1942): 606–9; Nathan Blackman, "Mental-Hospital Newspapers," *Mental Hygiene* 26, no. 4 (1942): 610–17; J. W. Klapman, "Public Relationships of the Mental Hospital," *Mental Hygiene* 28, no. 3 (1944): 381–96.

75. "Notes and Comments: National Committee Issues Annual Report," *Mental Hygiene* 25, no. 4 (1941): 680–81.

76. George S. Stevenson, "The National Committee's Part in the War Effort: A Report on the Year's Work," *Mental Hygiene* 27, no. 1 (1943): 38.

77. George S. Stevenson, "Review of the Year: A Report on the National Committee's Work in 1943," *Mental Hygiene* 28, no. 1 (1944): 8.

78. National Committee for Mental Hygiene, *Annual Report, 1944,* Reel 2, 0788, Eleanor Roosevelt Papers, 1945–1952, from the Franklin D. Roosevelt Library, Part 1: General Correspondence, 1945–1947 (hereafter Eleanor Roosevelt Papers), 26, 27, 28.

79. "This Shame," November 11, 1946, *Time* Magazine Archives.

9. "They Asked for a Hard Job"

1. Bennett, *Radical Pacifism,* 83–85.

2. Frank Olmstead, "They Asked for a Hard Job."

3. Ibid., 192.

4. NISBCO, *1996 Directory*, xxii–xxv.

5. Sareyan, *Turning Point*, 59.

6. Zigler in Frazier and O'Sullivan, *"We Have Just Begun,"* 11.

7. M. Head to All Employees, March 22, 1943, Reel 31, BHLA.

8. AFSC, *Experience of the American Friends Service Committee*, 31.

9. E. L. Hooper to Vernon H. Stinebaugh, July 1, 1943, Reel 25, BHLA.

10. Habegger, interview by Sprunger, August 13, 1974, MLA.

11. Sawyer, interview, January 2007.

12. *25 Men Needed at Lyons*, DG 002, Section 3, SCPC.

13. F. Nelson Underwood, "Information for Men in CPS Camps Concerning the CPS Unit, Augusta State Hospital, Augusta, Maine," May 8, 1943, 1, Reel 3, BHLA.

14. Ralph M. Delk to William H. Hammond, December 5, 1944, Reel 36, BHLA.

15. Handwritten notes on Delk's letter.

16. Barton to Weisbord, August 11, 1965, 4, Barton Manuscript Collections, CDGA, SCPC (brackets in original).

17. Sawyer, interview, January 2007; E. Schrag, interview by T. Schrag, September 13, 1974, MLA; Lord, interview, February 2007, Hostetler, interview by Miller, December 22, 1977, MLA; John Bartholomew, interview, January 2007; Hartman, interview, January 2007.

18. Diary of French, January 26, 1945, SCPC.

19. "Civilian Public Service Hospital Units, April 1, 1944," Reel 25, BHLA.

20. French, *Four Year Report*, 12.

21. Gingerich, *Service for Peace*, 214.

22. "Civilian Public Service Camp No. 86, Mt. Pleasant State Hospital," March 15, 1944, Camp no. 86, Personnel Records, IX-12-1, MCA.

23. G. L. C., "The History of CPS Unit #44," 12–16, CPS History Unit Write-Ups, 1945, ibid.

24. "Civilian Public Service Unit 109," February 20, 1945, Reel 39, BHLA.

25. COs at Byberry were identified from documents at the SCPC and primarily from CPSU Local 49 information (see chap. 6). These names were then checked against NISBCO's *1996 Directory*, which listed the religious affiliations, if any, of CPS men.

26. Harold Mishler to Robert Kreider, March 20, 1945, Mennonite Central Committee, CPS and other Corr. 1940–45, 86 Director, IX-6-3, MCA; E. H. Crawfis, "History of CPS Unit #69," 2, CPS History Unit Write-Ups, 1945, IX-12-1, MCA.

27. "Civilian Public Service Unit 109."

28. "CPS Unit 147," CPS History Unit Write-Ups, 1945, IX-12-1, MCA.

29. MCC, CPS, *Educational Director's Manual*, 13.

30. AFSC: CPS, DG 002, Section 3, SCPC.

31. CPS no. 49, *Dope Sheet*, December 15, 1944, ibid.

32. Gingerich, *Service for Peace*, 221–33. See, for example, CPS Unit 63, *P.R.N.*, and Civilian Public Service Unit no. 93, *Anniversary Review*, May 1945, DG 002, Section 3, SCPC.

33. P. Goering, interview by K. Goering, December 26, 1975, MLA.

34. Arthur Weaver, "The Story of CPS Unit No. 123, Union Grove, Wisconsin," 3, CPS History Unit Write-Ups, 1945, IX-12-1, MCA.

35. Habegger, interview by Sprunger, August 13, 1974, MLA.

36. Neil A. Dayton, "Open Letter to the Members and Wives of C.P.S. Unit #1," *Civilian Public Service 91, Mansfield State Training School and Hospital,* 7, DG 002, Section 3, SCPC.

37. Ralph M. Delk to W. Harold Row and Samuel A. Harley, "October–November Assistant Director's Report," December 6, 1944, Delk to Harley, "Events at Mansfield," March 15, 1945; Delk to Harley, "Events at Mansfield," March 16, 1945; Delk to Harley, "Events at Mansfield," March 17, 1945; Delk to Harley, "Events at Mansfield," March 21, 1945, Reel 36, BHLA.

38. Delk to J. M. Weaver, "Events at Mansfield—Special," March 24, 1945, ibid.

39. Ibid., 2.

40. Dayton to Delk, June 22, 1943, ibid.

41. Ibid., November 22, 1943.

42. D. Ned Linegar, "Training School Committee Meets to Plan Inter-agency Conference," December 30, 1944; Linegar to Training School Units in Civilian Public Service, January 2, 1945, ibid.

43. Dayton to Delk, December 29, 1944, ibid.; Mental Hygiene Program Civilian Public Service, "Report of the First Inter-agency Training School Conference," April 17, 1945, Barton Manuscript Collections, CDGA, SCPC.

44. C. H. Beahm Jr., "My Work at Mansfield Training School"; Ross Coulson, "A Report on My Work Here at Mansfield Training School"; Donald G. Holsopple, "My Impressions of Mansfield Training School"; Ralph S. Wolfe, "Work in Pandemonium Hall," Reel 36, BHLA.

45. Delk to the *Reporter* and Row, December 3, 1943, ibid.

46. Delk to Dayton, September 16, 1943, ibid.; Dayton to Delk, November 17, 1943, ibid.

47. NSBRO, *Congress,* 43.

48. Dayton to Delk, January 13, 1945, Reel 36, BHLA.

49. "Draft Objectors Hear Saito at Colony," March 22, 1944, news clipping, with no paper identified, Reel 39, ibid.

50. Ross Coulson to Freeman W. Meyer, March 10, 1945, Reel 36, ibid.

51. John H. Mosemann, "Memorandum of Information, Iowa State Hospital, Visited January 13, 1943," MCC C.P.S. and other Corr. 1940–45, 86 Director, IX-6-3, MCA; Underwood, "Information," 1.

52. "CPS Unit #74," March 1945, Periodicals; W. Jarrett Harkey, "Norwich State Hospital," October 26, 1945, Periodicals, DG 002, SCPC.

53. F. Nelson Underwood, "Administrative Report," February 3, 1945, Reel 3, BHLA.

54. Sawyer, Letters, September 27, 1942, August 16, 1943.

55. Sawyer, interview, January 2007.

56. "Description of C.P.S. #92," July 23, 1945, 2, CPS History Unit Write-Ups, 1945, IX-12-1, MCA; G. L. C., "The History of CPS Unit #44," 1.

57. Weaver, "The Story of CPS Unit No. 123," 3; Hartman, interview, January 2007; Ward Miles, interview, February 2007.

58. Harold Mishler, "A Brief Description of Mt. Pleasant State Hospital, Mt. Pleasant, Iowa, and Civilian Public Service Unit No. 86," July 17, 1945, 1, CPS Unit History Write-Ups, 1945, IX-12-1, MCA; Erving Goffman, *Asylums: Essays on the Social Situation of Mental Patients and Other Inmates,* xiii.

59. AFSC, *Women's Service in Mental Hospitals,* October 1944, Barton Manuscript Collections, CDGA, SCPC.

60. "Eastern Shore State Hospital, CPS Unit #74," March 1945, 1, DG 002, Section 3, SCPC; "Description of C.P.S. #92," July 23, 1945, CPS History Unit Write-Ups, 1945, IX-12-1; H. Mishler, "Mt. Pleasant State Hospital," 1; Dave Shank, "History and Evaluation of Civilian Public Service Unit 144,"

1, CPS History Unit Write-Ups, 1945, IX-12-1, MCA; Lotus E. Troyer to Albert M. Gaeddert, "Description of Unit and Hospital," July 6, 1945, 1, CPS History Unit Write-Ups, 1945, IX-12-1, MCA; Harkey, "Norwich State Hospital," 1.

61. Shank, "Civilian Public Service Unit 144," 1; E. Schrag, interview by T. Schrag, September 13, 1974, MLA.

62. Underwood, "Information," 1.

63. "CPS Unit 147," 1.

64. Ward Miles, interview, February 2007; Stark, interview, February 2007.

65. "Civilian Public Service, Mental Hospitals, CPS Unit #49—Byberry, CPS Quarters," DG 002, File 44c, SCPC.

66. Weaver, "The History of CPS Unit No. 123," 3.

67. G. L. C., "The History of CPS Unit #44," 1, 2.

68. "Description of Unit #71," stamped July 12, 1945, CPS History Unit Write-Ups, 1945, IX-12-1, MCA.

69. Clarence Kreider's diary, quoted in G. L. C., "The History of CPS Unit #44," 3.

70. Wolfensberger, *Origin and Nature,* 13, 43.

71. *Anniversary Review,* 13.

72. Weaver, "The Story of CPS Unit No. 123," 1.

73. Steven J. Taylor, "The Custodians: Attendants and Their Work at State Institutions for the Mentally Retarded."

74. Albert Gaeddert, "Description of CPS Unit #144—Hudson River State Hospital," July 9, 1945, 2, CPS History Unit Write-Ups, 1945, IX-12-1, MCA; H. Mishler, "Mt. Pleasant State Hospital," 1.

75. Weaver, "The Story of CPS Unit No. 123," 1; "Mansfield State Training School and Hospital," February 26, 1944, 3, Periodicals, DG 002, SCPC; "Eastern Shore State Hospital," 2; Harkey, "Norwich State Hospital," 2; Troyer to Gaeddert, July 6, 1945, 1; "CPS Unit #74, Eastern Shore State Hospital," April 1, 1944, 2, Reel 25, BHLA; Underwood, "Information," 2.

76. G. L. C., "The History of CPS Unit #44," 3, 5.

77. Diary of French, October 31, November 1, 3, 1945, SCPC.

78. Ibid., November 19, 20, 21, 1945.

79. Quoted in Weaver, "The Story of CPS Unit No. 123," 2–3.

80. Quoted in G. L. C., "The History of CPS Unit #44," 1.

81. Underwood, "Information," 4.

82. A. S. Imirie to Dr. F. C. Tyson, September 16, 1943, Reel 3, BHLA.

83. Van Dyck, *Exercise of Conscience,* 149.

84. Delk to Edelstein, August 4, 1945, Reel 36, BHLA.

85. Norwich State Hospital, "Program of Attendant Instruction for Conscientious Objectors," August 1943, Reel 25, ibid.; Harkey, "Norwich State Hospital," 1.

86. Barton to Weisbord, September 5, 1966, Barton Manuscript Collections, CDGA, SCPC.

87. Paul Wilhelm in Frazier and O'Sullivan, *"We Have Just Begun,"* 175.

88. P. Wilhelm, "Attendants' Class," Wilhelm Collected Papers, CDGA, Box 2, SCPC.

89. Untitled anonymous description of the CPS unit at Hudson River State Hospital (hereafter "Hudson River State Hospital"), 1–2, CPS History Unit Write-Ups, 1945, IX-12-1, MCA.

90. "Schedule for Lectures in Mental Hygiene and Psychiatry," Units, Poughkeepsie Educational, IX-12-1, MCA.

91. Barton to Weisbord, September 5, 1966, 12.

92. P. Goering, interview by K. Goering, December 26, 1975, MLA; J. Bartholomew, interview, January 2007; Lord, interview, February 2007; Miles, interview, February 2007; Stark, interview, February 2007.

93. H. Mishler, "Mt. Pleasant State Hospital," 1; Weaver, "The Story of CPS Unit No. 123," 1; "Hudson River State Hospital," 1.

94. Sawyer, interview, January 2007; Delk to Edelstein, August 4, 1945.

95. Shank, "History and Evaluation," 1.

96. Mosemann, "Memorandum of Information," 1.

97. Charles A. Zeller to Col. Lewis F. Kosch, April 8, 1943, reprinted in AFSC, *Experience of the American Friends Service Committee,* 28.

98. Delk to Edelstein, August 4, 1945.

99. Barton to Weisbord, September 5, 1966, 15.

100. Sawyer, Letters, August 6, 1945.

101. P. Goering, interview by K. Goering, December 26, 1975, MLA.

102. Ralph S. Wolfe, "Work in Pandemonium Hall," DG 002, Section 3, SCPC. This paper can be found at both the SCPC and the BHLA.

103. J. Willard Linscheid, "An Evaluation of the Work Done on Ward 41 Edgewood Service at Hudson River State Hospital," n.d., 2, CPS History Unit Write-Ups, IX-12-1, MCA; Underwood, "Information," 2–3; H. Mishler, "Mt. Pleasant State Hospital," 1.

104. Sawyer, Letters, October 17, 1942; Barton to Weisbord, September 5, 1966, 17.

105. Committee for Improvement of Patient Care, untitled paper, State Hospital, Howard, Rhode Island, DG 002, Section 3, SCPC; Barton to Weisbord, September 5, 1966, 11.

106. P. Goering, interview by K. Goering, December 26, 1975, MLA.

107. Untitled report, June 20, 1944, Barton Manuscript Collections, CDGA, SCPC.

108. Arthur Stevenson and Michael Marsh, "A Battle—yet to Win," May 15, 1943, DG 002, Section 3, SCPC.

109. Attendants in A Building to Dr. Charles A. Zeller, June 12, 1942, 1, Barton Manuscript Collections, CDGA, SCPC.

110. Stevenson and Marsh, "Battle," 4.

111. J. Bartholomew, interview, January 2007; Stevenson and March, "Battle," 3.

112. Sawyer, Letters, May 23, 1944.

113. Arthur M. Stevenson Jr. to L. E. Richards, R.N., Male Nursing Supervisor, September 11, 1943, Barton Manuscript Collections, CDGA, SCPC.

114. "Notes Prepared by F. Greenleaf," May 6, 1944, 2, ibid.

115. FB, "1B Building Notes," September 18, 1944, ibid.

116. Sawyer, Letters, March 22, 1944.

117. Sawyer, interview, January 2007; Sawyer, Letters, March 22, 1944.

118. Sawyer, Letters, September 5, 1944.

119. J. Bartholomew, interview, January 2007; Sawyer, Letters, August 6, 1945.

120. Sawyer, Letters, September 5, 1944; Sawyer Papers; "Notes Prepared by F. Greenleaf," May 6, 1944, Barton Manuscript Collections, CDGA, SCPC.

121. Sawyer, Letters, March 22, September 5, 1944, February 5, 1945.

122. Barton to Weisbord, September 5, 1966, 16, 15; Bill Marsh, interview, March 2007.

123. Sawyer Papers.

124. Thurston Griggs, February 4, 1946, ibid.; J. Bartholomew, interview, January 2007; Stark, interview, February 2007.

10. "Bughousers" and "Conchies"

1. Harold Maine, *If a Man Be Mad*, 340.

2. Delk to Edelstein, 1.

3. Ward Miles, interview, February 2007; Stevenson and Marsh, "Battle," 3.

4. David Patrick Lee, "The Bughouser Speaks—on What a Bughouser Was," *Psychiatric Aide* 5, no. 12 (1948): 3–4, Psychiatric Aide (The), IX-12-1, MCA; William and Wilma Ludlow in Frazier and O'Sullivan, *"We Have Just Begun,"* 190; Maine, *If a Man Be Mad*, 340; Sareyan, *Turning Point*, 63; William Seabrook, *Asylum*, 10.

5. Lee, "Bughouser Speaks," 4; Sareyan, *Turning Point*, 63; Habegger, interview by Sprunger, August 13, 1974, MLA.

6. Sareyan, *Turning Point*, 63; Lord, interview, February 2007; P. Goering, interview by K. Goering, December 26, 1975, MLA; Sawyer, Letters, December 5, 1945; Sawyer, interview, January 2007.

7. Ludlow and Ludlow in Frazier and O'Sullivan, *"We Have Just Begun,"* 190; Lee, "Bughouser Speaks," 3, 4.

8. Weaver, "The Story of CPS Unit No. 123," 4.

9. Sawyer, Letters, October 17, 1942.

10. Harold Barton, "Confidential," August 27, 1944, 1, Barton Manuscript Collections, CDGA, SCPC.

11. "Notes Prepared by F. Greenleaf," 2; Barton, "Confidential," 1.

12. Maechtle and Gerth, "Conscientious Objectors," 19.

13. "Observations and Evaluation of Experiences at Hudson River State Hospital, C.P.S. Unit #144," CPS History Unit Write-Ups, 1945, IX-12-1, MCA.

14. Maechtle and Gerth, "Conscientious Objectors," 20.

15. Eisen, *Pathways of Peace*, 214–15; Maechtle and Gerth, "Conscientious Objectors," 20.

16. Eisen, *Pathways of Peace*, 214–15.

17. Wilhelm in Frazier and O'Sullivan, *"We Have Just Begun,"* 175; Weaver, "The Story of CPS Unit No. 123," 4.

18. Ludlow and Ludlow in Frazier and O'Sullivan, *"We Have Just Begun,"* 190; Sawyer, interview, January 2007; Bill March, note to author, January 2007.

19. Zahn, *Another Part of the War*, 107.

20. Barton to Weisbord, September 5, 1966, 16.

21. Habegger, interview by Sprunger, August 13, 1974, MLA.

22. Ibid.

23. Delk, "October–November Report," 1; Linscheid, "Ward 41," 2; Wilhelm in Frazier and O'Sullivan, *"We Have Just Begun,"* 176.

24. Untitled, anonymous notes, June 20, 1944, 1, Barton Manuscript Collections, CDGA, SCPC.

25. Diary of French, March 19, 1943, SCPC.

26. Wolfe, "Pandemonium," 2–3; Holsopple, "Impressions."

27. See Chapter 9.

28. Van Dyck, *Exercise of Conscience*, 160.

29. See Goffman, *Asylums*.

30. AFSC, *Women's Service*, 3.

31. Taylor, "Custodians," 231.

32. Underwood, "Information," 3.

33. Harkey, "Norwich State Hospital," 2; Delk to Barton, February 8, 1945, Reel 36, BHLA.

34. Stevenson and Marsh, "Battle," 3.

35. Ibid., 5; Sawyer, Letters, February 5, 1945.

36. Sawyer, Letters, March 22, 1944.

37. Judith A. Bellafaire, "The Women's Army Corps: A Commemoration of World War II Service," CMH Publication 72-15, 20, http://www.army.mil/CMH/brochures/was/wac.htm.

38. "Women in War Jobs—Rosie the Riveter (1942–1945)," http://www.adcouncil.org/default.aspx?id=128.

39. DiBacco, Mason, and Appy, *History of the United States*, 1:421.

40. Nash, *American Odyssey*, 531.

41. Goossen, *Women Against the Good War*, 2–3.

42. Flynn, *Lewis B. Hershey*, 117–18.

43. NISBCO, *1996 Directory*, xv.

44. Goossen, *Women Against the Good War*, 129.

45. "Brethren Civilian Public Service, Personnel Data Summary," June 30, 1943, Reel 39, BHLA; Sawyer, Letters, July 2, 1945.

46. Dayton, "Open Letter."

47. *Anniversary Review*, 35.

48. Weaver, "The Story of CPS Unit No. 123," 2; H. Mishler, "Mt. Pleasant State Hospital," 2.

49. Ludlow and Ludlow in Frazier and O'Sullivan, *"We Have Just Begun,"* 187.

50. Van Dyck, *Exercise of Conscience*, 168.

51. Sawyer, Letters, March 22, 1944.

52. Stevenson and Marsh, "Battle," 2.

53. Mosemann, "Memorandum of Information," 1.

54. H. Mishler, "Mt. Pleasant State Hospital," 2; Dayton, "Open Letter"; Harkey, "Norwich State Hospital," 1.

55. "Civilian Public Service Unit 109"; F. Nelson Underwood, "Administrative Report for August–September 1944," October 13, 1944, 1, Reel 3, BHLA; Goossen, *Women Against the Good War*, 57–58.

56. Underwood, "Information," 3; Harkey, "Norwich State Hospital," 1; Goossen, *Women Against the Good War*, 57.

57. Goossen, *Women Against the Good War*, 101–2, 103.

58. AFSC, *Women's Service*, 1.

59. Goossen, *Women Against the Good War*, 104, 107.

60. Ibid., 107.

61. AFSC, *Women's Service*, 6.

62. Ibid., 2; Lois Barton, "The Sunnyside of Spencer Butte: A Different Peace," West by Northwest.org, October 5, 2005, http://westbynorthwest.org/artman/publish/printer_1226.shtml.

63. AFSC, *Women's Service*, 2; Alice Calder Miles, interview, February 2007; L. Barton, "Sunnyside," 2.

64. AFSC, *Women's Service*, 3–4.

65. Alice Calder Miles, interview, February 2007.

66. L. Barton, "Sunnyside," 2, 3.

67. Sawyer, Letters, March 22, 1944.

68. AFSC, *Women's Service*, 5.

69. L. Barton, "Sunnyside," 3.

70. Goossen, *Women Against the Good War*, 105.

71. Gingerich, *Service for Peace*, 229, 235; E. H. Crawfis, "History of CPS Unit #69," 2–3, CPS History Unit Write-Ups, 1945, IX-12-1, MCA; "Evaluation of the Women's Summer Service Unit Which Served at Hudson River State Hospital, Poughkeepsie, N.Y.," 2, Women's Service Unit Poughkeepsie, IX-12-1, MCA.

72. Goossen, *Women Against the Good War*, 101–2.

73. "Evaluation of the Women's Summer Service Unit," 2.

74. For information on the history of the Hudson River State Hospital women's unit, see ibid. and the following documents: "Interview with Dr. Ross, Superintendent of the Hudson River State Hospital," "Comments of Mr. Faust, R.N., Superintendent of Nurses, Hudson River State Hospital," and Bertran Smucker, "The Poughkeepsie Summer Unit," August 31, 1945, Women's Service Unit Poughkeepsie, 1945, IX-12-1, MCA.

75. "Evaluation of the Women's Summer Service Unit," 4.

76. Ibid., 5.

77. "Excerpts from the Daily Logs as Recorded by Poughkeepsie Women's Summer Service Unit Members," 3, Women's Service Unit Poughkeepsie Daily Logs, IX-12-1, MCA.

78. Ibid., 4.

79. "Response of Poughkeepsie Unit Members to the Mimeographed Questionnaire," 3, Women's Service Unit Poughkeepsie Questionnaire, IX-12-1, MCA.

80. Robert Bogdan and Steven J. Taylor, "Relationships with Severely Disabled People: The Social Construction of Humanness."

81. "Excerpts from the Daily Logs," 1.

82. "Poughkeepsie Questionnaire," 4.

83. Goossen, *Women Against the Good War*, 104–5.

84. "Poughkeepsie Questionnaire," 4.

85. "Evaluation of the Women's Summer Service Unit," 6.

86. "Hudson River State Hospital," 4; Gingerich, *Service for Peace*, 229, 235.

87. Kosch to Dayton, May 25, 1946, Reel 36, BHLA.

88. Gingerich, *Service for Peace*, 231.

89. Crawfis, "Unit #69," 3; Arthur Noyes, "History of Civilian Public Service Unit No. 66"; Silas W. Weltmer, "History of CPS Unit #143, State Hospital, Spring Grove, Catonsville, Maryland"; R. E. Bushong, "History of CPS Unit #71, Lima State Hospital," all in CPS History Unit Write-Ups, 1945, IX-12-1, MCA.

90. U.S. Selective Service, *Reports of Superintendents of State Mental Hospitals on the Work of Conscientious Objectors* (Washington, D.C.: U.S. Selective Service, 1950), 216–19, 271–78. Excerpts reprinted in Schlissel, *Conscience in America*, 234–41.

91. Quoted in Schlissel, *Conscience in America*, 237, 235–36.

11. "The Exposé as a Progressive Tool"

1. Sareyan, *Turning Point*, 71–76; Sibley and Jacob, *Conscription of Conscience*, 161–62; "Say Patients Suffered Cold: Rough Handling, Unsanitary Conditions Charged," undated newspaper article;

"Board Reports of Maltreatment at Williamsburg, Staunton Hospitals," *Roanoke Times,* August 4, 1943, Reel 39, BHLA. Newspaper articles on the controversy in the BHLA often lack the names of the newspapers and dates.

2. Rothman, *Discovery of the Asylum,* 43, 130.

3. "Brutal Treatment Shows Need of C.O.'s in Hospitals," *Catholic Worker,* MC#001, Box 1057, Folder 4, ACLU Records.

4. Diary of French, July 28, 1943, SCPC.

5. Letter from Van Cleve Geiger, quoted in Sareyan, *Turning Point,* 73.

6. G. L. C., "The History of CPS Unit #44," 4.

7. "Girl Assails Treatment at Hospital," August 25, 1943; "Grand Jury Indicts Hospital Attendant for Manslaughter," August 26, 1943, Reel 39, BHLA.

8. "Brown Launches Counter-attack: Charges War Foes Mistreated Hospital Patients," August 21, 1943, ibid.

9. Ibid.

10. "State Board Disagrees with Dr. George Brown: Says Conscientious Objectors Are Needed as Hospital Attendants," August 23, 1943, ibid.

11. Ibid.; "Legion Steers Clear of Fight on Hospital," August 24, 1943, ibid.

12. "Removal Asked for Employees: Attendants Say 'Objectors' Mistreat Patients," August 30, 1943, ibid.

13. "State Board Ousts Heads of Hospitals: Virtual Rebuilding of Two Mental Institutions Is Favored," *Roanoke Times,* September 9, 1943, ibid.

14. "Brown Assails Hospital Board: Says Action 'Insulting'—Dr. Ztass Resigns," September 16, 1943, Reel 39, BHLA.

15. "Plan Submitted to Governor: Davis Urges Increase in Medical, Nursing Staff," October 1943, ibid.

16. *On the Record,* Ohio State Department of Public Welfare, June 1946, MC#001, Box 1057, Folder 18, ACLU Records.

17. Leland Bullen to Robert Cox and Willard Hetzel, March 26, 1943, Robert Cox Papers.

18. Robert Cox, "Re: Cleveland State Hospital," February 1, 1944, Cox Papers.

19. Ibid.

20. Robert Cox, "An Approximation of My Testimony Before the Cleveland Grand Jury on March 9, 1945," March 15, 1945, 1, Cox Papers.

21. Maisel, "Bedlam, 1946," 115–16; Sareyan, *Turning Point,* 66–71.

22. Cox, "Approximation of My Testimony," 2; "Dr. Lee Loses a Patient," *Cleveland Press,* November 20, 1943, Cox Papers.

23. "For a Real Investigation," October 30, 1943; "Hospital Inquiry Committee Asked: Ministers Want Group to Study Institute Conditions," November 1, 1943; "Bricker Acts in Beating Quiz: Opposes Removal of Hospital Witnesses," November 11, 1943; "Hits State Hospital Report of Mooney: Baptist Leader Says Conditions 'Whitewashed,'" November 23, 1943, all *Cleveland Press,* in Cox Papers.

24. "Dr. Lee Should Be Removed," *Cleveland Press,* November 10, 1943, Cox Papers.

25. "Dr. Lee Loses a Patient."

26. Gingerich, *Service for Peace,* 223.

27. "Letter of Transmittal, Hal H. Griswold to Hon. John W. Bricker," November 20, 1944, in *Report of the Governor's Committee on the Mental Health Program for Ohio,* 1944, Cox Papers.

28. Justin to Bob and Martha, February 12, 1944, Cox Papers.

29. Ibid.; Cox, "Re: Cleveland State Hospital"; Martha Cox, "Re: Cleveland State Hospital," February 1, 1944; Justin to Bob, February 6, 1944, all in Cox Papers.

30. "Memorandum on Cleveland State Hospital," 1, 3, ibid.

31. Typewritten copy of newspaper article, "Church Leader Cites Brutality to Mentally Ill: Dr. Sharpe's Report Says State Hospital Conditions Worse"; typewritten copy of editorial, "The Committee Should Act," both *Cleveland Press*, March 7, 1944, Cox Papers.

32. Typewritten copy of article, "Claims Mentally Ill Undernourished: Charges Filed by Church Federation President," *Cleveland Press*, March 13, 1944.

33. Christine Conway Reese, interview, June 2004; Sareyan, *Turning Point*, 183.

34. "Lee Quits as Asylum Head: Woman Aide Cites Abuses," July 1, 1944; "Doctor Silenced by Ouster Threat: Says Lee Prevented Criticism of Mental Hospital," July 3, 1944, both *Cleveland Press*, in Cox Papers.

35. Albert Deutsch, "Shame of the States: Ohio Officials Bare Defects in Their Mental Hospitals," *PM*, April 26, 1946, 12, Cox Papers.

36. Editorial cartoon, "'You Tell 'Em, Governor!': Campaign Promises to People of Ohio to Institute State Hospital Reform," *Cleveland Press*, March 29, 1945, Cox Papers.

37. Cox, "Approximation of My Testimony"; "Grand Jury Subpoena, the State of Ohio, Cuyahoga Common Pleas to Mr. Robert Cox, 8th day of March A.D. 1945," Cox Papers.

38. "Jury Blasts State Hospital: Indicts 3 Former Attendants for Assault; Hits Brutality," *Cleveland Press*, March 28, 1945, Cox Papers.

39. "*Special Presentment* to the Honorable Samuel H. Silbert, Presiding Judge of the Criminal Branch of the Court of Common Please," Regular Grand Jury of Cuyahoga County, March 1945, 1–2, 7–8, Cox Papers.

40. "Jury Blasts State Hospital."

41. "*Life* Hails Press Exposé of Mentally Ill Care," *Cleveland Press*, May 4, 1946, Cox Papers.

42. Crawfis, "History of CPS Unit #69," 1.

43. Ibid.; P. Goering, interview by K. Goering, December 26, 1975, MLA; Wasser, interview by Kroeker, November 29, 1989, MLA.

44. Wasser, interview by Kroeker, November 29, 1989, MLA.

45. Vernon Rocke to Harmon Wilkinson, February 22, 1946; Leonard Boehs, "Work of National Importance," Cox Papers.

46. Crawfis, "History of CPS Unit #69," 1.

47. Rocke to Wilkinson, February 22, 1946.

48. P. Goering, interview by K. Goering, December 26, 1975, MLA.

49. "The ??? ???," Cleveland State Hospital, June 7, 1946, 3, Camp 69, DG 002, SCPC.

50. Deutsch, "Shame of the States: Ohio"; Albert Deutsch, *The Shame of the States*, 12–13.

51. John H. Mosemann, "Memorandum of Information" (see chap. 9, n. 51).

52. Earl Leinbach to Albert Gaeddert; Leinbach to Gaeddert; Gaeddert to Leinbach, all August 1, 1944, C.P.S. and other Corr. 1940–45, 86 Director, IX-6-3, MCA.

53. Leinbach to Gaeddert, July 31, 1944, ibid.

54. Typewritten letter, "To the Editor," *Des Moines Register*, July 31, 1944, ibid.

55. Leinbach to Gaeddert, July 31, 1944.

56. Copy of a statement "Dr. Soucek suggested we make to the press"; Leinbach to Gaeddert, August 2, 1944, ibid.

57. Leinbach to Gaeddert, July 31, 1944.

58. Leinbach to Board of Control of State Institutions, August 3, 1944, ibid.

59. Members of the C.P.S. Unit to all Mt. Pleasant State Hospital Employees, August 4, 1944, ibid.

60. Typewritten editorial, "Caring for Our Insane," *Davenport Paper,* August 2, 1944; typewritten letter to the editor, "Board of Directors Replies to Attack on a Hospital," *Des Moines Register,* August 4, 1944; typewritten editorial, "As Viewed from Here," *Iowa City Press-Citizen,* August 7, 1944; typewritten letters to the editor: Alton Koch, "Pastor Defends Insane Hospital," August 8, 1944, and F. E. Weitz, "Care of the Insane," *Des Moines Register,* August 8, 1944, all ibid.

61. Leinbach to Reuter, August 14, 1944, ibid.

62. Typewritten article, "Pastor Calls for Probe of Mental Care," *Des Moines Sunday Register,* November 26, 1944; Leinbach to Robert Kreider, November 28, 1944, both ibid.

63. Leinbach to Gaeddert, August 2, 1944; H. Mishler, "Mt. Pleasant State Hospital."

64. *Providence Rhode Island Bulletin,* 1943, quoted in Sareyan, *Turning Point,* 123.

65. G. D. S., "Description of CPS Unit #144—Hudson River State Hospital," July 9, 1945, 1, CPS Unit History Write-Ups, 1945, IX-12-1, MCA; Wasser, interview by Kroeker, November 29, 1989, MLA; Gingerich, *Service for Peace,* 242–46; Sareyan, *Turning Point,* 91–94.

66. Dave Shank, "Story and Evaluation of Civilian Public Service Unit 144," 4, CPS Unit History Write-Ups, 1945, IX-12-1, MCA.

67. Wasser, interview by Kroeker, November 29, 1989, MLA.

68. E. Schrag, interview by T. Schrag, September 13, 1974, MLA.

69. Ibid.

70. "Comments of Mr. Faust, Superintendent of Nurses, Hudson River State Hospital," Women's Service Unit, Poughkeepsie, Applications and Evaluations, Hudson River State Hospital, IX-12-1, MCA. These comments were recorded during an evaluation of the Women's Service Unit at Hudson River.

71. Sareyan, *Turning Point,* 93.

72. Habegger, interview by Sprunger, August 13, 1974, MLA.

73. Sareyan, *Turning Point,* 93. A note by Dennis Stoesz, MCA archivist, indicates that "Mary Ramseyer" was instrumental in inviting Eleanor Roosevelt to visit the hospital (Hist. Mss. 5-3 Small Archives Collection, MCA). Edna Ramseyer was director of the MCC women's summer service unit there. Ramseyer had been a faculty member at Mennonite Bluffton and Goshen colleges and had been a founder of the women's summer service unit program (Goossen, *Women Against the Good War,* 101).

74. E. Schrag, interview by T. Schrag, September 13, 1974, MLA.

75. "Mrs. Roosevelt Told COs Raised HRSH Standards: 'Practices' Uncovered, Writer Hears," *Poughkeepsie New Yorker,* July 11, 1945, 1.

76. "Dark Outlook," *Poughkeepsie New Yorker,* July 15, 1945, A10.

77. Ralph S. Lehman, "Observations and Evaluation of Experiences at Hudson River State Hospital, C.P.S. Unit #144," 1, CPS Unit History Write-Ups, 1945, IX-12-1, MCA.

78. "Evaluation of the Women's Service Unit which served at Hudson River State Hospital, Poughkeepsie, N.Y.," 4, Women's Service Unit, Poughkeepsie, Applications and Evaluations, Hudson River State Hospital; J. Willard Linscheid, "An Evaluation of the Work Done on Ward 41 Edgewood Service at Hudson River State Hospital," 3, CPS Unit History Write-Ups, 1945, both ibid.

79. Weisbord, *Some Form of Peace,* 49, 35.

80. Sawyer, Letters, January 21, 1946.

81. Ibid., February 5, 1946.

82. Lord, interview, February 2007.

83. Sawyer, Letters, February 5, 1946.

84. "Head of Byberry Says B Building Still Is Disgrace: Dank, Overcrowded Building Gets Dregs of Mental Cases," *Philadelphia Record*, February 10, 1946, 1–2.

85. Sawyer, Letters, February 19, 1946.

86. Sawyer to Miss Sophie O'Hara, February 17, 1946, ibid.

87. "The Mental Hygiene Program of the Civilian Public Service, Special Progress and Action Report #13," July 24, 1945, 1, Barton Manuscript Collections, CDGA, SCPC.

88. Albert Deutsch, "The Nation's Shame: Sick Minds on the Rack . . . Byberry Hospital: Case History in Barbarism"; "Mental Patients Rot in Philadelphia's 'Bedlam,'" *PM*, April 17, 1946, 10–13; Albert Deutsch, "Filth-Infested Byberry Cured Only Two Out of 5,900 Patients in Year: New Buildings, More and Better Attendants Needed for Hospital," *PM*, April 18, 1946, Barton Manuscript Collections, CDGA, SCPC.

89. Chapter 12 contains background on Deutsch's and Maisel's exposés.

90. "Convicts Fare Better than Insane: CO's Seeking to Ease Lives of Mental Patients," *Philadelphia Record*, May 9, 1946, Barton Manuscript Collections, CDGA, SCPC.

91. Quoted in Deutsch, *Shame of the States*, 45.

92. Ibid., 45–48 (quote on 47).

93. Weisbord, *Some Form of Peace*, 48.

94. Barton to O'Hara, May 20, 1946, Barton Manuscript Collections, CDGA, SCPC.

95. Weisbord, *Some Form of Peace*, 49.

96. U.S. Bureau of the Census, *Patients in Mental Institutions, 1946*, 209.

97. Stephen L. Angell, "Training Schools and CPS," *Reporter* 3, no. 2 (July 15, 1944): 3–5.

98. "Participation in MHP: Materials Received for Summary Statement and *The Attendant* to 1/24/46," January 24, 1946, IX-12-1, VII, MCA.

99. "Pennhurst Visit," November 9, 1945, Barton Manuscript Collections, CDGA, SCPC.

100. Quoted in Wilhelm, *Civilian Public Servants*, 21.

101. *Halderman v. Pennhurst State School and Hospital*, 446 F. Supp. 1295 (E.D. Pa. 1977); *Romeo v. Youngberg*, 457 U.S. 307 (1982). See also Chapter 15.

102. Angell, "Training Schools and CPS."

103. Trent, *Inventing the Feeble Mind*, 67, 166.

104. Review of *American Journal of Mental Deficiency* issues from 1944 through 1947 by the author.

105. Channing B. Richardson, "A Hundred Thousand Defectives," *Christian Century*, January 23, 1946, http://www.disabilitymuseum.org/lib/docs/1717.htm, Disability History Museum, http://www.disabilitymuseum.org.

106. Sareyan, *Turning Point*, 79–82.

107. "Comment: Newspaper Crusades," *American Journal of Psychiatry* 105, no. 12 (1949): 938–39.

108. Dain, *Clifford W. Beers*, 279–81.

109. Julius Schreiber, "Albert Deutsch—Crusader, 1905–1961," 473–82.

110. Tichi, *Exposés and Excess*, 3, 69, 76.

111. Albert Deutsch, review of *Jacob A. Riis: Police Reporter, Reformer, Useful Citizen,* by Louise Ware, *Mental Hygiene* 24, no. 4 (1940): 668; Karl A. Menninger, introduction to *Shame of the States,* by Deutsch, 15–24.

112. Deutsch, *Shame of the States*, 10–11.

113. Ibid., 11.

114. Deutsch, *Mentally Ill,* 449.

115. Schreiber, "Albert Deutsch—Crusader," 477, 473.

116. Albert Deutsch, "The Exposé as a Progressive Tool," 80, 84.

12. "They Were Fighting Everybody"

1. The profiles of Barton, Edelstein, Hetzel, and Steer are based on information in NISBCO's *1996 Directory.* NSBRO first published the directory in 1947. It was updated by NISBCO in 1996, with current addresses of CPS men, if available.

2. Weisbord, *Some Form of Peace,* 26–51; Weisbord, interview, July 10, 2006.

3. Barton to Weisbord, September 5, 1966, 14.

4. Harold Barton, "First Impressions," February 2, 1944, Barton Manuscript Collections, CDGA, SCPC; Barton to Weisbord, September 5, 1966, 14.

5. Report on a meeting on June 26, 1944, Mental Hygiene Program of the CPS, "Progress and Action Report #2," National Mental Health Foundation, IX-12-1, MCA.

6. Weisbord, *Some Form of Peace,* 35.

7. Mental Hygiene Program of the CPS, "Progress and Action Report #2," 1; Weisbord, *Some Form of Peace,* 35.

8. Edelstein to Assistant Directors, May 8, 1944, Mental Hygiene Program of the CPS, IX-12-1, MCA.

9. Mental Hygiene Program of the CPS, "Part I: The Monthly Inter-unit Publication," ibid.

10. Mental Hygiene Program of the CPS, "Part II: Summary Statement of Conditions," reprint, May 17, 1945.

11. Mental Hygiene Program of the CPS, "Progress and Action Report #1," May 26, 1944.

12. Mental Hygiene Program of the CPS, "Progress and Action Report #3," July 18, 1944, 1.

13. Mental Hygiene Program of the CPS, "Progress and Action Report #2," 1.

14. *Attendant* 1, no. 1 (June 1944): 7, DG 02, Sec. 3, Box 11, SCPC.

15. Weisbord, *Some Form of Peace,* 35–36.

16. Mental Hygiene Program of the CPS, "Report #3," 2.

17. Mental Hygiene Program of the CPS, "Progress and Action Report #4," August 4, 1944, IX-12-1, MCA.

18. Mental Hygiene Program of the CPS, "Progress and Action Report No. 6," October 21, 1944, ibid.

19. George Stevenson to Roger N. Baldwin, March 19, 1941, MC#001, Box 1057, Folder 2, ACLU Records.

20. Winfred Overholser to Clifford Forster, August 30, 1944, ibid., Folder 6.

21. *Attendant* 1, no. 2 (July 1944), DG 02, Sec. 3, Box 11, SCPC.

22. Weisbord, *Some Form of Peace,* 42.

23. Barton to Weisbord, September 5, 1966, 17; Weisbord, *Some Form of Peace,* 37–38.

24. Diary of French, August 10, 14, 1944, SCPC.

25. Richard W. Reuter, "Report CPS Hospital Conference," October 27, 1944, Barton Manuscript Collections, CDGA, SCPC.

26. National Mental Health Foundation, "Financial Development of the National Mental Health Foundation," January 30, 1948, National Mental Health Foundation (NMHF), IX-12-1, MCA.

27. "Mental Hygiene Program of CPS, to Unit Representatives," April 23, 1945, ibid.

28. Barton to Weisbord, September 5, 1966, 19; Weisbord, *Some Form of Peace*, 41.

29. Weisbord, *Some Form of Peace*, 39.

30. Hal Barton, "Unit Representatives Who Receive the *Exchange Service* and Other MHP Educational Materials," June 25, 1945, Mental Hygiene Program of the CPS, IX-12-1, MCA.

31. Mental Hygiene Program of the CPS, "Special Progress and Action Report #13," July 24, 1945, 2, Barton Manuscript Collections, CDGA, SCPC.

32. Mental Hygiene Program of the CPS, "Progress and Action Report #17," November 10, 1945, IX-12-1, MCA.

33. French to Barton, November 19, 1945, Barton Manuscript Collections, CDGA, SCPC; Diary of French, November 19, 1945, SCPC.

34. See, for example, Barton to Stevenson, "Re: Activities, May, 1945," June 11, 1945; "Pennhurst Visit," November 5, 1945; Barton to Claude Shotts, October 20, 1945, Barton Manuscript Collections, CDGA, SCPC; Barton to all hospitals and training schools, April 17, 1945, Mental Hygiene Program of the CPS, IX-12-, MCA.

35. Phil Steer, *Psychiatric Aid*, October 10, 1946, Mental Hygiene Program of the CPS, IX-12-1, MCA; National Mental Health Foundation, Board Meeting, October 11, 1946, Supplement 1, 3, Barton Manuscript Collections, CDGA, SCPC.

36. Mental Hygiene Program of the CPS, *CPS Attendant Handbook*, April 1945, IX-12-1, MCA.

37. Mental Hygiene Program of the CPS, *Handbook of Restraint*, preliminary draft, December 20, 1945, ibid.

38. Listings or copies of pamphlets may be found at the MCA: Mental Hygiene Program of the CPS, IX-12-1, MCA.

39. Leonard Edelstein to Orie Miller, February 22, 1946, MCC Corres., 1945–47, File 31, 1946, IX-6-3, MCA.

40. Harold Barton, "Guide to the Preparation of Material for the 'Summary Statement of Conditions,'" Barton Manuscript Collections, CDGA, SCPC; Mental Hygiene Program of the CPS, "Ways and Means to Increase Participation in Mental Hygiene Program of CPS," January 24, 1946; Mental Hygiene Program of the CPS, "Participation in MHP: Materials Received for 'Summary Statement' and the *Attendant* to 1/24/46," January 24, 1946, latter two in IX-12-1, MCA.

41. "All in the Day's Mail—Things That Need Not Be," July 13, 1945, Barton Manuscript Collections, CDGA, SCPC.

42. Phil Steer, "Interdepartmentals," Barton Manuscript Collections, CDGA, SCPC.

43. "The Mental Hygiene Program of Civilian Public Service," DG 02, SCPC; French, *Four Year Report*, 10.

44. Len, Wil, Hal, and Phil, "MHP on the Move—a Special Release," August 8, 1945, 1, Mental Hygiene Program of the CPS, IX-12-1, MCA.

45. Ibid., 2.

46. Leonard Edelstein, *We Are Accountable: A View of Mental Institutions*, Pamphlet no. 24 (Pendle Hill, 1945), Reel 2, 0788, Eleanor Roosevelt Papers.

47. Eleanore Price Mather, *Pendle Hill: A Quaker Experiment in Education and Community*.

48. Weisbord, *Some Form of Peace*, 43.

49. Ibid., 44.

50. Eleanor Roosevelt letter to seventeen persons, October 31, 1945; Thomas Parran to Eleanor Roosevelt, November 9, 1945, both Reel 2, 0788, Eleanor Roosevelt Papers.

51. "Mental Hygiene Program of CPS: Special Emergency Release," Reel 34, BHLA.

52. "The National Mental Health Foundation, Board Meeting—October 11, 1946, Supplement I," 2, Barton Manuscript Collections, CDGA, SCPC.

53. Barton to Weisbord, September 5, 1966, 19–21; Weisbord, *Some Form of Peace,* 41–42.

54. Barton to Weisbord, September 5, 1966, 19.

55. Ibid., 20–21.

56. "Interdepartmental," November 21, 1945, Barton Manuscript Collections, CDGA, SCPC.

57. *Psychiatric Aid* 3, no. 2 (February 1946): 1, IX-12-1, MCA.

58. National Mental Health Foundation, "Organization of the National Mental Health Foundation, Incorporated," ibid.

59. "Drive Opens to Assist Mentally Ill: Health Unit Asks Higher Standards," *Philadelphia Inquirer,* May 6, 1946, 17.

60. Sareyan, *Turning Point,* 148.

61. Maisel, "Bedlam, 1946," 102, 103.

62. Ibid., 103, 104–5.

63. Erika Doss, introduction to *Looking at "Life" Magazine,* edited by Doss, 7; Maisel, "Bedlam, 1946," 105.

64. Maisel, "Bedlam, 1946," 118.

65. Albert Q. Maisel, "The Shame of Our Mental Hospitals."

66. Terry Smith, "Life-style Modernity: Making Modern America," in *Looking at "Life" Magazine,* edited by Doss, 27.

67. Doss, introduction to *Looking at "Life" Magazine,* edited by Doss, 2–3.

68. James L. Baughman, "Who Read *Life*? The Circulation of America's Favorite Magazine," in *Looking at "Life" Magazine,* edited by Doss, 42, 45.

69. Doss, introduction to *Looking at "Life" Magazine,* edited by Doss, 11.

70. Weisbord, *Some Form of Peace,* 45.

71. Quoted in ibid., 45–46; Barton to Weisbord, September 5, 1966, 21.

72. Barton to Norman Whitney, September 8, 1946, Barton Manuscript Collections, CDGA, SCPC.

73. Mental Hygiene Program of the CPS, "Special Progress and Action Report #13."

74. Lord, interview, February 2007.

75. Diary of French, May 17, 1946, SCPC.

13. "Mental Hospitals Are Again under Fire"

1. Deutsch, *Shame of the States,* 166, 168.

2. "Herded Like Cattle," December 20, 1948, *Time* Magazine Archives.

3. Deutsch, *Shame of the States,* 177–78.

4. Mike Gorman, "Oklahoma Attacks Its Snake Pits," *Reader's Digest* 53, no. 317 (September 1948): 139–60.

5. Gorman, "Oklahoma," 143.

6. Maine, *If a Man Be Mad,* 415–16.

7. "Mad Man," April 28, 1947, 2, *Time* Magazine Archives.

8. Mary Jane Ward, *The Snake Pit,* 217.

9. "Snakes and Ladies," May 6, 1946, *Time* Magazine Archives.

10. "Shocker," December 20, 1948, 1, ibid.

11. Ibid., 1; Reese, interview, July 2004.

12. "Shocker," 3.

13. Samuel W. Hamilton, "Life in Our Mental Hospitals—Its Meaning for the Individual," *Mental Hygiene* 27, no. 1 (January 1943), 9.

14. Edith G. G. Graff, "Let Those Called Ex-Patients Speak: Tell the Facts to the Public, Says Physician," *Churchman,* January 15, 1945, MC#001, Box 1057, Folder 11, ACLU Records.

15. Deutsch, *Shame of the States,* 168–69.

16. Ibid., 169; George S. Stevenson, "Attacks on Mental Hospitals," *Mental Hygiene* 30, no. 3 (July 1946): 353–54.

17. Stevenson, "Attacks on Mental Hospitals," 353–54.

18. NCMH, *Annual Report, 1946,* 23–24, MC#001, Box 1057, Folder 14, ACLU Records.

19. Ibid., 24.

20. Ibid., 25.

21. "This Shame" (see chap. 8, n. 79).

22. Edith Stern, "Mental Hospitals, 1946," *Mental Hygiene* 31, no. 2 (April 1947): 185.

23. Frank Fremont-Smith, "New Opportunities for the Improvement of Mental Hospitals," *Mental Hygiene* 31, no. 3 (July 1947): 354–62 (quotes on 359).

24. George S. Stevenson, "Mental Health—a Look Ahead," *Mental Hygiene* 32, no. 3 (July 1948): 353–63.

25. "Fanning the Fire," August 30, 1948, *Time* Magazine Archives.

26. "Presentation of the Lasker Award in Mental Hygiene," *Mental Hygiene* 31, no. 1 (January 1947): 121.

27. "Standards for Psychiatric Hospitals and Out-Patient Clinics Approved by the American Psychiatric Association (1945–46)," *American Journal of Psychiatry* 102 (September 1945): 264–69.

28. Deutsch, *Shame of the States,* 170.

29. National Mental Health Foundation, "Current Developments in Mental Health," September 11, 1946, IX-12-1, VI, MCA.

30. Deutsch, *Shame of the States,* 170.

31. Ralph H. Chambers, "Inspection and Rating for Mental Hospitals," *American Journal of Psychiatry* 106 (October 1949): 251.

32. Deutsch, *Shame of the States,* 172; William L. Russell, review of *Shame of the States,* by Deutsch, *Mental Hygiene* 106 (February 1950): 636–37.

33. Deutsch, *Shame of the States,* 172; Karl M. Bowman, "Presidential Address," *American Journal of Psychiatry* 103 (July 1946): 15.

34. Bowman, "Presidential Address," 15, 16.

35. Leo H. Bartemeier, "The Psychiatric Foundation: Introductory Remarks," *American Journal of Psychiatry* 104 (September 1947): 145–47; Deutsch, *Shame of the States,* 173; Gerald N. Grob, *From Asylum to Community: Mental Health Policy in America,* 84.

36. "News and Notes," *American Journal of Psychiatry* 104 (February 1948): 582.

37. John C. Whitehorn, "Comment: The Central Inspection Board," *American Journal of Psychiatry* 107 (March 1951): 789.

38. Grob, *From Asylum to Community,* 84.

39. Ibid., 3, 28, 32.

40. Ibid., 32–33; Samuel W. Hamilton, "Presidential Address: Our Association in a Time of Unsettlement," *American Journal of Psychiatry* 104 (July 1947): 7.

41. Grob, *From Asylum to Community,* 33.

42. *APA Newsletter,* September 1949, APA Archives. "Historical APA Newsletters" from June 15, 1948, to November 15, 1949, were retrieved from the American Psychiatric Association's Web site (http://www.psych.org/public_info/libr_publ/) in 2007. These newsletters are no longer publicly available on this Web site.

43. *APA Newsletter,* April 1949.

44. "Program of the Mental Hospital Institute of the American Psychiatric Association, April 11–15, 1949," Barton Manuscript Collections, CDGA, SCPC.

45. *APA Newsletter,* September 1949, APA Archives.

46. Grob, *From Asylum to Community,* 42.

47. "Psychiatric Aide of the Year," *Psychiatric Aid* 4, no. 12 (December 1947): 3, IX-12-1, MCA.

48. "Rules Governing the Award," *Psychiatric Aid* 4, no. 7 (July 1947): 10, ibid.

49. National Mental Health Foundation, "The Psychiatric Aide of the Year Award for 1949," IX-12-1, VI, MCA.

50. "She Unlocked the Doors at Monson State," *Psychiatric Aide* 8, no. 3 (March 1951): 3, IX-12-1, MCA.

51. "Psychiatric Aide of the Year," 3, 4.

52. Grob, *From Asylum to Community,* 76, 90.

53. "Psychiatric Aide of the Year," 6.

54. "Presentation of the Lasker Award," 122.

55. Grob, *From Asylum to Community,* 25, 28.

56. "Are You Always Worrying?" October 25, 1948, 1, *Time* Magazine Archives.

57. Grob, *From Asylum to Community,* 74.

58. Menninger, introduction to *Shame of the States,* by Deutsch, 19, 24, 18.

59. Karl A. Menninger, "Letters to the Editor," *Psychiatric Aide* 8, no. 2 (February 1951): 7, IX-12-1, MCA.

60. Grob, *From Asylum to Community,* 83.

61. Your Oregonian Friend to Dick Hunter, November 9, 1948, Barton Manuscript Collections, CDGA, SCPC; Grob, *From Asylum to Community,* 85.

62. Your Oregonian Friend to Dick Hunter.

63. Grob, *From Asylum to Community,* 90; "History," Menninger, http://www.menningerclinic.com/about/Menninger-history.htm.

64. "Arousing Public Support for Improvement of Mental Health Facilities, NMHF Reprint No. 22," 2, IX-12-1, MCA.

65. "Psychiatric Aide of the Year," 6.

66. National Mental Health Foundation, "Report of the Executive Secretary, the National Mental Health Foundation, May 1948," IX-12-1, MCA; Bernard H. Hall et al., *Psychiatric Aide Education;* "The Menninger Foundation School for Psychiatric Aides," *Mental Hygiene* 33, no. 4 (October 1949): 678.

67. *Psychiatric Aid* 2, no. 10 (October 1947): 2, IX-12-1, MCA.

68. Hall et al., *Psychiatric Aide Education,* 15–16.

69. Ward Miles and Alice Calder Miles, interview, February 1, 2007.

70. Hall et al., *Psychiatric Aide Education,* 109–10; *Report of Psychiatric Aide Education Research Project, Conducted for The Rockefeller Foundation under the Auspices of the Menninger Foundation at Topeka, Kansas, 1 January 1948 to 1 July 1948,* Ward Miles Papers.

71. Hall et al., *Psychiatric Aide Education,* 16.

72. "Report of the Executive Secretary, May 1948."

73. Hall et al., *Psychiatric Aide Education*, 18.

74. Barton to Stevenson, June 11, 1945, 2.

75. Paul Harris to Barton, Barton Manuscript Collections, CDGA, SCPC.

76. Council of the American Psychiatric Association, "Psychiatric Aides Position Statement," approved November 1955, Document Reference no. 550001.

77. Hall et al., *Psychiatric Aide Education*, 18–19.

78. Grob, *From Asylum to Community*, 161–62.

79. Hall et al., *Psychiatric Aide Education*, 19.

80. Ibid., 20.

81. Ibid., 166.

82. Ibid., 109–10.

83. "History," Menninger.

14. "Another Growing Pain"

1. Lord, interview, February 2007; Ward Miles, interview, February 2007; Sawyer, interview, January 2007.

2. Weisbord, *Some Form of Peace*, 43.

3. Hetzel to Brothers, November 1, 1945, Barton Manuscript Collections, CDGA, SCPC; Len to Staff, "Complaints of Sending Out Material Before Cleared by Other Members of Staff" (a handwritten note at the top of this memo read "Oct. 1945?"), Barton Manuscript Collections, CDGA, SCPC.

4. Edelstein to Roy Kepler, October 10, 1945, Barton Manuscript Collections, CDGA, SCPC.

5. Hetzel to Brothers.

6. Lord, interview, February 2007; Ward Miles, interview, February 2007; Sawyer, interview, January 2007.

7. Steer to Len, November 12, 1945, Barton Manuscript Collections, CDGA, SCPC.

8. Barton to Whitney, September 8, 1946, Barton Manuscript Collections, CDGA, SCPC.

9. "Conclusions of Associates' Meeting, June 10, 1946," Barton Manuscript Collections, CDGA, SCPC.

10. Len to Wil, Hal, and Phil, June 5, 1946, ibid.

11. Ibid.

12. Ibid.

13. Barton to Whitney, September 8, 1946.

14. Ibid. See also Barton to Weisbord, "Answers to Questions to Hal Barton," October 29, 1966, Barton Manuscript Collections, CDGA, SCPC.

15. Barton to Whitney, September 8, 1946.

16. "Ex. Sec. Files—Personnel—R. M., Sept. '48," Barton Manuscript Collections, CDGA, SCPC.

17. "Board Meeting—October 11, 1946, Supplement I."

18. "Board of Directors, the National Mental Health Foundation, Minutes of Meeting of October 11, 1946," Barton Manuscript Collections, CDGA, SCPC.

19. Baldwin to Barton, October 8, 1946, MC#001, Box 1057, Folder 15, ACLU Records.

20. Stephen Thiermann to Mrs. Eleanor Roosevelt, August 20, 1946; Eleanor Roosevelt to Mrs. Harriman, September 12, 1946; Barton to Mrs. Eleanor Roosevelt, September 24, 1946, Reel 7, 0464, Eleanor Roosevelt Papers.

21. "Minutes of Meeting of October 11, 1946."

22. "Board Meeting—October 11, 1946, Supplement I."

23. "The National Mental Health Foundation," Barton Manuscript Collections, CDGA, SCPC. The prospectus is also contained in the Ward Miles Papers.

24. Barton to Weisbord, August 29, 1966, 18–19; Will to Hal, September 19, 1946, Barton Manuscript Collections, CDGA, SCPC.

25. "By-laws, National Mental Health Foundation, Incorporated," IX-12-1, MCA.

26. "Minutes of the Executive Council, October 9, 1946, Amending By-laws," ibid.

27. "By-laws, National Mental Health Foundation, Incorporated," January 8, 1947, ibid.

28. Board of Directors, "Minutes of Meeting of October 11, 1946," Barton Manuscript Collections, CDGA, SCPC.

29. "The National Mental Health Foundation," October 8, 1946, IX-12-1, MCA.

30. "Report of Dallas Pratt, M.D., to the First Annual Meeting of Members," February 14, 1947, 2, IX-12-1, VII, MCA.

31. "Board Meeting—October 11, 1946, Supplement I."

32. Barton to Mrs. Franklin Roosevelt, "1947 Financial Resume," March 25, 1947, Reel 16, 0134, Eleanor Roosevelt Papers.

33. "The National Mental Health Foundation, Inc., Summary of Income Expense January 1, 1946 Through July 31, 1946," IX-12-1, MCA.

34. Harold Barton, "Memorandum to Advisors and Supporters, December 5, 1946," IX-12-1, VII, MCA.

35. Harold Barton, "A Day of New Beginnings," January 29, 1947, Barton Manuscript Collections, CDGA, SCPC.

36. Bill Kenney to Staff, May 1947, IX-12-1, MCA; Harold Barton, "Proposed Budget for 1947," November 16, 1946, ibid.

37. Barton to Roosevelt, "1947 Financial Resume."

38. Barton to Mrs. Franklin Roosevelt, "Gifts and Contributions—1947," February 25, 1947, Reel 16, 0134, Eleanor Roosevelt Papers; Harold Barton, "Memorandum," September 19, 1947, IX-12-1, IV, MCA.

39. Barton to Roosevelt, "Gifts and Contributions—1947."

40. Barton, "Memorandum."

41. "Meeting of the Board of Directors, National Mental Health Foundation," September 28, 1948, IX-12-1, III, MCA.

42. National Mental Health Foundation, *Third Annual Report,* February 11, 1949, 2, ibid.

43. National Mental Health Foundation, "Minute [*sic*] of Board Meeting," March 19, 1948, IX-12-1, IV, MCA.

44. National Mental Health Foundation, *Third Annual Report,* 2.

45. Willard Hetzel, "Memorandum on Long-Term Objectives, Organizational Structure, Staff Responsibilities, Morale, and Compensation," May 9, 1948, Barton Manuscript Collections, CDGA, SCPC.

46. "The National Mental Health Foundation."

47. Barton, "Memorandum."

48. National Mental Health Foundation, *Third Annual Report,* 4–5.

49. National Mental Health Foundation, *Annual Report, 1949,* April, 1950, 6, IX-12-1, VI, MCA.

50. National Mental Health Foundation, *Third Annual Report,* 5.

51. National Mental Health Foundation, *Annual Report, 1949*, 12.

52. National Mental Health Foundation, *Third Annual Report*, 6–7.

53. Willard C. Hetzel and C. Lloyd Bailey, *The Mental Health Laws of Ohio: A Brief of the Statutes* (Philadelphia: National Mental Health Foundation, 1949), MC#001, Box 1058, Folder 5, ACLU Records.

54. National Mental Health Foundation, *Third Annual Report*, 7; National Mental Health Foundation, *Annual Report, 1949*.

55. National Mental Health Foundation, *Annual Report, 1949*, 13.

56. National Mental Health Foundation, "Analysis of Radio Project—Series I," October 10, 1946, IX-12-1, MCA.

57. National Mental Health Foundation, "Hats Off to Sarge!" Series I—Program 5, 1946, ibid.; "Columbia Broadcasting System Presents *Mind in the Shadow*," 1949, Barton Manuscript Collections, CDGA, SCPC.

58. Richard Hunter to Barton, March 30, 1948, Barton Manuscript Collections, CDGA, SCPC; Sareyan, *Turning Point*, 151, 173–74.

59. Sareyan, *Turning Point*, 152, 153.

60. Ibid., 175.

61. Harry S. Truman to Owen J. Roberts, July 26, 1948, IX-12-1, MCA.

62. Richard Hunter, "Margaret Carey Madeira," *Mental Hygiene* 35, no. 3 (July 1951): 465.

63. "Philadelphia Story," *Evening Bulletin*, October 28, 1948, Barton Manuscript Collections, CDGA, SCPC.

64. "Hal, Re: Madeira, 2/3/47, from ST" (most likely Stephen Thiermann), Barton Manuscript Collections, CDGA, SCPC.

65. Hunter, "Madeira," 465; National Mental Health Foundation, *Third Annual Report*, 2.

66. "Minute [*sic*] of Board Meeting," March 19, 1948.

67. "Minutes of Meeting of National Committee for Mental Hygiene, Psychiatric Foundation, Menninger Foundation and the National Mental Health Foundation, Conference in New York of Mental Health Organizations—May 16, '47," IX-12-1, IV, MCA.

68. "Memorandum of Action Taken by the Board of Directors of the National Mental Health Foundation," June 13, 1947, ibid.

69. Harold Barton, "Memorandum," September 19, 1947, ibid.

70. "Supplement to Minute [*sic*] of Executive Committee Meeting—October 31, 1947," ibid.

71. "Meeting in New York City of Representatives of the Menninger Foundation, the National Committee for Mental Hygiene, the National Mental Health Foundation, and the Psychiatric Foundation to Consider Merger," November 20, 1947, ibid.

72. Ibid.

73. Ibid.

74. Grob, *From Asylum to Community*, 83.

75. "Condensed Minute [*sic*] of Meeting of the Federation for Mental Health," March 13, 1948, IX-12-1, IV, MCA.

76. "Minutes of Meeting of American Federation for Mental Health," May 21, 1948, IX-12-1, MCA.

77. "Minute [*sic*] of Board Meeting," March 19, 1948.

78. Hunter quoted in Sareyan, *Turning Point*, 176–77.

79. Steer to Hal, November 18, 1948, Barton Manuscript Collections, CDGA, SCPC.

80. Hunter to Barton, December 17, 1948, ibid.

81. Hunter quoted in Sareyan, *Turning Point*, 177.

82. "Meeting of the Board of Directors," September 28, 1948.

83. Barton, "Memorandum," August 16, 1948, Barton Manuscript Collections, CDGA, SCPC.

84. "Meeting of the Board of Directors," September 28, 1948.

85. Ibid.

86. "Meeting of the Board of Executives," October 18, 1948, IX-12-1, III, MCA.

87. "Agenda of Meeting of Executive Committee," April 23, 1948, IX-12-1, MCA.

88. "Meeting of the Executive Committee of the Board of Directors," November 23, 1948, IX-12-1, III, MCA.

89. "Minute [*sic*] of Board Meeting," March 19, 1948.

90. "Notes Prepared for the Executive Committee Meeting of October 18, 1948, on Three Questions Now Before the Foundation Involving Other Organizations," IX-12-1, III, MCA.

91. "Notes Prepared for the Executive Committee Meeting of October 18, 1948."

92. Barton to Phil, December 30, 1948; Barton to Will, December 30, 1948; Hunter to Barton, November 11, 1948, Barton Manuscript Collections, CDGA, SCPC.

93. Steer to Hal, November 18, 1948, Barton Manuscript Collections, CDGA, SCPC.

94. Will to Hal, November 24, 1948, ibid.

95. Barton to Phil, December 30, 1948; Your Oregonian Friend to Dick, November 9, 1948, ibid.

96. "Meeting of the Executive Committee," November 23, 1948.

97. Hunter, "Report of the Executive Secretary, December," December 23, 1948, IX-12-1, III, MCA.

98. Ibid.

99. Ibid.

100. Hunter to Barton, December 17, 1948.

101. Hal and Lois, Edy and Davy to Dick, December 30, 1948, Barton Manuscript Collections, CDGA, SCPC.

102. "Report of the Executive Secretary, January–February 1949," IX-12-1, III, MCA.

103. National Mental Health Foundation, *Third Annual Report*, 1.

104. Hetzel to Barton, January 10, 1949, Barton Manuscript Collections, CDGA, SCPC.

105. Hunter to Barton, January 21, 1949, ibid.

106. Barton to Dick, March 24, 1949, ibid.

107. Hunter to Barton, March 30, 1949, ibid.

108. Richard Hunter, "Memorandum," October 20, 1949, IX-12-1, II, MCA; Paul to Hal, 1949, Barton Manuscript Collections, CDGA, SCPC.

109. Mildred Law to Barton, March 19, 1949, Barton Manuscript Collections, CDGA, SCPC.

110. National Mental Health Foundation, *Annual Report, 1949*, 4.

111. "National Voluntary Mental Health Association, Report of the Mental Health Study and Planning Committee," August 12, 1949, IX-12-1, II, MCA.

112. "Meeting of the Board of Directors," September 27, 1949, ibid.

113. "Report of the Staff to the Program Evaluation Committee," November 1948, Barton Manuscript Collections, CDGA, SCPC.

114. "Meeting of the Executive Committee of the Board of Directors," February 28, 1950, IX-12-1, II, MCA.

115. "Meeting of the Executive Committee of the Board of Directors," March 28, 1950, ibid.

116. National Mental Health Foundation, *Annual Report, 1949*, 4.

117. "Meeting of the Board of Directors," May 23, 1950, IX-12-1, II, MCA.

118. National Mental Health Foundation, "Minutes of Annual Meeting of Members—July 25, 1950," IX-12-1, MCA.

119. *Mental Hygiene* 34, no. 4 (October 1950).

120. *Mental Hygiene* 38, no. 4 (October 1954).

121. George S. Stevenson, "The National Association for Mental Health," *Mental Hygiene* 34, no. 4 (October 1950): 530.

122. Ibid., 529.

123. Hunter, interview by Keith Sprunger and John D. Waltner, May 7, 1972, 940.5316 #4a, MLA; Sareyan, *Turning Point*, 175–77.

124. Hunter, "Mrs. Percy C. Madeira," 465; Sareyan, *Turning Point*, 312.

125. Weisbord, *Some Form of Peace*, 50.

126. Will to Hal, February 17, 1951, Barton Manuscript Collections, CDGA, SCPC.

127. "Notice of Revocation of Bailment of All Files and Records and Correspondence," February 16, 1951, ibid.

128. Hunter, interview by Sprunger and Waltner, May 7, 1972, MLA.

129. "Where Are the Straight-jackets?" April 29, 1949, *Time* Magazine Archives.

130. Roy Simon, *Psychiatric Aide* 9, no. 2 (February 1951): 2.

131. Roy Simon, *Psychiatric Aide* 9, no. 3 (March 1952): 2; Oren Root, "An Open Letter to Our Readers," *Psychiatric Aide* 9, no. 3 (March 1952): 3.

132. Stevenson to Baldwin, March 19, 1941; Overholser to Forster, August 30, 1944.

133. Baldwin to Hetzel, May 1, 1950, MC#001, Box 1058, Folder 12; Baldwin to Robert Heininger, December 30, 1953; Baldwin to Stevenson, January 12, October 1, 1954; Stevenson to Baldwin, October 4, 1954; Baldwin to Stevenson, October 6, 1954, MC#001, Box 1059, Folder 8, ACLU Records.

134. Stevenson to Baldwin, October 14, 1954, Box 1059, Folder 8, ibid.

135. Hetzel to Board of Directors, March 27, 1950, ibid.

136. Nina Ridenour, *Mental Health in the United States: A Fifty-Year History*, 129.

137. Albert Deutsch quoted in Grob, *From Asylum to Community*, 86.

138. Albert Deutsch, "States Astir Against Mental Disease," 16, 17.

139. Grob, *From Asylum to Community*, 87.

140. Ibid., 20; Grob, *From Asylum to Community*, 88–90.

141. Mike Gorman, *Every Other Bed*, 293, 306.

142. Ibid., 305.

143. Grob, *From Asylum to Community*, 87.

15. "Scandal Results in Real Reforms"

1. Albert Q. Maisel, "Scandal Results in Real Reforms," 140.

2. See also Sareyan, *Turning Point*, 183.

3. National Mental Health Foundation, *Annual Report, 1949*, 7–8.

4. Deutsch, "States Astir," 15; Grob, *From Asylum to Community*, 90.

5. Grob, *From Asylum to Community*, 91.

6. Frank Bane, "The Governors' Study on Mental Hospitals," *Mental Hygiene* 35, no. 1 (January 1951): 13.

7. Deutsch, "States Astir," 14; Grob, *From Asylum to Community*, 91–92.

8. Deutsch, "States Astir," 13–23 (quote on 17).

9. Grob, *From Asylum to Community*, 92, 260.

10. Kathryn Alba et al., "Current Populations and Longitudinal Trends of State Residential Facilities (1950–2006)," in *Residential Services for Persons with Developmental Disabilities: Status and Trends Through 2006*, edited by Robert Prouty, Gary Smith, and K. Charie Lakin, 8.

11. Deutsch, *Shame of the States*, 187.

12. Grob, *From Asylum to Community*, 82.

13. "Meeting of the American Federation for Mental Health," May 21, 1948.

14. Thomas S. Szasz, *The Myth of Mental Illness: Foundations of a Theory of Personal Conduct, Ideology and Insanity: Essays on the Psychiatric Dehumanization of Man*, and *The Manufacture of Madness: A Comparative Study of the Inquisition and the Mental Health Movement*; R. D. Laing, *The Divided Self* and *The Politics of Experience*. Szasz's most recent book is *Psychiatry: The Science of Lies*.

15. Szasz, *Manufacture of Madness*, xix.

16. Ibid., xvii.

17. Thomas S. Szasz, "Science and Public Policy: The Crime of Involuntary Mental Hospitalization," 35.

18. Howard Becker, *Outsiders: Studies in the Sociology of Deviance*; Kai T. Erikson, *Wayward Puritans: A Study in the Sociology of Deviance*; Edwin M. Lemert, *Social Pathology: A Systematic Approach to the Study of Sociopathic Behavior*.

19. Becker, *Outsiders*, 9.

20. See especially Erving Goffman, *The Presentation of Self in Everyday Life*.

21. Erving Goffman, *Stigma: Notes on the Management of Spoiled Identity*, 137–38.

22. Goffman, *Asylums*, xiii, 74.

23. Ibid., xiii, ix–x.

24. Ibid., 384; Grob, *From Asylum to Community*, 284.

25. Michel Foucault, *Folie et déraison: Histoire de la folie*. 26. *One Flew over the Cuckoo's Nest* (1975), directed by Milos Forman, distributed by United Artists; Shorter, *History of Psychiatry*, 275.

27. *Titicut Follies*, directed by Frederick Wiseman (Cambridge, Mass.: Zapporah Films, 1967).

28. Doris Zames Fleischer and Frieda Fleischer, *The Disability Rights Movement: From Charity to Confrontation*; Fred Pelka, *The ABC-CLIO Companion to the Disability Rights Movement*.

29. Grob, *From Asylum to Community*, 209–38.

30. Deutsch, *Shame of the States*, 132–34.

31. Rothman and Rothman, *Willowbrook Wars*.

32. "Report of Executive Secretary, April–May 1950," IX-12-1, MCA.

33. Lee J. Marino, "Organizing the Parents of Mentally Retarded Children for Participation in the Mental Health Program," *Mental Hygiene* 45, no. 1 (January 1951): 14–18.

34. Trent, *Inventing the Feeble Mind*, 233–37.

35. Grob, *From Asylum to Community*, 219–20.

36. Trent, *Inventing the Feeble Mind*, 246–48, 250.

37. "Message from the President of the United States Relative to Mental Illness and Mental Retardation," House of Representatives, 88th Congress, 1st sess., doc. no. 88, February 5, 1963, 13, 12.

38. Trent, *Inventing the Feeble Mind*, 250–52.

39. See Steven J. Taylor, "Christmas in Purgatory: A Retrospective Look," *Mental Retardation* 44, no. 2 (2006): 145–49.

40. Burton Blatt and Fred Kaplan, *Christmas in Purgatory: A Photographic Essay on Mental Retardation*. *Christmas in Purgatory* was republished by the Center on Human Policy, a disability research, policy, and advocacy institute founded by Blatt at Syracuse University in 1971 and continues to be distributed by the center (Syracuse: Human Policy Press, 1974). I have been director of the center since 1983.

41. Burton Blatt and Charles Mangel, "Tragedy and Hope of Retarded Children," 96.

42. Burton Blatt, *Exodus from Pandemonium: Human Abuse and a Reformation of Public Policy*, 225–48.

43. Alba et al., "Current Populations," in *Residential Services*, edited by Prouty, Smith, and Lakin, 8.

44. Blatt, *Exodus from Pandemonium*, 258.

45. Marie Skodak Crissey and Marvin Rosen, eds., *Institutions for the Mentally Retarded: A Changing Role in Changing Times* (Austin: Pro-Ed, 1986), ix. Crissey and Rosen's book made a number of references to "dramatic pictorial indictments" that misrepresented most institutions but did not refer to Blatt by name.

46. Burton Blatt, "The Dark Side of the Mirror." The name of the American Association on Mental Deficiency was later changed to the American Association on Mental Retardation and then, most recently, to the American Association on Intellectual and Developmental Disabilities. *Mental Retardation* is now *Intellectual and Developmental Disabilities*.

47. Steven J. Taylor and Steven Blatt, eds., *In Search of the Promised Land: The Collected Papers of Burton Blatt*, 171.

48. Burton Blatt, Joseph McNally, and Andres Ozolins, *The Family Papers: A Return to Purgatory*, vi, 143.

49. Trent, *Inventing the Feeble Mind*, 244–47.

50. Dorothea D. Braginsky and Benjamin M. Braginsky, *Hansels and Gretels: Studies of Children in Institutions for the Mentally Retarded*; Louis A. Dexter, "On the Politics and Sociology of Stupidity in Our Society" (reprint of a paper presented at the American Association of Mental Deficiency in 1960); Robert Edgerton, *The Cloak of Competence*; Jane Mercer, *Labeling the Mentally Retarded: Clinical and Social Systems Perspectives on Mental Retardation*.

51. Robert B. Kugel and Wolf Wolfensberger, eds., *Changing Patterns in Residential Services for the Mentally Retarded*.

52. Burton Blatt, "Purgatory" and "Recommendations for Institutional Reform."

53. Bengt Nirje, "A Scandinavian Visitor Looks at U.S. Institutions," 53; Nirje, "The Normalization Principle and Its Human Management Implications," 181.

54. Nils E. Bank-Mikkelson, "A Metropolitan Area in Denmark: Copenhagen."

55. Wolf Wolfensberger, *The Principle of Normalization in Human Services*, 27.

56. Nirje, "Normalization Principle," 181.

57. Robert B. Kugel, "Why Innovative Action?" 10; Gunnar Dybwad, "Action Implications, U.S.A. Today," 385.

58. Dybwad, "Action Implications, U.S.A. Today," 386; Wolf Wolfensberger, "The Origins and Nature of Our Institutional Models," 65. Wolfensberger's chapter was reprinted as a monograph and is available from the Center on Human Policy (Syracuse: Human Policy Press, 1975).

59. Lloyd M. Dunn, "Small, Special-Purpose Residential Facilities for the Retarded," 214.

60. Wolfensberger, *Principle of Normalization*, 28. Wolfensberger acknowledged the contributions of Nirje and other Scandinavians in developing the concept of normalization, but maintained that

the Scandinavian version was overly simplistic, lacked precision and scientific validation, and invited misinterpretation. The Wolfensberger and Scandinavian formulations were never reconciled. Nirje and other Scandinavians considered Wolfenberger's version to be overly complex and inaccessible to average persons. See Steven J. Taylor and John O'Brien, "Normalization and Social Role Valorization," in *The Encyclopedia of American Disability History,* edited by Susan Burch (New York: Facts on File, in press). In the 1970s and '80s, the principle of normalization was criticized by some mental retardation professionals as being unrealistic for people with severe intellectual disabilities. More recently, many disability rights activists and disability scholars have maintained that normalization enforces conformity, limits individuals' choices about their lifestyles, and encourages people to try to disassociate themselves from a disability identity. For a good overview of a disability studies perspective, see Linton, *Claiming Disability.*

61. Wolf Wolfensberger, "Social Role Valorization: A Proposed New Term for the Principle of Normalization" and *A Brief Introduction to Social Role Valorization: A High-Order Concept for Addressing the Plight of Socially Devalued People and for Structuring Human Services.* The development of the principle of social-role valorization was motivated, in part, by Wolfensberger's belief that normalization had been misunderstood and misinterpreted. Everyone seemed to think they knew what "normal" meant and defined normalization in their own ways. Some people even tried to apply normalization to institutions. See Taylor and O'Brien, "Normalization and Social Role Valorization."

62. *O'Connor v. Donaldson,* 95 S. Ct. 2486 (1975), 11.

63. *Wyatt v. Stickney,* 344 F. Supp. 387 (M.D. Ala. 1972), 10.

64. Rothman and Rothman, *Willowbrook Wars,* 45.

65. *New York State Association for Retarded Children v. Rockefeller,* 357 F. Supp. 752 (E.D. N.Y. 1973), 6.

66. *Halderman v. Pennhurst State School and Hospital,* 446 F. Supp. 1295 (E.D. Pa. 1977), 24–25. Since the 1970s, federal courts have continued to consider the rights of people confined to institutions for people with intellectual and psychiatric disabilities. In *Romeo v. Youngberg,* 457 U.S. 307 (1982), the Supreme Court ruled that Nicholas Romeo, a resident of Pennhurst, had constitutional rights to freedom from undue restraint and safety as well as a limited right to treatment. In 1999, the Supreme Court ruled that unnecessary institutionalization was a violation of the Americans with Disabilities Act, which was passed in 1990. See *Olmstead v. L.C.,* 527 U.S. 581 (1999). According to the Court in *Olmstead,* people with disabilities had the right to the "most integrated setting appropriate."

67. Taylor and Blatt, *Promised Land;* Mary Ann Allard et al., eds., *Ahead of His Time: Selected Speeches of Gunnar Dybwad.*

68. William C. Gaventa and David L. Coulter, eds., *The Theological Voice of Wolf Wolfensberger;* David Race, ed., *Leadership and Change in Human Services: Selected Readings from Wolf Wolfensberger.*

69. Robert Krieder, foreword to *Turning Point,* by Sareyan, vii.

Conclusion

1. Richardson, *Writing Strategies,* 26–28.

2. Taylor, "Custodians."

3. See, for example, Nelly Bly, *Ten Days in a Mad-House.* This was based on a series of articles published in *New York World.*

4. Shorter, *History of Psychiatry,* 277; Grob, *From Asylum to Community,* 75, 83–85; Trent, *Inventing the Feeble Mind,* 227–30; Richard C. Anderson, *Peace Was in Their Hearts;* Keim, *CPS Story;* Vernon H. Neufeld, ed., *If We Can Love: The Mennonite Mental Health Story.*

5. John O'Brien, e-mail, May 2007; Don Forrest, e-mail, February 2007; Steven Mcfayden-Ketchum, e-mail, February 2007.

6. Nash, *American Odyssey*, 515.

7. Erikson, *Wayward Puritans*.

8. Dorcas Weaver Herr, *The Byberry 1-W Unit Story*.

9. Gilbert Goering, interview, January 2007; James Juhnke, quoted in Herr, *Byberry 1-W Unit Story*, 21.

10. S. Morgan Friedman, "The Inflation Calculator," http://www.westegg.com/inflation/.

11. Jacob H. Friedman, "An Organization of Ex-Patients of a Psychiatric Hospital," *Mental Hygiene* 23, no. 3 (July 1939): 415.

12. Grob, *From Asylum to Community*, 88–89.

13. National Alliance for Direct Support Professionals, http://www.nadsp.org/main/; College of Direct Support, http://info.collegeofdirectsupport.com/.

14. John O'Brien and Connie Lyle O'Brien, eds., *A Little Book about Person-Centered Planning*; John O'Brien and Connie Lyle O'Brien, *Implementing Person-Centered Planning: Voices of Experience*.

15. Sharon Barnartt and Richard Scotch, *Disability Protests: Contentious Politics, 1970–1999*; Fleischer and Fleischer, *Disability Rights Movement*; Pelka, *ABC-CLIO Companion*; Joseph P. Shapiro, *No Pity: People with Disabilities Forging a New Civil Rights Movement*.

16. Lennard J. Davis, *Bending over Backwards: Disability, Dismodernism and Other Difficult Positions* (New York: New York University Press, 2002); Linton, *Claiming Disability*; Paul K. Longmore, *Why I Burned My Book, and Other Essays on Disability*.

17. Linton, *Claiming Disability*, 11.

18. Titus William Bender, "The Development of the Mennonite Mental Health Movement, 1942–1971"; Neufeld, *If We Can Love*; Sareyan, *Turning Point*, 189–205, 229–34.

19. Bender, "Mennonite Mental Health Movement," 199–200.

20. Sareyan, *Turning Point*, 198–99.

21. Bender, "Mennonite Mental Health Movement," 164–65, 200–201.

22. Esther Jost, "Kings View," in *If We Can Love*, edited by Neufeld, 90–92.

Bibliography

Selected Sources

The primary sources for this book included manuscript collections maintained at the Swarthmore College Peace Collection (SCPC), the Mennonite Church USA Historical Committee and Archives (MCA), and the Brethren Historical Library and Archives (BHLA); taped interviews of World War II conscientious objectors maintained at the Mennonite Library and Archives (MLA); personal papers and letters provided to the author by individual former conscientious objectors or their family members; reports and microfilmed records obtained through interlibrary loan; online archival sources; journals maintained by the Syracuse University Libraries and the SUNY Upstate Medical University Library; and personal and phone interviews and e-mail communications between the author and former conscientious objectors and others. The archives maintained by the SCPC, MCA, and BHLA are extensive and include Civilian Public Service (CPS) records, camp and unit correspondence, letters and diaries, correspondence regarding the Mental Hygiene Program of the CPS and the National Mental Health Foundation, newspaper clippings, publications, and photographs. Most of the records at the MCA and the SCPC are original copies. The majority of the materials of the Brethren Service Committee maintained at the BHLA were transferred to microfilm in 1947 and 1948.

Secondary sources have been invaluable during this research. Leslie Eisen's *Pathways of Peace,* Melvin Gingerich's *Service for Peace,* and Mumford Q. Sibley and Philip E. Jacob's *Conscription of Conscience: The American State and the Conscience Objector, 1940–1947* were based on firsthand knowledge of the Civilian Public Service and written soon after the end of World War II. Eisen and Gingerich were associated with the Brethren Service Committee and Mennonite Central Committee, respectively, and their books documented the histories of those service committees. Sibley and Jacobs provided a comprehensive account of the CPS, including the activities of conscientious objectors who did not come from the historic peace churches. Sibley, who was affiliated with the Pacifist Research Bureau, was working on the history of the CPS as early as 1945. All three of these books contained excerpts of primary source materials and appendixes reprinting government and church committee documents. Alex Sareyan's *Turning Point: How Persons of Conscience Brought about Major Change in the Care of America's Mentally Ill* was directly relevant to this book. Sareyan was a former CO and had worked for the National Mental Health Foundation. Marvin Weisbord's *Some*

Kind of Peace: True Stories of the American Friends Service Committee at Home and Abroad gave the inside story of the formation of the National Mental Health Foundation and was based on the firsthand accounts of its founders. Taken together, these five books provided a road map to finding important primary source materials. Of course, these books were written from the authors' points of view.

Primary Sources

Manuscript Collections: Archives

Brethren Historical Library and Archives, Elgin, Ill.
 BSC-CPS-FU, Reel #3 (Microfilm).
 BSC-CPS-FU, Reel #16 (Microfilm).
 BSC-CPS-FU, Reel #23 (Microfilm).
 BSC-CPS-FU, Reel #25 (Microfilm).
 BSC-CPS-FU, Reel #31 (Microfilm).
 BSC-CPS-FU, Reel #34 (Microfilm).
 BSC-CPS-FU, Reel #36 (Microfilm).
 BSC-CPS-FU, Reel #39 (Microfilm).
Civilian Public Service Photographs
Mennonite Church USA Historical Committee and Archives, Goshen, Ind.
 Mennonite Central Committee, Civilian Public Service, Correspondence (IX-6-3).
 Mennonite Central Committee, Civilian Public Service, Individual Camps (IX-13-1).
 Mennonite Central Committee, 1920—Archives Collection (IX).
 Mennonite Central Committee, Photograph Collection, Civilian Public Service, 1941–1947 (IX-13-2.2).
 Mennonite Central Committee, Reports, 1940–1959 (IX-12-1).
 Mennonite Central Committee, Small Archives Collection (Hist. Mss. 5-3).
Mennonite Library and Archives, Bethel College, North Newton, Kans. Taped interviews (includes interviews available for direct quotation and for background information only). World War II, 1939–1945—Conscientious Objectors (Call Number: 940-5316).
 Berg, Lewis. Interview by Greg Phifer (background only). Aug. 12, 1986.
 Brandt, Waldo. Interview by R. Fleming (background only). Jan. 23, 1974.
 Diller, Victor. Interview by Howard Blosser. Nov. 1, 1989.
 Goering, Paul L. Interview by Kurt Goering. Dec. 26, 1975.
 Habegger, Loris. Interview by Keith Sprunger. Aug. 13, 1974.
 Hostetler, John. Interview by Joseph Miller. Dec. 22, 1977.
 Hunter, Richard. Interview by Keith Sprunger and John D. Waltner (background only). May 7, 1972.
 Miller, Orie, Henry A. Fast, and Elmer Ediger. Interview by James C. Juhnke (background only). Nov. 11, 1969.

Peachley, Laban. Interview by Joseph Miller. Apr. 4, 1978.

Schrag, Edwin J. Interview by Tim E. Schrag. Sept. 13, 1974.

Wasser, Marvin. Interview by Mark Kroeker. Nov. 29, 1989.

Wright, Frank L. Interview by Keith Sprunger and John D. Waltner (background only). May 7, 1972.

Swarthmore College Peace Collection, Swarthmore College, Swarthmore, Pa.

American Friends Service Committee: Civilian Public Service (DG 002).

Association of Catholic Conscientious Objectors. Collected Records (CDGA).

Barton, Harold. Manuscript Collections (CDGA).

Civilian Public Service Papers (DG 056).

Civilian Public Service Union Record, 1944–1946 (DG 008).

Diary (typescript) of Paul Comly French, 1940–1946 (CDGA: French, Paul Comly).

Photos (DG 002, DG 025, DG 056).

Wilhelm, Jayne Tuttle and Paul A. Collected Papers (CDGA).

Zahn, Gordon, WW II CO (CDGA).

Microfilmed Archives (Interlibrary Loan)

American Civil Liberties Union Records, Mental Health Issues, 1941–1978 (Gale).

MC#001, Box 1057.

MC#001, Box 1058.

MC#001, Box 1059.

Roosevelt, Eleanor. Papers, 1945–1952, from the Franklin D. Roosevelt D. Library, Part 1: General Correspondence, 1945–1947 (a UPA Collection from LexisNexis).

Reel 2, 0788.

Reel 7, 0464.

Reel 10, 0399.

Reel 16, 0134.

Online Archives

American Psychiatric Association. Position statements. Historical APA newsletters. June 15, 1948–Nov. 15, 1949. http://www.psych.org/public_info/libr_publ/.

Disability History Museum. http://www.disabilitymuseum.org.

Roosevelt, Eleanor. "My Day." http://www.gwu.edu/~erpapers/myday/.

Time Magazine Archives. http://www.time.com/time/archive/.

Journals

American Journal of Mental Deficiency. 1941–1947.

American Journal of Psychiatry. 1946–1950.

Mental Hygiene. 1917, 1939–1955.

Personal Papers and Letters

Cox, Robert. Papers.
Hartman, Neil. Papers.
Miles, Ward. Papers.
Sawyer, Warren. Papers and letters.
Wik, Harold. Papers.

Personal Interviews

Allen, Jack. 2007.
Bartholomew, Evert. 2007.
Bartholomew, John. 2007.
Berrigan, Jerry and Carol. 2007.
Burgess, Samuel. 2007.
Goering, Gilbert. 2007.
Hartman, Neil. 2007.
Johnson, Curtis. 2007.
Palmer, Stuart. 2007.
Sawyer, Warren. 2007.

Phone Interviews

Altman, W. Forrest. 2007.
Lord, Charles. 2007.
March, William. 2007.
Marsh, Caryl. 2007.
Miles, Ward and Alice. 2007.
Reese, Christine Conway. 2004.
Ruddell, Richard. 2007.
Siegel, Florence. 2007.
Stark, Leonard. 2007.
Weisbord, Marvin. 2006.

Written Reflections (E-mail)

Forrest, Don. 2007.
Mcfadyen-Ketchum, Steven. 2007.
O'Brien, John. 2007.
Schwartz, Michael. 2007.

Secondary Sources

Albrecht, Gary L. *The Disability Business: Rehabilitation in America.* Sage Library of Social Research, vol. 190. Newbury Park, Calif.: Sage Publications, 1992.

Allard, Mary Ann, Anne M. Howard, Lee E. Vorderer, and Alice I. Wells, eds. *Ahead of His Time: Selected Speeches of Gunnar Dybwad.* Washington, D.C.: American Association on Mental Retardation, 1999.

American Friends Service Committee. *The Experience of the American Friends Service Committee in the Civilian Public Service under the Selective Training and Service Act of 1940, 1941–1945.* Philadelphia: American Friends Service Committee, 1945.

———. *An Introduction to Friends Civilian Public Service.* Philadelphia: American Friends Service Committee, 1945.

———. *Projects and Incentives: A Study of the Work Projects and the Incentives for Work in the Civilian Public Service Camps and Units under the Administration of the American Friends Service Committee.* Grosvenor: American Friends Service Committee, n.d.

Anderson, Richard C. *Peace Was in Their Hearts.* Scottdale, Pa.: Herald Press, 1994.

Angell, S. L. "Training Schools and CPS." *Reporter* 3 (July 15, 1944): 3–5.

Bank-Mikkelson, Nils E. "A Metropolitan Area in Denmark: Copenhagen." In *Changing Patterns in Residential Services for the Mentally Retarded,* edited by Robert B. Kugel and Wolf Wolfensberger, 227–54. Washington, D.C.: President's Committee on Mental Retardation, 1969.

Barnartt, Sharon, and Richard Scotch. *Disability Protests: Contentious Politics, 1970–1999.* Washington, D.C.: Gallaudet Univ. Press, 2001.

Baynton, Douglas C. *Forbidden Signs: American Culture and the Campaign Against Sign Language.* Chicago: Univ. of Chicago Press, 1996.

Becker, Howard. *Outsiders: Studies in the Sociology of Deviance.* New York: Free Press, 1963.

Beers, Clifford W. *A Mind That Found Itself: An Autobiography.* 7th ed. 1908. Reprint, Garden City, N.Y.: Doubleday, 1956.

———. "Organized Work in Mental Hygiene." *Mental Hygiene* 1, no. 1 (1917).

Belknap, Ivan. *Human Problems of a State Mental Hospital.* New York: Arno Press, 1980.

Bender, Titus William. "The Development of the Mennonite Mental Health Movement, 1942–1971." D.S.W. diss., Tulane Univ., 1976.

Bennett, Scott H. *Radical Pacifism: The War Resisters League and Gandhian Nonviolence in America, 1915–1963.* Syracuse: Syracuse Univ. Press, 2003.

Berrigan, Philip, with Fred A. Wilcox. *Fighting the Lamb's War: Skirmishes with the American Empire.* Monroe, Maine: Common Courage Press, 1996.

Bérubé, Michael. *Life as We Know It: A Father, a Family, and an Exceptional Child.* New York: Vintage Books, 1998.

Blatt, Burton. "The Dark Side of the Mirror." *Mental Retardation* 6, no. 5 (1968): 42–44.

———. *Exodus from Pandemonium: Human Abuse and a Reformation of Public Policy.* Boston: Allyn and Bacon. 1970.

———. "Purgatory." In *Changing Patterns in Residential Services for the Mentally Retarded*, edited by Robert B. Kugel and Wolf Wolfensberger, 34–49. Washington, D.C.: President's Committee on Mental Retardation, 1969a.

———. "Recommendations for Institutional Reform." In *Changing Patterns in Residential Services for the Mentally Retarded*, edited by Robert B. Kugel and Wolf Wolfensberger, 173–77. Washington, D.C.: President's Committee on Mental Retardation, 1969b.

Blatt, Burton, and Fred Kaplan. *Christmas in Purgatory: A Photographic Essay on Mental Retardation.* Boston: Allyn and Bacon, 1966.

Blatt, Burton, and Charles Mangel. "Tragedy and Hope of Retarded Children." *Look Magazine* 41 (Oct. 31, 1967): 96–99.

Blatt, Burton, Joseph McNally, and Andres Ozolins. *The Family Papers: A Return to Purgatory.* New York: Longman, 1979.

Bly, Nellie. *Ten Days in a Mad-House.* New York: Norman L. Munro, 1887.

Bogdan, Robert, and Steven J. Taylor. "Relationships with Severely Disabled People: The Social Construction of Humanness." *Social Problems* 36, no. 2 (1989): 135–48.

———. *The Social Meaning of Mental Retardation: Two Life Stories.* New York: Teachers College Press, 1994.

Bowman, Carl D. *Brethren Society: The Cultural Transformation of a Peculiar People.* Baltimore: Johns Hopkins Univ. Press, 1995.

Braginsky, Dorothea D., and Benjamin M. Braginsky. *Hansels and Gretels: Studies of Children in Institutions for the Mentally Retarded.* New York: Holt, Rinehart, and Winston. 1971.

Brokaw, Tom. *The Greatest Generation.* New York: Random House, 1998.

———. *The Greatest Generation Speaks: Letters and Reflections.* New York: Random House, 1999.

Caldwell, Erskine. *Tobacco Road.* Athens: Univ. of Georgia Press, 1995.

Clark, Robert A., and Alex M. Burgess. "The Work of Conscientious Objectors in State Mental Hospitals During the Second World War." *Psychiatric Quarterly* 22, no. 1 (1948): 128–40.

Conrad, Peter, and Joseph W. Schneider. *Deviance and Medicalization: From Badness to Sickness.* Philadelphia: Temple Univ. Press, 1992.

Culp, G. Richard. *The Minority Report: A Behind-the-Scenes Story of Civilian Public Service.* Sugarcreek, Ohio: Carlisle Printing, 1999.

Dahlke, H. Otto. "Values and Group Behavior in Two Camps for Conscientious Objectors." *American Journal of Sociology* 51, no. 1 (1945): 22–33.

Dain, Norman. *Clifford W. Beers: Advocate for the Insane.* Pittsburgh: Univ. of Pittsburgh Press, 1980.

Danforth, Scot. "New Words for New Purposes: A Challenge for AAMR." *Mental Retardation* 40, no. 1 (2002): 52–55.

———. "On What Basis Hope? Modern Progress and Postmodern Possibilities." *Mental Retardation* 35, no. 2 (Apr. 1997): 93–106.

Davies, Stanley P. *The Mentally Retarded in America.* New York: Columbia Univ. Press, 1959.

Davis, Lennard J. *Bending over Backwards: Disability, Dismodernism and Other Difficult Positions.* New York: New York Univ. Press, 2002.

Day, Dorothy. *On Pilgrimage: The Sixties.* New York: Curtis Books, 1972.

Deutsch, Albert. "The Exposé as a Progressive Tool." *Mental Hygiene* 34, no. 1 (1950): 80–89.

———. *The Mentally Ill in America: A History of Their Care and Treatment from Colonial Times.* 2d ed. New York: Columbia Univ. Press, 1949.

———. Review of *Jacob A. Riis: Police Reporter, Reformer, Useful Citizen,* by Louise Ware. *Mental Hygiene* 24, no. 4 (1940).

———. *The Shame of the States.* Mental Illness and Social Policy: The American Experience. New York: Harcourt, Brace, 1948.

———. "States Astir Against Mental Disease." *Mental Hygiene* 40, no. 1 (January 1956).

Deutsch, Albert, and H. Fishman, eds. *The Encyclopedia of Mental Health.* Vols. 1–6. New York: Franklin Watts, 1963.

DeVault, Marjorie L. *Feeding the Family: The Social Organization of Caring as Gendered Work.* Chicago: Univ. of Chicago Press, 1991.

Dexter, Louis A. "On the Politics and Sociology of Stupidity in Our Society." *Mental Retardation* 32, no. 2 (1994): 152–55.

Dibacco, Thomas V., Lorna C. Mason, and Christian G. Appy. *History of the United States.* Vol. 2, *Civil War to the Present.* Evanston, Ill.: McDougal Littell, 1995.

Dix, Dorothea L. *Memorial of Miss D. L. Dix to the Senate and House of Representatives of the United States.* 33d Cong., 1st sess., Senate Report 57, 1850. Available at http://www.disabilitymuseum.org/lib/docs/1239.htm.

———. "Memorial to the Legislature of Massachusetts, 1843." In *The History of Mental Retardation: Collected Papers,* edited by Marvin Rosen, Gerald R. Clark, and Marvin S. Kivitz. Vol. 1. Baltimore: Univ. Park Press, 1976. Available at http://www.disabilitymuseum.org/lib/docs/737.htm.

Doll, Edgar. "Mental Defectives and the War." *American Journal of Mental Deficiency* 49 (1944): 64–66.

Doss, Erika. *Looking at "Life" Magazine.* Washington, D.C.: Smithsonian Institution Press, 2001.

Dunn, Lloyd M. "Small, Special-Purpose Residential Facilities for the Retarded." In *Changing Patterns in Residential Services for the Mentally Retarded,* edited by Robert B. Kugel and Wolf Wolfensberger, 211–26. Washington, D.C.: President's Committee on Mental Retardation, 1969.

Durkheim, Emile. *The Rules of Sociological Method.* Translated by Sarah A. Solovay and John H. Mueller. Edited by George E. G. Catlin. 8th ed. New York: Free Press, 1938.

Dybwad, Gunnar. "Action Implications, U.S.A. Today." In *Changing Patterns in Residential Services for the Mentally Retarded,* edited by Robert B. Kugel and Wolf Wolfensberger, 383–428. Washington, D.C.: President's Committee on Mental Retardation, 1969.

Edgerton, Robert. *The Cloak of Competence.* Berkeley and Los Angeles: Univ. of California Press, 1967.

Eisen, Leslie. *Pathways of Peace.* Elgin, Ill.: Brethren Publishing House, 1948.

Erikson, Kai T. "Notes on the Sociology of Deviance." *Social Problems* 9 (1962): 307–14.

———. *Wayward Puritans: A Study in the Sociology of Deviance.* New York: John Wiley and Sons, 1966.

Ferguson, Philip M. *Abandoned to Their Fate: Social Policy and Practice Toward Severely Retarded People in America, 1820–1920.* Philadelphia: Temple Univ. Press, 1994.

Fleischer, Doris Zames, and Frieda Zames. *The Disability Rights Movement: From Charity to Confrontation.* Philadelphia: Temple Univ. Press, 2001.

Flynn, George Q. *Lewis B. Hershey: Mr. Selective Service.* Chapel Hill: Univ. of North Carolina Press, 1985.

Foucault, Michel. *Folie et déraison: Histoire de la folie* [Madness and Civilization: A History of Insanity in the Age of Reason]. Translated by R. Howard. New York: Pantheon Books, 1965.

Franklin, Ursula M. *The Ursula Franklin Reader: Pacifism as a Map.* Toronto: Between the Lines, 2006.

Frazier, Heather T., and John O'Sullivan. *"We Have Just Begun Not to Fight": An Oral History of Conscientious Objectors in Civilian Public Service During World War II.* New York: Twayne Publishers, 1996.

French, Paul C. *Four Year Report of Civilian Public Service, March 15, 1941 to March 1, 1945.* Washington, D.C.: National Service Board for Religious Objectors, 1945.

Gaventa, William C., and David L. Coulter, eds. *The Theological Voice of Wolf Wolfensberger.* Binghamton: Haworth Pastoral Press, 2001.

Gering, Glenn, Richard Weaver, Gordon Engle, Gerhard Peters, and Ernest Lehman, eds. *Anniversary Review.* Harrisburg, Pa.: C.P.S. Unit 93, 1945.

Gingerich, Melvin. *Service for Peace.* Scottdale, Pa.: Herald Press, 1949.

Goffman, Erving. *Asylums: Essays on the Social Situation of Mental Patients and Other Inmates.* Boston: Prentice-Hall, 1961.

———. *The Presentation of Self in Everyday Life.* New York: Anchor, 1959.

———. *Stigma: Notes on the Management of Spoiled Identity.* Englewood Cliffs, N.J.: Prentice-Hall, 1963.

Goossen, Rachel Waetner. *Women Against the Good War: Conscientious Objection and Gender on the American Home Front, 1941–1947.* Chapel Hill: Univ. of North Carolina Press, 1997.

Gorman, Mike. *Every Other Bed.* Cleveland, Ohio: World Publishing, 1956.

———. "Oklahoma Attacks Its Snake Pits." *Reader's Digest* 53, no. 317 (1948): 140–60.

Gory, Adrian E., and David C. McClelland. "Characteristics of Conscientious Objectors in World War II." *Journal of Counseling Psychology* 11, no. 5 (1947): 245–57.

Grimes, John Maurice. *Institutional Care of Mental Patients in the United States.* Chicago: John Maurice Grimes, 1934.

Grob, Gerald N. *From Asylum to Community: Mental Health Policy in Modern America.* Princeton: Princeton Univ. Press, 1991.

———. *The Mad among Us: A History of the Care of America's Mentally Ill.* New York: Free Press, 1994.

————. *Mental Illness and American Society, 1875–1940*. Princeton: Princeton Univ. Press, 1983.

Hall, Bernard H., Mary Gangemi, V. L. Norris, Vivienne Hutchins Vail, and Gordon Sawatsky. *Psychiatric Aide Education*. New York: Grune and Stratton, 1952.

Hamilton, Samuel W., Grover Kempf, Grace C. Scholz, and Eve G. Caswell. *A Study of the Public Mental Hospitals of the United States, 1937–39*. Supplement no. 164 to the Public Health Reports. Washington, D.C.: U.S. Government Printing Office, 1941.

Herr, Dorcas Weaver. *The Byberry 1-W Unit Story*. Philadelphia: Philadelphia State Hospital, 1997.

Hincks, H. M. "Clifford Whittingham Beers." *Mental Hygiene* 27, no. 4 (1943): 654–56.

Keim, Albert N. *The CPS Story: An Illustrated History of the Civilian Public Service*. Intercourse, Pa.: Good Books, 1990.

Keim, Albert N., and Grant M. Stoltzfus. *The Politics of Conscience: The Historic Peace Churches and America at War, 1917–1955*. Scottdale, Pa.: Herald Press, 1988.

Kesey, Ken. *One Flew over the Cuckoo's Nest*. New York: Signet, 1962.

Kluger, Richard. *Simple Justice*. Vols. 1–2. New York: Alfred A. Knopf, 1975.

Komora, Paul O., Mary Augusta Clark, and Ralph A. Pierson. *State Hospitals in the Depression: A Survey of the Effects of the Economic Crisis on the Operation of Institutions for the Mentally Ill in the United States*. New York: National Committee for Mental Hygiene, 1934.

Kugel, Robert B. "Why Innovative Action?" In *Changing Patterns in Residential Services for the Mentally Retarded*, edited by Robert B. Kugel and Wolf Wolfensberger, 1–14. Washington, D.C.: President's Committee on Mental Retardation, 1969.

Kugel, Robert B., and Wolf Wolfensberger, eds. *Changing Patterns in Residential Services for the Mentally Retarded*. Washington, D.C.: President's Committee on Mental Retardation, 1969.

Laing, R. D. *The Divided Self*. Baltimore: Penguin Books, 1965.

————. *The Politics of Experience*. New York: Ballantine Books, 1967.

Leichty, Paul D. "Mennonite Advocacy for Persons with Disabilities." *Journal of Religion, Disability, and Health* 10, nos. 1–2 (2006): 195–206.

Lemert, Edwin M. *Social Pathology: A Systematic Approach to the Theory of Sociopathic Behavior*. McGraw Hill Series in Sociology. New York: McGraw-Hill, 1951.

Linton, Simi. *Claiming Disability: Knowledge and Identity*. Cultural Front. New York: New York Univ. Press, 1998.

Longmore, Paul K. *Why I Burned My Book, and Other Essays on Disability*. American Subjects. Philadelphia: Temple Univ. Press, 2003.

Longmore, Paul K., and Lauri Umansky. *The New Disability History: American Perspectives*. New York: New York Univ. Press, 2001.

Maechtle, Lowell E., and H. H. Gerth. "Conscientious Objectors as Mental Hospital Attendants." *Sociology and Social Research* 29 (Sept. 1944): 11–24.

Maine, Harold. *If a Man Be Mad*. Garden City, N.Y.: Doubleday, 1946.

Maisel, Albert Q. "Bedlam, 1946: Most U.S. Mental Hospitals Are a Shame and a Disgrace." *Life*, May 6, 1946, 102–18.

———. "Scandal Results in Real Reforms." *Life,* Nov. 12, 1951, 140–54.

———. "The Shame of Our Mental Hospitals." *Reader's Digest* 49, no. 291 (1946): 1–7.

Mason, Lorna C., William Jay Jacobs, and Robert P. Ludlum. *History of the United States.* Vol. 1, *Beginnings to 1877.* Boston: McDougal Littell, 1995.

Mather, Eleanore Price. *Pendle Hill: A Quaker Experiment in Education and Community.* Wallingford, Pa.: Pendle Hill, 1980.

Mellanby, Kenneth. *Human Guinea Pigs.* London: Victor Gollancz, 1945.

Mennonite Central Committee, Civilian Public Service. *Instruction Manual on Camp Records, Financing, and Procedures.* Akron, Pa.: Mennonite Central Committee, Civilian Public Service, 1943.

———. *MCC*CPS: Camp Director's Manual.* Akron, Pa.: Mennonite Central Committee, Civilian Public Service, n.d.

———. *MCC*CPS: Educational Director's Manual.* Akron, Pa.: Mennonite Central Committee, Civilian Public Service, 1942.

Mental Hospital Institute. *Better Care in Mental Hospitals: Proceedings of the First Mental Hospital Institute of the American Psychiatric Association Held at the Institute of the Pennsylvania Hospital, Philadelphia, Pa., April 11–15, 1949.*

Mercer, Jane R. *Labeling the Mentally Retarded: Clinical and Social System Perspectives on Mental Retardation.* Berkeley and Los Angeles: Univ. of California Press, 1973.

Mishler, Dorsa J., Harold L. Weaver, John E. Lehman, and Donald R. Weaver. *Our CPS Stories: Prairie Street Mennonite Church in Civilian Public Service, 1941–1946.* North Newton, Kans.: Mennonite Library and Archives, 1996.

Nash, Gary B. *American Odyssey: The United States in the 20th Century.* New York: Glencoe/McGraw-Hill, 2002.

National Interreligious Service Board for Conscientious Objectors. *1996 Directory of Civilian Public Service.* Scottdale, Pa.: Mennonite Publishing House, 1996.

National Service Board for Religious Objectors. *Camp Director's Manual: Civilian Public Service.* Washington, D.C.: National Service Board for Religious Objectors, 1945.

———. *Congress Looks at the Conscientious Objector.* Washington, D.C.: National Service Board for Religious Objectors, 1943.

Neefe, John R., Maj. James B. Baty, John G. Reinhold, and Joseph Stokes. "Inactivation of the Virus of Infectious Hepatitis in Drinking Water." *American Journal of Public Health* 37 (Apr. 1947): 365–72.

Neefe, John R., Joseph Stokes Jr., John G. Reinhold, and F. D. W. Lukens. "Hepatitis Due to the Injection of Homologous Blood Products in Human Volunteers." *Journal of Clinical Investigation* 23, no. 5 (1944): 836–55.

Neufeld, Vernon H., ed. *If We Can Love: The Mennonite Mental Health Story.* Newton, Kans.: Faith and Life Press, 1983.

Nirje, Bengt. "The Normalization Principle and Its Human Management Implications." In *Changing Patterns in Residential Services for the Mentally Retarded,* edited by Robert B. Kugel and Wolf Wolfensberger, 179–95. Washington, D.C.: President's Committee on Mental Retardation, 1969a.

———. "A Scandinavian Visitor Looks at U.S. Institutions." In *Changing Patterns in Residential Services for the Mentally Retarded*, edited by Robert B. Kugel and Wolf Wolfensberger, 51–57. Washington, D.C.: President's Committee on Mental Retardation, 1969b.

O'Brien, John, and Connie Lyle O'Brien. *Implementing Person-Centered Planning: Voices of Experience.* Toronto: Inclusion Press, 2002.

———, eds. *A Little Book about Person-Centered Planning.* Toronto: Inclusion Press, 1998.

Olmstead, Frank. "They Asked for a Hard Job." *Fellowship* (Nov. 1943): 192–94.

Parsons, Talcott. *The Social System.* New York: Free Press, 1951.

Parsons, Talcott, and Kenneth Clark, eds. *The Negro American.* Boston: Houghton Mifflin, 1966.

Pelka, Fred. *The ABC-CLIO Companion to the Disability Rights Movement.* Santa Barbara: ABC-CLIO, 1997.

Pernick, Martin S. *The Black Stork: Eugenics and the Death of "Defective" Babies in American Medicine and Motion Pictures since 1915.* New York: Oxford University Press, 1996.

Pierce, Franklin. *Franklin Pierce's 1854 Veto.* May 3, 1854. Available at http://www.disabilitymuseum.org/lib/docs/682.htm.

Prouty, Robert W., Gary Smith, and K. Charlie Lakin, eds. *Residential Services for Persons with Developmental Disabilities: Status and Trends Through 2002.* Minneapolis: Research and Training Center on Community Living, Institute on Community Integration/UCEDD, Univ. of Minnesota, June 2003. Available at http://rtc.umn.edu/risp02.

———, eds. *Residential Services for Persons with Developmental Disabilities: Status and Trends Through 2006.* Minneapolis: Univ. of Minnesota Research and Training Center on Community Living, 2007.

Race, David, ed. *Leadership and Change in Human Services: Selected Readings from Wolf Wolfensberger.* London and New York: Routledge, 2003.

Richardson, Laurel. *Writing Strategies: Reaching Diverse Audiences.* Newbury Park, Calif.: Sage Publications, 1990.

Ridenour, Nina. *Mental Health in the United States: A Fifty-Year History.* Cambridge: Harvard Univ. Press, 1961.

———. "The Mental Health Movement." In *The Encyclopedia of Mental Health*, edited by Alfred Deutsch and H. Fishman, 3:1091–1102. New York: Franklin Watts, 1963.

———. "The Mental Hygiene Movement 1948 thru 1952." In *A Mind That Found Itself: An Autobiography*, by Clifford W. Beers, 372–91. 7th ed. Garden City, N.Y.: Doubleday, 1956.

Roberts, Owen J. Foreword to *Out of Sight, Out of Mind*, by Frank L. Wright Jr. Philadelphia: National Mental Health Foundation, 1947.

Rothman, David. *The Discovery of the Asylum: Social Order and Disorder in the New Republic.* Boston: Little, Brown, 1971.

Rothman, David J., and Sheila M. Rothman. *The Willowbrook Wars: A Decade of Struggle for Social Justice.* New York: Harper and Row, 1984.

Russell, Marta. *Beyond Ramps: Disability at the End of the Social Contract.* Monroe, Maine: Common Courage Press, 1998.

Salmon, Thomas W. "Insane in a County Poor Farm." *Mental Hygiene* 1, no. 1 (1917): 25–33.

Sareyan, Alex. *The Turning Point: How Persons of Conscience Brought about Major Change in the Care of America's Mentally Ill.* Scottdale, Pa.: Herald Press, 1994.

Scheerenberger, Robert C. *A History of Mental Retardation: A Quarter Century of Promise.* Baltimore: Paul H. Brookes Publishing, 1987.

Scheff, Thomas J. *Being Mentally Ill: A Sociological Theory.* Chicago: Aldine Publishing, 1966.

Schlissel, Lillian, ed. *Conscience in America: A Documentary History of Conscientious Objection in America, 1757–1967.* New York: E. P. Dutton, 1968.

Schreiber, Julius. "Albert Deutsch—Crusader, 1905–1961." In *The Encyclopedia of Mental Health,* edited by Alfred Deutsch and H. Fishman, 2:473–82. New York: Franklin Watts, 1963.

Scull, Andrew. *Decarceration: Community Treatment and the Deviant—a Radical View.* 2d ed. New Brunswick: Rutgers Univ. Press, 1984.

———. *Social Order/Mental Disorder: Anglo-American Psychiatry in Historical Perspective.* Medicine and Society. Berkeley and Los Angeles: Univ. of California Press, 1989.

Seabrook, William. *Asylum.* New York: Harcourt, Brace, 1935.

Seibert, Michael. "Obituary: Don Charles DeVault." *Photosynthesis Research* 28, no. 3 (1991): 95–98.

Shamoo, Adil E., and David B. Resnik. *Responsible Conduct of Research.* Oxford: Oxford Univ. Press, 2003.

Shapiro, Joseph P. *No Pity: People with Disabilities Forging a New Civil Rights Movement.* New York: Three Rivers Press, 1993.

Shorter, Edward. *A History of Psychiatry: From the Era of the Asylum to the Age of Prozac.* New York: John Wiley and Sons, 1997.

Sibley, Mumford Q., and Philip E. Jacob. *Conscription of Conscience: The American State and the Conscientious Objector, 1940–1947.* Ithaca: Cornell Univ. Press, 1952.

Smith, J. David. *Minds Made Feeble: The Myth and Legacy of the Kallikaks.* Austin: Pro-Ed, 1985.

Stroman, Duane F. *The Disability Rights Movement: From Deinstitutionalization to Self-Determination.* Lanham, Md.: Univ. Press of America, 2003.

Szasz, Thomas S. *Ideology and Insanity: Essays on the Psychiatric Dehumanization of Man.* Garden City, N.Y.: Anchor Books, Doubleday, 1970.

———. *The Manufacture of Madness: A Comparative Study of the Inquisition and the Mental Health Movement.* New York: Delta, 1970.

———. *The Myth of Mental Illness: Foundations of a Theory of Personal Conduct.* New York: Delta, 1961.

———. *Psychiatry: The Science of Lies.* Syracuse: Syracuse Univ. Press, 2008.

———. "Science and Public Policy: The Crime of Involuntary Mental Hospitalization." *Medical Opinion Review* 4 (May 1968): 24–35.

Taylor, Steven J. "The Custodians: Attendants and Their Work at State Institutions for the Mentally Retarded." Ph.D. diss., Syracuse Univ., 1977.

———. "'You're Not a Retard, You're Just Wise': Disability, Social Identity, and Family Networks." *Journal of Contemporary Ethnography* 29, no. 1 (2000): 58–92.

Taylor, Steven J., and Steven D. Blatt, eds. *In Search of the Promised Land: The Collected Papers of Burton Blatt.* Washington, D.C.: American Association on Mental Retardation, 1999.

Taylor, Steven J., and Robert Bogdan. "Defending Illusions: The Institution's Struggle for Survival." *Human Organization* 39, no. 3 (1980): 209–17.

Taylor, Steven J., and Stanford J. Searl. "Disability in America: A History of Policies and Trends." In *Significant Disability: Issues Affecting People with Significant Disabilities from a Historical, Policy, Leadership, and Systems Perspective,* edited by E. D. Martin Jr., 16–63. Springfield, Ill.: Charles C. Thomas, 2001.

Terkel, Studs. *"The Good War": An Oral History of World War Two.* New York: Pantheon Books, 1984.

Tichi, Cecelia. *Exposés and Excess: Muckraking in America, 1900/2000.* Philadelphia: Univ. of Pennsylvania Press, 2004.

Trent, James W. *Inventing the Feeble Mind: A History of Mental Retardation in the United States.* Medicine in Society. Berkeley and Los Angeles: Univ. of California Press, 1994.

Tucker, Todd. *The Great Starvation Experiment: The Heroic Men Who Starved So That Millions Could Live.* New York: Free Press, 2006.

U.S. Bureau of the Census. *Patients in Mental Hospitals, 1944.* Washington, D.C.: U.S. Government Printing Office, 1947.

———. *Patients in Mental Hospitals, 1945.* Washington, D.C.: U.S. Government Printing Office, 1948.

———. *Patients in Mental Hospitals, 1946.* Washington, D.C.: U.S. Government Printing Office, 1948.

Van Dyck, Harry R. *Exercise of Conscience: A WW II Objector Remembers.* Buffalo: Prometheus Books, 1990.

Wagler, David, and Roman Rader, eds. *The Story of the Amish in Civilian Public Service.* Boonsboro, Md.: C.P.S. Camp No. 24, Unit III, 1945.

Ward, Mary Jane. *The Snake Pit.* New York: Random House, 1946.

Webb, Paul Frank. "Mennonite Conscientious Objectors and the Civilian Public Service Camps of World War II." Master's thesis, California State Univ.–Fresno, 1988.

Weisbord, Marvin R. *Some Form of Peace: True Stories of the American Friends Service Committee at Home and Abroad.* New York: Viking Press, 1968.

"The Wider Field of Work of the National Committee for Mental Hygiene." *Mental Hygiene* 54, no. 3 (July 1970): 425–26.

Wilhelm, Paul A. *Civilian Public Servants: A Report on 210 World War II Conscientious Objectors.* Rev. ed. Washington, D.C.: National Interreligious Service Board for Conscientious Objectors, 1994.

Winslow, C. E. A. "The Mental Hygiene Movement (1908–33) and Its Founder." In *A Mind That Found Itself: An Autobiography,* by Clifford W. Beers, 303–17. 7th ed. Garden City, N.Y.: Doubleday, 1956.

Wiseman, Frederick. *Titicut Follies.* New York: Grove Press, 1969.

Wolfensberger, Wolf. *A Brief Introduction to Social Role Valorization: A High-Order Concept for Addressing the Plight of Societally Devalued People, and for Structuring Human Services.* 3d ed. Syracuse: Training Institute for Human Service Planning, Leadership, and Change Agentry, Syracuse Univ., 1998.

———. "The Origin and Nature of Our Institutional Models." In *Changing Patterns in Residential Services for the Mentally Retarded,* edited by Robert B. Kugel and Wolf Wolfensberger, 59–171. Washington, D.C.: President's Committee on Mental Retardation, 1969.

———. *The Origin and Nature of Our Institutional Models.* Rev. ed. Syracuse: Human Policy Press, 1975.

———. *The Principle of Normalization in Human Services.* Toronto: National Institute of Mental Retardation, 1972.

———. "Social Role Valorization: A Proposed New Term for the Principle of Normalization." *Mental Retardation* 21, no 6 (1983), 234–239.

Wright, Frank L., Jr. *Out of Sight, Out of Mind.* Philadelphia: National Mental Health Foundation, 1947.

Zahn, Gordon C. "Abandon Hope." *Catholic Worker* 13, no. 8 (Oct. 1946): 1, 4, 6. Available at http://www.disabilitymuseum.org/lib/docs/1732.htm.

———. *Another Part of the War: The Camp Simon Story.* Amherst: Univ. of Massachusetts Press, 1979.

———. *Conscientious Objection: Catholic Perspectives.* Erie, Pa.: Pax Christi USA, 1991.

———. *A Descriptive Study of the Social Backgrounds of Conscientious Objectors in Civilian Public Service During World War II: Abstract of Dissertation.* Washington, D.C.: Catholic University of America Press, 1953.

———. "Slaves or Patients?" *Catholic Worker* 13, no. 7 (Oct. 1946): 1, 6. Available at http://www.disabilitymuseum.org/lib/docs/1720.htm.

———. "State School Unnatural, Maltreats Children." *Catholic Worker* 13, no. 6 (July 1946): 5–7. Available at http://www.disabilitymuseum.org/lib/docs/1733.htm.

Name Index

Italic page number denotes illustration.

Subject Index

Italic page number denotes illustration.